Prehistoric Russia
AN OUTLINE

Silver beaker from barrow grave
in Trialeti.

Prehistoric Russia

AN OUTLINE

Tadeusz
Sulimirski

JOHN BAKER
HUMANITIES PRESS

© 1970 Tadeusz Sulimirski

First published in 1970 by
John Baker (Publishers) Ltd
5 Royal Opera Arcade
Pall Mall, London S.W.1

s.b.n. 212 99831 5

Humanities Press Inc
303 Park Av South
New York, N.Y. 10010

Printed and bound in the Republic of Ireland by
Hely Thom Limited, Dublin

Contents

Illustrations   xi
Preface   xix

1. THE DAWN   I
   INTRODUCTION   I
   THE PLEISTOCENE AGE   6
   THE LOWER PALAEOLITHIC   8
     The Mousterian Period   8
   THE UPPER PALAEOLITHIC   13
     Stages in Evolution and Chronology   21
   THE MESOLITHIC   27
     The Pontic Province   34
       The Caucasus   34
       The Crimea   35
       The Lower Dnieper   37
       Other Pontic Mesolithic Groups   38
     Podolia   40
     The Forest Zone   41
     The East   44
       The Shigir Culture   45
     The North-West and North   48
       The Kunda Culture   49
   SUMMARY   52
   REFERENCES   54

2. THE NEOLITHIC (*The Fourth and Third
   Millennia B.C.*)   55
   NEOLITHIC REVOLUTION   55
   THE EARLY AND MIDDLE NEOLITHIC IN THE SOUTH   59
     The Danubian I Culture   61
     The Southern Bug Culture   64

The Tripolye Culture   66
Further Development   71
The Ancient Pontic Province   74
Transcaucasia   74
The Crimea   79
The Valley of the Dnieper   80
THE EARLY AND MIDDLE NEOLITHIC IN THE FOREST ZONE   84
The Comb-Pricked Ware Culture   86
East-Baltic Cultures   90
The Valdai Culture   92
The Volga-Oka Assemblage   93
THE NEOLITHIC IN THE EAST   98
Soviet Central Asia   98
The Kama-Ural Province   102
The South Urals   106
THE LATE NEOLITHIC IN THE SOUTH   107
The Tripolye Culture   108
The Dnieper-Donetz Culture   109
The Valley of the Dnieper   113
THE CAUCASUS   116
The Maikop Culture   117
The Abkhasian Dolmen Culture   125
THE STEPPE COUNTRY   127
The Yamnaya Culture   127
Steppe Settlements   133
The Settlement of Mykhailivka   134
THE LATE NEOLITHIC IN THE FOREST ZONE   136
The Kargopol Culture   138
The Karelian Culture   138
The East Baltic Area   140
SUMMARY   141
REFERENCES   145

3. THE BRONZE AGE (From 2000 to 1200 B.C. approximately)   147
THE AGE OF WESTERN PREDOMINANCE   147
THE TWO MAIN AGENTS   150
The Corded Ware Cultures   150
The Sub-Carpathian Barrow Graves   156
The Komarów Culture   158
The Trzciniec Culture   160
The Globular Amphora Culture   162

THE SOUTH-WEST   170
    The Tripolye Culture   170
    The Middle Dnieper Culture   176
    The Vykhvatyntsi Group   179
    The Usatovo Culture   180
    The Gorodsk Culture   184
    The Evminka-Sofiivka Groups   186
    The Voytsekhivka and Marianivka Cultures   188
THE FOREST ZONE   190
    The Dnieper-Desna Culture   190
    The Fatyanovo Culture   195
    The Balanovo Culture   199
    The Native Population   204
    The Volosovo Culture   205
    The Riazan and Balakhna Cultures   208
THE NORTH   209
    The Boat-axe Cultures   209
    The Kargopol Culture   212
    The Karelian Culture   213
    The White Sea Culture   215
    Northern Art   216
THE SOUTH EAST   221
    The Catacomb Culture   222
    The Caucasus   230
    The Trialeti Barrow Graves   237
SUMMARY   238
REFERENCES   242

4.   THE SHADOW OF THE RISING EAST (*The Second Millennium B.C.*)   244
THE COUNTRY EAST OF THE VOLGA AND THE URALS   244
    The Kazan Culture   245
    The Turbino Culture   249
    The Gorbunovo Culture   252
THE STEPPE   254
    The Poltavka Culture   254
    The Srubnaya Culture   256
    The Andronovo Culture   261
THE ROLE OF TRADE   266
    The Sea-borne Trade with the Aegean   270
EARLY METALLURGY IN THE KAMA-URAL REGION   276
    The Seima-Turbino Bronze Industry   281

The Origin of the Seima-Turbino Industry 284
The Expansion of the Eastern Bronze Industries 287
The Abashevo Culture 289
　The Abashevo Metal Industry 295
WEST SIBERIA 298
The West Siberian Bronze Industry 298
The Karasuk Culture 305
　The Consequences of Karasuk Expansion 308
The Account by Aristeas of Proconnesus 310
SUMMARY 313
REFERENCES 314

5. THE LATE BRONZE AND EARLY IRON AGES
　(*The Thirteenth to Seventh Centuries B.C.*) 317
THE FOREST ZONE 317
The Gorbunovo Culture 317
The Turbino and Kazan Cultures 320
The Country North of the Middle Volga 322
The Volosovo Culture 323
The Galich Culture 325
The Arctic Cultures 328
The Scandinavian Trade 331
THE EAST EUROPEAN STEPPE COUNTRY 335
The Srubnaya-Khvalinsk Culture 336
The Pozdniakovo Culture 339
The Country West of the Don 340
The Sabatynivka Culture 343
The Cimmerian Bronze Industry 346
THE SOUTH-WESTERN BORDERLAND 352
The Noua Culture 352
The Holihrady Culture 353
The Wysocko Culture 355
THE CAUCASUS 358
The Koban Culture 359
The Kayakent-Khorochoi and Late Kuban Cultures 362
Koban Trade 365
The Central Transcaucasian Culture 367
The Colchidic Culture 370
THE PONTIC LANDS AT THE END OF THE PREHISTORIC
　ERA 372
The Crimea 372
The Bilohrudivka Culture 375

The Chornii-Lis Culture   378
Thraco-Cimmerian Finds   383
The Country East of the Dnieper   384
SUMMARY   388
REFERENCES   390

6. CONCLUSION   393
    THE CIMMERIANS   395
    THE EARLY SCYTHIANS   397
    GREEK COLONIZATION   402
    REFERENCES   403
    BIBLIOGRAPHIES   429
    INDEXES   436

Illustrations

PLATES

Silver beaker from barrow grave in Trialeti *frontispiece*.
I   Female figurine carved in mammoth ivory from the site of Kostienki I.

II   Man of the Crô-Magnon racial type from the Magdalenian grave at Kostienki II.

III   Grave-chamber built of mammoth bones and skulls uncovered at the site of Kostienki II.

IV   Position of the early Upper Palaeolithic grave at the Markina Gora site, and a view of its tightly contracted skeleton.

V   Man from the double burial in the cave of Murzak-Koba in the Crimea.

VI   Young woman from the double grave in the cave of Murzak-Koba.

VII   Vessels characteristic of the Southern Bug culture.

VIII   A view of the 'ploshchadka' hut IV at Zhury on the Dniester.

IX   Vessels of the Tripolyan period B-1.

X   Vessels of the Tripolyan period B-2.

XI   Potsherds of the Lialovo culture.

XII   North-west Caucasian dolmens.

XIII   Pottery from the region of the Dnieper rapids.

XIV   Vase of the late stage of the Maikop culture.

XV   View of the steppe landscape of North-west Podolia, and vessels from Yamnaya barrow graves near Smiela.

XVI   Vessel from the Yamnaya barrow grave I at Novo-Nikolskoe.

XVII   Vessels from three superimposed levels of the settlement at Mykhailivka on the Lower Dnieper.

XVIII   Painted storage vase of period C-1 of the Tripolye culture.

XIX   Pottery of the Volhynian group of the Globular Amphora culture.

XX   Pottery of the Gorodsk culture from the settlement at Troyaniv near Zhitomir.

XXI Pottery of the Sofiivka culture from the cremation cemetery at Chernyn, north of Kiev.

XXII Bronze and bone daggers from the Tripolyan period C-1 site at Bilcze Złote.

XXIII Beakers and vases of the Middle Dnieper culture.

XXIV Vessels and gold ornaments of the early stage of the Komarów culture.

XXV Vessels of the developed Komarów culture from a barrow grave at Bukówna on the Dniester.

XXVI Pottery from barrow graves at Voytsekhivka on the Sluch in Central Volhynia.

XXVII Bronze tools found in the Ukraine.

XXVIII Pottery characteristic of the Fatyanovo culture.

XXIX Sherds of vessels characteristic of the Volosovo culture.

XXX A vessel characteristic of the early 'textile' pottery from Vorskla.

XXXI Examples of pottery of the three stages of the Balakhna culture.

XXXII Wooden ladle and a wooden sculpture of an elk, from the Gorbunovo peat-bog.

XXXIII Bronze knife or dagger, mace-head and 'arrow-straightener' characteristic of the Catacomb culture.

XXXIV Pottery characteristic of the Donetz group of the Catacomb culture.

XXXV Vessels from burials of the Catacomb period in the steppe west of the Dnieper.

XXXVI Vessel of the Poltavka culture, and a bowl from a secondary burial of the Srubnaya culture.

XXXVII Stone Battle-axes decorated in the 'Mycenanean' style.

XXXVIII Part of the bronze hoard from Sabancheevo, south-west of Kazan, with a pin of East Prussian type.

XXXIX Bronze daggers and a curved knife from the cemetery of Seima, and a curved knife from cemetery II at Turbino.

XL Grave 9 of the 'Late Volosovo' cemetery, with Scandinavian imported bronze tutulus and 'Mälar' celt.

XLI Pots from late Srubnaya barrow graves at Kalinovka on the lower Volga.

XLII Pottery and an iron knife from settlements of the Holihrady culture.

XLIII 'Villanova' bronze helmet found at Krzemienna near Kamenetz Podolskii.

XLIV Objects from the gold hoard of Michałków on the Dniester.

XLV Vessels characteristic of the cemeteries of the Wysocko culture.

XLVI Decorated bronze objects of the Koban culture.

XLVII A decorated vase of the Gandzha-Karabagh culture.

XLVIII Decorated oval bronze armbands of the Chornii-Lis culture.

XLIX Bronze grave goods and lance-heads made of iron from a cremation grave at Butenki on the Vorskla.

XLX An Urattian bronze helmet found in a cemetery of the Koban culture.

FIGURES

1 Chellean and Acheulian hand-axes from Satani-Dar in Transcaucasia, and points from Kiik-Koba in the Crimea.   [p. 9]

2 Plan of an Upper Palaeolithic (Solutrean) hut at Berdysh on the Sozh in Byelorussia.   [p. 18]

3 Plan of a Late Magdalenian hut at Moldova V, layer 3, and a reconstructed view of the camp.   [p. 20]

4 Flints of the Early Solutrean layer 10 of the Moldova V site. [p. 22]

5 Implements made of antler and mammoth tusks from the Upper Solutrean layer 7 of the Moldova V site.   [p. 23]

6 Flint and antler tools from the Magdalenian layer 4 of the Moldova V site.   [p. 24]

7 Final Palaeolithic flint tools from the upper horizon of site Borshevo II.   [p. 31]

8 Microlithic flint industry of the Late Mesolithic of the area between the Middle Dnieper and Upper Don.   [p. 33]

9 Plan and some burials of the Mesolithic Vasylivka I cemetery near the Dnieper rapids.   [p. 38]

10 Mesolithic flint industry of the country on the Middle Volga. [p. 43]

11 Bone arrow-heads of the 'Shigir' type from the Mesolithic and Neolithic sites of North-Eastern Europe.   [p. 46]

12 Burial (partial cremation) of the Danubian I culture at Nezvysko on the Dniester.   [p. 62]

13 Vessels and a slate chisel, or axe, from the burial of Danubian I culture at Nezvysko.   [p. 63]

14 Characteristic vessels and microlithic flints of the Southern Bug culture from Trifautskii Forest on the Dniester and from Hlynysche on the Boh (Southern Bug).   [p. 65]

15 Buttons, pendants, amulets, etc., made of bone, animal teeth, clay, and *Unio* shells, from the early Tripolyan settlement at Luka-Vrublivetska.   [p. 69]

16 Remains of a Tripolyan hut of period B-2 uncovered at Vladymirivka near Uman, and a reconstruction.   [p. 73]

17 Painted vessels of the Tripolyan period B-2.   [p. 75]

18 Pottery excavated at the settlement of Kyul-Tepe.   [p. 77]

19 Copper objects and fragments of moulds from Kyul-Tepe. [p. 78]

20 Potsherds characteristic of the second period of the Surskii culture found in the region of the Dnieper rapids.   [p. 81]

21 Plan and cross-section of the cemetery at Vilnyi in the valley of the Dnieper.   [p. 83]

22 Pottery from Neolithic sites of the Upper Dnieper basin. [p. 87]

23 Early Neolithic flint tools of the Dnieper-Donetz culture from sites on the Donetz near Izium.   [p. 89]

24 Flint industry and bone harpoons, arrow-heads, etc., from the Sakhtysh I and II sites.   [p. 94]

25 Plan of the lower and middle horizons of the Neolithic site excavated at Dolgoe on the upper Don.   [p. 97]

26 Pottery and tools of the Kelteminar culture.   [p. 101]

27 Vessels typical of the Kazan Neolithic culture from the Observatoria III site.   [p. 106]

28 Plan of a hut of the Kura-Araxes culture at Kvatskhelebi. [p. 110]

29 Examples of pottery and tools characteristic of the various regions of the Dnieper-Donetz culture.   [p. 111]

30 Objects from settlements of the Maikop culture.   [p. 119]

31 Decorated amphora from a barrow grave of the second stage of the Maikop culture.   [p. 120]

32 Plan and cross-section of barrow grave 5 at Ryżanówka (Ryzhanivka) west of Cherkasy.   [p. 128]

33 Vessels typical of the Sub-Carpathian barrow grave culture. [p. 158]

34 Vessels of Trzciniec derivation from Narodychi-Pishchane in Volhynia.   [p. 161]

35 Slab-cist grave from Voytsekhivka on the Sluch in Volhynia. [p. 163]

36 Flints found in a barrow grave at Orlivka near Berdyansk on the Sea of Azov.   [p. 168]

37 Decorated bone plaques, beaker and potsherds with an incised ornament, characteristic of the Globular Ampora culture. [p. 169]

38 Plan of the Tripolyan settlement of period C-1 at Kolomishchyna I.   [p. 171]

39 Examples of Tripolyan pottery of period C-1.   [p. 172]

40 Decoration on the upper part of a large vase from Petreny of Tripolyan period C-1.   [p. 175]

41 Clay cauldron and bronze 'Cypriot' pin from the Tripolyan settlement at Sabatynivka I.   [p. 177]

42 Vessels from the cemetery of Vykhvatyntsi.   [p. 181]

43 Pottery and other objects excavated at Usatovo.   [p. 182]

44 Copper tools, weapons and beads from the cremation cemetery at Sofiivka near Kiev.   [p. 187]

45 Vessels characteristic of the Marianivka culture and of the Sosnitsa culture.   [p. 189]

46 Grave goods from burial 1 in barrow grave 11 of the Dnieper-Desna culture at Moshka (Khodovichi).   [p. 192]

47 Three copper diadems and a clay vessel of Trzciniec derivation all of the Dnieper-Desna culture in Byelorussia.   [p. 193]

48 Grave goods of the Fatyanovo culture.   [p. 197]

49 Grave goods from burial 2 of a barrow grave of the Balanovo culture at Churachiki, south of Cheboksary.   [p. 203]

50 Remains characteristic of the Balakhna culture.   [p. 206]

51 Examples of vessels of the Corded Ware (Boat-axe) culture in the Baltic countries.   [p. 210]

52 'V' perforated amber buttons from Modlona I, East Baltic area and East Prussia; slate axes of Karelian type from Karelia, region of Kargopol and Siberia; 'pick-axes' of Karelian type from Karelia, region of Kargopol and Kostroma.   [p. 214]

53 Schematic figures of water birds incised on vessels of the Late Neolithic and Bronze Age from the northern part of the East European forest zone. Viper and human figurines carved in antler, bone and clay, from Olenii Ostrov, Tyrvala, and the region on Lake Ladoga.   [p. 216]

54 Human and animal figures carved in flint or engraved on rocks, from the East European forest zone.   [p. 219]

55 Characteristic niche graves of the Catacomb culture.   [p. 222]

56 Necklace from barrow grave 2 at Klynivka near Poltava. Flints and ornaments from graves of the Catacomb culture.   [p. 226]

57 Selected goods from burial 1 of barrow grave 5 at Ulskii. [p. 233]

58 Grave goods from a barrow grave at Solomenka.   [p. 235]

59 Pottery from settlements of the southern division of the Kazan Bronze Age culture.   [p. 247]

60 Grave goods characteristic of the Turbino cemetery.   [p. 251]

61 Pottery and ornaments typical of the Poltavka culture.   [p. 255]

62 Plan of barrow grave 5 at Yagodnoe near Kuibyshev.   [p. 256]

63 Vessels typical of the Middle Don group of the Srubnaya culture.   [p. 258]

64 Bronze tools and weapons characteristic of the Srubnaya culture of the steppe country on the Lower Volga and the country north of the Caucasus.   [p. 259]

65 Pottery of the Andronovo culture of West Siberia.   [p. 264]

66 Objects decorated in the 'Mycenaean' style.   [p. 275]

67 Socketed axes (celts) of common Andronovo types, found in the mountains east of Semipalatinsk.   [p. 286]

68 Reconstruction of an Abashevo woman's head ornament. [p. 290]

69 Bronze personal ornaments from Abashevo graves.   [p. 292]

70 Bronze tools of the Abashevo culture.   [p. 293]

71 Earliest bronze daggers, or knives, from West Siberia.   [p. 301]

72   Stone 'enclosures' round Karasuk tribal burial grounds in central Kazaakhstan and Karasuk sculptured menhir-statues from the central Siberian Minusinsk steppe.   [p. 304]

73   Bronze daggers and pottery of the Karasuk period in the valley of the Yenissey near Minusinsk.   [p. 306]

74   Hoard of Galich.   [p. 325]

75   Remains of the Galich culture.   [p. 327]

76   Pottery from late Volosovo settlements at Podboritsa-Shcherbininskaya and bronze weapons found in graves of the 'Late Volosovo' cemetery.   [p. 332]

77   Two bronze celts of the Mälar type from the regions of Kargopol and Kazan.   [p. 333]

78   Plan and cross-section of the largest hut in the settlement of the Late Srybnaya culture at Khutor Lyapichev on the R. Tsaritsa in the basin of the Middle Don, and plan of settlement.   [p. 338]

79   Burials with 'stone-covers' at Balka Bashmatka near the Dnieper rapids.   [p. 345]

80   Talc moulds from the settlement of the Sabatynivka culture at Novo-Oleksandrivka on the Lower Dnieper.   [p. 348]

81   Bronze lance-head of the Seima type and axe with an open socket, and objects typical of the 'Cimmerian' bronze industry from the Ukraine.   [p. 349]

82   Lusatian bronze objects found in the Ukraine.   [p. 351]

83   Bronze and iron ornaments characteristic of the Wysocko culture.   [p. 356]

84   Plan of a hut of the Wysocko culture.   [p. 357]

85   Bronze weapons, ornaments, and an iron dagger of the Koban culture.   [p. 360]

86   Weapons of iron, bronze, and parts of a horse harness of bronze and bone, from the Simferopol barrow grave and the burial from Butenki.   [p. 380]

87   Bronze boat-shaped brooch found at Hrebeny, in the district of Rzhyshchev south of Kiev, and a socketed axe of the Brittany type found in the Ukraine.   [p. 381]

88   Pottery of the Bondarykha culture.   [p. 385]

89   Plan and cross-section of a hut of the Bondarykha culture at Studenok 5.   [p. 386]

90   A shooting centaur from a Babylonian boundary stone of the thirteenth century B.C.   [p. 396]

91   Black polished pottery with white encrusted ornament.   [p. 398]

MAPS

I   Major vegetation zones of Eastern Europe.   [p. 4]

II   Distribution of Mousterian finds in Eastern Europe.   [p. 10]

III   The main Upper Palaeolithic sites in Eastern Europe. [p. 15]

IV   Late Mesolithic provinces and important sites in Eastern Europe.   [p. 29]

V   Distribution of bone arrow-heads of the 'Shigir' type. [p. 47]

VI   Scheme of the advance in Eastern Europe of the earliest agriculturalists, and of their contribution to spreading the knowledge of pottery.   [p. 56]

VII   The earliest agricultural communities in the south-west of Eastern Europe.   [p. 60]

VIII   Eastern Europe—first half of the third millennium B.C. [p. 85]

IX   Territories of the Valdai and Narva cultures.   [p. 92]

X   Settlements of the Liavolo culture.   [p. 95]

XI   Distribution in West Siberia and Central Asia of pre-Andronovo remains of the late third and early second millennia B.C.   [p. 100]

XII   Cemeteries of the Dnieper-Donetz culture.   [p. 114]

XIII   East European copper deposits exploited from the third to the first millennium B.C.   [p. 124]

XIV   Eastern Europe around 1700 B.C.   [p. 152]

XV   Distribution north-east of the Carpathians of bronze hoards.   [p. 159]

XVI   Distribution of flint sculptures in Eastern Europe.   [p. 217]

XVII   Distribution of North Caucasian bronze objects within the territory of the Catacomb culture.   [p. 228]

XVIII   The western drive, in the late second millennium B.C., of peoples of the 'Eastern assemblage' and West Siberia. [p. 241]

XIX   Territory of the Andronovo culture from about the fifteenth to the thirteenth centuries B.C.   [p. 262]

XX   Distribution throughout the eastern part of Central Europe, and in Eastern Europe, of Mediterranean goods in the mid-second millennium B.C., and the presumed routes of their diffusion.   [p. 272]

XXI   Diffusion of products of different metallurgical centres in Eastern Europe in the third and in the first half of the second millennia B.C.   [p. 278]

XXII   Diffusion of products of different metallurgical centres in Eastern Europe at the end of the second and early in the first millennia B.C.   [p. 279]

XXIII   Distribution of shaft-hole axes of the South Ural type. [p. 280]

XXIV Distribution of bronze socketed lance-heads of the 'Seima-Turbino' type with the pivot rhomboid in cross-section. [p. 282]
XXV Distribution of early 'Seima' bronze socketed axes. [p. 283]
XXVI Distribution of remains of the Abashevo culture. [p. 289]
XXVII Centres of the West Siberian bronze industry. [p. 299]
XXVIII Distribution in the Western Siberian steppe country and Soviet Central Asia of late Andronovo and early Karasuk bronze tools and weapons. [p. 303]
XXIX Eastern Europe around 1200 B.C. [p. 318]
XXX Distribution of sites of the Volosovo culture in the first half of the second millennium B.C. [p. 324]
XXXI Map showing the Swedish eastwards expansion in the Late Bronze Age, early in the first millennium B.C. [p. 330]
XXXII Koban trade about the eighth century B.C. [p. 366]

Preface

THE study of the archaeological remains of any country can take various forms. The description and classification of the actual archaeological material, the establishment of its date, connections, and stages in evolution, can be emphasized; or the economic base of prehistoric societies, their social evolution and technical progress, art and religion, may be stressed.

But there is another approach. The evolution of prehistoric peoples, like those whose history is well known from written records, has never proceeded without interruption, along a single track and in isolation. Archaeological material has presented many examples of a sudden break in the evolution of a people caused by external interferences, and which, in many instances, has been noticed throughout wider areas. Expansions, tribal migrations, conquests, and similar events of a political character, lay at the root of these occurrences.

The main object of the present book is the study of such changes in the prehistoric past of Eastern Europe, and their correlation with similar incidents in other parts of Europe and Asia; to determine their cause and study their effects; to find out, and explain, if possible and practicable, the general trends overlying these transformations. Special attention has been given to connections—commercial, warlike, and otherwise—with the countries of the ancient Oriental civilization, and its impact on the culture, technical progress, and the development of metallurgy, of the indigenous peoples of Eastern Europe.

The term 'Russia' has been used here only for the sake of convenience. It denotes the eastern part of Europe, which has been usually called by that name, and embraces principally the European part of the U.S.S.R. The western part of Siberia, up to the Yenissey, and Soviet Central Asia are referred to when their influence is felt in Eastern Europe. In any case, the steppe country of west Siberia up to the Yenissey, including the Minusinsk valley, and also Soviet Central Asia, were, up to the early Christian Era, a kind of eastern extension of Eastern Europe. The peoples of those areas at that time spoke eastern dialects of the Indo-European languages—Arian,

Iranian, Tokharian—and from the anthropological point of view represented a variety of the Europoid race.

The parts of the U.S.S.R. in Asia east of the Yenissey and the Minusinsk valley had only occasionally connections with the east European past. They belonged to a completely different world, the development of which proceeded along different lines and within a different cultural and chronological framework from that established for Eastern Europe.

The usual division into periods based on the technological progress of the material culture, and its terminology, have been applied here. But the denominations like the 'Neolithic', 'Bronze Age', and even the 'Iron Age', have a different meaning in various parts of Eastern Europe, owing to their differing geographic positions and the varying ecological conditions within them; in terms of absolute chronology they denote different periods. This circumstance often makes it difficult to correlate periods in different regions of the country. The traditional terminology therefore, has been applied here only conventionally—the 'Neolithic' meaning the fourth and third millennia, the 'Bronze Age' the second millennium, and the 'Early Iron Age' denoting the advanced stage of the first millennium B.C.

The few chronological horizons, easily discernible in the archaeological material of most regions of Eastern Europe, were the starting point for a uniform chronological scheme for the whole area. Special studies by several Soviet scholars, whether general or devoted to a particular period, were invaluable in working out such a scheme. The determination of an absolute chronology has been based on comparisons with the established chronology of Central Europe, the Mediterranean and west Asiatic countries. Carbon-14 dating has also been of the greatest importance.

This book deals with the prehistoric past of Eastern Europe up to the end of the seventh century B.C., to the Scythian conquest of the north Pontic area. This event, jointly with the Greek colonization of the northern coast of the Black Sea, which began at that time, brought the country into a close contact with the ancient civilized world. Written records relating to Eastern Europe and its peoples began to appear then in increasing numbers; and they are important in supplementing the archaeological material. The purely prehistoric age had come to an end, and the protohistoric era had begun, and that will be dealt with in a separate volume.

The book has been divided into six chapters. The Palaeolithic and Mesolithic are dealt with in the first of these. Chapters 2, 3 and 5 are devoted to the post-glacial development—the 'Neolithic', 'Bronze Age', and the 'Late Bronze Age' and 'Earliest Iron Age'. Chapter 4 deals with the development and the role of trade (especially the maritime trade with the Aegean), and with the east European and west Siberian metallurgy. Special tables at the end of the volume show the position within the chronological framework at any given period of the main cultures discussed in the consecutive chapters, and of the stages in the development of these, or of their industries. A series of smaller maps show the distribution of finds discussed in the text; and the aim of the few larger ones is to show conditions in Eastern Europe during some selected periods. Unfortunately, the picture shown by the latter is very incomplete, many areas being left blank owing to the insufficiency of research.

Several generally accepted abbreviations have been applied in this book. Those connected with Carbon-14 dates, e.g. LE-331, or RUL-185, etc., denote the symbol of the laboratory (Leningrad, Moscow, Tallin, Berlin, etc.), and its number of the sample taken from the respective site. Abbreviations: B.C. (before Christ), B.P. (before present), and A.D. (Anno Domini, the Christian Era), denote the date of the remains in question. Abbreviations relating to periodicals and serial publications (e.g. M.I.A., E.S.A., etc.) are quoted in the Bibliography at the end of the book.

This book was conceived several years ago. It is to some extent the result of my lectures on east European Archaeology, first at the Faculty of Archaeology and Anthropology of the University of Cambridge during the Lent Terms in 1953 and 1954, which I delivered on the kind invitation of Professor J.G.D. Clark, and then, since 1958, on my regular lectures on the same subject at the University of London Institute of Archeology. It has been based on the very large literature on the subject published by a great many Soviet authors in the U.S.S.R., and also by scholars working in the western countries. But my own excavations and research in many sites on the western borderland of the area dealt with here, within the limits of pre-war Poland, and the study of the relevant archaeological material in many museums and institutes in the U.S.S.R., which I had the opportunity to undertake during my visits, first in 1934, and then in 1961, 1963, and 1964, were essential for the study; and discussions on the various topics relating to the prehistoric past of the different parts of the U.S.S.R., which I had with several Soviet fellow archaeologists, many of whom have shown me unpublished materials from their recent excavations, were of great help. Important also were my pre-war and post-war studies in the museums of Finland (Helsinki) and Rumania, and discussions with Finnish and Rumanian colleagues, were also very valuable.

For their help and great willingness in providing me with information during the visits to the countries mentioned, I am very grateful particularly to Professors M.I. Artamonov and B.B. Piotrovskii, the former and present Directors of the Hermitage Museum in Leningrad, and to the late Dr B.A. Latynin, Keeper of the Neolithic Department there; to Mr S.S. Chernikov and Mrs N.N. Gurina of the Archaeological Institute of the Academy of the U.S.S.R. in Leningrad; Miss V.M. Raushenbakh, Deputy Director of the Historical Museum in Moscow; to the scholars working at the Archaeological Institute of the Academy of the U.S.S.R. in Moscow, in particular to the late Professor A.Ia. Briusov, and Messrs I.I. Artemenko, E.I. Krupnov, Iu.V. Kukharenko, V.S. Titov, and Mrs E.K. Chernysh; Professor S.N. Bibikov, Director of the Archaeological Institute of the Ukrainian Academy in Kiev; to the scholars working at that Institute, in particular Messrs V.M. Danylenko, M.L. Makarevych, M. Shmaglii, D.Ia. Telegin, Dr A.I. Terenozhkin, I.N. Zakharuk, and Mesdames V.A. Ilinskaya and O.G. Shaposhnikova; Miss T.G. Movsha and Miss T.F. Zaliska of the Historical Museum in Kiev; Dr M. Smishko, acting Director of the Institute of Social Sciences in Lwów-Lviv and Mr I.K. Sveshnikov of the same Institute; to the personnel of the Archaeological Section of the Historical Museum in Lwów-Lviv; I.T. Cherniakov, Director of the Archaeological Museum in Odessa and Mrs E.F. Patokova of the same Museum; Professor O.M. Dzhaparidze of the University of Tbilisi; Messrs T.N. Chubinishvili and A.I. Dzhavakhishvili of the Georgian Museum in Tbilisi; and to the personnel of other Museums visited both in 1934 and after the last war, at Minsk, in Byelorussia; Berdychev, Chernigov, Dnepropetrovsk, Kamenetz Podolskii, Kharkov, Kherson, Poltava, Vinnitsa and Zhitomir in the Ukraine; Sevastopol and Yalta in the Crimea; and Orjonikidze, Piatigorsk and Rostov-on-Don. I am similarly indebted to Mag. A. Erä-Esko and Mag. A. Kapisto of the National Museum in Helsinki, and to the many Rumanian colleagues for their help and discussions on topics relating to East European Archaeology during my several pre-war visits and a recent one in 1965, in particular to Professor V. Dumitrescu, Professor J. Nestor, Professor R. Vulpe and to Messrs D. Berciu, E. Comsa, Al. Vulpe and V. Zirra of the Institute of Archaeology of the Rumanian Academy in Bucharest; and Professor M. Petrescu-Dimbovița and Mr A. Florescu of the Moldavian Museum at Iași (Jassy).

Several plates have been reproduced from photographs very kindly given me or sent to me, for which I am very grateful to Professor B.A. Rybakov, Director of the Institute of Archaeology of the Academy of the U.S.S.R, Moscow; to Professor S.N. Bibikov, Director of the Institute of Archaeology of the Ukrainian Academy, Kiev, and to Dr. A.I. Terenozhkin of the same Institute; and to

Dr Wolfram Nadel of the Museum für Vor-und Frühgeschichte, Berlin-Charlottenburg.

Special grants, for which I am very grateful, received from the Pilgrim Trust Fund of the British Academy, the Calouste Gulbenkian Foundation, and the Gordon Childe Fund, enabled me to undertake the aforementioned visits.

I am greatly indebted to Mr Edward Pyddoke, Secretary and Registrar of the University of London Institute of Archaeology, for his insistence on my writing this book, his suggestion to give special attention to connections between Eastern and Western Europe, and for reading the typescript. I must also express my thanks to Miss J. du Plat Taylor and Miss G.C. Talbot, M.A., Librarians at the above Institute; to Mr H.M. Stewart, B.A., at the same Institute, for the preparation of most of the maps; to Miss B.J. Kirkpatrick, Librarian of the Royal Anthropological Institute; to Mr J. Hopkins, Librarian of the Society of Antiquaries of London; further to Mr F.N. Davis, A.L.A., Harlow, and Mr F.G. Thomas for correcting and improving my English text, and Mr D. Kidd of John Baker (Publishers) Ltd, for the great care shown in his editorial work.

T. SULIMIRSKI.

I

The Dawn

INTRODUCTION

EASTERN Europe is a vast plain more than nine times the size of France, and physically more like Western Siberia than Western Europe. It is essentially a country of low relief, with no protection from piercing northern or north-eastern winds; the Urals are too low to form an effective climatic barrier. In the south are the mountains of the Caucasus which rise to a height of 18,466 feet above sea level, exceeding the highest European Alps (Mont Blanc, 15,782 feet). In the north-west are the largest lakes in all Europe, the Ladoga and the Onega. The rivers of east Europe are on the same scale as its plains, its mountains and its lakes. The largest of these, the Volga, is the longest and widest river in Europe.

The northern expanse of Eastern Europe consists of forest land with a clay or sandy soil, but the south, extending from the Carpathians to the Urals and beyond, is a tract of great fertility, known as the black earth (chernozem) belt, much of which is treeless, except in the ravines and river valleys; and there are occasional marshes. In its natural state the steppe produces a large variety of grasses, some of which grow to a considerable height and have silvery plumes that wave in the wind. Under cultivation the black soil is capable of providing magnificent crops; it is rich in humus, absorbs moisture readily, and is more easily worked than the clay soil of the forest zone. North of the steppe and west of the Dnieper lie the Pripet Marshes, where conditions are very different. Here are vast morasses interlinked by a network of streams. In some parts these morasses are covered with reeds and rushes; elsewhere they are studded with pines and other trees. Stretches of sand-dunes form islands suitable for grazing cattle or for raising crops.

Movement across Eastern Europe was relatively easy. The boundless forests in the centre and the north, together with numerous swamps and ferocious beasts, would formerly have prevented men from wandering over great distances, if nature had not provided passages through the wilderness, whereby all obstacles might be circumvented; for over the plateau flow many slow-moving rivers forming 'the finest natural network of waterways in the world'. The watersheds from which these rivers flow northwards or southwards are low, and gradients are in general so gentle that except for a few occasional rapids the rivers are navigable in small boats far upstream. Their headwaters are so close together that it is relatively easy to drag boats overland across the watersheds from one river to another. Excellent waterways are thus provided from the Baltic to the Black Sea, the Urals and the Caspian Sea. These routes were followed by many prehistoric peoples, and by those of the later periods.

In the south, the steppe belt provided a natural highway for invaders from the east. In a description of Russia of the mid-nineteenth century we read that 'traversing the steppe one realizes how emphatically this is the undefended side of Europe; the open space through which all the Asiatic hordes entered; their cavalry darting over the steppe in search of enemies, of booty; their waggons following with their families and cattle; unchecked, except now and then by some great river, which, if it were too deep to ford, they crossed upon inflated skins'.

Eastern Europe has a continental climate: severe winters and burning summers. During the long winter the landmass becomes extremely cold and about half the country is frostbound for six months. Summer heat, on the other hand, is characteristic of the entire area. The strain on plant and human life to adapt themselves to these extreme conditions during the brief spring must be severe. But there are even greater extremes. The average summer temperature on the northern coast of Russia is lower than the winter temperature of the Crimea. The scantiness and irregularity of the spring rains and the variation in the duration of the snow-covering can have disastrous effects upon wide areas. If, owing to hot winds, the snow melts too soon in the southern steppe belt, or if the melting is delayed by a continuation of very cold winds, widespread damage to crops or the destruction of flocks may ensue.

Such extreme climatic conditions must have always prevailed in Eastern Europe. This is well attested by the classical authors, upon whom, without doubt, the cold made the deepest impression. Herodotus[1] in the fifth century B.C. says that, 'all this country is subject to such a severe winter that for eight months the frost is so intolerable that if you pour water on the ground you will not make mud'. 'Even the sea freezes'—the Cimmerian Bosphorus Straits of Kerch and the Sea of Azov—and the broad rivers 'so that people can drive and ride over them'. At the turn of the Christian Era, we read in Ovid that the people of the Black Sea countries protected themselves against the cold by wearing skins and sewn trousers, and of the whole form only the face was to be seen. 'Their hair often rattles from ice which hangs on it, and the beard shines with the frost which covers it.'

The lack of trees in the north Pontic region also made a great impression on those who came there from Greece and Italy. Herodotus says that the country is entirely bare both of cultivated and wild trees. Of the Scythians he relates how for want of wood they cook the flesh of animals with a fire which is made from their bones. Ovid mentions that there are no trees and that rarely in the open fields is there a bush.

Another factor that plays a considerable role in conditioning human activities is the soil, which shows great diversity in its quality throughout the whole vast territory. The very fertile loess and especially the black-earth (chernozem) covers almost the whole south, while heavy clay and poor sandy soils are typical of the regions further north. Physical conditions during the glacial and post-glacial periods were decisive factors in determining the nature of the various kinds of soil.

Climate and soil were chiefly responsible for the division of Eastern Europe into the series of vegetative zones, shown in Map I. This division has been based on present circumstances, but the study of peat-bogs and other survivals from the distant past reveals that the division was similar in prehistoric times, though some minor shifting of the zonal boundaries might have occurred in post-glacial climatic changes. The impact of some of these changes on vegetation was particularly strong in the south of the country.

All the zones marked on the map, their climates ranging from the arctic conditions in the extreme north to the almost Mediterranean weather in some regions of the extreme south (Southern Crimea, Western Transcaucasia), offered varied opportunities for the life and activities of the peoples who dwelt there. Accordingly, in each zone, different cultural groups developed different types of economy, adapted to local conditions. Thus climate, soil and landscape—the vast plain intersected by a network of large rivers and their tributaries—were the main factors responsible for the great variety of prehistoric cultures distinguishable in Eastern Europe. Many of these differed from each other in every respect—in origin, race, economy, way of life, and culture.

The social coherence of the various ethnical groups, and in particular their strong inborn conservatism, also led to differences between the various peoples living in this part of Europe. In many districts the way of life showed almost no change for centuries. The inhabitants of the deep Caucasian valleys are noteworthy in this respect: even today there is a great variety of races and tongues, as well as differences in religion and culture; a few villages will often

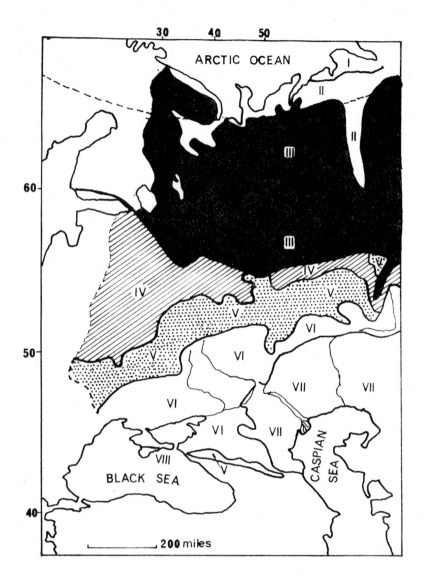

MAP I Major vegetation zones of Eastern Europe. After M. R. Shackleton (*Europe, a Regional Geography*. 6th edition, London 1958, p. 432, fig. 142) (I) (II) Tundra and Forest Tundra; (III) Coniferous Forest; (IV) Mixed Coniferous and Deciduous Forest; (V) Forest-Steppe; (VI) Steppe; (VII) Semi-Desert; (VIII) Mediterranean.

form a separate ethnical group. On the other hand, different but very complex conditions prevailed in many parts of the steppe country, at least up to the pre-Revolution period. In some regions different racial groups existed, often in the same village, interwoven yet each following its own way of life. The groups wore different dress. They buried their dead in distinct cemeteries, and their burial ritual differed according to their religion and customs inherited from the past.

Eastern Europe, therefore, cannot be treated as a uniform territory. This is why, in dealing with east European archaeology, we must take into account the fact that the variety of cultures within a given area does not always mean that they belonged to different periods; they may well have been contemporaneous. We must also be aware of the very slow development of some prehistoric tribes in Eastern Europe, of their conservatism in keeping to ancient cultural forms, especially in parts of the country away from the main routes and far from the leading centres of the periods in question.

The emergence of the leading centres, several of which have been distinguished in the prehistoric past of Eastern Europe, depended on many factors, one of the most important of which was a favourable geographical position—for example, on the junction of the great rivers, which secured them easy connections and relations with similar centres in other regions. It is interesting to note that nearly all the areas which became such centres continued to hold their position throughout almost the whole prehistoric past, and even later, in spite of the many upheavals and fundamental changes that occurred in the country.

Another leading factor in the emergence of important centres of industrial character was the natural resources of the region, especially the metalliferous resources.

Flint was the earliest indispensable raw material for making tools, and retained its position until the second millennium B.C. Flint is a rather common mineral but in several regions in Eastern Europe there were no deposits. It had to be imported into these regions or replaced by other varieties of stone less suitable for the purpose, e.g. quartz, quartzite or slate. Flint of excellent quality was restricted to a few areas and these became the earliest centres of the industrial production of flint tools and weapons intended for distribution to other areas. In some of these centres flint had to be mined.

Deposits of copper, the earliest metal known to man, were restricted to a small number of metalliferous regions (Map XIII). The earliest region to emerge was the Caucasus with its rich deposits of copper ore, lead, and arsenic—but no tin. Another region was the Urals and the adjacent country, especially on the Kama. Here copper and, in some areas, also gold and silver were available, but, as in the Caucasus, there was no tin. The absence of tin meant that substitutes, like arsenic, had to be used in alloying bronze. The richest deposits of all these metals, however, including tin, lie further east in west Siberia and the Altai Mountains. The metallurgical centres that sprung up there had a great bearing on the turn of events in Eastern Europe. Small and poor deposits of copper appear also in the region on the middle Donetz in the Ukraine, and in the central part of Volhynia; but these never played an important role (Map xxvii).

The knowledge of iron, the commonest metal, only came to Eastern Europe at the close of the period dealt with here. Iron objects which appeared then were all of southern origin. Not until the sixth century was iron smelted from local ores, when it became the most important metal in the production of weapons and subsequently of tools.

THE PLEISTOCENE AGE

Human history in Eastern Europe began, as elsewhere in Europe, in the Quaternary, or Pleistocene Age—the age of glaciations. Characteristic of this age, the duration of which has been estimated at over half a million years, were glacial periods—during which a large part of Europe lay under a very thick sheet of ice—separated by interglacial periods—when the climate was mild, usually much milder than that of the present time, and the ice-sheet completely vanished in Europe. Four glacial periods have been distinguished in Western and Central Europe, whereas in Eastern Europe only three glaciations have been established. The first of these periods is of no concern for us since no human traces have been found.

The earliest signs of human activity appeared in Eastern Europe, as in Western, in the interglacial preceding the penultimate glaciation, called the Mindel-Riss Interglacial in western terminology (Table 1).

The penultimate glaciation, called the Dnieper-Volga Glaciation, or the Saale-Riss Glaciation according to Western European sequence, was the greatest—the Maximal Glaciation. Most of Eastern Europe was under the ice cover and two wide salients extended far to the south: one, along the valley of the Dnieper, nearly reached the Dnieper bend, the region of the rapids; and the other, further east, penetrated along the valley of the Don and Volga, up to the region where the two rivers flow closest to each other.

The Maximal Glaciation was followed by a long interglacial period of about 60,000 years. During this mild period the whole country was covered with luxuriant vegetation and virgin forests. This interglacial, called the Riss-Würm Interglacial in western terminology, was ended by the last glaciation, known as the Valdai glaciation in Eastern Europe and the Würm glaciation in Western Europe.

The last glaciation lasted for over 100,000 years, from about 115,000 to about 8000 B.C. In Eastern Europe it affected an area considerably smaller than that of the Maximal Glaciation, only the north-western corner of the country being under the ice-sheet (Map III). Three stages of the glaciation have been distinguished in Central and Western Europe, separated by interstadials with mild climates. No such division has been worked out for Eastern Europe, but it has been commonly accepted by the scholars concerned that the glaciation in this area had at least two main stages with a milder interstadial between them. The latter evidently corresponded with the first interstadial, 'LG$_{11-2}$', in Central and North-West Europe.

In the west, the latter part of the last glaciation has been divided into a number of subsidiary stages. The most important for us are the last two of these: the Alleröd phase, an interval of milder climate; and the late Drias (III) time, the final cold period after which the Holocene, the present geological period, began. The two phases have been Carbon-14 dated at about 10,000 to 8800 B.C. and 8800 to 8000 B.C. respectively. No such division of the later part of the Valdai glaciation has been established in Eastern Europe, though geological surveys of the north Russian moraines confirmed four subsequent stages in the retreat of the glacier. These must have corresponded with the oscillations of the climate that marked stages of the glaciation.

The few Carbon-14 dates available for the Pleistocene are of no great help. The earliest of these, from the site of Shurskol near Yaroslav, north of Moscow, of 45,000 B.P. (RUL-185) possibly relates to the Riss-Würm interglacial. Carbon-14 dating of the interstadial of the Valdai glacial stage at Briansk and Mezin, both on the Desna, are 22,970 B.C. (Mo-337) and 22,250 B.C. (Mo-342) respectively. On the other hand, Carbon-14 dates of the 'interglacial deposits' from three sites in the region of Yaroslav are of a much later date and vary a great deal. The earliest site, Cheremoshnik, has been dated to 17,550 B.C. (RUL-8); the Levina Gora site to 15,250 B.C. (RUL-114); and the most recent, the Tutayevo site to 13,750 B.C. (RUL-197). Adding to the confusion is the date 13,130 B.C. (RUL-161) of a piece of wood from the lowest Holocene deposits near Zvenigorod, Moscow province.

THE LOWER PALAEOLITHIC

(Probably from about 400,000 to 140,000 B.P.)

The first traces of man in Eastern Europe are of the Pleistocene Age, considered to date from the Mindel-Riss Interglacial (Table 1). They are very scanty and restricted to Transcaucasia, though lately arti-facts probably of the same age have been found in west Podolia (Luka Vrublevetskaya on the Dniester). Those in Transcaucasia were found at Satani-Dar (Fig. 1) on the western slopes of Mount Aragats in Soviet Armenia. They consisted of very primitive tools made of obsidian and basalt, which are considered to be partly of Late Chellean and of Early Acheulian Age, that is, of the two earliest periods of the Lower Palaeolithic, or the Early Stone Age, according to the chronological scheme established for Western Europe.

Implements of an advanced stage of the Acheulian period have also been found in Transcaucasia, at Satani-Dar (Fig. 1) and in a score of sites in other parts of Transcaucasia, including Azerbaijan, but mainly on the Black Sea coast near Sukhumi, for example, in the Akhshtyrskaya cave. They have also been found north of the main Caucasian ridge, near Maikop in the north-west Caucasus and in Ossetia in the Central Caucasus. The geographic position of all these sites, and some characteristic features, link the Caucasian tools with those typical of the countries further south and suggest that the men who made them were Western Asiatic in origin.

By the end of the period the Acheulians had probably advanced beyond the Caucasus. Their traces have been found in the Crimea, in the lowest layer of the Kiik-Koba cave, east of Simferopol, along the northern coast of the Sea of Azov (Amvrosievka), on the Dnieper near the rapids (Nenasytets, Kruglyk), and on the Don and the Middle Volga (round Kuibyshev). In the west they were found at Luka Vrublivetskaya on the Dniester, near Kamenets Podolskii, but this site seems to have been connected with the Central European groups of the Acheulians. The northernmost site recorded in the Ukraine is near Zhitomir.

The Acheulians lived in small groups, usually close to river banks, and seldom sought shelter in caves. They were hunters and gatherers. Their tools were very primitive—flaked cores, rough choppers, and large, rough almond-shaped hand-axes. They were made of flint, obsidian, or other varieties of hard stone, such as quarts or quartzite.

THE MOUSTERIAN PERIOD

Remains of the subsequent Mousterian period (probably from

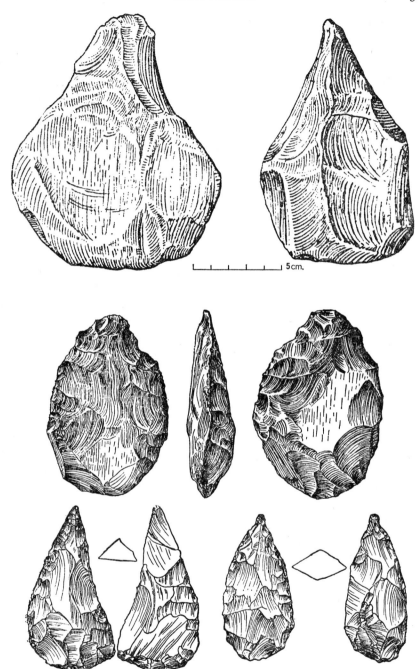

FIG. 1 Chellean and Acheulian hand-axes from Satani-Dar in Trans-caucasia, and points from Kiik-Koba in the Crimea.
After P.P. Efimenko (*Pervobytnoe Obshchestvo*. Kiev 1953, figs. 22, 37, 49, 50).

3

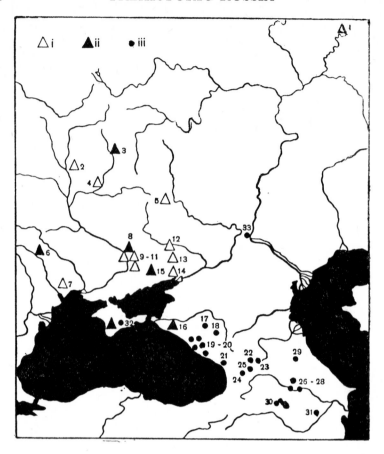

MAP II Distribution of Mousterian finds in Eastern Europe.
After A.A. Formozov (*Kamennyi Vek i Eneolit Prikubania*. Moscow 1965,
p. 40, fig. 11).
(I) Isolated finds of tools worked on both sides; (II) sites and larger finds
with similarly worked tools; (III) sites with tools of other types.
SITES MENTIONED IN THE TEXT: (1) Peshchernyi Log; (16) Ilskaya; (32)
Crimean sites, Kiik-Koba, etc.; (33) Sukhaya Mechetka.

about 140,000 to 70,000 B.P.) or the Middle Palaeolithic, are much
more numerous (Map II). The period began towards the end of the
Riss-Würm Interglacial (see p. 7). and terimated by the end of the
first stage of the Valdai glaciation (Table 1).

   Very severe climatic conditions prevailed during the Valdai glaciation despite its relatively small extent, and these greatly affected the
fauna and flora of the whole country. Close to the forefront of the

glacier extended the tundra belt with its very poor vegetation; further south was the cold steppe, with islands of northern forest. Polar fauna lived within the whole ice-free territory, including reindeer, musk-ox, bison, Saiga antelope, Przewalski horses, wild asses, polar rodents, and birds. During most of the glaciation the large shaggy mammoth, Siberian rhinoceros and cave bear also survived, though later they became extinct. However, the adverse climate did not discourage man; several human groups of hunters lived in all ice-free parts of the country.

The tools of the Mousterian period (of flint and other varieties of stone) were thick and made by an advanced process called the flake industry. They were found in many sites, in some of which were traces of ancient encampments (Map II).

The Mousterian flint industry differed considerably from that of the Acheulian period, the change being probably due to a new wave of population having entered the country from the south, from Western Asia. In a number of sites in Transcaucasia and in the Crimea (Kiik-Koba cave (Fig. 1)), and also in the region of the Dnieper rapids (Kruglyk, Nenasytets I), some flints, transitional in form between the two industries, have been found; they undoubtedly bear witness to the assimilation of the ancient Acheulians by the newcomers.

The earliest Mousterian finds occur in the Caucasus and the Crimea, and on the northern shore of the Sea of Azov, reaching eastwards to the Lower Volga, where a very important site was investigated near Stalingrad (Volgograd), which will be discussed later. All other sites, scattered over wide areas further north, are of later date, or Late Mousterian. They do not cross, however, the 49th parallel of latitude. The northermost site so far recorded was investigated at Peshchernyi Log near the town of Perm on the Kama. A distance of over 800 miles as the crow flies separates it from the site near Stalingrad (nos. 1 and 33 on Map II); its latitude corresponds with that of the Orkneys.

The Early Mousterian sites have been dated to the last interglacial, and the Late Mousterian finds to the early stage of the last glaciation, which seems to correspond with the first of its three stages distinguished in Central Europe. However, some scholars (P.P. Efimenko, and V.I. Gromov) erroneously place the Mousterian Age at the end of the Mindel-Riss Interglacial and the early stage of the Riss (Dnieper-Volga) glaciation.

The Mousterians do not seem to have led a purely migratory life. In the south—on the Black Sea coast of Transcaucasia, in the Crimean mountains and in some other regions—they took refuge in caves during the very severe winters of that time. Traces have been found of the seasonal occupation of these caves, probably by many successive generations. Further north, where no caves exist, large encampments of a semi-permanent character were set up, some of which have been uncovered. One of these investigated was at Sukhaya Mechetka on the Volga, near Stalingrad (Volgograd; no. 33 on Map II). It extended over quite a large area in which were found traces of shanties built of poles, and undoubtedly covered by hides originally. Numerous flint tools and chips, and broken animal bones —chiefly of aurochs, but also of mammoth and other species—lay around. Of particular importance was the geological position of these remains, which lay 65 feet below the surface, having been covered by a thick deposit laid down when the area was inundated by the Caspian Sea. As this event can be dated to the Valdai glaciation, the encampment must have been in existence before the glaciation.[3]

Another important Mousterian encampment was found at Moldova on the Dniester (west of no. 6, just outside the area of Map II) in North Bessarabia by A.P. Chernysh. Traces of a hut were uncovered there, the earliest known dwelling built by man in east Europe. It was twenty-three feet wide, thirty-three feet long, and mammoth bones, similar to those of the Upper Palaeolithic described later, were used in its construction. The Upper Palaeolithic huts evidently continued the old tradition established in the Mousterian period. The huge quantity of flints found in the remains of the hut implies a long occupation, and stone pestles suggest that the inhabitants must have supplemented their diet by gathering roots and the seeds of wild grasses.[4]

The Mousterians were hunters whose prey varied according to local conditions and seasons. In the Transcaucasian caves the cave-bear was hunted. On the northern side of the Caucasus, at Ilskaya (no. 16 on Map II) in the Kuban country, 60 per cent of the bones belonged to aurochs, representing over 2,400 individual animals killed. In the Crimean caves situated close to the steppe border, bones of Saiga antelope, wild horses and asses predominated.

The study of the Mousterian remains shows that man had adapted himself to the severe climate of the first stage of the last glaciation. The relatively large encampments, and the large number of animal bones found in the layers of occupation, indicate that he lived in groups, bound together by some kind of social structure. Graves also suggest that he believed in an after-life. In the Kiik-Koba cave in the Crimea, mentioned previously, the dead body was placed in a special cavity beaten into the rocky bottom of the cave.

The study of the implements of the successive superimposed layers of occupation found in a number of caves, especially in the Crimea, revealed some minor changes in the character and type of their tools, and four subsequent stages in the evolution of the Mousterian culture in that area have been established.

The Mousterians were of the Neanderthal racial type, and were not natives of Eastern Europe. They must have come from somewhere in Western Asia, pushing northwards through Transcaucasia. Minor differences noted in the Mousterian flint industry suggest the existence of a regional tribal division, which is well illustrated in Map II. A marked difference exhibited by the Podolian-Bessarabian remains seems to indicate that this region probably belonged to the Central European Mousterian province.

THE UPPER PALAEOLITHIC

At the close of the first stage of the last (Würm-Valdai) glaciation a new type of flint tool appeared. Some scholars maintain that this change had already occurred early in the interstadial. According to Carbon-14 dating, the change took place about 40,000 years ago in Western and Central Europe, and at the same time in Eastern Europe; it marks the beginning of the Upper Palaeolithic, a new era in the archaeological scheme (Table 1). Some authorities put the end of the Mousterian period and the beginning of the Upper Palaeolithic at about 70,000 B.P. The Mousterian flake industry disappeared, and its thick, rather clumsy tools were replaced by new tools in which the working of flint reached a high level. Elongated thin blades were struck off from one end of the conical flint core, and a variety of small and handy tools were made from these: knives, spearheads, scrapers, burins, etc. Some of these served for working wooden, bone or deer-antler tools; composite implements appear consisting of a flint edge set in a wooden or bone handle. There was likewise a fundamental change in the racial stock of the population, the primitive Mousterian Neanderthalers being replaced by people of the *Homo sapiens* species, considerably advanced in development. The Upper Palaeolithic men hardly differ from modern people; they were obviously direct ancestors of the people of our own time (Pl. II). A few groups of the Mousterians, who managed to survive the first stage of the glaciation, lived only in a few restricted areas and disappeared finally during the first interstadial.

The break between the Mousterian (Middle) and Upper Palaeolithic was clear-cut in most countries of Europe. It is generally supposed to have been caused by the influx of a new wave of hunters of a more evolved physical type, equipped with a fine advanced flint industry. Their origin is sought[5] in Western Asia, where the species had developed from an earlier, more primitive stage. They probably travelled north-westwards along the sea-shores and main rivers, through the Balkans into Europe. At the time of their advance the mild climate of the interstadial period was just beginning. The earlier population, the Mousterians, was not annihilated but gradually assimilated by the newcomers.

Most Soviet scholars hold a different view. They maintain that the change in physical appearance, and the difference between the flint industries of the Middle and Upper Palaeolithic, were the outcome of a progressive development, bolstered by the change in environmental conditions on the one hand and by social evolution on the other. This evolution was a gradual process lasting for several millennia. In support of their theories of the local evolution of the Upper Palaeolithic man, they cite the Neanderthal skull from the cave at Starosele in the Crimea, which shows some features proper to the Upper Palaeolithic racial type.

The presence of these features, however, might have been due to the hybridization of the two races. The same applies to the survival of the Mousterian type of tool in Upper Palaeolithic sites and to the adoption of the Mousterian type of huts mentioned previously. They attest to the absorption of the old population by the newcomers. The Mousterian substratum is reflected especially in the Upper Palaeolithic remains of the region of the Dnieper rapids. Furthermore, some Soviet scholars (for example, S.N. Bibikov) emphasize that in the Ukraine the connection between the Mousterian and the Upper Palaeolithic culture is hard to discern; it can be noticed only in the Crimea. On the other hand, tangible links associate the east European Upper Palaeolithic with the Upper Palaeolithic of Central Europe, and point to the origin of the Eastern hunters of that age.

The rise of the Upper Palaeolithic cultures of east Europe was clearly due to the arrival of new groups of people. They entered the country from the south-west, and this accounts for the ties binding their industry to that of the countries of Central and Western Europe. The archaeological material suggests that the Upper Palaeolithic population of Eastern Europe was not uniform, and must have consisted of several distinct tribes using different techniques in working their flint tools. The assimilation of the Mousterian survivors and also an admixture of new southern elements were probably responsible for the differentiation.

It seems, however, that the influx of southern immigrants advancing along the old-established route through the Caucasus was very restricted. The route was then closed by the Caspian Sea; its level was at that time about 160 feet higher than its present one, and a wide channel formed by the submerged valley of the Manych connected it with the Sea of Azov (Map III). The many Transcaucasian sites—mainly in west Georgia, plus a small group in the north-west

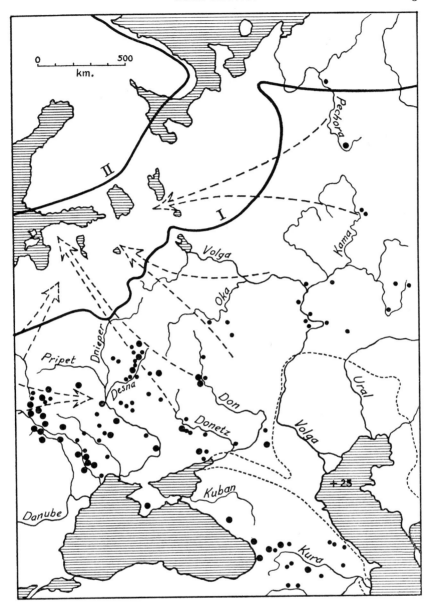

MAP III The main Upper Palaeolithic sites in Eastern Europe.
(I) Southern reach of the Valdai Glaciation; (II) South-Eastern reach of
the Fennoscandian Glacier.
Large points denote concentrations of sites; arrows denote migrations of
Upper Palaeolithic hunters in the areas freed of the ice-cover; the dotted
area round the Caspian Sea denotes the territory submerged at the late
Quaternary period, when the level of the Caspian Sea was 82 feet higher
than at present (25m).

Caucasus—and also the highland sites of the south Crimea, have features that link them with those of the Mediterranean and Caspian Upper Palaeolithic, and distinguish them from other east European sites. They evidently belonged to a distinct province of the Upper Palaeolithic.

In spite of the severe climate the density of the population in the areas further north had evidently increased, as suggested by the number of Upper Palaeolithic sites, well over two hundred of which have been recorded. They were diffused mainly in the south and south-west of Eastern Europe, as shown on Map III, which is based on the work by N.A. Beregovaya. There are a few gaps in their distribution, especially between the Don and the Volga, which are due mainly to insufficient investigation of these areas. The sites were distant from the glacier, and in the north-east, in the regions which were outside the reach of the Valdai glacier, they stretch far to the north along the Urals.

The sites form a number of concentrations, evidently in regions offering the most favourable conditions for Upper Palaeolithic man (Map III); they appear in regions that had been preferred by the Mousterians (Map II). One such site existed in the Crimean mountains, where the lowest Upper Palaeolithic layer of occupation of cave Siuren I revealed that the Mousterian culture became extinct gradually. Another concentration, on the Middle Dniester, is perhaps the most characteristic. In this area many sites have been uncovered whose several superimposed Palaeolithic layers illustrate remarkably well the gradual evolution of the culture of the local Palaeolithic hunters and the sequence of their changing flint industry.

Other larger concentrations have been discovered on the Middle Dnieper and its tributaries; in the region of the rapids of the Dnieper; in the area of Novgorod Severskii on the Middle Desna, which includes several famous sites like those of Mezin, Pushkari, Timonovka, etc.; on the Middle Donetz; on the Middle Don near Voronezh—the Kostienki-Borshevo group—with a series of well known sites, about twenty in all; and, finally, in the Southern Urals. All these groups represent different but kindred tribes.

In recent years investigations have revealed that the Upper Palaeolithic man advanced far to the north along the western slopes of the Ural mountains. Several sites have been discovered east of Perm, in caves of the Middle Urals, and traces of an encampment with quadrangular dwellings have been investigated on the Chusovaya close to its junction with the Kama; the site had been formerly visited by the Mousterians. Further north at least thirty sites have been found along the river Pechora and its tributaries by B.I. Guslitzer, V.I. Kanivets and E.M. Tymofeev. They were all in caves, among which was the

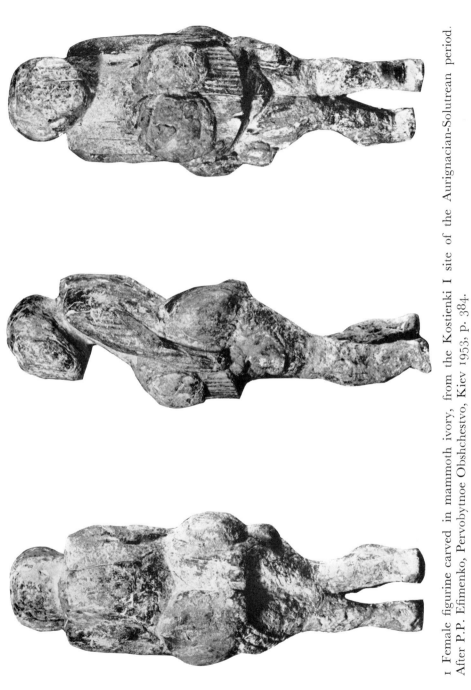

1 Female figurine carved in mammoth ivory, from the Kostienki I site of the Aurignacian-Solutrean period. After P.P. Efimenko, Pervobytnoe Obshchestvo, Kiev 1953, p. 384.

II Man of the Crô-Magnon racial type, from the Magdalenian grave
(Upper Palaeolithic) at Kostienki II. Reconstructed by M.M.
Gerasimov, *Liudy Kamennogo Veka*, Moscow 1964, pl. xiv.

III Grave chamber built of mammoth bones and skulls uncovered at the
Kostienki II site, of the Magdalenian period.
After M.M. Gerasimov (as pl. i, p. 152.).

IV *Upper:* Position of the early Upper Palaeolithic grave at the Markina Gora site (Kostienki XIV). *Below:* View of its tightly contracted skeleton of the Negroidal racial type.
After M.M. Gerasimov (as pl. I, p. 123.).

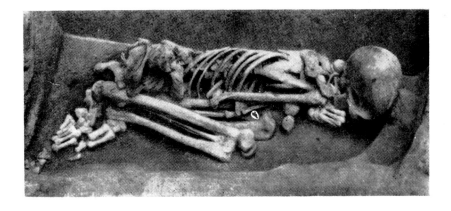

vi Young woman from the double grave in the cave of Murzak-Koba in the Crimea. Reconstructed by M.M. Gerasimov (as pl. i, pl. xvi.).

v Man of the Mesolithic Age from the double burial in the cave of Murzak-Koba in the Crimea. Reconstructed by M.M. Gerasimov (as pl. i, p. 167.).

'Bear' cave (Medvezha) on the Upper Pechora, where traces of a hearth and thousands of broken bones of the cold fauna typical of the Upper Palaeolithic were found; also among these were bones of the Saiga antelope, common in the steppe country but rarely found in the north.

The northernmost site so far recorded was that investigated at Byzovaya, on a terrace on the right bank of the river Pechora, north of the town of Pechora and north of latitude 65°. Remains of a hut built of mammoth bones were uncovered. A large quantity of mammoth bones lay over the whole area of the encampment, and those of a reindeer and a white bear. Implements were mostly of flint, a few of slate. According to V.I. Kanivets, who investigated the site, the flint industry bears some resemblance to that of the fifth layer of Kostienki I on the Don, and may accordingly be considered as of the Aurignacian-Solutrean age.

The east European Upper Palaeolithic tribes must have crossed the Urals and entered Siberia. The flint industry of west Siberia, reaching up to the valley of the Yenissey, was closely related to that of Eastern Europe but exhibits nevertheless a distinct character of its own. According to A.P. Okladnikov, contributions by the east European tribes were decisive for the formation of the west Siberian Palaeolithic, among the best known sites of which are those of Malta and Bireti. The territory east of the Yenissey already constituted a part of the east Siberian/Chinese province of the Upper Palaeolithic.

Concentrations of Upper Palaeolithic sites appear in areas which could best accommodate life in the glacial period; sites were placed mainly on the edge of valleys that provided shelter against cold winds, and close to hunting grounds and to outcrops of flint. In the Crimea, Transcaucasia, and the Southern Urals, rock-shelters and caves were occupied. Where no caves existed, semi-permanent winter camps were established with ingenious huts sunk about three feet into the ground.

Over forty Upper Palaeolithic huts have been uncovered in the south of Eastern Europe, usually marked by an accumulation of large mammoth bones and tusks. The vertical position of large bones shows that they originally formed part of the structure of huts, serving as poles in the then treeless country. The huts were either round or oval in plan, conical in shape and presumably covered by skins. The lowest part of the wall of skins was strengthened by mammoth skulls and other heavy bones, one end of which was sunk into the ground (Fig. 2). Reindeer antlers and mammoth tusks were laid on the upper part of the hut-cover to prevent the skins being torn by winds. Towards the end of the glacial period, when the climate grew warmer, rods and poles were used in their construction. Huts had one or more

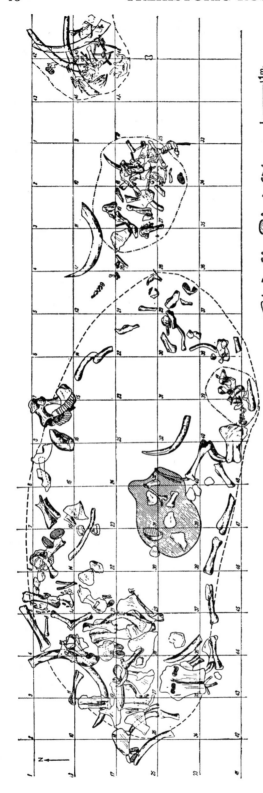

FIG. 2 Plan of an Upper Palaeolithic (Solutrean) hut at Berdysh on the Sozh in Byelorussia, built on a paling of mammoth tusks. After V. D. Budko (KSIAM No. 101, p. 32, fig. 7).

hearths, either in the centre or along the axis. Larger encampments consisted of several huts which were sometimes adjacent, and also lighter huts of shanty type, which were probably summer dwellings. Encampments covered an area of six to ten acres (for example, Timonovka, Pushkari I, Pogon). Superimposed layers of occupation uncovered in many sites, especially on the Middle Dniester and the Middle Don, imply that by the end of the Palaeolithic there was a semi-settled way of life and a preference for keeping to well known regions.

The results of excavation at the Moldova V site on the Dniester in Northern Bessarabia, already referred to in the preceding section, are of special interest. Remains of three huts were uncovered at various levels of this stratified site, all of them belonging to various stages of the Late Upper Palaeolithic period (the Magdalenian period). The first of these, belonging to the final stage of the period, found in Layer 2, was marked by an accumulation of 275 reindeer antlers. The second one, in Layer 3 (Fig. 3), was about one foot deeper; around it, at various distances, were scattered traces of sixteen camp-fires and of temporary shanty-like constructions. Still deeper, in Layer 6 of the Early Magdalenian period, remains of the third dwelling of a semi-permanent character were discovered. All huts were of nearly the same size and construction, and were of the same type as those uncovered in the Upper Palaeolithic sites on the Upper Don (for example, Gagarino), or on the Desna (for example, Mezin).

Tools were made of flint, stone or bone. Some were household utensils, for cutting meat and hides, for sewing garments of skins like awls and needles; others were connected with hunting. Large mammoth shoulder-blades served as shovels for digging pit-dwellings and traps.

The Upper Palaeolithic men of Eastern Europe led a semi-settled life, probably in tribes. Their social organization must have been strong enough to keep them together, and to arrange hunts for big game. Their whole life centred around these huts. Bones of animals typical of the cold climate of the last glaciation—reindeer, aurochs, bison, wild horses, and above all the mammoth—were found in large quantities in the kitchen refuse of the encampments. At Amvrosievka in the south of the Ukraine, over one thousand bison were killed, and bones found in the lower layer of the site of Kiev-Kirillovskaya accounted for sixty-seven mammoths. Hunting must have been a collective enterprise, the animals being run into mud, or driven into pitfalls, or over precipices. Fire was undoubtedly used for this purpose. Excavations reveal that often whole herds of animals were trapped and killed. Roots and wild fruits supplemented the diet.

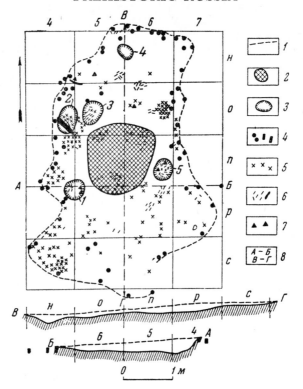

FIG. 3 *Upper:* Plan of a Late Magdalenian hut at Moldova V, layer 3.
Lower: A reconstructed view of the camp.
After A. P. Chernysh (*Pozdnii Paleolit Srednego Pridnestrovia.* Moscow 1959,
p. 99, figs. 48, 49).

Several sites of the latest period (the Magdalenian period) yielded figurines, which were chiefly female (Pl. I) but also included those of various animals, carved in ivory (mammoth tusks) or bone. Ethnographic parallels among recent primitive peoples suggest that they served some magic purpose. This was undoubtedly also true of the animal figures engraved on bone plaques, and of the paintings in red ochre of mammoths, horses, and rhinoceroses found in the Kapova cave on the river Belaya in the Southern Urals. The decoration of a few female figurines gives details of dress. Similar objects were likewise found in Upper Palaeolithic sites in Central and Western Europe. In a few cases, traces of a mammoth cult, or some kind of magic ceremony, are discernible, for example, at Eliseevichi, where an accumulation of thirty mammoth skulls was uncovered.

A few Upper Palaeolithic graves were excavated in various parts of the U.S.S.R. Skeletons in a hunched-up position and sprinkled with ochre were unearthed, and suggest that belief in the after-life was common. Anthropological study of their bones revealed that the Upper Palaeolithic men were all of the *Homo sapiens* species, mostly of the Crô-Magnon type. Among these was a man aged about fifty, from a grave of unique construction, uncovered at the site of Kostienki II on the Don, of the Magdalenian period (Pl. II). The grave, which adjoined a hut of the common Upper Palaeolithic type, consisted of a chamber built of mammoth bones and skulls (Pl. III), with a floor strewn with yellow sand. The skeleton was sitting, facing south, with knees hunched up. No grave goods were found near it. Of a different, Negroid type, was a tightly contracted male skeleton from the Kostienki XIV site (Markina Gora), of an early stage of the Upper Palaeolithic (Pl. IV).

The picture of Upper Palaeolithic man that emerges from the descriptions above—their way of life, dress, personal ornaments of bone and ivory, their huts and encampments—suggests that they were similar to the modern Arctic hunting tribes.

STAGES IN EVOLUTION AND CHRONOLOGY

It has already been mentioned that, according to Carbon-14 datings, the Upper Palaeolithic period began about 40,000 years ago and lasted until about 10,000–8000 B.C. During the 30,000 years of this period many climatic fluctuations took place, and consequently the natural conditions in which the man of that time had to live also underwent considerable changes. During that tremendous span there was ample time for the progress and evolution of man's culture, and many occasions for tribal movements over the wastes of Eastern Europe. However, only a few hundred sites have been recorded and their theoretical ratio throughout the entire country is less than one

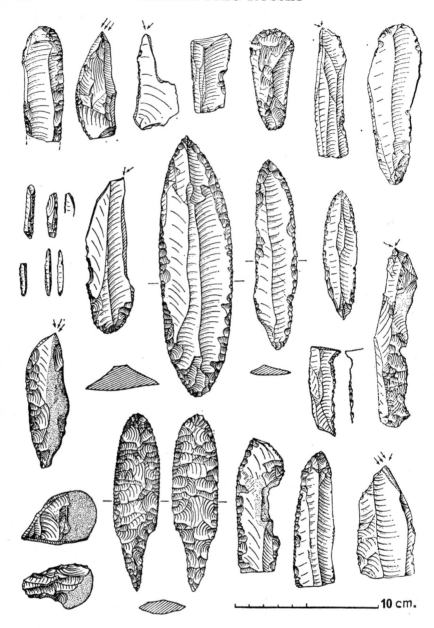

FIG. 4 Flints from the Early Solutrean layer 10 of the Moldova V site. After A. P. Chernysh (as fig. 3, p. 71, fig. 33).

site for every one hundred years of the Upper Palaeolithic. It is understandable that in these circumstances no proper synthesis can be expected of the changes in the Upper Palaeolithic, and that even the date and classification of related finds in different parts of the country are disputable.

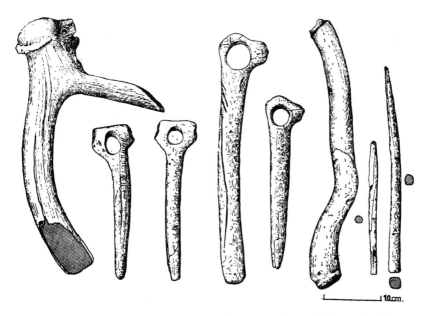

FIG. 5 Implements made of antler and mammoth tusks from the Upper Solutrean layer 7 of the Moldova V site.
After A.P. Chernysh (as fig. 3, p. 82, fig. 39).

Stratified sites with several superimposed layers of occupation, investigated in various parts of the country, give the opportunity of establishing the local sequence of cultures and flint industries. But the differences between these, due to the somewhat different ecological conditions in regions lying hundreds of miles apart, do not facilitate the establishment of an universally acceptable chronological scheme.

The scheme devised by P.P. Efimenko distinguishes six consecutive periods in the development of the Upper Palaeolithic, beginning with the Riss-Würm Interglacial. On the other hand, P.I. Boriskovskii lays down seven periods (Table 1), naming them after the main sites attributable to these periods. An attempt in 1961 by a group of Soviet geologists to attribute the earliest Upper Palaeolithic sites to the Last Interglacial (LIG 1), and not to the Würm-Valdai Interstadial (LG l_{1-2}), does not seem convincing.

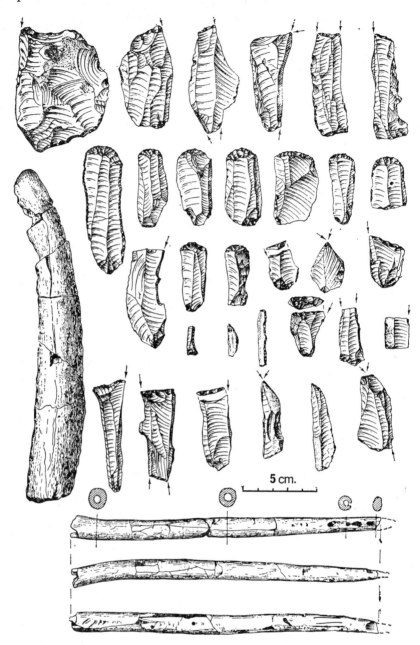

FIG. 6 Flint and antler tools from the Magdalenian layer 4 of the Moldova V site.
After A. P. Chernysh (as fig. 3, p. 95, fig. 45).

The western terminology of the Upper Palaeolithic periods—the Aurignacian, Solutrean and Magdalenian—has been commonly applied by Soviet authors. However, the respective cultures differ in many respects from those in the west, and Aurignacian-type industry is almost non-existent in Eastern Europe. Accordingly, in current usage, only two periods have been distinguished, called the 'Aurignacian-Solutrean' and the 'Magdalenian', although their flint industries, especially that of the 'Magdalenian' type, differ from those of the standard sites of Western Europe. A good example is shown in the results obtained by A.P. Chernysh at Moldova V, mentioned previously. Twelve superimposed layers of occupation have been uncovered: the earliest (Layers 11 and 12) were of Mousterian period; they were overlaid by four 'Aurignacian-Solutrean' strata (Layers 7–10, Figs. 4 and 5), and five of the 'Magdalenian' period (Layers 2–6, Figs. 3 and 6); the top layer (Layer 1) was early Mesolithic. The Carbon-14 date of Layer 7 (at a depth of eleven feet six inches) is 23,000 ±800 B.P. (Mo. 11). The layer is considered to equate with the west European late Solutrean.[5]

In some of the sites investigated, such as Kostienki IV (Alexandrovskaya), remains proper to the Magdalenian period (according to Western designation) lay in the reverse sequence to that in the west, under a layer where the findings were characteristic of the Solutrean period. Some scholars are of the opinion that a sequence of this kind need not always signify the start of a new period in the evolution of the Upper Palaeolithic; it might have been caused by the successive occupations of the same area or site by different tribes who roamed the country during the same period.

The time of the Pleistocene, however, was running out. The glacier gradually retreated northwards, and a chain of moraines south of the Baltic coast—the Pomeranian Glacier—mark its last halting-place on the European mainland. The next step in its retreat began at about 13,000 B.C. and its final stage—the Fennoscandian Glacier, which covered Middle Sweden and part of Finland—ended at about 8000 B.C. (Map III). This phenomenon is considered to mark the end of the Pleistocene and the beginning of the Holocene, the present geological period. The halts of the retreating glacier were the outcome of the change of the late Pleistocene climate, which alternated between milder and cooler phases. The cold phase of the Pomeranian Glacier stage was followed by the milder phase of the Alleröd stage (from about 10,000 to 8800 B.C.). Then came the final cooler phase, called Drias III (from about 8800 to 8000 B.C.), after which the Holocene began (Table 2).

In archaeology, the beginning of the Holocene has been commonly accepted as the termination of the Palaeolithic, after which began

4

the new era, the Mesolithic. In Soviet archaeological literature, however, the end of the Upper Palaeolithic is usually placed at about 10,000 B.C. to exclude all the final Palaeolithic cultures and to include them in the Mesolithic. Carbon-14 dates for the deposits of the earliest Holocene have been given as 13,130 B.C. (RUL-161) at the site of Zvenigorod near Moscow, 10,930 B.C. (RUL-168) at the site of Gremyachee near Kaluga, and 10,850 B.C. (RUL-205) at the site of Debolovskoe near Yaroslav. The term 'Mesolithic' seldom appeared in the literature until recently. A different terminology, and also a different chronology of the relative periods, were used instead. The name of 'Epi-Palaeolithic' has been given to the period that corresponded with the final stages of the Pleistocene, and the cultures of that period have been called 'Epi-Palaeolithic'. The subsequent period, the Mesolithic of the early Holocene of Western terminology, has been called the 'Early Neolithic'. It is only in recent literature that the term 'Mesolithic' has been used in the west European sense.

The 'Epi-Palaeolithic' cultures differ in many respects from the true Upper Palaeolithic cultures of the same region, and were evidently transitional to the Mesolithic. They developed in different climatic conditions. Ecological and climatic conditions also varied with different geographical latitudes. One example is that the late Pleistocene cultures of the Crimea and the Caucasus are regarded as Mesolithic. A mild climate must have prevailed for some time in these regions; for the centre of the Crimea lies 900 miles south-east of the nearest Pomeranian moraines, and over 1,100 miles south of the Fennoscandian moraines in Finland.

With the transformation of the climate and vegetation, the fauna also underwent a considerable change. This is well reflected in the remains found in a number of stratified sites in the southern part of the country—at Siuren and other Crimean caves, at Kamiana Mohyla north of Melitopol, Osokorivka in the region of the Dnieper rapids, and Vladimirovka on the Siniukha, a tributary of the Boh (Southern Bug). In the lowest, Upper Palaeolithic layers of occupation of these sites the bones of mammoths were discovered, but they do not appear in the superimposed strata; no bones of reindeer or other species typical of the cold, or cool, climate were found in the upper layers. These animals must have migrated northwards or north-eastwards, and bison, wild horses and the contemporary fauna took their place.

Man followed the retreating animals. A wide strip of land south of the retreating glacier was peopled by tribes moving up from the south. Their gradual movement northward is well attested by the close association of the flint industry of several sites in the basin of the Upper Dnieper—Podluzhie III and the lowest horizon of Grensk (both near Gomel)—with that of the Kostienki-Borshevo sites on the Don; these similarities seem to point to the original country of the Late Upper Palaeolithic hunters of the region around Gomel Map III). But at the same time, the flint industry of the western (regions of the east European forest zone, which did not differ from that of the Late Swiderian culture of Poland, suggests that larger groups of Late Upper Palaeolithic hunters must have arrived there from the west. According to the chronology established in Poland, finds of this type belong to the final stage of the Pleistocene; but in the Soviet literature they are considered as Mesolithic. Recently published Carbon-14 date of the lower occupation layer of site Grensk is 18,620 B.C. (LE–450).

Man had to adapt himself and his way of life to the new ecological conditions with considerable change to his material culture. These changes jointly mark the beginning of the new age, the Mesolithic.

THE MESOLITHIC

The term 'Mesolithic', the Middle Stone Age, denotes the post-glacial—post-Palaeolithic—Era; it preceded the 'Neolithic'—the New, or Late, Stone Age—whose beginning marked fundamental changes in the economy and life of primitive man.

The growing warm climate, which caused the glacier to retreat and disappear, underwent further changes in the post-glacial Era, the Holocene. At first, a relatively cool 'Pre-Boreal' climate prevailed for 600 to 700 years and was followed by a hot and dry continental or 'Boreal' climate, which lasted for nearly two thousand years. A further evolution took place by the middle of the sixth millennium, when the warm but damp 'Atlantic' climate set in, and that lasted until about the end of the fourth millennium B.C.

At the same time important changes took place in the water level of the Baltic and the White Seas, and of the lakes in the northern part of the country. The Baltic Ice-Lake of the time of the Fennoscandian glacier became the 'Yoldia' sea, a cold sea, during the retreat of the glacier. The next stage was the 'Ancylus' lake, which corresponded with the period of warm Boreal climate; finally, the warm 'Litorina' sea developed through the isostatic rise of Fennoscandia, which coincided with the Atlantic climate.

The north-western part of Eastern Europe, freed from the ice sheet, was soon covered with tundra vegetation. Under the impact of the warm climate the tundra retreated (as in other areas of the northern part of the country) before the advancing coniferous forest, which, in the central zone, in turn, gave ground to mixed deciduous and coniferous forests. In the south a rich grassland at first developed but deteriorated as soon as the climate became drier. The very hot and dry Boreal climate, advantageous to the northern areas, must have been disastrous for life in the south, large parts of which often suffer from drought even during the present temperate climate. At the peak of the Boreal period the wide steppe belt must have been a semi-desert. No suitable conditions for the growth of virgin forest ever prevailed there. In the early post-glacial period only the valleys of the large rivers were afforested. The position there changed later with the spread of the Atlantic climate, when the forest began to encroach upon the steppe.

Ecological conditions differed considerably in various parts of Eastern Europe during the Mesolithic. The growing warm climate of the final Pleistocene forced large tribal units, characteristic of the Upper Palaeolithic, to break up and migrate northwards in the wake of those retreating animals adapted to live in a cool climate. The central and northern parts of Eastern Europe, with their forests teeming with game, and rivers and lakes with fish, offered comfortable conditions for these peoples. Traces of their northern migration have been noted in the remains of some regions of the forest zone (Map III).

In the meantime, conditions in the south, within the present steppe belt, greatly deteriorated. The advent of the dry and hot Boreal climate gradually turned the country into a semi-desert, and thus compelled the tribes that did not migrate northwards to move into the river valleys. There they kept to the lowest river terraces, or lived on river islands. They hunted small game, but depended chiefly on fishing and gathering molluscs, snails, edible roots and berries. It is only in some restricted areas that living conditions allowed the Palaeolithic hunters to survive into the subsequent Era, the Mesolithic, and to retain their ancient culture almost unmodified. One area was in the Caucasus, another one in the Crimean mountains,

---

MAP IV *(Opposite)* Late Mesolithic provinces and important sites in Eastern Europe (based on maps by O. N. Bahder, G. M. Burov, A. A. Formozov, L. Jaanits, V. P. Levenok, H. Moora, D. Ia. Telegin).
(I) Suomusjärvi culture; (II) Kunda culture; (III) Swiderian culture; (IV) the 'Western province'; (V) the area of the 'Small tranchet'; (VI) Podolian province; (VII) 'Donetz-Volhynian' culture; (VIII) Pontic province, Dnieper-Crimean branch; (IX) Pontic province, Crimean Highland branch; (X) Pontic province, Caucasian group; (XI) Central Russian province; (XII) East Russian (Kama-Ural) province; (XIII) sites on the Usa; (XIV) the area of the 'Arctic Palaeolithic'.
(A) Extension of the Kunda culture; (B) the northern border of the Tardenoisian industry (after V. P. Levenok); (C) Caucasian and Volga-Kama connections.
Asterisks: sites with Swiderian elements; *Crosses*: Epi-Palaeolithic sites mentioned in the text; *Squares*: Kunda finds outside their proper territory; *Points*: Late Mesolithic sites quoted, and *(circles)* not quoted, in the text.

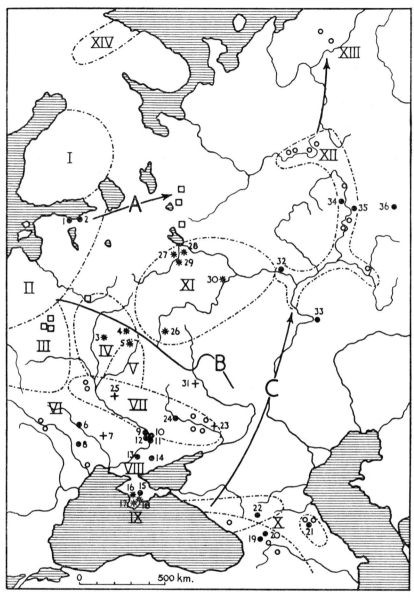

SITES: (1) Kunda; (2) Narva; (3) Grensk; (4) Pishchanyi Riv (Pesochnyi Rov); (5) Smyachka; (6) Zankivtsi; (7) Vladimirovka; (8) Rezina; (9) Kizlevyi Island; (10) Vasylivka; (11) Osokorivka; (12) Voloske; (13) Kaury; (14) Kamyana Mohyla; (15) Kukrek; (16) Siuren; (17) Murzak-Koba; (18) Shan-Koba; (19) Pogrebennaya; (20) Gvardzhilas-Klde; (21) Chokh; (22) Sosruko; (23) Rogalik; (24) Mesolithic sites near Izium; (25) Zhurovka; (26) Gremyachee; (27) Sobolevo; (28) Skniatino; (29) Zolotoruchie; (30) Elin-Bor; (31) Borshevo; (32) Russo-Lugovskaya; (33) Kuibyshev-Postnikov Ovrag; (34) Pogurdino; (35) Nizhnee Adishchevo; (36) Shigir.

and there are other probable areas in Podolia and the South Urals.

There was a marked difference between the Mesolithic archaeological material and that of the late stages of the Upper Palaeolithic, including the Epi-Palaeolithic, especially in the central and northern parts of Eastern Europe, where owing to the entirely different natural conditions, the material culture of the descendants of the Palaeolithic hunters must have undergone considerable changes. In the south of the country, as mentioned previously, the Late Palaeolithic traditions survived longer.

Mesolithic remains are not uniform throughout the whole country. Six main Mesolithic provinces may be distinguished (Map IV), some of which, especially in the south, were subdivided into smaller areas. The cultures of each of these provinces evolved in their own way, with their own problems. The provinces, which will be briefly reviewed later, were the Pontic province in the south; the Podolian; the 'Western' of the forest zone and the east Baltic in the west; the Central Russian in the centre of the country; and the east Russian or Kama-Ural province in the east. The people of some of the regional groups were related to, and successors of their Upper Palaeolithic predecessors in the area, but some, especially in the north, in the lands which during the Palaeolithic were under the ice-sheet, had no roots in the past of the region.

A characteristic feature of the Mesolithic which was already apparent by the end of the Palaeolithic was the diminution in size of flint tools. This tendency reached its peak during the Late Mesolithic, the 'Tardenoisian' period (Fig. 8). Bone or wooden tools and weapons came into common use; many of these were either provided with inlaid microlithic flint blades or flint tips. The universal weapon was now the bow with flint-tipped arrows, and bone harpoons, sometimes flint-barbed, were used for fishing. A new invention was the axe, an indispensable tool for the forest dwellers, and very useful for the inhabitants of the afforested river valleys. Another new feature was the domestication of the dog.

During the five odd millennia of the Mesolithic Era, the rate of change in material equipment differed throughout the country, especially in its western division. In some areas subsequent periods in local evolution have been distinguished and equated with those established in North-Western and Central Europe. The correlation of these periods often meets with difficulties. Nevertheless, an attempt has been made in Table 2 to present a chronological scheme of the Mesolithic development within the whole country. At the present stage of research this scheme is incomplete and liable to alterations.

The Mesolithic development within Eastern Europe has been divided here into three main periods. The earliest of these, the

'Epi-Palaeolithic', is distinguishable only in some parts of the country; in fact, it was the final stage of the Upper Palaeolithic development (Fig. 7). In the south, in the Caucasus and the Crimea, the Azilian kind of flint industry was characteristic of this period. This was the very end of the Pleistocene—the Alleröd stage with its somewhat warmer climate, and the final cold phase of the Upper Drias (Drias III).

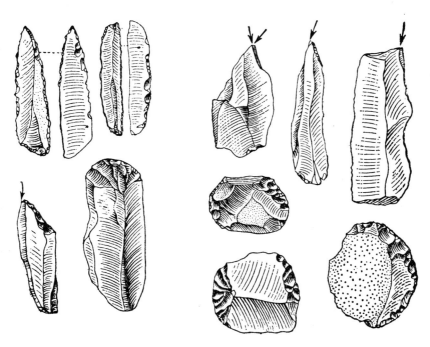

FIG. 7 Final Palaeolithic flint tools from the upper horizon of site Borshevo II.
After P. P. Efimenko (*Pervobytnoe Obshchestvo*, 1953, p. 613, figs. 311, 312).

Clearly discernible in the remains of almost the whole territory are also two other periods, called the Early and the Late Mesolithic. The beginning of the first of these may be put at the end of the ninth millennium B.C.; it approximately covered the whole period of the Pre-Boreal and Boreal climate. It was marked by the spread of the Swiderian, or Swiderian-type, flint industry, named after a final Palaeolithic site in Poland. However, according to Polish archaeologists[7], the east European 'Swiderian' industry differs considerably from the genuine one by its different flint technique, and also by the fact that only a few of its implements (such as arrow-points; Fig. 8

top row) are reminiscent of their Western Swiderian prototypes. Some west Swiderian elements might have been included among the formative factors of the industry of the east European forest zone, but the latter bears a much stronger and clearer imprint of the Siberian industry.

The Eastern 'Swiderian' industry, with its tanged arrow-heads (Fig. 8), differed considerably from that of the southern part of the country, with its typical 'Pontic' industry of Azilian character. It also differed from the Upper Palaeolithic industry of the east European forest zone (Table 1): Mezin, Pushkari on the Desna, Karachanovo on the Oka, or Gagarino on the Upper Don, etc. It evidently advanced from the west, as indicated by the age of the relative finds. It seems that its spread was partly due to reciprocal contact with neighbouring tribes, but it was mainly propagated by the eastward movement of small Swiderian groups that were subsequently absorbed by the indigenous population of the relative regions. The industry affected almost the whole western and central parts of the forest zone and influenced many other areas (Map IV). According to G.I. Matiushin, flints related in some way to the Swiderian types have been found even near Ufa (site Ilmurzino) at the foot of the Urals.

The second, 'Late Mesolithic', period coincided with the Atlantic climate. The Tardenoisian microlithic flint industry with its segmented microlithic tools (Fig. 8), introduced probably around the middle of the sixth millennium, was characteristic of this period. The industry was not uniform throughout the whole country, being of two main types. In the south, within the Pontic province, it was of southern, Mediterranean or west Asiatic type; and in the west was the Central European Tardenoisian industry. The Tardenoisian industry, whether southern or western, did not extend over the whole of Eastern Europe, being unknown in the central and northern divisions of the country; its northern limit is marked on Map IV. The Central Russian province was not affected by the Tardenoisian current; there the culture of the Early Mesolithic with its Swiderian elements continued. This area, lost to the western assemblage, was subsequently exposed to strong influences from the cultures of Eastern Russia and west Siberia.

The opinions of the scholars concerned differ as to whether the Tardenoisian industry was brought to east Europe by a new wave of western or southern immigrants, or whether it spread to the indigenous population from their kindred tribes living further to the west or south.

It has been assumed that the Late Mesolithic, and the Mesolithic Age as a whole, ended when the earliest agricultural communities

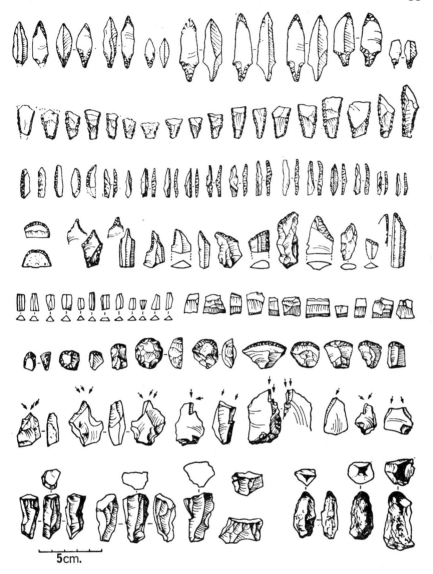

FIG. 8 Microlithic flint industry of the Late Mesolithic of the area between the Middle Dnieper and Upper Don.
After V. P. Levenok (MIA 126, 1966, p. 95, fig. 4).

appeared in the south-west of the country—by the end of the fifth millennium. However, the Mesolithic culture and the ancient mode of life continued in most parts of the country, and in some regions it survived for at least another millennium.

It has been mentioned previously that considerable differences existed in the Mesolithic cultures of the various regions of Eastern Europe and their development. These and the main topics involved will be briefly reviewed.

THE PONTIC PROVINCE

This was the largest Mesolithic province, embracing the Ukrainian steppe country, the Crimea, and also the Caucasus (Map IV). Ukrainian sites were concentrated especially in the valley of the Dnieper near the rapids, and another concentration has been recorded on the Donetz and the Lower Don. The western-most sites have been found on the Lower Dniester. Those on the Lower Don and the Manych seem to have been connected with the Northern Caucasus. The fact that the flint industry of the sites discovered as far north as the region of Perm, on the Kama in east Russia, shows some relation to that of the Pontic-Caucasian province is worthy of mention. These southern links may go back to the Upper Palaeolithic, but they might have also been due to some connections between the Urals and the region on the Kama with Soviet Central Asia, the culture of which at that period belonged similarly to the west Asiatic-Mediterranean Mesolithic assemblage.

Conditions in all the three groups of the north Pontic province were different, though three main periods in the local evolution of each have been distinguished. The flint industry of the two earlier groups shows some affinity with the Mediterranean Azilian culture, and accordingly the relative sites have been sometimes called 'Azilian'. The flint industry of the last period, the Late Mesolithic, was microlithic, of the Tardenoisian type. Most common were 'geometric' flints, chiefly 'trapeze' shaped. The Southern Tardenoisian industry, however, differs from the Central European Tardenoisian, and exhibits links with the late Mesolithic industry of Western Asia.

The Caucasus

Three distinct groups of Mesolithic remains have been distinguished in the Caucasus by O.N. Bahder. The largest of these, the Georgian group in Transcaucasia, consisted of twelve sites, including the caves of Pogrebennaya and Gvardzhilas-Klde; it was the northern extension of the west Asiatic Mesolithic. Only a few sites belonged to the second group—in Dagestan in the north-east Caucasus—called the Chokh group after the respective site; the group was closely related to that of the north-west Caucasus. A representative site of the latter, the third Caucasian group, was the rock-shelter of Gubskii-Naves. Another important site was the cave of Sosruko in Kabarda, with its superimposed occupation-layers. Two upper ones, M 1 and M 2 (Table 2), yielded flint tools of the Tardenoisian type, and represent two stages of the later part of the Mesolithic. The lower layers, M 3 and M 5, of the 'Azilian' type, belonged to the Early Mesolithic. The culture of all layers shows close relations with Crimean sites. Table 7 shows examples of the flint-industry characteristic of the subsequent stages in the local development in the three regions mentioned above.

The Crimea

The Mesolithic of the Crimea, like that of the Caucasus, had no connection with the Upper Palaeolithic cultures; no flint industries of the Aurignacian, Solutrean, or Magdalenian type reached there. The origin of the Crimean Mesolithic is obscure, but its roots evidently go southwards to Transcaucasia and Western Asia.

Crimean Mesolithic has been divided into two main periods called 'Azilian' and 'Tardenoisian', each subdivided into two stages. The Azilian type of industry probably appeared there at a much earlier date than further north; the 'Azilian' stage possibly began in the final Glacial period, being at least partly 'Epi-Palaeolithic'. The Tardenoisian microlithic flint industry typical of the two stages of the Late Mesolithic may have likewise appeared there earlier than in the areas situated north of the Crimea. Crimean industry represents a southern variety different from that of the latter regions.

Over 100 Mesolithic sites have so far been recorded. They form two distinct groups—the open-air stations in the Crimean steppe country, and cave or rock-shelter sites in the mountains.

Several superimposed layers of occupation have been uncovered in the caves and rock-shelters. The 'Upper Azilian' layer (the lower layer) of Shan-Koba cave was typical of the earliest Mesolithic. Bones of reindeer found alongside those of red deer imply a rather cool climate; the region was covered with coniferous forests. The period seems to correspond with the final stage of the Pleistocene (Drias III) and the beginning of the Holocene; the character of the remains was already post-Palaeolithic, and definitely Mesolithic. It partly equates the site with the early Mesolithic of the north-west Caucasus—with layers M 3 and M 5 of the site of Sosruko (Table 2).

The flint industry of the upper layer of the Shan-Koba cave was

Tardenoisian, of the Late Mesolithic age. The period has been called the 'Murzak-Koba' period, after another site of the same age. Conditions at that time were entirely different from those of the preceding 'Azilian' period; for the climate was very mild, probably Atlantic, as indicated by oak charcoal found in the remains of hearths, and bones of boars, lynxes, and stags were found.

Graves uncovered in the caves of Fatma-Koba and Murzak-Koba belonged to this period. The skeleton from Fatma-Koba, which was of the Late Mesolithic, lay in a contracted position. Its skull had Negroid features. At Murzak-Koba a double burial of a man and a woman was uncovered (Pls V, VI), both skeletons supine. They were of the Crô-Magnon racial type but the female skull was more delicate. The woman was killed on the man's grave, as indicated by a bone point found in her skull. She had had the middle fingers (Phalanges) of both hands amputated in childhood—a practice connected with some magical beliefs recorded among modern primitive tribes like the Bushmen of Africa, and noted also, in the Upper Palaeolithic of Spain, in handmarks found in the Altamira cave. Recently similar handmarks have been found by J. Mellaart on the walls of the lower layers of the settlement of Chatal-Hüyük in Anatolia, of the sixth, or even seventh, millennium B.C. and contemporary with the burial of Murzak-Koba. The handmarks in the Crimea represent another link with the Mediterranean.

The most important sites of the Crimean steppe Mesolithic were those of Kukrek, Siuren I and Siuren II. The latter two, both stratified, were in fact a rock-shelter and a cave situated on the lowest foothills of the Crimean Mountains near Simferopol. The upper layer of Siuren I and the lower layer of Siuren II were typical of the Early Mesolithic. Their flint industry differed from the 'Azilian' of the Crimean caves, and the nearest analogies may be found in the lower layers (M 3 and M 5) of the north-west Caucasian site Sosruko, already referred to. The Crimean steppe sites belonged to a larger province that extended northwards over the Ukrainian steppe country east of the Lower Dnieper and north of the Sea of Azov.

Of special importance was the Swiderian industry found in the lower layer of Siuren II. Its appearance in the Crimea must have been due to the arrival of north-western immigrants, though the route by which they travelled remains obscure; the immigrants seem to have soon been absorbed by the natives. The Swiderian flint industry of Siuren II is reminiscent of that of Witów in Poland.[8] The latter site flourished at the end of the Alleröd phase, Carbon-14 dated to about 8800 B.C. A few Swiderian forms of flint tools have also been found in the Crimean caves further south (Shan-Koba, Murzak-Koba). Skeletons of the Crô-Magnon racial type from the two

Crimean caves mentioned above, likewise point to the arrival of northern immigrants; they belonged to the racial type characteristic of the east European Palaeolithic (see p. 21).

The Lower Dnieper

The steppe part of the Crimea, as mentioned before, was only a southern extension of the larger group which, according to D.Ia. Telegin, extended from the Lower Dnieper (including the region of the rapids) to the Sea of Azov. A number of sites have been investigated in various parts of that area: one of these, at Kaury near Kakhivka on the Dnieper, was of Early Mesolithic, whereas the lowest layers of the stratified site of Kamyana Mohyla were Late Mesolithic.

The most exhaustively investigated in this group were a number of its northernmost sites in the valley of the Dnieper, near the rapids. They all lay on the lowest terraces or islands of the river, and usually had several layers of occupation. The lowest layers of some of these (for example, Osokorivka) were of the Upper Palaeolithic age, overlaid by 'Epi-Palaeolithic' or 'Azilian' layers exhibiting some Upper Palaeolithic features (Table 2). The Late Mesolithic sites, typical of the Pontic Tardenoisian, were similarly placed, several being on river islands like the Kizlevyi Ostriv. Their flint industry was microlithic and 'geometric', with characteristic long and narrow segmented blades.

Several cemeteries of the group were uncovered. They belonged to two periods. A few, considered as Epi-Palaeolithic by their investigators, seem to have been still in use in the Early Mesolithic; whereas others, called Early Neolithic, were in fact Late Mesolithic (Table 2). See also p. 82.

The earlier, the 'Epi-Palaeolithic' cemeteries, situated quite near each other, consisted of up to forty-four burials. Skeletons lay in rows in a strongly contracted position, and were sometimes strewn with ochre (Fig. 9). In the cemeteries of Vasylivka III and Voloske flint arrow-heads have been found sticking in the bones, and the tip of a spear-head was found in another skeleton.

The flint arrow-heads were evidently the cause of the death of the persons buried, and some scholars suggest that the graves bear witness to tribal struggles, the final outcome of which was the change in population of the region of the Dnieper rapids.[9] These struggles are thought to mark the beginning of the new period, the 'Early Neolithic', which in fact means the Late Mesolithic.

Cemeteries of the Late Mesolithic differed in many respects from those of the Early Mesolithic. Their burial ritual was different, all

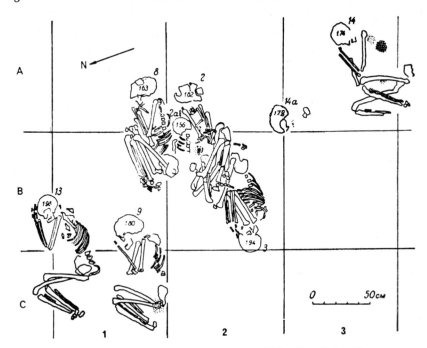

FIG. 9 Plan and some burials of the Mesolithic Vasylivka I cemetery
near the Dnieper rapids.
After A. D. Stolyar (ASE vol. I, 1959, p. 89, fig. 12).

skeletons being in an extended position; and they belonged to a
different racial type. Those of the Epi-Palaeolithic cemeteries were
of the Mediterranean racial type; those of the later cemeteries were
almost exclusively of the 'Crô-Magnon' type, related to the population of the regions extending further to the north. There was evidently an influx of northern immigrants who superseded the former
inhabitants of the country. The difference between the culture of the
Early and the Late Mesolithic was probably the outcome of the
change of population. However, the new inhabitants continued to
live in the country during the Early Neolithic period (see p. 84).

    The size of the Mesolithic cemeteries implies a settled mode of life
for the dwellers of the Dnieper valley, who must have lived mainly on
fishing. The sites are concentrated exclusively in the valley near the
river, which suggests the dry Boreal climate of Western Europe
(Table 2).

Other Pontic Mesolithic Groups

    In recent years several Late Mesolithic sites with the Tardenoisian
flint industry have been recorded and partly investigated[10] in the

country along the Dniester up to Odessa, and east of the river probably up to the Dnieper along the present forest-steppe and steppe border (Kazanka near Krivoy Rog). Their microlithic flints are related to those of the Crimean sites, but they also have features in common with the Rumanian sites further to the south-west. They probably mark the western limit of the Pontic province of the Mesolithic.

A larger concentration of Mesolithic sites has been recorded on the Middle Donetz in the region of Izium, an area in which many Upper Palaeolithic sites have been found. The Mesolithic sites of this area, like those in other regions, represent two chronological periods, the material equipment of which differed to a great extent. Characteristic of the earlier of these are the Rogalik-Yakimovskaya and Beregovaya sites, both of Epi-Palaeolithic type. Sites of the later period lay on sandy soils or sand-dunes, and always kept to the river terraces. Their flint industry was microlithic with the characteristic 'trapeze' forms, high or very wide. A.A. Formozov considers these sites as belonging to the Pontic assemblage and connects them with those of the Dnieper rapids and the coast of the Sea of Azov. On the other hand D.Ia. Telegin associates them with sites on the Middle Dnieper near Kiev and with a few further west in east Volhynia; and he calls them all the 'Donetz-Volhynian' group, which he classes in the western group of the forest-zone cultures. This was evidently a border group containing elements of the two different Mesolithic assemblages. This group possessed hewing or axe-like flint tools, which implies that the country, at present steppe, was covered with woods at that time. It was probably the period of the warm and damp Atlantic climate. There is no connection between the remains of the Early and Late Mesolithic. Different peoples must have lived in the country during these periods. Presumably, during the greater part of the dry Boreal climate, the country was an uninhabited semi-desert.

The basin of the Don in the region of Voronezh, nearly 200 miles north of the former group, was a densely populated area during the Upper Palaeolithic, within which several famous sites of the Kostienki-Borshevo group were investigated (see p. 27). Surprisingly, however, no Mesolithic sites have been reported there nor Mesolithic or 'Epi-Palaeolithic' layers in stratified sites. The only exception was perhaps the upper layer of site Borshevo II (Fig. 7), considered to be either final Palaeolithic or early post-Palaeolithic. The region was again well populated at an early stage of the Neolithic.

This phenomenon was probably the outcome of circumstances similar to those on the Donetz already mentioned. It is of interest to note that the latest Upper Palaeolithic sites of the Kostienki-

Borshevo group, including site Borshevo II (Fig. 7), kept to the lowest river terrace close to the stream, a pattern unlike that of the earlier stages of the Upper Palaeolithic, when the sites lay outside the river valley. This may have been connected with the gradual change in the climate, which had increased by the end of the Palaeolithic. Significant also is the fact, emphasized by some authors,[11] that the flint industry of the earliest Mesolithic sites on the middle Desna and in Northern Byelorussia exhibit many features in common (tools and flint technique) with that of the Late Palaeolithic sites of the Kostienki-Borshevo region. These similarities perhaps testify to the northward and westward migration of the Palaeolithic hunters, who, at the end of the Glacial Era, followed the game as it retreated northwards.

Further south, on the Lower Don and the Western Manych, a number of Mesolithic sites very similar to those of the 'North Pontic' type were discovered. Their flint industry was of the Pontic Tardenoisian type. Similar remains also occur further north, on the Middle Volga (Kuibyshev–Postnikov Ovrag—Fig. 10), and even in the basin of the Kama and the Chusovaya near Perm. These eastern sites do not seem to have represented an outpost of the north Pontic population, but rather a distinct province connected with the north Caucasian, and perhaps also with the west Asiatic, branches of the large complex to which the north Pontic Mesolithic likewise belonged.

PODOLIA

Podolia, particularly west Podolia, formed another Mesolithic province, distinct from that of the 'North Pontic Mesolithic'. According to several scholars[12] the local Palaeolithic population and its culture survived there up to the Neolithic, which means that they must have lived there throughout the whole Mesolithic. The ancient Palaeolithic traditions in the flint industry were carried on into the subsequent period, showing only minor changes, but there are no features characteristic of the Mesolithic flint industry; this is well illustrated by finds from the upper layers of a number of Upper Palaeolithic sites (for example, Vladimirovka). Furthermore, the flint industry of the Neolithic settlements of the province, especially of the Tripolye culture (see p. 70), exhibits close links with that of the local Upper Palaeolithic; Palaeolithic traditions evidently continued there up to the Neolithic.

No sites of the microlithic flint industry of the Tardenoisian type have been recorded in Podolia, except for a few sites on its southeastern confines, close to the border of the forest-steppe and steppe zones, and the lowest layer of occupation at Zankivtsi near Haisin belonged to these. The site lies in the valley of the Southern Bug (the Boh), less than seven feet above the present summer level of the river, in a position implying a dry climate at the time of its occupation. The site may be assigned to the second stage of the east European Mesolithic. The Tardenoisian microlithic flint industry was likewise characteristic of the earliest agricultural communities of the valley of the Southern Bug (see p. 64); it was of the Pontic Tardenoisian type (Fig. 14).

THE FOREST ZONE

Ecological conditions within the east European forest zone during the Mesolithic were basically different from those in the south. Virgin forests full of game—elk, deer, bear, etc.—covered the country, and the dense river network and countless lakes were rich in fish. However, the area has been very unevenly investigated, so that some parts show fairly large numbers of sites and the rest are large blanks on the map (Map IV).

The western division of this area, which extended mainly over Byelorussia, embraces the whole basin of the Upper Dnieper and those of its main tributaries, the Pripet and the Desna. Over one thousand sites have been discovered on the Upper Dnieper and the Sozh, and hundreds on the Middle and Upper Desna; but in other regions of the country their number is considerably less.

Sites were mostly small in size, 50 to 250 square yards in area, and had usually a single layer of occupation; this points to the migratory mode of life of temporary residents. Camp sites were dry places on the sandy slopes of low river terraces, or on the top of sand-dunes, and close to rivers and lakes. Traces of light shanties have been found.

The flint industry was not uniform, showing chronological differences. Accordingly, two periods of Mesolithic development have been distinguished, in some sites well attested by stratigraphic evidence.

The western section of the basin of the Pripet and the basin of the Upper Niemen formed the eastern province of the Swiderian culture of Poland (Map IV). It must have been peopled soon after the retreat of the Pomeranian Glacier, as indicated by a number of early Swiderian finds. No Upper Palaeolithic sites have been recorded in that area. Late Mesolithic remains were entirely different, being of Tardenoisian type, characteristic of which was the microlithic flint industry of Central European character.

Further east, the largest number of sites were found in the area on the Sozh near Gomel, particularly important being the stratified site of Grensk. The flint industry of its lower layer carried on Late Palaeolithic traditions, but Swiderian tools also appear there,

5

especially arrow-heads; a tendency towards smaller tools was also evident. The Swiderian tools were of an advanced type, reminiscent of those of the Swiderian III period. The layer has been dated by V.D. Budko as belonging to the final Glacial period. However, late Swiderian elements imply a later date, at the earliest the Boreal age. Carbon-14 dating of the upper layer of the Grensk site, 4690–4150 B.C. (LE 274), places it in the Atlantic Age, or in other words the Late Mesolithic (Table 2).

Most sites in the area, mainly on sand-dunes, belong to the Late Mesolithic period; their flint industry was microlithic—typical Tardenoisian of Central Europe. But alongside these sites, probably founded by newcomers to the country, are other sites evidently belonging to the indigenous population. Their flint industry carried traditions of the preceding period. Hewing tools, called 'small tranchets' in the Soviet literature, which subsequently developed into the neolithic flint axes, were characteristic, and the presence showed that the people lived in a forest region. The two populations of the country lived side by side but gradually mingled, and by the Early Neolithic had formed a single people.

The next group, on the Middle Desna, south-east of the sites described above, was very similar. The same division of the Mesolithic into two periods can be seen here. Typical of the earlier period is the Smyachka XIV site, near Novgorod Severskii. Its flint industry was 'Epi-Palaeolithic', with many Swiderian features. Many large blades and tools made of these—scrapers, burins, etc.—were found, but no microlithic implements were present. These were found in the Smyachka XIII site alongside those characteristic of Site XIV. Site XIII must have been transitional to the Late Mesolithic. Another important site, Pishchanyi Riv in the same region, yielded both types of flint industry, but the microlithic industry was already preponderant (Table 2).

The hewing tools, 'small tranchets', were very characteristic of this region and the group has even been called after them.[13]

The flint industry of the advanced stage of the Swiderian culture also reached further east. It has been recorded in sites of the Central Russian Mesolithic province (Map IV). Among these were sites on the Oka (Gremyachee) and on the Upper Volga north of Moscow (Skniatino, Sobolevo). Most of these were of the Late Mesolithic age (Table 2), and some even Early Neolithic,[14] as indicated by pottery of the Lialovo type associated with 'Swiderian' sites, for example, at Zolotoruchie I, west of Yaroslav (see p. 93). Isolated 'Swiderian' elements have been recorded even as far east as on the Middle Volga and the Vychegda (see p. 45).

The Central Russian province extended eastwards, probably to

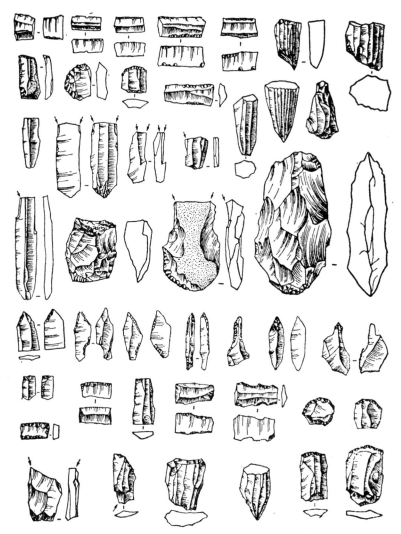

FIG. 10 Mesolithic flint industry of the country on the Middle Volga. After A. Kh. Khalikov (MIA 126, 1966, p. 188, fig. 3).

the Middle Volga. Several sites have been recorded in that territory, and the stratified site of Elin Bor, near Murom on the Lower Oka, counts among the more important ones. Its lowest (third) Early Mesolithic layer yielded several tools of Upper Palaeolithic character. The flint industry of the middle (second) layer was Late Mesolithic, similar to that of other sites in the province of this period, in particular those on the Upper Volga. The upper layer of Elin Bor was already Neolithic.

The Central Russian province was not affected by the Tardenoisian culture. The industry of the earlier period survived during the Late Mesolithic, and no marked changes have been recorded there. In no other part of east Europe did the Swiderian elements last for such a long time.

The East

A different Mesolithic province extended over the wide country west of the Urals up to the Middle Volga. It included the basin of the Kama and its tributaries, the Belaya and Chusovaya; the area on the Upper Vychegda; and even the tundra forests further north in the basin of the Pechora, in the north-eastern corner of Europe (Map IV). Over one hundred Mesolithic sites have been listed within this large strip of land extending nearly 1,000 miles. These sites form several very unevenly diffused groups. Several sites were excavated. At the peat-bog site Vis I in the basin of the Vychegda, scores of flints and of bone implements were found. Among the latter were many points of the 'Shigir' type. The site has been dated as the seventh or sixth millennium b.c.[15] There are a few important stratified sites, some near Ufa in the south, but the best known are those on the Kama near Perm. In all these two stages in the Mesolithic development have been distinguished.

The site of Ogurinskaya on the Kama is representative of the earlier stage; it has been compared with the Skniatino site on the Volga (Table 2). The site of Nizhnee Adishchevo, at the junction of the Chusovaya with the Kama, is characteristic of the later stage, which in this region has been dated to the fifth and the fourth millennia b.c.; it may be compared with site of Sobolevo on the Upper Volga. No sites have been recorded with any similarities to the early Mesolithic of the south of the Central Russian forest zone.

The two provinces, the Central Russian and the Eastern overlapped in the region of Kazan on the Middle Volga. There, several sites have been investigated by A.Kh. Khvalikov (Fig. 10). The Russo-Lugovskaya site showed three layers of occupation, the upper one being Neolithic. In the lowest, the Mesolithic, layer a semi-pit dwelling was uncovered; it was quadrangular in plan, nearly twenty-three feet by eighteen feet in area, sunk about three feet into the ground. A similar hut was uncovered at Elin Bor on the lower Oka (Table 2). The flint industry of this layer was mainly microlithic, like that of the Ogurinskaya site. The middle layer, likewise Mesolithic, has not only much in common with the final Mesolithic Sobolevo site on the Upper Volga, but also with the site of Nizhnee Adishchevo on the Kama.

The flint industry of all these eastern sites has some similarity with the Late Mesolithic industry of the country on the Upper Volga, but no characteristic arrow-heads of Swiderian type have been found there; though they reached the sites on the Vychegda further north. The culture of the whole area had no roots in the local Palaeolithic;[16] some connections, and many common features, suggest that it must have been brought there by immigrants from the south, from the region on the Lower Volga and the Caucasus. In its further development some Central Russian, but also west Siberian, elements must have been included, and, ultimately, the culture of the area west of the Urals acquired a distinct character of its own.

A few sites have been recorded in the south Urals. At one of these, site Yangelka in the basin of the Upper Ural river, remains of a mesolithic hut and a few thousands of flint implements and blades were uncovered; the latter were chiefly microlithic of the 'geometric' type. The technique of their flint industry exhibits close analogies to that of the Mesolithic of the east Caspian Djebel cave.[17] The region was inhabited during the Upper Palaeolithic. Mesolithic drawings found on the walls of the Idrisovskaya cave on the Iuriuzan imply the survival of the local hunters into the Mesolithic. It seems very likely that the upper occupation layers of a number of caves of the area, considered to be of Upper Palaeolithic age (Buranovskaya, Sukhodolskaya, etc.) in which only the bones of recent fauna were found, were already post-glacial. The caves were probably visited by the post-Palaeolithic hunters who continued their ancient mode of life and kept to their ancient culture during the Mesolithic.

The Shigir Culture

Mesolithic remains found on the eastern side of the Urals bear a different character. They have been called the 'Shigir' culture, after a peat-bog north of Sverdlovsk in which they were excavated. In the earlier archaeological literature, this term was applied likewise to a large group of Neolithic and Bronze Age remains found in the area. Recently, the name of the 'Gorbunovo' culture (after another peat-bog investigation) was given to all these later remains, and under the term of 'Shigir' culture are grouped only the earliest, Mesolithic remains (see p. 103).

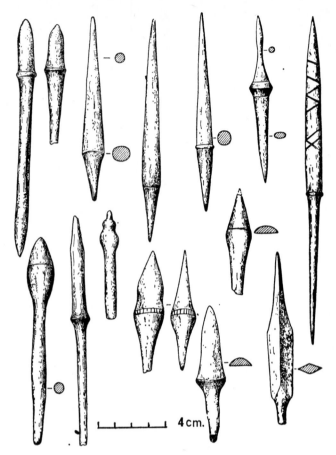

FIG. 11 Bone arrow-heads of the 'Shigir' type from the Mesolithic and Neolithic sites of North-Eastern Europe.
After M. E. Foss (MIA 29, 1952, p. 45, fig. 15).

The Shigir peat-bog was excavated commercially, and quite insufficient data exist concerning the objects found there. This has often caused confusion as regards the chronology of the objects found in the site. Only a relatively small number of bone objects were Mesolithic. They are known to have been found on the bottom of the bog, under the peat, and are well recognisable by their colour, which differs from that of other specimens found in higher strata; the latter were evidently of a later date.

Mesolithic finds consist almost exclusively of bone weapons; harpoons and three types of arrow-head. All the arrow-heads are very long, about twelve inches in length; one type has flint inlays, the second is very thin and needle-shaped, and the third has a conical

MAP V Distribution of bone arrow-heads of the 'Shigir' type.
After M. E. Foss (MIA 29, 1952, p. 46, fig. 16).
SITES: (1) Kubenino; (2) Kinema; (3) Nizhnee Veretye; (4) Karavaikha;
(5) Pogostishche; (6) Modlona; (7) Olenii Ostrov; (8) Fedorovskaya;
(13) Volosovo; (14) Maloe Okulovo; (17) Shigir; (21) Kunda; (23)
Pärnu-Pernau; (27) Zedmar; (35) Dolgoe.

tip. The latter have been called the 'Shigir' type (Fig. 11). Except
for the points with flint inlays, all the other types survived to the subsequent Neolithic period, the first period of the Gorbunovo culture.
Later specimens differ somewhat from those of the Shigir culture,
and were shorter (Fig. 11). Similar ones were also found outside the
area of the Gorbunovo culture, near the Baltic in Estonia (Map V).

The two other sites of the Shigir culture so far known are burials.
One of these was a grave near Kurgan on the Tobol, about 250 miles
south-west of Shigir; its furniture consisted of bone weapons of the
Shigir type. The other was also a grave uncovered near Miass, about
fifty miles east of Cheliabinsk.

Besides the two burials just mentioned, a female skull was found in the Shigir peat-bog itself. It was associated with weapons of the earliest type and evidently belonged to the Shigir culture. Anthropological study revealed that all three skulls of the Shigir culture were of the same hybrid racial type, basically Europoid with a Mongoloid admixture. They exhibit traits similar to those known in Central Russia, and also to the Laponoid racial type proper to Eastern Europe.

Not much can be said about the Shigir culture because of the scarcity of archaeological material. The men were chiefly fishermen, who led a settled life close to the shores of lakes. They also hunted, using weapons made of the bones of deer, and hides for clothing.

The origin of the culture is disputable. Most Soviet scholars believe that it evolved locally, in the Trans-Ural area, out of the Palaeolithic culture of the Southern Urals. Its chronology is also debatable. The earliest stratum of the Shigir bog, in which the Mesolithic objects were found, is considered to date to the end of the Boreal period, though no pollen-analytical date exists in this respect. The time of change from the Boreal to the Atlantic climate in North-Western Europe has been Carbon-14 dated, either to the middle of the sixth millennium B.C. or to about 6000 B.C. Recently, the relative Mesolithic layer of the Shigir peat-bog has been dated to the sixth–fifth millennium B.C. The sixth millennium B.C. may, accordingly, be considered as the earliest date for the beginning of the Shigir culture, provided that its climatic age has been properly established.

The culture is thought to have come to an end in the third millennium B.C., when it was succeeded by the Gorbunovo culture (see p. 103).

The North-West and North

The improvement of the climatic conditions in Northern Europe began at the time of the melting away of the Fennoscandian glacier, from about 8000 B.C. onwards. During the warm Boreal and its subsequent Atlantic periods, the climate of the Eastern Baltic and White Sea regions differed from the present one, being much milder. At that time the mixed forests spread far to the north, to Finland and Northern Russia, beyond their present limit. The chief fauna of the forests became the aurochs, boar, and, above all, the elk. The level of the seas and lakes was also different, for they were much larger then than now.

Man entered this part of Eastern Europe at the very end of the Glacial period, early in the Mesolithic, or Epi-Palaeolithic (see p. 28). Carbon-14 datings of the two superimposed Mesolithic layers at Kunda, in the Gulf of Finland in Northern Estonia, are 6390 B.C.

(TA-14) and 4065 B.C. (TA-16); of another Estonian site, at Narva, of the lowest (III) Mesolithic layer, 5690 B.C. (TA-53), 5630 B.C. (TA-25), and 5140 B.C. (TA-41); of the middle (II) layer, 5365 B.C. (TA-52), 4790 B.C. (TA-40), and 4070 B.C. (TA-17); and of the upper Mesolithic (I) layer, 3870 B.C. (TA-33) and 3350 B.C. (TA-7). The earliest sites were from the second half of the Boreal period, those of the later Mesolithic being all of the Atlantic period.

The Kunda Culture

All the sites above belonged to the 'Kunda' culture, called after the site. The culture formed part of a large homogeneous complex extending over a wide strip of land along the southern coast of the Baltic, east of the Vistula. Sites of the culture were also found further north, in the Karelian Isthmus (site of the Antrea peat-bog), and in Finland; and eastwards they reached the region of Kargopol. Its Finnish branch, called the Suomusjärvi culture, extended along the northern shore of the Gulf of Finland and spread northwards into Central Finland. The Finnish sites were of a later date than the earliest ones in Estonia. The Suomusjärvi culture mainly developed during the early Atlantic period, and its earliest sites at the end of the Boreal age (Map IV).

The sites of the Kunda culture and of its related groups kept exclusively to ancient sea and lake beaches, and to river banks. Some were found under a thick layer of peat. The people were fishermen and hunters, the chief game animal being the elk. Deposits consisted of tools made of flint, quartz and quartzite, and of bone and antler, the latter amounting to 40 per cent of the total. Among these were axes made of antler, barbed harpoons, fishhooks, ice-picks, spearheads, and conical projectile points, a weapon widespread in the north of Eastern Europe but unknown further west (Map V).

Controversial views have been expressed about the origin of the Kunda culture. Many scholars consider it to be an eastern branch of the Maglemose culture, to which it was evidently related. Others seek its origin somewhere in the east, in Siberia, and many Soviet scholars[19] regard the Shigir culture as its parent.

The latter assumption is based on the diffusion of weapons and tools made of bone and antler, especially of conical projectile points of the 'Shigir' type, which were found in several sites in the northern part of Russia, and in sites of the Kunda culture in Estonia, and further west (Map V). However, the relative finds in north Russia were mainly Neolithic, except two Mesolithic specimens later than the date of the Kunda period in Estonia. Most of the Shigir points, whether Mesolithic or Neolithic, were found in the western division of the area of their diffusion, and those from the Shigir and Gorbunovo peat-bogs lay on the extreme east of it. The chronology of these objects may even completely reverse the Soviet scholars' assumption.

The cranial material from a series of assumed Neolithic graves in north Russia has often been quoted in support of an early Eastern (Asiatic) racial expansion into Europe. G. Debets says that groups of Mongoloid stock must have penetrated the northern forest zone during the Neolithic or perhaps in the Mesolithic. Mongoloid skulls, or at least skulls basically Europoid with apparent Mongoloid features, were found in Neolithic graves of Northern Russia. A.Ia. Briusov thinks that the Asiatic features are the heritage from the early Mesolithic settlers who advanced into the country from the Urals, and who were later absorbed by a new wave of Neolithic immigrants from Central Russia.

However, the origin of the Mongoloid racial type, and of the brachycephalic racial elements in Eastern Europe in general, is a complicated question calling for further research. The population of the Shigir culture, of the supposed parent culture of the whole east Baltic Mesolithic complex, inclusive of the Kunda culture, was—as mentioned previously—of Europoid not Mongolian stock, and had only a slight admixture of Mongoloid features. It should also be borne in mind that brachycephalic Laponoid, not Mongoloid, elements appeared early in Europe. The skull from the Tardenoisian grave at Janisławice in Central Poland was Laponoid, and greatly resembles the modern Lapp crania of the Scandinavian north. Objects of Maglemose character were found in this grave, which was of the Boreal (Ancylus) period. On the other hand, in some north Russian burials Mongoloid crania were found which can hardly be regarded as connected with the Shigir culture. A definitely eastern Siberian wave of population has been attested to in north Russia at a much later date, in the second half of the second millennium B.C. (see p. 317); it penetrated westwards up to the Baltic coast.

It seems that a proper answer to the dilemma may be found in the suggestion by R. Indreko. He points to remarkable similarities between Kunda flint tools and their technique and those of the Upper Palaeolithic sites in the south, especially Borshevo I, but not to those of the Epi-Palaeolithic time (Borshevo II), and concludes, therefore, that the roots of the Kunda culture have to be sought in the south. Similarities may have also been recorded between Kunda flint tools and those of Early Mesolithic on the Desna, and in north Byelorussia (see p. 41). In the light of these observations, it seems very likely that the Upper Palaeolithic hunters of the region on the Don, and possibly also those of other regions, had moved gradually to the north by the end of the Upper Palaeolithic. They ultimately reached the Baltic coast, but there they seem to have met other, different groups. Some of these advanced there probably from the south-west, along the Baltic coast. Another group of hunters, which must also have contributed to the formation of the Kunda culture, reached there from the east. This is suggested by the diffusion of the bone and antler tools of special east European types, already mentioned; they might have been connected with the Upper Palaeolithic hunters whose sites have been discovered as far north as the Pechora (see p. 44). They belonged to a different stem from those who came from the south.

Investigations of a series of peat-bogs further east, in Northern Russia, north of the town of Vologda, in the area of Lake Vozhe, revealed that early in the post-glacial era the region was covered by dense forests. Early in the third period of the development of forest cover in that region,[20] pine and birch forests with some admixture of fir, spruce and willow, were dominant; the stage probably coincided with the Boreal period of North-Western Europe. During the next stage, which seems to have coincided with the Atlantic period, the percentage of spruce markedly increased, and trees common to a warm climate appeared—oak, lime, elm, and even alder. Site Pogostishche I belonged to this period; the list of bones found there is of interest: there were beaver, reindeer, elk, marten, roe-deer, maral (*Cervus elaphus*), wild bull (*Bos latifrons*), and wolf. Remains of this site, and also those of the Neolithic sites of the region, lay under the present level of the nearby river. By the end of the period, the water level began to rise gradually, and the formation of peat-bog started. This development was entirely different from that recorded further west, in the east Baltic area.

The origin of the earliest inhabitants has not been established. They might, however, have been the descendants of the Upper Palaeolithic hunters whose sites were discovered along the Urals, the Kama and the Pechora.

Favourable post-glacial climatic conditions encouraged small groups of hunters and fishers to proceed still further north. By the end of the Boreal period (about the middle of the sixth millennium B.C.) Northern Finland, Eastern Karelia, and even the shores of the White Sea and the Arctic Ocean on the Kola Peninsula, were reached. Several sites of these expanding groups have been investigated. Their flint and stone industry (quartz) was based upon flakes and blades, and no organic material was found. The culture has been called the 'Arctic Palaeolithic'; it was closely related to the 'Komsa' culture of the north Norwegian Atlantic coast. The culture was approximately contemporaneous with the Kunda culture of Estonia and Southern Finland. Some similarities of the stone industry suggest that the culture represents an immigration from the south, from the area of the east Baltic complex (Map IV).

SUMMARY

The earliest traces of man in Eastern Europe consist of a small number of very primitive stone tools considered to be of the Early Palaeolithic Age, of the Late Chellean or Early Acheulian period, found in Soviet Armenia in the southern part of Transcaucasia. Similar stones found in Western Podolia were also possibly of the same age. They all probably dated from the penultimate Mindel-Riss Interglacial. The Acheulian period had lasted through the whole Riss-Volga Glaciation and part of the last Interglacial. During that time early man must have enlarged his territory; Acheulian sites, or stray stone tools, were found in several parts of Transcaucasia, and even north of the main Caucasian ridge, in the Crimea, and in the areas on the lower Dnieper and the lower Volga.

During the later part of the Riss-Würm Interglacial and the first stage of the last, the Würm-Valdai Glaciation (the Mousterian Age), small groups of Mousterian people, of the Neanderthal race, lived throughout the whole southern and central part of Eastern Europe, and in the east they reached as far north even as the region of Perm on the Kama (Map II).

A fundamental change in the culture of Palaeolithic man took place at the very end of the first Interstadial of the last Glaciation, or at the beginning of the first Interstadial, around 40,000 B.P. The Mousterian Neanderthal man was replaced by man of the *Homo sapiens* species, equipped with a much more advanced flint industry; the new age, the Upper Palaeolithic, began. The change was due to the arrival, probably mainly from the south-west, of a wave of new tribes, which soon spread over the whole ice-free territory of Eastern Europe and probably also advanced further east into Siberia. The largest concentrations of Upper Palaeolithic sites have been recorded in the south-western part of east Europe, in the basins of the Dniester, the Middle Dnieper and the Desna, and the Donetz and the upper Don (Map III). The Upper Palaeolithic hunters, like their Mousterian predecessors, advanced far to the north along the Volga, the Kama and the western foothills of the Urals, reaching the regions on the upper Pechora. Remains of semi-permanent winter huts, many of which have been uncovered, give an idea of the material culture of the people of that time, and the burials give an insight into their belief in after-life. The Upper Palaeolithic man of Eastern Europe was for the most part of the Crô-Magnon racial type.

A series of stratified sites with several superimposed layers, investigated in various parts of the country, illustrate the subsequent changes in the culture of Upper Palaeolithic man, and especially the sequence of the changing flint industry. The west European chronological scheme and its terminology have been usually applied to the Palaeolithic sequence in Eastern Europe. However, this scheme does not fit in properly with the local conditions. Actually, only two main periods have been distinguished in the east European Upper Palaeolithic (Table I)—the Aurignacian-Solutrean and the Magdalenian periods—though the flint industries characteristic of these periods differ in many respects from those known under these names in the west.

The change of climate, which by the end of the Pleistocene steadily grew warmer, resulted in a general shifting of the late Palaeolithic (Epi-Palaeolithic) hunters northwards, into the areas freed from the ice cover. This process accelerated during the post-Glacial era, the Holocene, which began about 8000 B.C.; tribes from the south, but also advancing from the west, from Central Europe (the Swiderians) and possibly also from the east, from the Urals and beyond these (Map II), spread over the whole north of Eastern Europe. In the meantime, however, conditions considerably deteriorated in the south, in the present steppe zone, and during the hot and dry Boreal climate of the early Holocene, during the Early Mesolithic period, these regions became almost semi-deserts, inhabited only by small human groups living in the deep valleys of the main rivers.

A new development took place early in the sixth millennium B.C., when the climate changed again, and the warm but damp Atlantic climate set in. It seems that new groups of people entered Eastern Europe, especially its southern and south-western regions, and introduced their characteristic Tardenoisian flint industry. Their arrival inaugurated the Late Mesolithic period, during which the various ethnic elements blended in various parts of the country; consequently several distinct provinces were formed, each differing in culture from its neighbours (Map IV). The provinces exhibit close links with the countries in which, presumably, the bulk of their population used to live. Those in the west, including the east Baltic area, the basin of the Upper and Middle Dnieper, the country further east up to the upper Don, and Podolia, were closely tied to various parts of Central Europe. The south, the Caucasus, the Crimea, and the country along the northern coast of the Sea of Azov, were bound to the Eastern Mediterranean, to the west Asiatic *Kulturkreis*. The eastern areas show an intermixture of Central Asiatic, Caucasian and Central Russian connections, but those with the neighbouring west Siberian cultures were the strongest. Although absorbing many Western, Central European elements, the Central Russian province retained many elements of the local culture of the preceding period, and this gave it a character of its own.

It has been commonly accepted that the Mesolithic came to an end by the close of the fifth millennium B.C., at the time of the appearance in the south-west of the earliest agricultural communities. However, their presence, and the new food-producing economy they introduced, at first affected only a small region of Eastern Europe. Most of the country still kept to the ancient Mesolithic economy, way of life, and culture for further centuries; in some areas at least for another millennium. But the Mesolithic had left a very important and durable legacy—the division of Eastern Europe into a series of distinct provinces. These provinces, within their nearly unchanged boundaries, are distinguishable in the many subsequent periods of the whole Prehistoric and Protohistoric Eras of Eastern Europe.

References

1 Herodotus IV, 28, 21, 61.
2 Bone charcoal from site Anosovka (Kostienki) has been Carbon–14 dated as 7890 B.C. (LE–409), and that from site Kostienki I as 6750 (LE–451); both sites are considered to be of late Würm Age.
3 See: KSIAM 82, 1961, articles by S.N. Zamyatnin (pp. 5–36); A.A. Chiguryaeva and N.Ia. Khvalina (pp. 37–41); and V.N. Gromov (pp. 42–48).
4 A.P. Chernysh, KSIAM 82, 1961, pp. 77–85; and Idem, *Pozdnyi Paleolit Srednego Pridnestrovia*, 1959.
5 E.g., by E.S. Coon, *The Origin of Races*. London, 1963.
6 The following are a few recently published Carbon–14 dates: Moldova V: layer 10, late Solutrean, 21, 150 B.C. (GIN–106); layer 5, Middle Magdalenian, 15, 150 B.C. (GIN–52); layer 4, late Magdalenian, 15, 150 B.C. (GIN–147) and 9,950 B.C. (GIN–8); Mesolithic layer 8,990 B.C. (GIN–54) and 8,640 B.C. (GIN–7). Markina Gora (Kostienki XIV), 12,350 B.C. (GIN–79). Kostienki II, mammoth bones, 9,050 B.C. (GIN–93).
7 R. Schild, *Archaeologia Polona*, Vol. III, 1960, pp. 7–64.
8 M. Chmielewska, *Huttes d'habitation epipaléolitiques de Witów*. Tódź, 1961.
9 E.g., A.D. Stoliar in ASE, vol. I, 1959, and IA; and D.Ia. Telegin, KSIAK 7, 1957, and AK, vol. XIII, 1961.
10 P.I. Boriskovskii, KSAMO, 1964.
11 P.I. Boriskovskii, MIA 121, 1963; N.N. Gurina, MIA 126, 1966; and D. Budko, MIA 126.
12 E.g., M. Rudynskii, AP, vol. II, 1949; and A.Ia. Briusov, *Mezoliticheskaya neuryaditsa*.
13 M. Rudynskii, *Antropologiya* I, Kiev.
14 D.A. Kraynov, KSIAM 97, 1964.
15 The Carbon–14 dates, recently published, of four pieces of wood from site Vis I, from the depth from 1.2 to 1.9 m, oscilate between 5,870 and 5,140 B.C. (LE–616, 684, 685, 713).
16 O.N. Bahder, MIA 79, 1960.
17 G.I. Matiushin, KSIAM 97, 1964.
18 S.N. Tyuremov, KSIAM, 75, 1959.
19 A.Ia. Briusov, V.M. Raushenbakh.
20 Established by G.N. Lisitsyna, SV, 1961.

2

The Neolithic

NEOLITHIC REVOLUTION

A far-reaching step in human development was the so-called 'Neolithic' revolution—the change from an economy based on hunting, fishing and gathering, typical of the Palaeolithic and Mesolithic, to a new economy based on food production, agriculture, and animal husbandry.

The new economy was not a European invention, and still less an east European one. Its original centre, or centres, lay somewhere in Western Asia, whence it gradually spread northwards and north-westwards into Europe. The very beginning of agriculture in Western Asia has been Carbon-14 dated as far back as the eighth, or end of the ninth, millennium B.C. It took about three millennia to reach Eastern Europe.

There were three potential ways for the northern spread of the new economy (Map VI). The nearest of these was across the Caucasus; and agriculture was introduced into Transcaucasia, in the country bordering on the ancient centres, some time in the fifth millennium B.C. Another way, leading towards the eastern part of Eastern Europe, ran from the Iranian centres around the Caspian Sea through Soviet Turkestan. In fact, the earliest agricultural communities appeared in the southern part of Soviet Turkestan, close to the Iranian border, as early as in the fifth, or perhaps in the sixth, millennium B.C.

However, these two spearheads of the new economy played only a restricted role in its diffusion through Eastern Europe. The west Siberian steppe barrier, unfavourable to primitive agriculture, barred its further advance. The position was similar in the area north of the Caucasus. The most effective and important way by which the new economy was introduced to Eastern Europe proved to be the longest one—the Black Sea route. By this route, across the Balkans, it reached Central Europe and also, through Rumania, the south-western part of Eastern Europe. The earliest agricultural communities discovered in the South-Western Ukraine were probably founded in the late part of the fifth millennium, but possibly in the middle of that

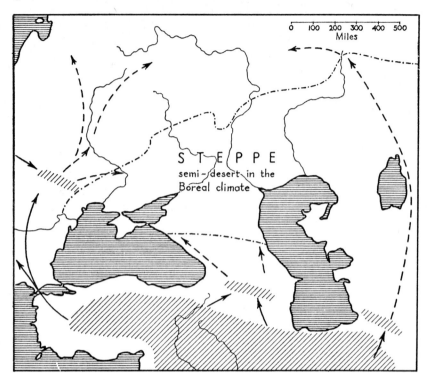

MAP VI Scheme of the advance in Eastern Europe of the earliest agriculturalists (*plain arrows*), and of their contribution to spreading the knowledge of pottery (*broken lines*).
Continuous hatching: the area of the earliest agriculture in Western Asia; *Small hatched areas:* the earliest (primary) agricultural communities in Eastern Europe and in Soviet Central Asia.

millennium; they were, therefore, of a similar date to that of the earliest agricultural communities in the areas already mentioned.

The spread of agriculture, and of the food-producing economy in general, was a long process, which proceeded at varying rates in different parts of the country. It affected at first only a relatively small section of Eastern Europe. Within the whole forest zone, by far the largest part of the whole territory, the old Mesolithic mode of life and economy survived almost unchanged for further millennia. New types of tools and weapons, pottery unknown to the Mesolithic, and other objects characteristic of the Neolithic or of later periods, which have been found besides the old types in the respective sites, are usually the only indication of their age. The great differences in climate and in ecological conditions within that huge territory were responsible for considerable backwardness in some areas, where cul-

VII Vessels characteristic of the Southern Bug culture (second stage), from Sokoltsy and Mytkiv Ostriv. Institute of Archaeology of the Ukrainian Academy, Kiev.

VIII A view of the 'ploshchadka' hut IV at Zhury on the Dniester near Rybnitsa, situated close to the river; excavated by Prof. S.N. Bibikov in 1952.

IX Vessels of the Tripolyan period B–I with painted and grooved decorations, from the settlement at Zhury on the Dniester; excavated by Prof. S.N. Bibikov. Institute of Archaeology of the Ukrainian Academy, Kiev.

tures of the Mesolithic type survived much longer, and where also Neolithic cultures developed long after the end of the Neolithic, even up to the first millennium B.C.

Some areas, particularly the northern coniferous forest zone (the Taiga) offered no suitable conditions for the expansion of primitive agriculture (Map I). In the south, for example, in the wide steppe country, the local environment and resources were suitable to the development of a different type of food-producing economy, which evolved in the third millennium and was based on stock-rearing and pasturage.

There was no change in population at the transition from the Mesolithic to the Neolithic. This is well evidenced by the survival in most areas of old types of tools and weapons, and by the continuation in the Neolithic of the ancient provinces distinguishable in the Mesolithic. It seems that small groups of southern agriculturalists progressively advanced northwards, assimilating the aboriginal population, which adopted the new economy.

The term Neolithic has a wide and undefined meaning in Eastern Europe. As mentioned in the preceding chapter, some authors apply the name of Early Neolithic to the whole Mesolithic proper. In some regions, such as Transcaucasia, no Neolithic has been distinguished, the earliest Neolithic agriculturalists having been already acquainted with the use of copper; accordingly, the term Charcolithic was applied to their cultures. Similarly, in the south-west, the earliest agriculturalists also used copper, and their culture has been called 'Aeneolithic'. Furthermore, copper was also in use among the earliest steppe pastoralists of the second half of the third millennium B.C., and their age has been called, therefore, the 'Copper Age' or the 'Early Metal Age'.

Taking these circumstances into account, there was no period in Eastern Europe as a whole to which the term Neolithic could be applied in its proper meaning. In our study, this customary term has been used to denote the important formative age, the fourth and third millennia, during which foundations were laid for the future development of this part of the continent. In the light of the above, the beginning of the Neolithic is difficult to establish. It has been fixed arbitrarily at about the end of the fifth millennium, the approximate time of the appearance of the earliest agriculturalists in the southern regions of Eastern Europe, though other areas were affected by the new development much later. Its end has been put about 2000 B.C., the time at which further far-reaching changes began.

At the dawn of the east European Neolithic, the warm and damp Atlantic climate was characteristic of Western Europe. This lasted from about the middle of the sixth millennium B.C. to about the end of the third millennium, and was followed by the drier 'sub-Boreal' climate. We notice, however, that up to the third millennium B.C., the earliest agricultural settlements in the south-western part of Eastern Europe kept chiefly to the deep river valleys. They usually lay on the lowest river terraces close to the stream, three to seven feet above the present summer level of the river. This position implies a spell of dry climate, during which the inhabitants of the hamlets had no fear of river inundations; today, the rise of flood water above the summer level is quite common. These circumstances do not fit in with the contemporaneous climatic conditions in Western Europe, so it seems that geographic factors must have been responsible for the discrepancy. There is a marked difference between the present climate of Western Europe and the continental climate in the east. Similar differences, which undoubtedly affected the vegetation, particularly of the southern part of Eastern Europe, must have existed also during the remote past. The change of climate might soon have changed the vegetation in the West, but in the south of Eastern Europe it probably took much longer to become effective; the consequences of the changes are well discernible in the remains of later stages of the Neolithic and Bronze Age.

During the two thousand years of the Neolithic, Eastern Europe was divided into several provinces, which on the whole corresponded with those of the Mesolithic (see p. 54). In this age, pottery mainly determined the areas of the provinces and smaller local groups, whereas in the Palaeolithic and Mesolithic it had been various types of flint industry. The great variety in the make and shape of the vessels, the style of their decoration, etc., denote both chronological and regional differences. However, within smaller areas pottery was to a great extent homogeneous and is considered, therefore, to denote tribal units and their areas.

The Neolithic development was not uniform throughout the whole country, and marked differences have been noticed in this respect in the various provinces. Nevertheless, the two Neolithic millennia form a well defined age in which three consecutive periods may be discerned—especially in the western division of the country—called the Early, Middle and Late Neolithic (Table 3).

The Early Neolithic, which began about the end of the fifth millennium with the appearance of the first agricultural communities, may be divided into three stages, based on the development in the south-west (of the Tripolye culture and its predecessors). During the first stage, the Neolithic was in fact restricted to the south of the country; in other regions of Eastern Europe, by far the larger part, the Mesolithic way of life and culture continued uninterrupted. During the second stage, the Neolithic features of the material culture, pottery, polished stone tools, etc., spread further north in the Ukraine, and in the third stage, in the second half of the fourth millennium B.C., cultures of the Neolithic type, although still based on the ancient, Mesolithic type of economy, spread to large areas of the western part of the east European forest zone.

The second period, the Middle Neolithic, began approximately at the end of the fourth millennium B.C. and lasted for 500-odd years till the middle of the third millennium. The main difference between this period and the Early Neolithic consisted partly of a few changes in the culture of a few regions (Transcaucasia and the south-west), but mainly in the marked spread of Neolithic-type cultures over larger areas.

A clear-cut division existed, however, between the Middle and Late Neolithic (Table 3). It was marked by considerable expansions and tribal movements around the middle of the third millennium B.C., and felt over almost the whole country. Several new cultures suddenly appeared at that time, in various parts of the country. During this period cultures of the Neolithic type already covered the major part of Eastern Europe, though the Neolithic food-producing economy was still restricted to the south of the country. The Late Neolithic lasted for over half a millennium, till the early second millennium B.C. Its established order was then shattered in most regions by a new outbreak of disturbances. In consequence, tribal dislocations and considerable changes mark the end of the Neolithic and the beginning of a new era.

The development that took place during the three periods of the Neolithic will be discussed later. The Early and Middle Neolithic will be dealt with jointly, as the first of these related mainly to restricted areas in the south, and there was no sharp division between them. The development in the different parts of Eastern Europe did not follow the same pattern nor did it proceed at the same pace. All the separate provinces must, therefore, be treated separately. In Table 3 an attempt has been made to correlate the stages in the development of the many cultures in various regions. Their chronology has been based on the very insufficient framework of the Carbon-14 dates available, and on the established connections with the well dated cultures in other regions. The chronological scheme produced here must, therefore, be treated as approximate only.

THE EARLY AND MIDDLE NEOLITHIC IN THE SOUTH

The earliest agricultural communities in Eastern Europe appeared north-east of the Carpathians (Map VII), in the south of the former

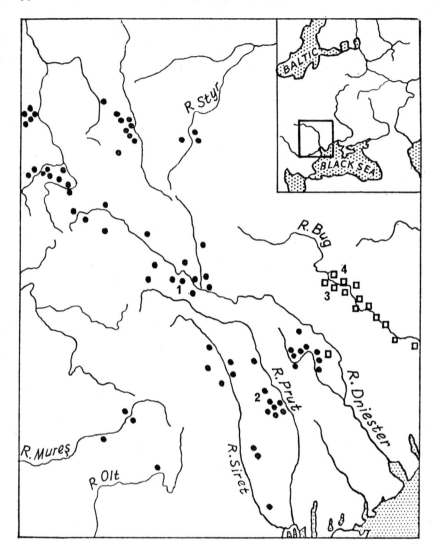

MAP VII The earliest agricultural communities in the south-west of Eastern Europe (after T. Sulimirski, *Chambers's Encyclopaedia World Survey.* 1965, p. 73. With the kind permission of the Editors).

Points: sites of the Danubian I culture; *Squares:* sites of the Southern Bug culture.

SITES: 1 Nezvysko; 2 Floreşti; 3 Hlynyshche; 4 Bashkiv Ostriv-Samchyntsi.

Podolian province of the Mesolithic (see p. 40). The earliest agriculturalists were the bearers of the Central European 'linear-band' pottery, or the 'Danubian I' culture. Their priority in this respect has been revealed by stratigraphic evidence of the remains at Nezvysko in West Podolia (Table 3), and at Floreşti in Bessarabia.[1] At both sites, Danubian I remains lay on the bottom of the occupation layer, overlaid by those of other early Neolithic cultures (Tripolyan B-1 at Nezvysko, Boian-Giuleşti at Floreşti).

THE DANUBIAN I CULTURE

Well over fifty sites of the Danubian I culture have been recorded north-east of the Carpathians, east of the San, including those in Transylvania, Moldavia and Bessarabia (Map VII). Diffusion of the culture was due to the migration of its people, but was also the result of the newcomers absorbing into their culture some local tribes of Palaeolithic and Mesolithic origin. The starting point of the migration might have been somewhere in the region of Cracow or Sandomierz in Southern Poland, whence they may have proceeded eastwards along the Carpathian foothills. But Rumanian sites, and the position of many sub-Carpathian sites on the approaches to the Carpathian passes, suggest that the ancient home of at least a section of the newcomers must have been on the other side of the mountains. Obsidian tools found in Danubian I sites imply relations—across the Carpathians—with the Hegyala region in North-Eastern Hungary, which was rich in obsidian deposits. Connections existed between the two cultures as early as the Upper Palaeolithic; the early Danubian I settlers may, therefore, have moved along old and well established tracks.

No Carbon-14 dates exist for eastern Danubian I sites. Their chronological position is indicated indirectly by Carbon-14 dates for Danubian I settlements in Central Europe, which are placed between 4500 and 4000 B.C. It seems that a date at the end of the fifth millennium B.C. can safely be assumed for the appearance of the earliest Danubian I settlers in Podolia.

The settlements, or rather hamlets, of the Danubians were small. Huts were of the semi-pit dwelling type, slightly sunk in the ground. In a few cases post-holes for the posts supporting the roof were found. But large huts built on the surface, with the floor fired, were uncovered also; one of the huts of this type, at Nezvysko, was about forty feet long and twenty-three feet wide. Tools were made of flint or obsidian. Stone implements also appear—small polished axes, polished chisels, etc.—made of slate. In most hamlets fragments of primitive saddle-querns were excavated. Pottery was of two types (Table 8: A): either (1) a well made ware, consisting of mainly semi-spherical medium-sized bowls with the surface smoothed and decorated by incised angular bands, or by wavy lines with small holes at the junctions—the so-called 'note-head' decoration; or (2) a kitchen ware consisting of large spherical vases with short cylindrical necks and flat, often high, bases. The latter were made mostly of a clay paste tempered with some organic matter, and decorated with raised warts, finger-tipped bands, etc. Their shape and decoration are strikingly reminiscent of pottery of the Criş-Körös culture, the earliest agricultural culture of east Hungary, Transylvania and Moldavia.

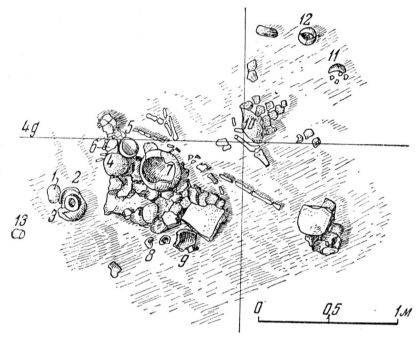

FIG. 12 Burial (partial cremation) of the Danubian I culture at Nezvysko on the Dniester.
After E. K. Chernysh (кsпмк No. 63, 1956, p. 52, fig. 21).

Many animal bones were found in all the sites investigated, approximately half of them of domesticated animals (cows, goats, sheep, pigs), and the other half of wild beasts (boars, stags, roe-deer, *Bos primigenius*). Wheat and peas were cultivated, and grains of wheat were found at Nezvysko.

A grave, a partial cremation on the spot, was uncovered at Nezvysko, close to a hut built on the surface (Fig. 12). The skeleton was crouched, its head to the north-west. Several vessels were found around it, and also among the grave-goods were a slate chisel and a bone awl (Fig. 13).

FIG. 13 Vessels and a slate chisel, or axe, from the burial of Danubian I culture at Nezvysko.
After E. K. Chernysh.

The Southern Bug Culture

Another group of the earliest agriculturalists lived in the valley of the Southern Bug (the Boh) below Vinnitsa, and on its tributaries up to the steppe border near Pervomaisk. Recently, a few settlements of the culture were discovered on the middle Dniester. The remains have been called the 'Southern Bug' culture,[2] and recently the 'Southern Bug-Dniester' culture (Map VII).

Sites consisting of a few huts lay on the lowest river terrace in a topographical position similar to that of the Danubian I sites in the valley of the Dniester, which again implies a period of dry climate at the time of their occupation. Sites were mostly stratified, and their lowest occupation layer was between five feet and six feet eight inches above the present summer level of the river, though in a few cases it was as little as sixteen inches above it (Hlynyshche near Bratslav).

Stratigraphic evidence implies three stages in the development of the culture, followed by the early Tripolyan period. The earliest occupation layer of the culture was disturbed in several sites, and partly ruined by subsequent floods. Sometimes it overlay the Mesolithic remains (Hlynyshche, Zankivtsi, Soroki on the Dniester) to which the name of 'pre-pottery Neolithic' has been given by some authors.

The men of the Southern Bug culture were acquainted with agriculture and stock-breeding, but hunting and gathering must have still played a considerable role in their lives, as indicated by the large number of bones of wild animals and mollusc (*Unio*) shells found at their sites.

The flint industry of the earliest stage of the culture was microlithic, of the Pontic Tardenoisian type (see p. 41), like that of the Mesolithic layers of the same area (Fig. 14). The Mesolithic industry was later replaced by the Neolithic; tools made of bone, such as hoes, were also found.

Pottery was in use from the outset, but there was no uniformity in the pottery of the earliest stage. Vessels generally had rounded or pointed bases, but in some sites only flat-based pottery appeared (Pl. VII), as in sites of the later periods. Many incised decorative patterns (rows of small incisions, zig-zag lines, cross hatching, curved motifs, etc.) point to close connections with the Criş-Körös culture of east Hungary and Rumania.

Sites of the Criş-Körös culture were recorded in Middle Bessarabia, but none were found north-east of the Dniester in the Ukraine. It seems, however, that isolated groups may have reached the valley of the Dniester in west Podolia and there met the Danubians. This is suggested by the Danubian I 'kitchen ware' found at Nezvysko, which exhibits many features characteristic of the Criş-Körös culture.

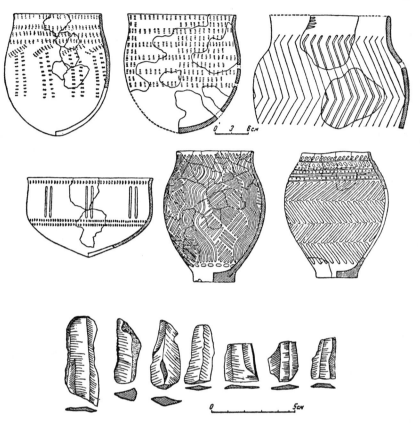

FIG. 14 *Upper:* Characteristic vessels and microlithic flints of the first stage of the Southern Bug culture from Trifautskii Forest on the Dniester. *Lower:* The second stage from Hlynyshche on the Boh (Southern Bug). After V. I. Markevich (KSIAM No. 105, 1965, p. 88, fig. 17) and P. I. Khvalyuk (KSIIMK No. 75, 1959, p. 170, fig. 60).

The men of the latter must have also crossed the Dniester and reached the valley of the Southern Bug; and there, in mixing with the indigenous Mesolithic population, they contributed to the formation of the Southern Bug culture. They arrived there before the Danubians.

The spread of the Criş-Körös culture up to the Podolian border,[3] had far-reaching consequences within a very wide territory in Eastern Europe. According to some scholars[4] the earliest pottery of the area of the Dnieper rapids, that of the Surskii culture discussed later, shows traces of an influence emanating from some centre of the Criş-Körös culture; and the area lay nearly 200 miles east of the territory of the Southern Bug culture. It seems very probable that the tribes of the forest zone further north (see p. 88) up to the Baltic were also affected by the Criş-Körös influence, either through the Southern Bug culture or the Surskii culture of the Dnieper rapids.

Carbon-14 dates for Hungarian sites of the Criş-Körös culture range between 5140–5100 (Bln. 75) and 4420–4100 B.C. (Bln. 57). Consequently, the beginning of the Southern Bug culture has been dated to the fifth millennium B.C.[5]

The decoration of pottery in the second stage of the Southern Bug culture, called the 'Samchyntsi' period after the corresponding site, consisted mainly of rows of alternating slanting grooves or comb impressions arranged in parallel horizontal strips (Fig. 14). The latter call to mind the 'comb-pricked ware' (Fig. 22) of the forest zone further north (see p. 86). Several potsherds of genuine Danubian I ware, found at Bashkiv Ostriv on the Southern Bug in the layer of this stage, are important for the establishment of the relative chronology. They imply that the Danubians reached the region of the Southern Bug after the men of the Criş-Körös culture. Remains of the third stage of the Southern Bug culture, called the Savran stage, are stated to have been overlaid by those of Tripolyan period B-2; this implies that the remains must be dated to the third millennium B.C.

Huts of the two earlier stages of the culture, a few of which were uncovered, were small in size, built of wattle and clay daub, and supported on a frame of wooden posts. Huts of the third, the Savran stage, had stone foundations to their timber walls, and were divided into two apartments; the roof was supported by posts placed along the middle of the hut.

THE TRIPOLYE CULTURE

Stratigraphic evidence in a series of sites (such as Nezvysko; Table 8) indicates that both the Danubian I and the Southern Bug cultures were succeeded by the 'Tripolye' culture, called after a settlement in the region of Kiev; in Rumania it has been called the 'Cucuteni' culture, after a settlement in the northern part of Moldavia. The Tripolye culture was one of the most important Neolithic cultures of Eastern Europe. It was formed in Moldavia during the first half of the fourth millennium B.C.[6]

Once formed, the Tripolye culture soon spread northwards into the territory of the west Podolian branch of the Danubian I culture, and further east into the domain of the Southern Bug culture; and initiated in these areas the second stage of our Early Neolithic (Table 3). Both local cultures were soon assimilated entirely, and the Tripolyan culture began to expand gradually still further north and north-east. Ultimately, it extended over the whole forest-steppe zone, the fertile black-earth territory west of the Dnieper. A study of its remains in the newly acquired territories reveals that an important feature in its diffusion was the conservative character of its advance groups; for they kept to ancient forms, though these had already changed in the homeland. This occurrence has often been over-looked, hence misleading conclusions have been drawn as to the Tripolyan chronology in some areas.

Tripolyan remains within this wide area were not uniform, and exhibit both regional and chronological differences. The diffusion of the Tripolye culture, due mainly to the acculturation of local tribes by small bands of Tripolyan colonists, resulted in the formation of regional groups in which some elements of the local cultures were included. Five main provinces of the Tripolye culture may thus be distinguished: the original Moldavian or Rumanian province (the Cucuteni culture); the west Podolian; the Central Bessarabian, or Middle Dniester; the Uman, or Southern Bug (Boh); and the Kiev provinces. Tripolyan influence also penetrated deep into the adjacent territories; potsherds of Tripolyan character were found as far away as Nikolaev, at the mouth of the Southern Bug. In the Late Tripolyan period, the second millennium B.C., a number of hybrid groups were formed in the peripheral areas (see p. 179).

During the two millennia or so of its existence, the Tripolye culture underwent several changes, that mark consecutive stages in its evolution. They are important for the understanding of the Neolithic and Bronze Age development of the whole south-west of Eastern Europe, and also to a considerable extent for the study of conditions in the neighbouring areas. These changes were, for the most part, the outcome of occurrences affecting wide parts of the country.

The accepted chronological scheme of the Tripolyan evolution, worked out by T.S. Passek about thirty years ago, distinguishes three main periods, each with its own decorative style of pottery: the Early Tripolyan period 'A'; the Middle Tripolyan period 'B', sub-divided into two stages 'B-1' and 'B-2'; and the Late Tripolyan period 'C', likewise subdivided into two stages, 'C-1', and 'C-2' in the northern part of the Tripolyan territory, and 'γ-1' and 'γ-2' in the south. The scheme, based chiefly on the evolution of the decora-tive style of pottery of the Kiev and Uman groups, and partly on stratigraphic evidence offered by pre-war Rumanian excavations, was a considerable achievement. However, it treats the whole Tri-polyan territory as a nearly uniform entity, within which evolution had proceeded in the same way and at the same rate, and also includes in the Tripolyan sequence hybrid groups formed outside genuine Tripolyan territory.

The scheme was partly revised by T.S. Passek, in order to adjust it to the results of post-war excavations of a series of stratified settlements in west Podolia and Bessarabia [Nezvysko (Table 8), Polivaniv Yar, Solonceni, etc.]. But their evidence calls for further revision, and especially for a proper correlation of the Tripolyan stages with the periods distinguished in the evolution of contemporary cultures in other parts of the country. The consequences of the new achievements have to some extent been worked out here.

The earliest Tripolyan remains (period A) in our territory were recorded exclusively within the areas previously held by the two early Neolithic cultures—the Danubian I and Southern Bug. They formed three somewhat differing groups—the west Podolian, Middle Dniester, and Uman groups—the differences between which were presumably due to the uneven acculturation by the expanding Tripolyans of the natives, who were of different origins in each of these regions.

The settlements, or more precisely hamlets, of the west Podolian and Middle Dniester groups were small, the largest ones being only about 220 by 270 yards square. They were kept to the river valley and were placed, like those of their preceding cultures, almost exclusively on the lowest river terrace (Pl. VIII), and only exceptionally appearing on the edge of the valley (Lenkivtsi, Solonceni). Those on the Boh, which seem to have been of a slightly later age, were rather larger, and lay mainly on the slopes of higher terraces of the river. Many were placed on steep, not easily accessible elevations (Pechora), on sites encircled by a meandering river (Krasnostavka), or on sites often selected later for hill-forts because of their topographical position (Borisovka).

Hamlets usually consisted of a few huts (eight at Luka Vrublivetska).[7] Huts were mostly of the pit-dwelling type sunk about three feet in the ground. They were either round, oval, or oblong in plan; some were only about eleven feet six inches in diameter, a few nearly twenty-three feet by sixteen feet six inches square. An exceptionally large pit-dwelling was uncovered at Luka Vrublivetska; it was 141 feet long, six to ten feet wide, with eleven hearths placed along the middle of it. There were also huts built on the surface. They were of the 'ploshchadka' type, characteristic of settlements of later periods; they were built of wattle and clay daub supported on a frame of wooden posts, with a large oven built of osier covered with a thick layer of clay. The floor was paved with rolls of fired clay (Pl. VIII).

In the occupation layer of the hamlets and in the remains of the huts, many objects were usually found; among these were tools made of flint and bone, especially flint scrapers and knives, ornaments, amulets, etc. (Fig. 15). Larger axe-type implements evidently served for felling and working wood. Flint inlays of composite sickles, and

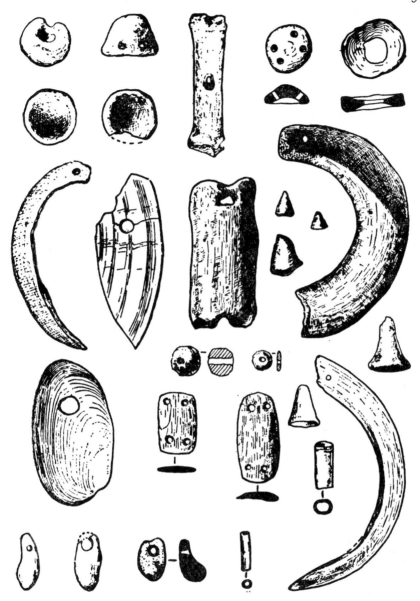

FIG. 15 Buttons, pendants, amulets, etc., made of bone, animal teeth, clay, and *Unio* shells, from the early Tripolyan settlement at Luka-Vrublivetska.
After S. N. Bibikov (MIA 38, 1958, p. 363, Pl. 71).

also actual corn (charred) witness to the knowledge of agriculture; wheat and millet were cultivated. Small copper objects were sometimes found, the largest number (twelve in all), mostly fish-hooks and a few beads, at Luka Vrublivetska in west Podolia. They were made of native cold-wrought copper of Balkan or Transylvanian origin. It is important to note that the flint industry in west Podolia evidently relates to the local Upper Palaeolithic industry (see p. 40); in the Uman group it was mainly microlithic, inherited from the Southern Bug culture of the preceding period (see p. 64).

Pottery was of two types. Kitchen ware was rather poorly fired, coarse, sand-gritted, thick-walled, and was poorly decorated with stamped impressions, and nail-tipped and incised rows. The second category was well made and fired, its clay paste either silted or slightly grog-gritted. Vessels were either large and thick-walled, used mainly for storage of food, or consisted of fine cups, bowls and vases. Their decoration consisted of rills, dots, wide flat furrows, etc.; the surface was either grey or black, sometimes polished. No painted vessels appeared in this period (Table 8B).

Clay figurines of various domesticated animals, and above all human figurines, give insight into the religious beliefs, which seem to show a great similarity to those of Minoan Crete. Of particular interest were female figurines made of clay paste to which grains of wheat were added (Luka Vrublivetska). At Oleksandrivka, about one hundred female figurines, mainly in a sitting position, and also their 'chairs' were excavated; they were evidently a borrowing from the Balkans.[8] A vase in the shape of a large bird, from Luka Vrub-livetska, calls to mind similar vessels from Danubian II (stroked) pottery in Central Europe.

Early Tripolyans kept cattle, goats and sheep, pigs and dogs; bones of horses were sometimes found among the kitchen refuse. Bones of wild animals amounted to up to 60 per cent of the whole osseous material excavated, which points to the important role played by hunting in the supply of meat.

The placing of early Tripolyan sites implies that they were set up during a period of relatively dry climate, like that in the preceding periods. However, thin layers of sand found in a series of huts (Luka-Vrublivetska, Bernovo-Luka) indicate that the settlements on the lowest terraces had been flooded from time to time. With the climate getting progressively damper, the settlements had to be moved to higher terraces. Oak and hazel charcoal found in a series of settle-ments, points to a warm but rather damp climate (Atlantic), and elk bones found at Luka Vrublivetska point to the increase of the forest areas, enabling the elk, an animal characteristic of dense woods, to reach the Dniester.

Further Development

There was no great change in conditions during the subsequent period of Tripolyan development, called the 'B-1' period (or 'Cucuteni A' in Moldavia), which marks the third stage of our Early Neolithic (Table 3). It probably began soon after the middle of the fourth millennium B.C. Settlements had not been moved and tools and weapons remained unchanged. Huts were of the same type, but those built on the surface of the 'ploshchadka' type (Pl. VIII) increased in number. The ratio of bones of domesticated animals to those of wild beasts increased significantly, and this process was greatly accelerated in the subsequent period. It shows the steady decline of the importance of hunting in the economy of settled societies.

The main difference between the cultures of the two periods was the appearance of painted pottery. Vessels were mainly painted in white, but black was also applied, the spiral and its derivative being the main decorative motifs (Pl. IX); deep incised ornament was also common. Kitchen ware decoration changed also, and impressions by a comb-like stamp (Pl. X:1) were introduced.

The new style of painting pottery was evidently introduced from the south, from Moldavia, where painted ware had appeared by the end of the preceding 'pre-Cucuteni II' period, though its style and technique were different. It should be noted, however, that north of the Dniester the new decorative style was adopted within a restricted territory only. The so-called Cucuteni A, or Tripolyan B-1 painted decoration, appears exclusively in the southern part of west Podolia and in a narrow strip of land along the middle Dniester, up to the steppe border (Zhury on the Dniester (Pl. IX), Solonceni in Bessarabia), and also on the Southern Bug (the Boh). There, the old decorative style, characteristic of the preceding Tripolyan A period, survived much longer. This is well illustrated by the pottery of the settlements of Sabatynivka II on the Boh, and Oleksandrivka (Alexandrovka in Russian) on the steppe border between the Dniester and the Boh, the late age of which has been emphasized by their investigators.[9]

At Oleksandrivka several potsherds were found bearing a painted and incised decoration characteristic of the Hamangia culture.[10] The centre of the latter lay in the Dobruja and in the southern part of Bessarabia near the Danubian delta. It developed parallel to the Cucuteni A (Tripolye B-1) culture in Moldavia, which bordered it on the west. Its Carbon-14 date, 3930 B.C. (GrN. 1966), seems to relate to an early stage in its development.

An important hoard of copper objects excavated in a Tripolyan settlement at Corbuna,[11] near Kishinev, on the steppe border in

Bessarabia, also points to a late date for eastern settlements of Cucu-teni A (Tripolye B–1) type. The hoard consisted of 444 copper objects: copper and stone battle-axes; an axe; spiral bracelets; personal orna-ments and pendants made of *Spondylus* shells; and, most important, several perforated pendants, some of which may represent very rudimentary anthropomorphic figures, made of a thin copper plate. The hoard was found in a vessel of the Tripolyan A period, but was evidently of Tripolyan B–1 age, as indicated by the objects of which it consisted. There are many replicas of the 'anthropomorphic' pen-dants in clay, silver and copper, in settlements of the Cucuteni A (Tripolyan B–1) period in Moldavia (Hăbăşeşti,[12] Truseşti). A similar hoard was found in the settlement of Hăbăşeşti[13] character-istic of the Cucuteni A (Tripolye B–1) period. The final stage of this settlement was Carbon-14 dated to about 3400 B.C.

The hoard from Corbuna, like that from Hăbăşeşti, suggests that metal tools were beginning to play an increasing role among the early Tripolyans, though actual finds of copper objects in the respective settlements were rather rare. The metal was evidently too precious to be wasted.

It is worth mentioning that in the southermost part of Bessarabia, north of the Danube, a number of settlements have been discovered of the Rumanian Gumelniţa culture (Aldeni II type). In one of these, at Bolgrad, a child's grave was found under a stone cover. The sites have been dated to the Tripolyan period B–1.

A new period of the Tripolyan development, called B–2, had begun by the very end of the fourth millennium and continued for about one thousand years, till the end of the third millennium. It lasted, therefore, throughout the whole Middle and Late Neolithic (Table 3). No stages have been distinguished so far in the development of the culture during this very long lapse of time. There are, however, a few special features in the archaeological material that seem to date it to a later age, presumably Late Neolithic. This will be discussed later (see p. 108).

During the Middle Neolithic, the first half of the third millennium, the Tripolye culture greatly enlarged its territory in reaching the Middle Dnieper south of Kiev, nearly to Cherkassy. Almost the whole very fertile black-earth country west of the Dnieper was now its domain (Map VIII).

In spreading eastwards the Tripolyans evidently assimilated the small local tribes. Their absorption undoubtedly contributed to the formation of the two new groups of the culture within the newly acquired territories, the Kiev group in the region of the Middle Dnieper south of Kiev, and the Uman group on the Middle Boh (the Southern Bug) and its tributaries. At the same time differences de-

x Vessels from the Tripolyan period B–2: comb decorated vase (kitchen ware) from Buczacz in West Podolia; excavated by Prof. L. Kozłowski.
Historical Museum, Lwów-Lviv.
Three unpainted vessels from Pieniżkowa (Penizhkova) of the Uman group; excavated by M. Himner.
State Archaeological Museum, Warsaw.

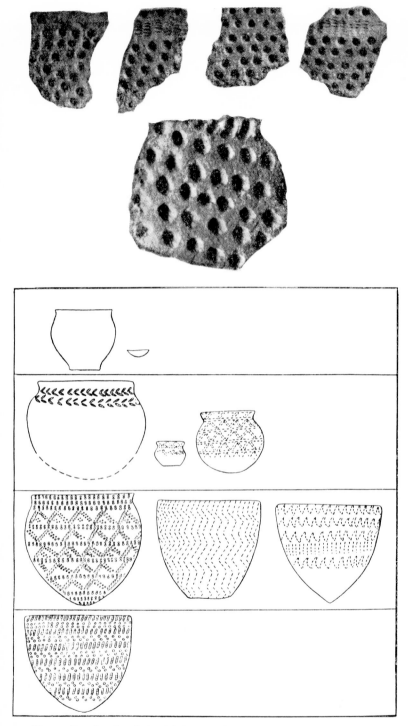

xi *Upper:* Potsherds of the Lialovo culture—the earliest of the Volga-Oka Assemblage, from the country on the upper Volga.
After V.M. Raushenbakh, sa vol. 1964–2, p. 189, fig. 1.

Lower: Pottery characteristic of the subsequent stages in the Neolithic and Bronze Age history of the Volga-Oka country. The Lialovo pottery is in the lowest row.
After M.P. Zimina, sa vol. 1968–2, p. 144.

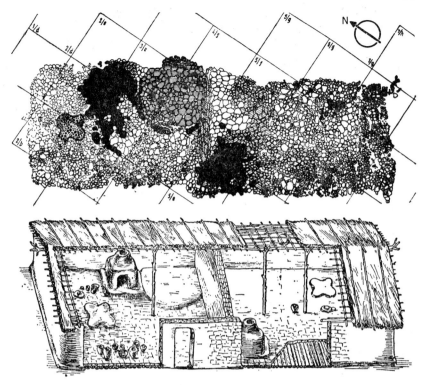

FIG. 16 *Upper:* Remains of a Tripolyan hut of period B-2 built on the original surface ('ploshchadka' type), uncovered at Vladimirovka near Uman. *Lower:* A reconstruction with the cross-shaped 'offering site' clearly visible.
After T. S. Passek (MIA 10, 1949, pp. 82, 83, figs. 38 a, b).

veloped between the western groups of the culture that had existed since the preceding period—the Bessarabian, and especially the west Podolian and Cucuteni groups—on the one hand, and the newly formed Kiev and Uman groups on the other. The differences are well reflected in the decorative styles of pottery and also in the type of settlements. In Podolia, hamlets still kept to the river valleys, though now they were more often placed on higher terraces; but in the east, settlements were set up almost exclusively on the plateau, near the edge of river valleys or near smaller streams. They were large in size and some, such as that at Volodymirivka (Vladimirovka in Russian) in the Uman group with over 200 huts, rank among the largest Tripolyan settlements yet recorded.

Huts were mostly of the 'ploshchadka' type (Fig. 16), built on the surface, of wattle and daub mounted on a frame of oak posts. Floors were paved with irregular bricks or lumps of fired clay, evidently to counter the dampness of the soil. Few semi-pit dwellings appear, and then mainly in sites in the river valleys.

Pottery was still of a high quality, very well made and baked. It was mainly a trichromatic ware—red, black and brown being the usual colours. But the decorative style of the eastern and western groups of the culture differed considerably. In the west—Nezvysko (Table 8:C), Polivaniv Yar, Zaleszczyki—it evolved directly out of the preceding period B–1 (Fig. 17:B). The decorative style B–2[14] was exclusively characteristic of the eastern groups (Volodymirivka of the Uman group; Kolomishchyna II of the Kiev group (Fig. 17:A); it had no connection whatever with the Tripolyan B–1 style, or its successive western style of the B–2 period. It was related to that of the eastern monochromatic decoration of period A (Penizhkova) and evidently evolved out of it (Pl. X). In many eastern sites pottery of styles A and B–2 was found in the same occupation layer; there was no break in the continuity of settlement there, nor in the evolution of the local groups of the Tripolye culture, in spite of the fact that there was no B–1 intermediary.

Flint axes were very common, replacing those of slate, which were characteristic of the earlier periods. Other tools were made either of flint, or bone and antler. The art of weaving was developed. Impressions of fabrics on the base of several vessels revealed two kinds of technique in use; some textiles were knitted, others had two separate systems of woven thread. The linen was probably made of hemp fibre; for grains of hemp were found in some settlements. Impressions of woollen thread were also identified. Looms were of a primitive type, about four feet wide.

The economy was based on agriculture; wheat, barley and millet were cultivated. The greatly increased number of bones of domesticated animals point to the growing importance of animal husbandry; chiefly cattle and pigs were reared, goats and sheep being of lesser importance. Hunting played a very subordinate role, a change from the earlier periods.

The Ancient Pontic Province
Transcaucasia

The ancient Pontic province of the Mesolithic, or more precisely its southern part, Transcaucasia, lay nearest to the original centres of agriculture in Western Asia. In spite of that, the knowledge of agriculture does not seem to have reached there much earlier than in distant Podolia. Furthermore, the role of Transcaucasia in the early propagation of the new economy in the countries further north was negligible.

The earliest archaeological traces in Transcaucasia of a people

FIG. 17 Painted vessels of the Tripolyan period B-2.
(A) Volodymirivka; (B) Nezvysko.
After T. S. Passek (KSIIMK No. XXVI, 1949, p. 53, fig. 19) and E. K.
Chernykh (KSIIMK No. 63, 1956, p. 54, fig. 22).

acquainted with the new economy have been called the 'Kyul-Tepe I' culture, after the lowest layer of a site investigated near Nakhichevan, on the Araxes in Western Azerbaijan.[15] The culture extended eastwards over parts of Eastern Azerbaijan between the Kura and the Araxes, where several sites were recorded. The remains of the culture, particularly its pottery, show marked connections with central Iranian sites of Tepe-Gavra type, and it is there that the origin of the culture must be sought.

The Kyul-Tepe culture developed during the fourth millennium B.C., our Early Neolithic. Remains of its settlements in the lowest, first layer of the standard site at Kyul-Tepe (Figs. 18, 19) were Carbon-14 dated to 5770 ±90 B.P. (LE. 477), about 3800 B.C.; they were overlaid by an occupation layer of remains typical of the Kura-Araxes culture of the Transcaucasian Late Neolithic, our Middle Neolithic, dealt with later, and Carbon-14 dated to 2930 ±90 B.C. (RUL. 163). Houses of the lowest layer were built of stone and clay, and each was provided with a stove or an open hearth. Its inhabitants cultivated wheat, barley and millet, and reared cattle and sheep; they also hunted and fished. Their tools were made of obsidian and stone; a few objects (awls, beads) were of native copper.

Pottery consisted mainly of undecorated, thick-walled pots, basins, jars, bowls, etc., reddish or yellowish-grey in colour. Alongside there were a score of potsherds in a well fired sand-gritted ware made of clay paste with some organic (straw) admixture; the slightly polished surface of the vessels was decorated with simple geometric patterns painted in red, brown or black. This pottery is believed to have come from some centre further south.

About the end of the fourth millennium B.C. an important change occurred in Transcaucasia. The earliest Transcaucasian agriculturalists of the Kyul-Tepe I culture, of Central Iranian parentage, were replaced, or superseded, by a new wave of early farmers of an entirely different origin, who advanced there from Eastern Anatolia. They initiated a new period in the development of Transcaucasia.

The culture of the newcomers has been called the 'Kura-Araxes' culture after the two main Transcaucasian rivers. The culture extended over most of Transcaucasia, and only small areas near the Black Sea coast in the west, and the Azerbaijan steppe in the east, were outside its influence (Map VIII). Its pottery and metal objects are closely connected with Anatolia and with Troy II, giving a good clue to the culture's place of origin. It has been estimated that the culture developed between 3200 and 2400 B.C., during our Middle and the beginning of our Late Neolithic (Table 3). Three consecutive stages of this period have been defined by stratigraphic evidence in a few settlements investigated.

FIG. 18 Pottery excavated at the settlement of Kyul-Tepe, characteristic of the lowest layer (Kyul-Tepe I culture; *two lower rows*), and of layer II (Kura-Araxes culture; *two upper rows*).
After O. A. Abibulaev (s.a. vol. 1963–3, pp. 163, 165, figs. 5, 7).

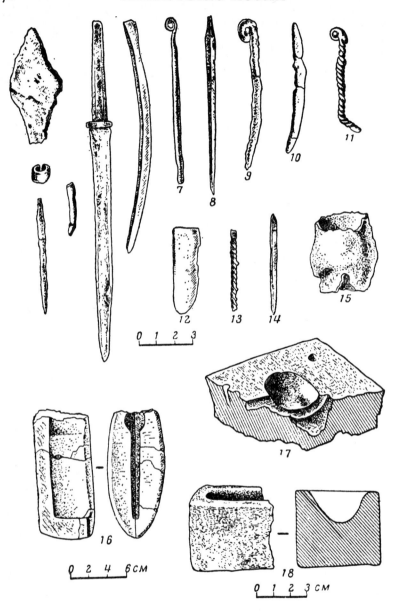

FIG. 19 Copper objects from layers I and II at Kyul-Tepe, and fragments
of moulds from layer II.
After O. A. Abibulayev (as FIG. 18, p. 162, fig. 4).

The men of the Kura-Araxes culture were farmers and breeders of sheep, but they also kept cattle. Hunting was of minor importance. Metallurgy was well developed, and from the outset arsen-bronze rather than pure copper was used for making objects of personal adornment and tools. Among the latter were shaft-hole axes, a mould for casting them having been found in one of the settlements. The pottery, of a high quality, was a hand-made, black or red monochromatic ware, decorated in relief.

The people lived in large villages or in hill-forts; and their houses were built of pisé, or of wattle and clay daub. One of the most important settlements was that excavated at Kvatskhelebi on the Kura, north-west of Tbilisi.[16] It had three occupation layers, the two lower ones belonging to the Kura-Araxes culture (C, B) and the upper one the Christian era (A). Each layer of the settlement had three building levels or horizons. The lowest layer, C, has been Carbon-14 dated to 2810 ±90 B.C. (RUL. 157), and the layer B has been provisionally dated to 2300 B.C. The houses in this settlement were nearly square and kept the same design throughout the existence of the Kura-Araxes settlement. Of special interest was the hearth, which was about three feet in diameter (Fig. 28), sunk in centre of the floor, and thoroughly coated with fired clay; it had four (occasionally five) rounded prominences, made of fired clay, also jutting towards the centre over the hole, giving the hearth the shape of a clover leaf.

A few graves of various stages in the settlement were uncovered, some richly furnished with personal ornaments made of bronze.

Amiranis Gora, near the town of Akhaltsike in Georgia, was another large settlement of the culture, investigated recently.[17] It lay 3,200 feet above sea level.

A number of sites along the Black Sea coast, in Western Georgia, Abkhasia and further north, probably belonged to the same period. Some of these were stratified, and yielded two layers of occupation (Odishi). A.A. Formozov distinguishes two periods in the Neolithic development of this area, the later one being of the 'Late Neolithic' period; a characteristic feature of the earlier period was its microlithic flint industry, a survival from the Mesolithic. The people of the culture, which was related to that of the Crimea, were evidently direct descendants of the local Mesolithic hunters.

The Crimea

The old Mesolithic population also survived in the other region of the ancient Pontic province, the Crimea, in the mountains and their northern foothills. It still kept to its old mode of life and economy based on hunting and fishing, and still lived in caves and rock-shelters, though traces of encampments outside these have also been found. Typical of that period, our Early and Middle Neolithic, were the upper occupation layers in caves—the Shan-Koba cave, well known from the Mesolithic, or Zamil-Koba—and also in sites in the Yaila Mountains, like At-Bash. The culture, and its microlithic flint industry found in all these sites, was of Mesolithic tradition, and remained almost unchanged during the Neolithic and Bronze Ages. A few flint tools of Neolithic character and a few potsherds attest to the age of these sites. The Crimean population of the Early Neolithic, like that of the Mesolithic, was related to that of the valley of the Dnieper—the Surskii culture dealt with later.

Lately, several Early Neolithic sites have been discovered in various parts of the Crimean steppe country, for example, at Alekseevskaya-Zasukha on the Sivash Sea, a part of the Sea of Azov.[18] They all kept to the streams and springs, and their remains bear a close resemblance to those of the steppe country further north, including the valley of the Dnieper; its people must have belonged to the same stock.

A similar development is shown by the archaeological material of the Early Neolithic in the northern confines of the Pontic province, in the valley of the Dnieper including the region of the rapids. There again, the Mesolithic tribes survived to the new age with only gradual changes in their culture.

The Valley of the Dnieper

Several Early Neolithic sites have been uncovered in the valley of the Dnieper (Map VIII). They lie exclusively on low terraces and on sandy river islands, like those of the Mesolithic of the region, and their remains often overlay the latter. The stratigraphic evidence at Ihren 8 and Surskii Island on the Dnieper, at Kamiana Mohyla on the Molochna, and at a series of other sites, implies the existence of three early periods of occupation. The earliest was of the Mesolithic age, followed by two Neolithic periods that mark two consecutive stages in the development of the local Early Neolithic, the remains of which have been called the 'Surskii' culture. The later of these, the Surskii II period, seems to have been contemporary with our Middle Neolithic (Table 3).

Traces of hearths were usually found in the Early Neolithic layers and occasionally traces of shanties, but only a few huts of a semi-permanent character. The sites were evidently visited seasonally. Vessels of the earlier stage were mostly small and made of talc, pottery was scarce, and its decoration consisted usually of cross-hatched lines, though many vessels were undecorated. They had a pointed base. In the later stage no stone vessels appeared, and pottery was differently decorated, its patterns being more elaborate—small triangular impressions, incisions and grooves (Fig. 20). The flint

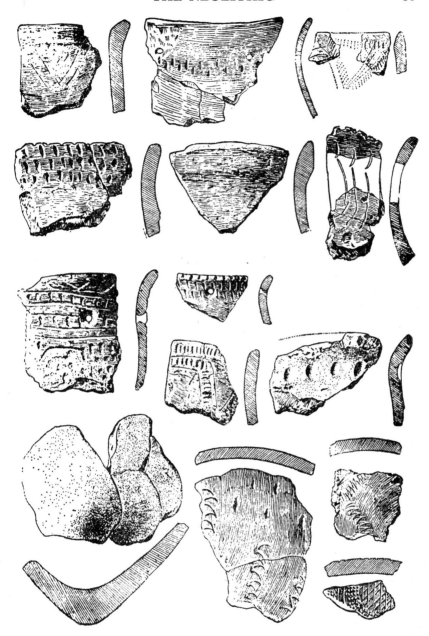

FIG. 20 Potsherds characteristic of the second period of the Surskii culture found in several sites in the region of the Dnieper rapids. After V. M. Danylenko (AK, vol. III, 1950, p. 143, pl. V).

industry was microlithic of Mesolithic character, but with a few examples of the Neolithic. Large implements, many polished, made of local varieties of stone—granite, slate, and talc—were in use concurrently with flint implements. Bone tools were also found, such as points, awls, and fish-hooks.

The economy of the inhabitants of the valley was based on fishing, and, to a lesser extent, on hunting. A large number of bones of freshwater fish and fish scales were excavated in all sites. Animal bones were identified as those of red-deer, aurochs (*Bos primigenius*), boar, hare, fox, wolf, river tortoise, various marsh birds, and beaver. No domesticated animals were in evidence, except dogs at a later stage. There were no signs of any knowledge of agriculture or any animal husbandry; they appear only later, in the remains of the subsequent period, the Late Neolithic.

Often the remains had been flooded, and so were covered by alluvial deposits. At Surskii Island, the Early Neolithic layer was overlaid by accumulations of *Paludina* shells and a sterile layer six to eight inches thick; above this layer were remains of the next period, the Middle Neolithic. The flooding was evidently concurrent with similar floods recorded in the valley of the Dniester and the Southern Bug. According to some authorities, the level of the Dnieper rose at that time about thirteen feet above the level of the Early Neolithic sites, and this was obviously the cause of their abandonment. The inhabitation of the sites was contemporary with that of the low-placed sites in the river valleys further west in the Ukraine.

During the Early Mesolithic, the region was linked to west Asiatic culture and the Caucasus. Caucasian connections were also apparent during the later stages of the Neolithic, but they are not discernible in the archaeological material of the local Early Neolithic. At that time, particularly during the second stage of the Early Neolithic, the region, at least the area of the Dnieper rapids, was connected with the cultures of the south-west Ukraine. The decorative patterns of the Surskii culture of that stage are reminiscent of those of the Criş-Körös culture, and especially of the Boian-Giuleşti layer at Floreşti in Bessarabia, the site mentioned previously (see p. 61). These connections suggest that pottery was introduced into the area from the west, presumably by the middle or the second part of the fourth millennium B.C. Local conditions were probably unsuitable for the introduction of agriculture at that time.

Several 'flat' cemeteries of this period have been investigated.[19] The graves had no markers. The skeletons lay flat on their backs, usually sprinkled with red ochre, in groups of two to seven in a single pit. These pits were at a distance from each other. Several of the skeletons lacked a number of bones, and skulls were often damaged, evidently

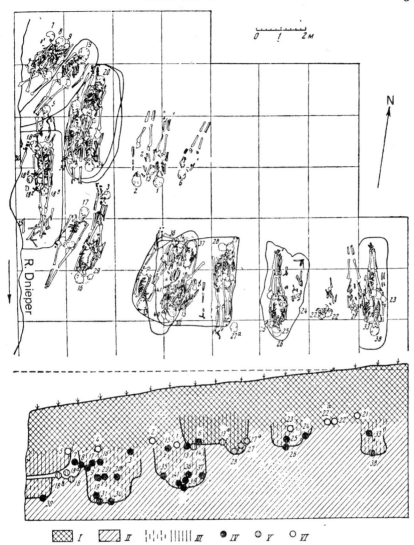

FIG. 21 Plan and cross-section of the cemetery at Vilnyi in the valley of
the Dnieper, with its overlapping burials.
After D. Ia. Telegin (S.A. vol. 1966–1, p. 5, fig. 2).

when the person in question was killed. Grave goods consisted mainly of objects of adornment, in the form of pendants of stag fangs and fish teeth; and sometimes microlithic scrapers and 'trapezes' were found, the latter probably serving as arrow-heads. In several cemeteries graves overlapped, which gave the opportunity of establishing their relative chronology (see p. 37 and Fig. 21). Many cemeteries were in use during two or three subsequent periods. The people buried were mostly brachycephalic, and of the late Crô-Magnon racial type, like those of the latest phase of the Mesolithic of the same region.

THE EARLY AND MIDDLE NEOLITHIC IN THE FOREST ZONE

The 'Neolithic' in the forest zone differed in many respects from that of the southern part of the country. There was no change in the economy of the population, which, as in the Mesolithic, was still based on hunting and fishing, at least in most parts of the forest zone. The main marks of the Neolithic age at the sites in question were pottery, flint or stone tools, and weapons of a new 'Neolithic' type. Such advances did not occur at the same time all over the country, and considerable backwardness has been noticed in some regions. Still later the food-producing economy, based on stock-rearing usually combined with rudimentary agriculture, was introduced into some provinces.

The pottery and other Neolithic remains of the east European forest zone were far from being uniform. The several varieties point to distinct cultures or their assemblages, each situated in a different region within the four main provinces. Each assemblage represented a distinct racial or ethnic group. The four provinces roughly cover the areas of the Mesolithic provinces (see p. 30), and they were evidently a continuation of these.

MAP VIII *Opposite:* Eastern Europe in the first half of the third millennium B.C. (I) Sperrings culture; (II) Narva culture; (III) Valdai culture; (IV) Lialovo culture; (V) Belev culture; (VI) Dnieper-Elbe (Masovian) culture; (VIa) Dnieper-Donetz branch of Dnieper-Elbe culture; (VII) Tripolye culture of the early B-2 period; (VIII) Surskii culture; (IX) pre-pottery Kazan culture; (X) pre-pottery Middle Kama culture; (XI) Early Gorbunovo culture; (XII) Chebarkul—South Ural Early Neolithic culture; (XIII) Kelteminar culture; (XIV) Yamnaya culture; (XIVa) newly acquired Yamnaya territory; (XV) Maikop culture; (XVI) Abkhasian and West Georgian Neolithic; (XVII) Kura-Araxes culture: (XVIII) North-East Causcasian extension of Kura-Araxes.

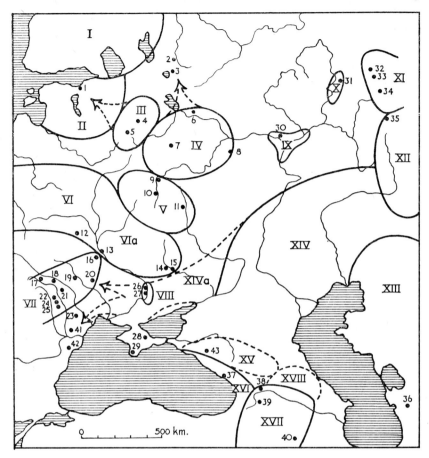

sites: (1) Narva; (2) Veretie; (3) Pogostishche; (4) Lake Piros; (5) Lake Seliger; (6) Boran; (7) Lialovo; (8) Arzamas; (9) Gremyachee; (10) Belev; (11) Dolgoe; (12) Kalenske on the Mostva; (13) Mykilska Slobidka; (14) Bondarykha; (15) Ustie Oskola; (16) Tripolye; (17) Horodnica; (18) Polivaniv Yar; (19) Pechora; (20) Volodymirivka; (21) Floreşti; (22) Truşeşti; (23) Corbuna; (24) Cucuteni; (25) Hâbâşeşti; (26) Vovnykh; (27) Surskii Island; (28) Alekseevskaya Zasukha; (29) Shan-Koba; (30) Observatoria III; (31) Nizhnee Adishchevo; (32) Poludenka; (33) Gorbunovo peat-bog; (34) Shigir peat-bog; (35) Chebarkul; (36) Djebel; (37) Odishi; (38) Kvatskhelebi; (39) Amiranis Gora; (40) Kyul-Tepe; (41) Bolgrad; (42) Hamangia; (43) Maikop.

The main indication of the Neolithic age of the sites was pottery, which was not an east European invention. Its diversity in shape, decoration and make indicates that it must have been introduced from outside the forest zone, though the original centres of its many varieties are difficult to trace. Nevertheless, recent studies of the cultures of these areas throw some light on the origins of the Neolithic of the east European forest zone.

The first Early Neolithic cultures of the forest zone were the 'Dnieper-Elbe' assemblage, also called the 'Comb-Pricked Ware' culture in the south and west, and the 'Finnish Sperrings' culture in the north (Karelia). Later, in the Middle Neolithic, several cultures appeared—the Volga Oka assemblage in Central Russia, the Valdai and Narva culture in the north-western regions, the Gorbunovo culture in the Urals, and some others. Larger parts of the country were, however, still peopled by tribes who kept to the Mesolithic traditions; the culture of some of these, which adopted a few Neolithic tools or other items, acquired the character of the 'pre-pottery' Neolithic. We shall briefly review the main cultures of that period.

THE COMB-PRICKED WARE CULTURE

Sites of the Comb-Pricked Ware culture were spread over a very large territory from the Middle Donetz, in the region of Izium, westwards along both sides of the forest and forest steppe border up to regions of Kiev. They occur in the forest zone west of the Desna, in the Basin of the Upper Dnieper (Fig. 22), and still further west in Central and Western Poland, until in east Germany they even reach the Elbe. The northernmost sites in Eastern Europe have been discovered on the Western Dvina near Polotsk[20] (Map VIII).

Various names have been given to these remains: the Proto-Finnish, Masovian, or the Dnieper-Elbe culture,[21] and the Comb-Pricked Ware culture.[22] Lately the term of the Dnieper-Donetz culture has been proposed;[23] but this term can be applied only to the second, Late Neolithic stage of the culture, remains of which have been found only within the eastern areas of the assemblage.

A large number of sites of the assemblage have been recorded in Eastern Europe. They lie mainly on the tops of sand-dunes, on the edges of the lower river terraces, and on the banks of lakes that are now mostly peat-bogs. Their remains were also found in the fossil humus or beneath it, sometimes under the layer of peat (Kalenske on the Mostva in east Volhynia). Among the other most important sites are Bondarykha 2, the lower layer of site Ustie-Oskola, Studenok 5, etc. on the Donetz, Vita-Litovska, and Mykilska Slobidka etc. near Kiev; plus a series of peat-bog sites in East Prussia, such as Zedmar (now renamed Serovo[24]).

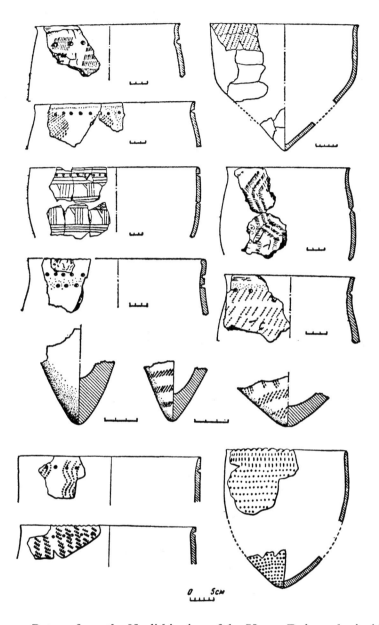

FIG. 22 Pottery from the Neolithic sites of the Upper Dnieper basin (the Comb-pricked ware culture).
After I. I. Artemenko (S.A. vol. 1963–2, p. 33, fig. 6, and KSIAM No. 88, 1962, p. 72, fig. 19).

The sites on sand-dunes usually contained traces of hearths, flints, and small pieces of potsherds. No bones survived, except in a few sites protected by a layer of peat in which a series of bone and antler weapons and tools were excavated. They closely resembled those of the east Baltic culture dealt with later. Flints were mainly microlithic of Tardenoisian tradition, highly developed in manufacture. But alongside these were frequently found large tools, especially axe-like hewing tools, of the 'tranchet type', which probably served for working bone and wood. The earliest flint axes, lenticular in section, were found in sites of the advanced stage. Only their edge was polished (Fig. 23).

The pottery of the assemblage was not uniform. Excavation of a few stratified sites in the region of Kiev (such as Mykilska Slobidka) and on the Donetz revealed that the pottery of the earlier layers differed somewhat from that of the later strata. The earlier pottery was made of a clay paste with vegetal (straw or grass) admixture, often slightly sand-gritted; and it was insufficiently baked. Vessels had a rounded or pointed base and their decoration consisted of rows of finger-nail impressions, small dimples, rows of impressions made by the tip of a stick drawn back, and sparse impressions of a short fine comb-like stamp, etc. Vessels of the later stage were in the main decorated all over their surface by impressions of a similar, but longer, fine comb-stamp and by small incisions arranged in horizontal rows. This pottery was typical of the Late Neolithic (see p. 112).

The people of this culture were undoubtedly descended from the local Mesolithic tribes, and their economy was similarly based on hunting and fishing. Animal bones had disintegrated in most sites, but those that survived all belonged to wild beasts. Remains of hearths, and sometimes traces of shanties, were uncovered, but never traces of any dwellings of a more permanent character. This points to a migratory mode of life.

The origin of the culture poses a problem. The earliest pottery differs from Danubian I ware and evidently represents another tradition in the potter's craft. Similarities connecting it with the early Neolithic ware of the south Ukraine suggest that it may have developed from pottery of the Surskii culture of the Dnieper valley, but more likely from that of the Southern Bug culture. D.Ia. Telegin[25] points to the connections of the earliest pottery of the assemblage with that of the Southern Bug culture and he accordingly equates the early stage of the Comb-Pricked Ware culture with the latter. In any case the origin of the Comb-Pricked Ware may ultimately be traced back to the Criş-Körös pottery (see p. 65). Presumably the pottery was adopted by the tribes of the forest zone from their southern neighbours in the first half of the fourth millennium, and it then spread further north and north-west.

XII North-west Caucasian dolmens. *Upper:* Beregovaya; *Lower:* Pshad. After A.M. Tallgren, ESA IX, p. 9.

XIII Pottery from the region of the Dnieper rapids. Comb-pricked vase from the cemetery of Mykilske (after D.Ia. Telegin, KSIAK 11, 1961, p. 23); *lower left:* Staryi Kodak, Serednii Stog stage; *right:* Khortytsia, Sobachky stage; both at the State Historical Museum, Kiev.

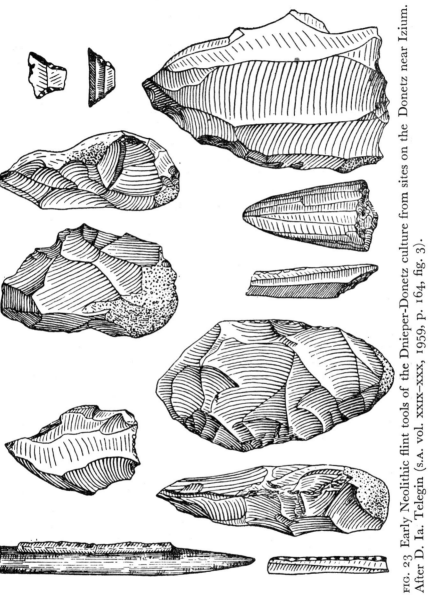

FIG. 23 Early Neolithic flint tools of the Dnieper-Donetz culture from sites on the Donetz near Izium. After D. Ia. Telegin (S.A. vol. xxix–xxx, 1959, p. 164, fig. 3).

EAST-BALTIC CULTURES

North-west and north of the Dnieper-Elbe assemblage extended the ancient east Baltic province, the domain of the Kunda culture and its related groups in the Late Mesolithic (see p. 49). It embraced the countries along the south-eastern coast of the Baltic up to the line marked by Lake Onega, Lake Ilmen and the Valdai Hills, and included parts of Finland (Map VIII: I, II).

Investigations in Finland revealed that the Neolithic developed there during the time of the Litorina Sea, when the sea level in the Gulf of Finland and the Gulf of Bothnia (and also that of the larger lakes) was 65 to 105 feet higher than today. The southern and western coast of Finland and a strip of the western coast of Estonia were then submerged. The relative age of the sites is shown by their position on the ancient beaches: those of the Mesolithic Suomusjärvi (Kunda) culture lie on the highest beaches of the Litorina Sea, whereas those of the Neolithic are confined to the lower beaches; the lower the beach line the later the age of the respective sites. The Litorina Sea lasted from about 6000 to 2000 B.C.[26]

Three consecutive periods have been defined in the development of Finnish Neolithic. Characteristic of the first of these was pottery of 'Sperrings' type. The territory covered by that ware extended eastwards over Karelia, reaching the Gulf of Onega (Map VIII: I). Its origin and initial date are debatable. Most Finnish scholars consider the makers of the Sperrings pottery as newcomers in the countries on the Eastern Baltic, who assimilated their predecessors, the indigenous fishers and hunters of the Mesolithic Suomusjärvi and Kunda cultures. Their original country has been sought somewhere in the western part of the Baltic, and they have often been connected with the Ertebølle culture of Denmark (from about 6000 to 3000 B.C.).

Estonian and Russian scholars[27] seek the origin of the Sperrings pottery, and, implicitly, of its makers, in the Urals. They point out that similar decorative motifs appear on the earliest pottery of the Gorbunovo culture (see p. 103), and are of the opinion that Finnish pottery derived from the latter. However, a distance of about nearly 1,000 miles in which no early pottery has been found separates the two regions. Furthermore, R. Indreko, in analyzing features characteristic of pottery of both regions, emphasizes that neither the Sperrings nor the Narva pottery of Estonia, discussed later, had anything to do with that of the Urals and Central Asia. However, he erroneously seeks the origin of the Sperrings pottery in East Prussia; he thinks that it was formed there through a blending of elements of the Danubian I ware with those of the west Baltic Køkkenmødding culture. The chronology of the east Baltic sites and those of the

Gorbunovo culture in the Urals does not favour the eastern theories either. The Strelka site of the Gorbunovo peat-bog, in which the earliest pottery of the region was excavated, has been Carbon-14 dated to 2850 ± 200 B.C. (Mo. 2). On the other hand, the position of sites that contained the Sperrings pottery, on ancient beaches in Finland, implies that they were of the fourth millennium, and definitely earlier than that of the Gorbunovo culture.

The earliest pottery of Estonia, of the Narva type (Table 12), called after a group of settlements on the river near the town of Narva, was characteristic of the Narva culture. According to N.N. Gurina[28], who devoted it a special study, the culture extended over the former territory of the Mesolithic Kunda culture (see p. 49), over Estonia, Latvia and Lithuania up to East Prussia; it also formed isolated groups in north-west Russia and northern Byelorussia. Its people were hunters and fishers whose tools were mostly of bone; these were evidently of Kunda derivation. Only a very few small scrapers and similar implements were of flint and quartz. Pottery of the culture calls to mind the Ertebølle ware of Denmark, but it also shows unmistakable similarity to that of the earliest ware of the Dnieper-Elbe assemblage. The latter feature should be taken into account when considering the origin of the Narva pottery. It seems very probable that this pottery had been introduced into the northern area by small groups of hunters and fishermen who had proceeded northwards from some southern region before the expansion of the Pit-Comb Ware culture of Central Russia. The origin not only of the Narva but also of the Sperrings pottery may possibly be traced back to one of the South-Ukrainian cultures, and ultimately to the Criş-Körös culture.

Several Carbon-14 dates have been published for the Narva culture. Four of these are relative to the settlement at Käpää in Estonia: peat from the lower part of the settlement 2915 ± 234 B.C. (TA. 5); elk bone from the cultural layer 2530 ± 255 B.C. (TA. 6); charred wood from the cultural layer 2400 ± 220 B.C. (TA. 4); and the fourth date quoted by N.N. Gurina 2385 ± 220 B.C. Dates for another settlement of the culture, at Sārnate in Latvia, are as follows: charcoal from the relative layer 2540 ± 250 B.C. (TA. 24); animal bones 2750 ± 250 B.C. (TA. 26); and a date mentioned by N.N. Gurina 2935 ± 250 B.C. The dates suggest the end of the fourth millennium B.C. for the formation of the culture.

THE VALDAI CULTURE

East of the area of the Narva culture, and north-east of the culture of the northern confines of the Dnieper-Elbe assemblage, lay the Valdai Upland, within the area of which a large group of sites have recently been discovered. The Early Neolithic culture of these sites shows many distinctive features. It has been called the Valdai culture[29] (Map IX). Sites on Lake Piros and on Lake Seliger (such as Kochishche) were among the excavations. The people of the culture were fishermen and hunters, and evidently descended from the local Mesolithic population.

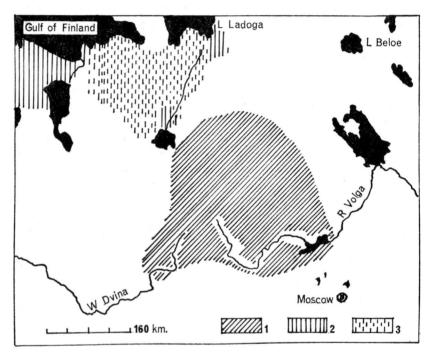

MAP IX Territories of (1) the Valdai culture and (2) (3) the Narva culture. After N. N. Gurina (S.A. vol. 1958–3, p. 42, fig. 6).

The flint industry included many microlithic tools of Mesolithic tradition, but also exhibited several more archaic features that link it with the Byelorsussian Mesolithic sites of the Grensk type (see p. 42). The flint industry links the culture with a wide region extending over the basins of the Upper Volga, Upper Dnieper and the Upper and Middle Desna.[30]

The pottery of this culture was closely allied with that of the region to the south, the Dnieper-Elbe assemblage. It was for the most part made of clay paste tempered with some organic admixture, but a slightly sand-gritted ware was also found. Vessels had a pointed base, and their decoration consisted of irregularly scattered thin comb impressions, incisions, etc. It differed markedly from that of the Volga-Oka assemblage.

The formation of the Valdai culture was undoubtedly connected with the same current that contributed to the formation of the Dnieper-Elbe assemblage, and possibly also of the east Baltic cultures discussed previously.

THE VOLGA-OKA ASSEMBLAGE

The Central Russian plain, enclosed by the Upper Volga, the Oka and the Desna, which lay entirely within the forest zone, was the homeland of the Neolithic 'Pit-Comb Ware' culture, also called the 'Pit-Marked Ware' culture. This culture extended over the territory of the former Central Russian Mesolithic province (see p. 42). Mainly the southern regions of the culture have been investigated —near the southern border of the forest zone, along the Klyazma east of Moscow, and along the Oka—over a distance of about 300 miles. But recently scores of sites, several of them stratified like Zolotoruchie, Seltso and Sakhtysh (Fig. 24), have been discovered in the territory north of Moscow, south of the Upper Volga.[31] The collective name of the 'Volga-Oka Neolithic' culture has been given to these remains. It did not form a uniform assemblage. A.Ia. Briusov distinguished several groups and discussed their reciprocal relations; but new discoveries have considerably altered his scheme.

The culture was distinguished by its pottery, of which elongated, baggy vessels with a pointed or rounded base were characteristic. Their decoration, from which the name of the culture derives, consisted of deep pits—round, semi-circular or rhomboid—covering the whole surface of the vessels (Fig. 25, lowest row). They were arranged in horizontal zones divided by comb impressions, or in checkerboard patterns. The decorative style of each region has its own specific motif; it also shows chronological differences between the regions.

The flint industry of the early sites displays strong Mesolithic traditions. Larger, well formed tools and weapons of the Neolithic type appear later, retouched on the whole surface, especially arrow and dart-heads. Of interest also is the bone industry found in some sites on the shores of lakes, or in peat-bogs. At Sakhtysh (Fig. 24) in the region of the Upper Volga, many bone awls, piercers, points, chisels, daggers, harpoons, fish-hooks, and also arrow-heads, including those of the 'Shigir' type (Fig. 11) were excavated.[32]

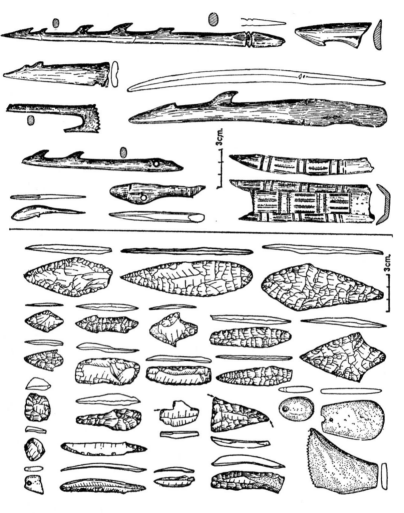

FIG. 24 Flint industry and bone harpoons, arrow-heads, etc., from the Sakhtysh I and II sites.
After O. S. Gadzyatskaya and D. A. Kraynov (KSIAM No. 100, 1965, pp. 32, 33,

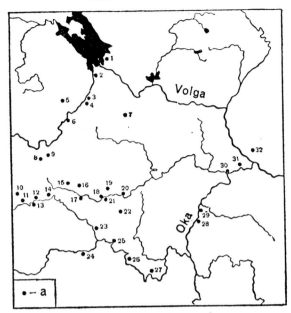

MAP X Settlements of the Lialovo culture.
SITES: (6) Zolotoruchie; (7) Seltso; (15) Lialovo.
After P. N. Tretiakov (KSIAM No. 106, 1966, p. 11, fig. 4).

The people of the Pit-Comb Pottery culture were undoubtedly direct descendants of the local Mesolithic population, like those of the groups hitherto described. However, the origin of their pottery remains unknown. Some scholars[33] consider it to be of Siberian origin, others[34] connect it with the comb-pricked ware and seek its origin in East Prussia, whence it spread eastwards. It seems, however, that the pottery had developed locally in Central Russia out of the early comb-pricked ware of the Dnieper-Elbe culture. No agriculture nor animal husbandry were practised by this culture during the Neolithic, its economy being based on hunting and fishing.

The encampments of the culture kept to the river banks and shores of lakes, but many lay on sand-dunes. The accumulated layers of the sites on lakes point to a rather settled way of life among the fishing population. On the other hand, the sites on sand-dunes gave evidence of seasonal camps, which suggest a migratory way of life. It is interesting to note that potsherds found in the latter often belonged to a single vessel; it could have been shattered when breaking up the camp, and its sherds scattered over a wide area.

The earliest of all groups of the Volga-Oka assemblage was the Lialovo culture[35] (Pl. XI). The culture covered a much wider area than previously assumed, and was the basic Neolithic culture of the whole Volga-Oka territory, except its south-western region on the upper Oka, south of the river Moskva (Map X). The latter was the domain of the Belev culture another Early Neolithic culture of the assemblage. The Lialovo culture originally also extended over areas outside the territory defined above, east of the Lower Oka, south of the Middle Volga; and a site near Arzamas, east of Murom, has been investigated.[36] The culture is supposed to have reached eastwards up to the Volga below the junction of the Kama.

The Lialovo culture also extended north of the Upper Volga (Map VIII: IV). Sites yielding pottery of the culture were investigated in the region of Kostroma, for example at Boran;[37] they have been considered to be of the middle of the third millennium.

The second half of the fourth millennium may be assumed as the time when the pottery and a series of tools of neolithic character were adopted by the local Mesolithic tribes, and the Neolithic Lialovo culture formed. This is suggested by circumstances in the areas bordering on the culture to the south and south-west and by Carbon-14 dates of sites Pleshcheevo IV, 2770 B.C. (GIN–115), and Pleshcheevo II, 1920 B.C. (GIN–116); the latter represents the second stage in the development of the Pit-comb pottery. The culture continued almost unchanged up to the end of the third millennium.

Another early group of the Volga-Oka assemblage was the Belev culture (Fig. 25), considered by some authors to form an independent culture (Map VIII: V). It centred on the area on the Upper Oka, but is said to have reached northwards along the Desna into the area of the Upper Dnieper, thus being wedged in between the Byelorussian sites of the Dnieper-Elbe Assemblage and the territory of the Lialovo culture in the east. Eastwards, it extended approximately to the Upper Don. The site of Gremyachee[38] was typical of the culture, and interesting also is the easternmost site at Dolgoe, on the Upper Don near Dankov,[39] nearly 200 miles south-east of Moscow. The Dnieper-Donetz culture bordered on the Belev culture to the south.

Three horizons have been distinguished in the occupation layer at Dolgoe. The upper one, of the Catacomb period (see p. 222), lay over a sterile intercalation. The two lower horizons were Neolithic (Fig. 25). In the lowest one, *Unio* and *Anadonta* shell-middens were uncovered, and many animal and fish bones and flint tools and much pottery excavated. In its superimposed, middle horizon pottery and flint tools were also found, and many bone harpoons, halberds, daggers, arrow-heads, etc. The bone weapons and tools were of the same kind, and represented the same types, as those found in sites in the region on the Upper Volga such as Sakhtysh,[40] and in Mesolithic sites on the east Baltic coast. The inhabitants of the site were fishermen and hunters. According to the investigator, the site was

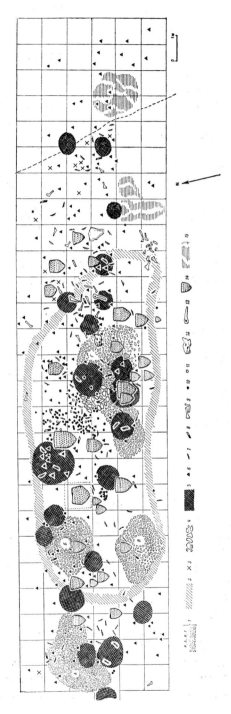

FIG. 25 Plan of the lower and middle horizons of the Neolithic site excavated at Dolgoe on the upper Don. *Smaller roundels*: concentrations of shells in the lower horizon; *Larger roundel in the centre*: a concentration of flint pebbles; *Points*: hearths of the middle horizon. The pottery of the lower layer occurred almost exclusively within the area encircled by the hatched band; all the reconstructed vessels were of the middle horizon. Other signs, triangles, etc. denote flint and bone objects. The larger object marked in the centre was a bear's skull. After V. P. Levenok (MIA 131, 1965, p. 224, fig. 1).

inhabited from the end of the fourth to the end of the third millennium B.C.

The Belev culture resembles the Lialovo culture, to which it was related, but shows many features of its own. Its pottery, consisting of elongated vessels of the same shape and similarly decorated as those of the Lialovo culture, differed in that the pits which also covered the whole surface of the vessels were predominantly rhomboid in shape, whereas those of the Lialovo culture were almost exclusively round or rounded. The flint industry also differed; it retained many archaic types going back to the Early Mesolithic. Large hewing tools and massively bladed knives were peculiar to the Belev culture. A similar flint industry has been found in the sites of the Valdai culture.

Presumably the late fourth millennium B.C. saw the formation of the Belev culture. Probably by not later than the middle of the third millennium, pottery typical of the culture appeared in the region on the Middle Donetz (see p. 112). It marks the southern migration of the Belev tribes. Some authors[41] place this occurrence at about 2000 B.C.

THE NEOLITHIC IN THE EAST

An entirely different province of the Neolithic extended over the area on both sides of the Urals, the Middle Volga being its approximate western limit. It has been called the 'Kama-Ural' province (Map VIII). Several distinct cultures have been distinguished within the province, the roots of which lay for the most part further south, in Soviet Central Asia. Some attention, therefore, should be given to the Early Neolithic of the latter area.

SOVIET CENTRAL ASIA

The earliest settlements, or rather small hamlets, in the area east of the Caspian Sea appear exclusively within a narrow strip of land in the southern part of Soviet Turkestan, on the foothills along the Iranian border. This was the area nearest to the ancient Oriental centres that originated the new Neolithic economy (see p. 55).

The occupation layers up to twenty feet deep imply that the inhabitants of the hamlets enjoyed a settled way of life. They lived in huts built of pisé, and farmed on irrigated plots situated close to the streams in the valleys. They cultivated wheat and barley. Bones found were exclusively those of wild animals; this was probably the time at which domestication had just began. The flint industry was 'geometric', microlithic of Mesolithic tradition, and consisted mainly of inlays, blades, etc., fitted to wooden or bone sickles and other tools.

The name of the Jeitun culture has been given to these remains,[42] and their date estimated as the fifth, or even the sixth, millennium. The culture, as suggested by its pottery, was closely related to that of the early settlements in Iran, of the Tepe-Sialk type. The culture formed the northernmost outpost of the early agricultural centres of Western Asia.

The Jeitun culture seems to have developed in a dry climate, probably contemporary with the Boreal climate of Western Europe.[43] Later, a damp climate set in, which enabled the agricultural communities to spread over larger areas in Southern Turkestan. The Anau and the Namazga cultures were their archaeological equivalents, the further development of which, up to the second millennium B.C., has been divided into several stages.

Further north, and along the eastern coast of the Caspian Sea, lived tribes which still kept to the Mesolithic culture with its microlithic flint industry and ancient mode of life. The best known, and one of the earliest sites was the Djebel cave, after which this group of remains has been called. In the cave several occupation layers were uncovered, the Mesolithic Layer 4 being Carbon-14 dated as 4070 ±240 B.C. (LE. 1). Bones of domesticated animals were found in its Neolithic layers, predominantly those of sheep and goats.

The Mesolithic sites kept almost exclusively to the region close to the sea coast. However, a change took place in this respect later, owing to the change of climate. Pollen analysis of ancient peat-bogs in the valley of the Uzboi, a river which has disappeared, revealed that the area, now a desert, was afforested; fir, pine, birch, alder, oak, beech, hazel, etc. grew there. These conditions were characteristic of the fifth and fourth millennia;[44] their date equates them with the period of the damp Atlantic climate of Western Europe.

A considerable expansion of the area inhabited by the Caspian tribes has been noted at that time. Traces of their seasonal visits (no permanent settlements were found) then appeared in the country— almost a desert at present, and undoubtedly a desert during the preceding period of the Boreal climate (or of its Central Asiatic equivalent)—along the banks of streams and rivers that have long since ceased to exist, in the area south-west of the Sea of Aral and on the shores of many lakes that are now empty. The economy of the people was dependent on hunting, but fishing also formed an important activity. Bones found in the sites were identified as those of boar, red-deer, roe-deer, etc.—all species characteristic of a wooded country.

Remains similar to those mentioned were found within a very large territory extending over ancient Chorasmia and west Kazakhstan, in the country north-west and north of the Sea of Aral. The name of

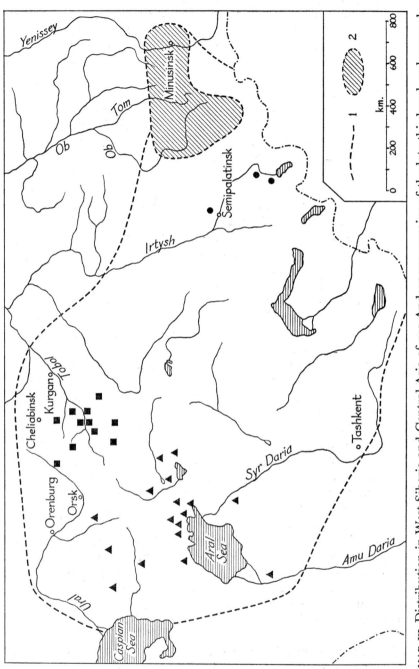

MAP XI Distribution in West Siberia and Central Asia of pre-Andronovo remains of the late third and early second millennia B.C.

(1) Area of the Andronovo culture of the second millennium B.C.; (2) territory of the Afanasievo culture. *Squares*: sites of the South Ural Neolithic culture; *Triangles*: sites of the Kelteminar culture; *Points*: other sites of the period.

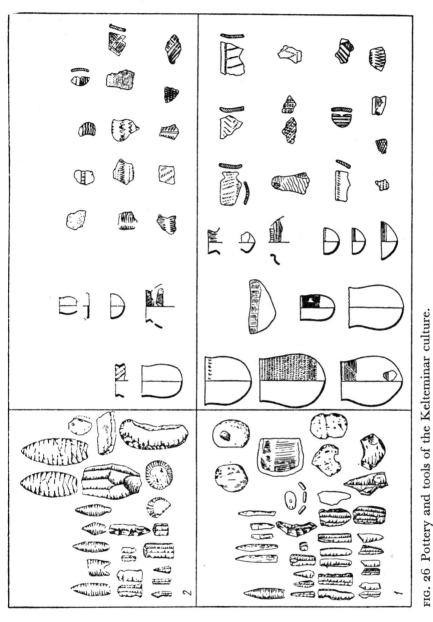

FIG. 26 Pottery and tools of the Kelteminar culture.
(1) the earlier stage; the third millennium B.C.; (2) the later stage; the late third and early second millennia B.C.
After V. M. Masson (*Srednyaya Aziya i Drevnii Vostok*. Moscow-Leningrad 1964, p. 175, fig. 31).

the Kelteminar culture was given to them (Map XI). The flint industry was microlithic, of Mesolithic derivation; pottery consisted of large bag-shaped vessels with a pointed base, covered with short incisions, arranged in rows and forming other patterns. A thin comb-stamp was also used (Fig. 26). The knowledge of the potter's craft was undoubtedly acquired through contact with the agricultural tribes further south.

The people of the Kelteminar culture were at first engaged only in hunting and fishing, but later some of its tribes gradually took to a settled life and to stock-breeding, which they evidently adopted from southern settlers. Several settlements with large huts have been investigated.

The culture is considered to have been formed in the fourth millennium. No Carbon-14 dates for the culture are available, but its coeval Namazga III culture, in Turkestan further south, has been Carbon-14 dated as 2750 ±220 B.C. (LE. 2). The culture had developed till the end of the third millennium. Its importance lies in the fact that it had exercised a considerable influence on the culture that developed further north, in the Southern Urals, and also on those in the forest-steppe and forest zones of Western Siberia. It passed on the knowledge of the potter's craft; and several flint tools popular among west Siberian Neolithic cultures seem to have been taken over from the Kelteminar culture (Map VIII: XI–XIII). The Neolithic cultures of the Kama-Ural province were also among those influenced by the Kelteminar culture, which must have reached them through the Neolithic groups of the south Urals bordering it to the north (Map XI). During the fourth millennium, the period of the Atlantic climate, the area north of the Sea of Aral up to the Urals does not seem to have been an arid steppe as it is at present.

THE KAMA-URAL PROVINCE

The large east Russian Neolithic province, usually called the Kama-Ural province, extended over the forest zone on the middle Volga, over the basin of the Kama, and also over a wide stretch of land on the other, eastern side of the Urals (Map VIII: IX–XI). It also embraced the sparsely populated virgin Taiga forests further north; a closely related group, which perhaps also formed part of the assemblage, developed on the Upper Ob in Western Siberia. The province approximately covered the area of the 'Eastern Province' of the Mesolithic.

The Neolithic cultures of this huge territory differed from those of the Central Russian forest zone. A few distinct regional groups have been distinguished there, but they all show sufficient common features to unite them into a wider assemblage. They were formed in the main

during the second half of the third millennium B.C., our Late Neolithic, and only a few—the Gorbunovo culture and a few sites in the
south Urals investigated in recent years—go back to the first half of
the third millennium or even the end of the fourth, to our Middle
Neolithic.

The best known of all eastern groups was the Gorbunovo culture,
called after a peat-bog near Sverdlovsk, on the eastern side of the
Middle Urals. Some scholars call it the 'Poludenka' culture, after
another peat-bog in the region of Nizhne-Tagil. The culture followed
the Shigir culture of the Mesolithic (see p. 45), and formerly was even
called the Shigir culture. It extended over an area about 190 miles
long and 125 miles wide, east of the Middle Urals (Map VIII: XI).
Three consecutive periods in its development have been distinguished
by V.M. Raushenbakh, but other scholars[45] divide the first of these
into two distinct stages corresponding with our Middle and Late
Neolithic (Tables 3, 17).

The Strelka sites of the Gorbunovo peat-bog and Poludenka I are
typical of the earlier stage of the Early Gorbunovo culture of the
Middle Neolithic, whereas the lowest layer of the site 'Section 6' of
the Gorbunovo bog may be regarded as characteristic of its second
stage, the Late Neolithic. In fact, however, there was no marked
difference in the material culture of the two periods.

The inhabitants of the Gorbunovo sites, like their Mesolithic predecessors and ancestors, led rather a settled life, living close to the
shores of lakes, now mainly bogs. Their dependence on fishing is
shown by the amount of fishermen's tackle discovered—harpoons,
net-sinkers, bone needles for making nets, etc. Hunting was also
important; a simple wooden bow was excavated at Gorbunovo. Bone
arrow-heads with flint inlays, characteristic of the Mesolithic Shigir
culture, went out of use, but those of the 'Shigir' type (Fig. 11) were
still made, though they were now shorter than before. Arrows with
flint points preponderated in this period, suggesting that smaller
animals and birds were hunted as well as big game (mainly the elk).

Larger tools were mainly of schist and only small tools like scrapers
or points were made of a local variety of poor-quality flint. Sled
runners, of the same type as those excavated in Finland in Early
Neolithic deposits, were also found. Sledges were about six feet six
inches long and had a single runner, but at the end of the period
sledges with two runners appeared; they were presumably drawn by
the hunters themselves, and were used to carry game. Bird-cherry
stones found in the occupation layer attest to gathering. Wooden
sculptures were found at the Section 6 site, representing figures of elk,
primitive human idols, and, once, a dipper in the shape of a duck,
with its head forming the terminal.

Pottery was made of clay paste with an admixture of talc, mica and some organic matter. Large, straight-sided vessels were made with a rounded base, their surface entirely covered with wavy lines incised by a sharp stick and often combined with thin comb impressions. Pottery was frequently decorated also by impressions made by a thin toothed stamp arranged in parallel rows or in zig-zags. This pottery calls to mind the Sperrings type of the Finnish Early Neolithic, and on this account, as previously mentioned (see p. 90), some scholars consider the latter to be derived from the Gorbunovo ware; however, the chronology of the respective sites in Finland and the Urals seems to be against such a theory.

Data furnished by pollen analyses of a number of peat-bogs containing remains of the Gorbunovo culture revealed that it existed through the late part of the Atlantic period, but developed mainly during the dry and warm sub-Boreal climate. The Carbon-14 date of the Strelka site, 2840 $\pm$200 B.C. (Mo. 2) implies that the culture must have been formed, at the latest, at the turn of the third and fourth millennia, in our Middle Neolithic. The first stage of the early period must have ended by the middle of the third millennium, as indicated by another Carbon- 14 date, 2400 $\pm$200 B.C. (Mo. 1), for the lowest layer of the Section 6 site of the same Gorbunovo peat-bog; it already belonged to the second, our Late Neolithic (Table 3).

The origin of the Gorbunovo culture remains obscure. Its bone industry, which includes several types characteristic of the Shigir culture, suggests that it developed out of its Mesolithic predecessor. Many scholars emphasize that the early Gorbunovo pottery, and especially its decoration, are comparable to those of the Kelteminar culture—which seems to show that the latter contributed to the development of the former. Others think, however, that the Gorbunovo and Kelteminar cultures were two parallel, independent branches of a larger assemblage that extended over Russian Central Asia and west Siberia, including the Urals; and believe the fact that both developed out of the same substratum accounts for their similarity.

Two cultures with pottery closely related to that of the earliest stage of the Gorbunovo culture extended along the western side of the Urals—one, the Early Kama Neolithic culture, in the basin of the Middle Kama mainly in the region of Perm and on the lower Chusovaya; and the other, the Early Kazan Neolithic culture, further west on the Middle Volga. The first of these cultures is typified by the lower layer of the Borovoe Ozero I site, and the second by the lowest occupation level (horizon) of Observatoria III. Their pottery differed substantially from that of the Central Russian (Volga-Oka) pit-comb ware. On the other hand, the shape of the vessels of both cultures, and above all their practice of impressing their ornamentation by a

xiv Vase of the late stage of the Maikop culture, from a habitation site under a rock-shelter at Khadzhokh I in the North-west Caucasus. After A.A. Formozov, Kamennyi Vek, 1965, p. 118, fig. 57.

xv *Upper:* View of the steppe landscape in North-west Podolia, at present unde
cultivation; in the foreground is a Neolithic barrow grave, considerably ploughe
down (Lisieczyńce near Zbaraż).
Lower: Vessels from Yamnaya barrow graves near Smiela in the region of th
Middle Dnieper; barrows nos. 56, 251, 362; excavated by Count A.A.Bobrinskoy
State Historical Museum, Kiev.

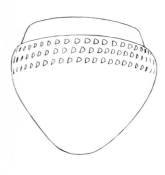

0   5 cm

thin toothed stamp, is strikingly similar to that of the comb-pricked ware of the Dnieper-Donetz culture, dealt with later.

The two cultures belonged to the wider 'Eastern Assemblage' together with the Gorbunovo culture and its related groups further east in west Siberia. Both cultures, or more exactly their standard sites, have been dated to the end of the third millennium B.C., our Late Neolithic, in spite of the similarity of their pottery with that of the early Gorbunovo Strelka of our Middle Neolithic.

The Kazan Neolithic culture, extended mainly over the areas along the Middle Volga near Kazan and around the junction of the Kama. Many sites have been recorded and several investigated,[46] among which the site of Observatoria III must count as one of the most important. It had two main occupation layers, one Neolithic, the other Bronze Age (Fig. 27). The lower of these had three levels (horizons), which denote three stages of the Kazan Neolithic (Table 4).

Huts of the lowest level, which represents the first period of the Kazan Neolithic, were round in plan. The pottery found there and in similar sites was closely related to that of the first period of the Kama Neolithic and to that of the earliest stage of the Gorbunovo culture. In spite of that, the period cannot be considered as Early Neolithic, but already Late Neolithic—of the middle and the second half of the third millennium B.C. This is indicated by the presence of pottery typical of the Balakhna culture of the Volga-Oka assemblage (see p. 208) in a site of this period belonging to the Kazan culture in the area west of Kazan. According to several scholars, this was due to the influx of the Balakhna tribes which, from their former seat somewhere on the Lower Oka, retreated eastwards about the eighteenth century B.C. under the pressure of the advancing Fatyanovians, in fact of the proto-Balanovo tribes (see p. 204).

The other group was the Kama Neolithic culture. A few sites of the period have been investigated, mainly in the region of Perm, along the Kama and near the junction of the Chusovaya (Map VIII). There lay the Late Mesolithic site of Nizhne Adishchevo, which dated from either our Early or Middle Neolithic. To the earliest Neolithic sites proper belonged Borovoe Ozero I on the Chusovaya (N.O. Bahder). Its well baked pottery was a sand-gritted ware decorated with toothed-stamp impressions, small dimples, and straight or wavy lines. It was related to the early Gorbunovo pottery, though it was most probably of a later date, our Late Neolithic or the very end of the Middle Neolithic. Its flint industry was of Mesolithic character, but its flint arrow-heads, which were of a type common in the remains of the Volga-Oka Assemblage, point to a Late Neolithic date for the site.

9

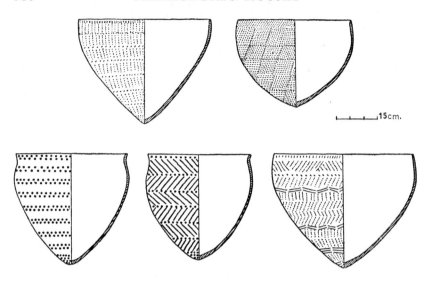

FIG. 27 Vessels typical of the Kazan Neolithic culture from the Observatoria III site.
Lower row: lowest horizon; *Upper row:* middle horizon.
After A. Kh. Khalikov (MIA 61, 1958, p. 15, fig. 4).

In three sites copper objects, the earliest in this region, were found (a copper knife at Levshino). They were all of north Caucasian origin, of the turn of the third and second millennia B.C.

THE SOUTH URALS

The earliest Neolithic sites of the South Urals were of a late Mesolithic character (e.g. the site of Akbuta on the upper Belaya near Yumaguzino), and only an admixture of tools belonging to the Neolithic indicates their age,[47] most likely our Early and perhaps also Middle Neolithic. The blade flint industry connected the sites with the wide Mesolithic province of the forest zone of the Volga-Kama-Ural region, reaching eastwards up to the Irtysh in western Siberia.

The position during the Neolithic was different, in fact our Middle and Late Neolithic. According to L.Ia. Krizhevskaya,[48] the South Urals were then the westernmost province of a large assemblage to which also belonged cultures of western and eastern Kazakhstan, and of the west Siberian forest-steppe zone. They jointly covered the territory within which the Andronovo culture had developed in the second millennium B.C. (Map XI; see p. 261).

The South Ural Neolithic culture consisted of two somewhat different branches, one in the 'Transural' country east of the main

Ural ridge, and the 'Preural' branch in the country west of the latter, which extended westwards up to the middle Belaya river. Their differences relate to both flint industry and pottery.

Typical of the Transural branch was its flake flint industry with some admixture (mainly during the early stage) of the survivals of the local Mesolithic blade industry. Its pottery was not uniform. The earliest seems to have been the 'wavy line' and 'pricked' ware, which links and equates the culture with the Kelteminar culture of Central Asia, and suggests the date of its early stage, our Middle Neolithic (Table 3). The southernmost South Ural sites lay quite close to the northernmost sites of the Kelteminar culture (Map XI). Typical of this stage was the lower occupation layer of the stratified site of Chebarkul II on Lake Chebarkul south-west of Cheliabinsk. Its flint industry was very archaic in character, and was related to the local Mesolithic industry; its pottery was mainly of the category with the 'pricked' stamped decoration. The 'comb' decorated ware was another kind of pottery typical of the Transural branch; its decoration consisted of impressions made by a thin comb-like stamp. The pottery of the upper layer of Chebarkul II was mainly of this type; it has been considered to be of a later date than that of the 'pricked' ware. It shows many points of similarity with that of the Early Gorbunovo culture.

Only a few sites of the western, Preural branch of the culture have been investigated, mainly seasonal flint workshops in the valley of the river Ufa. The contact of this branch with Central Asia was weak and indirect. Several Transural elements are discernible in the content of this branch; they are reflected mainly on pottery. The vessels were thick-walled, large in size, and their character were akin to those of the Kama Neolithic culture. Their 'wavy-combed' decoration was somewhat different from that of the Transural branch. Its flint industry carried on the traditions of the local Mesolithic industry.

THE LATE NEOLITHIC IN THE SOUTH

There is a well marked distinction in most parts of east Europe between the remains of the Middle and Late Neolithic. One of the most characteristic occurrences marking the division between the two periods, around 2500 B.C., was the westward expansion of the steppe people of the Yamnaya culture (Map VIII). Yamnaya graves at Baia-Hamangia near the Danubian delta in Rumania, on the western fringe of the steppe, have been Carbon-14 dated to 2500 B.C.[49] which implies that the Yamnaya people must have crossed the whole steppe prior to that date. West Siberian pottery, with an admixture of talc in the clay paste, and a west Siberian flint industry also appear about this time in the regions west of the Ural mountains. Archaeological material of the Late Neolithic, of the second half of the third millennium, points to the emergence of a new culture in Eastern Europe, and the displacement and change in the areas covered by the earlier ones; these changes were evidently connected with the great events just mentioned and probably their outcome. The period, the Late Neolithic, ended early in the second millennium B.C.

All the main cultures of the period will be briefly reviewed. As before, we shall first concentrate on the southern division of Eastern Europe, starting from its south-western corner, where the leading culture was still the Tripolye culture (see p. 71).

THE TRIPOLYE CULTURE

The very long-lived period B-2 of the Tripolye culture, which started at the end of the fourth millennium, lasted nearly up to the end of the third, covering both our Middle and Late Neolithic. There were only minor changes during that time. One of the features characteristic of the later part of the period, that of the Late Neolithic, was the appearance of a coarse comb-decorated kitchen ware, evidently of alien origin (Pl. X). Some scholars seek its origin in the northern forest zone, within the area of the Comb-Pricked Ware culture. The spread of this pottery, which differed considerably from Tripolyan kitchen ware of the preceding period, was possibly connected with the western migration of small groups of eastern forest dwellers who ultimately mingled with the Tripolyans.

The archaeological material well illustrates the contacts of the Tripolye culture of the later part of period B-2 with the existing cultures in other areas. In this respect, again, a marked difference existed between the eastern and western groups. The Kiev group must have maintained close relations with the Dnieper-Donetz culture: Tripolyan potsherds of B-2 (but also of the subsequent C-1) period were found in sites belonging to that culture in east Volhynia (Kalenske on the Mostva), and in the region of Kiev (Mykilska Slobidka)—and also further south in settlements in the valley of the Dnieper up to the region of the rapids, where they occur in sites (Fig. 29) of the Seredni Stog period (see p. 133).

The ramifications of the Uman group were different. A peculiar type of remains, found exclusively in this group, seems to reveal that Transcaucasian influences implanted some religious beliefs or practices. This relates to 'sanctuaries', smooth-faced, four-foil clover-leaf-shaped elevations, about three feet in diameter, found in the central part of each dwelling of the Volodymirivka (Vladimirovka) settlement and also marked on clay models of huts excavated in the debris of settlements of the following period (C–1) of the same region (Popudnia); these elevations were evidently connected with some form of worship. This otherwise inexplicable phenomenon seems to derive from hearths characteristic of the huts of the Kura-Araxes culture (see p. 79) of Transcaucasia (Fig. 28), the shape of which was strikingly similar to that of the Tripolyan 'sanctuaries' (Fig. 16). Hearths of this type survived in Transcaucasia (Kvatshelebi) to the second half of the third millennium B.C., the time of the above-mentioned Tripolyan huts. It may be that the proximity of the Uman group to the steppe country, the ancient north Pontic province, enabled the Transcaucasian influence to reach it. On the other hand, a genuine Tripolyan clay female figurine of period B–2 or C–1, was found in a barrow grave at Urup in the North-West Caucasus; it must have been brought there from the Ukraine.

The links of the western branches of the culture, the west Podolian and Bessarabian, with the Moldavian group (the Cucuteni culture) were always much closer than those with the Eastern Tripolyan branches. The age-old contact with Transylvania is attested by copper objects, and especially by copper axe-adzes found within the area of the west Podolian branch. On the other side of the Carpathians, the axes or adzes were associated mainly with the Bodrog-Keresztur culture, but, apart from these axes, no other traces of any contact of the Podolian group with that culture are discernible in the archaeological material. It is of interest to note that no connections are visible at that period either with the cultures bordering the Tripolyan territory on the west, nor with the 'Lublin Painted Pottery' culture in particular (Fig. 17).

The copper axes-adzes were probably used as battle-axes. Specimens found within the Tripolyan territory all belonged to the end of period B–2, as indicated by the copper hoard from Horodnica II. They were possibly connected with the upheaval that ultimately resulted in the change of cultural and commercial relations of the west Podolian branch, and marked the beginning of the new period (C–1) in Tripolyan development in the second millennium B.C. The period fell within the subsequent age in east European evolution.

THE DNIEPER-DONETZ CULTURE

A noticeable difference developed in the Late Neolithic between the various regions of the Dnieper-Elbe assemblage (see p. 86), especially between those in the south-eastern and western areas.

Excavation of a few stratified sites in the region of Kiev, like Mykilska Slobidka (see p. 88), revealed that pottery of the later stage of the Dnieper-Elbe assemblage differed from that of the earlier period. The earlier pottery was the 'classic' comb-pricked ware,

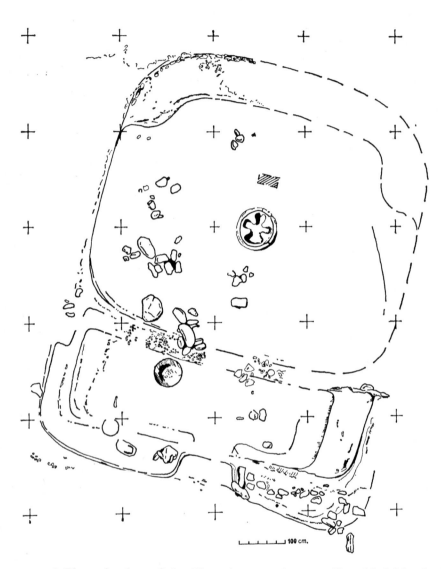

FIG. 28 Plan of a hut of the Kura-Araxes culture at Kvatskhelebi, of level B-1 (about 2300 B.C.), with the 'clover-leaf shaped' hearth (see p. 79). After A. I. Dzhavakhishvili and L. I. Glonti (*Urbnisi I.* Tbilisi 1962, pl.VI).

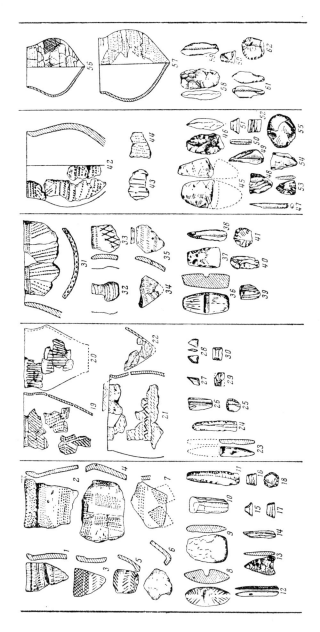

FIG. 29 Examples of pottery and tools characteristic of the various regions of the Dnieper-Donetz culture. After D. Ia. Telegin (s.A. vol. 1961–4, p. 35, fig. 7).

vessels of which were made as before of a clay paste with vegetal admixture and had a pointed base; however, the decoration of the later pottery covered the whole surface (Fig. 29). It consisted of impressions made by a fine comb-like stamp, longer than that used previously, usually arranged in horizontal rows. This pottery appears mainly in sites of the region between the Dnieper and the Donetz, hence the name of 'Dnieper-Donetz'[50] culture given to these remains. This pottery was also found in east Volhynia (Kalenske on the Mostva), and north of the Pripet, in Western Polesia,[51] but not further west; a large group of sites with a similar pottery has recently been investigated[52] in the basin of the Sozh and the Upper Dnieper. The northernmost sites were those in the region of Mogilev and Rogachev (such as Khodovichi, Zavalie). The pottery was likewise found in several settlements and cemeteries near the Dnieper rapids.

The date of the 'classic' comb-pricked ware is indicated by discoveries at Kalenske and Mykilska Slobidka (Fig. 29) associating it with Tripolyan B-2 ware. The sites in Byelorussia were likewise all of the third millennium B.C., and the comb-pricked pottery found in the region of the Dnieper rapids was of the same date. The pottery, and implicitly the culture of which it was characteristic, survived to the first part of the second millennium B.C. This is shown by the decorative patterns typical of the Globular Amphora culture (see p. 167) that appear on a few pots of the culture in the region of Kiev and in east Volhynia, and also by vessels belonging to the above culture found in association with those of the Comb-pricked Ware culture—for example, at Pilava north of Kiev, on the junction of the Teterev with the Dnieper (see Fig. 37).

The archaeological material of the region of Izium on the Donetz, the easternmost periphery of the culture, shows that it was overrun by the representatives of the Belev culture, one of the Volga-Oka assemblage (see p. 98), soon after the presumed evolution of the pottery. Part of the population was driven out by the newcomers and probably moved westwards and southwards, and part of it remained and adapted themselves to the new conditions; this is indicated by the fact that the comb-pricked ware remained in use alongside the new pit-comb ware characteristic of the northern newcomers.

The date of the expansion of the Belev culture can be deduced from the appearance of the comb-pricked ware in the region of the Dnieper rapids, evidently taken there by the retreating Dnieper-Donetz tribes. It was by the middle of the third millennium B.C. The Dnieper-Donetz culture must have been, therefore, in existence already in the first half of the third millennium B.C.

The economy of the Dnieper-Donetz population was, as before, based on hunting and fishing; but possibly a few domestic animals, cattle and goats, were reared, this being the only advance towards a new food-producing economy. No traces have been found of any knowledge of agriculture. The new pottery embodied many elements of the preceding Dnieper-Elbe pottery, differing from it chiefly in its decoration.

The appearance of a new kind of pottery poses several problems. Did it evolve locally? If so, in which region of the eastern division of the Dnieper-Elbe assemblage did this transformation take place?

The characteristic comb-pricked pottery was not restricted to the country west of the Donetz. It has been found at sites east of that river up to the Don. It also appears in the sites of the Kazan and Kama Neolithic cultures, and also in the early stage of the Gorbunovo culture, of the Middle Neolithic. A similar decoration has been also noted on the Neolithic pottery of South Urals, Kazakhstan and on the Kelteminar pottery. The eastern pottery cannot have derived from the west (see p. 104).

Two alternatives arise. Was the typical comb-pricked pottery introduced into the region around the Urals and into Central Asia by tribes migrating eastwards from the Donetz country? Or were the Urals and Central Asia the original home of the pottery, whence it was spread over parts of Eastern Europe by eastern tribes round the middle of the third millennium? The latter seems more likely.

This question, however, cannot be settled in the present state of research, though the archaeological material of the southern part of Eastern Europe implies that important tribal movements must have taken place at that time and the new type of comb-pricked pottery moved with them. The western migration of the Yamnaya people was also one of the manifestations (see p. 129). This was the beginning of a new period in Eastern Europe, of the Late Neolithic in our reckoning. The date of these events differed in various parts of the country, oscillating round the middle of the third millennium.

THE VALLEY OF THE DNIEPER

The arrival of the Dnieper-Donetz tribes in the area of the Dnieper rapids and in the country further south, on the lower Dnieper (the site at Kaury) up to the coast of the Sea of Azov (the cemetery of Mariupol), began a new period in the development of the region. It was called the Sobachky period after the corresponding site, and was of a relatively short duration.

The sites of the Sobachky period, like those of the Early Neolithic, lay on low terraces of the Dnieper or on islands in the river. Their remains overlay those of the Surskii culture. The flint industry was mainly microlithic, but larger implements were also in use. Axes were made of local varieties of stone (granite, slate), and some were

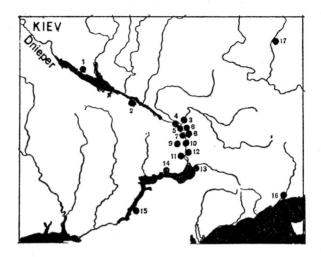

MAP XII Cemeteries of the Dnieper-Donetz culture, concentrated mainly in the valley of the Dnieper, in the region of the rapids.
SITES: (3) Chapli; (7) Mykilske-Nikolskoe; (8) Marievka; (9) Vovnykhy (11) Sobachky; (15) Kaury; (16) Mariupol; (17) Aleksandriya.
After D. Ia. Telegin (S.A. vol. 1966–1, p. 4, fig. 1).

polished. Flat rocks almost certainly used for polishing stone implements were found in several sites close to the stream and sand deposits. The fishing implements found were made of bone.

The use of pottery had greatly increased, and differed from that of the preceding period. It was of the 'comb-pricked' type with the usual decoration of that sort of ware, but differed from it in being mainly flat-bottomed (Pl. XIII: 1). Wide-bottomed beakers were typical. No traces of any agricultural activity were recorded, but animal husbandry must already have been developed at that period, for bones of cattle, pigs and goats were found in the sites, besides those of the dog.

Single graves were uncovered in a few sites, but most important for the study of the culture is a series of cemeteries such as Vovnykhy I and Mykilske (Nikolskoe in Russian), each containing 30 to 130 burials (Map XII).

The cemeteries consisted of 'flat' graves, mostly in large pits or in trenches. Skeletons lay on their backs in an extended position, and were richly sprinkled with ochre. In some cemeteries (e.g. Mykilske) the skeletons were mostly incomplete or partly ruined. Grave goods, mainly for personal adornment, were scarce except for a few graves. They consisted of a few copper rings, beads and pendants made of perforated stags' teeth or of limestone (150 of these were found in one of the graves), and also of the perforated teeth of a variety of carp (a grave at Vovnykhy yielded 400 of these). Occasionally there were *Unio*-shell ornaments and ornaments made of boars' tusks, and sometimes beads of carnelian and rock-crystal. Small flint knives and scrapers and similar small tools were often excavated, but pottery was seldom found. A custom restricted to a few cemeteries was that of shattering vessels (probably during the funeral feasts) and scattering the sherds all over the cemetery. The anthropological study of the skeletons revealed that the people buried in these cemeteries belonged to a heavily built type (men five feet seven inches tall) with a large, heavy, wide-faced head—the Crô-Magnon type.

The cemeteries were in use for several generations. Superimposed and overlapping graves (Mykilske, Vilnyi, Fig. 21) enabled D.Ia. Telegin to distinguish three periods in their use. The earliest graves, those of the Early Neolithic (see p. 82), and also those of the Seredni Stog stage (see p. 133), the final Neolithic stage of the Dnieper rapids area, were all very poorly furnished. The greatest number, and among them several better equipped burials, were of the Sobachky stage. Their date is indicated by their pottery, which was the comb-pricked ware of a late type (Pl. XIII: 1), and in particular by the objects of adornment found in graves. Among the grave goods of importance for dating were serpentine mace-heads and a fragment of a stone ring; these items link the graves with the Maikop culture of the north-west Caucasus (see p. 121) of the second half of the third and the beginning of the second millennia.

The cemetery of Mariupol, situated near the coast of the Sea of Azov, which was excavated nearly forty years ago,[53] also belonged to the culture. Its burials yielded a large number of flints, pendants, and beads made of stags' teeth, bone, shells, etc., but no pottery. Objects of alien origin were frequent, such as mace-heads and pendants of porphyry, beads of carnelian and rock crystal, and copper spiral bracelets. They were imported from, or via, the Caucasus. A few graves that differed in both burial ritual (crouched skeletons) and grave goods (mace-heads, copper bracelets) from those usual in the Late Neolithic were of the subsequent Catacomb period.

The arrival in the area of a new wave of alien people of the Yamnaya culture (see p. 133), who settled in the surrounding steppe, marks the beginning of a new stage of the Neolithic, called the Seredni Stog period and considered to be Late Neolithic or Final Neolithic, in the region of the rapids. Some of the new groups entered the valley and mingled with the natives. Their presence affected the local culture, which was gradually converted into that of the subsequent 'Early Metal' period of the region, dating to the early second millennium B.C. (Pl. XIII).

The Dnieper-Donetz people seem to have also retreated westwards and north-westwards. The appearance of their typical pottery in the forest zone on the Middle and Upper Dnieper in our Late Neolithic was undoubtedly connected with their retreat to that area. The same applies most likely to the Tripolyan kitchen ware of the B–2 period, which has some of the characteristics of the comb-pricked ware mentioned previously (see p. 86).

THE CAUCASUS

The evolution that took place in Transcaucasia during our Late Neolithic was of great importance for the development of the cultures north of the main Caucasian ridge. The ancient Kura-Araxes culture (see p. 76) lasted till about 2400 B.C., but then its relative uniformity began to falter, regional differences grew, and new cultures emerged in various parts of the country.

One of the new cultures of the new period of the Transcaucasian Bronze Age was the Sachkhere culture, called after a town north-west of Tbilisi, and this extended over parts of Western Georgia. Three periods in its development have been defined,[54] each about two centuries in duration. The last one ended about 1800 B.C. Typical of the culture were stone mounds, each a family or clan burial ground, which grew gradually with subsequent interments. Pottery and bronze objects were the usual grave goods. The graves of the mound at Sachkhere contained many more bronze objects than other burial places.

The pottery found in the graves, mostly black in colour with a pink slip, was closely related to that of the Kura-Araxes culture and had many of its characteristic features. This relation implies that the Sachkhere culture was a further development of the Kura-Araxes culture of the preceding period. But the most characteristic feature of the new culture was its advanced bronze industry. The most common bronze grave goods were shaft-hole axes, with long tubular shafts and long, bent, narrow blades, forged, tanged daggers, and long pins with T-shaped heads, and pins with double spirals giving their heads the shape of a ram's head.

Most of these objects were cast or forged locally, the west Georgian bronze industry of that period being the most advanced of all Transcaucasian centres; it was based on the rich copper deposits of that area. Almost all bronze implements of the Sachkhere culture had their parallels in Iran or Anatolia, and a number of weapons, such as spear-heads, were even of west Asiatic origin. The culture and its bronze industry had evidently been strongly influenced by west Asiatic centres. The same influence also affected the peoples of the metalliferous region on the other side of the main Caucasian ridge.

By the middle of the third millennium, the Kura-Araxes culture crossed the Caucasus (Map VIII: XVIII). In the new areas, the culture retained its ancient character to some extent, though in the meantime a further evolution has taken place in its original home in Transcaucasia. Its earliest sites north of the mountains were recorded in Dagestan, near the approaches to the main passes. Settlements and cemeteries were also found in the area east of the river Terek, up to the Caspian Sea. Those in the western part of the area were of a somewhat later date. Remains of the eastern division, in Dagestan, are considered[55] to date from the twenty-sixth to twenty-fourth centuries B.C., whereas those in the west date from the twenty-fourth to twenty-second centuries. To the latter belonged the Lugovoe settlement on the western border of the culture, many remains of which exhibit features characteristic of the Maikop culture bordering it to the west.

Burials of the northern group were either 'flat' graves found in settlements or nearby, or barrow graves, especially in Dagestan. Skeletons in both types of grave placed in deep pits flat on their backs, were strewn with a little ochre, and usually covered with a thick layer of stones. Grave goods consisted of personal ornaments, mainly copper beads, and a single vessel, sometimes a single potsherd, was found in most graves. In the Novi Arshi barrow grave, about 400 small beads of white paste were excavated; they had probably been sewn on to a garment. In some barrow graves secondary burials were uncovered.

THE MAIKOP CULTURE

The Kura-Araxes culture and the Bronze Age Sachkhere culture of Transcaucasia which followed it greatly affected the primitive tribes in the western part of the north Caucasus. The Maikop culture was formed there under their impact.

The culture, to which a special study has recently been devoted,[56] owes its name to the famous, very richly furnished 'royal' barrow grave. Over forty sites have been recorded, mainly barrow grave cemeteries, but including also several settlements. They form two main, somewhat differing groups, the western one in the area south of the river Kuban, and the eastern group in the region of Pyatigorsk-Nalchik. A few sites have been discovered on the Black Sea coast and on the Taman peninsula (Map VIII: XV).

The culture has been dated to the second half of the third millennium; some scholars put its initial date at 2500, others at 2400 B.C., and terminate it at 2100, 2000 or 1900 B.C. Two periods of development are confirmed by the stratigraphic evidence in some barrow graves and settlements, especially at Meshoko in the valley of the Belaya, about fifty miles south of Maikop, in the mountains.

The standard sites of the two periods were (1) the 'royal' barrow, grave of Maikop, and (2) those at Tsarskaya-Novosvobodnaya.

Several settlements were investigated, and they all lay in the south- in the lower part of the mountains; whereas only barrow graves were found further north. All the settlements were placed either on elevated ground surrounded by deep ravines, on rocky promontories over the river valley, or on similar positions. They had some de- fensive constructions, such as a ditch with a fence, or even a stone wall; the latter at Meshoko was thirteen feet wide and six feet six inches high, built of irregular blocks. Some settlements were large, Meshoko, for instance, extending over an area of three and three- quarter acres. The centre served as a cattle enclosure, dwellings being built around it. Huts were rectangular in plan, twenty to forty feet long and thirteen feet wide. They were light, probably of wattle plastered with clay, and supported by posts; post-holes were un- covered. The occupation layers were five to six feet thick, implying a long period of habitation. A mass of potsherds, hundreds of stone and bone implements, fragments of animal bones, and occasionally a copper object were the usual content of the occupation layers (Fig. 30; Pl. XIV).

The people were stock-breeders who also knew agriculture; bones of domesticated animals amounted to 90 per cent of the whole osseous material. At Meshoko bones of 217 pigs were found, making up 52 per cent of the domesticated animals identified; next were 119 cattle (28 per cent); and 73 sheep or goats (18 per cent). Clay strainers were found, pointing to the production of cheese.

Burials were generally under mounds, but 'flat' graves have also been found, mainly in settlements. Some of these were slab-cists (as at Skala near Meshoko). The usual type were square shafts, their sides lined with stones or timber. In the earlier period stone rings (cromlechs) appear round the grave or the perimeter of the mound, or as cairns over the burial. In the later period slab-cist graves were quite common. Burials were mostly poorly furnished—one or two vessels, and occasionally a small copper knife being their grave goods —though some better equipped graves contained a few metal objects and some imported goods. Exceptions to this rule were the famous very richly endowed 'royal' barrow graves, one at Maikop and two at Novosvobodnaya (formerly Tsarskaya), all in the western division of the culture. Many of their gold and silver objects, and beads made of semi-precious stones were imported from distant countries.

There was a marked difference between the 'royal' graves of the two standard sites in the metal objects found and in the pottery. The construction of their graves also differed. The barrow graves of the two sites denote two different periods in the development of the

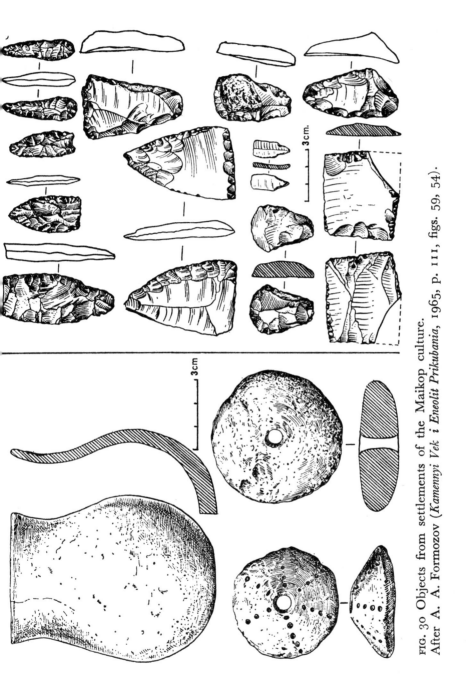

FIG. 30 Objects from settlements of the Maikop culture. After A. A. Formozov (*Kamennyi Vek i Eneolit Prikubania*, 1965, p. 111, figs. 59, 54).

3 cm.

FIG. 31 Decorated amphora from a barrow grave of the second stage of the Maikop culture.
After A. A. Formozov (as fig. 30, p. 69, fig. 30).

culture, which have been called after them. The pottery found in these graves, and also other grave goods, correspond with the respective finds in two superimposed layers of the stratified settlements.

The pottery of the earlier period was thin-walled, reddish-yellow or greyish in colour, with the surface polished and undecorated. Typical vessels were ovoid in shape with a rounded or slightly flattened base, and an everted collar. This was a local ware, but alongside it also appeared pottery decorated in relief, like that of the Kura-Araxes culture of Transcaucasia. The pottery of the later period was a greyish sand-gritted ware, thin-walled, with an unpolished surface. The vessels were more globe-shaped than the earlier form, with a straight collar, and their characteristic decoration consisted of small regular bosses pressed from inside, usually arranged in a row or parallel rows (Fig. 31). Sometimes incised double-hatched zig-zag lines appear, a motif of Transcaucasian origin.

Tools were made of stone—thin polished triangular axes or chisels—or of flint—scrapers, the blades of composite wooden or bone sickles, and large segmented blades made in a thoroughly Mesolithic technique. A few obsidian tools were found in the remains of the early period, to which the segmented flints also belonged. Many stone querns and grinders attest to a knowledge of agriculture. A few settlements of the early period yielded stone rings, a type characteristic of the Neolithic of the Mediterranean regions. A large quantity of tools were made of bone: awls, a variety of points, arrow-heads, etc. Archaic types of pendant were found, made of perforated stags' teeth; in the later period imitations of these in bronze were frequent. Also from the later period were ornaments made of boars' tusks—small plaques with perforations on their corners. Metal objects found in the remains of the earlier period were imported, whereas those of the later period were for the most part made of locally smelted copper.

The earliest remains of the culture were found in its western division. Those further east, in the region of Pyatigorsk and Nalchik, were mostly of the second period. Among the latter was the earliest settlement of the culture to be investigated, at Dolinskoe, and the barrow grave at Nalchik, which was of special interest.

The Nalchik mound was ninety-eight feet in diameter and only two feet nine inches high, but it contained 120 burials. A small mound was raised over each burial, which ultimately resulted in the formation of a larger mound covering the whole burial ground; similar growths of mounds has been observed in some Yamnaya barrow graves on the Lower Volga (see p. 131). The skeletons lay on their backs with legs contracted, in shallow oval holes, but in later graves a crouched position prevailed. The graves were poorly furnished, with a few exceptions. Pendants and beads made of animals' teeth (stag, fox, bull, goat or sheep, boars' tusks), marble, carnelian, and other stones were most common. Of particular interest were nineteen bracelets made of marble, similar to those found in the settlements of the earlier period in the western division. Some graves contained flint arrow-heads of an archaic type, and one stone mace-head and a female figurine, also made of stone, were found.

The cemetery, or the barrow grave of Nalchik was most probably the burial place of the common people. It was first used late in the second half of the third millennium, by the end of our Late Neolithic, and was in use for several generations, as indicated by graves ruined by later exhumations. In one of the latest burials, which also was one of the most richly furnished, over 1,000 beads made of glassy paste (faience) were found, along with two copper ear-pendants or temple ornaments, and a clay vessel typical of the subsequent period; the grave dates to the middle of the second millennium B.C. Only two vessels were excavated in the cemetery.

Opinions vary as to the origin of the Maikop culture. A.A. Formozov emphasizes that it developed out of the local Neolithic.

10

But no Neolithic sites have been found within the Maikop territory. Those referred to by this author (such as Nizhne Shilovskaya) lay on the Black Sea coast, over ninety miles from the Maikop centre and separated from it by a chain of mountains. Their inhabitants might have migrated northwards and settled on the lower northern ranges of the mountains where all the settlements were found, but it does not seem likely that they moved further north to the plain, where only barrow graves but no settlements have been found. Were those buried in barrow graves the descendants of the Mesolithic hunters who were influenced by the Transcaucasian settlers? Or were they perhaps a branch of the Yamnaya people who lived in the steppe north of the river Kuban? A few graves of Yamnaya type have been found within the Maikop territory, and the burial ritual of the Maikop burial was like that of the Yamnaya culture—the skeleton lying on its back with legs contracted. Noteworthy is also the barrow-grave of Uch-Tepe in Azerbaijan[57], the earliest one known so far. A few finds of Maikop type, on the other hand, were recorded in the area north of the Kuban, in the Yamnaya area.

In discussing the origin of the Maikop culture, and other related topics, special attention should be given to the 'royal' barrows; for their character is entirely different from that of the other, mostly modest, burials of the culture. All these barrows have been the subject of many studies; their furniture has been described and published in western languages,[58] and their connections, date, etc. discussed. Several of the problems raised by these burials are of great significance and importance for wider areas of Eastern Europe. Nevertheless, these are many vital questions to which no satisfactory answer can be found in the literature on the subject.

The great wealth displayed by the 'royal' barrow graves, and especially by the Maikop burial, with its human offerings (two persons offered to the buried chief), implies that the society was already divided into sharply differentiated classes—the common people, buried in poorly furnished graves, and the rulers, chieftains or kings. This fact, in turn, poses immediate problems relating to the origin of the ruling class and to the source of its wealth.

There are scholars who believe that the emergence of chieftains or divine kings was a frequent by-product of the impact of higher civilizations on barbarous tribes. But such an emergence could have taken place within a society that had already been in existence for a long period; the social division of the Maikop society had existed from the outset. Furthermore, the territory of the culture lay far from the centres of the ancient Oriental civilization; and a process similar to that in the Maikop culture, the emergence of wealthy chieftains, has not been noticed in the Kura-Araxes culture lying on the verge of the civilized world.

The pottery of the Maikop culture has close affinities with the Transcaucasian Kura-Araxes culture. Some scholars even consider the Maikop culture to have been closely related to the latter, and look upon it as the northernmost outpost of the Anatolian-Transcaucasian assemblage of the third millennium B.C.[59] The furniture of the main grave of the Maikop barrow also seems to have southern connections; its 135-odd gold and silver ornaments; its beads of carnelian, agate, meerschaum, etc.; its canopy decorated with golden figures of bulls; its gold and silver vessels, two of which have an animal decoration; and its many copper implements and weapons, among them a transversal axe and an axe-adze. This rich hoard of metal and semiprecious stones was all imported, some of it from Anatolia and Syria, some from Iran and India. A number of objects, and especially the decoration of gold and silver vases, are reminiscent of Sumerian art, and a similarity with Troy II has also been pointed out.[60]

It seems very strange indeed that a ruler of a remote country inhabited by a primitive people nearly Neolithic in their culture could have entered into such wide connections at the very early date of the development of the culture. The fact must be also borne in mind that no similar finds have been recorded for the same period in Transcaucasia, nor in any neighbouring country. Furthermore, the imported weapons and luxuries must have been paid for. What was given in exchange for them, at a time when no organized trade in agricultural products or cattle was in existence? How could a ruler of a small obscure country accumulate such a fortune—substantial even if measured by present standards?

The northern slopes of the north-west Caucasus, close to the southernmost settlements of the Maikop culture known at present, are metalliferous (Map XIII). Copper, gold and silver ores have been found, and traces of ancient exploitation recorded in several points. According to V.G. Childe,[61] this remarkable tomb may well illustrate the conversion of the autochthonous food-gatherers to food production by agents of Oriental civilization, seeking in this metalliferous region copper, gold and silver in order to satisfy the demand of west Asiatic cities. The nearest points in which copper ores were found lie about sixty miles south and south-west of Maikop. The copper region belonged to a different culture, the Abkhazian dolmen culture described later. It seems that the Oriental prospectors, most probably those from Troy II, must have arrived by sea at the mouth of the river Kuban, and then proceeded along that river and its tributaries to the highland region. This was the easiest route to the metalliferous regions. At that time the rich copper deposits of the Central Caucasus probably had not been discovered.

The wealth displayed by the early Kuban barrows, the Maikop

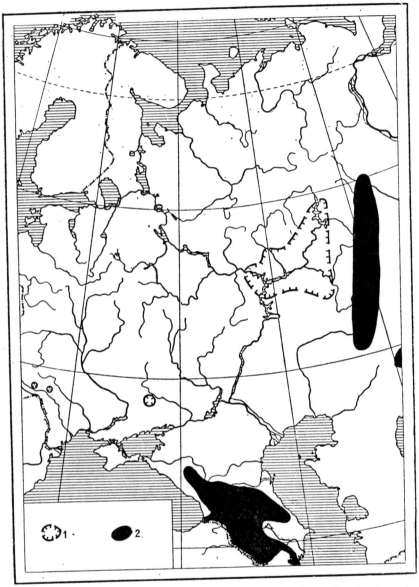

MAP XIII East-European copper deposits exploited from the third to the
first millennium B.C.
(1) Sandstone copper ores; (2) copper ores of other kinds.
After E. N. Chernykh (MIA 132, 1966, p. 4, map 1).

burial in particular, seems to have its sources in treaties concluded between the local chieftains and foreign prospectors, and in the protection provided by the former, for which the latter had to pay.

The conditions were different during the second period of the culture, the Novosvobodnaya period. A large proportion of the metal objects found in graves and settlements consisted of local products, evidently of locally smelted copper. Imported grave goods, found especially in the two barrows at Novosvobodnaya, came from different sources to those of the Maikop tomb. They have affinities with Tepe Hissar III in Iran and sites in Mesopotamia, while some of the weapons correspond to those of the Mediterranean coast of Syria.

Evidently a change in the commercial and cultural relations must have taken place at the turn of the two periods of the culture. Some authors[62] connect the change with the destruction of Troy II, about 2300 B.C., a consequence of which was the cessation of the maritime export of Caucasian copper, and of the connections established at the early stage of the Maikop culture. But also of importance was the fact that mined copper now remained in the country and was available for local needs. Thus the local metal industry began to develop those products which have been found in settlements and graves of the second period of the culture, the Novosvobodnaya period.

THE ABKHAZIAN DOLMEN CULTURE

Finally, a small group of remains in the mountains of the north-west Caucasus, called the Abkhazian dolmen culture, deserves mention. Its territory extended on both sides of the main ridge south of the territory of the Maikop culture, over the north-west Caucasian metalliferous region. (Map XIV: XXIX).

Only graves of the culture have been recorded. They were all slab-cists built of stone slabs, scattered exclusively over the west Caucasian mountains—on the southern slopes of Abkhazia and Western Georgia, and also on the northern slopes, chiefly between the rivers Laba and Belaya, where their largest concentrations occur. In the latter area they usually formed groups of up to 200 or even 500 dolmens. They were mostly built on the surface, being easily visible and accessible, which accounts for most of them having been looted. Dolmens varied in size, many being small. The largest, and presumably the latest ones, were built of squared heavy slabs very well fitted together. A circular or oval hole was usually found in the front slab, often covered with a stone disc. A number of dolmens were built of boulders and rough stone blocks (Pl. XII).

The dolmens were used as burial chambers for a very long period, and in some undisturbed examples up to forty burials have been uncovered in a single dolmen. They lay in superimposed layers, and belonged to three different periods: (1) the earliest ones were of the beginning of the Metal Age, the end of the third millennium; (2) the next were of the Middle Bronze Age, of the 'Eshery' culture, called after a cemetery with well equipped dolmen burials; and (3) the latest ones were of the Early Iron Age. Cists were evidently tribal or family vaults, the construction and the large concentrations of which suggest a rather settled mode of life. However, no settlements have been uncovered in the area except those on its northern border, which have been attributed to the Maikop culture.

Bones of sheep and, in later graves, horses point to a developed animal husbandry. But it seems that in the first place the population was engaged in copper mining. This is suggested by their concentration in the metalliferous areas, in the region where copper mining first began in the Caucasus. It is of interest to note that the decline of the group began in the second millennium B.C., at a time when the main centre of Caucasian copper mining shifted further east into the central part of the highland.

The origin of the Abkhazian dolmen culture is enigmatic. It was probably formed late in the third millennium B.C. Its dolmens differ from the slab-cists of Central Europe; the earliest ones were of an earlier date than the easternmost slab-cist graves of Central European parentage in the Ukraine and Rumania. Their origin must be sought somewhere in the eastern Mediterranean area. Their design might have been brought into the country by Mediterranean prospectors and the earliest miners. Nevertheless, the builders of the dolmens mostly seem to have been the descendants of the ancient Neolithic population of Abkhazia and Western Georgia (see p. 79).

The reciprocal relations between the Dolmen culture and the Maikop culture remain rather obscure. The cultures bordered on each other, and the Novosvobodnaya 'royal' mounds lay close to the largest concentration of dolmens, about 1500. The graves of the latter mounds were in fact large slab-cists, 'dolmens' of the Caucasian type. Some scholars[63] include the Dolmen group in the Maikop culture, which does not seem correct. Both cultures extended over different areas, the construction of their graves was different, and, although some Maikop burials were in slab-cists under mounds, the burial ritual was different. However, the Maikop rulers might have taken advantage of the circumstances that the easiest access to the metalliferous region was through the Kuban territory, and might have either levied tribute for free passage on the copper traders, or perhaps even subdued the country of the Dolmen culture, at least its northern division.

THE STEPPE COUNTRY

North of the Caucasus and south of the forest zone lay a different type of country—the open steppe or grassland (Pl. XV). During the Mesolithic, when the dry and hot Boreal climate prevailed, the country was probably uninhabited, or was an extremely thinly populated desert, especially in the Caspian depressions. No Early Neolithic remains have been found there either, though conditions during the Atlantic climate must have been much more favourable. By the end of that period a distinctive steppe population already lived there, and left behind many traces of its presence.

THE YAMNAYA CULTURE

The earliest post-Mesolithic remains of the steppe proper are known under the name of the 'Yamnaya' culture, or the 'Pit-grave' culture. The most remarkable feature of the culture was the raising of mounds of various sizes over the graves. The custom of raising a mound ('kurgan') over the grave was still observed by the steppe peoples up to the fifteenth century A.D. The kurgans, thousands of which are scattered over the grasslands of Eastern Europe and Western Siberia, are one of the most characteristic features of the steppe landscape. Thousands were excavated, but hundreds were robbed by treasure-seekers in various periods of the past.

The Yamnaya graves were deep square or rectangular shafts, often lined with timber, and usually covered with timber planks or beams. Skeletons lay on their backs with legs contracted, knees often upright, in a position seldom observed in graves of other cultures; we shall call it the 'Yamnaya' position (Fig. 32). Burials were richly strewn with ochre, and, accordingly, the name of 'Ochre' graves has often been given to them. In the east, in the steppe on the Volga, many secondary burials were uncovered in a single mound, usually fifteen to thirty, often well over fifty. Several of these were of the Yamnaya type, which indicates that mounds were used there as family or tribal burial grounds. Further west, secondary burials of the Yamnaya type were less numerous. In the steppe in the area on the Lower Dnieper and further north, west of the river, a few contemporary graves have been found under a single mound; a man was buried in these, and his wife and children sacrificed to him.

The graves of the Yamnaya culture were poorly furnished and in many no grave goods were found, possibly because they were made mainly of perishable material; in a few cases traces of wooden vessels were noticed. In the sixty-eight Yamnaya graves investigated in the region on the Middle Donetz, a total of thirteen flint knives, scrapers and arrow-heads, a few bone awls, and some other small objects were

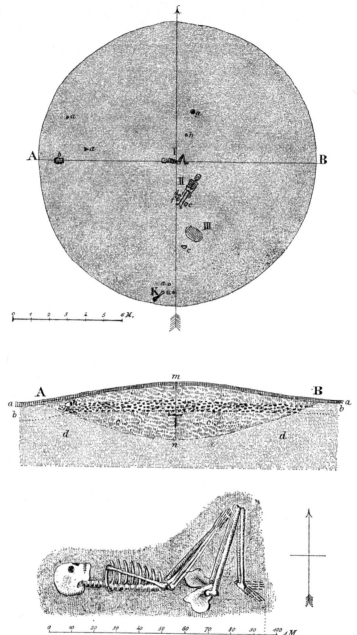

FIG. 32 Plan and cross-section of barrow grave 5 at Ryzanówka (Ryzhan-ivka) west of Cherkasy, with its Yamnaya primary grave (lowest figure), which contained no grave goods. Two secondary burials were of the pre-Scythian and Scythian periods.
After G. Ossowski (*Zbiór Wiadom. do Antropol. Krajowej*, vol. XII, Kraków 1888, pl. VII).

excavated. The position was similar in other regions, such as the Lower Volga, where only a few objects of adornment like beads, pendants, etc. made of bone or stone were found. Copper objects (small knives, small rings) were an exception, and seem to have belonged only to a later stage of the culture. Sometimes, especially in graves of children, there were ovoid vessels with a rounded or pointed base (Pl. XVI).

Yamnaya barrow-grave cemeteries appear all over the whole east European steppe country, from the Urals in the east to the Dnieper and Ingulets in the Ukraine in the west. The forest zone was their northern limit, and in the south they reached the Caucasian foothills and the Crimean steppe.[64] Yamnaya graves are said to have been found even in the oasis of Bukhara (Zaman Baba I) in Soviet Central Asia.[65] At a later stage, the culture expanded northwards into the forest-steppe country. Single Yamnaya graves, or small groups of them, were also recorded further west—west of the Dnieper in the Ukraine, in Rumania and north-west Hungary (Map VIII). Graves of the earliest stage of the sub-Carpathian barrow-grave culture were of the Yamnaya type, and so were graves under mounds investigated further west in Central and North-Western Europe up to Jutland.

The burial ritual displayed by Yamnaya graves within the wide east European steppe belt, and also their furniture, was astonishingly uniform;[66] only relatively small local differences have been observed.

Six regional groups of the culture have been defined.[67] Barrow-graves of the steppe on the Lower Dnieper, one of these groups, and also those in the region north of the Sea of Azov, differed in some respects from those of the eastern groups. Their characteristic feature was a shaft faced with stone slabs and covered by a single large slab; in a few graves anthropomorphic *stelae* were found, and several had a stone circle, called a cromlech in Soviet archaeological literature, built around the main, central burial. The cromlechs appeared chiefly in mounds of a late period, contemporary with the early period of the Catacomb culture east of the Dnieper of the second millennium B.C. (see p. 222).

The Yamnaya people were engaged mainly in animal husbandry; sheep were mostly reared in the eastern division, and cattle in the west on the Ukrainian steppe. Hunting seems to have been of importance, too, at least in the early stage. Tribes lived within restricted areas, probably moving around on two-wheeled carts of the 'arba' type drawn by oxen, similar to those used by steppe dwellers up to modern times. Remains of such carts were found in Yamnaya barrow graves on the Lower Dnieper (Staryi Kodak) and north of the Sea of Azov (Akkermen). Carts and timber-lining of graves imply acquaintance with timber working.

A number of sand-dune sites on the Volga and settlements investigated in the valleys of the main steppe rivers, the Volga, the Don and the Dnieper, have usually been attributed to this culture. Both settlements and barrow-graves were for the most part of the same age; but those in the west at least, on the Dnieper, had undoubtedly belonged to a different people, who led a different life and were of a different origin. Both peoples of the country must have been in mutual contact, and at some later date they may have blended into a single people.

The origin of the Yamnaya culture and its initial date have often been argued. No remains known so far can be considered as belonging to its primary state; at the earliest stage known to us the culture appears as an already formed complex. According to some scholars, mainly Ukrainian, the culture began in the areas between the Dnieper and the Donetz. Recent excavations in the steppe country east of the Volga, up to Orenburg,[68] and the discovery of Yamnaya barrow graves on the eastern side of the Urals, support the view[69] that the original centre of the culture lay in the steppe between Saratov and Volgograd (Stalingrad), east of the Volga.

The Yamnaya culture extended over the same territory as the north Pontic province of the Mesolithic, including its eastern division on the Urals (see pp. 34, 40). Many features characteristic of the earliest Yamnaya graves link them with the Mesolithic assemblage of the same area. In the earliest Yamnaya burials of the steppe on the Lower Volga, microlithic flints were excavated typical of the Pontic Neolithic, and in many instances skeletons were not in the 'Yamnaya' position but lay extended like those in graves of the Middle and Late Neolithic in the western division of the Pontic province (see p. 114), or in early shaft graves of the north Caucasus.

The Mesolithic population, which kept to its ancient mode of life and culture, seems to have survived on the Volga up to the time of the appearance of the Yamnaya culture, and constituted the main substratum on which this culture developed. Once formed, the culture was gradually adopted by many kindred tribes of the ancient north Pontic province.

Some scholars[70] suggest that the Yamnaya culture emanated from the south of Soviet Central Asia; graves of Zaman-Baba I, Djebel, etc. have been mentioned in this context. The influence emanating from the Kelteminar culture (see p. 102), the northernmost sites of which have been recorded on the river Turgau close to the south Urals (Map X; A.A. Formozov), had evidently reached the South Ural culture (Chebarkul II) of the Middle Neolithic (see p. 107). The tribes who lived in the area bordering on the Urals to the west, the presumed ancestors of the Yamnaya people, were most probably influenced as well.

The final formation of the Yamnaya culture, at least of its Lower Volga group, was undoubtedly greatly influenced by the north Caucasian Maikop culture, though some Yamnaya elements were probably among the original people of the latter culture (see p. 122). An anthropological study of the cranial material excavated in the steppe on the Lower Volga (Kalinovka) revealed that the population of that region was closely related not only to that of the Yamnaya group on the Lower Don and the Manych, but also to that of the north-west Caucasian Kuban country. On the other hand, the people of the steppe further north and east, towards the south Urals and the Middle Ural river, were of a different racial type.

The original territory of the Yamnaya culture lay within the area of the Pontic Mesolithic to which the Caucasus had also belonged, and there was quite easy access to the Lower Volga from the Caucasus along the rivers Egorlyk, Manych and Don. The two most characteristic features of the Yamnaya culture—the specific position of the skeletons in a rectangular shaft, and the mound raised over the grave—recorded in the early north-west Caucasian graves point to a very early contact between the Volga steppe peoples and the north Caucasus. The Nalchik barrow grave may also be mentioned (see p. 121): many mounds (kurgans) of the steppe on the Lower Volga (as at Berezhnovka 9) with a larger number of Yamnaya secondary burials grew only gradually, in the same way as the Caucasian mound grew; they also were family or clan burial grounds. The Yamnaya graves on the Lower Volga are definitely linked with the Caucasus by grave goods: the pendants and beads made of shells, bone and stone, and the polished stone rings are of the same type as those of the Maikop culture.

Another link is the flat grave of Krivoluchie near Kuibyshev, about 250 miles north of the barrow graves on the Lower Volga and about 750 miles north of Nalchik. The grave, containing a crouched skeleton, was richly furnished: its inventory consisted of lumps of ochre; over 200 beads made of deer teeth and of *Pectunculus* and *Dentalium* shells; wide-tanged flint dart-heads retouched over their whole surface; decorated bracelets made of polished talc, replicas of those found in the cemetery (barrow) of Nalchik; mace-heads of black stone; a perforated lugged axe made of porphyry; and a few flint tools.

Caucasian connections imply that the culture must already have been in existence before the middle of the third millennium B.C. This is corroborated by Carbon-14 dates, 2262 ±160 B.C. (Bln. 29) and 2716 ±65 B.C. (GrN. 1995)—a piece of wood from the same grave—relating to the Yamnaya-type graves excavated at Baia-Hamangia on the Danubian Delta in Rumania.[71] A distance of nearly 900 miles separates these graves from the original centre of the Yamnaya culture on the Lower Volga, and a sufficient time must be allowed for the Yamnaya people to reach the Danube. Another age indicator is the wooden cart with plain wheels. Such double-wheeled carts were found in Yamnaya barrow graves of an advanced stage on the Lower Dnieper; their date has been estimated as the turn of the third and second millennia B.C. These carts originated somewhere in Western Asia, and must evidently have reached the steppe and been adopted by the Yamnaya people at an earlier date. It is worth mentioning in this context that the massive wooden cart-wheels found in the peat-bogs in the Netherlands were Carbon-14 dated to 2120–2010 B.C. These carts seem to have reached Western Europe via the east European steppe, and the Yamnaya people seem to have been the men who travelled in them.

Four periods have been distinguished in the development of the culture by N.Ia. Merpert; however, the development had not proceeded uniformly within the whole of its territory. In the northern part of the Volga steppe, the culture gradually changed to a new one to which the name of the 'Srubnaya' culture (Timber grave culture) has been given (see p. 256), and further south to the 'Poltavka' culture. West of the Volga and the Don, the 'Catacomb' culture was formed at the beginning of the second millennium B.C. (see p. 222), and subsequently replaced the Yamnaya culture there.

It is only in the region on the Lower Dnieper, and in the steppe west of that river up to the Inguletz, that the Yamnaya culture survived into the second millennium, the period of the Catacomb culture. In that area niche ('catacomb') graves appeared very seldom, and pottery of the late Yamnaya burials, the 'Catacomb' period and the Middle Bronze Age of the Ukraine, consisted mainly of somewhat evolved types of vessels familiar to the Yamnaya culture of the earlier period; they were sometimes provided with one or two lugs or handles. The old Yamnaya tradition survived also in the steppe north of the Sea of Azov. Vessels were found there similar to those mentioned above, alongside those typical of the Catacomb culture. The strength of the ancient traditions is also illustrated by the so-called 'transitional' type of grave, with the shaft divided by a threshold into two parts—precursors to the shaft and niche of the proper 'Catacomb' graves—or shafts with a small cavity instead of a proper niche. The graves combined the age-old burial custom with the new and alien ideas.

The lot of the small outlying gangs of the Yamnaya people which reached into countries further to the west and south-west (e.g. Rumania),[72] was everywhere the same. They succumbed relatively quickly to the local population, or were absorbed by the expanding groups of the Corded Ware people. They handed down some of the elements of their culture to these new people, especially some of their burial customs and ritual (shaft graves, mounded over, ochre strewn over the corpse, etc.).

STEPPE SETTLEMENTS

In various parts of the Yamnaya territory settlements or traces of seasonal encampments have been attributed to the culture. Some of these, in the region on the Lower Volga and also further east—for example, at Novaya Kazanka, over 200 miles east of the river— yielded microlithic flints and a few potsherds of Yamnaya type. They were evidently traces of the seasonal camps of small migratory groups.

Some settlements uncovered in the river valleys of the Don (Khutor Repin), and especially in the region of the Dnieper rapids, which were well investigated and possess an established chronology, were different in character. They succeeded the settlements of the earlier periods, and belonged to the very end of the Late Neolithic and the Early Metal Age ('Copper Age') of the region. The name of Seredni Stog has usually been given to the period, after the standard site on a rocky island in the Dnieper (see p. 115). Its contemporary sites also lay on high rocks or high river terraces, in topographical positions, different from those of the sites of the Early and Middle Neolithic in the valley.

Two occupation layers were uncovered on the Seredni Stog site. The earlier one is considered to be of the Late Neolithic. More important was the upper layer, called Seredni Stog II, of the final stage of the Late Neolithic but mainly of the local Early Metal Age. It yielded flint scrapers and arrow-heads, perforated stone axes, bone awls, and 'polishers', etc. In both layers of the settlement bones of domesticated animals (cattle, sheep or goats, and dogs) were found besides those of wild beasts. Huts were of the light shanty type. The pottery was a shell-gritted ware, mainly vases with a pointed base decorated by furrows, small pits, thin comb-impressed patterns and twisted-cord impressions (Pl. XIII, bottom left). A few Tripolyan potsherds of period C–1 (see p. 108), and those of the Globular Amphora culture (see p. 167) are of importance for chronological reasons. In another site of the same type (Strelcha Skela), Tripolyan potsherds of period B–2, with polychrome decoration, were excavated.

The continuity of settlement of the valley has been well established by the use during the Late Neolithic of the cemeteries of the preceding period. In the latest graves, according to the stratigraphic evidence, of the cemetery at Mykilske, Yamnaya vessels with a pointed base appear. In some cemeteries several skeletons lay in the specific 'Yamnaya' position, on the back with legs contracted, knees upwards. Besides the traditional grave goods—adornments made of bone, necklaces of wild animal fangs and teeth, etc.—perforated stone axes were found, like those in the burials of the Corded Ware/Battle Axe assemblage (see p. 151). A Tripolyan vessel of period C–1 was excavated in a double grave at Ihren near the female skeleton in the 'Yamnaya' position. These burials suggest the emigration to the Dnieper valley during an early stage of the Seredni Stog period (the end of the third millennium B.C.) of small groups of the Yamnaya people who settled amongst the indigenous population. The latter must have been influenced by the newcomers, but there is no reason to maintain, as some scholars do, that the whole population of the valley at that time belonged to the Yamnaya culture. After all, a peaceful coexistence of peoples of different origin and culture within the same region was a common occurrence in the Eurasiatic steppe, recorded by historical sources, and still in existence up to the present century.

The Settlement of Mykhailivka

Some attention should be given to the stratified settlement at Mykhailivka (Mikhailovka in Russian) on the right bank of the Lower Dnieper.[73] It lies about thirty-one miles south-west of Nikopol. The two upper layers (II and III) of the settlement are considered to belong to the Yamnaya culture, and its stratigraphic evidence has often been referred to for establishing the successive periods in the development of that culture[74] and its characteristic features. But the fact that the site lay on the extreme western edge of the Yamnaya territory has not been taken into account; the conditions there cannot be regarded as indicative of the evolution in other, remote groups of the culture.

Three superimposed layers of occupation were uncovered, each with somewhat different remains (Table 10). Pottery from the lowest layer was a shell-gritted ware; vessels were flat-based with a slightly polished dark-brownish surface, covered with comb-stamped or cord-impressed decorative patterns. Kitchen ware was Tripolyan in type, presumably of period B–2. A large, cord-decorated amphora of 'Thuringian' type, characteristic of the Corded Ware assemblage (see p. 154), was important since, according to the excavators of the site, it equated the layer with the Seredni Stog II period of the region of the Dnieper rapids.

The second occupation layer was similarly equated with Seredni Stog II, and has commonly been attributed to the early stage of the Yamnaya culture. A sand-gritted ware of high-necked vessels with a pointed or narrow, flat base, and decorated with comb or cord impressions or stamped patterns, was typical of the layer. This pottery has links with that of the latest stage of the Late Neolithic of the Dnieper rapids (the site of Durna Skela) and with combed ware of the Dnieper-Donetz culture (see p. 113). A 'Thuringian' cord-decorated amphora of a debased type, and sherds of painted ware of the Usatovo type (see p. 182) are important for dating the layer with the respective cultures, which were all of the second millennium B.C. (Pl. XVII).

Remains of the upper, third layer of Mykhailivka were evidently of a late date, corresponding to an advanced stage of the Catacomb culture east of the Dnieper (see p. 222). Its pottery was a sand-gritted ware, and vessels with a pointed or rounded base were most common. Their decoration consisted of comb and cord-impressed lines and bands, most frequent being rows of hanging-hatchet triangles, a motif very popular in the Catacomb culture. Several decorated and unde-corated three-or-four-legged (or cross-legged) saucers or 'lamps' (Table 10) were identical with those characteristic of the Mostičarska (Laibacher Moor) and Slavonian cultures on the Middle Danube;[75] they differed from those typical of the Catacomb and North Caucasian cultures of the second millennium B.C. only through lack of a curved septrum. Twenty-six copper objects were excavated—awls, knives, a flat axe, a chisel; and flint daggers, their surface covered with a fine retouch, were imitations of metal archetypes.

Neither the pottery nor the other objects found in Mykhailivka were typical of the Yamnaya culture. Only the burial ritual displayed by the majority of the 'flat' graves uncovered outside the settlement reflects the Yamnaya tradition. Skeletons lay in the 'Yamnaya' position, but some were crouched, a position typical of the Corded Ware culture. Some burials were encircled by stones (cromlechs), or were covered by a layer of stones. Such constructions were typical of the Bronze Age on the Lower Dnieper, a period which corresponded with the Catacomb period of the steppe country east of the Dnieper, the first half of the second millennium B.C.

The inhabitants of the settlement were engaged in animal hus-bandry and fishing; agriculture was of secondary importance. Domesticated animals supplied up to 96 per cent of the meat diet, and among these were cattle (44 per cent), goats or sheep (32 per cent), horses (18 per cent) and pigs (2 per cent). The position was similar with the osseous material found in the contemporaneous settlement at Durna Skela in the region of the Dnieper rapids, but there instead of pigs' bones there were those of dogs. It is interesting to note that in the settlement of approximately the same period at Repin on the Don, in the steppe nearly 500 miles east of Mykhailivka, the horse was the main animal reared (80 per cent of the osseous material).

Copper objects found in the upper layer of Mykhailivka were of Caucasian origin. A number of finds such as a fragment of a stone bracelet similar to those of the Maikop culture, also point to Caucasian connections at that period. The lowest layer of the settlement seems to have belonged to the late third millennium B.C. The settlement of the second (middle) layer was in existence during the early second millennium, as shown by the Slavonian connections that began at that time (pedestalled saucers). Metal objects of the third (upper) layer suggest the second quarter of that millennium. The defensive constructions—a stone wall around the settlement—were built during the latest stage of its existence. They are convincing evidence of the disturbances which affected the Ukraine at that time, a subject to which we shall return later (see pp. 230, 241).

THE LATE NEOLITHIC IN THE FOREST ZONE

Tribal movements corresponding to those further south, discussed in the preceding sections, show up also in the archaeological material of some regions of the east European forest zone, but it seems that the local peoples were less affected by these than those further south. No great changes have been recorded at the turn of the Middle and Late Neolithic, at the end of the fourth millennium, in the Central Russian province, where the Lialovo culture (see p. 95) continued to develop almost unchanged during the Late Neolithic. Some changes occurred, however, within its peripheral area, near the junction of the Oka and the Volga. There the ancient pit-comb ware underwent changes which mark the formation of a new culture, called the Balakhna culture after the region in which it centred.

The Balakhna territory extended over a relatively narrow strip of land west and south of the Middle Volga near the junction of the Oka, and further south along the Oka. The southernmost part of the latter region, south of Murom, was lost to the Volosovo culture in the second millennium (see p. 205). The pottery of the Balakhna culture did not differ much from that of the Lialovo culture, which predominated in that area in the preceding period, the Middle Neolithic (Fig. 50). It was also a gravel-gritted ware, and the main difference consisted in a different style of pit-comb decoration.[76]

The Balakhna people led a peaceful life, fishing and hunting, and had little contact with other peoples. Later, however, in the second millennium, in the subsequent period, a radical change took place in their lives (see p. 208).

The huge territory north of the Upper Volga and east of Lake Ladoga, the northern coniferous forest zone called the Taiga, did not offer much opportunity for widespread settlement or agriculture either in Neolithic or in later prehistoric periods.

By the end of the Mesolithic, the southern regions of the area were invaded by small groups of early hunters and fisherman, who lived there undisturbed in the Early and Middle Neolithic. Three of the most important sites were (1) the site on the river Yagorba, which was of Late Mesolithic age; (2) those at Pogostishche on the river Modlona (of the Early Neolithic), and (3) at Veretie on the river Kinema (of the Middle Neolithic), which was the northernmost of the three. The remains on all sites were found to be similar; flint and stone tools, and wooden and bone implements, were of the same type, in spite of the considerable time lag between them. Among these were needle-shaped and 'Shigir' type bone arrow-heads (Fig. 11), harpoons, hooks, etc., but no pottery. The name of the 'Pre-Pottery Neolithic' has been given to these remains.

The country must have been extremely thinly populated at that time by small groups, as suggested by the very small number of finds, even in regions relatively well investigated[77] and in which several sites of the succeeding periods have been recorded.

By the end of the fourth millennium or by the beginning of the third, early in the Middle Neolithic, the southernmost part of the country was colonized by men of the Lialovo culture, who crossed the Volga near Kostroma; the Boran site (see p. 96) was typical of that region. By the end of the third millennium, early in the Late Neolithic, this culture had moved further north, and eventually reached the coasts of the White Sea.

The increased number of sites in these regions implies an increase in the density of population during the Late Neolithic. They covered the huge territory northwards up to the White Sea, and spread also on to the Kola Peninsula. The culture of the whole territory, however, was not uniform, and four main groups have been distinguished —the 'Kargopol' culture in the south; the 'Karelian' culture northwest of it, mainly in Russian Karelia; the 'White Sea' culture in the north, along the southern shore of the White Sea and on the eastern coast of the Kola Peninsula; and, finally, the 'Kola' culture in the south and west of the peninsula. Several stages have been distinguished in the development of each of these. In fact, however, the content of the culture of each stage differed considerably from that of its preceding period, which indicates that there was no continuous development of a single culture. Each stage of all the cultures distinguished, except that of the Kola peninsula, represents a different culture; the common name given to all subsequent cultures in each area is, therefore, rather misleading. Only two, the Kargopol and Karelian cultures, were formed in the third millennium and continued their existence in the second millennium B.C. The other cultures belonged entirely to the later period.

11

The Kargopol Culture

The Kargopol culture, called after a town at the northern end of Lake Lacha, was the southernmost of the 'Arctic' cultures, extending over a large territory south-east of Lake Onega. Sites investigated lay mainly in the area between Lake Vozhe and Lake Beloe. Recently, however, several sites have been discovered and some excavated in the region south of the latter lake, up to Lake Rybinskoe.[78] They lay close to the northern reach of the Volga-Oka culture, sites of which have been investigated near Kostroma; and mark the route by which the southern immigrants moved northwards.

The Kargopol culture, or rather the culture of the earliest stage of the area, was formed by immigrants from Central Russia. This is reliably indicated by the pottery found in the earliest sites, whether in the south (Vaskin Bor II), in the central part (Karavaikha in the region of Lake Vozhe), or in the northernmost site (Kubenino on Lake Lacha) about 190 miles north of the southern border of the culture; the pottery was closely related to that of the Lialovo group of the Volga-Oka assemblage (Table 14).

A few unfurnished graves of this period were uncovered at Karavaikha.[79] Skeletons, some slightly sprinkled with ochre, lay in shallow pits, variously orientated, and covered with stones. Of particular interest was a female burial; the skeleton lay facing the bottom of the grave pressed down by three large stones, the largest on its head. Small fish bones and scales lay heaped near the position of its stomach. A firebed of stones with a little charcoal and three large bones of a bear, elk and beaver extended over the burial.

Pollen analyses have shown that sites of the early stage of the Kargopol culture could all be dated to the end of the Atlantic period.[80] The southern immigrants, therefore, must have arrived in the country at the latest by the end of the third millennium. The aboriginal hunters and fishermen of the local 'Pre-Pottery Neolithic' were submerged and assimilated, but some elements of their culture, such as the bone projectile-points of Shigir type, were taken over by the new Kargopol culture, which cannot be looked upon as of purely Central Russian character. During the first period in its development bone implements were more common than those made of stone.

The culture developed almost unchanged until about the middle of the second millennium. A new period then began, and the culture was probably superseded by a new wave of immigrants.

The Karelian Culture

The other 'Arctic' culture, called the Karelian (Tables 15, 16), after the country in which it developed, differed from the Kargopol culture, which it bordered to the north-west. It extended over a broad strip of land about 300 miles wide, north-east of the region around Lake Ladoga up to the White Sea (Gulf of Onega). The largest concentration of sites, nearly 500 of which have been recorded in all, occurred in the central part of the area around Lake Onega.

Three main periods can be distinguished in the development of Karelia during the Neolithic and the Bronze Age. The first of these, called the Early Neolithic,[81] lasted probably from the fifth to the middle of the third millennium B.C., corresponding with our Early and Middle Neolithic (Table 3). The Sperrings pottery of the period gave the whole country, up the Gulf of Onega, the character of an eastern province of the Sperrings culture of Finland (Tables 15, 16). The second Neolithic period of Karelia, which lasted till about 1700 B.C., was begun by a wave of southern immigrants soon after the middle of the third millennium. This was the period of the First Karelian culture, formed by men belonging to the Pit-comb ware culture of Lialovo derivation; they arrived in Karelia from the area of the Kargopol culture. Elements of the Belev culture—rhomboidal pits covering the whole surface of the vessels—have also been distinguished. The southern immigrants evidently met their predecessors of the Sperrings culture, and at first both populations seem to have lived side by side, seldom mingling with each other. An example of this is the Ust-Rybezhno I site, south of Lake Ladoga. Another example is the cemetery Sandermokha at Povenets on the southern shore of Lake Ladoga, in which a few potsherds were found of both types Sperrings and Lialovo,[82] The cemetery consisted of eleven burials with supine skeletons bestrewn with ochre and surrounded by large boulders. The sole equipment were splinters of quartz.

The large cemetery of Olenii Ostrov (Stag's Island) on Lake Onega is among the best known of the culture. Over 170 burials were uncovered. Skeletons lay mainly in an extended position on their backs, but some were crouched. All were richly strewn with ochre. Grave goods consisted of tools made of bone; objects of personal adornment, made of perforated animal teeth, boars' tusks, etc.; and flint arrow-heads, bone and antler harpoons, axes made of slate, etc. No pottery was found in any grave. There were a few burials in deep shafts with skeletons in a standing position; they were exceptionally richly endowed, and besides a large number of the usual personal ornaments and arrow-heads, they were equipped with bone daggers. Chieftains or *shamans* were undoubtedly buried there. The cemetery must have been a burial place of several clans living near the island, on the shores of Lake Onega, and was evidently used for a long period.

Opinions vary as to the date of the cemetery and the people buried in it.[83] Some authors put it at the turn of the fourth and third millennia, others consider it as Early Neolithic and date it to the first half of the third millennium. It has been connected with the spread of the Sperrings pottery, which is regarded as of Ural origin, and support for these theories has been sought in some Mongoloid features of the preponderant Crô-Magnon cranial material from the cemetery. But these Mongoloid features might have been the outcome of the arrival in the area of small groups of eastern tribes by the mid-third millennium B.C., early in our Late Neolithic; they may have been connected with the tribal movements recorded at about the same time in the countries further south. The character of many grave goods of the Olenii Ostrov cemetery, and its Swedish parallels (Västerbjers on Gotland)[84] suggest its use until our Late Neolithic, the second half of the third millennium B.C.

THE EAST BALTIC AREA

The culture of the second Neolithic period (our Late Neolithic) in the regions further to the west, the East Baltic countries, differed from that of its preceding period (see p. 90). In Estonia[85] it lasted over the second half of the third millennium (Tables 3, 12). The second Neolithic layer of the stratified site at Akali on the river Emajögi was typical of the period. The site was set up in the first period and was continuously inhabited for over 1000 years. Another stratified site of the same region, at Kullamägi, was later, its earliest layer dating to the end of the second period.

Flint and bone implements, arrow-heads, spear-heads, fish-hooks, harpoons, axes, etc. found at Kullamägi were almost the same as those of the first period, but the pottery was entirely different. Typical of the second period was the 'Combed' ware, which, unlike the Pit-comb ware of the Volga-Oka assemblage, showed more emphasis on combed motifs than on pits. The same type of pottery was characteristic of Finland and the north-western part of Russia south of Leningrad.

The culture of which this pottery was characteristic was not native to the east Baltic area. Its homeland was probably the Valdai Upland and the region north of it. Objects made of flint, which was of Valdai origin, reinforce this point of view. Such objects were not found in the remains of the first period. However, the relation of the culture to the Valdai culture (see p. 92), and the pottery of both, need further study. It seems, however, that besides the Valdai culture, other contributors to the formation of the 'Combed' ware culture were the Pit-comb pottery of the Volga-Oka assemblage and the 'Comb-pricked' ware of the Dnieper-Donetz type, the northernmost outposts of which have been recorded not far away from the southern border of the Valdai culture.

The Combed ware culture travelled further west along the Baltic coast and reached East Prussia. The great initial uniformity of the pottery and of its decorative motifs within the whole reach of the culture, from Finland to the Vistula, suggests its swift expansion.

A large number of amber pendants, beads, V-perforated buttons, and other ornaments found in sites of the culture was characteristic of the late stage of the Second Neolithic period in Estonia. At about the same time amber ornaments also appeared in the adjacent areas of Russia and Finland, but exclusively within the reach of the cultures to which the Combed ware was characteristic. The amber probably came from east Prussia, this country being within the range of the same culture, though some scholars think that amber deposits on the western coast of Latvia were also exploited at that time. This exploitation and trade were evidently in the hands of the Combed ware people. The period ended with the invasion of the country by the Battle-axe (Boot-axe) people around the middle of the second millennium B.C. (see p. 209).

SUMMARY

The beginnings of the Neolithic in Eastern Europe were very modest. By the end of the fifth millennium B.C., the earliest agricultural communities appeared there in two distant regions, one in Podolia, represented by the Danubian I culture, and further east, by the Southern Bug culture; one of the main formative elements of this culture was the Criş-Körös culture. The second centre was formed in the southernmost part of Transcaucasia, and is represented by the Kyul-Tepe I culture. To these two, a third centre should be added, though it lay outside Europe, in the southernmost part of Soviet Central Asia on the border of Iran; it also played an important role in the diffusion of the Neolithic in Eastern Europe (Map VI).

The share of these three centres in the spread over wider areas of the new food-producing economy, and consequently of the new 'neolithic' type of culture, was very uneven. The most important in this respect was the Podolian centre, which ultimately affected the whole western half of Eastern Europe. Its two cultures, of the earliest husbandmen, were soon absorbed by the newly formed Tripolyan culture, which was for the following 2,000 years, up to the end of the third millennium, the only large farming community of Eastern Europe north of the Caucasus.

The spread of the new economy based on agriculture, however, was a very slow process. Local conditions were not suitable everywhere for the adoption of primitive agriculture as the basis of an economy. The Tripolyans kept to the fertile black-earth regions (chernozem) west of the Dnieper; and up to the end of the Neolithic, the end of the third millennium, agriculture had not spread eastwards beyond the Dnieper, nor northwards into the forest zone. In no region of the east European forest zone, except perhaps its westernmost part, was any form of food-producing economy introduced during that period. The forest dwellers kept to the ancient mode of life based on fishing and hunting. Nevertheless, the impact of the more highly evolved culture of the agriculturalists on the neighbouring tribes led the latter gradually to adopt some changes—in particular pottery and some new forms of tool. This was the case with the inhabitants of the valley of the Lower Dnieper, who belonged to the Surskii culture, and with the Dnieper-Elbe tribes. It seems very likely that the men of these two areas passed the knowledge of pottery further north and west. The pottery of the Valdai and Narva cultures, possibly also that of the Sperrings, and maybe even that of the Volga-Oka assemblage, might have ultimately been of Southern Bug and Criş-Körös parentage.

The role of the second, Transcaucasian foothold of the earliest agriculturalists, those of the Kyul-Tepe I culture, in the diffusion in Eastern Europe of the new economy and culture was of lesser importance. The activities of the Kyul-Tepe I people were restricted to a small region of Transcaucasia until the end of the fourth millennium, when the country was taken over by the people of the Kura-Araxes culture. The latter subsequently crossed the Caucasus, spreading their agriculture to several North Caucasian tribes. A branch of the Kura-Araxes culture and its kindred Maikop culture was formed there.

The Caucasus was cut off by a wide steppe belt from the forest zone (Map I); no marked traces have been recorded of Caucasian influence on the forest dwellers. On the other hand, it seems very probable that the steppe peoples were affected by the Caucasian centre. The Yamnaya culture in the steppe north of the Caucasus and further north in the lower Volga adopted a special type of food-producing economy based on stock-breeding. Unlike agriculture, it was adapted to the conditions in the east European grassland, and the culture subsequently evolved a purely pastoral economy.

Stock-breeding was not an invention of the Yamnaya people. They may have learnt it from the west Siberian tribes, their eastern neighbours, and, if so, it was of Central-Asiatic, Iranian derivation. But it is more likely that they acquired their knowledge from the north-west Caucasian agriculturalists, who, in turn, adopted it from Transcaucasian stock-breeders.

The Central Asiatic centre of the early agriculturalists was probably the earliest of the three. But only very late in its development did it influence the neighbouring Mesolithic tribes in the country further north. The earliest of the latter peoples to learn about pottery were the men of the Kelteminar culture, which was formed about the beginning of the third millennium. A pottery closely related to that of the Kelteminar culture, and presumably taken over from that culture, appeared soon in the region of the south Urals, further north in the Gorbunovo culture, and also in the Kama and Kazan cultures west of the Urals. All these cultures belonged to a wider Ural/West-Siberian *Kulturkreis*. The Kelteminar pottery, which seems to be the earliest of all, was probably adopted from the Anau or Namazga cultures of the southern part of Soviet Central Asia. Lately, however, opinions have been expressed that the Kelteminar pottery was not of Central Asiatic origin, but was taken over from the west, from some east European centre. Further studies and research will undoubtedly answer this question.

The spread of the new economy, and especially the adoption of pottery by the fishing and hunting tribes of the forest zone, led to the formation of a large number of local cultures (and larger assemblages), which differed from each other by a somewhat different type of vessel, or a different style of decoration. Most of them were formed at the turn of the fourth and third millennia; and this date, therefore, marks a turning-point in the development of Eastern Europe—the beginning of a new period, the Middle Neolithic.

The chronological position of the main Neolithic cultures distinguished in Eastern Europe, and described in this chapter, is shown in Table 3. The chronological framework proposed there is based on a study of the relations between cultures; on stratigraphic evidence of their sequence; on the well established chronology of some of the cultures; and on the available Carbon-14 dates of a few important sites. The two Neolithic millennia have been divided into three periods, the Early, Middle and Late Neolithic, which do not always correspond with the terminology applied in works dealing with the Neolithic in various parts of the country.

During the first of these periods, the Early Neolithic, by far the largest part of the country was inhabited by tribes that kept to the ancient Mesolithic mode of life and economy. A new period, the Middle Neolithic, began in fact late in the fourth millennium when there was an increase in the number of cultures of Neolithic character appearing in many parts of the forest zone (Map VIII).

The conditions during the Middle Neolithic seem to have been stable and no great changes have been noticed in the development of the cultures of that period. However, the middle of the third millennium witnessed the end of this stable period. Considerable changes took place in many regions of the country, and in some areas a complete break with the past has been recorded. The archaeological material from the southern part of Eastern Europe, and from many regions of the forest zone, implies that the tribal movements of that time largely reshaped the east European Neolithic. They mark the beginning of the last Neolithic period, the Late Neolithic; it lasted until the end of the third millennium and terminated with a new outbreak of unrest.

The ultimate cause of all these changes cannot be established. The evidence available suggests that the starting point of the tribal movements of that time, which constitutes a kind of chronological horizon, lay somewhere in west Siberia. One of its agents—or perhaps just one of the peoples affected—were the men of the Yamnaya culture, some tribes of which seem to have been forced to move out of their original country on the Lower Volga. They possibly advanced southwards towards the Caucasus and may have been among the founders of the Maikop culture. Their advance into the region on the Lower Dnieper and that of the rapids, at about the middle of the third millennium, has been well attested by the archaeological material. At about the same time they must have reached the steppe near the Danubian delta, where their Carbon-14-dated burials have been uncovered.

More important, maybe, were the movements of the Comb-pricked were people belonging to the Dnieper-Donetz culture. The starting point of their expansion cannot be established definitely, but it seems unlikely that the movement began in the area between the Dnieper and the Donetz, which was more likely seized by the culture of a later date. The starting point, as suggested by many pieces of evidence, was probably somewhere in west Siberia, and the cause of the move was possibly the same as that which provoked the migration of the Yamnaya people.

The expansion of the Comb-pricked ware people probably proceeded along the southern border of the forest and steppe zones. The sudden appearance of west Siberian elements in sites on the western side of the Urals seem to confirm the advance of these peoples. There is also evidence of their seizure of the country between the Dnieper and the Donetz and their advance into the regions of the Lower Dnieper and further south. They seem to have also advanced northwards into Byelorussia in the basin of the Middle and Upper Dnieper. The adoption of Tripolyan B-2 kitchen ware, akin to the Comb-pricked pottery, was probably also in some way the result of these movements.

The eastern elements seem also to have penetrated north into the forest zone, though they might have proceeded by another more northerly route. This is suggested by the appearance of Mongoloid elements in the cemeteries of the north-west part of Eastern Europe

—in the settlements of the Kargopol culture, and, above all, in the famous cemetery of Olenii Ostrov. The archaeological material of the Neolithic of Eastern Europe does not reflect any great social differences, nor differences in wealth, between the members of the many tribes throughout the country, except for the 'royal' barrow graves of the Maikop culture. These are the earliest signs of the emergence in many parts of the country later of a distinct, wealthy and powerful class of local rulers.

References

1 T.S. Passek and E.K. Chernysh 1963; E.K. Chernysh, MIA, 102, 1962.
2 V.M. Danylenko, KSIAK 9, 1947; T.S. Passek, *Symposium*.
3 M. Petrescu-Dimboviţa, *Acta Archaeologica Hungarica*, Vol. IX, 1958, p. 53 ff.
4 V.M. Danylenko, KSIAK 9, 1947.
5 According to the information kindly given by Dr J. Nandris, recent Carbon–14 determinations of the Mesolithic layer at Soroki III are 5480 and 5220 B.C., and of its superimposed Southern Bug layer is 4990 B.C.
6 V. Dumitrescu, *Studii şi Cercetări de Istorie Veche*, Vol. XIV, 1963, pp. 51 ff., 285 ff. *Idem, Archeologia-Warszawa*, Vol. XIV, 1963, p. 1 ff. The hut at Varvarovka in Bessarabia, Carbon–14 dated as 5140 B.C. (LE–391), does not seem to have been Tripolyan.
7 S.N. Bibikov, 1961.
8 V. Dumitrescu, IPEK, Vol. 8, 1932–3, pp. 49–72.
9 V.M. Danylenko; A.P. Esipenko, KSIAK 4, 1955; M.L. Makarevych, KSAMO for 1962.
10 D. Berciu, *Cultura Hamangia*. Bucharest, 1966.
11 G.P. Sergeev, SA 1963–1. L.S. Klein, *Problemy Arkheologii*, Vol. I, Leningrad 1968.
12 V. Dumitrescu, *Hăbăşeşti*. Bucharest, 1954, p. 410 ff. Fig. 36, Pl. CXXII.
13 V. Dumitrescu, *op. cit.*, p. 434 ff., Figs. 41, 42, Pl. CXXIV; and also in *Dacia*, Vol. NS I, 1957, p. 73 ff.
14 Defined by T.S. Passek.
15 A.A. Yessen, KSIAM 93, 1963; O.A. Abibullaev, MIA 67, 1959; SA 1963–3.
16 A.I. Dzavakhishvili, L.I. Flonti, 1962.
17 T. Chubinishvili, 1963. Carbon–14 dates of its Early Bronze Age layer are: 1770 B.C. (TB–3), 2285 B.C. (TB–4), and 2340 B.C. (TB–9).
18 Iu.G. Kolosov, KSIAK 7, 1957.
19 D.Ia. Telegin, SA 1966–1.
20 N.N. Gurina, MIA 131, 1965.
21 A. Gardawski, *Wiadomości Archeologiczne*, Vol. XXV, 1958, p. 287 ff.
22 D.Ia. Telegin, AK, Vol. XI, 1957.
23 D.Ia. Telegin, MIA 70, 1960; SA 1961–4.
24 M. Gimbutas, *Prehistory of Eastern Europe*, Part I. Cambridge, Mass., 1956, Pl. 6; and R. Indreko, *Mesolithischen Kulturen in Osteuropa und Westsibirien*. Stockholm, 1964, Fig. 64.
25 D.Ia. Telegin, SA 1961–4.
26 F.E. Zeuner, *Dating the Past*. 4th ed., London, 1958, p. 84.
27 H. Moora, L. Jaanits, 1959.
28 N.N. Gurina, 1967.
29 N.N. Gurina, I.V. Gavrilova, L.Ia. Krizhevskaya, SA 1958–3.
30 P.N. Tretiakov, MIA 131, 1965.
31 D.A. Kraynov, KSIAM 97, 1964; O.S. Gadzyatskaya, KSIAM 100, 1965.
32 O.S. Gadzyatskaya, KSIAM 106, 1966.
33 A.Ia. Briusov.
34 R. Indreko.

35 A.Ia. Briusov, N.P. Tretiakov, KSIAM 106, 1966.
36 A.E. Alikhova, KSIIMK 75, 1959.
37 N.N. Gurina, MIA 79, 1960.
38 I.Ia. Briusov.
39 V.P. Levenok, MIA 131, 1965.
40 O.S. Gadzyatskaya, see notes 31, 32.
41 I.G. Rosenfeldt, KSIIMK 75, 1959.
42 V.M. Mason, 1964.
43 Layer II at Chagally, considered to belong to a late stage of the Jeitun culture, has been Carbon–14 dated as 5050±110 B.C. (RUL–592).
44 S.P. Tolstov, 1962.
45 V.N. Chernetsov, MIA 35, 1953; M. Gimbutas, PPS, Vol. XIX for 1953.
46 G.N. Matiushin, Bashkirskii Arkheologicheskii Sbornik, 1959.
47 L.I. Krizhevskaya, 1968; KSIAM 97, 1964.
48 A.Kh. Khalikov, MIA 61, 1958.
49 V. Dumitrescu, 'The Date of the Earliest Western Expansions of the Kurgan Tribes', Dacia, Vol. NS VII, 1963, p. 500.
50 D.Ia. Telegin, SA 1961–4.
51 Iu.V. Kukharenko, 1962.
52 I.I. Artemenko, 1967.
53 By N. Makarenko, ESA, Vol. IX, 1934.
54 O. Dzhaparidze, 1961.
55 R.M. Munchaev, 1961.
56 A.A. Formozov, 1965.
57 Its burial ritual, ochre and metal objects link it with the Maikop culture, although its pottery is Transcaucasian, reminiscent of the Kura-Araxes and Beli-Kent wares. Its Carbon–14 dates are 2880±230 B.C. (LE–300) and 2550±120 B.C. (LE–305).
58 A.M. Tallgren, F. Hančar, M. Gimbutas.
59 E.I. Krupnov, SA 1964–1; A.A. Formozov, 1965.
60 A.A. Yessen, SA, Vol. XII, 1950.
61 V.G. Childe, The Dawn of European Civilization, 5th ed., London, 1950, p. 149.
62 A.M. Tallgren, ESA, Vol. IX, 1934, p. 31 ff.
63 A.M. Tallgren, as above.
64 N.Ia. Merpert, Symposium.
65 K.F. Smirnov, MIA 78, 1960.
66 I.V. Spitsyn, KSIAK 7, 1957; MIA 60, 1959.
67 N.Ia. Merpert, op. cit., note 64.
68 K.F. Smirnov.
69 N.Ia. Merpert.
70 N.Ia. Merpert.
71 V. Dumitrescu, 'The Date of the Earliest Western Expansions of the Kurgan Tribes', Dacia, Vol. NS VII, 1963.
72 Op. cit. in ref. 71, p. 495 ff.
73 O.F. Lahodovska, O.G. Shaposhnikova, M.L. Makarevych, 1962.
74 N.Ia. Merpert, see note 64.
75 Op. cit. in ref. 61, p. 155.
76 I.K. Tsvetkova, MIA 110, 1963.
77 M.E. Foss, MIA 29, 1952; N.N. Gurina, MIA 87, 1961.
78 S.V. Oshibkina, SA 1966–1; I.K. Tsvetkova, sv.
79 A.Ia. Briusov, sv.
80 G.N. Lisitsina, sv.
81 N. N. Gurina, MIA 87, 1961; MIA 20, 1951. Charcoal from the occupation layer of site Ust-Rybezhno I has been Carbon–14 dated as 4430±220 B.C. (LE–405); see SA 1969–1, p. 254.
82 G.A. Pankrushev, 1964.
83 N.N. Gurina: 1956.
84 M. Stenberger, Sweden. London, 1962, p. 48. Ancient Peoples and Places series.
85 L. Jaanits.

3
The Bronze Age

From 2000 to 1200 B.C. approximately

THE AGE OF WESTERN PREDOMINANCE

DURING the second half of the third millennium changed conditions in Eastern Europe signalled the end of the Neolithic and the rise of a new, entirely different epoch. The archaeological material of the turn of the third and second millennia reflects considerable disturbances. One by one the ancient cultures disappeared and new cultures displaced them in all parts of the country; those which survived, such as the Tripolye culture, underwent important changes.

One of the most significant events of that period was the appearance on the stage of history of the earliest Indo-European peoples. Ancient written records register their presence at that very time in Asia Minor; the destruction of the second city of Troy, about 2300 B.C., was most probably connected with their expansion. A plausible suggestion is that the catastrophe was the outcome of tribal movements and disturbances in the south of Eastern Europe that preceded this event; likewise advancing Indo-Europeans, who came from the north, may perhaps be linked with the western expansion of the Yamnaya culture discussed in the preceding chapter.

During the first half of the second millennium B.C. either the food-producing economy of agriculture and stock-breeding, or stock-breeding alone, spread throughout the whole country, except its northernmost part, where conditions were unsuitable. Metal, and particularly bronze, became common, and so the name of the Metal Age, or Bronze Age, has been given to the period. Commercial relations were established with distant countries, and trade in fact played a very important role in the development of the prehistoric peoples of the country by fostering new ideas and new inventions, and in spreading higher forms of culture. The expanding east Mediterranean maritime trade, represented mainly by the sixth city of Troy, penetrated deep into the continent, leaving its imprint on local cultures and bringing about considerable social changes.

All these factors were important in transforming the life of Eastern

Europe; but the most important of all was the eastward drive of the two Central European cultures, the 'Corded Ware' or 'Battle-axe' assemblage and the 'Globular Amphora' culture. The first of these was partly rooted in the westernmost region of the east European forest zone, and the other was an alien newcomer. In some areas the two cultures expanded independently, in others they mingled, but ultimately they reached all parts of Eastern Europe. Map XIV shows the many directions and extent of their influence.

The expanding groups of the Corded-Ware/Battle-axe assemblage established themselves within the almost unchanged boundaries of several ancient provinces of the country. The true nature of the expansion can in most cases hardly be established. In some areas the newcomers imposed themselves over the natives; they seldom drove them from their territories. Generally the natives merged with their rulers, and either adopted their culture or absorbed their conquerors. The drive ultimately resulted in the formation of several new groups inside the assemblage.

The Globular Amphora culture, a much smaller but very influential group, also left traces of its presence in Eastern Europe. Local groups in Volhynia and Podolia belonged to it; vessels and potsherds covered with decorative patterns characteristic of the culture were found in many sites belonging to local cultures in the Central and east Russian forest zone, as far east as the basin of the Lower Ob beyond the north Urals.

In the second half of the millennium, the Corded Ware expansion was followed by that of the Trzciniec and Komarów cultures, both of Central European parentage.

The Trzciniec culture evolved out of the Corded Ware culture in Central and Eastern Poland. Around the fourteenth century B.C., its remains appeared on the western border of the east European forest zone and subsequently its influence spread far to the east, affecting the cultures of the southern border of the forest zone west of the Dnieper, those of the Valley of the Middle Dnieper, and those of the forest-steppe further east. Its traces extend at least to the Don, and very likely to the north Caucasus.

The other expansion, improperly called that of the Komarów culture, originated either in the Hungarian Plain or, more likely, in Transylvania (the Füzesabony-Otomani culture); it affected the whole forest-steppe zone and to a lesser extent the steppe west of the Dnieper. It partly overlapped the area influenced by the Trzciniec culture.

The second millennium up to about 1200 B.C. was, then, the age of the preponderance in Eastern Europe of cultures of Central European parentage. The period was closed by the expansion of the steppe people of the Srubnaya culture in the thirteenth century B.C., which will be discussed in Chapter IV. During the 800-odd years that the period lasted, many fundamental changes and transformations occurred in Eastern Europe; by its end conditions greatly differed in all respects from those of a thousand years before. Many changes were the outcome of the drive of the cultures of Central European origin mentioned before, but there were other important factors. Among these we have already listed commercial connections with distant countries, and especially the maritime trade. This development led to the growth of several centres of the metal industry in Eastern Europe, and consequently was a cause of change itself. Trade and the metal industry will be discussed in Chapter IV.

All the transformations and changes brought about by the various factors mentioned above occurred at different times in different areas; and some areas changed more than others. Accordingly, different chronological schemes have been established for the evolution of local cultures in different parts of the country, and they often do not correspond with each other. Nevertheless, three main stages in the development of Eastern Europe as a whole are discernible in the period under review, which roughly corresponds with the Early and part of the Middle Bronze Age of Central and Northern Europe.

Table 4 presents the new division proposed here. All the main cultures allocated to the three stages of the period are quoted and some of the more important Central European and other cultures are equated. The division suggested and the dating of a number of cultures do not entirely conform to current opinions in the Soviet archaeological literature. However, the scheme has been based on the evidence available. The periods, or stages, distinguished in the development of the various cultures of that time have been fitted into the framework and, what is of importance, the picture that emerges offers a reasonable explanation of many otherwise hardly explicable occurrences.

The stages are easily seen in the western part of the territory, in the areas most strongly affected by the western cultures. Some regions were noticeably backward, and others—within the area of the Catacomb culture, for example—changed imperceptibly during some of the stages. On the other hand, the scheme is not nearly so positive as regards the conditions in the east—in the Kama-Ural region, and to some extent also in the steppe east of the Volga. In the Kama-Ural area the period, divided into two stages only, began approximately a century later than further west, if the present dating of the respective remains is correct, and seems to have ended earlier. The earlier ending was evidently due to pressure from west Siberia, which soon affected the neighbouring areas of the Urals and regions further west of the mountains, and also the steppe country east of the Volga. The pressure of the west Siberian peoples on those in Eastern Europe brought about considerable tribal movements, which ultimately resulted in great changes throughout most of the country, and initiated a new epoch in its history. The new age has been called the Late Bronze Age, or the Early Iron Age in some restricted areas, or the Pre-Scythian period.

These events will be discussed in Chapter IV, with an examination of the culture of the easternmost part of Eastern Europe in the second millennium B.C. which was the mainspring of this development. Here we shall first examine the two main cultures of the period—the Corded Ware and the Globular Amphora cultures; then, we shall consider various regional cultures on similar lines to those in Chaper II.

THE TWO MAIN AGENTS

The Corded Ware Cultures

The first of the two agents, the Corded Ware or Battle axe assemblage, was among the most important and widespread of the Late Neolithic in Europe. Its constituent cultures differed in various degrees from each other, and were not all of the same age. Their unifying factor was pottery adorned by cord-impressed horizontal lines round the neck and upper part of the vessels, and later by more sophisticated decorative patterns. The assemblage owes its name to this decoration, but the shape of the vessels and the sand or grog-gritted clay paste of which they were made were also peculiar to it. A very large literature exists on the assemblage, and many controversial opinions have been expressed with regard to its nature, chronology and origin.

In various parts of Europe corded ware was associated with stone battle-axes, and this accounts for the other name of the assemblage, the 'Battle-axe' culture. Some scholars, however, are of the opinion that these two were originally different cultures.[1] In fact, battle-axes and toll beakers with an S-profile were found together mainly in the west and north of Europe, while in the south battle-axes appear only in graves of a moie advanced stage of the Corded Ware cultures. In most areas, however, both groups are hardly distinguishable.

The archaeological remains of the assemblage fall into two main categories. Those of the first group of cultures consisted almost entirely of sepulchral remains; no settlements or encampments are attributable to them. The burial ritual was fairly uniform, the skeletons being mostly crouched, with their heads to the west, and occasionally sprinkled with ochre. A difference exists between areas in which 'flat' graves were typical (mainly in the north), and those where a mound was raised over the burial. Graves of the latter type, endowed with corded ware and/or battle-axes, occur only within the northern border of the east European forest-steppe zone; further west, in Central Europe, they were found only along the northern fringe of the loess soils, reaching Jutland in the north-west. Their distribution suggests that the custom was in some way connected with similar practices of the steppe population of the Yamnaya culture, or simply adopted from it.

The second category of remains of the Corded Ware assemblage consists of sites on sand-dunes within the Central European forest zone, west of the Dnieper and reaching as far as the Elbe. They were traces of temporary encampments of migratory groups of people; remains of settlements of a more permanent character have seldom been recorded there. Burials furnished with the corded-decorated pottery tend to be an exception in the area. A few groups or remains of a similar character were found outside the above territory, close to its southern border—the Strzyżów and Gorodsk cultures (see p. 184), and on the Baltic coast—the Rzucewo culture;[2] they were hybrids of a later date, in the formation of which other cultures merged with the Corded Ware element.

Originally, the remains of the two categories formed one entity, their division and differences having arisen through their later development in different areas and in different conditions. The light sandy soils of the Central European forest zone and of the western part of east Europe, west of the Dnieper, seem most likely to have been the original home of the Corded Ware assemblage. The culture in its earliest stage extended mainly over the area of the Masovian (Dnieper-Elbe) culture (see p. 86), from which possibly it descended; in many sites pottery of both cultures appeared together. The close relation between these two cultures is reflected also in the shape and style of decoration of their vessels.

Stone battle-axes, very common grave goods of many groups of the Corded Ware assemblage, do not seem to have been their original weapon. They do not occur in the earliest barrow graves of several Corded Ware groups of the Central European loess belt, that is, in the Sub-Carpathian area dealt with later in Thuringia, and also further west. They seem to have been modelled on copper axes.[3] Several copper axe-adzes, associated with settlements of the Tripolyan period B-2, were found in west Podolia and near Kiev; a few simple copper shaft-hole axes, and a hammer-axe, were found in sites along the southern border of the original country of the Corded Ware culture, east of the Bug up to the region of Berdychev. They might have served as prototypes of the stone specimens.

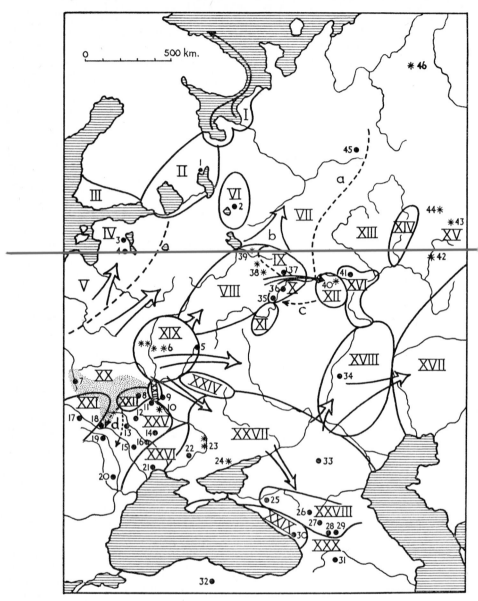

MAP XIV Eastern Europe *c.* 1700 B.C.

(I) White Sea culture; (II) Karelian culture; (III) Finnish Boat-axe culture; (IV) Estonian Boat-axe culture and conquered local groups of the Pit-comb ware culture; (V) East Baltic Late Neolithic cultures; (VI) Kargopol culture; (VII) territory of small local groups of the Pit-comb ware assemblage extending eastwards up to the dotted line 'a'; (VIII) Fatyanovo culture and conquered Pit-comb ware culture; (IX) Balakhna culture; (X) early Volosovo culture; (XI) Riazan culture; (XII) Balanovo culture; (XIII) territory of small local groups of the Eastern Assemblage; (XIV) Kama-Turbino culture; (XV) Gorbunovo culture; (XVI) Kazan Neolithic culture; (XVII) Andronovo culture; (XVIII) Poltavka culture; (XIX) Dnieper-Desna culture; (XX) Strzyzów culture and other groups of the Corded Ware assemblage; (XXI) Sub-Carpathian barrow graves; (XXII) Gorodsk culture; (XXIII) Evminka-Sofiivka group; (XXIV) Marianivka culture; (XXV) Tripolye C-1 culture and Middle-Dnieper barrow grave culture in the north-eastern part of the area; (XXVI) Usatovo culture; (XXVII) Catacomb culture; (XXVIII) North Caucasian Bronze Age culture; (XXIX) Abkhazian and Eshery Dolmen culture; (XXX) Transcaucasian Bronze Age culture.

Arrows mark the presumed expansions, or spread of influence; hatching in the south-western part of the map denotes the area of the Eastern Globular Amphora culture. (a) Approximate boundary between the Eastern assemblage and the Pit-comb ware assemblage; (b) approximate direction of the northern retreat of the Central Russian Pit-comb ware groups; (c) presumed migration of the proto-Volosovo tribes; (d) presumed migration of the Gorodsk and Volhynian Globular Amphora peoples; asterisks indicate sites in which decorative patterns of pottery or/and other elements characteristic of the Globular Amphora culture have been found. SITES: (1) Olenii Ostrov; (2) Modlona; (3) Akali; (4) Tamula; (5) Rechitsa; (6) Strelitsa; (7) Gródek Nadbużny; (8) Gorodsk; (9) Krupol; (10) Kanev; (11) Kolomishchyna; (12) Jackowica; (13) Pechora; (14) Volodymirivka-Vladimirovka; (15) Vykhvatyntsi; (16) Sabatynivka; (17) Komarów; (18) Bilcze Złote; (19) Horodiştea; (20) Folteşti; (21) Usatovo; (22) Mykhailivka-Mikhailovka; (23) Seredni Stog; (24) Orlivka; (25) Ulskii; (26) Piatigorsk; (27) Nalchik; (28) Verkhnaya Rutkha; (29) Verkhnaya Koban; (30) Eshery; (31) Tsalki-Trialeti; (32) Alaca-Hüyük; (33) Elista-Stepnoe; (34) Poltavka; (35) Elin-Bor; (36) Volosovo; (37) Balakhna; (38) Sakhtysh; (39) Fatyanovo; (40) Balanovo; (41) Zaimishchi; (42) Ust-Ayskaya; (43) Gorbunovo-Beregovaya; (44) Kalmatskii Brod; (45) Vis; (46) Ches-Tyi-Iag.

12

The Corded Ware people were originally hunters and fishermen, but at an early date they adopted a food-producing economy based on stock-rearing and pastured their cattle on the meadows of the deciduous forests of their homeland. The character of their sites suggests that they had no permanent settlements and led a semi-migratory mode of life within restricted areas. At some early date, small groups of the people seem to have left their country in search of better pastures than the forest meadows could provide at the onset of the hot and dry sub-Boreal climate. Perhaps the pressure of the Globular Amphora people was also one of their reasons for emigrating. In entering new countries the Corded Ware people encountered the indigenous population; the mutual contact and mingling with these ultimately resulted in the formation of a number of local groups of the Corded Ware culture.

The earliest remains of the culture in Central and Eastern Europe have not yet been Carbon-14 dated. But the expansion of the culture must have taken place in the second part of the third millennium B.C., as suggested by Carbon-14 dates of the Single-grave culture in Lower Saxony (2200–2100 B.C.) and of its branch in the Netherlands, the Tumulus culture (2230 ±140 B.C.).

The hallmark of the earliest expanding groups were the so-called 'Thuringian' amphorae, or amphorae of 'Schraplau' type (Fig. 33). These vessels, which appear in almost all groups in their early stage, bear a striking resemblance to each other, either in shape or decoration or in both, in spite of the very distant countries in which they have been found. In the western part of Central Europe, those in their pure form, usually associated with the S-shaped beakers and stone battle-axes, were probably all about the same date and denote the 'Corded Ware' horizon; those of the more evolved or 'debased' forms, and also various local hybrid types, must be placed in a period soon after this horizon. The relative date of the horizon in Eastern Europe is given by the amphorae from the lowest settlement of Mykhailivka on the Dnieper (Pl. XVII), and also by the Tripolyan vessels modelled on these amphorae found in settlements of period C–1 (Kolomishchyna I). They equate the advanced stage of the horizon with the early part of period C–1 of the Tripolyan sequence. Later, but still of the Early Bronze Age, our Stage I (Table 4), were the Thuringian amphorae of a more or less debased type found in the graves of Vykhvatyntsi (Fig. 42) and Usatovo (Fig. 43), and those of the Fatyanovo (Fig. 48) and Balanovo cultures (Fig. 49) in the Central Russian forest zone.

The Corded Ware/Battle-axe cultures have been looked upon by many authors as the archaeological equivalent of the earliest Indo-Europeans, and their expansion connected with the spread of the

Indo-European peoples. Some attention should therefore be given now to the racial or ethnical complexities of the prehistoric past of Eastern Europe.

The forest zone of Eastern Europe has always been considered as the original homeland of the Finnish, or Finno-Ugrian, peoples, with the Pit-comb ware cultures as their earliest archaeological equivalent. The ancient Finno-Ugrian territory, at present for the most part Russianized, embraced the three prehistoric provinces of (1) the east Baltic region including Finland; (2) the Central Russian province with its northern extension; and (3) the Kama-Ural territory, which also extended over a large strip of land on the eastern side of the Urals. In each of these, distinct though related cultures developed, but the respective position of the people of these cultures among the Finno-Ugrian peoples as a whole has not been definitely established.

The position is different as regards the peoples of the Indo-European stock. The question of their original homeland, which has been variously placed in north-west or Central Europe, in south-east Europe or further east in Asia, is very disputable. Accordingly, opinions on the prehistoric cultures attributable to these peoples are controversial, the crucial point at issue being their country of origin. There are in fact two main competitors for the distinction of representing the earliest Indo-Europeans. The obvious choice of the followers of a Western or Central European origin is the Corded Ware/Battle-axe assemblage, whereas those who seek their origin in the east single out the Yamnaya culture. An attempt to combine both ideas by deriving the Corded Ware cultures from the Yamnaya culture proved to be futile.

The results of linguistic research must be decisive in this dilemma. According to many scholars, linguistic data suggests that the earliest homeland of the Indo-Europeans should be placed somewhere within the grassland of the Eurasiatic border. These views favour the Yamnaya people as representatives of the proto-Indo-Europeans, and archaeological material and historical records seem to support this theory. Stratigraphic evidence in Rumanian barrow graves implies that the burials of Yamnaya type were the primary ones, whereas interments containing cord-decorated vessels were secondary burials. Furthermore, the earliest wave of the Indo-Europeans seems already to have arrived in Anatolia around the middle of the third millennium B.C., and definitely not later than 2300–2200 B.C.; they must have come from the north, from the Balkans and Rumania. They can only be connected with the advance of the Yamnaya pastoralists. The Corded Ware people, the other contestants, have been recorded only in Greece, at the beginning of the second millennium B.C., and do not seem to have entered Anatolia, the country in which the earliest Indo-European speaking peoples have been reported.

Linguistic data and, above all, the circumstances in the Aegean just mentioned are against the theories of North-Western, or even Central European origin for the Indo-Europeans. These areas might have been their secondary centres, the Corded Ware/Battle-axe assemblage representing a later stage in their evolution and history.

However, there may be still another solution of the Indo-European enigma. Neither the Yamnaya, nor the Corded Ware assemblage were uniform at the time of their first appearance—the middle and the end of the third millennium respectively. Within each of these cultures, especially the Corded Ware, many regional groups have been distinguished, differing considerably from each other. This circumstance means—irrespective of which of the two groups of remains is taken into account—that the Indo-Europeans were already split at that time into several basic groups. Their origin may, perhaps, be put back to the Early Neolithic or even the Mesolithic, as some authors do,[4] though there is no answer yet as to which of the early Neolithic or Mesolithic cultures might be considered their earliest archaeological equivalent.

The Corded Ware/Battle-axe groups in the east European forest zone may indeed be looked upon as Indo-European, irrespective of the final issue of the question of origin. They entered an alien territory inhabited by peoples most probably of Finno-Ugrian stock. Linguistic research[5] revealed a number of very ancient Indo-European, namely proto-Baltic (Latvian-Lithuanian), borrowings in the west Finnish and Estonian languages, relating chiefly to animal husbandry and agriculture. It implies a very ancient contact, which may be put back to the time of the expansion of the Battle-axe (Boat-axe) people and connected with it (see p. 209). Very ancient Indo-European borrowings have also been recorded in the language of east Finnish tribes of the region on the Volga near its junction with the Kama, in the 'Balanovo' territory (see p. 199), but these might also have been due to the contacts of the ancestors of the indigenous Finnish tribes with the Indo-European peoples of another branch, the Arian (Scythian-Sarmatian) peoples, who at that time inhabited the steppe further south, and were in close contact with their Finno-Ugrian neighbours.

The Sub-Carpathian Barrow Graves

In this context attention should be given to the Sub-Carpathian barrow-grave culture, one of the assemblage. It was one of the earliest to be formed outside the original territory of the assemblage, and was hardly affected by any other culture than the Yamnaya culture of the east European grassland. The study of its development gives some insight into the evolution of other groups of the assemblage that expanded into territories of Eastern Europe inhabited by alien peoples.

The sub-Carpathian barrow-grave culture (Map XIV: XXI) extended over the Carpathian foothills and their adjacent regions east of the San up to the Podolian plateau, and partly over the north-western corner of Podolia and the bordering part of Volhynia. The major part of that area belongs to Central Europe.

Shaft graves covered by a mound, characteristic of the Yamnaya culture but unknown to the Corded Ware/Battle-axe groups in the north, were characteristic of this group also. Skeletons were seldom found because they had decomposed; but those that were found were mostly crouched, seldom in a supine position. At a later stage, burials were placed on the ground, one series of these consisting of cremations on the spot. Graves were mostly poorly furnished and several, especially at the earliest stage, had no grave goods at all. The furniture often consisted of one or more vessels (Fig. 33), a few small flints, and a flint axe; in later stages the number of vessels increased in some graves, and stone battle-axes, flint daggers, personal ornaments and metal objects (copper, gold, bronze) appeared. In a few cases faience beads were excavated. All the grave goods are characteristic of the Central European Late Neolithic and the Early Bronze Age.

In relation to the duration of the period to which they belonged, the number and size of burials suggests that only the chiefs, or persons of a high social standing, were buried in barrow graves.

The pottery of the sub-Carpathian barrow-graves was a genuine corded ware. The 'Thuringian' amphorae (Fig. 33), vessels with a large, almost spherical body, two or four horizontally perforated lug-handles, short necks, and flat bases, were typical of the early graves. The most striking characteristic is their decoration; it consists of a horizontal band running round the middle of the body and of a similar one on the base of the neck, both connected with a number of vertical bands symmetrically distributed over the vessel. The later specimens gradually lose their proper shape, and their decoration becomes simpler or even disappears.

In a few graves of the western division of the group there was pottery typical of the Funnel Beaker culture, which bordered on it to the north; and in some regions potsherds of the Globular Amphora culture appeared in burials. These finds are of importance for a proper equation of the periods in the development of all these cultures.

The sub-Carpathian group, including its north-west Podolian extension, was probably founded by the end of the third millennium. The main contributors to its formation were the Corded Ware people of the forest zone east of the Oder and the Vistula, who found good pastures for their cattle in this then rich grassland, and the Yamnaya

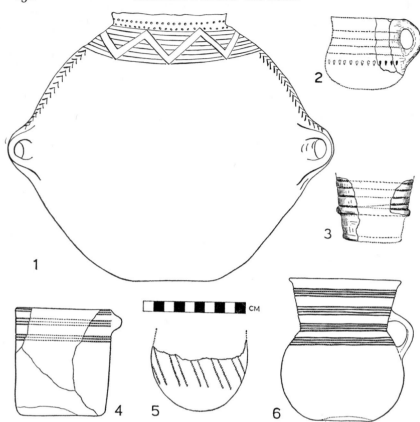

FIG. 33 Vessels typical of the Sub-Carpathian barrow grave culture. After T. Sulimirski, *Corded Ware and Globular Amphorae*, 1968, fig. 10.

people advancing westwards and presumably mingling with them. The custom of burying the dead in shafts under barrows was probably taken over from the latter.

The evolution of the sub-Carpathian barrow-grave culture has been divided into three stages, each with its specific set of grave goods. The earliest of these stages was final Neolithic; the second and the third stages correspond with our Stages I and II of the Bronze Age. the Alpine periods A–1 and A–2 of the Bronze Age respectively (Table 4).

The Komaрów Culture

During the last stage of the barrow-grave culture a significant development began in the region of Halicz, south of the Dniester, near the approaches to the Carpathian passes. Under a strong influence from the other side of the Carpathians, emanating from the Otomani

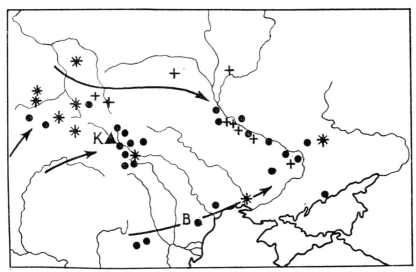

MAP XV *Asterisks:* Distribution north-east of the Carpathians of bronze hoards of Koszider type. *Points:* stray objects of 'Hungarian' Koszider type of the Middle Bronze Age. *Crosses:* bronze objects connected with the Trzciniec culture. (B) hoard of Borodino; (K) cemetery of Komarów.

and Füzesabony cultures, the ancient barrow-grave culture of the Neolithic type was gradually transformed into the new Komarów culture, named after a barrow-grave cemetery excavated by the author.

The Komarów culture that originally developed within the territory of the ancient barrow-grave culture also used barrow graves, most of which formed part of the cemeteries of its Neolithic predecessor. At least one, but more often up to six vessels were found in all the graves. This pottery, the most characteristic feature of the culture, was a reddish-brown slipped ware. There were tulip-shaped pots and similar smaller beakers; deep bowls, some single or double-lugged; and sometimes handled cups and other small vessels. (Pls. XXIV and XXV). They were decorated by incised horizontal lines, rows of shaded triangles, or other similar motifs. Fluting was characteristic of the later pottery. Other grave goods were mainly personal ornaments, bronze bracelets, temple ornaments, pins, etc. Weapons were rare— a small bronze dagger, a few stone battle-axes of a special type, and flint arrow-heads. All the metal (bronze and a few gold) ornaments excavated in the Komarów barrow graves were of 'Hungarian' origin; so were most of the stray bronze objects and hoards found within the Komarów territory and in the area further to the east in west Podolia. Thanks to these, the sub-Carpathian area and west Podolia acquired the character of a 'Hungarian' Bronze Age province (Map XV).

Four stages in the development of the Komarów culture are distinguishable in the sub-Carpathian area. Graves of the earliest of these (our Stage II of the Bronze Age) were found within a restricted area only, and they were contemporary with the graves of the third stage of the sub-Carpathian 'Neolithic' barrows in other regions. The next Komarów stage, the period of the Hungarian 'Koszider'-type bronzes,[6] belonged to our Stage III, and the two later stages belonged to the Late Bronze Age and Early Iron Age. Iron bracelets were found in a grave of the latest stage—Horodyszcze near Sambor. The mode of life and economy of the people do not seem to have differed from that of their ancestors, the men of the preceding Neolithic barrow graves.

The 'Hungarian', or more correctly Transylvanian, current that transformed the sub-Carpathian barrow-grave culture into the Komarów culture also strongly affected the northern part of Moldavia, where the Costişa culture[7] was formed. The results of its impact on the cultures of Western Podolia and of the chernozem country further east will be discussed later (see p. 354).[8]

The Trzciniec Culture

The transformation of the Corded Ware culture in Poland was rather like that of the sub-Carpathian barrow-grave culture. The Trzciniec culture[9] evolved out of the Corded Ware culture in east Poland around the fifteenth century B.C. The new culture was typical of the second period of the Polish Bronze Age. It extended over the territory of the eastern groups of the Polish Corded Ware culture, and traces of its subsequent drive, or at least of its strong influence, are plainly discernible in countries situated far to the east.

There is some similarity between the pottery of the Trzciniec and Komarów cultures, which was due mainly to their common Corded Ware background. Both cultures were formed under similar conditions. There were, however, considerable differences between them. The southern current, the important formative factor in the Komarów culture, only slightly affected the Trzciniec culture.

In some regions the two cultures, or their spheres of influence, overlapped—in the northern part of west Podolia and south Volhynia, for instance, where elements of both are discernible in the furniture of local barrow graves. The best guide to their spheres of influence is the bronze objects. Those of the Koszider type, characteristic of the 'Hungarian' bronze industry and connected with the Komarów culture, have been found east of west Podolia along the northern coast of the Black Sea up to Melitopol. They also extend along the valley of the Dnieper nearly up to Kiev. However, no bronzes of this type appear in Volhynia and in the country west of

xvi Vessel from the Yamnaya barrow grave I, burial 17, at Novo-Nikolskoe on the lower Volga in the province of Volgograd-Stalingrad; excavated by V.P. Shilov, 1954. The Hermitage Museum, Leningrad.

1

2

II Vessels from three superimposed levels of the
settlement at Mykhailivka on the lower Dnieper.
Institute of Archaeology of the Ukrainian Academy,
Kiev; published by O.F. Lahodovska, O.G.
Shaposhnikova and M.L. Makarevych, *Mykhail-
ivske poselennya*, Kiev 1962.

xviii Painted storage vase of period C–i of the Tripolye culture, with the encircled cross motif, from Petreny, Bessarabia. After E. v Stern, *Reallexókon-Ebert*, vol. xiii, pl. 20.

xix Pottery of the Volhynian group of the Globular Amphora culture. After O.N. Bahder, Balanovskii Mogilnik, 1963, p. 126, fig. 63.

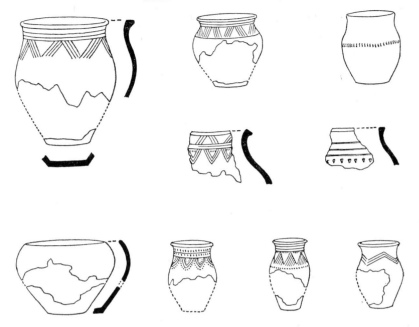

FIG. 34 Vessels of Trzciniec derivation from Narodychi-Pishchane in Volhynia. After I. Levytskii (*Antropologiya* vol. IV, Kiev 1930, pp. 227 ff., fig. 36).

Kiev—the domain of the Central European bronze industry diffused by the Trzciniec culture (Map XV, Pl. XXVII).

The westernmost culture affected by the Trzciniec within the territory with which we are concerned was a small local group, the Voytsekhivka culture, called after a barrow-grave cemetery on the Sluch. Its pottery bears marked Trzciniec features, though it also shows some traces of Komarów influence (Fig. 34; Pl. XXVI). The Voytsekhivka culture extended mainly over the area held previously by the Central and east Volhynians groups of the Globular Amphora culture (see p. 188).

Pottery closely related to that of the Trzciniec culture, and evidently evolved under its influence, was found in a series of sites in the vicinity of Kiev and in the valley of the Dnieper southwards up to the steppe border (such as Moshna near Cherkassy). They were incorrectly attributed to the Komarów culture.[10] Of a similar character was pottery of the Sosnitsa culture in the forest-steppe country east of the Dnieper (Fig. 45), extending along the lower Desna and the Seim up to Putyvl. Furthermore, vessels which call to mind the Trzciniec ware, both in their shape and decoration, were found in graves of the Dnieper-Desna culture further north

(Fig. 47), and also in those of the early Srubnaya culture in the region of Voronezh and even further east.

Much more significant is the eastern diffusion of a series of bronze objects of Central European type. They were found roughly along the track by which the Trzciniec-type pottery was diffused, and may likewise be connected with the eastern drive of that culture. Among these objects were over fifty flanged axes, and armlets with spiral terminals. Some of these were undoubtedly imported from Central Europe, but most were evidently cast locally, though under the influence of the Trzciniec people. It also seems very likely that the bronze armlets with spiral terminals, found in several Srubnaya-Khvalinsk graves of period 'B' on the Lower Volga (see p. 339) were modelled on prototypes current within the Trzciniec territory. A similar origin may even be sought for a number of personal ornaments of the early Koban culture of the Central Caucasian highland; they are strikingly reminiscent of Central European types of the second Bronze Age period, the time of the Trzciniec culture in Poland.

THE GLOBULAR AMPHORA CULTURE

This was the other Central European culture of the early second millennium B.C. that played an important role in the development of a new order in Eastern Europe and, together with the cultures of the Battle-axe assemblage, also affected large sections of the country further east. The culture has been dealt with in many archaeological works. Its large and important centre was Kuyavia in northern Poland,[11] from which it expanded eastwards and south-eastwards—along the Vistula and the Bug into Volhynia, Podolia, and the northern part of Rumania, even reaching Bulgaria. In the Soviet archaeological literature, the name of 'Volhynian' megalithic culture has been given to its Volhynian branch, on account of its slab-cists, the characteristic grave form.

The diffusion of Globular Amphora remains within this vast area appears to be very uneven (Map XIV). About 150 graves in about 120 sites have been recorded east of the Bug, including Rumania; they form several groups, with scattered graves between them. The route which must have been followed by the migrants involved a distance of nearly 500 miles from Kuyavia to West Podolia; an even greater distance, some 530 miles to the easternmost graves in Volhynia; and over 930 miles to the southernmost grave in Bulgaria at Pekliuk.[12]

The West Podolian group, by far the largest, consisted of about sixty graves in forty sites; the next largest, the Central Volhynian group, included about thirty graves in twenty-five sites; and the smallest, near Vinnitsa further south, had only six graves. Each of

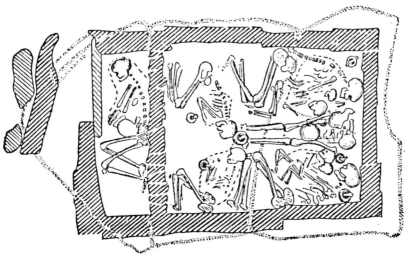

FIG. 35 Slab-cist grave from Voytsekhivka on the Sluch in Volhynia, in which a man was buried accompanied by two women, four children, two adolescents, and a slave in the adjoining compartment. After I. Levytskii (*Zapyski Vseukr. Akad. Nauk* vol. 1, Kiev 1931).

these groups developed in a different geographical environment; and each was surrounded by a different set of existing cultures, which in a different way influenced its local development.

Burials were almost exclusively in slab-cists sunk in the ground, with no mound or other external mark. Skeletons lay mostly in the supine position, but a crouched position was not infrequent. Double burials of a man and woman prevailed, but many cists, especially in Volhynia, contained a number of skeletons of persons buried together. In these cases the dead male was attended in his journey beyond the grave, usually by members of his family—two women with small children in one instance. The largest number, ten skeletons, was encountered in the large slab-cist grave at Voytsekhivka on the Sluch near Polonne (Fig. 35). The main male skeleton was sitting and leaning against the shorter side of the cist. Along the longer sides of the chamber, facing each other, lay skeletons of two women, each with two small children, and a young boy and a young girl, all in a crouched position; at the entrance to the main chamber, in a special annexe, lay a contracted skeleton of a serf. All the skeletons, except that of the main male, were richly strewn with ochre. In the easternmost group of the Globular Amphora culture, in Volhynia near Zhitomir, cremation burials were found almost exclusively in the cists, either in urns or heaped on the floor; and each cist contained several cremations.

The usual grave goods in slab-cists consisted of a few vessels (Pl.

XIX) and flint axes and chisels. The most characteristic vessels were amphorae of two main types, ovoid and 'Kuyavian', provided with lugs at the junction of the neck and shoulder. Another common vessel was a semi-spherical bowl. The decoration consisted of deeply incised horizontal zig-zag lines, separated by rows of very regular short vertical incisions. The pottery of the Podolian group was ornamented generally with rows of hanging triangles made by small semicircular incisions, the 'fish-scale' ornament. The latter ornament, and also the incised patterns, were usually filled in with white paste. Axes characteristic of the culture, made of white flint, were flat, were shaped like an elongated trapeze, and were very well polished all over their surface. Small chisels, square in section, were also characteristic of the culture and similarly polished.

At first sight the remains of the eastern Globular Amphora culture seem to exhibit a remarkable uniformity, in spite of the distance separating them. The basic shape of their pottery, and its decorative patterns (Pl. XIX) relate them to the Kuyavian centre in Poland. However, these vessels in their pure form (especially the ovoid and the 'Kuyavian' type amphorae), which do not seem to differ in any particular from the respective specimens in Kuyavia, have been found in a relatively small number of graves; they can be regarded as the earliest in each group, and date approximately to the early second millennium.

Some remains, however, do not occur in the central and eastern parts of Volhynia or in the south of West Podolia. Most numerous in all the groups in these areas were slab-cist graves, evidently of a somewhat later date; their inventories reflect in various degrees the influence of the surrounding indigenous cultures, which resulted in the formation of specific local variations, or distinct local groups of the culture. Remains of this sort have been found within an area larger than that covered by graves of the first category, especially in the areas that extended further to the east and south. They imply a further expansion of the culture from the newly established centres, and the formation of a new series of local groups still farther from the original centre of the culture.

In most areas the local groups of the culture did not develop any further. The next stage was their disappearance as distinct groups as they merged with the local cultures. It is only in Podolia, and in the central part of Volhynia (near Dubno) that the third stage of the culture is distinguishable. However, considerable changes took place at this stage: the traditional Globular Amphora pottery and other grave goods were replaced by those typical of the late stage of the Corded Ware culture. Stone battle-axes appeared for the first time in burials of the culture. Only the grave form (the slab-cist) and the

burial ritual, the essential elements of the ancient culture, bear witness to the identity of the groups; and this identity is further confirmed by the geographic diffusion of the late graves, which were
confined to the same area as before.

It is not easy to establish dates for all the groups of the culture.
They were formed at different times, and were obviously not long-
lived. It seems that a time-span of more than 250 years (five generations?) at the most cannot be given to any of the eastern groups in
their genuine form. So they must have come to an end around 1600
B.C., the end of our Stage I (Table 4). In some areas, as emphasized
in the previous paragraph, the groups continued for a few centuries
more, during our Stage II. The east Volhynian group of the Sluch
may be included among these, in spite of the fact that it ceased to
exist within the confines of its own area. Its representatives had
migrated southwards and ultimately reached Transylvania, their
route marked by pottery of the Volhynian type found in several sites
and graves near Vinnitsa on the Southern Bug, in the southern part
of West Podolia close to the Dniester, and further south in the Bucovina and Rumania (Moldavia), where several slab-cist graves of the
culture have been recorded. In all the latter graves the traditional
Globular Amphora pottery was to a great extent replaced by cord-
decorated ware.

In West Podolia, the descendants of the Globular Amphora people
were still to be found in the following period, our Stage III. In a
number of West Podolian slab-cists pottery and other grave goods
were found, and they did not differ in any respect from such remains
found in the barrow graves of the second and third periods of the
Komarów culture. The name of the Biały Potok group has been given
to these remains, which are considered to constitute a small local
group of the Komarów culture. The persons buried in the slab-cists
were evidently descendants of the ancient Globular Amphora people
of the west Podolian group.

The Biały Potok group was formed in our Stage III, evidently
under the impact of those factors that fostered the formation of the
Komarów and Costişa cultures (Pl. XXV: 2, 4, 5). The group, like
the sub-Carpathian Komarów culture, survived into the Early Iron
Age; this is indicated by iron objects found in the late slab-cists.

The survival into the later period of the descendants of the Globular Amphora people can likewise be traced in Transylvania. Slab-
cist graves that appeared there early in the second half of the second
millennium have been attributed to the later ('B') stage of the
Schneckenberg culture.[13] The form of the grave and the decorative
motifs of the sepulchral pottery identify them as descendants of the
Globular Amphora people. Slab-cist graves of the Bronze Age found

in the Ukraine along the Middle Dnieper west of the river undoubtedly belong to the same category.

The Globular Amphora culture was an intrusion in the east. The
very small number of graves in relation to the territory they cover,
and the fact that no settlements of the culture have been discovered
east of the Bug, are cogent arguments in favour of its alien, intrusive
character. Its pottery was almost without exception a sephulchral
pottery. The anthropological study of the cranial material from the
slab-cists revealed that the people were of the 'Nordic' type, except
the serf in the grave at Voytsekhivka (see p. 163), and some female
skulls from Podolian graves, which were brachycephalic.

The men of the culture have often been regarded as hunters and
swineherds, engaged in casual robbery and trade.[14] The character of
their grave goods and their geographic diffusion suggest, however,
that they were primarily warriors who invaded countries already inhabited. They most probably imposed their rule over the regions in
which they settled, but they did not exterminate the indigenous
population; they do not even seem to have interfered to any extent
in the further evolution of the native cultures. Their position as
members of the ruling class is indicated in particular by slab-cist
graves in which slaves, or serfs, were buried together with their
masters, and, above all, by the different racial stock to which the
serfs belonged, obviously that of the subdued population.

The Globular Amphora people ruled over the representatives of a
small local group of the Corded Ware people, in West Volhynia and
west of the Bug, called the Strzyżów culture; in East Volhynia the
subdued population seems to have been of the Gorodsk culture (see
p. 184), a hybrid of the Tripolyan culture with a preponderant element of the local group of the Corded Ware culture. In West Podolia
they ruled the West Podolian group of the Tripolye culture. The very
small number of Globular Amphora graves in each of the regions,
usually one or two slab-cists, but never more than four in one site,
suggests that their population was not numerous. No settlements
attributable to the Globular Amphora culture were found in these
regions, which shows that they must have lived in settlements of the
subdued population; and Globular Amphora potsherds have actually
been found in a number of settlements of the local cultures.

The diffusion of the globular amphorae in Volhynia suggests that
their representatives were the founders of a large number of flint
workshops discovered in the country; these workshops specialized in
the production of very fine daggers, spear-heads, curved knives
('sickles'), etc. Most probably the Globular Amphora people were
also engaged in the distribution of these products over wider areas.
Within their territory lay rather poor Volhynian copper deposits,

which seem to have been exploited at this time. The southern drive of the Central Volhynian group of the Globular Amphora people, which ultimately reached the metalliferous region in Transylvania about the middle of the second millennium B.C. (in our Stage II), suggests that the migrants or their immediate descendants intended to seize the rich copper, and possibly also gold, mines.

It is of interest to note that the diffusion of the remains of the Gorodsk culture outside its territory, which seems to have been ruled by the Central Volhynian Globular Amphora people, is exactly the same as that of the latter. They appeared at the very same time near Vinnitsa (Pechora), in the southernmost part of West Podolia (Kasperowce, Koszyłowce-Tovdry, etc.), where they brought down the local branch of the Tripolyan culture around 1600 B.C.—as suggested by the date of the Tripolyan remains in Werteba cave at Bilcze Złote, discussed later. Settlements of Gorodsk type were also recorded in Rumania, where they are known as the Horodiştea type in Moldavia, and the Schneckenberg culture in Transylvania (see p. 186). The coincidence in time and direction of both expansions suggests that the people of the Gorodsk culture were led south by their rulers, the Globular Amphora people.

The eastern Globular Amphora culture was in close contact with several other cultures. Its potsherds were found in early sub-Carpathian barrow graves. Deeply incised decorative motifs, the zigzag lines characteristic of the culture, appear on a series of Tripolyan vessels of period C–1. Genuine Globular Amphora potsherds and flint chisels have been found in the valley of the Dnieper north and south of Kiev (Kanev); those excavated in the settlement of Seredni Stog II date the expansion of the Globular Amphora culture to the period called after that settlement. It seems very likely that the Scandinavian flint dagger from a barrow grave at Orlivka, near Berdyansk on the Sea of Azov (Fig. 36), found its way by means of the Globular Amphora culture. The site lay about 110 miles south-easte from Seredni Stog (Map XIV: 24) (see p. 133).

Traces of penetration, possibly by small groups of Globular Amphora traders, may be followed eastwards along the Upper Dnieper and the Upper and Middle Volga up to the Urals, over a distance of about 1,400 miles (Map XIV: asterisks). Potsherds typical of the culture (Fig. 37) have been found in several sites in Byelorussia —in the regions of Gomel and Rogachev on the upper Dnieper, in settlements of the Dnieper-Desna culture (Zavalie) and at Dubosishche east of Smolensk.[15] Decorative patterns characteristic of the Globular Amphora culture, or at least very reminiscent of them, adorn a series of vessels from various sites on the Upper Volga (Sakhtysh, Malyi Ostrovok);[16] and from the cemeteries of the

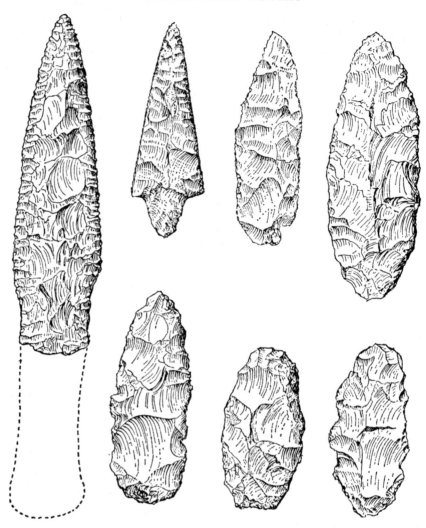

FIG. 36 Flints, including a dagger of Scandinavian type, found in a
barrow grave at Orlivka near Berdyansk on the Sea of Azov.
After O. Ia. Ohulchanskii (A.P. vol. IV, 1950, p. 137, fig. 5).

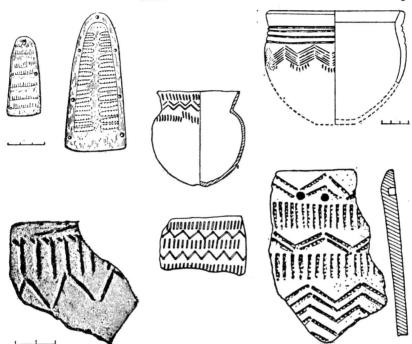

FIG. 37 Decorated bone plaques, beaker and potsherds with an incised ornament, characteristic of the Globular Amphora culture, from Balanovo, Balanbash, Lake Sakhtysh, Zavalie, Ches-Tyi-Iag (see Map XIV).

Fatyanovo culture, especially of its Yaroslav-Kalinin group, where also sherds of a decorated vessel typical of the Globular Amphorae were excavated in the settlement Stanok II near Kostroma, north of the Volga.[17] A small debased amphora, with the characteristic deeply incised decorative patterns, was found in a grave (see p. 201) of the Balanovo cemetery (Pl. XIX) and in other graves of that cemetery two decorated bone plaques excavated were likewise characteristic of the Globular Amphora culture (Fig. 37). It seems very likely that the Globular Amphora people contributed jointly with the Corded Ware assemblage to the formation of both the Fatyanovo and Balanovo cultures, though its share in it was evidently the smaller. Again, the typical motif of single or double horizontal zigzag lines separated by a row of short vertical incisions appears in the area of the Upper Ufa river in the Middle Urals (Balanbash; Ust-Ayskaya);[18] on pottery of the second period of the Gorbunovo culture (Beregovaya, Kalmatskii Brod); and perhaps in its most pronounced form on pottery from the site of Ches-Tyi-Iag,[19] on the Northern Sosva in the Northern Urals (Fig. 37: 3, 5).

Except for the last, all these finds fall into a single line extending

13

from East Volhynia in the west to the Middle Urals in the east, which seems to imply that this particular motif was of western derivation. It does not seem to appear outside this rather narrow strip. The finds are of importance for the establishment of chronological correlation of cultures in distant regions of the country; they also illustrate the extent of the western penetration into Eastern Europe.

THE SOUTH-WEST

THE TRIPOLYE CULTURE

By the end of the third millennium, towards the end of its period B-2, the Tripolye culture must have met the Yamnaya culture, which had expanded at that time and reached the Danubian delta; it also penetrated into the forest-steppe, the black-earth region west of the Dnieper belonging to the Tripolyan territory. Some mounds raised over the debris of Tripolyan settlements of period B-2 have been investigated; but contact with the Yamnaya pastoralists left no notable traces in the culture of the Tripolyan agriculturalists.

Different was the effect, however, produced by the Corded Ware and Globular Amphora cultures. Their expansion greatly interfered with the development of the Tripolye culture, the territory of which they entered and crossed in several points. The considerable changes caused by the intrusions mark a new period in the development of the culture, called period C-1. It belonged to our Stage I of the east European Bronze Age (Table 4).

The significant feature of the new period was the position of settlements (Fig. 38). They lay exclusively on the plateau, and there was a marked preference for placing them on its edge. Mostly sites were chosen in well protected positions, surrounded by deep and steep ravines and valleys, with an easy access from one side only. Defensive constructions, moats and ditches, were often built across this side, and sometimes also round the whole settlement. It was a turbulent period.

There was no major difference in the content of the culture from that of the preceding period: tools and huts were similar, the latter all of the 'ploshchadka' type built on the surface, and the economy continued unchanged. But there are well marked changes in the Tripolyan pottery. A common feature throughout the whole Tripolyan territory was the decline of spiral motifs and the frequent use of linear patterns in the decorative style of pottery, whether painted or incised (Fig. 39). In this respect considerable differences developed between the styles of the various groups within the culture; and in some of these different types of vessel appeared the shape of which calls to mind those of their neighbouring cultures.

The differences in the Tripolyan decorative style of the period, and

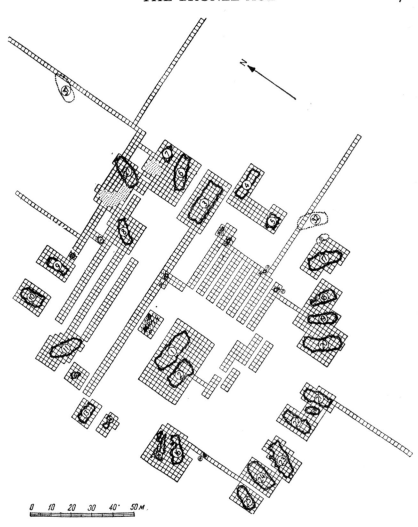

FIG. 38 Plan of the Tripolyan settlement of period C-1 at Kolomishchyna I.
After T. S. Passek (MIA 10, 1949, p. 132, fig. 70).

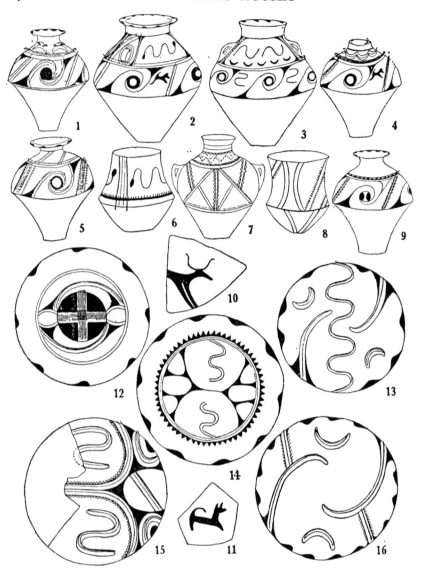

FIG. 39 Examples of Tripolyan pottery of period C-1; Bilcze Złote, West Podolia.
After L. Kozłowski (Zarys pradziejów . . ., Lwów 1939, pl. X).

other occurrences restricted to its various groups, were mainly the outcome of the interference of the two expanding Central European cultures. But the effects of these was not as strong everywhere, the most affected being the West Podolian group. The establishment of the Globular Amphora group within its confines cut it off from other Tripolyan groups and accounted for its somewhat different development.

The break with old traditions is clearly marked. There was a weakening of the age-old links of the West Podolian group of the Tripolye culture with Moldavia (the Cucuteni culture) and with the Bessarabian group, and the change in commercial relations is reflected by the replacement of Transylvanian copper, almost the only metal in the remains of earlier periods, by north Slovakian or east Alpine metal. The decorative style of West Podolian pottery of that period shows the strong influence of the Funnel Beakers alongside that of the Corded Ware. This was due to close and reciprocal relations between the group and the easternmost outpost of the Central Polish Funnel Beaker culture, the 'Gródek Nadbużny' group (on the Bug).[20] Potsherds and a few complete vessels of Tripolyan character with painted decoration were excavated in a series of settlements of the latter culture on the Bug and in West Volhynia. And, vice-versa, perforated stone axes with a knobbed butt, typical of the Funnel Beakers, were found in sites situated in the centre of the Podolian group of the Tripolye culture. Two-lugged vessels of painted Tripolyan ware, excavated in some West Podolian settlements (Koszyłowce, Bilcze Złote-Werteba), were simply replicas of the amphorae of the Funnel Beaker culture, made in a different technique (Fig. 39: 7) and differently decorated.

Relations between these two cultures developed during our Stage I. The Funnel Beakers in Central Poland (Ćmielów) have been Carbon-14 dated to 2725 ±100 B.C. (H.566–592), but the Gródek Nadbużny group on the Tripolyan border was definitely of a later date. Copper objects of Slovak origin excavated in the standard site of the group place its destruction, and the downfall of the group, about 1800 B.C.

The shape of a series of vessels provided with two lugs on their bodies, found in some West Podolian settlements of the period (Koszyłowce, Bilcze Złote) and in particular their painted decoration are strikingly reminiscent of the 'Thuringian' amphorae, typical of the early stage of the Corded Ware culture; they are evidence of the contact of the local Tripolyan group with the latter culture.

By the middle of the second millennium B.C. the West Podolian branch of the Tripolye culture declined, most probably under the impact of an invading alien people. A remarkable find in the Werteba cave at Bilcze Złote could place the destruction of the group at around 1600 B.C. The cave was inhabited for a short period, presumably by the inhabitants of a large settlement of period C–1 nearby, who took refuge there in unsettled times. Traces of hearths, potsherds, whole vessels, implements made of stone, flint, bone and antler, and a few copper objects were found. Of particular interest were several daggers of bone and a three-riveted copper specimen, and also a dark blue glass bead. A similar bead was found in a grave in Austria of Reinecke's Bronze Age period A2 (about 1600–1500 B.C.).[21] The copper dagger is of a type common in the Alpine region during the A2 period and the following period B (up to about 1400 B.C.) (Pl. XXII).

A feature peculiar to the cave was the presence of disordered heaps of human bones; they apparently belonged to persons slain on the spot. Human bones, weapons and other circumstances suggest that the occupation of the cave ended in a massacre. The dagger and the glass bead give its date. A flint axe characteristic of the Globular Amphora culture that was found there seems to indicate that the assailants were most probably men of the Central Volhynian group of that culture. Presumably they advanced there jointly with the people of the Gorodsk culture, settlements of the latter having been recorded at several points in the south of West Podolia. The newcomers most probably put an end to the local Tripolyan group, though they do not seem to have annihilated the population.

Pottery from settlements of a later date than these events was of a decadent Tripolyan type, a poor, 'soft' grog-gritted undecorated ware. Pottery of the same type was found in a few barrow graves and in the settlements at Komarów, all of the Neolithic barrow-grave culture. Pottery of West Podolian settlements of the next stage (and also of those in the Bucovina) was already the typical Komarów ware. The development was similar further south, in the northern part of Moldavia (see p. 160), where the Costişa culture[22] was the equivalent of the Komarów culture of Podolia. It has already been emphasized that this development was the outcome of a strong influence emanating from the cultures of the other side of the Carpathians. The local West Podolian group of the Globular Amphora people succumbed to the same influence and its new embodiment was the Biały Potok group. Traces of this influence may be also followed further east, up to the Dnieper. The name of the Komarów culture has been lately extended to embrace all these remains, and even remains of evident Trzciniec lineage have been often included.

A change in conditions occurred again about the thirteenth century B.C. It marks a new period in the development of the whole country, and will be dealt with in Chapter IV.

There was a different evolution during the period C–1 for the Middle Dniester-Bessarabian group of the Tripolye culture. Its decorative style of painted pottery was closely related to that of the Moldavian group (the late Cucuteni culture); it was distinct from that of the West Podolian group and from the decorative style of the two other groups further north, the Uman and Kiev groups. It has been called 'style γ–1'.[23]

Characteristic decorative motifs often appearing on large storage vessels of the group (Pl. XVIII), and also on those of the late Cucuteni culture, are encircled crosses and similar patterns (Fig. 40). The same motifs were typical of the Mostičarska culture (Laibacher Moor) and Vučedol; basically the decorative style of the pottery of these distant areas was similar if not identical, in spite of the different techniques used in producing it. Remarkable parallels to these motifs, emphasized by several authors, occur in the Middle Bronze Age pottery of Cyprus, dated 1800–1600 B.C. Such parallels and points of agreement date the settlements of the Middle Dniester group to our Stage I (Table 4).

FIG. 40 Decoration (course of the solar disc) on the upper part of a large vase from Petreny of Tripolyan period C-1.
After B. A. Rybakov (SA vol. 1965–1, p. 42, fig. 21).

The links with the Aegean countries, and possibly also with the Middle Danubian area, that influenced the decorative style of pottery were not isolated instances in that period. Maritime trade connections were then maintained by the inhabitants of the Usatovo settlement with Anatolia and the Aegean countries; they are well attested by a number of objects found in the settlement and its cemetery that originated in those areas (see p. 183).

The Middle Dniester Tripolyan group seems to have suffered the same fate as its neighbouring West Podolian branch. In their southern drive the Gorodsk-Globular Amphora wave must have crossed the country, and the Tripolyan groups affected do not seem to have survived the trial. Later, the Komarów-Costişa culture took over the whole area.

The two other Tripolyan groups, the Kiev and Uman groups, do not show any great changes in their development during the period C–1. Both must have been in contact with the Yamnaya pastoralists as the latter advanced into the steppe country west of the Dnieper and into parts of the forest-steppe zone. Their subsequent contact with the early Corded Ware culture is well illustrated by the decoration of a few vessels of the Kiev group, a genuine Tripolyan ware, which follows patterns characteristic of the 'Thuringian' Amphora (Kolomishchyna I). Stone battle-axes found in the settlement of the Uman group (Popudnia) were also types belonging to the Corded Ware assemblage; the settlement was of Tripolyan period C–1. A number of vessels in settlements of this period of the Kiev (Khalepie) and Uman (Volodymirivka) groups bear incised decorative patterns characteristic of the Globular Amphora culture. They imply the intrusion of the latter into Tripolyan territory not later than about the eighteenth century B.C.

The growing importance of stock-breeding is well reflected in the plan of the settlement of Kolomishchyna I (Fig. 38), with the cattle enclosure in its centre. The steppe breeders of the Yamnaya culture undoubtedly influenced this development, but its main cause was most probably the change of climate, which at that time entered into its hot and dry sub-Boreal phase.

The Uman group seems to have been a junction for various influences. At Sabatynivka I on the Southern Bug (the Boh), a knot-headed 'Cypriot' bronze pin and a clay cauldron were excavated in the Tripolyan layer (Fig. 41). The pin was of a widespread and long-lived style. Similar specimens were current during the Early Bronze Age in Central Europe, Reinecke's period A1; such a specimen formed part of a Middle Bronze Age hoard found in Kolodnoe in the Carpatho-Ukraine.[24] They were also found in Moldavia in a settlement of the 'Proto-Noua' culture (Gîrbivaţ) of the thirteenth century B.C.[25] The clay vessel from Sabatynivka I was evidently modelled on Transcaucasian bronze cauldrons of the middle of the second millennium B.C.

The Tripolye culture did not cease to exist at the same date throughout its whole territory. But the middle of the second millennium B.C. may be taken to be the approximate terminal date of the Tripolyan groups, except perhaps the Uman group. The latter, situated in rather a backwater during that turbulent period, may have survived a few centuries longer, during our Stage II (see p. 377).

THE MIDDLE DNIEPER CULTURE

During the second millennium B.C. a series of local cultures appeared in the country west of the Dnieper, south of the southern border of the forest zone up to the Black Sea coast. They were mainly hybrids formed from amalgamations between the Tripolye culture and others which about that time entered the country. The hybrids

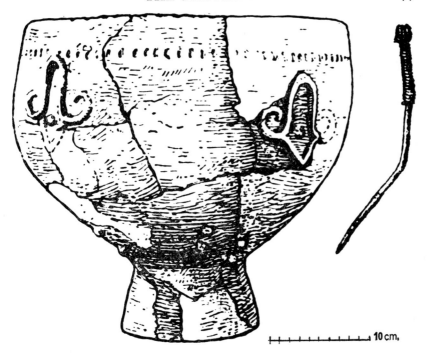

FIG. 41 Clay cauldron and bronze 'Cypriot' pin from the Tripolyan settlement at Sabatynivka I.
After A. V. Dobrovolskii (A.P. vol. IV, 1952, pp. 82 ff., fig. 2, pl. II: 17).

were mostly short-lived, but the role of some of them in the development of the country was of importance.

The earliest of the local cultures was the Middle Dnieper culture. Its origin goes back to the turn of the third and second millennia, the time at which the Yamnaya people, after crossing the Dnieper, spread northwards into the forest-steppe zone. There they met the Tripolyans and both peoples seem to have lived side by side without intermingling (see p. 170). But in some regions, in particular nearer to the Dnieper-Boh watershed, the area of the preponderant steppe, the Yamnaya people established themselves as the only occupants; no Tripolyan settlements have been recorded in this area at all.

Soon afterwards the Corded Ware people advanced into the area from the west or north-west. The intermingling of the two elements resulted in the formation of a hybrid, the Middle Dnieper culture.

The newly formed culture extended over the black-earth region west and south-west of Kiev, nearly up to the Southern Bug (the Boh), and included part of the territory of the Kiev group of the Tripolye culture. A number of barrow graves attributable to the culture have also been investigated south-east and east of Kiev and east

of the Dnieper, in the forest-steppe zone near the border of the Catacomb culture. In the earlier archaeological literature the culture was
called the 'Jackowica' (Yatskovitsa) group or the 'Kiev group of
Corded Ware'. It consisted solely of barrow graves, which usually
appeared in small groups, though in the semi-steppe on the watershed
between the Dnieper and the Boh they formed larger cemeteries of
up to 200 mounds (Jackowica). Such large cemeteries showed a considerable chronological variety, ranging from the final Neolithic to
the Scythian period.

The stratigraphic evidence reveals that graves of the Yamnaya
type were the earliest, implying that the Yamnaya culture must have
been the substratum on which the Middle Dnieper culture was
formed (Pl. XVI). The formative element was evidently represented
by immigrants of the Corded Ware assemblage.

Burials of the earliest stage, those of the Yamnaya type, were in
shafts, where supine skeletons with legs contracted lay strewn with
red ochre. Later burials were mostly on the surface, with skeletons
crouched and heads mostly turned to the west as in the majority of
the Corded Ware groups. Graves were poorly furnished and about
one in ten had no grave goods at all. Single vessels, or occasionally
two or three in one grave, were the commonest grave goods (Pl.
XXIII). The standard vessels were deep bowls with a wide, slightly
rounded and decorated base; and ovoid beakers with a pointed or
rounded base and a short funnel-shaped neck. Ornaments consisted of
various incisions, chevron patterns, single cord impressions, hatched
triangles arranged in bands, etc. An early stage of the group was
exemplified by one grave in which a 'Thuringian' amphora was
associated with a flint axe (Grishchintsy), by another containing an
almost perfect 'globular' amphora (Losiatyn), and by a third in
which a Tripolyan vessel was found with a stone battle-axe (Grechaniki). Pottery from later graves was different, showing the influences
of the Late Bronze and Early Iron Ages of the neighbouring regions.

Other grave goods consisted of stone battle-axes, flint axes,
flint arrow-heads and a few spear-heads or daggers. Two 'arrow-
straighteners', equated the relative graves with the Catacomb culture
(see p. 223). Personal ornaments were frequent: necklaces made of
animal teeth (wolf fangs); amber beads; tubular beads made of spiral
bronze wire or imitations made of thin tubular bird bone; boar tusks;
bronze and silver rings and temple ornaments with hooked and
flattened terminals typical of the Central European Early Bronze
Age; hammer-headed pins made of bone, typical of the Catacomb
culture, etc.

The influence exercised by the Catacomb culture was of importance during the later stages of the development of the Middle

Dnieper culture (see p. 229), but also that of the Dnieper-Desna culture (see p. 194). The latter extended over the sandy soils of the forest zone, and has been incorrectly considered to be a late offspring of the Middle Dnieper culture.

The Middle Dnieper culture is supposed to have been post-Tripolyan. However, many circumstances point to the fact that mounds of the early stage at least could be equated with the Tripolyan period C–1. Furthermore, the larger barrow-grave cemeteries lay in areas in which no Tripolyan settlements were recorded; so it seems that the two peoples lived side by side, the Tripolyans close to the streams, and the Middle Dnieper people on the open grassland.

The Middle Dnieper culture seems to have been formed at a later date than the sub-Carpathian group, probably early in the second millennium B.C. Its development, several stages of which can be distinguished, ran parallel to that of the Catacomb culture east of the Dnieper. The group continued during the later part of the Bronze Age and its descendants probably survived to the middle of the first millennium B.C., though their culture underwent considerable changes under the influence of their neighbours (Table 4).

A number of settlements in the valley of the Dnieper south of Kiev have been attributed to the culture. In fact, their inhabitants were direct descendants of the Neolithic population of the valley (see p. 115). They always adapted themselves to new conditions as soon as changes, caused by the influx of new groups population or otherwise, occurred in the neighbouring areas. Accordingly, their 'Middle Dnieper' pottery was soon replaced by that of the Trzciniec (or 'Trzciniec-Komarów') type of the Middle Bronze Age (see p. 160).

THE VYKHVATYNTSI GROUP

The expansion of the Corded Ware at the turn of the third and second millennium B.C. was similarly directed southwards; some of its groups proceeded along the Dniester, ultimately reaching the Black Sea and the region of the Lower Dnieper further east. Traces of their advance by that route are plainly visible on the Middle Dniester, on the northern border of the steppe country where the Vykhvatyntsi group was formed, and called after a village near Rybnitsa. They contributed to the formation of the Usatovo culture in the steppe east of the Lower Dniester and on the Black Sea coast; the settlement of Mykhailivka (see p. 134) on the Lower Dnieper bore strong marks of the advancing Corded Ware people.

The Vykhvatyntsi group consisted of a number of 'flat' cemeteries, the burial ritual and grave goods of which imply that several different elements were responsible for its formation. The cemetery of Vykhvatyntsi[26] contained over sixty graves; skeletons were supine with legs contracted, in the characteristic 'Yamnaya' position. Stones laid around the graves or encircling them (cromlechs) connect them with burials belonging to the settlements of the valley of the Lower Dneiper and the region of the rapids; many Yamnaya graves of that region also had stone rings round the graves under the mound. On the other hand, grave goods of the Vykhvatyntsi cemeteries were mostly typical of the Corded Ware assemblage; they did not much differ from those of the sub-Carpathian barrow graves, in particular the stone battle-axe, flint 'sickle', bone daggers and awls, flint flakes, beads and pendants of *Unio* shells, boar tusks, etc. Pottery was of two categories (Fig. 42). One of these was a genuine corded ware with several vessels representing somewhat debased 'Thuringian' amphorae. The second category was made up of black-painted Tripolyan vessels, deep bowls and a few other types. There were also large two-lugged amphorae, evidently modelled on the 'Thuringian' ones both in their shape and their painted decoration. Clay figurines found in several graves were also Tripolyan.

The Vykhvatyntsi group, placed on the border of the true steppe (Map XIV: 15) was a hybrid to which several cultures must have contributed. Its substratum was Tripolyan or Yamnaya or both, but the organizing element was evidently the newcomers of the Corded Ware assemblage advancing south-eastwards along the Dniester. The group is considered to belong to the Tripolyan culture and to have been of period C–2. However, the size of the cemetery implies a longer period than that, and the Thuringian amphorae found in its graves equate it with Stage II of the sub-Carpathian barrow graves, and suggest the early second millennium B.C., Stage I of our east European Bronze Age sequence.

THE USATOVO CULTURE

A somewhat similar group had developed at about the same time further south, in the steppe east of the Dniester, reaching eastwards approximately to the Boh (Southern Bug). It has been called the Usatovo culture, after a village on the outskirts of Odessa where barrow graves, two flat cemeteries, and a settlement were investigated.

Barrow graves were typical of the culture. According to stratigraphic evidence, the earliest burials, which appear, however, in a limited number, were of the Yamnaya type; they were most probably connected with the westward drive of that culture. The most numerous were primary and secondary burials of a characteristic type. Skeletons lay crouched in shafts, though later burials were often laid on the surface of the ground and many graves were dug into the already existing mounds. Slab-cist graves under a mound were re-

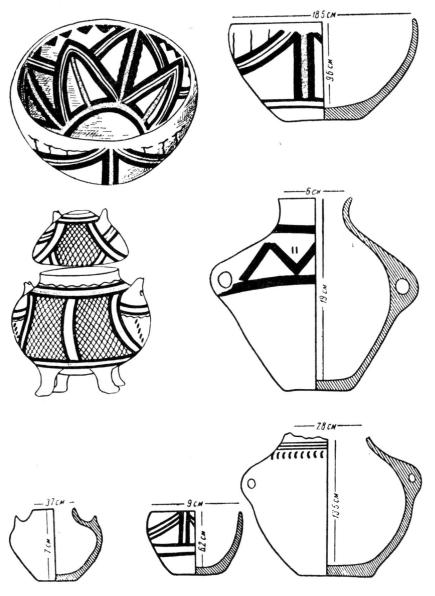

FIG. 42 Vessels (mainly painted) from the cemetery of Vykhvatyntsi,
except the pedestalled vase covered with a lid from a barrow grave of the
Usatovo culture at Tiraspol.
After A. E. Alikova (KSIIMK No. XXVI, 1949, pp. 73, 74, figs. 28, 29) and
T. S. Passek (*Trypilska Kultura*. Kiev 1941, fig. 33:2).

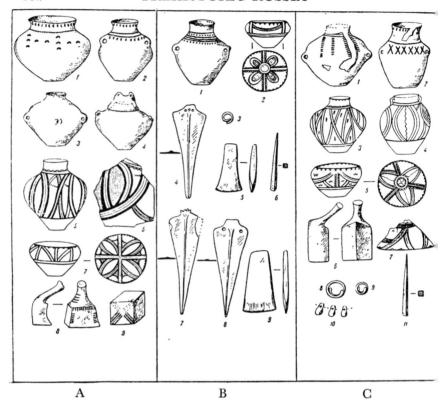

               A   B   C

FIG. 43 Pottery and other objects excavated at Usatovo.
(A) settlement; (B) barrow grave cemetery I; (C) barrow grave cemetery
II. After T. S. Passek (MIA 10, 1949, p. 192, fig. 97).

latively frequent, especially at Usatovo. Under many mounds stone
rings or cromlechs have been uncovered round the main grave; there
were sometimes two or three concentric rings, often built of vertical
slabs. At least one slab of the cromlechs has either human or animal
figures (horse, stag) incised on it, or some geometric patterns. A few
typical 'Catacomb' graves, shafts with a niche, seem to have belonged
to an advanced stage of the culture.

Burials were rather poorly furnished, except a series of barrow
graves at Usatovo (Fig. 43). Grave goods consisted of one or two pots,
a few objects of personal adornment, and weapons. Pottery was of
two types. About 8 per cent of it was a kind of Tripolyan black-
painted ware, similar to that found in graves of the Vykhvatyntsi
group. The bulk was a sand or shell-gritted ware with cord/or stamp-
impressed decoration; it was either corded ware or Central European
character (found mainly in the steppe barrow graves), or a special
variety, a local corded ware, found mainly in graves and in the settle-

ment of Usatovo, and only seldom in barrow graves in the steppe. 'Thuringian' amphorae of a somewhat debased form were common among both kinds of corded ware (Fig. 43: top row).

Other grave goods, found chiefly in graves of a later stage, consisted of a few stone battle-axes, some of which (Horozheno) had an incised 'Mycenaean' ornament (Pl. XXXVII); a bronze dagger with four rivet holes (Sukleia); and a few bronze ear or temple pendants. Once a bone imitation of a Unetice bronze pin was found (Tiraspol). Most of the objects, typical of period A–2 of the Alpine Bronze Age, were presumably of Central European origin.

Usatovo and the adjacent region seem to have held a unique position within the remains of the culture called after it. It lay close to a liman at present cut off from the sea by a strip of land about two miles wide, but which was connected with the sea at the time of the Usatovo culture and the settlement. There richly furnished barrow graves were found with copper weapons, silver-plated daggers, flat axes, knives and awls, etc. The settlement was surrounded by a stone wall, and there were quadrangular houses built of stone slabs and blocks.

Many objects found in Usatovo graves and in the settlement were of foreign origin and point to wide commercial relations. Amber beads imply links with the Baltic coast, and silver temple ornaments with Central Europe. But the most important trade connections must have been with the Aegean and Anatolia, probably through the intermediary of the sixth city of Troy during its early stage of existence. Copper objects, especially daggers (some silver-plated), represent Aegean types current by the end of the third and the beginning of the second millennia (Fig. 43). They were either imported or cast locally; bronze slag and lumps of Anatolian antimony imply the existence of local foundries. A corbelled grave chamber built of small stone slabs, uncovered under one of the Usatovo mounds, was evidently inspired by the Aegean tombs; and the cult of the bull, traces of which have been found, must also have been introduced from the south. Skulls of bulls have been found deposited in special offering holes in a few barrow graves; stelae with bull's head sculptured on them were also excavated from these. In the settlement of Usatovo a rock was uncovered disclosing a cavity to which the shape of a bull's head has been given; it was found close to an offering site.

Animal husbandry was well developed at Usatovo, but agriculture was of lesser importance. The chief domestic animal was the sheep, but bones have also been found of cattle, goats and dogs. Hunting was evidently practised. Horses were kept, for their bones have been found, and they figure on a few stelae. A bone cheek-piece suggests that horses were used for drawing chariots.

The two types of cemetery uncovered at Usatovo—one consisting of richly furnished barrow graves with elaborate stone constructions, the other formed of 'flat' and rather modestly endowed burials— indicate the social stratification of the Usatovo society, at the head of which evidently stood a wealthy and powerful ruling class. It is also significant that many barrow graves were ransacked soon after the funeral; the looters were obviously not members of the same class to which those buried in the respective graves belonged. The wealth of the rulers undoubtedly came from their commercial activities, especially the maritime trade with Troy VI (see p. 271).

The substratum of the whole Usatovo population was probably the descendants of the local Mesolithic hunters and fishermen who had been joined later by the Yamnaya pastoralists gradually advancing from the west. Next were the immigrants of the Corded Ware culture, who arrived in small numbers from the north-west, possibly from the Vykhvatyntsi group; they seem already to have been mixed with the Tripolyans. The stone constructions, slab-cist graves of a type proper to the Globular Amphora culture, a few vessels of a special type reminiscent of those of the latter culture, and the finding of amber, suggest that an important element in the final formation of the culture must have been the men of the Globular Amphorae. They seem to have been the main organizing element responsible for the development of overseas commercial relations, and the backbone of the Usatovo ruling class.

The evidence available suggests that the culture was formed early in our Stage I (Table 4).[27] It developed parallel to the Catacomb culture of the steppe east of the Dnieper (see p. 228). In its development two periods are distinguishable, the first characterized by the settlement of Usatovo. It flourished contemporaneously with the early stage of the sixth city of Troy (1800–1600 B.C.), with which it seems to have had important commercial connections (see p. 270). The settlement had probably ceased to exist by the middle of the millennium, in the second period of the culture which bears its name (our Stage II). The culture continued for a few centuries more, as indicated by barrow graves in which objects characteristic of the Alpine Bronze Age A–2 were found. The final ending cannot yet be dated with certainty. The culture might still have been in existence during our Stage III, some barrow graves of a late date seeming to suggest it. But it definitely lasted no later than the thirteenth century B.C., when the Srubnaya culture advanced into the country from the east.

THE GORODSK CULTURE

In turning to the north of the area under review, further north than the Tripolyan territory, the first local culture to be met with is the

XX Pottery of the Gorodsk culture from the settlement at Troyaniv near Zhitomir; excavated by M.M. Shmaglii, vol. XIII, 1961, pp. 20–37. Institute of Archaeology of the Ukrainian Academy, Kiev.

xxi Pottery of the Sofiika culture from the cremation cemetery at Chernyn, north of Kiev, except the urn on the right (amphora), which is from the cemetery of Chervonyi Khutor; excavated by V.I. Kanivets, AP, vol. VI, 1956, p. 107, pl. II.
Institute of Archaeology of the Ukrainian Academy, Kiev.

xxii Bronze and bone daggers from the Tripolyan period C–I site in the Werteba cave at Bilcze Złote, West Podolia.
Archaeological Museum, Kraków, Poland.

Gorodsk culture (Map XIV: XXII). This was the most important of the hybrids in that region, and was called after a fortified settlement on the Teterev, east of Zhitomir, within the forest zone. The remains of the culture, mainly settlements, have been recorded within a relatively large area extending over the southernmost part of the sandy soils within the forest zone on the Teterev and westwards up to the river Sluch, and over the northern border of the fertile loess soils south and south-west of Zhitomir; southwards it reached to the Upper Boh (the Southern Bug).

Huts of the Gorodsk culture were of two types. Those of Tripolyan 'ploshchadka' type, built on the surface, were uncovered in its southern settlements, placed mainly on the fertile loess soils; but further north, on the sandy soils, pit-dwellings were usual (for instance, at Gorodsk). The inhabitants of the settlements were engaged in agriculture and stock-rearing. Pottery in 80 to 90 per cent of cases was mostly a crude and heavy sand-gritted, cord-decorated ware. Quartz, crushed shells, or some organic matter were often added to the clay paste; and many vessels had a red slip (Pl. XX). Large storage vessels, and smaller bowls and vases were typical. The other category, which formed between 10 and 20 per cent, was a kind of Tripolyan ware decorated with black-painted geometric patterns, very similar to that of the Vykhvatyntsi and Usatovo cultures.

The decorative style of the painted Tripolyan ware has been called the Tripolyan C–2 style, and considered to be characteristic of the latest stage of the Tripolye culture. Accordingly, the Gorodsk culture is thought[28] to have represented the last stage of the Tripolyan development, stage C–2.

In fact, however, there is sufficient evidence to equate the Gorodsk style C–2 with remains of the Tripolyan period C–1. The labels C–1 and C–2 denote two different decorative styles of Tripolyan pottery that were in use at the same time in different regions. They do not signify two different Tripolyan periods, at least not in the area west of Kiev. The Gorodsk culture may be regarded as a distinct group, or branch, of the Tripolye culture if the character of its settlements and, to a lesser extent, the economy of their inhabitants, are considered as decisive for its identification. However, the local non-Tripolyan Corded Ware element was by far the most common, and it seems that the remains ought to be looked upon as a local branch of the Corded Ware assemblage that had developed under a strong impact from the Tripolye culture; an influx of small groups of Tripolyans from the neighbouring Kiev and Uman groups cannot be ruled out.

The culture was formed not later than the early part of our Stage I (Table 4). This is indicated by objects characteristic of the Gródek

14

Nadbużny group of the Funnel Beaker culture excavated in several settlements of the Gorodsk culture—small clay models of stone shaft-hole axes with a semi-spherical butt. On the other hand, painted Tripolyan ware akin to that of the Gorodsk culture was found in settlements of that group. These points of agreement also corroborate the equation of the Gorodsk decorative style C–2 with the Tripolyan period C–1.

At a later period, settlements of the Gorodsk culture appeared south of its original territory (see p. 167)—south of Vinnitsa (Pechora), in West Podolia (Kasperowce), in North Moldavia (Horodiştea), and further south in Rumania (Folteşti; Map XIV). They evidently demonstrate the southward migration of the Gorodsk people, most probably under the leadership of the Globular Amphora people of the central Volhynian branch; for remains of the latter culture of the same age follow the same track.

This migration took place around 1600 B.C. and initiated a new period in the local development of West Podolia. The cause of the migration and the relation of the culture with the Volhynian Globular Amphora culture need further study. The migration presumably meant the end of the local Globular Amphora group. It cannot yet be established whether the same applies to the Gorodsk culture, and the question remains open whether within its own territory the latter had survived in the post-Tripolyan age, our Stage II.

THE EVMINKA-SOFIIVKA GROUPS

Settlements similar to those of the Gorodsk type, and likewise erroneously considered to be late Tripolyan of period C–2, were also found east of the Gorodsk territory—around Kiev, mainly on sandy soils east of the Dnieper, and further north on the Lower Desna. They have been called the 'Evminka' group, after a settlement on the Lower Desna. The bulk of the pottery of this group was a local ware, and only a fraction, about 5 to 10 per cent of the pottery excavated, was a kind of Tripolyan painted kitchen ware. In a few sites huts of Tripolyan 'ploshchadka' type were uncovered. The non-Tripolyan pottery differed from that of the Gorodsk group, being evidently allied to the pottery of the local culture of the preceding period. The Evminka group must have been formed under the impact of the Tripolye culture, in similar conditions to those that gave rise to the Gorodsk culture. The different background caused the disparities between the two similar and kindred groups. The Evminka group was connected with the Catacomb culture of the steppe country east of the Dnieper.

No graves of the Evminka group have been discovered, but another group of remains of the same area consisted exclusively of

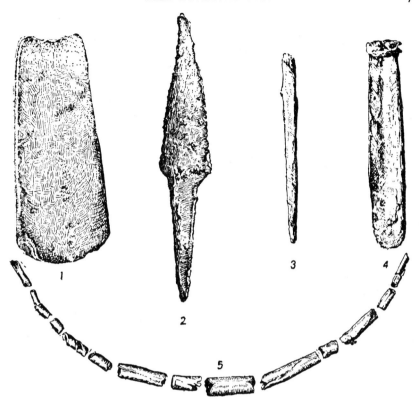

FIG. 44 Copper tools, weapons and beads from the cremation cemetery at Sofiivka near Kiev.
After *Narysy Starodavnoy Istorii Ukrainskoy RSR*, Kiev 1957, p. 68.

cemeteries. These were cremation cemeteries, the cremations being deposited either in urns or in unprotected pits in sand-dunes. They have been called the 'Sofiivka' type after a cemetery east of Kiev, and are considered to be one of the late Tripolyan groups. The cinerary urns, some decorated, others with a simple cord-impressed ornament, are a kind of a Tripolyan ware (Pl. XXI). A number of these vessels call to mind a debased form of 'Thuringian' amphorae (see p. 154). Grave goods consisted of weapons and ornaments (Fig. 44). Many stone battle-axes of a special type were found. Riveted copper daggers, flat copper spear-heads or daggers, flat copper axes, and small rings, temple ornaments and other objects of personal adornment made of copper, were relatively numerous. Copper beads (often forming necklaces), and single amber and turquoise beads were common. The copper objects were made of Transylvanian copper and in style they belong to the Central European Early Bronze Age.

These objects, in particular a dark blue glass bead similar to that found in the Werteba cave at Bilcze Złote (see p. 174), date the group to 1800–1600 B.C., our Stage I. The group was evidently an offspring of the Corded Ware assemblage, evolved under a strong influence from the Tripolye culture. The origin of its cremation ritual remains obscure. It seems that the rite of incineration, common in the easternmost group of the Volhynian Globular Amphora culture, was taken over from the Sofiivka group.

The final date of all these northern hybrids has not yet been established, nor has that of the Kiev group of the Tripolye culture. Conditions during our Stage II in the chernozem (Tripolyan) country west of the Dnieper need further study and investigation. It seems that the culture and the hybrids gradually disintegrated during our Stage II and were replaced by the new cultures of the subsequent period.

The Voytsekhivka and Marianivka Cultures

The Trzciniec influence (see p. 161) reached the country most probably before the end of our Stage II. Its traces are well marked in the remains of the subsequent Stage III, especially in the border area of North-west Podolia and Volhynia, in barrow graves from the region of Izaslavl-Krzemieniec (Siwki, Radzimin), and in settlements (Kostianets).[29] They have also been recorded further east, on the Sluch (barrow-grave cemetery of Voytsekhivka) (Pl. XXVI) and in the region of Zhitomir (settlements of Rayki, Troyaniv; flat cemetery of Narodychi (Fig. 34) etc.). Grave goods of some of these cemeteries also reflect the southern influence of the Komarów culture; again at a later date the Noua influence reached the region (I.K. Sveshnikov) (Pl. XXVI, bottom). Pottery excavated in some of the settlements illustrates a gradual evolution that ultimately led to the formation of pottery typical of the Bilohrudivka culture (see p. 375).

It has been mentioned previously that traces of the Trzciniec current have also been recorded east of the Middle Dnieper, and that they may be followed nearly up to the Volga, or even to the Caucasus. In the forest-steppe zone east of Kiev, a series of local cultures of the second half of the second millennium B.C. have been distinguished, and they are more or less distinctly marked by the Trzciniec culture; but they have all retained a character of their own and cannot be regarded as of Trzciniec parentage. They seem to have developed from the ancient local cultures of the Neolithic and Early Bronze Ages: their remains indicate that they must have been affected subsequently by the several larger cultures of the area on which they bordered—the Corded Ware assemblage, and the Middle Dnieper, Dnieper-Desna, and Catacomb cultures.

FIG. 45 *Lower row:* Vessels characteristic of the Marianivka culture. *Upper row:* Vessels characteristic of the Sosnitsa culture. After S. S. Berezanskaya (KSIAK No. 10, 1960, p. 37, fig. 1 and p. 42 fig. 3).

The earliest of these was the Marianivka culture[30] (Map XIV: XXIV) of the middle of the second millennium, probably of our Stage II (Table 4; Fig. 45); it does not seem to have been influenced by the Trzciniec culture. It extended over a relatively large area, reaching the Upper Donetz; its southern branch on that river has been considered by some scholars to form a separate culture called the Studenok culture. The Marianivka culture produced high pots with a rounded body, decorated in a manner reminiscent of the local Dnieper-Donetz culture of the preceding period, the late Neolithic.

Its successor was the Sosnitsa culture (Fig. 45) which extended over the basin of the Middle Desna and the Lower Seim, a tributary of the Desna. Over twenty settlements of the culture have been recorded in that region and a few have been excavated.[31] They all lay on sandy soils, on elevated sites close to the river banks. Their huts were about twenty-three feet by nineteen feet six inches, sunk a little in the ground, with a hearth in the centre. High, wide-based and clumsy tulip-shaped pots were most typical of the pottery. Their decoration, confined to the upper part of the vessel, consisted of a few horizontal incised lines, hatched triangles, pricked lines, etc. These vessels are strikingly reminiscent of the Trzciniec culture; they evidently owe their shape and decoration to the Trzciniec influence, which probably reached the country early in our Stage III. Remains of a similar type, likewise influenced by the Trzciniec current, found further north along the Upper Dnieper and the Sozh in Byelorussia, have recently been attributed to the Sosnitsa culture and considered to form its northern branch (see p. 194).

THE FOREST ZONE

During the second millennium B.C. a great variety of cultures developed in the east European forest zone. They differed in many respects from those of the steppe and forest-steppe zones further south, in particular because their mode of life was adapted to different ecological conditions.

THE DNIEPER-DESNA CULTURE

This culture, which belonged to the Corded Ware/Battle-axe assemblage, is dealt with first (Map XIV: XIX). Its homeland was the basin of the Upper Dnieper, and its centre lay somewhere near Gomel in Byelorussia. Southwards, it extended to the limits of the forest zone, where, in the vicinity of Kiev, it bordered on the Middle Dnieper culture.

Over seventy sites, traces of ancient encampments, and semipermanent settlements, have been recorded;[32] they lay mainly on sand-dunes in the valleys of the rivers. Huts were built on the surface of the ground; a large number of potsherds, flint implements, and other traces were found in their remains. 'Flat' graves were excavated near some of these huts. A few barrow-grave cemeteries have also been investigated.

The culture was long-lived. Three periods in its development can be distinguished, though an accurate attribution of all its remains among them is hardly practicable, especially as regards the settlements. Barrow graves of the earliest period were situated at the eastern limits of the culture, on the border of the steppe and forest-steppe zones. Their situation points to contact with the Yamnaya culture, and is confirmed by the custom of raising a mound over the grave, and by skeletons in the early graves lying on their backs with legs contracted. These graves, and also the 'Thuringian' amphora from the Rechitsa barrow grave (near Briansk), give the date of the earliest period as the turn of the third and second millennia B.C., our Late Neolithic.

The next period produced a few flat graves, but mostly barrow graves, which formed cemeteries of up to twenty mounds. Most of these contained several subsequent interments. One or two vessels were found in most graves. Both the sepulchral pottery and that from the settlements was homogenous. There were ovoid beakers and bowls with a rounded base, a low, nearly spherical body, and usually a high, cylindrical or funnel-shaped neck. Their decoration, restricted mainly to the upper part of the vessel, consisted of impressions of cords, twisted cords, short impressions, and sometimes short incisions; the most common decorative patterns were horizontal lines, herring-bone designs, hatched triangles, etc. The pottery differed from the 'comb-pricked' ware of the preceding period in this area, though both were found together in a number of sites. The shape and decoration of many vessels are reminiscent of those found in graves of the Middle Dnieper culture.

Other grave goods consisted of flint knives and arrow-heads, 'arrow-shaft smoothers', polished flint axes, stone battle-axes mainly of the Fatyanovo type, and some copper awls or personal ornaments, but few weapons (Fig. 46). A flat cemetery at Strelitsa consisted of twenty-four graves, mainly cremations.[33] Besides the usual objects— flint darts and arrow-heads, a few pots, flint axes, etc.—two copper 'diadems' or, more accurately, collars were excavated. They were about eight inches in diameter, and made of copper sheet one inch wide, thinning out towards the terminals. Another collar was made of amber beads. A faience bead found in the cemetery dates it to the middle of the second millennium B.C.

Such a collection of grave goods reflects various contacts. Two copper shaft-hole axes and a number of tools and personal ornaments represent types characteristic of the North Caucasian metallurgical centre (Map XXI). Spectral analysis of these also suggests their North Caucasian origin. On the other hand, relations with the Central European countries were probably very close during the later part of the period. Faience beads (Strelitsa) must have been brought there via Poland (Map XX). Amber beads point to trade with the east Prussian amber coast. A socketed spear-head made of poor arsenic bronze may have been of Caucasian origin, but it seems more likely to have been East German (Thuringian). Similar specimens, all of the Early Bronze Age, have been found in East Prussia and in Pomerania. No close analogies have been found in the neighbouring countries in Eastern Europe for the copper collars (or diadems) excavated in a few flat graves at Strelitsa (Fig. 47). However, specific comparisons may be made with several Early Bronze Age necklaces

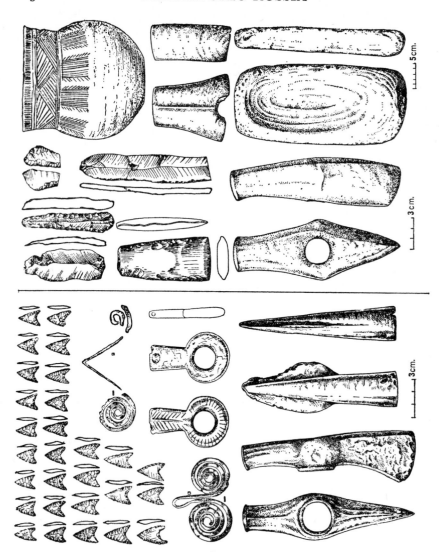

FIG. 46 Grave goods: polished stone plaque and axe, flints, copper weapons and ornaments, beaker from burial 1 in barrow grave 11 of the Dnieper-Desna culture at Moshka (Khodovichi).
After I. I. Artemenko (*Pamyatniki Kamennego i Bronzovogo Vekov v Evrazii.* Moscow 1963, pp. 46, 47, figs. 10, 11).

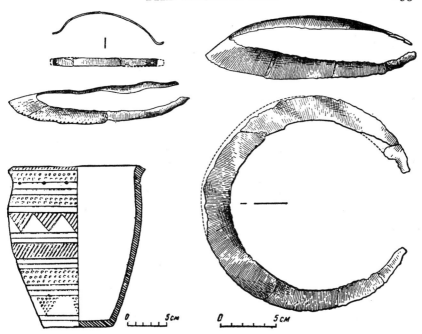

FIG. 47 Three copper diadems (collars?) from flat graves at Strelitsa, and a clay vessel of Trzciniec derivation from a flat cremation burial at Moshka, all of the Dnieper-Desna culture in Byelorussia. After I. I. Artemenko (MIA 130, 1965, p. 113, fig. 2; and *Pamyatniki Kamennego* . . . as FIG. 46, p. 35, fig. 2).

and bronze collars found in the northern part of Poland, in Germany, and in the British Isles. The penetration at that period of traders from the British Isles is well illustrated by several British imported objects, mostly of gold, found in Poland (ear-pendants, lunula); one of these had reached as far as west Podolia (barrow grave at Rusiłów), within 220 miles of Strelitsa. Connections with the Catacomb culture have also been recorded, and also with the Globular Amphora culture; potsherds adorned with patterns characteristic of the latter have been found and also some of its typically small and flat flint axes, polished all over their surfaces.

Most of the metal objects and other grave goods, and the implied connections with other cultures arising from these, tend to date the burials of the second period of the Dnieper-Desna culture to our Stages I and II of the east European Bronze Age. Their further subdivision between these two stages is not practicable, for neither the shape nor the decoration of the sepulchral pottery shows any marked chronological differences. The third period of the culture, which belonged to our Stage III, can be more easily differentiated. Its poorly decorated vessels differ markedly from those of the earlier graves, and tend to be baggy-shaped. They exhibit many features characteristic of the pottery of the Milograd culture of a later period in the same region. Cremations seem to have prevailed in this period; they were exclusive, for example, in a barrow-grave cemetery of that time at Belynets on the eastern periphery of the culture. The date of the period is well indicated by a flat-based beaker found in a 'flat' grave at Moshka, which was evidently modelled on Trzciniec beakers and decorated with their typical motifs (Fig. 47). Elements of the Trzciniec culture, discernible also in other remains of this period in that region, connect them with the Sosnitsa culture (see p. 190).

The Dnieper-Desna culture has been erroneously considered[34] to have formed a local variation of the Middle Dnieper culture (see p. 175), which at a later stage of its evolution had expanded northwards into the forest country. The character of each is utterly different. The Dnieper-Desna culture kept almost exclusively to the sandy soils, except for its easternmost section, east of the Middle Desna near Briansk, and this section may have formed a distinct culture. Several settlements, many traces of encampments on sandy soils, and a few 'flat' cemeteries of the Dnieper-Desna culture have been recorded; barrow graves appear only in the afore-mentioned eastern section, and exceptionally in the central part of the territory of the culture. On the other hand, the Middle Dnieper culture consisted only of barrow-grave cemeteries or of isolated graves under mounds, all within the black-earth region west of the Dnieper. The settlements that have been attributed to the culture appear only in the valley of the Dnieper, in fact outside the territory of the culture, and can hardly be considered as forming an integral part of it. Furthermore, the burial ritual and the pottery of the two cultures were different, though a few related types of vessels may be found in both. The cultures were contemporary, and there are no grounds for assuming that the Middle Dnieper culture was earlier.

The origin of the Dnieper-Desna culture remains obscure. Its pottery was often made of a clay paste with an admixture of some organic matter, a feature characteristic of the Masovian-Elbe-Dnieper assemblage of the same region. On the other hand, the pottery of the culture differed in many respects from that of its immediate local predecessor, the 'comb-pricked' ware of the Dnieper-Donetz culture, though potsherds of both have been found together in many sites. It seems very likely that the western section of the culture's territory formed part of the original area of the Corded Ware culture. The culture seems to have been formed at the turn of the third and second millennia and developed during the first half of the latter.

H. Moora considers the Dnieper-Desna culture to have been the most important of the eastern groups of the Corded Ware assemblage; he is of the opinion that it contributed considerably to the formation of its kindred groups north (Estonian and Finnish Boat-axe cultures) and east of its territory; the culture seems to have played an important role in the formation of the Moscow group of the Fatyanovo culture. It also influenced the Middle Dnieper culture, as was shown by the appearance of some of its vessels in the graves of the latter.

THE FATYANOVO CULTURE

Another group of the Battle-axe assemblage within the forest zone was the 'Fatyanovo' culture, called after a flat cemetery near Yaroslav, north of Moscow (Map XIV: VIII). It was in many respects similar to the Dnieper-Desna culture and evidently related to it. It extended approximately over the territory of the ancient Volga-Oka assemblage, the Pit-comb ware cultures (see p. 93). Hitherto it has been known only from over 100 cemeteries, but lately remains of the culture such as pottery and occasionally battle-axes have been found in settlements.[35]

Two quite distinct groups of the culture have been distinguished: the Moscow group in the southern part of the territory, and the Yaroslav-Kalinin group in the north, with a smaller Ivanovo-Vladimir branch embracing the eastern sites. Hundreds of stray stone battle-axes, characteristic of the culture, have been found all over the area.

Graves were shallow shafts with no mounds over them. Skeletons lay crouched, men's heads mostly to the south-west and women's to the north-east. Double burials of a man and a woman, or a woman with a child, have often been found. Stone battle-axes of the Fatyanovo type, many with a drooping blade projecting backwards, copper or bronze shaft-hole axes and flint axes were found in male burials (Fig. 48). Bone tools, chisels, daggers, etc., and amulets made of perforated bears' teeth or boars' tusks were common. Grave goods in female burials consisted mainly of personal ornaments—copper temple ornaments with overlapping terminals, small ear-rings, bracelets, necklaces of perforated animal teeth, beads made of small tubular bird bones, etc. Bone and copper awls were also found.

Some light is thrown on their religious or magical beliefs by some special burial practices. Fire must have played an important role in these; for traces of a hearth have been found over more lavishly furnished burials, evidently of outstanding members of the society. Other graves often contained lumps of charcoal and occasionally lumps of ochre. Flint flakes found in almost all graves must have played some role in the ritual. But of special interest were the graves of a kid and a bear. The latter was buried in the cemetery (Vaulovo near Rybinsk) like a human being, with lumps of ochre, flint flakes, etc., but no other grave-goods.[36]

Almost all graves contained at least one vessel, more often two or three, but never more than five. The pottery of the two groups differed (Pl. XXVIII). Low, wide-mouthed, semi-spherical bowls with a short neck were typical of the Moscow group; also ovoid vessels reminiscent in their shape and decoration of those of the Dnieper culture. The usual decorations consisted of horizontal bands of incisions, stamped horizontal lines, zigzags, etc. Pottery of the Yaroslav group shows a greater variety. Besides bowls similar to those of the Moscow group, but usually more elongated and with a higher neck, some other types of vessel appear, the most characteristic being large spherical amphorae decorated with patterns characteristic of the 'Thuringian' amphorae of the Corded Ware assemblage (Fig. 48); the only difference between these vessels and the genuine 'Thuringian' amphorae is that they had no lugs on the body, though some were provided with small nipples reminiscent of these. In shape the amphorae of the Fatyanovo culture corresponded with those of the settlements of the Rzucewo culture on the Baltic coast near the mouth of the Vistula.

In most graves of the Fatyanovo culture animal bones have been found, but here, again, a difference existed between the two groups of the culture: the Yaroslav group generally provided mutton for the journey beyond the grave, while the Moscow group generally provided pork. No cattle bones were found, though they appear in the graves further east.

Grave goods of the Fatyanovo culture reflect connections with several distant cultures. Personal ornaments found within the Yaroslav group include many Central European, Unetice types—bronze temple ornaments or wide bronze wrist-bands (Fig. 48; Map XX). In some graves bronze or copper shaft-hole axes of north-west Caucasian type were found, and they equate the culture with the second stage of the North Caucasian culture (see p. 232). Close connections with the Baltic coast, most probably with East Prussia, are shown by amber beads. These were also found in the contemporary settlements of the subdued local population; in a grave of the latter, at Sakhtysh VIII, about 100 amber beads and buttons were found, evidently sewn on to a garment.[37] The so-called 'arrow-straighteners', or 'arrow-shaft smoothers', point to connections with the Catacomb culture.

The Fatyanovo culture had no roots in the country. Its burial ritual, mainly single graves with no mounds over them, and grave goods reveal close connections with the groups of the Corded Ware/

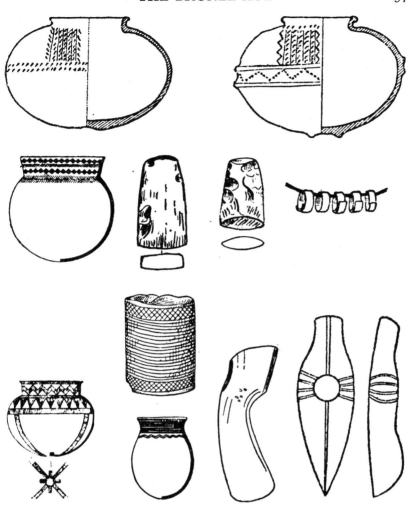

FIG 48 Grave goods of the Fatyanovo culture: pottery including amphorae of the 'Thuringian' type, flint axes, copper shaft-hole axe, a stone battle-axe of the 'Fatyanovo' type, and ornaments including the wide decorated bronze wrist-band from Mytishchi.
After O. A. Krivstova-Grakova (KSIIMK No. XVII, 1947, pp. 22, ff., figs. 7–9), and P. M. Kozhin ('Thuringian' type amphorae, S.A. vol. 1963–3, p. 36, fig. 6).

Battle-axe assemblage of the forest zone further to the west. The differences in the pottery, and also in some other grave goods, between the two Fatyanovo groups suggest their somewhat different origin. The pottery of the Moscow group was to some extent related to that of the Dnieper-Desna culture, which seems to imply that the latter contributed to the formation of the former. But the immigrants who were responsible for the formation of the Yaroslav group seem to have come from the region on the Upper Dnieper, perhaps somewhere near Smolensk, and Northern Byelorrussia. They must also have had close contact with the peoples on the Baltic coast, those in East Prussia in particular. Another element, besides the Battle-axe assemblage, which contributed to the formation of the Fatyanovo culture, but especially to the Yaroslav group, must have been the Globular Amphora culture. Decorative motifs of a number of vessels found in the cemetery of Fatyanovo, and also potsherds found in settlements associated with the Fatyanovo pottery (Malyi Ostrovok on Lake Sakhtysh) are evidently derivative from those characteristic of the Globular Amphora culture, as were the small and flat entirely polished flint axes (see p. 167).

Battle-axes and other weapons found in graves imply that the Fatyanovians were a warlike people. In invading the country they must have met the native population, hunters and fishermen belonging to the Volga-Oka culture of the Pit-comb ware assemblage. The Fatyanovians were of a different anthropological type from the latter, being closely related to the people of the east Baltic region and the Scandinavian countries. They probably displaced some of the local tribes, but the bulk of the native population did not leave its homeland and lived side by side with the newcomers.

In many settlements recently investigated in various parts of the area, pottery characteristic of the Fatyanovo culture, and sometimes stone battle-axes, were found in the occupation layers together with pottery typical of the indigenous inhabitants of the country. Several settlements were stratified (Sakhtysh, Zolotoruchie I, II). It has been established[38] that the Fatyanovo pottery has never been found in the lowest layer, pottery of the Lialovo culture being characteristic of this stratum. Instead, it always lay in the next layer up, associated with pottery of the second stage in the development of the country— the early pottery of the Volosovo and the early Pozdniakovo cultures, and the early 'textile' pottery (see p. 207). Arrow-straighteners (Zolotoruchie II) equate the settlements with the Catacomb culture.

The culture was a long-lived one. The date at which the Proto-Fatyanovians entered the country was about 1800 B.C., the beginning of our Stage I. The culture developed during the whole Bronze Age, during the three stages distinguished by us. However, no division of

the culture into subsequent stages has been carried out. The stratigraphic evidence of two overlapping graves at Mytishchi, south of
Kostroma, implies that graves containing vases of the 'Thuringian'
type were of an earlier period, evidently corresponding to our Stage I.
In the later grave of Mytishchi, a wide, richly decorated copper (or
bronze?) armband of Unetice type was found; it has been reproduced
in several publications. And graves in which metal objects more
or less of the Unetice type were excavated belong to our Stage II.
Copper objects of Caucasian origin confirm this dating.

The final date of the culture cannot yet be established. However,
the newcomers seem to have retained their identity for several generations; a small copper disc, probably an amulet, found in one of the
graves had the surface covered with iron. In the long run, probably
early in the first millennium B.C., the descendants of the newcomers
ultimately merged with the local population, represented by the
Volosovo culture.

The economy of the Fatyanovians was based chiefly on stock-
breeding, but they evidently had some form of primitive hoe agriculture. Pigs, sheep or goats, and cattle, were kept, but fishing and
hunting were also important. They had no settlements of their own,
but must have lived in those of the native population.

Some scholars connect the formation of the 'Arctic' cultures with
the northern migration of the Volga-Oka (Lialovo) tribes who retreated under the pressure of the Fatyanovians. However, the chronology of the respective finds disproves such theories. The formation
of the Arctic cultures, the Kargopol and the Karelian cultures in
particular, took place in the middle of the third millennium (see p.
137), whereas the Fatyanovians or the Proto-Fatyanovians entered
Central Russia over 500 years later.

THE BALANOVO CULTURE

One of the branches of the Battle-axe intruders that entered the
Volga-Oka territory did not remain in that country. They crossed it,
and, advancing along the Middle Volga, reached the region inhabited by peoples of the Eastern Kama-Ural assemblage. They
settled there on the Sula, a southern tributary of the Volga, south-
west of the Volga bend, and south-west of Kazan. A new group of
the Battle-axe assemblage, the easternmost of all, was thus established,
and was called the Balanovo culture after a large 'flat' cemetery
(Map XIV: XII).

Well over seventy sites have been attributed to the culture, mainly
graves and cemeteries, with a few settlements. Some of these, considered to be of a later stage in the development of the culture, lay
north of the Volga, and north of Kazan; they lay within the territory

that was previously the westernmost section of the Kama-Ural Neolithic culture. In the south the territory of the culture bordered on the steppe.

A few barrow grave cemeteries were found, but it was mainly the larger 'flat' cemeteries of the culture that were investigated. Among the latter was the cemetery of Balanovo, which consisted of seventy-five graves containing nearly 120 interments. Skeletons lay mostly crouched, seldom in the 'Yamnaya' position. About one-third of the graves were double burials, of a man and his wife, sometimes accompanied also by small children who evidently could not survive after the death of both parents. Many secondary burials of children have also been uncovered. The very hard conditions of life at that time have been revealed by the fact that 44 per cent of all persons buried in the cemetery were children under twelve years of age; no man lived over fifty years, and no woman over sixty.[39]

The Balanovo pottery was closely related to that of the Fatyanovo culture, and many scholars[40] consider the culture as a branch of the latter. The most common vessels, bowls or beakers, differed only slightly from those of the Yaroslav group, and many were similar to those of the Moscow group, and even to those of the Dnieper-Desna culture. In another category were the large bulky amphorae reminiscent of the Thuringian amphorae; they are very similar to those of the Yaroslav group in style and decoration, but differ in that the bodies are provided with two lugs, most of which are unperforated. These amphorae were very like those found in the Rzucewo sites on the Baltic coast near the mouth of the Vistula.

Other grave goods included stone battle-axes of the Fatyanovo type, and a few crooked specimens were strikingly reminiscent of the north Caucasian 'Piatogorsk' type. Copper shaft-hole axes of Caucasian type were found in a few graves, and in a barrow grave at Churachiki, west of Kazan, two moulds for casting them were excavated (Fig. 49). A copper spear-head with an open socket was Caucasian. Flint axes, mainly lenticular in section, were very common. Flint-tanged arrow-heads were of the same type as the dart-heads from the Krivoluchie grave. There were many flint knives, bone awls and points, and copper awls; and several personal ornaments in copper—tubular beads made of thin copper sheet, long spiral beads, small rings, temple ornaments of the Unetice type, pendants made of perforated fangs of wild animals, etc. Small clay models of wheels of a type found sometimes in the steppe graves of the Catacomb period were also discovered. And small clay spoon-shaped vessels with a handle were found in children's graves. Similar 'spoons' appear in graves of the Corded Ware people in Central Europe.

Of special interest are finds that point to connections with the

XXIII Beakers and vases of the Middle Dnieper culture. *Left:* Vase and its decorated base from a barrow grave at Hatne (Gatnoe), and a vase from Netrebka (no. 43593). *Right:* Two beakers from barrow graves at Stretivka; the lowest one from barrow grave V at Yankovichi (no. 1029).
State Historical Museum, Kiev and Historical Museum, Moscow.

XXIV Vessels and gold ornaments of the early stage of the Komarów culture, from barrow graves at Komarów excavated by the author.

I

2

xxv Vessels of the developed Komarów culture from a barrow
grave at Bukówna on the Dniester (1, 3), and of the Biały-Potok
group from Zeżawa (2), Horodnica (4), and Czernelica (5) in
West Podolia.
After R. Rogozińska, *Materiały Archeologiczne*, vol. 1, Kraków
1959, pl. 1, 3, 5; VIII 1, 3; IX: 6.

3

4

5

XXVI Pottery from barrow graves at Voytsekhivka on the Sluch in Central
Volhynia. Excavated by O. Lahodovska and Iu.M. Zakharuk (AP VI, 1956,
pp. 69 ff.); and by S. Hamchenko (O. Lahodovska, AK 11, 1948, pp. 62 ff.)

XXVII Bronze tools found in the country on the middle Dnieper in the Ukraine.
State Historical Museum, Kiev.

Globular Amphora culture, and even suggest that the latter culture was one of the formative elements of the Balanovo. A small debased amphora typical of the Globular Amphorae was excavated in the grave at Balanovo (Pl. XIX) already mentioned previously (see p. 169). It had rows of short and deep vertical incisions round it and they were separated by similar incised horizontal lines—a characteristic decoration of the culture. The same patterns appear on the decoration of several bowls and beakers typical of the Balanovo culture (Fig. 37). Another link with the Globular Amphora culture is two decorated bone plaques, probably parts of a belt buckle (Fig. 37). Plaques of this type have been found in several graves of the Globular Amphora culture in Poland and Rumania, and also in Scandinavian slab-cists.[41]

The Balanovians were a settled population engaged in animal husbandry and in a primitive form of agriculture. The rather densely wooded country—mixed forest zone—allowed only the river valleys and clearings to be inhabited. Only a few settlements have been recorded and some have been investigated. They usually yielded two or three Balanovo occupation layers belonging to the subsequent periods in the development of the culture. It is of interest to note that those of the later periods were situated on well protected sites, which points to the turbulence of the time. Mainly pottery was found, and only a few stone and copper tools. Animal bones were identified as those of cattle, sheep, horses, pigs and dogs; wild animals were represented by reindeer, bears, wild boars, *Bos primigenius*, wolves and beavers. The men obviously hunted. Fishing seems to have been also been of some importance.

The Balanovo culture is regarded by many scholars as an extension of the Fatyanovo culture; however, it has been emphasized by others[42] that it must be considered as a culture in its own right owing to many features that distinguish it from the Fatyanovo. Its character, burial ritual and many grave goods—especially stone battle-axes and 'Thuringian' amphorae—link it decisively with the Battle-axe assemblage. It was an intrusive culture with no roots in the country.

It may be mentioned that O.N. Bahder claims a southern or Caucasian origin for the Balanovo culture, but this claim does not seem to be well founded. He bases his assumption on the racial considerations discussed below, and on some items of the culture showing similarities to the north Caucasian types. These items include the large bulky vases from the Novosvobodnaya barrow graves (see p. 120), which he considers to be prototypes for the vessels of the 'Thuringian' amphora type in the Balanovo cemeteries. However, Caucasian vessels stem from the same Central European current as the 'Thuringian' amphorae, and that current had not only reached

15

the region on the Middle Volga, but also the North-west Caucasus. Another pointer to the culture's antecedents is the physical type of the Balanovo population. Soviet scholars are of the opinion that the cranial material of the Balanovo cemeteries was similar to that from the Early Iron Age graves in Transcaucasia, and belonged to a racial type common among the modern population of Iran, East Turkey and North Iraq; accordingly, O.N. Bahder claims that the Balanovians were southern, Pontic or Caucasian immigrants, though he admits that no such racial type is represented in the Neolithic material from these areas. However, the study of the published cranial material reveals the striking similarity between the skulls from the Balanovo cemeteries and the Neolithic skull from the Swedish mega-lithic culture; and this similarity leaves no doubt that the Balanovians were mainly of the Nordic racial type and of western origin. A number of skulls from poorly furnished graves, evidently those of the indigenous population, exhibit some Mongolian features.

The population of the Balanovo culture was socially stratified. The richly furnished graves of 'warriors' and some graves of old women, likewise richly endowed, were those of the western immigrants. They imposed their Battle-axe culture on the local population, just as similar groups did in the areas further to the west. Men of the Globular Amphora culture seem also to have been among the western immigrants, as suggested by the debased amphora, decorative motifs and bone plaques mentioned previously. The newcomers were probably soon assimilated by the local population, and their western connections gradually replaced by those with the neighbouring cultures and countries to the east and south. This is reflected especially in the copper objects of north Caucasian type and their east Russian derivatives. Similar tubular beads and other personal ornaments, copper awls, flint arrow-heads, etc., appear in the Andronovo culture of the west Siberian steppe country. The socketed bronze spear-head with the open socket forms an exception, to which analogies can be found in the north-west Caucasian (Abkhazian) Dolmen culture.

The Balanovo culture was formed at the beginning of the second millennium B.C., early in our Stage I, soon after the formation of the Fatyanovo culture. It survived up to the beginning of the first millennium B.C., though only within a small area along the river Sura.[43] Four main periods in the development of the culture have been distinguished (Table 18). Graves with the 'Thuringian' amphorae and pottery decorated with 'Globular Amphora' patterns (Figs. 37, 49) belong to the first of these, our Stage I. During the second period, the fifteenth and fourteenth centuries B.C., approximately our Stage II, the culture attained its greatest geographical extent. It crossed the Volga, and stretched nearly 125 miles to the north of Kazan. The

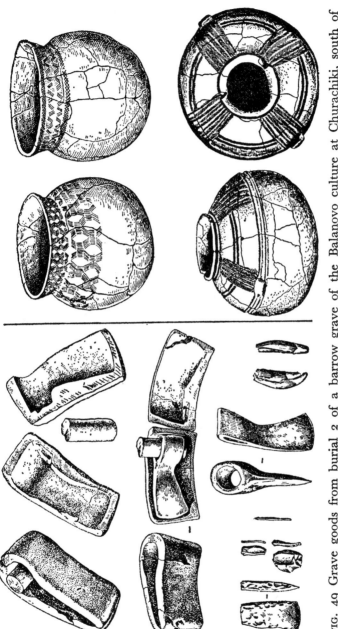

FIG. 49 Grave goods from burial 2 of a barrow grave of the Balanovo culture at Churachiki, south of Cheboksary.
After V. F. Kakhovskii (s.a. vol. 1963–3, p. 176, figs. 6, 7).

northern expansion was presumably the outcome of the migration of a number of Balanovo tribes under the pressure of the advancing Abashevian and Srubnaya tribes. In the third period, the fourteenth to twelve centuries B.C., our Stage III, the southern part of the country was seized by the Srubnaya culture, and the Abashevians settled in many parts of the country further north. In consequence, many elements of the two invading cultures were adopted by the Balanovians. Ultimately, during the fourth period, our Late Bronze Age (the eleventh to ninth century B.C.), dealt with in Chapter IV, the Balanovians were gradually absorbed by the Abashevians.

The Native Population

The intrusion of the Corded Ware/Battle-axe peoples, that is, the Proto-Fatyanovians and Proto-Balanovians, into the territory of the cultures of the Volga-Oka assemblage had a tremendous influence on the evolution of the indigenous population of the country. The native hunters and fishermen whom the invaders had not annihilated remained in their homeland and still kept to their former mode of life. But under the impact of the newcomers, and due to tribal displacements caused by the invasion, a gradual disintegration took place in the ancient Volga-Oka assemblage.

One of the consequences of the western invasion was the appearance on the Lower Oka of the Volosovo culture, one of the Eastern assemblage. The reason for this may be traced back to the time of the eastern drive of the Proto-Balanovians early in our Stage I. The invaders crossed the territory of the Balakhna group (see p. 105), the easternmost of the Volga-Oka assemblage, at the junction of the Oka with the Volga and advanced eastwards into the country inhabited by the peoples of the Eastern assemblage. The Balakhna tribes survived their passage, but some of them retreated eastwards and reached the area of the Kazan Neolithic culture where they seem soon to have been absorbed by the local population.

However, their movement along the Middle Volga and, above all, the seizure of the region on the Sura and within the bend of the Volga by the advancing Battle-axe folk (the Proto-Balanovians) had provoked larger tribal movements. Some of the native tribes of the area of the newly established Balanovo culture submitted to the newcomers and were subsequently assimilated by them. But most of the natives, who were closely related to those of the Kazan Neolithic culture of the Eastern (Kama-Ural) assemblage, gave way before the invaders. They moved westwards and took over the country on the Lower Oka, south of Murom, hitherto inhabited by the southern branch of the Balakhna tribes of the Volga-Oka assemblage. Consequently a new culture, the Volosovo, one of the Eastern assemblage, appeared in the area early in the second millennium, during our Stage I (Table 4; Map XIV: X).

So two new cultures were formed early in our Stage I on alien territories: the Balanovo culture of the Battle-axe assemblage in the area previously settled by tribes of the Eastern assemblage, and the Volosovo culture of the Eastern assemblage in the region previously held by the Volga-Oka cultures. They both found themselves cut off from their kindred cultures, both absorbed elements of the culture of the local tribes, and ultimately in the new environment they both acquired sufficient features of their own to differentiate them from other cultures of the assemblage to which they originally belonged. Both greatly influenced the further development of their neighbours.

THE VOLOSOVO CULTURE

The Volosovo culture extended over an area on the Lower Oka near Murom and south of that town, and also along the Klyazma, a tributary of the Oka.[44] Its intrusive character is well attested by stratigraphic evidence in a series of sites (for instance, Elin Bor, Zolotoi Bugor). The earliest sites yielded pottery of the Balakhna type of the Volga-Oka assemblage (Fig. 50; Pl. XXXI); pottery of the subsequent period—the Early Bronze Age (Stage I)—was of the Volosovo type, entirely different from its predecessor and closely related to that of the Kazan Neolithic culture of the Eastern assemblage.

A characteristic feature of the Volosovo culture was the thickness of its occupation layers, literally stuffed with stone and bone tools and other remains. They imply a long period of habitation for the sites investigated. The culture's pottery changed as time went by, and its three somewhat different varieties mark three periods in the development of the culture.

The earliest Volosovo pottery (Pl. XXIX), of our Stage I, was closely related to that of the Kazan Neolithic culture (Table 4); its clay paste had some organic admixture. The period lasted till about the middle of the second millennium. Vessels of the second period, which ended around 1300 B.C. and roughly corresponded with our Stage II, did not differ much from those of the preceding period. They were ovoid with a rounded base, and often large; they were adorned with impressions of whipped cords, cross hatching made by a combed stamp, or zigzags impressed by a toothed stamp. Many tools were found in settlements of both periods: flint chisels and axes, daggers and stone shaft-hole axes. Several pendants made of schist and figurines of bone were found. Figurines in chipped flint (Fig. 54), typical of the 'Arctic Neolithic' (see p. 216) were of special interest;

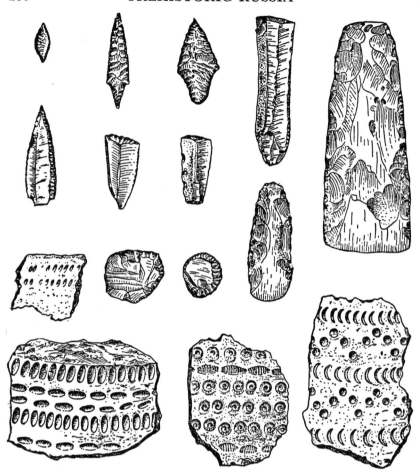

FIG. 50 Remains characteristic of the Balakhna culture.
After A. Ia. Briusov (OCHERKI. 1952, p. 87, fig. 14).

they belonged to the late period of the culture, our Stage III (Map
XVI).

One of the most important sites was at Volosovo, after which the
culture was named. Two settlements and two cemeteries have been
uncovered there. Graves in the 'early Volosovo cemetery' were
shallow pits; skeletons were supine, accompanied by a few flints, and
globe-shaped vessels considered to be similar to those of the early
Srubnaya culture. This cemetery has been dated to the third quarter
of the second millennium, the end of our Stage II and the beginning
of Stage III. The other, the 'late Volosovo' cemetery, was of the
subsequent period (Fig. 76) (see. p. 323).

Huts excavated at Volosovo and in other settlements of the culture (such as Pamfilovo, Volodary) were quadrangular, a shape characteristic of the Eastern assemblage and quite the opposite of the circular huts of the Volga-Oka cultures. They were of the semi-subterranean type, between twenty-six and thirty-three feet long and twenty-six and thirty feet wide, sunk up to forty inches into the ground. The entrance was on one of the shorter sides, and most huts in the settlement were interconnected by corridors dug in the ground.

Fish bones and scales and bones of wild animals point to the importance of fishing and hunting. But the relative density of population during the later periods, illustrated by the larger size and number of dwellings in settlements, points to the need for other means of subsistence. Domesticated animals, including horses, were kept, though actually bones of these beasts were seldom found. It seems that the people were already acquainted with some sort of primitive agriculture. The adoption of new forms of economy was presumably due to the influence of the Srubnaya culture, which in the fourteenth century B.C. began to advance westwards and reached the borders of the Volosovo culture.

The invasion of the Fatyanovo people, and the seizure of the southern section of the Balakhna territory by the eastern newcomers of the Volosovo culture, resulted in the gradual disintegration of the ancient Volga-Oka culture. Elements of the Fatyanovo culture seldom appear in the remains of the surviving groups of the Volga-Oka assemblage. But perhaps the most marked feature of the new period in the history of that assemblage was the growing impact of the Eastern cultures, the earliest representative of which, during the early second millennium B.C., was the Volosovo culture. Among the results of the new conditions were the loss to the assemblage of large parts of its southern territory, and increasing differences between its local groups. The differentiation had began in the preceding period, the Late Neolithic, but now some of the groups actually lost their identity and were divided from other branches of the assemblage.

The pit-decorated pottery characteristic of the cultures of the assemblage, especially of the Lialovo culture of the Late Neolithic, was gradually replaced by 'textile' pottery (Pl. XXX). The name of the latter derives from the decoration of the vessels, which were covered with impressions of some rough cloth or linen. This pottery was a further development of the old ware: it was made by the same technique, its vessels were still round-based, and, besides the 'textile' patterns, there remained many features of the ancient pit-decoration.

The new decorations seem to have evolved in the northern part of the culture, on the Upper and Middle Volga north of Moscow, but it soon spread over almost the entire territory still in the possession of the Volga-Oka cultures. But in the middle of the millennium, during our Stage II, it also appeared outside it—in Estonia, in the areas north of the Upper Volga, and in Karelia and South Finland. In its further development, the 'textile' pottery underwent some changes, partly under the influence of the Volosovo culture, and later of other cultures of the Eastern assemblage. The result was that the textile pottery of our Stage III (the Late Bronze Age), differed in many respects from the early 'textile' pottery, and became the characteristic ware of the later periods.

THE RIAZAN AND BALAKHNA CULTURES

A very marked feature of the development of the various groups of the ancient Volga-Oka cultures during the second millennium B.C. was their growing saturation by elements of the Volosovo culture, and by those of other groups of the Eastern assemblage that expanded westwards at a later date. This is clearly reflected by the remains of the Riazan group on the Middle Oka,[45] which at first showed a close association with the Belev culture bordering on it to the west. Its western connections are indicated by several imported objects: a perforated *Cyprea moneta* shell found in one of the sites; early Unetice wide and decorated bronze wrist-bands found in graves at Mytyshchi and Vladichino (Map XX) were evidently imported from Central Europe. A polished stone axe was of Scandinavian origin. Connections with the Catacomb culture have also been noted. However, connections with distant countries were in fact the outcome of the supremacy of the Fatyanovo culture; for in their remains similar objects were often recorded.

The Riazan culture (Map XIV: XI) was exposed to the strong and most persistent impact of the Volosovo culture, the intensity of which increased during our Stage II (Table 11). Pottery characteristic of the Volosovo culture was found in several sites in the border area between the two cultures. Later it spread all over the Riazan territory and finally during our Stage III the Riazan culture became simply a local group of the Volosovo culture.

A similar development may be observed in other parts of the Volga-Oka territory, especially in that of the Balakhna culture around the junction of the Kama with the Volga. This culture originally extended over the whole area on the Lower Oka, but its southern division, south of Murom, was seized early in the second millennium B.C., in our Stage I, by eastern immigrants of the Volosovo culture (see p. 204). The country further north, probably up to the region of Kostroma, remained in the possession of the Balakhna people. Pottery of this period, the second in the local development (Pl. XXXI), did not much differ from that of the early stage of the culture, during our Late Neolithic. Its best examples have been excavated in the lower occupation layer of the Balakhna site, after which the culture has been named (Fig. 50). At Sakhtysh VIII, north-east of Moscow near Ivanovo (see p. 196), remains of a settlement of that period have been uncovered. A semi-pit dwelling and a rectangular surface shelter, twenty-three feet by five feet, were excavated. There were remains of posts and the back wall, and also ten burials. Skeletons were supine except one which was crouched. Near one of these were about 100 amber beads and buttons that had been sewn on a garment.

The Balakhna culture reached westwards up to Ivanovo, and long retained the character of one of the Volga-Oka assemblage. It was only later, probably about the end of the fourteenth century B.C., that considerable changes marked the final break with ancient traditions, and the beginning of the third stage in the local development. Under new pressure from the eastern tribes and the Volosovo people, the culture of the Balakhna population became progressively saturated, chiefly with Volosovo elements, and the influx of a larger wave of eastern immigrants finally changed its character completely.

Some of the Volga-Oka tribes seem to have yielded to the Volosovo pressure and migrated north-eastwards into the taiga, the territory peopled by tribes of the Eastern assemblage (Map XIV: VII, b). In a number of sites excavated on the Upper Vychegda, a tributary of the Northern Dvina, there was pottery (as at Vis III) that showed many characteristics of Central Russian ware alongside pottery typical of the Kama region (Table 13).

THE NORTH

THE BOAT-AXE CULTURES

One section of the Battle-axe assemblage moved north-eastwards, towards the east Baltic coast. Its traces have been found in all the east Baltic countries, but they are most numerous in Estonia and in the south-western part of Finland. They form two closely related groups that have been called the 'Boat-axe' cultures, on account of the shape of their stone (diabase) battle-axes, of fine design and admirable execution (Map XIV: III, IV). Both were established about 1700 B.C.

Both the Estonian and Finnish groups of the Boat-axe culture are known mainly from graves, which were exclusively single graves with no mounds over them. Only a few settlements were recorded. Grave goods—besides the boat-axes—consisted of flint axes, personal ornaments, and pottery. Wide beakers or bowls with a rounded base were typical of the latter; their incised, occasionally cord-impressed, de-

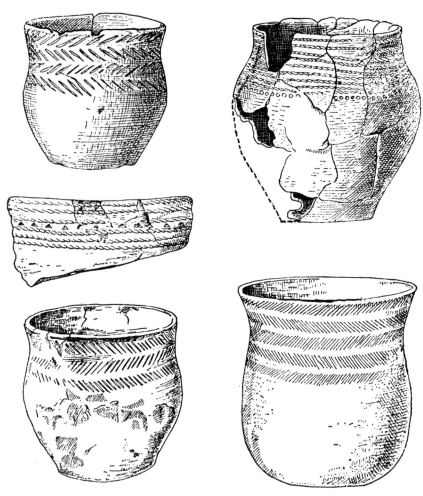

FIG. 51 Examples of vessels of the Corded Ware (Boat-axe) culture in the Baltic countries.
After H. A. Moora (S.A. vol. XXI, 1954, p. 99, fig. 2).

coration shows chevron patterns, rows of slanting incisions, etc., around the neck and the upper part of the vessel (Fig. 51).

These groups, but more particularly the Finnish, were closely related to the corresponding Boat-axe culture in Sweden. They were all parallel but independent groups, formed by immigrants from the same centre, probably somewhere in East Prussia, and this accounts for their similarity. The Estonian group must have been formed in association with its related Yaroslav group of the Fatyanovo culture, as indicated by many points of similarity between these two groups. Some authors[46] are inclined to seek the original country of the invaders in the region of the Upper Dnieper, and consider the Dnieper-Desna culture as an ancestor of the Estonian Boat-axe culture.

The Boat-axe people invaded the countries inhabited by tribes of the western Combed Ware culture (see p. 141). Cranial material revealed that the newcomers were of the 'Nordic' racial type, and differed from that of the native population; later, both peoples mingled, as indicated by cranial material from later periods. The invasion marks the beginning of a new period in the development of the areas affected, which corresponds with our late Stage I and Stage II (Table 12). It is of interest to note that the invading culture covered almost exactly the territory of the ancient Kunda culture and its related groups in Finland; it also extended further south-west in the east Baltic countries.

The expansion of the Boat-axe people in the east Baltic countries brought about considerable changes in the culture of the indigenous population. The cord-decorated pottery, typical of the newcomers, was found henceforth not merely in the burials but also in the settlements of the local population alongside their own combed ware. The hitherto well marked uniformity of the Combed Ware culture began to disintegrate and several new local groups evolved. In the western division, up to East Prussia, most of the groups soon disappeared, being probably absorbed into the culture of the newcomers, though a number of small pockets survived for a very long period.

The development was different in the eastern division, in Estonia. There, in the long run, the newcomers of the Boat-axe culture were absorbed by the local population, as is shown by the results of excavation in a few important sites (Akali-Komsa, Kullamägi).[47] The newcomers introduced new forms of economy, agriculture and stock-breeding into the country; their innovations also spread further north and north-east, into parts of Finland and the neighbouring regions of Russia, provided that conditions were suitable for their adoption. However, hunting and fishing still retained their leading role there, though the decrease in importance of fishing, especially in Finland, is illustrated by the fact that sites of the period were no longer as near the sea coast as they were in the preceding periods.

Close connections were maintained during this period with the Karelian culture, partly because some of the Estonian Combed Ware tribes retreated northwards before the Boat-axe invaders. The reciprocal relations between these two countries are well illustrated by the relatively large number of tools made of the greenish slate found in Estonia; for they originated from workshops in the vicinity of Lake Onega, which belonged to the Karelian culture. On the other hand, the earliest bronze objects found in Estonia and the adjoining regions, mainly stray flanged axes, were of Central European origin, of Bronze Age period II;[48] they point to the south-western contacts of the culture.

The appearance soon after the middle of the second millennium B.C. of the early 'textile' pottery in Eastern Finland and Eastern Estonia indicates that contacts must have existed between these countries and Central Russia. However, the spread of this type of pottery may also suggest that some Central Russian groups had retreated westwards under the pressure of a new wave of eastern peoples invading their own country.

THE KARGOPOL CULTURE

Events and changes in the second millennium B.C. in Central and east Russia also affected to a greater or lesser extent the peoples of the 'Arctic' cultures in the northern part of the forest zone, the taiga and tundra.

The Kargopol culture, the southernmost of the northern area, set up by immigrants of the Volga-Oka culture, had maintained its Central Russian character till about the second quarter of the second millennium (Table 14). By that time it had absorbed many elements of the east Baltic Combed Ware culture, especially the 'western' decorative patterns for its pottery, amber personal ornaments, etc. This was the beginning of the second period of the culture, which lasted over the later part of our Stage I and the whole of Stage II (Table 4). The country was invaded by small groups of east Baltic people who were retreating before the advancing Boat-axe invaders; probably they were not very numerous and were ultimately absorbed by the native people of the Kargopol culture.

The 'pile' settlement on the river Modlona, about halfway between Lake Beloe and Lake Vozhe, may be attributed to these western newcomers. The pottery of its lower layer (Modlona I) is very different from that of the Kargopol culture, and closely resembles that of the Estonian Combed Ware culture of the time immediately preceding the arrival of the Boat-axe people. The east Baltic origin of the Modlona settlers is also corroborated by over twenty specimens of amber ornaments, pendants, V-perforated buttons (Fig. 52), etc., found on the floor of the huts investigated. The huts, which stood in two rows, were built of wattle, supported by piles; they were quadrangular but irregular in plan, had wooden floors and two-eaved roofs. Wooden pavements connected them. No pit-dwellings or huts partly sunk in the ground have been found in the area; only traces of light shanty-like structures were uncovered.

The settlement of Modlona, and those on other sites, were long-lived; almost all had more than one occupation layer, or a few occupation horizons, which denote changes in the culture and new periods in the history of the country. However, this circumstance cannot be considered to prove the continuity of settlement;[49] for the very conveniently situated sites were always chosen by different tribes or peoples who settled in the country during the several periods of the 'Arctic Neolithic'.

A third period may have begun as early as the fourteenth century B.C., but more likely later, and lasted presumably to the early first millennium B.C. To this period belonged the upper layer of the 'pile settlement' on the Modlona, called Modlona II, the middle occupation level of the settlement of Karavaikha, and a number of other sites. The pottery of this period differed from that of the preceding one. Vessels were still ovoid in shape and round-bottomed, but their decoration consisted of geometric and zonal patterns, combining rows of oblique impressions, rows of pits, etc. New decorative motifs were schematic figures of water birds, and also human beings (Fig. 53). Sculptures of animals and water birds in stone and flint (Fig. 54), or carved in wood, were new features; the handles of wooden ladles were often shaped like an animal head or a bird.

Sculptures of this kind, and the bird motif in the decoration of pottery, were common to almost all cultures of the northern forest zone, from Finland to West Siberia. They were characteristic of the second period in the development of the Early Gorbunovo culture (see p. 103), which terminated in the thirteenth century B.C., and approximately corresponded with our Stage II. It seems that both the new type of pottery and the sculptures bear witness to the arrival of a wave of eastern peoples; this was the time at which larger tribal movements seem to have started in west Siberia (Map XVIII).

THE KARELIAN CULTURE

The culture of Karelia and of the area south of the great lakes (Ladoga, Onega) differed from its neighbouring Kargopol culture, though both were formed by immigrants of the Volga-Oka assemblage. The early stage of the development of the Early Karelian culture proper has been discussed in Chapter II (see p. 139); it lasted until about 1700 B.C.[50] This date is corroborated by the relations of the culture of that period with the east Baltic Estonian Combed Ware culture, which evidently preceded the invasion of the Boat-axe culture (Table 4).

The culture lasted until about 1300 B.C., throughout the east European Bronze Age. Its development during that period has been subdivided into three stages (Tables 15, 16). The first of these stages can be equated with the Early Unetice culture of Central Europe

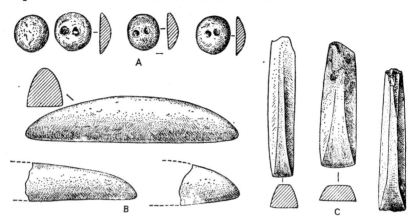

FIG. 52 'V' perforated amber buttons from Modlona I, East Baltic area and East Prussia; slate axes of Karelian type from Karelia, region of Kargopol and Siberia; 'Pick-axes' of Karelian type from Karelia, region of Kargopol and region of Kostroma.
After M. E. Foss (MIA 29, 1952, p. 195, fig. 100).

(1700–1600 B.C.), our Stage I of the east European Bronze Age (Table 4), and the second stage to the time of the expansion of the Mycenean trade in Central Europe (see p. 273). This corresponds with Stage II of our scheme. Conditions during the third stage will be discussed in Chapter V.

A very distinctive feature of the culture was large, well polished implements made entirely of greenish slate. They include axes, gouges, chisels, arrow and spear-heads, points, etc. (Fig. 52; Table 15). Only small implements, scrapers, and some arrow-heads, were made of the local variety of flint, which was of a very poor quality. Slate was probably quarried in the area close to the north-western shore of Lake Onega, where its outcrops occur and traces of work-shops have been recorded. These products were widely diffused: they were found throughout the area of the Karelian culture (Fig. 52; Table 14), also in Finland, Estonia, and in the adjoining part of North-west Russia. They found their way to the Kargopol culture and the White Sea culture in the north. The industry seems to have already been in existence in the period of the Early Karelian culture and tools were still manufactured in the early first millennium B.C. The earliest bronze objects probably reached the country by the turn of our Stage II and III of the east European Bronze Age, about 1300 B.C.

The Karelian culture was famous for its flint and stone sculptures (Fig. 54). The flint sculptures appeared in Stage III of our scheme, evidently under eastern influence. The best known are engravings on rocks close to the shores of Lake Onega, and further north on rocks along the Gulf of Onega (Map XVI). They mostly belong to the early first millennium B.C.

THE WHITE SEA CULTURE

The northernmost of the 'Arctic' groups was the White Sea culture. Its sites extended along the southern shore of the White Sea, the Gulf of Dvina, and the Gulf of Onega, and contained a large number of flint objects—well made lancet-shaped arrow-heads, various points, knives, scrapers, etc.—and also many potsherds. Their earliest pottery was a pit-decorated ware of Lialovo type, evidently brought by immigrants from the area of the Kargopol culture during the first part of the second millennium B.C.; for they were the first occupants of the country. At a later stage, perhaps in the fourteenth century B.C. but more likely later, a new wave of immigrants from west Siberia entered the area and overwhelmed its earlier inhabitants. A similar development has been noticed in the area of the Kargopol culture further south.

The men of the White Sea culture must have been keen seafarers. They sailed round the Kola peninsula, 125–185 miles north of their habitations on the southern shores of the White Sea; traces of their passage have been recorded on the eastern and southern shores of the peninsula (Map XIV: I). They were engaged mainly in seal and whale hunting, to a lesser degree in hunting elk and other land animals, and to a minor degree in fresh-water fishing.

The people of the White Sea culture always maintained contact with the Kargopol culture further south. During the first half of the first millennium (see p. 329), they also established contact with the Kama region.

The southern and western shores of the Kola Peninsula were not inhabited until the end of the Neolithic. The settlers were of mixed origin, mainly immigrants of the Karelian culture who mingled with the men of the old east Finnish and north Scandinavian Arctic cultures. Their summer sites were on the seashore or river banks in the western part of the peninsula, and winter habitations, larger in size, were situated further inland. The economy was based on sea fishing. Implements were made of granite, quartzite or slate, no flint being available in the area. Of special interest are the 'labyrinths', circles or spirals thirty-three to forty-three feet in diameter of granite stones. They were built on small islands or peninsulas, always close to the seashore, in the vicinity of a gulf with plentiful fish, and were evidently connected with magic rituals. The culture survived to the end of the arctic Bronze Age, about the middle of the first millennium B.C.

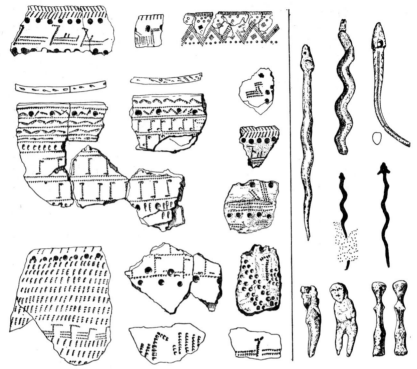

FIG. 53 *Left:* Rows of schematic figures of water birds incised on vessels of the Late Neolithic and Bronze Age from the northern part of the East European forest zone. *Right:* viper and human figurines carved in antler, bone, and clay, from Olenii Ostrov, Tyrvala, and the region on Lake Ladoga, and engraved (black) on Karelian rocks.
After N. N. Gurina (MIA 87, 1961, pp. 141, 147, figs. 19, 23).

NORTHERN ART

Commonly found in the remains of most of the cultures of the northern forest zone, including the arctic region, were sculptures in stone, wood, bone, antler or amber, and clay. Some of these represent human heads or figures, but most are figures of animals, or of their heads—elk, bear, water birds, fish, serpents and lizards. Some seem to be idols, and many others were perforated and evidently used as amulets, or other magical symbols. Larger objects like stone shaft-hole axes with a bear or elk head on the butt, must have been used either for some ceremonial purpose or as signs of distinction.

Another large group of designs form schematic representations of the human figure and of the elk, but mostly of water birds (ducks, and less frequently swans), impressed in rows on vessels and included in their decorative patterns (Fig. 53). Finally, there is a special group

xxviii Pottery characteristic of the Fatyanovo culture from the Volosovo-
Danilovskii cemetery.
After D.A. Krainov, sa vol. 1964–4, p. 75, fig. 6.

xxix Sherds of vessels characteristic of the Volosovo culture from the settlement of Volosovo.

xxx A vessel characteristic of the early 'textile' pottery from Vorskla.

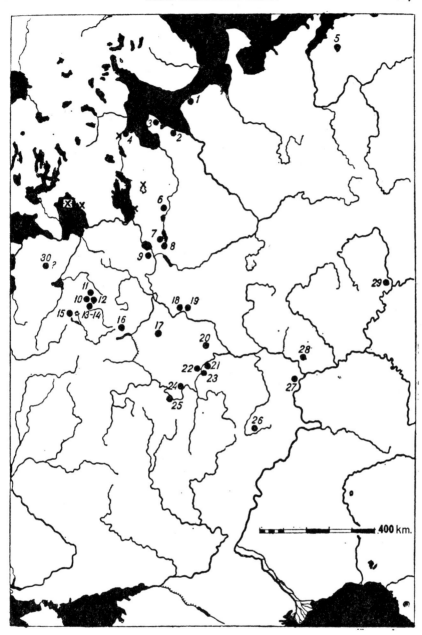

MAP XVI Distribution of flint sculptures in Eastern Europe.
SITES: (6) Kubenino; (7) Modlona; (11) Piros; (18) Boran; (21) Volosovo;
(26) Penza; (28) Kazan; (X) petroglyphs.
After S. N. Zamyatnin (S.A. vol. x, 1948, p. 89, fig. 1).

16

of rock engravings, but these are restricted to the area of the Karelian culture (Map XVI: X).

In the west the earliest designs to appear were small, often crude schematic human figurines and human heads (Fig. 54). In Estonia (Akali), small figurines or heads of this type, carved in bone, antler, or clay, were found in deposits dating to the end of the third and the early second millennium B.C.—the Late Neolithic, the period preceding the invasion of the Boat-axe people. Similar sculptures were found in Finland, and in sites of the Kargopol culture; the latter were of a somewhat later date—the first half of the second millennium, our Stage I of the East European Bronze Age—and seem to have been introduced by the newcomers retreating from the east Baltic area. One of the most remarkable was a schematic human figurine with elk legs, found in the upper layer of Modlona II, which was dated to our Stage III.

Far more numerous were groups of zoomorphic figures, some of excellent workmanship, which appeared mainly within restricted areas. They show chiefly static animals, either carved in amber, stone, flint, and clay, or cut out of bone plaques. They were probably used as amulets or pendants. Some display naturalistic animal heads to decorate axe butts, the handles of ladles (Pl. XXXII), or the heads of bronze pins (Table 15).

The largest group of all contained pendants or amulets in the shape of bears, birds or vipers, carved in amber or antler, or cut out of bone plaques. They were found in Estonia and in some sites of the Kargopol culture, and also in the countries further west, along the southern coast of the Baltic up to North Poland. Among the earliest was a head of a bird (duck?) carved in amber, found in the settlement of Akali in Estonia, in a layer dated around 2000 B.C. Amber figurines of bears and figurines of birds and vipers in bone or antler were also found in later layers of the same settlement and in other sites, and were among the grave goods of a series of burials uncovered in another settlement of the Combed Ware culture, at Tamula in Estonia. In one of these a remarkable small bone spoon was found with a bird figurine at the end of its handle. The earliest zoomorphic sculpture of this region seems to have been a large well executed and decorated figure of a viper carved from antlers. It was found near Narva in Estonia, in a Litorina period layer, and so must have been from the third millennium B.C.

Another group of zoomorphic sculptures are very fine elk or bear heads on the butts of large stone ceremonial shaft-hole axes (Table 15); sometimes the shape of an animal head was also given to the stone mace-head, as in an example from Esbo in Finland. Some of these sculptures were objects of excellent workmanship, well polished

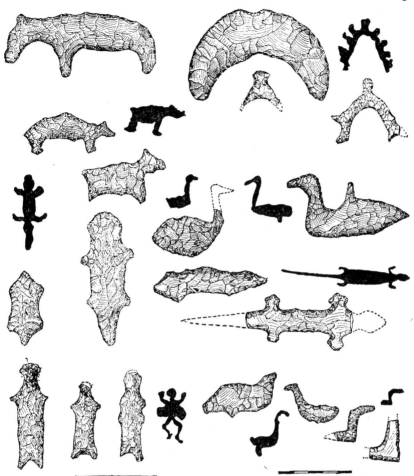

FIG. 54 Human and animal figures: elks, boars, reptiles, vipers, ducks, fish and symbolic signs, carved in flint or engraved on rocks (represented in black), from the East European forest zone.
After S. N. Zamyatnin (S.A. vol. x, 1948, pp. 103, ff, figs. 2–6).

all over their surface. They appear mainly in Finland and Karelia, and belonged mostly to the period of the Boat-axe culture, the first half of the second millennium B.C.

The third large group consisted of figurines chipped in flint (Fig. 54). They are surprisingly naturalistic representations of animals, birds, lizards, and some human beings—in spite of the very unsuitable material used for this purpose. The sculptures in flint were found mainly in the remains of the Kargopol and White Sea cultures, the regions most affected by the wave of West Siberian peoples in our Stage III (Map XVIII). The sculptures were much less frequent in the remains of the adjoining areas, the southernmost specimens deriving from the settlement of the Volosovo culture on the Lower Kama. The flint sculptures were typical of the later part of the second millennium, our Stage III.

A different type of art is represented by the rock engravings found in two regions within the reach of the Karelian culture. The earlier group consists of rock engravings on the north-western side of Lake Onega; the other group, slightly different in style, are petroglyphs near the mouth of the river Vyg in the White Sea. All petroglyphs show single human figures or groups of them, skiing, hunting or just together; figures of bears and elks, birds (mainly ducks) fish, and reptiles; and geometric signs and figures. They are like the Scandinavian petroglyphs, and both are of the third period of the Scandinavian Bronze Age, the very end of the second and the early first millennia B.C., our east European Late Bronze Age (Fig. 54).

No anthropomorphic or zoomorphic figurines were found in the remains of other cultures of the Eastern assemblage west of the Urals, that is the Kazan, the Kama Neolithic, or Bronze Age cultures. They appear, however, even before 2000 B.C. on the other side of the Urals, in the peat-bog sites of the Gorbunovo culture. A large primitive wooden idol was found in the lower layer of the Section Six site, together with wooden sculptures of elks and a viper; the layer dated from our Late Neolithic (Table 3). Human figures carved in wood were also excavated in the middle layer of Section Six, and were dated to late Stage I and early Stage II of the east European Bronze Age.

Remarkably fine sculptures are wooden ladles (Pl. XXXII) shaped to resemble the figure of a duck, whose handles are shaped to resemble the neck and head of these birds. One such ladle was found in the lower layer of Section Six, and others came from the middle layer of the same site of the Gorbunovo bog. No great time lag could have separated these objects, though they were found in different layers. It is important to note that wooden ladles, almost identical in shape, were found in the western section of Eastern Europe, in Finland, and in a site of the Kargopol culture (Modlona). They differ from those of the Gorbunovo culture in that they have animal (not bird) heads carved at the end of the handle. There is one of a dog from Modlona II, and of an elk from Kittilä in Finland. The pollen-analytical date of the latter has been given as 1500–1000 B.C., approximately our Stages II and III, and the date of the ladle from Modlona was similar. These specimens were evidently later in date than those from the Urals, and their appearance in the west seems to have been due to the western drive of the eastern forest dwellers around 1400 B.C. The duck's head, an essential part of the shape given to the ladle by the Gorbunovo sculptors, was replaced in the west by that of larger animals, a motif which was more to the taste of the local artists, though in no way bound up with the shape of the object.

Finally, there was a large group of schematic figures—mainly ducks, sometimes swans, seldom larger animals or human figures—impressed on many vessels of almost all the cultures of the Eastern assemblage, from the Gorbunovo culture in the east to the Kargopol and White Sea cultures in the west (Fig. 53). The figures were usually arranged in rows and formed part of the decorative patterns of the vessels. These decorative motifs probably originated in the east, their westward spread being due to the advance of the eastern tribes.

This short review of the art of the Eastern European forest zone shows that its two different stems, western and eastern, are clearly discernible. The west contributed schematic, mainly small anthropomorphic and zoomorphic figurines that usually served as amulets. They appear chiefly within the territory of the ancient mesolithic Kunda culture and the adjoining areas that were affected by the subsequent east Baltic cultures. Some scholars suggest a connection with the mesolithic art of Western Europe, and others compare the figurines with the clay figurines and idols of the agricultural peoples of Central Europe and the Ukraine; though the latter were predominantly female figurines, whereas those of the Baltic area in the north were exclusively male.

The naturalistic sculptures and other representations of the eastern stem were native to Finland and the arctic cultures of north Russia, in particular Karelia; they also appeared, at about the same time, in the Gorbunovo culture of the Urals. There is, however, some difference between the sculptures of these two regions; in Finland, Karelia and neighbouring areas animal sculptures predominate, the bear (often only its head) being the favourite motif along with the elk. No bear figures have been recorded so far in the Gorbunovo area, where the water-bird (duck) figures predominate in the sculptures. The two branches, though closely related, seem to have developed independently of each other. Nevertheless, some contacts must have existed between them, especially in the second half of the second millennium B.C.

THE SOUTH EAST

Significant changes that mark the beginning, early in the second millennium B.C., of a new era (our east European Bronze Age) also took place in the south east, throughout the steppe country between the Dnieper and the Urals and down to the Caucasus. New cultures emerged there as successors to the Yamnaya culture. The name of

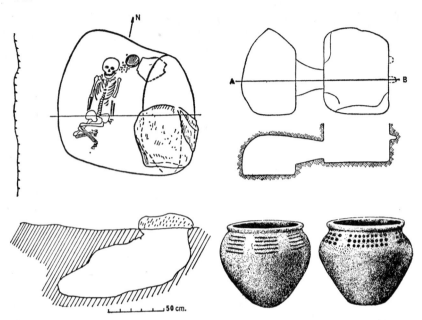

FIG. 55 Characteristic niche ('catacomb') graves of the Catacomb culture. *Left:* A flat grave of the second cemetery at Leontiivka near Kakhivka on the lower Dnieper (after O. G. Shaposhnikova, AP vol. x, 1961, p. 8, fig 9); *Upper right:* grave 17 of barrow grave 3 on the Chyngul, north of Melitopol (after V. F. Peshchanov, AP vol. vi, 1956, p. 88, fig. 2); *Lower right:* two vessels typical of the Azov group of the Catacomb culture (after T. B. Popova, *Plemena Katakombnoy Kultury.* Moscow 1955, p. 85, fig. 19).

the 'Catacomb' culture has been given to one of these on account of a special form of grave, a shaft with a niche dug into one of its sides in which the corpse was laid (Fig. 55). This was an important culture which for many centuries held a key position in the south-east.

THE CATACOMB CULTURE

The Catacomb culture extended over the steppe east of the Dnieper up to the Lower Volga (Map XIV: XXVII). Several local groups of the culture have been distinguished,[51] but the three most important were the Western or Donetz group; the Southern group on the Sea of Azov; and the Eastern or Don-Manych group, called also the 'Fore-Caucasian' steppe group.[52] The groups show a considerable diversity in their burial ritual, orientation of skeletons, and grave goods. Nevertheless, their pottery and its decorative patterns exhibit some basic likeness, and many grave goods, weapons and objects of personal adornment, did not differ substantially, though they were not evenly diffused over the whole area of the culture. Bronze or copper objects were relatively frequent (Fig. 56)—temple ornaments with thickened and overlapping terminals, cast bronze pendants of north Caucasian origin with a 'cord decoration', and tubular beads or imitations made of small tubular bird bones with an incised spiral ornament. Bone hammer-headed pins (Fig. 56), beads made of bone or bronze, and also imported beads of faience, carnelian and rock-crystal, were characteristic. Flat bronze knives or small daggers, flint arrow-heads (once a wooden bow survived), and stone battle-axes were common; no polished flint axes were found in any grave. In several burials there were 'arrow-straighteners', or 'smoothers'; they were small sandstone plaques with a furrow along the whole length, a type common in Central Europe but also in the Aegean area (Pl. XXXIII).

Many of the grave goods demonstrate the wide commercial connections of the respective groups of the culture. Metal objects found throughout the territory were mainly of North Caucasian origin (Map XVII). Later, however, simple metal objects like flat knives or spearheads might have been produced locally from the native copper of the region on the Middle Donetz. Also of Caucasian, or Transcaucasian, origin were a number of battle-axes made of serpentine and nephrite and carnelian beads. Faience beads were imported from the Mediterranean countries.

The Catacomb people were pastoralists. Sheep bones account for 65 to 75 per cent of the osseous material excavated in the graves, and often entire skulls were found; and up to 35 per cent were bones and skulls of cattle. Horse bones were rarely found. It seems that the Catacomb people were not a horse-breeding tribe, and there is no indication in the graves that they evolved a nomadic life. They moved around in carts with heavy plain wheels drawn by oxen. Remains of such carts have been found in the Yamnaya graves (see p. 129), and in several burials of the Catacomb culture (such as Elista in the Astrakhan steppe). Pestles and querns found in some graves point to some agriculture in the regions, which were in fact suitable for it; charred grains of millet, or their traces, were found in a few instances.

The difference in the endowment of graves suggests social stratification within the Catacomb society, and graves looted soon after the funeral point to the same conclusion; such looting has not been observed either in the Yamnaya graves nor in those of the subsequent Srubnaya culture. Another indication of social differences is human sacrifice: the buried man was frequently accompanied by his wife and her small children, and often one or more of his serfs was sacrificed on his grave.

There was a special burial ritual in some of the barrow graves. In one near Elista (Stepnoe), a shaft-grave of the Catacomb period was uncovered in which a person of high social position was buried, probably a chief or prince. In the centre of the area covered by the mound, over the grave-shaft, traces of a great fire were plainly distinguishable, below which lay bones of three cows and sheep, and near these two clay vessels, bone tubular beads and a clay model of a two-wheeled cart. The large square shaft was covered with timber planks or logs; around it lay stones, and on its corners were the plain wooden wheels of a cart. A fifth wheel and the remains of a yoke were found in the shaft itself. At the bottom of the shaft was a male skeleton in a sitting position; it was strewn with ochre, and near it lay two bronze awls, a bronze knife, one wooden and two clay vessels, and two skeletons of vipers. The grave was dated to about 1500–1400 B.C. and belonged to the Don-Manych group. In another site of the same group (Remontnoe) the grave was surrounded by a stone circle nearly twenty-three feet in diameter, and a bone hammer-headed pin was found among its grave goods.

The Don-Manych group differed in some respect from other groups of the Catacomb culture. The number of secondary burials of the period uncovered in a single mound—eight to twenty-five—implies that the barrows served as a family burial ground, a practice also observed in the Yamnaya barrow-graves east of the Volga and in the successive cultures of that area; the Nalchik barrow grave in the North Caucasus (see p. 131) was one of the earliest of this type. Further west, mounds were raised mainly over a grave of a single person, evidently if he was of a sufficiently high social position. Another distinguishing feature of the Don-Manych group was that skeletons with deformed skulls were found in a relatively large number of burials, a fact rarely observed in other groups. The custom of deforming skulls survived in the area up to the Sarmatian period, that is to the first centuries of the Christian era.

The available anthropological evidence relates only to the northwestern graves of the culture. The people buried in them were about five feet eight inches tall, and strongly built; about 71 per cent of them were dolichocephalic, though brachycephalic skulls were also found. In the barrow graves of the region north of the Sea of Azov most of the skulls were of the 'Caucasian' type (brachycephalic).

Several Bronze Age settlements have been attributed to the Catacomb culture, mainly on account of the pottery; however, these settlements lay mainly in the valley of the Dnieper on the western border of the culture or already outside its limits, or to a lesser extent along its northern periphery; no settlements have been recorded in the steppe, the area in which most graves of the culture were excavated. The main decorative motif of the pottery excavated in the settlements mentioned above was cord-impressed rows of hatched triangles, a pattern very popular among Central European cultures of the period, and also the Komarów culture, and adopted by all groups of the Catacomb culture and those bordering on it. This motif cannot be regarded as exclusive to the Catacomb culture, but rather as indicative of the range of the western influence on the east.

There is no common agreement as to the origin of the Catacomb culture. The substantial difference between its content and that of its predecessor, the Yamnaya culture emphasized by M.I. Artamonov and by several authors after him, implies that the transition from one to the other was not a simple process. Their grave forms were different, as was the position of the corpse (crouched with the Catacomb people as in the cultures of the Battle-axe assemblage, instead in the 'Yamnaya' position). Other differences were the orientation of the heads, and in most regions the pottery and its decoration. Stone battle-axes, never found in Yamnaya burials, were placed in Catacomb graves. The differences among the main groups of the Catacomb culture itself add to the complexity of its origin, though the evidence available suggests that the culture was the immediate successor to the Yamnaya.

Both the Donetz and Don-Manych groups may be claimed as the originators of the culture, but it seems that the claims of the latter are the stronger. On the Lower Don, graves characteristic of the Don-Manych group are said[53] to have been preceded by those of the Donetz group, which would imply the earlier origin of the latter, but such graves appear only within the border area of the two groups. In the steppe south of the Lower Don and on the Volga, the Catacomb culture appears in its earliest and purest form.[54] The Don-Manych group undoubtedly played an important role in the adoption and fostering of the 'catacomb' type of grave, which was most probably of Mediterranean origin. The catacomb graves were very common in the Don-Manych group up to the Caucasus. In the west they appear in the Donetz group, but did not spread to the neighbouring areas, not even to the area of the Lower Dnieper; they were reluctantly accepted in the group north of the Sea of Azov, where many hybrid forms of grave developed, one being a cross of the old shaft with the niche grave. The local, conservatively minded, community evidently tried to preserve part of its traditional burial forms and usages.

Pottery was another important element in the identification of the culture (Figs. 55, 56; Pls. XXXIV, XXXV). That found in the earliest graves of the Don-Manych group was of two different types. The first consisted of vessels of north-west Caucasian type, attributable to the early stage of the North Caucasian culture (see p. 120).

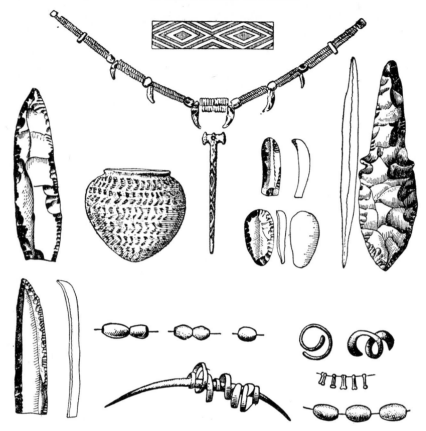

FIG. 56 Necklace made of grooved tubular bone beads, animal teeth, a decorated bone hammer-headed pin, and a vessel, from barrow grave 2 at Klynivka near Poltava (after M. Rudynskii, *Korotke Zvidomlenia za* 1926 *rik*. Kiev 1927, pp. 144, 150, fig. 1, pl. XXXI: 2). Flints and bronze ornaments from graves of the Catacomb culture (after T. B. Popova, as fig. 55, pp. 104, 127, figs. 23, 30).

These were mainly large vessels with a rounded body and an everted rim, usually undecorated. Close analogies may be found in the pottery of the settlements (Dolinskoe) and graves of the second stage (Novosvobodnaya) of the Maikop culture (Fig. 31). Vessels of the north-west Caucasian type were also found west of the Don in the graves of the Donetz group and in those north of the Sea of Azov, and they lend considerable support to the theory of the eastern, Don-Manych origin of the culture.

The so-called 'lamps' or 'incense-burners', saucers with cruciform feet divided into two unequal compartments by a curved septum which did not differ from the North Caucasian specimens (Table 20), also point to the Don-Manych origin of the culture. They were usually richly adorned with impressions of simple cord, whipped or braided cords, comb-stamps, etc. Similar vessels were found in the Donetz group, and also a few in the steppe on the Lower Dnieper and north of the Sea of Azov. They appear also in the graves of the North Caucasian culture. They were most numerous in the latter region and in the territory east of the Don, and it is there that their gradual evolution has been established by stratigraphic evidence. The vessels seem to have been of alien origin, as were the graves of the 'catacomb' type. V.G. Childe[55] remarks that the 'incense-burners' are remarkably like vessels of the Slavonian or Pecsel cultures of north Yugoslavia and Hungary, where burial in pit-graves (niche-graves) was also practised, and concludes that the points of agreement are too close to be fortuitous. All these cultures were of the early second millennium B.C.

The second group of pottery consisted of vessels closely related to and evidently derivative from the Corded Ware assemblage. There is the same relation to their incised or cord-impressed decoration, consisting mainly of fish-bone motifs and of rows of hatched triangles; the exuberant decoration characteristic of the Donetz group of the culture appears here only on the 'incense-burners'.

Close connections evidently existed between the Don-Manych group and the north Caucasus, especially the Piatigorsk country. Caucasian bronze objects were found in graves of the steppe up to the Don and the Volga, and a large part of the pottery found in them is of Caucasian character. North Caucasian bronze objects were also found in graves of other groups of the Catacomb culture west of the Don (Map XVII); they point to the important role played by the Don-Manych group in the formation of the western groups of the culture.

According to some scholars the marked Caucasian features exhibited by the remains of the Don-Manych group were due to a northern migration of some North Caucasian tribes. However, the area seems always to have been inhabited by tribes closely related to those of the North-west Caucasus, and this circumstance, not a Caucasian expansion, accounts for the close ties between the two countries.

The original centre of the Don-Manych group, and implicitly of the Catacomb culture as a whole, seems to have been restricted to the region on the Lower Don, close to the border of the Donetz group. In later periods the area was known for centuries as a strong commercial centre with a wide 'Hinterland'. It seems very likely that it had already begun to play this role early in the second millennium B.C., at the time of the formation of the Catacomb culture. Prospectors and merchants from distant overseas countries had probably visited

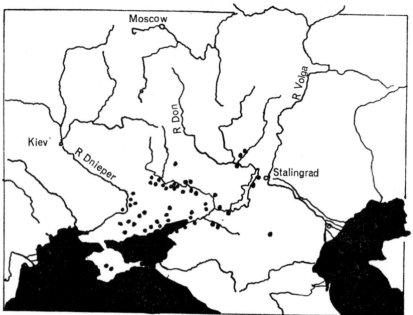

MAP XVII Distribution of North Caucasian bronze objects within the
territory of the Catacomb culture.
After T. B. Popova (*Plemena Katakombnoy Kultury*. Moscow 1955, p. 99,
fig. 21).

this region and had presumably implanted some elements of their
culture (niche or catacomb graves, the practice of the deformation
of skulls, the 'incense burners', etc.). Sea connections with the Usatovo
culture are confirmed by the discovery of a wide beaker with a narrow
neck, typical of that culture in a catacomb grave of the early period
in one of the barrow graves on the Manych; its decoration, consisting of a row of semi-circular impressions by whipped cord stamp, was
likewise characteristic of the Usatovo culture.

The other important factor in the formation of the Catacomb culture was the western influence. Pottery of the non-Caucasian type in
the Don-Manych group reveals strong 'western' connections with
the Corded Ware assemblage. The introduction of stone battle-axes
points in the same direction. The western current must have reached
the area via the territory of the Donetz group. Pottery of western
type, similar to that characteristic of the Donetz group, was actually
found in the earliest graves of the Don-Manych group in the region
on the Lower Don, and several burials in that area yielded an inventory of a mixed character. In this area, Caucasian and western
elements blended with overseas influences to give birth to the Catacomb culture.

The Donetz group, centred round Izium and in the steppe further to the west and south-west, seems to have been formed a little later than the Don-Manych group. Its substratum was the local Yamnaya culture, but its two formative elements—the western and the eastern one emanating from the region on the Lower Don—are easily discernible in its remains. The impact of the western current, however, was much stronger here than further east. The most characteristic feature of this group was its flat-bottomed bulging vessels, with an exuberant ornament consisting of impressions of cords, whipped or braided cords, comb-stamps or shells (Pl. XXXIV). Neither the shape of these vessels nor their decoration had anything in common with pottery of the preceding Yamnaya culture. Flat-bottomed pottery was common to the 'Comb-pricked ware' culture of the valley of the Dnieper and to the forest-steppe zone north and north-west of the Donetz group. It was also characteristic of the Corded Ware assemblage and the Globular Amphora culture, both of which considerably affected the neighbouring territories. Decorative patterns consisting of rows of triangles appear first on the vessels of the Globular Amphora culture; the motif of rows of hatched triangles, usually down-pointed, was popular in several groups of the Corded Ware in Central Europe and on pottery of its derivative cultures, such as the Bronze Age Komarów culture of the sub-Carpathian area (Pls. XXIV, XXV). The motif gradually spread eastwards, possibly propagated by small advancing groups of the Battle-axe folk. It appeared on pottery from the settlements in the valley of the Dnieper, it was subsequently adopted by the Catacomb culture and then reached the Caucasus where it was applied to the decoration of vessels of the north Caucasian culture. Many vessels of the early Srubnaya culture on the Volga also bear this decoration.

Stone battle-axes were another link with the Battle-axe assemblage, from which they were adopted. Their early specimens either do not differ from those of Central Europe, or were closely related to them; it is only later that some local forms appeared, some of them with a carved decoration. Flint blades and small flint implements made of Volhynian flint, found in many burials, point to the close contact of the Donetz group with the regions further to the north and north-west. A cord-decorated single-lugged beaker ('Zapfenbecher'), characteristic of the 'Oder' group of the Corded Ware and excavated from a barrow grave east of the Dnieper (Krupol), close to the border of the Donetz group, illustrates the eastern drive of the Corded Ware cultures. The Donetz group must have been formed under the impact of the Middle Dnieper and Dnieper-Desna cultures, but the share of the Globular Amphora culture must also have been considerable. This is suggested by the characteristic decorative motif of rows of concentric semi-circles, or similar figures, usually directed downwards with a point in the centre, which appears on the richly decorated pottery of the Donetz group (Pl. XXXIV). It was typical of the Globular Amphora culture.

The most conservative of all groups of the culture seems to have been that which extended north of the Sea of Azov. There the ancient traditions of the Yamnaya culture were preserved, as is shown in both the burial ritual and grave form, which differed from the genuine 'catacombs', and in the local pottery (Fig. 55). The same conservatism was to be found in the steppe west of the Dnieper where the grave form and sepulchral pottery differed considerably from that of other groups of the culture (Pl. XXXV).

The Catacomb culture lasted for about 600 years, from the beginning of the second millennium to the fourteenth and thirteenth centuries B.C., being then gradually superseded by the Srubnaya culture advancing from beyond the Volga. The first to disappear was the Donetz group, and the area on the Lower Don was almost simultaneously overrun. In other parts of the country, such as the Crimea and the region north of the Sea of Azov, the culture survived longer; but its remains in these regions show a strong admixture of the Srubnaya culture, which finally overcame it. The tribes of the Don-Manych group found a refuge in the Astrakhan steppe and in the North-west Caucasus, where they survived up to the early centuries of the first millennium B.C., that is, to the beginning of the Iron Age. The position was similar in the Astrakhan steppe west of the Caspian Sea, where the Catacomb burials lingered on up to the end of the second millennium B.C. in spite of the surrounding Srubnaya culture. In this context, a find in that area deserves mention. It is a flat iron dagger, or point, found in a barrow grave at Elista in association with pottery and metal objects characteristic of the Catacomb culture; it is the earliest iron object so far found in Eastern Europe. However, the iron from which the dagger was made was of meteoric origin and is of no importance for dating purposes.

Three periods have been distinguished in the development of the various groups of the Catacomb culture.[56] The second period was the 'classic' period, and the third and final period was clearly a period of decline.

THE CAUCASUS

During the second millennium B.C., the North Caucasus became an important centre that considerably affected the steppe peoples further north. The growth of this centre was to a great extent connected with the development of the Caucasian metallurgy, based on local deposits, mainly of copper; no tin deposits exist in the Caucasus, except for a small region in Southern Ossetia, and arsenic was used instead for making bronze (arsenic bronze).

The population of North Caucasus was not uniform at this period, and the cultures of the various regions differed in some degree from each other. They were divided into three main groups, considered to have been branches of a single culture, to which the name of the 'North Caucasian' culture has recently been given.[57] In the earlier archaeological literature, its western group was known under the name of the Kuban culture, after the country on the river Kuban; the next, the Central Caucasian group, was subdivided into two sections—the north-western, which was closely connected with the Kuban group, and the eastern one, the highland section; and the third, the Eastern group of the culture, embraced the area around the towns of Groznyi and Dagestan. The northern boundary of the culture cannot be definitely established; remains were found within a wide strip of the steppe north of the Caucasus foothills, but they were intermingled with barrow graves of the Don-Manych group of the Catacomb culture. The latter ultimately replaced the North Caucasian culture in the steppe, and also took over a large portion of its territory in the mountains.

All the groups of the North Caucasian culture evolved out of the local substratum of the preceding period—the Maikop culture in the west, and some survival of the Kura-Araxes culture in the east. But the main formative element of the new culture was the steppe cultures, especially the Catacomb culture, or, more exactly, the impact of the Corded Ware/Battle-axe assemblage on the Catacomb culture, the repercussions of which have been noticed even further south, in the Caucasus. The Corded Ware was responsible for the introduction of a number of very characteristic features into the North Caucasian culture—the cord-impressed decoration of pottery, its style and common patterns including rows of hanging hatched triangles, stone battle-axes, etc. Previously during the period of the Maikop culture, only copper shaft-hole axes were used; and the stone axes were evidently no substitute for metal specimens, which continued to be used alongside the stone axes. The latter must have been brought by the newcomers to the country, but were obviously not used as weapons, still less as tools; they undoubtedly served as a sign of distinction, or a symbol of power and dignity.

The western current seems already to have reached the Caucasus during the Novosvobodnaya stage of the Maikop culture. The very large, nearly spherical, amphorae with short cylindrical necks, excavated in the Novosvobodnaya graves, are very different from the local ware of southern, Transcaucasian parentage. Their decoration consisted of incised herring-bone patterns round the neck and arranged in vertical bands running from the neck down the greatest extent of the body. In their shape and decoration these vessels correspond with amphorae from the Yaroslav group of the Fatyanovo culture (see p. 196), and like these they are strikingly reminiscent of the 'Thuringian' amphorae, vessels characteristic of the early stage of the Corded Ware culture. The likeness between the Novosvobodnaya amphorae and those of the Fatyanovo culture has often been pointed out, but it has been wrongly considered to be due to a Caucasian influence reaching Central Russia. Some authors[58] even seek a Caucasian origin for both the Fatyanovo and Balanovo cultures (see p. 201). In fact, however, the same Central European current seems to have reached both areas, Central Russia and the Caucasus, at approximately the same time. Debased cord-decorated 'Thuringian' amphorae were found in some graves of the North Caucasus culture.

The North Caucasian culture was probably formed in the region of Piatigorsk, in the western division of the central group (Table 19). The earliest remains of the culture were found in this area, and there also appeared the earliest examples of the North Caucasian cord-decorated pottery. The earliest of its barrow graves (Solomenka near Nalchik; Fig. 58) seem to have been partly contemporary with the Novosvobodnaya stage of the Maikop culture in the Kuban area. In the latter region the new development started a little later than around Piatigorsk, but still relatively early in the second millennium. It was marked by barrow grave 5 at Ulskii (grave 1), in which one clay and two alabaster figurines were found, plus a number of bronze ornaments. A crouch-headed bone pin links the grave with the last phase of the preceding Maikop culture (Fig. 57).

The remains above represent the first stage of the three distinguished in the evolution of the culture. The survival of ancient traditions in the burial ritual was shown by contracted skeletons orientated mainly to the south, lumps of ochre thrown into the graves, crouch-headed pins, and some types of vessels. To this period also probably belonged the upper layer of the settlement at Dolinskoe. But outside the original area and the Kuban country, in the highland zone and in the eastern part of the North Caucasus, local cultures of the preceding period continued to exist, and only a few items adopted from neighbouring groups indicate the dates of the respective finds.

The three consecutive stages in the development of the North Caucasian culture in the region of Nalchik-Piatigorsk, and their typical stone and metal objects and pottery are shown in Table 19. The first, the formative period of the culture was of a rather short duration. But once formed, the culture spread all over the North Caucasus. This heralded the second stage, the summit in the develop-

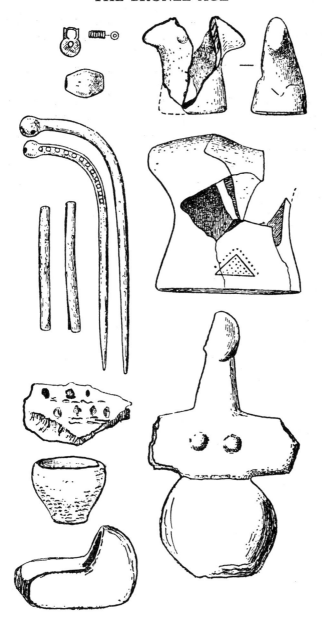

FIG. 57 Selected grave goods from burial 1 of barrow grave 5 at Ulskii.
After V. I. Markovin (MIA 93, p. 31, fig. 2).

ment of the culture, which began around 1700 B.C. From then on any features inherited from the culture of the preceding period gradually died out.

Some changes occurred in the construction of graves. Mounds were often built entirely of heaped stones; this was especially common in the central group, where slab-cist graves or tombs built of small stone slabs laid in layers were very common. In the highland zone the usual type was the slab-cist sunk in the ground with no mound raised above it. Slab cists, especially those provided with a porthole, might have continued the ancient local tradition. But most were of a different type, and seem to have been related to those of the Crimea and the region on the Lower Dnieper, which were of Globular Amphora derivation. It seems very likely that the same current eventually reached the Caucasus also, especially the metalliferous area of the Central Caucasus.

The grave goods, especially of the Piatigorsk-Nalchik and the Kuban regions, closely connect the culture with the neighbouring group of the Catacomb culture; and some scholars even consider these remains to represent a branch of the Catacomb culture. The steady thrust of the Catacomb culture resulted in a gradual shrinking of the territory of the North Caucasian culture. Ultimately, in the third stage of its development, the Caucasian culture was confined mainly to the southern part of its former central division and to the highland zone.

The North Caucasian pottery of the second stage had already departed from ancient prototypes. Bowls and bulging vessels, usually provided with lugs under the rim, were most common; the decorative patterns consisted mainly of cord-impressed or incised rows of hatched triangles, a typical decoration of the Catacomb culture. Richly decorated 'lamps' or 'incense burners' were popular (Table 20), they were of the same type as those of the Don-Manych group of the Catacomb culture. Many other grave goods were similar to those of the Catacomb culture—'arrow-straighteners' (Pl. XXXIII), stone battle-axes, ornaments, etc. The stone battle-axes evolved locally into a specific 'Piatigorsk' type, markedly bent with a drooping blade, and made very accurately of serpentine. Another link with the Catacomb culture was the hammer-headed pin, made at first of bone, but later of bronze.

The metal industry was considerably advanced and knew the technique of casting à cire perdue; and it displays Transcaucasian influences. Its main centre was in the region of Nalchik and Piatigorsk, close to the metalliferous area in the mountains; another centre, later to grow in importance, was in the central highland zone. The industry copied some Oriental and Anatolian types—shaft-hole axes,

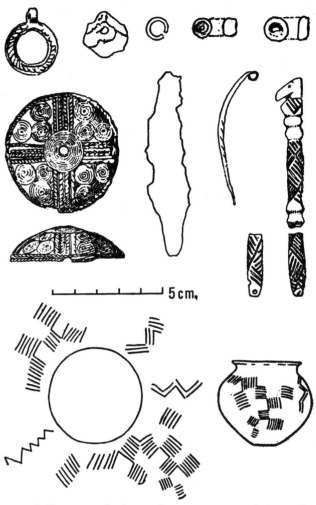

FIG. 58 Grave goods from a barrow grave at Solomenka near Nalchik.
After A. P. Kruglov and G. V. Podgaetskii (MIA 3, 1941, p. 195, fig. 33).

hammer-headed pins, disc pendants, daggers, etc.—but it developed them into its own forms. The most spectacular were a variety of personal ornaments, and a special feature was the 'braided cords' ornament applied in cast to the decoration of plaques, pendants and similar objects (Fig. 58), pins, and even shaft-hole axes (Table 19). 'Ram-horn'-headed and double-spiral-headed pins were common. Hammer-headed pins evolved into bizarre forms provided with two or three pairs of large knobs, or their heads took the shape of two or three wide-stretched prongs. Some late specimens of these attained an unusual size, being up to twenty-eight inches long, with heads up to six inches wide. Silver and gold ornaments were rather an exception.

Trade relations were maintained with many distant countries and regions. Products of the North Caucasian bronze industry were widely distributed over the whole steppe further north (Maps XVII and XXI), beyond the Catacomb territory, reaching the Middle Volga and the Middle Kama countries; a 'Piatigorsk' stone battle-axe was even found near Omsk, on the Irtysh in West Siberia, nearly 1,200 miles north-east of Astrakhan. Single North Caucasian shaft-hole axes and personal ornaments found their way westwards as far as West Podolia, the region on the Upper Dnieper in Byelorussia and Central Russia. Trade relations with Transcaucasia, especially with Georgia, and with the countries further to the south, are indicated by a number of imported objects: carnelian beads probably of Georgian origin, lapis lazuli beads brought from Persia, and bronze daggers imported from Western Asia. Of special interest was a damaged bronze lance-head from a grave at Galashi-Pervomaiskoe, similar to that from barrow grave XV of Trialeti. Faience beads found at Galashi and in graves at Verkhnaya Rutkha were all approximately of the fifteenth century B.C., as was also a Syrian haematite seal found near Verkhnaya Koban. The ram-horn-headed pins have their Transcaucasian and Anatolian parallels, and the alabaster figurine from the Ulskii barrow grave, probably a local product, was copied from some Mediterranean example.

The territory of the north Caucasian culture began to shrink gradually during the second stage of its development, and in the third stage, which began in the fourteenth century B.C., it was restricted to the Nalchik-Piatigorsk region and the highland zone. The area further west was lost to the Catacomb culture, which retreated southwards under the pressure of the Srubnaya culture. Further east, the Srubnaya culture encroached deep into the Caucasian territory. In its residuum, the central part of its former territory, the North Caucasian culture continued for a few centuries more; and during this third and last period the culture was gradually transformed into the Digorian culture, the predecessor of the Koban culture and the culture of the Early Iron Age of the central North Caucasian highland. The beginning of the Digorian culture has usually been put about 1200 B.C.

The economy of the North Caucasian culture was based chiefly on animal husbandry, though its people also knew some form of primitive agriculture. Sheep or goats supply 56 per cent of the bones found, but cattle were kept also. Bones of dogs and horses were rarely found. The tribes in the North-west Caucasian steppe must have led a partly migratory life, as is indicated by the clay model of a covered cart or waggon found in one of the barrow graves at Ulskii. A few settlements have been recorded in the hilly region. Metallurgy must have been in the hands of trained specialists who worked in special workshops, and copper mining and smelting must also have been specialized. Society was evidently stratified—some graves were considerably better equipped than others—but the differences never attained such a degree of ostentation as was displayed by the 'royal' barrow graves of the preceding period, like Maikop or Novosvobodnaya.

THE TRIALETI BARROW GRAVES

During the first half of the second millennium B.C. a number of smaller groups developed on the other, southern, side of the main Caucasian ridge, in Transcaucasia. Among these was the Abkhazian dolmen culture, a continuation of the culture of an earlier period called the Eshery group, after a village in which a larger number of slab-cist graves were investigated.[59] Grave goods of this group, which was of no wider importance, resemble those of the second, developed stage of the North Caucasian culture, mainly of its central group; they must have been approximately of the same age.

However, another group of Transcaucasian remains is important for our study, although they lay not far from the border of Turkey. This was a group of forty-two barrow graves excavated[60] in the valley of the river Khram, about 7,200 feet above sea level, in the province of Trialeti west of Tbilisi; they have accordingly been called the Trialeti group. Some of the barrow graves of the Early Bronze Age belonged to the end of the third millennium B.C., but the majority were of the first half and, mainly, of the middle of the second millennium B.C. Many precious objects of Oriental origin found in them are helpful in establishing the precise chronology of the graves. The close relations of the group with the countries of the ancient Oriental civilizations were undoubtedly connected with trade in the Caucasian metals, and one of these was perhaps gold.

The Early Bronze Age graves, mostly poor in content, were all in burial pits under mounds. One or two pots in a grave, a flat copper spear-head, a dagger, a gold band, a haematite mace-head like the one from Alishar II in Anatolia (1900–1600 B.C.), an awl, and a silver cup, were all the objects excavated in these barrows. It is important to note, however, that the objects of Anatolian origin were of the same age as those found at Usatovo (see p. 183); trade obviously flourished at that time within the basin of the Black Sea. A second, even more flourishing, period is reflected by the grave goods of the Trialeti Middle Bronze Age of about 1500–1350 B.C., and also by the grave goods of the same period found in several points of Eastern Europe.

The Trialeti mounds of the Middle Bronze Age were made of heaped earth and stones. Burials were in pits or on the surface. Up to twenty-four vessels were discovered in a single burial, and pottery appeared in almost all graves. The metalwork included plain silver or gold cups, awls, personal ornaments, and a few weapons. Among the most surprising are a gold cup with curls and friezes outlined in double filigree and set with carnelians and turquoises, a silver bucket with a hunting scene on its surface, pierced silver pins with gold heads set with carnelians and turquoise and granulation, and a necklace of big gold beads with a central piece of agate mounted in gold. Perhaps the most important was a silver cup decorated with several stags and men and a sitting figure of a god, and all the human figures were wearing animal masks and tails. The men's profile and the general look of the scene are distinctly Hittite of the middle of the second millennium B.C. (frontispiece). In one large and deep burial pit a four-wheeled waggon was uncovered; it was drawn by oxen, for their skeletons lay near it. Weapons consisted of flint arrow-heads, stone mace-heads, silver and bronze daggers, and a bronze lance or spearhead with a silver ferrule from the east Mediterranean, and another one with an open socket.

The finest pieces of metalwork from Trialeti burials point to relations with the south, Anatolia, Troy VI, and even Syria. The bronze lance-head with a silver fastening ring found in barrow grave XV was evidently a Mycenean or Syrian imported weapon, dated 1550–1400 B.C.[61] Of Mycenean derivation were decorative motifs of a number of ornaments and other objects (beads, discs, etc.). We have here[62] a civilization rich in gold, apparently not far removed in time or place from the Golden Fleece.

It is of interest to note that no human sacrifices were found in any of the Trialeti barrow graves. Furthermore, the circumstance that the richly equipped barrows were found side by side with the poorly furnished ones suggests that no marked class distinction existed in the Trialeti society of that period.

SUMMARY

The speed of development and rate of change in Eastern Europe during the Palaeolithic and Mesolithic greatly accelerated in the fourth and third millennia, the Neolithic, and speeded up even more in the second millennium B.C., the Bronze Age. There were various reasons for this, but one of the most important was the expansion of the Central European Corded Ware and Globular Amphora cultures, and the consequent spread of new ideas (Map XIV). The expansion of these cultures which we have followed in this chapter resulted in the formation of several new groups of both cultures and hybrids in various parts of the country. It seems that the main drive of the Corded Ware assemblage was directed towards the centre of Eastern Europe, into the forest zone. The first culture formed in that territory was the Dnieper-Desna culture in the basin of the Upper and Middle Dnieper north of Kiev and of the Desna; it extended over the western part of the territory of the former Dnieper-Donetz culture (Map XIV). Next was the Fatyanovo culture, established within the central and northern part of the Volga-Oka assemblage, and the drive further east along the Middle Volga resulted in the formation of the Balanovo culture, the easternmost outpost of the assemblage. Meanwhile the northern advance of another branch of the assemblage led to the establishment within the territory of the East Baltic Combed Ware culture of the Boat-axe cultures of Estonia and Finland.

In spreading southwards and south-eastwards the peoples of the assemblage came into contact with both the Yamnaya pastoralists and the Tripolyan farmers. Their mingling with these resulted in the formation of a series of hybrid groups. In the sub-Carpathian region the Barrow-grave culture appeared, and east of it, up to the Dnieper, appeared the Middle Dnieper Barrow-grave culture with the Gorodsk and Sofiivka groups to its north. In the south the Vykhvatyntsi group emerged on the steppe border on the Middle Dniester, and further south, in the steppe, the Usatovo culture was established. The formation of the Catacomb culture must be looked upon as having developed under a strong impact from the Corded Ware assemblage, and the same happened with the North Caucasian (Kuban) culture. The formation of all these groups and cultures marks the break with ancient local traditions, irrespective of whether the formative intrusive element ultimately gained the upper hand over the native one or was absorbed by it.

The Globular Amphora people was another contributor to the changes of the period, though its share in this respect is less tangible. Its expansion resulted in the establishment of the Volhynian and Podolian groups, all formed on alien territories in the south-western part of Eastern Europe. But unlike the Corded Ware migrants, the Globular Amphora invaders did not interfere with the evolution of the native population. At a later date one of the Volhynian groups presumably provoked the southern expansion of the Gorodsk culture, which brought about the decline of the western groups of the Tripolye culture.

The Globular Amphora culture did not expand eastwards beyond the Dnieper. However, traces of its penetration have been found in very distant regions, far beyond the reach of the Corded Ware/ Battle-axe assemblage—in the area of the Kama culture and in the Urals, and even east of the mountains (Map XIV). Their eastern penetration, which proceeded along a relatively narrow track—the Middle Volga and the Kama and its tributaries—seems to have been connected with trade, in particular in trade in copper.

The eastern drive of the Corded Ware assemblage was later followed by another Central European current, that of the Trzciniec culture of the Middle Bronze Age plus elements of the 'Hungarian' Komarów culture. This current also penetrated deep into Eastern Europe. Ultimately, nearly the whole central and southern parts of Eastern Europe and the western regions of its northern part were more or less affected by the western cultures just mentioned. And their secondary influence, through the medium of the Catacomb culture, may be traced even to the Altai mountains of West Siberia, about 1,750 miles east of the eastern border of the Catacomb culture, and in Soviet Central Asia; for remains of the Catacomb culture were found in those areas (see p. 266; 300).

Apart from the eastern drive of the Central European cultures, there were other factors behind the changes during the second millennium. There was trade, especially the maritime trade with the Aegean countries, and the development of metallurgical centres in some parts of Eastern Europe and Western Siberia (see Chapter IV).

Three stages are distinguishable in the development of most regions of Eastern Europe during the Bronze Age, the period from about 1800 to 1200 B.C. presented in Table 4. The main cultures of the period have been quoted there and stages in their evolution marked. It has been already emphasized that in some regions the triple division is not always distinguishable and that in several instances development was held up. Nevertheless, the diagram illustrates the trends in the general evolution of the whole country, and agreement in the dates of stages in the evolution of cultures in different parts of Eastern Europe implies that similar causes lay at the basis of the changes.

The period of the second millennium up to at least the thirteenth century B.C. was the age of western preponderance in Eastern Europe. The various groups that sprang up there early in the millennium bore a more or less marked imprint of either the Corded Ware/Battle-axe assemblage or the Globular Amphora culture. In most regions the influence of the western cultures was lasting, in spite of later events and later tribal movements.

The northern part of the east European forest zone was not affected by the western cultures, except for the east Baltic region, where the

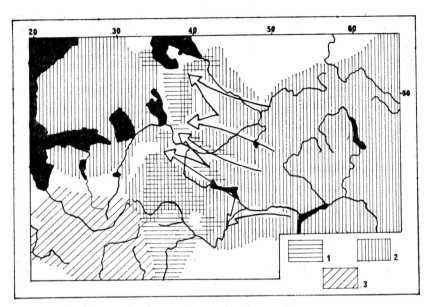

MAP XVIII The western drive, in the late second millennium B.C., of peoples of the 'Eastern assemblage' and of West Siberia.
(1) Volga-Oka tribes mostly submerged by the expanding eastern peoples; (2) expanding Kama-Ural peoples and (in the East Baltic area) peoples of the Combed Ware culture, both of Finno-Ugrian stock; (3) the Dnieper-Desna culture, presumably of Baltic peoples of Indo-European stock. After P. N. Tretiakov (*Sovetskaya Etnografiya*, vol. 1961–2, p. 88, fig. 2).

Boat-axe cultures were formed. However, discussion on the 'Arctic' cultures of these regions has shown that around the fourteenth and thirteenth centuries B.C., or perhaps still later, they were affected by an influx of new eastern tribes, who advanced into their territories by some northern route from the west Siberian forest zone.

The western drive of these tribes was not an isolated phenomenon. It formed part of the advance of the eastern peoples into Europe along the whole Eurasiatic border, from the Northern Urals to the Caspian Sea, which took place during the last quarter of the second millennium B.C. A map by P.N. Tretiakov (Map XVIII) illustrates well its final effect within the east European forest zone. The whole 'Arctic' region and the Volga-Oka territory, except for the area of the Belev culture in the south-west, were occupied by the eastern newcomers. Further south, in the steppe country, the expansion reached the Lower Dnieper, and its effects were felt as far west as Central Europe (Map XXI).

It is of interest to note that the territory seized by the eastern wave at the end of the second millennium B.C., including the East Baltic area within which the Boat-axe people were absorbed by the natives of the Combed Ware culture, corresponds almost exactly with the area peopled by the Finno-Ugrian tribes before the great Slavonic expansion in the second half of the first millennium of the Christian era.[63] On the other hand, the early typonymy of the territory of the Dnieper-Desna culture, as shown by recent studies,[64] bears a marked 'Baltic' character. This circumstance suggests that the people of the Dnieper-Desna culture must have been some proto-Baltic tribes; this formerly large group of Indo-Europeans is at present represented only by the Lithuanians and the Latvians.

References

1 E. Sturms, *Bericht über den V. internationalen Kongress f. Vor und Frühgeschichte.* Berlin, 1961. p. 779 ff.
2 L. Kilian, *Haffküstenkultur und Ursprung der Balten.* Bonn, 1955; and J. Żurek, 'Osada z młodszej epoki kammiennej w Rzucewie i kultura rzucewska' ('The Settlement of the Late Stone Age at Rzucevo and the Rzucewo culture'). *Fontes Archaeologicae Posnanienses*, Vol. IV, 1953.
3 V.G. Childe, in the *7th Annual Report of the Institute of Archaeology*, London, 1951.
4 A.Ia. Briusov, in *Rapports et Informations*, 1962.
5 H. Moora, in *Voprosy etnicheskoy istorii*, 1956.
6 I. Bona, 'Chronologie der Hortfunde vom Koszider Typus'. *Acta Archaeologica Ac. Sc. Hungaricae*, Vol. IX, 1958.
7 A. Vulpe, *Dacia*, Vol. NS V, 1961, p. 105 ff.
8 I.K. Swiesznikow, *Archeologia Polski*, Vol. XII, 1967, pp. 39–107.
9 A. Gardawski, 'Plemiona kultury trzcinieckiej w Polsce' ('Tribes of the Trzciniec Culture in Poland'). *Materiały Starożytne*, Vol. V, 1959.
10 V.A. Ilinskaya, KSIAK 10, 1960.
11 T. Wiślański, *Kultura amfor kulistych w Polsce północno-zachodniej.* Wrocław-Warszawa-Kraków, 1966.
12 N. Petkov, *Arkheologiya*, Vol. III-4, Sofia 1961, p. 67 ff.
13 A. Prox, *Die Schneckenbergkultur.* Kronstadt, 1941.
14 V.G. Childe, *The Dawn of European Civilization*, 5th ed., London, 1950, p. 191.
15 I.I. Artemenko.
16 A.F. Dubynin, MIA 130, 1965.
17 D.A. Kraynov, SVOD; N.N. Gurina, MIA 110, p. 135, fig. 36.
18 L.Ia. Krizhevskaya, SA 1962-2.
19 V.N. Chernetsov, MIA 35, 1953.
20 J. Kowalczyk, *Wiadomości Archeologiczne*, Vol. XXIII, Warsaw, 1956, p. 47, Fig. 18 (map).
21 R. Pittioni, *Urgeschichte des österreichischen Raumes.* Vienna 1954.
22 *Istoria Romíniei*, Vol. I. Bucharest 1960, p. 98, Pl. IX (map).
23 T.S. Passek, 1949.
24 K. Bernjakovič, Slovenská Archeológia, Vol. VIII-2. Bratislava 1960, p. 390, Pl. XIII.
25 A.C. Florescu, *Archeologia Moldovei*, Vols. II-III, Iaşi 1964, p. 178, Fig. 22.
26 T.S. Passek, MIA 84, 1961.
27 Carbon–14 date of a hut at Maiaki near Odessa, supposed to have been Usatovian, is 2390 B.C. (LE–645); however, the type of the hut (a pit-dwelling) and its date are against such an attribution.
28 M.M. Shmaglii, AK, Vol. XX, 1966. T.S. Passek and others.
29 I.K. Svieshnikov, AP, Vol. IV, 1952.
30 V.A. Ilinskaya, AK, Vol. X, 1957; S.S. Berezanska, KSIAK 10, 1960.
31 S.S. Berezanska, AK, Vol. XI, 1957.

32 I.I. Artemenko.
33 I.I. Artemenko, MIA 130, 1965.
34 T.S. Passek, I.I. Artemenko.
35 D.A. Kraynov.
36 D.A. Kraynov, SVOD 20, 1964.
37 D.A. Kraynov, AO for 1965.
38 D.A. Kraynov, SVOD, 1964.
39 O.N. Bahder.
40 O.A. Krivtsova-Grakova, KSIIMK 17, 1947; P.M. Kozhin, SA 1963-3; P.D. Stepanov, MIA 80, 1960.
41 M. Stenberger, *Swiatowit*, Vol. XXIII, 1960, p. 201 ff.
42 O.N. Bahder.
43 O.N. Bahder.
44 A.Ia. Briusov, I.K. Tsvetkova.
45 A.Ia. Briusov.
46 H. Moora.
47 L. Jaanits.
48 Montelius.
49 M.E. Foss.
50 M. Gimbutas, PPS, Vol. XIX, 1953, p. 112.
51 T.B. Popova.
52 A.A. Yerusalimskaya, SA 1952-2
53 A.A. Yerusalimskaya, as above.
54 M.I. Artamonov, SA, Vol. XI, 1949.
55 V.G. Childe, *The Danube in Prehistory*. Oxford, 1929, p. 212.
56 T.B. Popova.
57 E.I. Krupnov; V.I. Markowin.
58 O.N. Bahder.
59 A.M. Tallgren, ESA IX, 1934.
60 V.A. Kuftin; O.M. Dzhaparidze, SA 1964-2.
61 C.F.A. Schaeffer, *Antiquity*, Vol. XVII, 1943, p. 183 ff.
62 E.H. Minns, 'Trialeti', *Antiquity*, Vol. XVII, 1943, p. 129 ff.
63 P.N. Tretiakov. *Istoria, Folklor, Iskusstvo Slavyanskikh Naradov*. Moscow 1963. 5th Internat. Congress of the Slavists in Sofia.
64 V.N. Toporov and O.N. Trubachev, *Lingvicheskii analiz gidronimov verkhneg Podneprovia*. Moscow, 1962; and several contributions by V.V. Siedov in various periodicals. See also: P.N. Tretiakov, *Finno-Ugry, Balty i Slavyane na Dnepre i Volge*. Moscow-Leningrad, 1966; and J. Antoniewicz, 'Tribal Territories of the Baltic Peoples in the Hallstatt-La Tène and Roman Periods in the Light of Archaeology and Typonymy', *Acta Baltico-Slavica*, Vol. 4, Białystok, 1966.

4

The Shadow of the Rising East

The Second Millennium B.C.

THE COUNTRY EAST OF THE VOLGA AND THE URALS

CHAPTER III covered the development of east Europe during the Early and Middle Bronze Age, the second millennium up to about the thirteenth century B.C. The hallmark of the period was the expansion of the Central European Corded Ware/Battle-axe assemblage and Globular Amphora culture, which reached most parts of the country and left a lasting influence.

In the thirteenth century B.C. events occurred with far-reaching consequences for the cultural evolution and history of Eastern Europe. At that time several West Siberian tribes crossed the border and penetrated deep into the country, displacing the local tribes and causing considerable changes. They affected the easternmost part of Europe, the forest zone of the Kama-Ural region, and the steppe on the Lower Volga further south.

The starting point of unrest must be sought somewhere deep in Siberia, but its roots most probably lay in the South Urals. That country and West Siberia are very rich in deposits of copper, tin and other metals. These were presumably sought by the Aegean or Trojan prospectors and traders, who seem to have been chief agents in the development of the metal industry in the Urals and West Siberia that subsequently became the source of power of the local peoples.

One of the specific features of the second millennium was the considerable expansion of trade. The diffusion and concentrations of objects of alien origin, often imported from distant countries, found in graves and settlements indicate the main trading centres of the past and the main trading routes. Besides the overland trade, ample evidence exists for a sea-borne trade that provided foreign luxuries for the members of the ruling classes of the regions concerned. The special importance of the overseas trade lay in the very fact of the contact of the native population with foreign traders, or prospectors, who were representatives of the much higher Aegean civilization. Their impact on the local population and also on the further development in Eastern Europe was undeniably deep and far-reaching.

The territory of the Kama-Ural cultures, which were the core of the Eastern assemblage, extended over the east Russian forest zone from the river Vetluga, a northern tributary of the Middle Volga, in the west beyond the Middle and Northern Urals in the east. The huge but sparsely inhabited north-east European virgin forests—the 'Taiga' forests between the Pechora and its tributaries and the Ob east of the Northern Urals—also formed part of this territory (Map XIV).

Several local groups have been distinguished there during the second millennium B.C., but only the three most important of these are of interest here; they are the Kazan culture on the Middle Volga and the Lower Kama in the west, the Middle Kama (Turbino) culture in the centre, and the Gorbunovo culture east of the Middle Urals. A characteristic feature of these cultures, and also of the smaller groups further north in the taiga, was their almost purely Neolithic character, which they maintained up to the end of the second millennium. By the middle of the millennium, however, some of the southern tribes had learned animal husbandry and some forms of primitive agriculture. But these new forms of economy were still of secondary importance to fishing and hunting.

THE KAZAN CULTURE

The domain of the Kazan culture was the area along the Lower Kama and the Middle Volga (Map XIV: XVI). Southwards it extended along the Volga up to Ulianovsk, though originally it probably reached the Samara bend of the Volga. The change of climate, from the Atlantic to the dry and warm sub-Boreal phase resulted in the gradual advance of the steppe, the northern boundary of which moved some 90–125 miles north of its present position. The consequential advance of the steppe peoples forced the forest dwellers to retreat, and during the first half of the second millennium B.C. large parts of the southern division of the culture were lost to the Poltavka culture.

The gradual retreat of the fishermen and hunters of the Kazan culture continued during the later part of the second millennium. The impact of the Srubnaya culture, which in the meantime had replaced the Poltavka culture, on the Kazan tribes[1] is well reflected by the Kazan pottery of the third period; for it shows a marked tendency towards a flat-based type of vessel, often decorated only on the upper part in the Srubnaya fashion.

According to stratigraphic evidence (at the sites of Observatoria III, and Zaimishchi IIIa) the development of the Kazan Neolithic culture (see p. 105) was divided into three periods. The first dates entirely to the third millennium and the beginning of the second, and the two later periods to the first half of the second millennium (Table 4). The appearance in sites of the two latter periods of pottery characteristic of the early stage of the Balakhna culture is important for the dating of these periods (see p. 105); according to the scholars concerned there was an influx in the eighteenth century B.C. of the Balakhna tribes, which retreated eastwards from their former base somewhere on the Lower Oka, under the pressure of the advancing 'Fatyanovians', in fact proto-Balanovian tribes (Map XIV: IX).

The Upper Neolithic level (horizon) of site Observatoria III and the lower horizon of Zaimishchi were characteristic of the third period of the Kazan Neolithic, approximately the second quarter of the second millennium B.C. (Fig. 27). Its semi-pit dwellings differed from those of the preceding stages, being quadrangular in plan; they often had two hearths and were inter-connected with corridors sunk in the ground. The pottery was still Neolithic in character; vessels had a rounded or pointed base. The characteristic decorative patterns consisted of cross-hatched lines impressed with a toothed stamp, and zonal patterns were also popular. However, the influence of the pressing Srubnaya culture is already reflected in this pottery.

The economy of the Kazan population was also affected by the Srubnaya culture. It was still, as before, based on fishing and hunting, but in the third period traces of animal husbandry and agriculture have been noticed, evidently adopted from the Srubnaya culture.

The earliest copper objects found in the area were of North Caucasian origin, probably of the eighteenth century B.C. (Table 9). They belonged to the second period of the Kazan Neolithic culture. During the third period the local industry had begun to develop, evidently under the North Caucasian influence. At that time two local types of copper shaft-hole axes appeared, called the 'Fatyanovo' and the 'Kama' types, and both were derived from North Caucasian prototypes. The centre of their production lay probably somewhere on the Middle Volga east of Kazan and on the junction of the Kama with the Volga. The axes were cast of copper smelted from local ores.

About the middle of the second millennium the Kazan Neolithic culture gradually changed into the Kazan Bronze Age culture, which continued to the early first millennium B.C.[2] About the middle of the second millennium the whole south of the former Kazan Neolithic, south of the Lower Kama and its junction with the Volga, was lost partly to the Srubnaya culture and partly to the Andronovo culture. The remaining territory of the culture was also considerably influenced. The adoption of the flat-based pottery (Fig. 59), of some decorative motifs, and some other elements characteristic of the Srubnaya culture, were among its results. According to many scholars

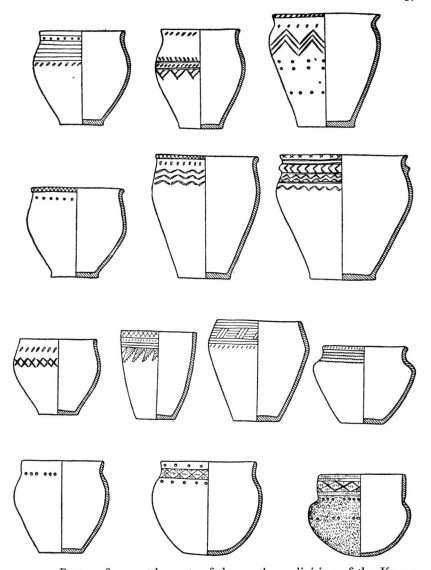

FIG. 59. Pottery from settlements of the southern division of the Kazan Bronze Age culture, with a strong Srubnaya imprint. After N. F. Kalinin and A. Kh. Khalikov (MIA 42, 1954, p. 182, fig. 13).

the transformation of the Kazan Neolithic culture into that of the Bronze Age was due to the impact of the Srubnaya culture.

Some Andronovo influence in the formation of the Kazan Bronze Age culture must also be taken into account. The Andronovo tribes, like those of the Srubnaya culture, also advanced northwards into the area east of the Volga along the Urals. They reached the Volga at some points, but were later driven off by the Srubnaya tribes. In this respect, the site at Khriashchevka, close to the junction of the Susnak with the Volga and situated within the former territory of the Kazan Neolithic culture, is of interest. The settlement, which was well protected by the meandering river and the defensive construction around it, had two occupation layers. The pottery of the lower one was a genuine Andronovo ware, whereas in the upper layer both Andronovo and Srubnaya pottery appeared together. A bronze socketed arrow-head found in the upper layer indicates its date, the early first millennium B.C. The settlement had two cemeteries; in the earlier of these only Andronovo burials were uncovered, but the dominant type in the other were Srubnaya graves.

The turbulence of the period during which the Kazan Bronze Age culture developed is indicated by significant changes in the positions of several of its settlements. Sites to which the access was rather difficult were often selected, and some also had defensive constructions. The great number of copper and bronze weapons (mainly of the 'Seima' type) found in hoards or as isolated stray objects, is also significant of a troubled period. In the Kazan territory—in contrast to the area on the Middle Kama (the Turbino culture) or further west (the Seima cemetery)—they were never found in graves or settlements.

Over 100 sites of the culture have been recorded. In Zaimishchi III two occupation levels have been distinguished, both of the Kazan Bronze Age culture. The lower horizon, dated approximately to the middle of the third quarter of the second millennium, and the remains of the upper horizon were of the last quarter of the second and the beginning of the first millennium B.C.

During the early period, traditions of the local Neolithic were maintained. Hunting and fishing were still as important to the economy of the population as stock-breeding and primitive agriculture, but importance of the latter two steadily increased. Cows, sheep, and horses were reared. The huts were semi-subterranean arid quadrangular in plan, as before, and had a two-eaved roof supported by one or two rows of posts placed along the axis of the hut. Huts were often interconnected.

The impact of the Srubnaya culture affected almost all areas of the culture. The local egg-shaped vessels were gradually replaced by

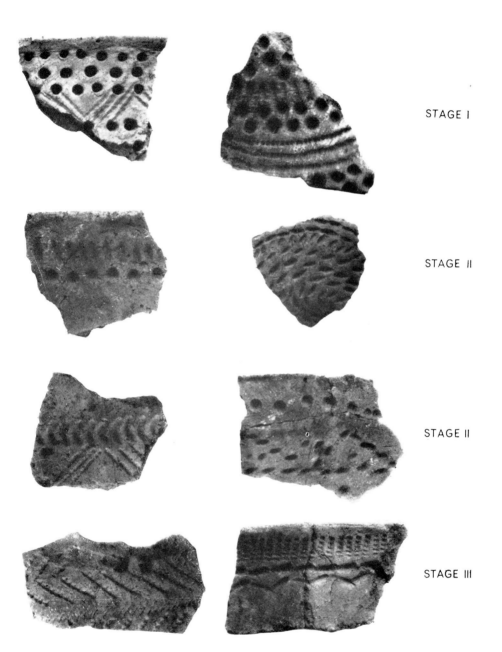

STAGE I

STAGE II

STAGE II

STAGE III

xxxi Examples of pottery of the three stages of the Balakhna culture.
National Museum, Stockholm.

xxxII Wooden ladle and a wooden sculpture of
an elk, from the Gorbunovo peat-bog.
After A.Ia. Briusov, *Po sledam drevnikh kultur*,
Moscow, 1954, p. 152.

xxxIII Bronze (copper) knife or dagger, mace-head
and 'arrow-straightener' characteristic of the Catacomb culture.
After T.B. Popova, *Plemena Katakombnoy Kultury*, 1955,
pl. VII, VIII.

flat-based pots, and in the southern area the Srubnaya influence was supplemented by Andronovo elements. Tools were made of flint and of other varieties of stone, and did not differ substantially from those of the preceding 'Neolithic' culture; though some new types appeared, such as arrow-heads of the Srubnaya type. There was a gradual decline in flint technique as the use of metal implements increased. Local metallurgy continued to develop, and copper was smelted from local copper ores. Copper slag and small clay crucibles were discovered in a series of Bronze Age sites.

The metal industry of the Kazan culture has often been mistaken for that of the Abashevo culture (see p. 295), or simply called the Abashevo industry. Both industries concentrated on copper objects, bronze objects being a rarity. Abashevo influence has been detected in the remains of the Kazan Bronze Age culture, but relations between them remain obscure.

Lumps of iron have been found in sites of the latest stages of the Kazan Bronze Age culture, and these findings indicate that the respective sites could not have been earlier than the eighth century B.C. The culture survived until the formation of the Ananino culture, which occupied the area in the Early Iron Age. This culture was formed around the eighth century, and embraced the territories of the Kazan culture and the adjoining kindred Middle Kama (Turbino) culture. The Kazan culture, however, was the main substratum out of which the Ananino culture evolved, together with various outside influences, one of which was the Abashevo culture.

THE TURBINO CULTURE

The eastern neighbour of the Kazan culture was the Middle Kama Neolithic culture, and that was followed by the 'Turbino' culture, called after an important site (Map XIV: XIV). The culture was a development of its Neolithic predecessor and extended approximately over the same area—mainly along the Middle Kama and the Lower Chusovaya, a tributary of the Kama, reaching southwards nearly to the junction of the Belaya with the Kama about 200 miles south of Perm (see p. 105). Over eighty habitation sites and cemeteries of the culture have been recorded so far.

The population was engaged in fishing and hunting, no traces whatever have been found of animal husbandry or agricultural activities, and lived in small hamlets consisting of a few huts. They formed two large groups—one in the region of Perm, the other in the region of Osa further south. Huts were rectangular in plan, of semi-pit dwelling type, and often interconnected by sunken corridors. They were of the same type as those of the Kazan culture on the Middle Volga.

18

The development of the Turbino culture has been divided into two periods[3]—the 'Garinskii' period (after the site at Gari), and the 'Borskii' period (after sites II, III and IV at Bor). The earlier period lasted from the fifteenth to the thirteenth centuries B.C. Its pottery retained a Neolithic character alongside a new variety made of clay paste tempered with some organic substance. A talc-gritted ware was also found in a series of sites; it was evidently brought from the other side of the Urals, from the territory of the Gorbunovo culture. Tools, made of flint, schist and other varieties of stone, do not differ substantially from those of the preceding Neolithic period.

The country on the Middle Kama has plenty of poor-quality copper ores, but it was only by the very end of the period that smelting of local ores began; this was revealed by spectral analyses of copper objects excavated in the habitation sites of Bor I and Vystelizhna. Metal objects appeared in the Garinskii period mainly in the cemeteries (Table 9). The most richly endowed was the cemetery of Turbino. The metal ornaments and weapons found in its graves differed from those excavated in settlements.

The cemetery of Turbino was one of the most important remains of East Europe at that time. In fact, there were two distinct cemeteries situated on low hills facing each other. One of these, Turbino II, was almost completely ruined by the modern village set up on its site; it was of a later date than the other one, but there could not have been a great time lag between them.

The cemetry consisted of about 200 graves, the skeletons of which had decayed entirely. Graves were richly furnished with metal objects (Fig. 60). Among these were twelve bronze or copper lance-heads and one of silver, all of the Seima type, some with an open socket; forty-four socketed celts with no loop, some of them decorated; some flat axes of the Andronovo type; shaft-hole axes of the Kama type; gouges; and forty knives and daggers, many of them of the Srubnaya type though considered to have been produced locally. There was a large group of objects of personal adornment: bracelets similar to those of the Abashevo culture, some made of silver; and many ear-rings or temple ornaments, some of these very similar to those of the hoard from Verkhnii-Kizil of the Abashevo culture. There were also thirty-six rings of nephrite and serpentine, one axe of diorite and many flint arrow-heads and knives. No pottery was found in any grave, but a few indefinable potsherds, which are considered to have been contemporary, were found within the area of the cemetery. Once traces of a tissue of white wool were found, the wool being of Andronovo origin.

The famous inward-curved bronze knife with figures of three rams on the handle, found in the cemetery II, was of the Karasuk type

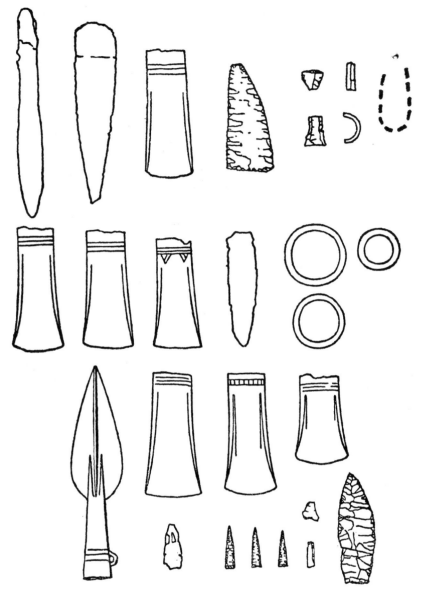

FIG. 60 Grave goods characteristic of the Turbino cemetery (from burials 62, 70, 108).

After O. N. Bahder (*Drevneyshie Metallurgi Priuralia*. Moscow 1964, p. 54, fig. 32).

(Pl. XXXIX) and was evidently of south Siberian or Altai origin. There will be further references to these bronze objects, which were mainly of the 'Seima' type, in the section devoted to the development of Ural and west Siberian metallurgy (see p. 310).

The first Turbino cemetery was in use in about the fourteenth and the thirteenth centuries B.C. O.N. Bahder is incorrect in dating it to the sixteenth and fifteenth centuries B.C. Both cemeteries have been considered to belong to the culture called after them. The spectral analysis of all metal objects found there implies, however, that the earliest specimens were exclusively of Siberian origin, and only the later ones were cast of copper smelted from local ore. The people buried in the cemeteries were eastern newcomers in the country[4] and alien to the local population who lived in the 'Turbino' settlements.

THE GORBUNOVO CULTURE

Further to the east, on the other side of the Middle Urals, lay the territory of the well known Gorbunovo culture (Map XIV: XV), dealt with already (see p. 103). The second stage of the Early Gorbunovo culture survived until about 1700 B.C. The changes which took place from that time up to about the thirteenth century B.C. occupied the Middle Gorbunovo period (Table 4). During the dry sub-Boreal climate of this period the steppe border gradually shifted about 90 to 125 miles northwards, just as it did on the western side of the Middle Urals; consequently the area was lost to the southern steppe peoples who entered it. The level of the lakes sank, and many of them became marshy bogs in which peat grew. In these circumstances fishing began to lose its predominance in the economy to hunting. This is demonstrated by tools found in the sites of the culture of the period, for objects connected with hunting considerably increased in number. Elk, reindeer and water birds were hunted. Gathering played an important role in providing additional food; hazel-nut shells were found in quantities, but mushrooms and fruits were undoubtedly collected.

Only a few semi-pit dwellings were uncovered (Kalmatskii Brod, Makushinskoe). In the middle layer of 'Section Six' of the Gorbunovo peat-bog, the standard site of the culture, there were the remains of wooden floors on which lay many tools, potsherds and also a number of carved wooden objects. Among the latter were a few primitive human figures, viper and water-bird sculptures, a wooden paddle, hooks, and a boomerang. Stone and bone tools were similar to those of the preceding period, flint scrapers being the most numerous. Many flint arrow-heads were of the Seima type. Also common were unperforated stone axes; and at Kalmatskii Brod there were stone 'arrow-straighteners' that differed somewhat from those of the Catacomb culture (see p. 223), though of the same period.

Among the few metal objects was a shaft-hole axe excavated in the middle layer of 'Section Six', and a copper awl of the 'Srubnaya' type. At Beregovaya 1 in the Gorbunovo peat-bog, a mould for casting socketed axes of the Seima type was found, as was a similar one at Tolstik on Lake Osetskoe. Some sites near the easily accessible outcrops of copper contained tools for crushing ore and crucibles for smelting (see p. 277). A number of stray socketed axes of the Seima type, and awls and knives of the Srubnaya and Andronovo types also belonged to this period (Table 17).

Flat based vessels differed from those of the preceding Early Gorbunovo period, and their decoration was new—striated bands, and small triangles and lozenges filled in with parallel impressions made by a toothed stamp. These motifs resemble those of the Andronovo culture.

Close connections were maintained, as before, with kindred tribes, in particular those of the Turbino culture on the Middle Kama. Contact with the Abashevo culture and the influence of the Andronovo culture are reflected on the decorative motifs of Gorbunovo pottery.

Remains very similar to those of the Gorbunovo culture also have been found further east, in the West Siberian forest zone on the Irtysh and the Ob (Table 17). Another small group of these extended along the Northern Sosva, a western tributary of the Ob. The northernmost settlement of this group[5], situated in the Northern Ural mountains at Ches-Tyi-Iag, consisted of a score of large, nearly square pit-dwellings. They ranged from twenty-nine feet six inches square to eight-two feet by eighty-five feet in size, and were ten to thirteen feet deep. Some vessels were sixteen to twenty inches in diameter; all had a pointed base, and neither in their shape or decoration did they differ much from those of the Gorbunovo culture. However, the decorative patterns of some vessels were characteristic of the Globular Amphora culture—horizontal zigzag lines separated by rows of short vertical incisions (Fig. 37). Another link with the Globular Amphorae (see p. 169) were flint chisels, nearly square in section, which were rare in these regions.

The settlement and other sites of the group have been dated to the second half of the third millennium B.C., but this date is doubtful. They may have been founded in the late third millennium, but the undeniable Globular Amphora elements indicate that the group must have still been in existence in the first half of the second millennium. The conditions in this remote northern region during the period of the warm sub-Boreal climate were undoubtedly much more favourable than they are at present. Furthermore, the Northern Ural mountains were most probably a tin-bearing region,[6] the deposits of which may have been completely worked out in the remote prehistoric past; this would, perhaps, explain the presence of the Globular Amphora elements.

THE STEPPE

THE POLTAVKA CULTURE

Traces of western influence are plainly discernible on the remains of the second millennium B.C. in the steppe country on the Lower Volga, and even further east up to the Altai. There, especially in the area between Saratov and Volgograd (Stalingrad), the ancient Yamnaya culture (see p. 132) underwent considerable changes under the impact of the Catacomb culture, its western neighbour. Consequently, around the eighteenth century B.C., the 'Poltavka' culture was formed (Map XIV: XVIII). It was named after a barrow-grave cemetery in the steppe on the Lower Volga, halfway between Saratov and Volgograd. The culture usually has been considered to have been the first stage in the development of its subsequent Srubnaya culture. Recently, however, it has been considered to be a distinct culture, and a predecessor, to the Srubnaya culture.[7]

Vessels characteristic of the Poltavka culture (Fig. 61; Pl. XXXVI: 1) evolved from those characteristic of the preceding Yamnaya culture, but at the same time show many influences from the Catacomb culture (flat bases), especially as regards their ornamentation. The latter consisted of impressions made by cord, twisted cords, or combed stamps, covering the whole surface of the vessel. Several pots have a slightly carinated body, a feature—in its more marked form—characteristic of the Srubnaya culture of the subsequent period. Flint axes, metal objects like gouges, flat knives or spear-heads, spiral ear-rings, and beads, mainly came from North Caucasian centres (Map XXI). However, a few graves like Kalinovka and Koltubanka, in which local foundry masters were buried, attest to a developed local foundry work. In these burials, moulds and crucibles were found among the grave goods; the moulds were for casting shaft-hole axes and other objects typical of the culture. The pottery found in these graves was typical of the Poltavka culture.

Other grave goods found in Poltavka burials—bone hammer-headed pins, beads, discs, arrow-heads, including those made of flint —do not differ from similar specimens found in graves of the Catacomb culture. However, stone battle-axes were an exception, being found only in a few burials.

The burial ritual differed from that of the Catacomb culture. Graves were mostly square or quadrangular shafts, very seldom pro-

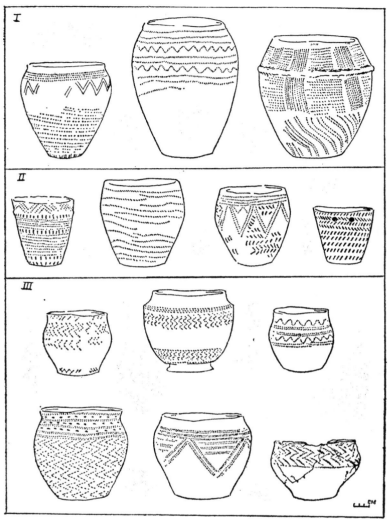

FIG. 61 Pottery typical of the Poltavka culture.
After N. K. Kachalova (ASE vol. 5, 1961, p. 38, fig. 2).

vided with a niche ('catacomb'), and were lined with oak planks or logs. A thin layer of ochre or chalk was spread over the floor, and often the corpse was similarly sprinkled. Corpses, heads mostly to the east, lay either in the 'Yamnaya' position on the back with legs contracted, or crouched. Besides the few grave goods mentioned and one or two vessels, the burials were also accompanied by bones of domesticated animals, mostly of sheep but also of cattle. Horse skulls were found in a few graves.

The economy of the population was based on stock-breeding and

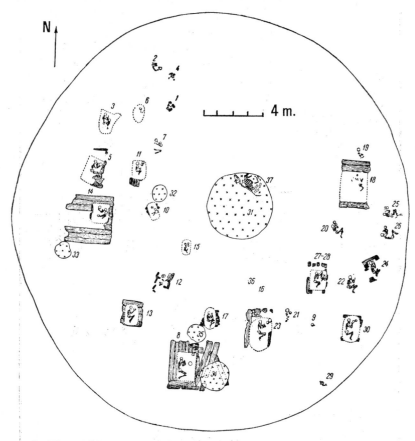

FIG. 62 Plan of barrow grave 5 at Yagodnoe near Kuibyshev, with its timber-lined graves of the Srubnaya culture. After N. Ia. Merpert (MIA 42 1954, p. 70, fig. 15).

pasturage. Traces of small settlements have been discovered in a number of sites situated close to the river banks, the remains imply the knowledge of a primitive form of agriculture. The population must have led a semi-settled mode of life. Anthropological study has revealed a rather mixed character—it was mainly of the 'Europoid' racial stock but included brachycephalic elements.

THE SRUBNAYA CULTURE

A notable change took place in the steppe on the Lower Volga around the fifteenth century B.C. The Poltavka culture gave way to the Srubnaya culture, and a new period in the development of the region began. The Russian name of the culture has often been rendered into English as the 'Timber-graves' culture[8] or the 'Timber-frame' culture[9] on account of the timber construction or lining of the tombs (Fig. 62). The name 'Srubnaya-Khvalinsk' culture has also been used, but only in relation to the remains of the culture on the Lower Volga.

We have already said that many scholars consider this period as the second in the development of the Srubnaya culture, the Poltavka culture representing its first stage. Those who look upon the Poltavka culture as a distinct culture seek the origin of the Srubnaya somewhere on the northern border of the steppe, in the region of Kuibyshev on the Samara bend of the Volga.

The development of the Srubnaya culture has been divided into three post-Poltavka stages, only the first of which concerns us here. It began in the fifteenth century and lasted till the thirteenth century B.C. (Table 4). The subsequent stage, usually called the Srubnaya-Khvalinsk culture, belongs to another age in east European development and will be dealt with in Chapter V.

The territory of the culture extended over an area larger than that of the Poltavka culture (Map XXIX: XV), and two main regions have been distinguished, the main one on the Lower Volga, the other extending eastwards over the region of Orenburg on the southern fringe of the South Urals. At a later date new groups of the culture were formed in consequence of the migration of Srubnaya tribes, or a gradual spread of Srubnaya colonists, into the neighbouring areas. One such group was a small one on the Lower Don to which the earthwork of Kobiakovo also belonged; its culture has many Catacomb elements, probably because it has assimilated the native population of the region.

The burial ritual of the Srubnaya culture during the first period does not show any marked difference to that of the preceding Poltavka culture (or period), but the grave goods are very different. The commonest vessel of the Poltavka pottery, a flat-based pot with a rounded body, fell from favour and was gradually replaced by wide-mouthed bowls or vases and pots with carinated bodies and everted rims (Fig. 63; Pl. XXXVI). Some were strikingly reminiscent of bowls from the Trzciniec and Komarów cultures. Their decoration consisted mainly of incised comb-stamped geometric patterns, horizontal lines, zigzags, and rows of hatched triangles and lozenges. Other grave goods were small tanged bronze knives (or daggers) of the Srubnaya type, awls, flint and bone arrow-heads, occasional temple ornaments, and bracelets (Fig. 64). Almost all graves had the remains of food in them, in the form of the bones of cattle, sheep or horses. Skeletons of horses were uncovered in a few graves.

The Srubnaya people evidently began to evolve a horse-riding steppe culture, undoubtedly under the influence of their eastern

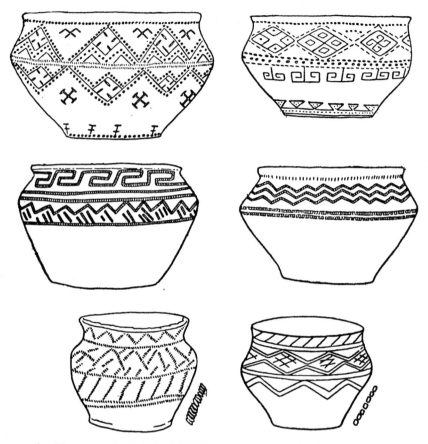

FIG. 63 Vessels typical of the Middle Don group of the Srubnaya culture. After O. A. Krivtsova-Grakova (MIA 46, 1945, p. 88, fig. 17).

neighbours, the Andronovo people of the west Siberian (Kazakhstan) steppes.

A number of settlements have been attributed to the early Srubnaya culture.[10] However, they all lay in the peripheral areas of the culture, in the forest-steppe zone, mainly near Kuibyshev in the valley of the Volga and the Samara and a number of smaller rivers of the region. Some other centres lay in the region south of Penza in the valley of the Upper Khoper, and still further west, on the Upper Don near Voronezh; both these concentrations were also within the forest-steppe zone. No settlements have been recorded further south among the pastoralists of the true steppe country; but barrow-graves have been investigated in the region of Saratov and further south, 185–370 miles from the northern settlements.

The earliest settlements were rather small in size, like Suskan II

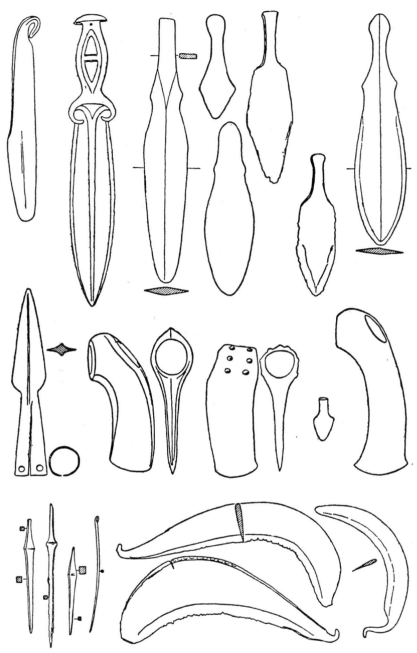

FIG. 64 Bronze tools and weapons characteristic of the Srubnaya culture of the steppe country on the Lower Volga and the country north of the Caucasus.
After O. A. Krivtsova-Grakova (as FIG. 63, pp. 55, 61, figs. 12, 14).

(Map XXIX: 25). The houses, about sixteen feet square, were sunk about twenty-eight inches into the ground, and had a hearth in the centre. The roof was supported by poles placed in the central part of the dwelling. The later settlements were larger, rectangular in plan, about twenty-nine feet six inches by twenty feet in size, and were also sunk in the ground; their walls were sometimes lined with timber, and they had two hearths each. Huts of three small hamlets at Mokshan, thirty-seven miles south-west of Penza were also sunk in the ground, and each had a hearth built of stones. Many cattle bones were found in these, and stone hoes and grain grinders proved the inhabitants' knowledge of a primitive agriculture.

The bowls reminiscent of the Komarów-Trzciniec type seem to suggest that a later, second western current had reached the territory of the Srubnaya culture on the Volga. Several personal ornaments of bronze were modelled on Central European types, for example, elongated temple ornaments with flattened and overlapping terminals, or bracelets with spiral terminals; the latter were very popular in the next period, but they differed from their western prototypes in that the spirals there were wound differently. These ornaments, like other metal objects found in Srubnaya graves, were products of the South Ural metallurgical centre.

Strong links connected the culture with its eastern neighbour, the Andronovo culture of west Siberia. Similar bronze objects appeared in both, from the same south Ural centre. Genuine Andronovo pots were found in several Srubnaya burials on the Lower Volga, and many vessels were decorated in the Andronovo style. On the other hand, traces of Srubnaya penetration have been recorded in several sites in the South Urals, in the Andronovo territory. All these finds bear witness to tribal movements, probably warlike, which, however, did not result in major boundary changes between the two cultures. Traces of Srubnaya penetration have also been found in Southern Turkestan;[11] the migrants must have reached there along the eastern side of the Caspian Sea.

The Andronovians were evidently the aggressors. The advance of the Srubnaya tribes into the country of the Kazan Bronze Age culture (see p. 245), and their pressure on the Don-Manych group of the Catacomb culture (see p. 230), were undoubtedly caused by the activities of the Andronovians, as was the Srubnaya drive into the central territory of the Catacomb culture west of the Don and into the forest zone further north, which took place in the thirteenth century B.C. The upheaval that followed these tribal movements destroyed the Trojan or Mycenean trade (see p. 287) and cut the age-old connections of the North Caucasus with the East European steppe (Map XXII).

THE ANDRONOVO CULTURE

The eastern neighbour of the Srubnaya culture was the Andronovo culture, called after a village north-west of Krasnoyarsk in Siberia, in which a few graves were investigated. The site lay close to the north-eastern border of the culture called after it. The culture extended over a huge territory, which included the entire West Siberian steppe east of the river Ural up to the Altai mountains and the Yenissey valley, a distance of about 1,700 miles, and reached southwards to the river Amu-Daria, and even to Tashkent and the Pamir mountains (Maps XI and XIX). The culture spread southwards, however, later in its existence, when under pressure from the Karasuk culture (see p. 309) it had to abandon the areas east of the Irtysh up to the Yenissey. A smaller branch moved northwards into the forest-steppe zone between the rivers Tobol and Irtysh.

The Andronovo culture was a West Siberian culture, which developed outside Europe, the territory with which we are mainly concerned here; but the culture influenced the Srubnaya culture and had a bearing on the turn of events in East Europe, and so some attention should be given to it (Tables 4, 5).

The culture is considered to have flourished from the eighteenth or seventeenth centuries B.C. to the eighth century B.C., and four periods have been distinguished in its development.[12] The earliest of these, up to about 1500 B.C., was the formative period. Its sites have been recorded[13] only in three small areas, in Northern Kazakhstan, on the Yenissey in the east, and near the sources of the Irtysh. During the next, the 'Fedorovskii' period, the culture spread over a considerable area from the Urals in the west to the Altai mountains in the east; the period lasted from the fifteenth century to the thirteenth, and was followed by the 'Alakulskii' period (twelfth to ninth centuries), and the 'Zamaraevskii' period (ninth to eighth centuries). Pottery typical of the Fedorovskii and Alakulskii periods from Western Siberia is shown in Fig. 65. The beginning of the latter period was marked by a great upheaval which affected the whole steppe country; the eastern part of the territory was lost and the Andronovo culture spread southwards; but these periods are not of our concern here.

There was no uniformity in the burials ritual of the Andronovo culture, and its pottery shows both chronological and regional differences. Burial ritual and pottery also show tribal movements and displacement, though scholars differ as to their time and extent. Barrow graves are typical of the steppe country; and flat graves prevail in the forest-steppe zone, though they also appear in parts of the steppe close to its northern border and in the southern areas. Mounds

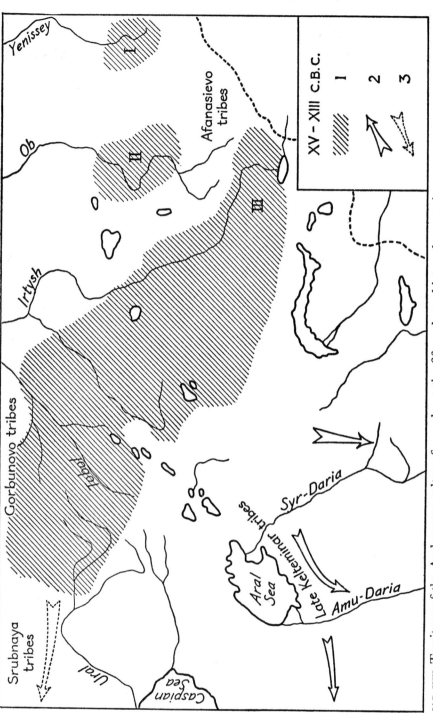

MAP XIX Territory of the Andronovo culture from about the fifteenth to thirteenth centuries B.C. (1) territory of the Andronovo culture of the Fedorovskaya type in the west; (2) direction of the southern expansion (or retreat) of the Andronovo tribes; (3) direction of the retreat of the Srubnaya tribes.

were mostly low, and in the west many had a stone circle, or 'cromlech', around the centre. Slab-cist burials were common. Skeletons were in a contracted position, and cremation was also practised. Grave goods consisted of pottery, personal ornaments and, only occasionally, tools and weapons. High pots similar to those of the Poltavka and Srubnaya cultures were common; they had well marked necks and everted rims. Another common vessel, the bowl, was similar but lower, and had an everted rim also. The usual decorative motifs consisted of triangles, rows of lozenges, meanders, and zigzag motifs (Fig. 65). In most graves bones of sheep, cattle, horses and even dogs were excavated, and often the entire skeleton of an animal.

A number of settlements were investigated, mostly in the forest-steppe zone or along the river valleys. Two were Carbon-14 dated: a grave in the settlement of Bobrikino near Shadrinsk north-west of the town of Kurgan, on the border of the Gorbunovo culture, was dated 1410 ±65 B.C. (LE. 276); and a settlement at Tasty-Butak near Aktiubinsk, near the bend of the Upper Ural river on the western confines of the culture, was dated 1250 B.C. (LE. 213) and 1550 B.C. (LE. 614) (another hut). All were of the Fedorovskii period.

Huts were of the semi-subterranean type and round, with the roof supported by a central post. Pottery, stone implements and animal bones were most common in the settlements excavated, with occasional bronze objects. The inhabitants were engaged in hoe agriculture and stock-breeding; cattle enclosures adjoined the dwellings. But the meat diet could not have been very plentiful as suggested by the material from the remains in the important settlements like Alekseevskoe on the Upper Tobol. Bones excavated were identified as those of twelve bovidae, eight horses, twenty-three sheep or goats, and one camel. There were also a few wild animals: a bison, red-deer, beaver, fox, two hares and three dogs. The settlement lasted for two or three centuries during the later stage of the culture, and the number of animals identified seems to be very small for such a long period.

A very important branch of the economy of several groups of the Andronovo people was metallurgy. Several metalliferous regions lay within the reach of the culture: part of the Southern Urals; the steppe along the Upper Ural river; the Western Altai mountains; and also the smaller Kazakhstan mountain ranges (Dzhekagan, Karatan). In all these regions rich deposits of copper, and in some also tin and gold (Stepnyak), were exploited, and traces of ancient mining operations and foundries have been recorded (Map XXVII). In some of these, metallurgical activities seem to have begun early in the second millennium B.C., in the pre-Andronovo period. This is suggested by a copper object, perhaps an awl, found at Karabalykty IX near

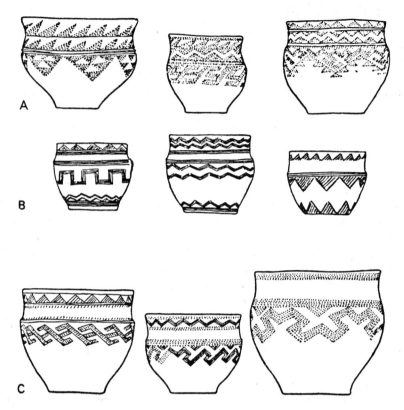

FIG. 65 Pottery of the Andronovo culture of West Siberia.
(A) Pottery of the Fedorovskii period of the Cheliabinsk steppe; (B)
pottery of the Alakulskii period of the same region; (C) pottery of the
Alakulskii period of Western Kazakhstan.
After M. N. Komarova (ASE vol. 5, 1961, p. 56, fig. 5).

Magnitogorsk in the Southern Urals, which lay on a bed of copper
ore together with pottery of the local late Neolithic type. In several
settlements (such as Alekseevskoe) moulds for casting bronze objects,
copper slag, various tools, pestles, crucibles and lumps of copper were
excavated, showing that copper was smelted there from local ores.
At the Shandasha site east of Orsk, also in the Southern Urals, remains of an Andronovo foundry have been found dating to the second
half of the second millennium B.C. A semi-pit dwelling, about twenty-
six feet by fifty-six feet and twenty inches deep, had its sides lined
with stone slabs; and two large hearths, sunk in the ground and
plastered with stones, were in the centre. The area was filled in with
cinders, charcoal, slag and drippings of copper, copper ore, stone

xxxiv Pottery characteristic of the Donetz group of the Catacomb culture. After T.B. Popova (as pl. xxxiii, p. 49, pl. ii.).

xxxv Vessels from burials of the Catacomb period at Snigurievka on the Ingulets, in the steppe west of the Dnieper.
Institute of Archaeology of the Ukrainian Academy, Kiev; excavated 1951.

XXXVI *Upper:* Vessel of the Poltavka culture from a burial at
Srednaya Akhtuba (no. 2039–141). *Lower:* Bowl from a secondary
burial of the Srubnaya culture in a barrow grave at Kalinovka
(no. 1741–57).
Institute of Archaeology of the Academy of the U.S.S.R. in Leningrad. V.P. Shilov, MIA 60, 1959, p. 409, fig. 35: 8.

moulds for casting the Srubnaya-Andronovo type of knives or daggers, and various stone implements. Little pottery was found in the hut. There must have been special social classes of miners, foundrymen and traders who were engaged in the diffusion of the products of the various centres.

The differences in the remains of the various regions of the Andronovo territory divide it into several regional groups, some of which differed considerably from each other. However, some authors[14] emphasize that there was a great uniformity in these remains throughout the whole territory, which was the outcome of the ancient connections between the cultures of this area in the period preceding the formation of the Andronovo culture. Connections between the Kelteminar culture in the region south of the Sea of Aral, within which the Tazabagyabskaya culture subsequently developed (considered as one of the Andronovo assemblage), and the Afanasievo culture on the Yenissey have been attested by beads made of *Curbicula fluvialis* shells found in the graves of the latter; the mollusc lives only in the river Amu-Daria. The Afanasievo culture is looked upon as one of the parent cultures of the Andronovo culture. Also, in the remains of the Afanasievo culture there were stone tools of Ural origin, which points to connections with that region. The Afanasievo pottery is reminiscent of that of the Yamnaya culture.

Recent investigators, however, consider that the 'Andronovo' culture was in fact only an assemblage of more or less distinct cultures; and that the groups or cultures of the Andronovo assemblage, after which periods in its development have been named, never extended over the whole territory attributed to the culture.[15] It is said that some of them developed during two subsequent periods but in different areas (for example, the Fedorovskaya group), which evidently implies tribal migrations. The differences in the archaeological material suggest that the Andronovo culture was the equivalent of two distinct ethical groups, the Indo-Europeans (Arians-Iranians) in the steppe country, and the Ugrians in the forest-steppe zone further north. It is said that a third group bordered them to the north-east, the Samoiedes, with whom the Samus culture[16] is connected (see p. 300).

Nevertheless, the distinctive 'Andronovo' features of the 'Andronovo' assemblage indicate that there must have been a unifying factor. This was evidently a western current, the source of which can be found in the Early Catacomb and the Poltavka cultures. Traces of this current have been recorded in all parts of the Andronovo territory.[17] The shape of a number of vessels and especially their decorative patterns, whether of the Tazabagyabskaya culture or found on the Yenissey, show unmistakable links with the Catacomb-

19

Poltavka pottery and its characteristic decorative patterns. Copper daggers and 'arrow-straighteners' of the Catacomb type were also found throughout the Andronovo territory. The rampart metal industry of the culture, based on extremely rich deposits, also developed under the western impulse, at first under that of the North Caucasian centre; the North Caucasian prospectors must have arrived before the Poltavka-Catacomb current, which followed the same route.

It has been emphasized[18] that the Tazabagyabskaya culture round the Sea of Aral showed only northern and north-western connections —those with other branches of the Andronovo and with the Srubnaya culture; it had no relations whatever with the highly developed agricultural communities in the south of Soviet Central Asia, Iran, or other countries of the ancient civilization of Western Asia. The elements of the Poltavka culture found in the Tazabagyabskaya culture imply that the latter must have been founded before the transformation of the Poltavka into the Srubnaya culture, before 1600 B.C. In the east, elements of the Catacomb culture have been found mainly in the remains of the late stage of the Afanasievo culture, which preceded the formation of the Semipalatinsk branch of the Andronovo culture.

The importance of the Andronovo culture lies also in that within its confines there was a development that later had far-reaching consequences. The Andronovians of the steppe country were the first people who kept horses not solely for the supply of meat but to ride; they gradually evolved a new type of steppe life, a highly mobile nomadism, which in the forthcoming millennia became a great menace not only to the ancient Oriental civilizations, but also to the settled peoples of Eastern and Central Europe.

THE ROLE OF TRADE

The significance of wide commercial connections crossing the borders of many prehistoric cultures and peoples has already been emphasized. The existence of prehistoric trade in this part of the Continent has often been mentioned by various authors. However, they have concentrated either on some of its aspects or dealt with it within very restricted areas in attributing trade activities to some undefined local inter-tribal relations.

The second millennium was a period of considerable growth in trade. Eastern Europe was widely travelled by Aegean traders and prospectors, or their Trojan agents, in search of raw materials, in particular metals, which were in great demand by the expanding Bronze Age cultures of the ancient Orient. Knowledge of the main trends and routes of this 'international' trade, traces of which are plainly distinguishable in many parts of the country, is indispensable for a proper understanding of the changes in the development of some local cultures, and especially for a proper understanding of the turn of events in the eastern section of Eastern Europe; otherwise many happenings will be unintelligible.

Archaeological material reveals that some forms of rudimentary trade must already have existed in Eastern Europe during the fourth millennium B.C. Trade then crossed the boundaries of smaller regions, but kept strictly within the limits of the larger provinces distinguished in the Early Neolithic. The main commodities were flint, obsidian in some regions, and copper. Small copper objects (fish-hooks, awls, sometimes beads) were found in several early Tripolyan settlements of period A. By the end of the fourth millennium the earliest copper hoards appeared in the south-western part of the Cucuteni-Tripolye territory (Hăbășești, Corbuna).[19] Transylvanian copper was later, during the third millennium, widely diffused over the whole greatly enlarged Tripolyan territory (Table 6). By the end of the millennium, large copper objects—flat axes, hammer-axes, axe/adzes—were found as far as Kiev on the Dnieper, and formed part of hoards (Horodnica).

Traces of early trade, which go back to the second half of the third millennium, are likewise plainly discernible in the countries east of the Dnieper, within the ancient 'Pontic' province (see pp. 115, 136). Several objects of Caucasian and west Asiatic origin were found in the cemetery of Mariupol, close to the coast of the Sea of Azov, and also further north in the region of the Dnieper rapids (Mykilske-Nikolskoe); there were pendants and mace-heads of porphyry, beads of marble, carnelian, and rock crystal, marble bracelets of the Nalchik type (Mykhailivka), and copper rings. They were also distributed along the Volga (Krivoluchie).

The four-foil clover-leaf shaped 'sanctuaries' characteristic of the Tripolyan huts of the Uman group (Fig. 16) may have been connected in some way with this trade. As already mentioned, they are strikingly similar in shape to the hearths in the huts of the Kura-Araxes culture of Georgia (Fig. 28); furthermore, their date tallies with that of the Caucasian trade of the third millennium (see p. 109).

The wealth displayed by the well known barrow graves of Maikop and Novosvobodnaya, recorded by many authors, was most probably the outcome of trading activities. It seems that the trade was based on the exploitation of North-west Caucasian copper deposits (Map XIII), and possibly also on the delivery of copper north of the Caucasus. Grave goods found in these burials show a wide range of connections with the west Asiatic countries: Iranian turquoise, lapis lazuli and probably carnelian; Mesopotamian imported axe/adzes and other weapons; and meerschaum and silver vases from Anatolia. Connections between Maikop and Troy II have been pointed out by many scholars, and they are useful for dating the Maikop grave, which must have been earlier than 2200 B.C., thus preceding the destruction of the city. Copper was probably the main commodity exported to the southern countries; from the North-west Caucasus it was probably transported along the river Kuban, through the territory held by the Maikop princes.

The cessation of the Trojan trade did not affect the overland connections of the North-west Caucasus with Iran and other west Asiatic countries. Imported objects originating from these countries formed part of the equipment of the richly endowed Novosvobodnaya 'royal' graves, and a number of weapons have a Sumerian or Mesopotamian pedigree, though they were probably made locally by North Caucasian coppersmiths.

The sudden break of North Caucasian trade relations with the west Asiatic countries, which occurred at the beginning of the second millennium, was most probably caused by the influx of the northern peoples who were responsible for the formation of the North Caucasian culture. It was only in the highland zone of the central part of the North Caucasus that connections with Transcaucasia were still maintained. It is of interest to note that the break had no effect in the areas on the other side of the main Caucasian ridge, where west Asiatic imported goods were found in the Trialeti barrow graves of the second millennium B.C. though the origin of the latter culture poses a problem.

The exploitation of North Caucasian copper deposits was not affected. It continued in new conditions and its centre seems to have gradually shifted towards the central part of the Caucasus. This was a period of boom for the North Caucasian metal industry (copper and arsenic bronze). It was at first worked on traditional lines, as indicated by objects in the copper hoard from Privolnoe, one of the earliest of the new period. Its products—flat axes, shaft-hole axes, massive gouges—closely related to those of the Maikop culture, were still exported northwards into the countries along the Volga. They also followed the ancient route along the northern coast of the Black Sea (Feodosiya) to the region on the mouth of the Dnieper liman (Adzhiask), and then further inland along the Dnieper (near Kherson, the settlement of Mykhailivka) up to the region of the Dnieper rapids (Mikhailovka near Dnepropetrovsk).[20]

From the second quarter of the second millennium B.C. onwards, the industry probably developed on new lines. Objects were cast in arsenic bronze as no tin was available. A series of specific North Caucasian types evolved, called 'Middle Kuban' types in the earlier archaeological literature; shaft-hole axes and objects of personal adornment decorated by a cast 'cord' ornament were characteristic of it. They were widely diffused over the whole territory of the Catacomb culture (Map XVII) and also reached countries beyond it (Map XXI). They have been found in graves of the Poltavka culture near Saratov, in the Fatyanovo and Balanovo burials in Central Russia and the Middle Volga, and even in the Gorbunovo peat-bog (middle layer of Section Six). North Caucasian shaft-hole axes and smaller objects were excavated from graves of the Dnieper-Desna culture in Byelorussia, and penetrated westwards to West Volhynia (hoard of Stubło), West Podolia (barrow grave of Ostapie), and even into the Bucovina (hoard of Prelipce); the latter hoard, which consisted of objects of Koszider type, dates the western expansion of the North Caucasian trade late into our stage II, and the 'cord-decorated' ornament from Ostapie dates the same period.

In the south-western part of Eastern Europe the turn of the third and second millennia marked a break in ancient trade relations similar to that noted in the Caucasus at about the same time. The flow of Transylvanian copper to the countries north and north-east of the Carpathians ceased altogether, probably because of events of a political character, as in the east. Possibly the drive of the Yamnaya tribes (see p. 129) across North Rumania and the Carpathians into the Hungarian Plain cut off the ancient supply route; but most probably migrations of the Corded Ware tribes were the cause.

The fact that Slovakian and east Alpine metal, and even metal (via Poland) from Saxony and Thuringia, appeared in the countries of the ancient 'western province' and the western part of the forest zone, seems to support rather the latter view. Central European Unetice-type flanged axes, silver, bronze or copper lock-rings, temple pendants, ear-rings, pins, and wide wrist-bands (Fig. 48) spread over the whole territory affected by the Battle-axe/Corded Ware assemblage up to the Volga (Map XX), and were adopted by local workshops. In the east, they were made of Caucasian metal or that from the Urals and the country on the Kama, or were often locally imitated in bone. They illustrate well the extent and the strength of the western impact on the East European cultures of the first half of the second millennium B.C.

Nothing is known of the organization of prehistoric trade in Eastern Europe. Its extent and volume imply that, at least from the end of the third millennium B.C., it could not have been—as suggested by some authors—a primitive form of barter between neighbouring tribes. It must have been in the hands of professional traders who had a good knowledge of the sources of supply; who were well aware of the value of the merchandise, especially of the semi-precious stones, gold and silver; who knew the outlets; who knew what east European products were in demand in the Mediterranean markets; and who were able to organize the transport and distribution of their commodities over wide areas. Evidently, they must have collaborated closely with, and bribed, the local chiefs in the countries concerned and in the countries through which they passed.

THE SEA-BORNE TRADE WITH THE AEGEAN

The second half of the third millennium B.C. witnessed the development of a new factor, the sea-borne trade of Eastern Europe with overseas countries, especially with Anatolia and the Aegean. The Maikop trade with Troy II seems already to have been sea-borne. But it was in the early second millennium that the sea-borne trade greatly expanded; its far-reaching consequences are reflected in the evolution of several important cultures of the North Pontic area and beyond it.

There were two main periods of expansion of the Aegean trade.[21] The first of these, the Cretan major expansion, occurred about 1850–1700 B.C. (MM I–II periods) when Crete enjoyed far-flung foreign contacts. The second period was that of the Mycenean trade, about 1550–1425 B.C. (LM I-II periods). Both expansions reached the North Pontic countries and left traces in their archaeological remains. The main agent of this trade to the Black Sea countries must have been the sixth city of Troy, which came into existence about 1800 B.C., presumably to handle this trade, and continued to about 1300 B.C.[22]

A.M. Tallgren, V.G. Childe[23] and several other scholars have often pointed out striking features in common between the Catacomb culture and the Aegean countries and Anatolia, which could only have reached the North Pontic area through Aegean or Trojan prospectors. Thus the idea of the 'catacomb' grave, just a pit-cave like the Aegean rock-cut chamber tombs, may have been introduced by traders who settled on the coast somewhere near the mouth of the Don or the Kuban. They also could have introduced the models for the winged beads of copper found in some Catacomb and North Caucasian graves, and perhaps also for the figurines of stone from North Caucasian tombs (Ulskii barrow grave). There may be connections with Iran, Hissar II, and also with the Cycladic settlements. It deserves mention in this context that Baltic amber, possibly of East Prussian origin, was found in the settlement Hissar IIIc,[24] which usually has been dated as c. 2000–1900 B.C. The 'arrow-straighteners' (Pl. XXXIII) found in several graves of the North Caucasian and Catacomb cultures, in graves of the Middle Dnieper and Fatyanovo cultures, and even in sites of the Gorbunovo culture in the Middle

Urals, may have been made locally after Aegean models. Hammer-headed pins may have been derived from Anatolia; they were very common in the Caucasus where they were cast in bronze (Table 19), and in the Catacomb culture where they were imitated in bone (Fig. 56). The latter have been often wrongly attributed to the Yamnaya culture. Hammer-headed pins have been found in the royal tombs of Alaca Hüyük in Anatolia, which date to the late third millennium B.C.

Other derivative items are the 'lamps' or 'incense burners' (Table 20), characteristic of the Catacomb and North Caucasian cultures. They have close parallels in the Slavonian and Pecsel cultures of Yugoslavia and Hungary, but the latter have no curved septum dividing the saucer into two compartments. On the other hand, cross-footed saucers excavated in the middle and upper layers of the settlement of Mykhailivka on the Lower Dnieper (see p. 135) do not differ in any respect from those of the Middle Danubian countries. Undecorated quadruped saucers were found in several settlements of the Uman group of the Tripolye culture of period C–1 (Toma-shivka, Popudnia), but no such vessels appear in earlier Tripolyan settlements (Table 10).

These vessels, whether Central or east European, were all approximately of the same period, 1800–1600 B.C., which suggests that they must all have been derived from a common source. Southern Aegean (Cypriot) and Middle Danubian (Mostičarska and Vučedol cultures) connections are also reflected in the striking similarities between the Tripolyan decorative style 'γ1' and the Middle Danubian pottery, but there are even more striking similarities between the Tripolyan and the Cypriot painted ware of the Middle Bronze Age (1800–1600 B.C.). The animal figurines painted on many Tripolyan vessels of period C–1 of the southern groups of the culture were perhaps also the result of the Aegean impulse (Fig. 39).

In the western part of the North Pontic area, the settlement of Usatovo (see p. 183) must have been an important centre of sea-borne trade with the Aegean, and especially with Troy VI, during the early stage in the development of that city (Map XX). The size of the settlement, its stone houses, the earliest in the North Pontic area, and the defensive wall round the town, point to its unique and outstanding position. Imported objects found in the ruins of the settlement and in the richly furnished barrow graves of its ruling class (Fig. 43), reflect wide overseas connections with the Aegean and Anatolia. The very strong ties linking the Usatovo settlement with these countries have been emphasized,[25] but it is difficult to ascertain what commodities were exported from the North Pontic lands.

The impact of the Cretan culture on the Usatovians, or at least on

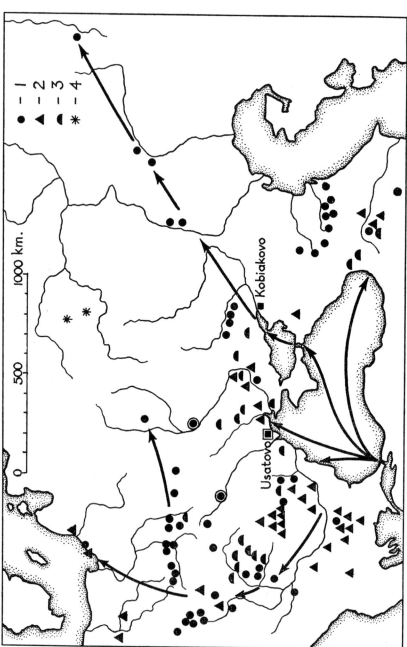

MAP xx Distribution throughout the eastern part of Central Europe, and in Eastern Europe, of Mediterranean goods in the mid-second millennium B.C., and the presumed routes of their diffusion.
(1) Faience and early blue glass (encircled) beads; (2) swords, daggers, shaft-hole axes, helmets, etc., and the Hittite figurine from Sernai (Schernen) on the Baltic coast; (3) objects of lead made decorated in the 'Myom

their ruling class, is illustrated by their acceptance of the cult of the bull; the corbelled grave chamber in one of the barrows also reflects the strength of the Aegean influence.

The second major expansion of the Aegean trade, this time of the Mycenean trade (1550–1425 B.C.), also left traces in the North Pontic lands, but more in Central Europe. In Eastern Europe, unlike the Cretan expansion, it only slightly affected the local cultures. The few decades during which the trade might have flourished were probably too short a period for any deeper penetration of the cultural influence. Nevertheless, in some parts of the country the Mycenean penetration had a far-reaching effect. The main agent of this trade must have been, as before, the sixth city of Troy.

Faience beads were one of the objects exported by the Trojans to Central and Eastern Europe (Map XX). The fact deserves mention that 157 faience beads of Mycenean or east Mediterranean derivation were found in Troy VI in levels dated around 1425 B.C.[26] Faience beads, including segmented specimens, were found in several graves of the Strzyzów culture in West Volhynia on the western border of Eastern Europe, and further east in a barrow grave of the Dnieper-Desna culture near Gomel; they were evidently distributed via the Danubian amber route, first being carried to Poland and then eastwards by the distributive channels of the trade in Central European (Unetice) bronze.

In the east, faience beads appear in North Caucasian and Catacomb graves, and further east in the Srubnaya burials on the Lower Volga and Andronovo burials in the Urals. They were concentrated in the centre of the North Caucasian metallurgical area of the period, around Nalchik and in the highland zone (Map XX). There, near Koban, a haematite seal of Syrian origin of about 1400 B.C. was also found. The other concentration of beads appears in the metalliferous region on the Donetz in the Ukraine, within the territory of the Catacomb culture. Their diffusion suggests that the main commodity sought by the Mycenean or Trojan traders was copper. There are many reasons to believe that these traders reached the metalliferous regions of the Southern Urals, and possibly some regions of West Siberia;[27] the rich deposits of these regions had previously been discovered by the North Caucasian metallurgist-prospectors and most probably exploited by them in the first half of the second millennium B.C. (Fig. 71). The overseas traders probably wanted mainly tin and gold. The sudden expansion of the South Ural bronze industry around the middle of the millennium was undoubtedly connected with the presence and activities of the overseas prospectors.

Faience beads found on the Lower Volga near Pokrovsk, in barrow graves near Uralsk on the river Ural, and on the Upper Tobol in

West Siberia (Map XX), point to the route followed by the presumed Mycenaeans or Trojans from its starting point somewhere near the mouth of the Don. Perhaps the earthwork of Kobiakovo, but more likely the earthwork of Liventsovka, or another Bronze Age settlement in the delta of the Don, was in some way connected with this trade and served as the main transit port.

Only a preliminary report has been published, so far, on investigation of the Liventsovka earthwork at Rostov-on-the-Don.[28] This was a fortress c. 660 by 500 feet in size, with strong defensive constructions built of stone on a very well conceived plan. On the outer side of the walls, in moats, over 500 flint arrow-heads have been found, which attests to an assault by a foe. The date of the fortress has been established at the mid second millennium B.C., precisely the time of the Mycenaean-Trojan penetration; the elaborate plan of the defensive constructions suggests that it was of Mediterranean origin.

The faience beads are of importance for the establishment of the date of the seizure of the Catacomb territory by the advancing Srubnaya tribes. At the time at which they were imported, at the latest by the end of the fifteenth century B.C., the Catacomb culture must have been still in possession of its homeland. Its ousting by the Srubnaya culture could have taken place at the earliest in the fourteenth century B.C.

Mycenaean weapons, and armour—swords, helmets—were found in many sites outside our area; in Rumania, where a golden sword was found, and further west in Central Europe.[29] A few were also recorded in Transcaucasia: an Early Mycenean sword from a grave at Samtavro, and a bronze lance from Trialeti (see p. 236). Connections of Western Transcaucasia with Syria and Eastern Mediterranean countries are to be found in a series of grave goods from the Trialeti barrow graves—golden discs, beads, and decorative motifs.[30]

Another group of imported Late Mycenaean goods of a different type consisted of a few stray double-axes found in the south of the Ukraine, and similar specimens that formed part of two hoards in the same area along with the bronze sickles and other objects. The traders all kept to the river Dnieper: some near the estuary, others along the valley up to the region of the rapids or the Dnieper bend. They must have reached the region before the expansion of the Srubnaya culture disrupted the age-old connections with the Aegean.

A number of stone battle-axes (Pl. XXXVII) and bronze weapons found in the Ukraine were decorated in the 'Mycenaean' style, or its derivative (Fig. 66). Among these was a socketed spear-head from Tsiurupinsk near Kherson, a tanged spear-head found near Dnepropetrovsk, and decorated objects from the silver hoard of Borodino (Map XX). A few more were mentioned by A.M. Tallgren who also

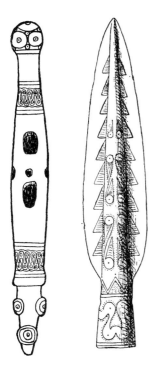

FIG. 66 Objects decorated in the 'Mycenaean' style. Bone cheek-piece from Bełz
north of Lwów (Lviv) (after T. Sulimirski,
Wiener Prähist. Zft vol. xxv, 1938, p. 143,
fig. 7). Bronze spear-head from Tsiurupinsk
near Kherson (after A. M. Tallgren, ESA
vol. xi, 1937, p. 117, fig. 7).

pointed out that the early east European steppe was subject to a strong prehistoric Oriental influence.

The Aegean, Mycenaean, or Trojan, trade mainly in metals with the remote parts of Eastern Europe, and also possibly with the centres in West Siberia, was most probably organized like the old Assyrian trade in Anatolia in the twentieth to eighteenth centuries B.C., which is well known from the cuneiform tablets from Kültepe in Central Anatolia.[31] The Assyrian traders had no influence on the local people in political and administrative matters, and were obliged to pay the local rulers a custom duty. Imports and exports were handled entirely by the Assyrians, but the princes in return for custom duty took measures to safeguard their life and property along the caravan routes. Nevertheless, they must have, in various ways, affected the culture of the indigenous peoples on their trade routes. K.F. Smirnov, in a special study points out that the pastoral tribes of the steppe country east of the Volga and of Kazakhstan had already used the horse as a draft animal put to the chariot in the Bronze Age. A relatively large number of cheek-pieces of that period, made of bone and antler were found in this area. The earliest ones, of the fifteenth and fourteenth centuries B.C., found in graves of the Srubnaya and Andronovo cultures, closely resemble those current at that time in the West Asiatic countries and Iran and Mycenae. Graves in which a pair of horses accompanied the buried chieftain point to the same conclusion. The same relates to cheek-pieces round in shape, made of antler, found at Balanbash in Bashkiria and near Kanev in the Ukraine.[32]

The question remains open as to the kind of goods sought by the Mycenaean or Trojan traders in the Ukraine, and what they received in exchange for imported metals and luxuries. Amber does not seem to have been among these. Amber beads and pendants have been found in several sites in the Ukraine: in Volhynian slab-cist graves, graves of the Sofiivka group near Kiev, barrow graves of the Middle Dnieper culture, and also in the settlement of Usatovo. But all these finds were of the early second millennium, and the Globular Amphora people seem to have been responsible for their distribution. The date of these finds tallies with that of the first expansion of the Aegean trade, and it seems that at that time amber might have been one of the commodities exported via Usatovo to Troy VI and the Aegean countries.

The amber trade with the Mediterranean flourished during the Mycenaean period, the middle of the second millennium. But at that time the Usatovo settlement was either no longer in existence, or had lost its importance; the main amber route led from the Baltic coast in East Prussia across Poland, and Moravia and along the Danube and the Black Sea to Troy VI. A bronze figurine of a Syrian god found at Šernai (Schernen) near Klaipeda (Memel), and a copper or bronze double-axe of the late Mycenaean trade from Sambia, both of the late fifteenth century B.C., point clearly to a Mycenaean trade in East Prussian amber.

EARLY METALLURGY IN THE KAMA-URAL REGION

Copper and tin, and their alloy, bronze, played an important role in the development of East European cultures in the second and first millennia B.C. Several scholars[33] have recently devoted special studies to the origin and diffusion of the various types of metal objects of that period, to the peculiarities of the technical processes of their production, and to the main metallurgical centres in East Europe and Siberia.

Copper was found in many regions of East Europe, some of which we have already dealt with (Map XIII). In the Caucasus, some areas of the South-eastern Ukraine, and almost everywhere in the Urals, copper ore was easily accessible, though ore of satisfactory quality was found in certain regions only. Traces of ancient mining have been recorded in several sites. There were wide artificial caves on the steep banks of the river Kama and its tributaries, which have been dug out in the search for ores. Traces of mining were found in the main ridge of the south Urals west of Magnitogorsk; ancient shafts up to sixty-six feet deep, and galleries up to 220 yards long, were uncovered.

Copper was smelted on the spot, close to the mines or outcrops; copper slag, moulds, crucibles and also pestles and hammers for crushing ore have been found at such sites or in hamlets nearby.

Ores from the various regions mentioned had impurities which the ancient founders were unable to eliminate. The impurities differed in various regions, and this factor enables the present-day specialists to distinguish the origin of copper or bronze objects found in various countries. The most common impurity was arsenic, a characteristic especially of Caucasian copper.

Copper was not hard enough for tools and weapons, and already in the third millennium B.C. it was alloyed with other metals to form bronze. Tin was the usual alloy, and the best; but tin, unlike copper, was not available in the Caucasus, and only in small quantities in the South Urals (mainly ninety-odd miles west of Cheliabinsk). Its richest deposits lay about 950 miles further east in the Altai mountains. In the Caucasus, arsenic was employed as a substitute, and thus Caucasian bronze objects are easily distinguishable. In many regions where no suitable substitute could be found, objects were still cast of pure copper up to the end of the second millennium B.C. One such region lay on the Middle Volga and the Kama, and included the metal industry of the Abashevo culture.

In this respect Table 6 showing the development of the metal industry (copper, arsenic and tin-bronze) in various parts of Eastern Europe is very instructive. Also instructive is the map of the diffusion of the products of the different East European metallurgical centres during the third and first half of the second millennia B.C. (Map XXI). The country west of the Dnieper, where no copper is available except for the meagre deposits in the westernmost part of Volhynia, was dependent mainly on Transylvanian or Balkan metal (as in the Tripolye culture); the areas further north were supplied by the Central European bronze industry. East of the Dnieper up to the Urals and beyond those mountains was the territory of the North Caucasian metallurgical centre; within this area objects made of impure arsenical copper, or cast of arsenic bronze, were widely distributed. All small flat knives, flat axes, square awls, and shaft-hole axes, found in the remains of the Catacomb and Poltavka cultures were of North Caucasian origin. Also Caucasian were the earliest copper objects of the Kazan Neolithic culture and the Kama culture (see p. 106), and a small copper knife found in the Shigir peat-

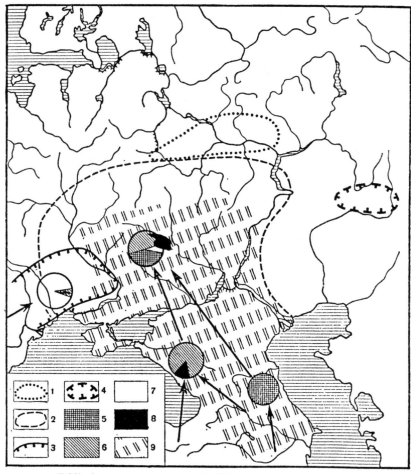

MAP XXI Diffusion of products of different metallurgical centres in Eastern Europe in the third millennium B.C. and the first half of the second millennium.

(1) Fatyanovo culture; (2) northern reach of the North Caucasian imported objects of arsenic bronze; (3) area of the predominantly Transylvanian copper objects (Tripolye culture); (4) area of the South Ural copper; (5) North-east Caucasian (Terek) copper; (6) North-west Caucasian (Kuban) copper; (7) so-called 'pure' copper; (8) Maikop copper with an admixture of nickel; (9) territory within which predominantly Caucasian metal objects were distributed.

After E. N. Chernykh (MIA 132, 1966, p. 88, map 3).

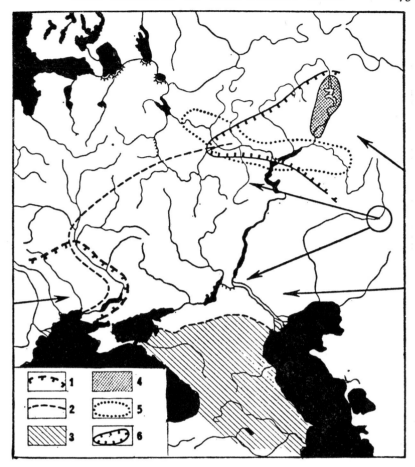

MAP XXII Diffusion of products of different metallurgical centres in Eastern Europe at the end of the second and early in the first millennia B.C.
(1) the so-called 'Cimmerian' group; (2) Srubnaya industry; (3) Caucasian industry; (4) metal objects of the Turbino settlements; (5) Abashevo industry; (6) Seima-Turbino industry.
After E. N. Chernykh (as MAP XXI, p. 89, fig. 4).

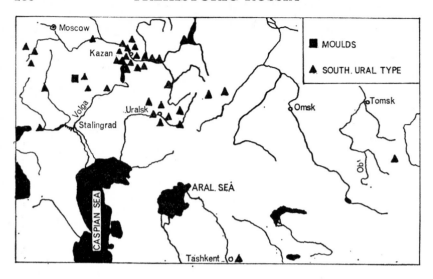

MAP XXIII Distribution of shaft-hole axes of the South Ural type.
Squares: a find of moulds for casting these axes.
After B. G. Tikhonov (MIA 90, 1960, p. 112, Pl. XIX).

bog in the layer of the second stage of the Early Gorbunovo culture
(see p. 103).

Of special interest are two burials, uncovered in barrow graves at
Kalinovka on the Volga, belonging to the Poltavka culture of about
1500 B.C. Foundry-masters were buried in these, along with the equipment needed for their craft: moulds of shaft-hole axes and flat axes,
nozzles, crucibles, etc. The graves imply that at that early time
itinerant foundry-masters had been working in some regions remote
from the metalliferous areas. They worked in Caucasian metal, according to the type of objects cast in their moulds.

A metal industry based on local ores began to develop in the
Southern Urals probably not later than 1800–1700 B.C. The earliest
centre seems to have been the region of Cheliabinsk, on the border
of the steppe and forest-steppe zones. The early products of this centre
were a further development of North Caucasian types—shaft-hole
axes (Map XXIII), and a variety of flat knives called the 'Srubnaya'
type. These products were diffused among the Srubnaya tribes on
the Lower Volga and the Andronovo tribes in West Siberia. This
suggests an early penetration by some Caucasian prospectors into the
Southern Urals. A series of Andronovo foundry settlements of the mid
second millennium B.C. have also been discovered south of the river
Ural, in the region of Orsk.[34]

THE SEIMA-TURBINO BRONZE INDUSTRY

Early centres of metallurgy, similarly based on copper smelted from local ores, developed on the Middle Volga and the Lower Kama, and also in the Middle Urals on the eastern side of the mountains. They were undoubtedly started by North Caucasian prospectors or traders, and their beginning cannot be put back beyond the second quarter of the second millennium B.C. Their products were at first a further development of North Caucasian types (Table 9). They were wrought or cast of almost pure copper. Among the most remarkable products of the centre on the Middle Volga were shaft-hole axes of two varieties called the 'Fatyanovo' and 'Kama' types after their westernmost and easternmost diffusion. They differ slightly from each other, though both were a development of the North Caucasian axes of similar type. An axe of Kama type was found in the middle layer of the Section Six site at the Gorbunovo peat-bog, of the Middle Gorbunovo culture; it is thought to have been a local Middle Ural product.

The Middle Ural industry was centred mainly in the southern part of the country. It worked on copper smelted from local ore, which was of a different type from that available on the western side of the Urals, on the Kama and the Middle Volga, being of a much higher quality and of a greater yield. The same raw material was available further south where, in the neighbouring area, the aforementioned South Ural centre developed.

Considerably later, by the end of the thirteenth century B.C. (see p. 321), the exploitation and smelting of local ore and the casting of copper tools was begun in the region on the Middle Kama. The industry of that region had only poor quality ores, and was always a kind of cottage industry working for local needs only.

The fifteenth century B.C. witnessed a great boom in the metallurgical industries of the Urals and the adjoining regions up to the Middle Volga, which is illustrated clearly by Table 9. However, as shown in Table 6, most areas still produced pure copper, or arsenic bronze in the Caucasus and the Ukraine; but in the South Urals, West Siberia, and the region on the Lower Volga, tin-bronze had already made its appearance. The demand for metal tools, weapons, and ornaments was undoubtedly one of the factors that fostered this development. However, it cannot satisfactorily explain the sudden progress of the industry, shown by newly acquired ability to produce the tin bronze, the appearance of entirely new products requiring high skill in making, and the use of an evolved casting technique hitherto completely unknown in the Urals or the neighbouring countries. No such advanced bronze industry, which was

20

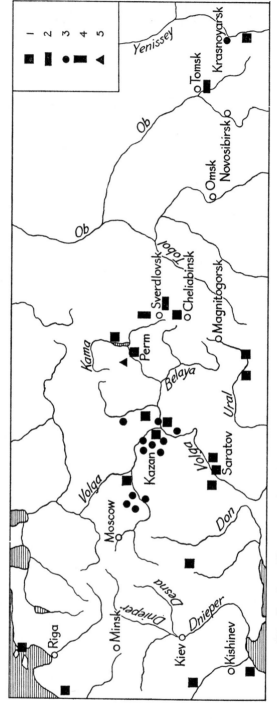

MAP XXIV Distribution of bronze socketed lance-heads of the 'Seima-Turbino type' with the pivot rhomboid in cross-section. (1) Lance-heads of 'group A'; (2) their moulds; (3) lance-heads of 'group b'; (4) their moulds; (5) lance-heads of 'group B'.
After B. G. Tikhonov (as MAP XXIII, p. 105, Pl. VI).

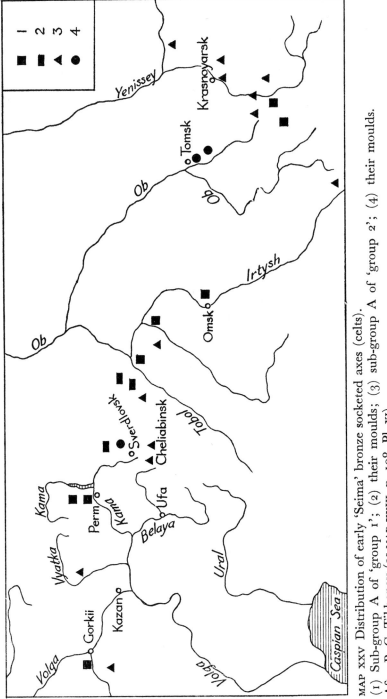

MAP XXV Distribution of early 'Seima' bronze socketed axes (celts).
(1) Sub-group A of 'group 1'; (2) their moulds; (3) sub-group A of 'group 2'; (4) their moulds.
After B. G. Tikhonov (as MAP XXIII, p. 108, Pl. XI).

also acquainted with silver, was in existence at that time in any region of Eastern Europe (except perhaps the Caucasus) or in West Siberia and the Minusinsk valley.

Large socketed lance-heads ten to sixteen inches long, of Seima type (Fig. 81) and socketed axes ('celts') of the so-called 'Turbino-Seima' type (Fig. 60) were among the most typical products of the Ural bronze industry. Other products were flat axes, wedges, shaft-hole axes, knives, daggers, bracelets and temple ornaments. We shall call this industry the 'Seima-Turbino' bronze industry, which does not mean that the objects were necessarily produced at these sites. Spectral analysis of the objects indicates that they were cast of copper of East Ural or West Siberian origin. The products of the industry differed from those of the Abashevo culture (see p. 295), but similar objects were produced by several foundries in West Siberia.

The original centre of the Seima-Turbino industry[35] must have been situated on the border of the South and Middle Urals, somewhere west of Cheliabinsk and Magnitogorsk (Maps XXI: 4; XXVII). This was a region rich in easily accessible deposits of copper, zinc, arsenic, gold and silver. Fuel for processing the ores and metals was available on the spot in this well wooded country. Small quantities of tin were available in the neighbouring region in the South Urals. The Chusovaya, Belaya and other rivers tributary to the Kama, the sources of which lay on the border of the area, provided easy connections with the countries on the western side of the Urals, on the Kama and the Middle Volga. Furthermore, the cast ornament of the Seima celts follows the decorative patterns characteristic of the local pottery of the region, which also support the suggestion that there was the original centre of the industry (Figs. 65, 67).

The products of the industry were widely diffused over the forest zone of Eastern Europe (Map XXII: 6) and spread also to West Siberia, where they were produced in local foundries. Their diffusion is shown in a series of maps by B.G. Tikhonov (Maps XXIV, XXV). However, the largest and most varied concentration of metal objects appears in the cemetery of Turbino on the Chusovaya near Perm (see p. 250).

The cemetery poses some important problems, some of which will be discussed later (see p. 321); our concern here is the origin of the Seima-Turbino metal industry and its main products, so well represented in the Turbino cemetery.

THE ORIGIN OF THE SEIMA-TURBINO INDUSTRY

It seems the necessary clue to the origin of the industry lies in the

Seima socketed lance-heads. They represent the earliest products of the new progressive industry in the Urals, as shown further below.

The lance-heads have been wrongly considered as local inventions of the Ural or Altai metallurgical centres. In fact no early socketed lance-heads, nor weapons which could be looked upon as their prototype, have been found in those regions; all known specimens discovered in East Kazakhstan are regarded as of 'western' (Ural) origin.[36]

On the other hand, very similar lance-heads or spear-heads and similar specimens with a folded (open) socket that were also produced in the Urals, were already well known and widely used in the Mediterranean countries—Syria, Palestine, etc.—at the end of the third millennium.[37] Childe points out that the folded sockets had been translated into cast sockets soon after 2000 B.C. in North Syria, and the improvement was soon adopted in Greece. It also gradually spread northwards. Socketed lance/or spear-heads were found at Alishar II in Anatolia (1900–1600 B.C.) and in Persian Talysh in the middle of the millennium. East Mediterranean socketed bronze lance-heads similar to those of the Seima type have also been found in Transcaucasia (as in the barrow grave XV at Trialeti), and it seems very likely that they reached the Urals not later than the mid-second millennium B.C. A decisive factor for establishing the origin of the Seima type is that its specimens have been found in barrow graves of the Poltavka culture, in the area presumably reached by the Trojan or Mycenaean trader-prospectors; the fact that these prospectors reached the area is indicated by faience beads found in the same region (Map XX) in graves, a little later in date, of the earliest stage of the Srubnaya culture or transitional from the Poltavka to the Srubnaya stage.

Three varieties of Seima lance-heads have been distinguished.[38] Those found in the remains of the Poltavka culture belonged to the variety 'A' and were evidently the earliest of all. These specimens, with the pivot of the blade rhomboid in section (Fig. 81), were found almost exclusively in the steppe country (Map XXIV) within reach of the Poltavka and Andronovo cultures. They seem to have been products of the South Ural centre.

Other varieties of the Seima type lance-heads have not been found in the steppe country, and were diffused only over the forest zone. None of these have been found in remains of a date comparable to that of the Poltavka culture, which implies that they must have been a further development of the original type. The Seima-Turbino socketed lance-heads of the mid-second millennium found in Eastern Europe (Fig. 60, Table 9), were undoubtedly an East Mediterranean type, introduced most probably by Trojan or Mycenaean prospectors,

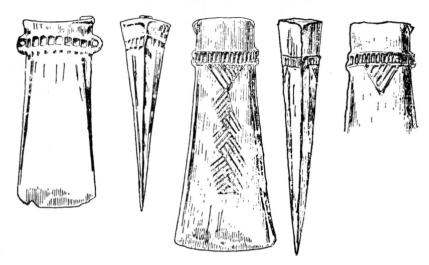

FIG. 67 Socketed axes (celts) of common Andronovo types, found in the mountains east of Semipalatinsk. After S. S. Chernikov (MIA 88, 1960, p. 254, pl. LXI).

which took root in the Urals and also in the West Siberian metallurgical centres and then followed its own line of evolution.

Another type characteristic of Ural and West Siberian metalwork were socketed axes or 'celts' (Fig. 67, Table 17). The earliest of these[39] (Fig. 81) had folded sockets, and they made their appearance in the Urals in the second quarter of the second millennium B.C. Axes of this type evolved somewhere in Iran[40] at the turn of the third and second millennia, a socketed gouge of this type formed part of the Privolnoe hoard in the North-west Caucasus and was dated around 2000–1700 B.C. These axes were a development of flat axes, the long edges of which were hammered thin and flat and wrapped round the shaft (Figs. 64, 70). Later specimens of this type were cast with a normal socket, but their decoration, on one side of the axe only, was always reminiscent of the former open socket.

A different type is represented by the Seima-Turbino celts, which were octagonal in section and were later often provided with a loop (Fig. 60). They were usually decorated with hatched triangles and lozenges, designs evidently taken from the pottery of the Andronovo culture. The axes, the earliest proper socketed axes, seem to have been a genuine local invention in the Urals (Map XXV). However, their production implies that the foundry-masters knew the complicated process of casting sockets by inserting a movable core in the mould; and they must have learned this knowledge of core-casting from those who introduced the socketed lance-head, produced in the same manner, into the area.

The invention of the socketed bronze celt was epoch-making; it was the first metal instrument cheap enough to be used for rough work like tree-felling, even in areas remote from ore deposits. 'As such it must have revolutionized the economy of the woodland zone of Eurasia and initiated that transformation of the landscape that the iron axe was a few centuries later to accelerate.'[41]

The newly invented tools spread rapidly over large areas of the East European forest zone, but moulds for casting them were found only in the Urals and in a series of settlements along the southern border of the West Siberian forest zone. A fragment of a mould for casting Seima-Turbino celts was found at Beregovaya 1 in the Gorbunovo peat-bog; it came from the advanced stage of the second period of the Gorbunovo culture (the fourteenth to twelfth centuries B.C.).[42] The axes developed a large variety of long-lived types. Later, the idea spread westwards, and all European socketed axes seem to have been derived from this East European prototype.[43]

THE EXPANSION OF THE EASTERN BRONZE INDUSTRIES

The development of the Seima-Turbino industry in the Urals undoubtedly stole the market from the Caucasian products, which at that time ceased to reach the Urals and the country on the Volga. But more important and far-reaching changes occurred in approximately the thirteenth century B.C. (Map XXII). At that time the South Ural industrial area was seized by the advancing Andronovo tribes, and soon afterwards West Siberian products appeared in the Urals and in the countries further west. These products already showed the strong influence of the Karasuk bronze industry.

Tribal movements and displacements in the West Siberian steppe country at that time also considerably affected the East European steppe. The western drive of the Srubnaya tribes destroyed the trade of the Caucasian metal industry in the area up to the Dnieper (Map XXI), and replaced it with the Ural and West Siberian industries (Map XXII).[44]

The products of the newly evolved Seima-Turbino industry of the Urals and its related centres in the West Siberian forest zone were diffused mainly along a relatively narrow strip of land across the central part of Eastern Europe—along the Volga and then the Upper Dnieper, the Dvina and the Niemen to the East Baltic coast.[45] Stray bronze lance-heads of Seima type have been found in Latvia and Estonia, and six specimens were found still further west in Lithuania and East Prussia.[46] A bronze pin of Seima type with an elk head at its terminal was discovered in Polesia (Kruchowicze).

The diffusion of these objects does not seem fortuitous; it must have been through trade. Some amber finds of this period along one route support this assumption; among them were amber beads from a grave at Strelitsa near Gomel in Byelorussia, an amber pendant from the cemetery of Seima on the Lower Oka, and an amber bead excavated in the settlement of Borovoe Ozero I on the Kama, of the Garinskii period of the Turbino culture (fifteenth to thirteenth centuries B.C.). This must also have been the route by which the bronze pin of east Baltic type found its way to the region about 155 miles south-west of Kazan. This pin formed part of the bronze hoard of Sabancheevo (Pl. XXXVIII), which can probably be dated around 1200–1100 B.C., possibly the date at which the advance of the Srubnaya culture up to the region near Kazan broke the contact with the Baltic area.

The most remarkable relic of this period in Central Russia is the cemetery of Seima, which is situated close to the junction of the Oka with the Volga. Its skeletons had nearly all disintegrated and traces of them were noticed in a few graves only. Its grave goods were very similar to those of the Turbino cemetery. There were copper shaft-hole axes, flat copper axes and awls, a score of bronze socketed axes, large bronze lance-heads, some with a loop on the socket, and over thirty copper daggers with handles in open-work or topped with a carved elk head. One dagger had a viper carved on its handle (Pl. XXXIX). There were also flint weapons, a dagger, 'sickles' or knives, and arrow-heads. Once a stone 'arrow-straightener' was found, typical of the Catacomb culture. Rings of nephrite or serpentine, pendants made of clay, and an amber pendant, were on the list of personal ornaments.

The amber pendant, as mentioned previously, was of East Prussian origin, but all the metal objects were of eastern, mainly Ural and Siberian, origin. They closely resemble those found in the cemeteries of Turbino on the Middle Kama. The name of the 'Seima' types has been given to these bronzes after the cemetery, since that is where they were first discovered and described.

The cemetery of Seima was contemporary with the Turbino cemetery and the final stage of the Middle Gorbunovo culture of the Middle Urals. It might have been set up at the end of the fourteenth century, but its latest graves must have been of the twelfth or even eleventh centuries B.C., as suggested by a bronze inward-curving knife with a handle in open-work having two figurines of small steppe horses at its top; it was very similar to the one found in the second cemetery of Turbino that was adorned with three figurines of rams (Pl. XXXIX). Both knives were of Siberian origin, from the region near the Altai mountains, and closely resemble the Karasuk

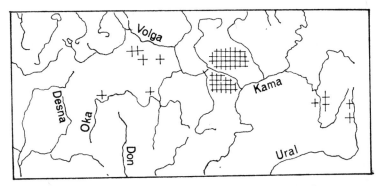

MAP XXVI Distribution of remains of the Abashevo culture.
After P. N. Tretiakov.

knives. Knives of this type did not appear prior to the eleventh century B.C.[47] (see p. 321).

The Seima cemetery, as emphasized by many investigators, had no roots in the country. It was unique in the area, even lying outside the territory of the culture often called after it, which extended north of the Middle Volga. Those buried in the cemetery were evidently alien to the local population. They left no traces of their existence in the remains of the subsequent period. It was a warriors' cemetery, packed with weapons. The eight socketed axes found there were cast in two moulds only, but they were not local products; no traces of any metallurgical activities have been found in the area, and no moulds for casting 'Seima' socketed celts were found west of the Urals. The bronze used for their manufacture came from the East Urals, which points to the centre of their production. The nephrite rings were also of Ural or West Siberian origin.

All the facts seem to indicate that the people buried in the cemetery of Seima have had some connection with the trade in eastern bronze products. The grave goods suggest that they were well armed eastern traders of the time when the Seima-Turbino industry was at its height—the fourteenth-thirteenth centuries B.C., who founded there a small colony, a centre of east-west trade. It is possible, however, that they were refugees from the southern part of the Middle Urals, the centre of the Middle Ural metallurgy, who had left their country under the pressure of the advancing Andronovians.

THE ABASHEVO CULTURE

Some attention should also be paid to a relatively small but widespread group of remains called the 'Abashevo' culture, after a barrow grave cemetery near Cheboksary on the Middle Volga (west of

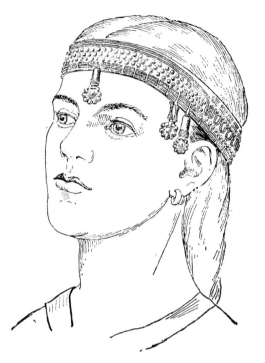

FIG. 68 Reconstruction of an Abashevo woman's head ornament (decorated bronze band), from a barrow grave at Vtoraya Vilovatovskaya near Cheboksary.
After A. Kh. Khalikov (MIA 97, 1961, p. 216, fig. 70).

Kazan). The culture is known mainly from barrow graves, well over fifty of which have been recorded, stray bronze objects, and some hoards and settlements. There are two main concentrations—the central and most important one being south of the Middle Volga and enclosed by the bend of that river and the Sura in the west, within the former territory of the Balanovo culture (Map XXVI); and the other concentration, the 'Volga-Vyatka' group, lying north of the Middle Volga. A less coherent group of Abashevo remains, the 'Balan-Bash' group, appears in the Urals on the river Belaya south of the town of Ufa, and also near the sources of the river Ural. Finally, scattered finds and isolated graves have been recorded in Central Russia north of Moscow, and also north of the Middle Oka; and a number of barrow graves have been investigated in the area on the Upper Don. In spite of their dispersion the remains of these groups show some degree of uniformity, except perhaps those of the Balan-Bash group, which exhibit many features of their own.[48]

Barrow graves usually contained two to four burials; the small ones a single grave. In the largest mounds up to fifteen burials have been uncovered. They were all in shafts. Skeletons lay on the back with knees upwards in the 'Yamnaya' position, and, exceptionally, in a supine position. Heads were mostly turned to the south-east or east. No ochre was strewn in the graves. One or two vessels and personal ornaments were the usual grave-goods; weapons and tools were never found, except for a clay mould for a shaft-hole axe excavated in a barrow grave (Penkino) north of the Middle Volga and north-west of Kazan. A number of burials were richly furnished with bronze ornaments, the most remarkable in this respect being female graves at Algaski west of Cheboksary; there were elaborate head-dresses (Fig. 68) and clothes adorned with a mass of small various shaped plates, of bronze or of silver of poor quality, sewn on them (Fig. 69).

Among the manifold bronze personal ornaments were double-spiral temple pendants, tubular spiral beads, and ear-pendants with flattened ends overlapping, the latter a type known from the burials of the Catacomb, Srubnaya, and North Caucasian cultures (Fig. 69). The most characteristic were slightly oval bracelets thinning out towards pointed terminals. The pottery shows variations, especially in decoration, throughout the culture. The main vessels were tulip-shaped pots with small flattened or rounded bases, and wide-mouthed bowls and similar carinated bowls, both with rounded bases (Table 21). Their decoration consisted of horizontal rows of hatched triangles, lozenges, zigzag lines, and meanders. Vessels of the Don-Oka group show many points of similarity with those of the Yamnaya culture, and the carinated vases of other groups show an unmistakable likeness in their shape, and partly in their decoration, to the carinated vases of the Srubnaya culture. Decorative motifs characteristic of the Andronovo culture appear on pottery of the easternmost remains.

Some settlements of the culture have been investigated[49] in the valley of the Belaya, an area belonging to the Balan-Bash group. Huts were built on the surface. Various implements, pottery, broken bones of cattle, sheep and pigs, point to a settled mode of life based on agriculture and animal husbandry. The Balan-Bash group seems to have been formed by the invading Abashevians, who assimilated the indigenous population of the area.

A large number of stray metal objects and hoards are attributable to the culture. The metal objects were cast of 'pure' copper, as tin was not within reach of the culture. They indicate a variety of types: socketed lance-heads, socketed axes, daggers, and sickles with a hooked shaft tang (Fig. 70). The most important was the hoard from Verkhnii Kizil in the South Urals (Map XXIX: 24).[50] It consisted of personal ornaments, among which were eleven bracelets with pointed

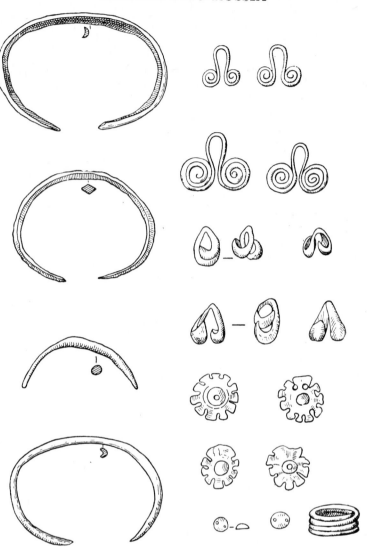

FIG. 69 Bronze personal ornaments; bracelets, temple ornaments, buttons, pendants from Abashevo graves.
After O. N. Evtiukhova (MIA 130, 1965, p. 141, fig. 3).

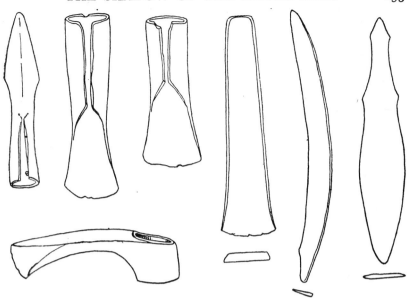

FIG. 70 Bronze tools of the Abashevo culture.
After P. N. Tretiakov (*Památky archaeologické* vol. LII, 1961, p. 375, fig. 2).

terminals and 'spectacle' temple ornaments, small plates of the same type as those found in Abashevo graves in other areas, copper beads, small thin knives, a sickle, a fish-hook, a socketed spear-head, and a dagger of the Srubnaya type, all deposited in clay vessels characteristic of the Abashevo culture.

Of special interest was the settlement at Urniak on the Belaya, where crucibles, stone slabs, pestles and stone hammers for crushing copper ore, copper slag, lumps of smelted copper, and some copper objects were found. The settlement and other finds in the area suggest that the Abashevian economy was based on metallurgy and that the South Ural bronze industry was in their hands. The products of this industry were exported westwards, and, as indicated by the relative finds, even reached as far as the region on the Middle Dnieper. There was, however, no contact with the Srubnaya tribes in the country further south on the Lower Volga.

Controversial opinions have been expressed as regards the origin of the Abashevo culture. It was rather a short-lived group, which developed between the fifteenth and the twelfth centuries B.C. Many authors[51] believe that it developed in the country south-west of Kazan, under a strong influence from the Srubnaya culture bordering it to the south, out of the Balanovo culture and local elements going back to the Neolithic. Other scholars emphasize, however, that the essential difference between these cultures precludes such theories. One says that the Abashevo culture was not native to the territory mentioned earlier,[52] but had developed out of a northern branch of the Yamnaya culture of the forest zone in the area between the Upper Don and the Middle Oka. This is suggested by the burial ritual, the 'Yamnaya' position of the skeletons in the Abashevo graves, and by simple forms of pottery showing Late Yamnaya influences. Several decorative motifs and other features point to connections with the Catacomb culture in the country further south. The Abashevians were forced to migrate north and north-eastwards under the pressure of the Srubnaya tribes.

Other scholars[53] place the original Abashevo country some 185–250 miles further west in the forest-steppe country east of the Dnieper and south-east of the Desna. They consider the Middle Dnieper culture as the main formative element, which, in spreading eastwards, absorbed many elements from the local branches of the Yamnaya culture. The Abashevo culture appears then to have been a hybrid. Its basis was undoubtedly the Yamnaya culture, as indicated by its burial ritual. The formative element seems to have been one of the groups of the Corded Ware/Battle-axe complex, but the decisive factor must have been the share of the Globular Amphorae (Fig. 37). Decorative patterns characteristic of the latter appear on Abashevo vessels, especially those of the Volga-Vyatka group. Srubnaya decorative motifs are also easily distinguishable in the decoration of the pottery of the southern remains and of the Andronovo group in the Balan-Bash section (Table 21). Close relations must have also been maintained later with the west, as is shown in the bronze temple ornaments of the same type as those found in early graves of the Komarów culture in the sub-Carpathian area. The elaborate head-dress found in female graves of the central group consisting of a richly decorated bronze band (diadem) (Fig. 68), was probably taken over from the west; such a head-dress appeared at that time, about the fourteenth century B.C., in the burials of the Trzciniec culture in Poland.

The migrations of the Abashevo people and the spread of their culture were presumably due to the pressure of the Srubnaya tribes, who seized the whole forest-steppe zone west of the Middle Volga. The northward retreat of the Abashevians first displaced and then absorbed the Balanovo tribes. According to many scholars, the Abashevo culture was one of the basic formative elements of the Early Iron Age Ananino culture, which extended over the areas of the Kazan Bronze Age culture, the Turbino (Middle Kama) culture, and the neighbouring regions.

The Abashevo Metal Industry

The Abashevians appear to have been skilled metallurgists, at least in their central area between the Middle Volga and the Sura, and in the Urals (the Balan-Bash group). Their metal industry was well developed, its typical products being flat axes, chisels, daggers of the Srubnaya type, shaft-hole axes, and wrought spear-heads and axes with open, folded sockets. All these objects were found, some loose and some in hoards. The industry specialized in the production of the variety of objects of personal adornment.

Traces of metallurgical activities have been recorded in several settlements of the South Ural branch excavated along the river Belaya on the western side of the mountains—at Balan-Bash, Urnyak, etc.[54] Huts were built on the surface. The remains included a large number of potsherds, a variety of stone tools, fragments of saddle-querns, crucibles, stone hammers and pestles for crushing copper ore, lumps of ore, copper drippings, slag, characteristic Abashevo bronze (copper) bracelets, sickles, and knives. The pottery adopted many features from the local indigenous population of the Ural forest zone, which was akin to the Gorbunovo population, but many decorative patterns were evidently borrowed from the Andronovo culture. The bones found in settlements were all of domesticated beasts.

The Ural branch of the Abashevo culture extended over the whole metalliferous area of the South Urals (Maps XXVI and XXIX: XIII, 24). There the large and important hoard was found on the Verkhnii Kizil, a small river twelve and a half miles south-west of Magnitogorsk, which has been described previously. The remains of a settlement were uncovered a few miles from this site, on the Malyi Kizil river, and adjoining it were a small cemetery, and a special offering site with the sacred constructions burnt away. The ritual burials of beheaded calves and skeletons of three burnt cows were found there; and a dissected human skeleton near a hearth and, in another site, a child's skull bear witness to human offerings. A few copper objects such as ornaments and a knife were of typical Abashevo work, but others, like a copper axe, were characteristic of the forest zone cultures. The pottery of the settlement was characteristic of the Abashevo culture of the South Ural group (Table 21, upper row), but vessels were also found that were shaped and decorated like those of the forest zone cultures of the Urals further north. Many decorative motifs of the Abashevo pottery were taken over from the latter, though the culture had its own distinctive patterns.

The Abashevians arrived in the Ural area at a late date and wedged themselves in between the Srubnaya and Andronovo tribes in the south and those of the fisherman-hunter population of the forest zone.[55] Their relations with the latter were peaceful, but not with the pastoral tribes. The easternmost traces of the Abashevo advance have been found in the Alekseevskoe settlement of the Andronovo culture near Kustanai on the Tobol. The Abashevians were ultimately absorbed by the Andronovo people in the east, and probably by the Srubnaya tribes on the western side of the Urals.

Stratigraphic evidence from the Abashevo settlement at Beregovskoe in the western part of the South Urals seems to imply that the culture appeared rather early in that area. In this settlement the Abashevo layer was overlaid by Srubnaya remains dated from the fourteenth and thirteenth centuries B.C. They give the date for the beginning of the Ural branch of the Abashevo culture, and also of its ending.[56]

The other centre of the Abashevo metal industry lay on the Middle Volga, in the region of Kazan and the junction of the Kama. The area is rich in copper deposits, and products cast from this copper are easily distinguishable because of their impurity, which is caused by the presence of more than $1 \cdot 6$ per cent of aluminium. The beginnings of the local metallurgy go back to the second quarter of the second millennium. In the early pre-Abashevo period its main products were two or three varieties of shaft-hole axes (Fig. 70). It seems that the real development of the industry began only after the arrival of the Abashevians, probably in the fourteenth century, by the end of the fifteenth. All the Abashevo personal ornaments common to all its groups (Fig. 69), and presumably also the sickles of Abashevo type found on the Volga and the South Urals, must have been produced then. The main aim of the Abashevian advance in that area may have been the seizure of the rich metalliferous region.[57] The relation of the culture to the Kazan Bronze Age culture, however, is not at all clear. Abashevo elements have been distinguished in the remains of the latter, but the entire metalliferous area of this region does not seem to have been seized by the Abashevians. The industry of the Kazan/Lower Kama region has been sometimes called the Abashevo industry, but excavations have uncovered many weapons and tools of the Seima-Turbino type—lance-heads, socketed celts, etc.—and spectral analysis has shown them to be Middle Ural or West Siberian products. Relationship between the two industries in that area, and the role of the Abashevians in the production and in the diffusion of all these bronzes will only be properly established by further investigation.

Early in the twelfth century B.C., the Abashevo tribes were probably forced to abandon the area south-west of Kazan and migrate northwards. The bronze hoard from Sabancheevo (Pl. XXXVIII), about 155 miles south-west of Kazan, seems to give the date of the

xxxvii Stone battle-axes decorated in the 'Mycenaean' style from a late Catacomb grave at Beshevo in the Sea of Azov group (left), and from a barrow grave at Horozheno north of Kherson (right).
After I. Fabricius, *Antropologia-Kiev*, vol. III, 1930, pp. 171 ff, figs. 1–3.

xxxviii Part of bronze hoard from Sabancheevo, south-west of Kazan, with a pin of East Prussian type.
After N.Ia. Merpert, MIA 130, 1965, pp. 149 ff., figs. 1, 3.

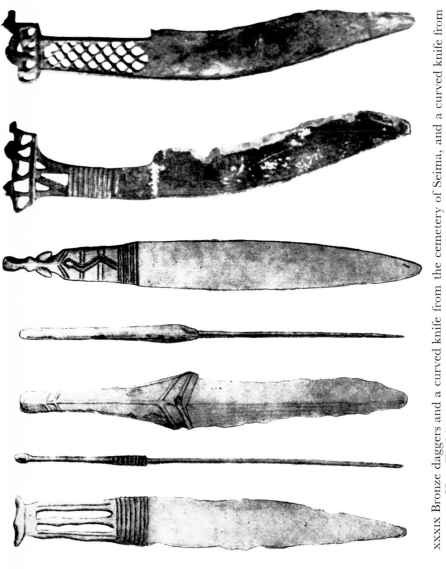

XXXIX Bronze daggers and a curved knife from the cemetery of Seima, and a curved knife from cemetery II at Turbino.
After A. M. Tallgren

Srubnaya advance. It consisted of two double-looped celts and one with no loops, a socketed spear-head with openings on the blade, three knives, a neck-ring of thick wire with spiral terminals, and a pin with a large spiral flat hammered head; it has been dated to the turn of the second and first millennia,[58] but it seems that the twelfth century B.C. is more likely. The decoration of the celts is very reminiscent of the Seima celts, and suggests a similar date. The neck-ring was Central European in type of Period III of the Bronze Age; and the pin, which was of East Baltic (East Prussian) origin, was of the same date, 1200–1100 B.C. The presence of the latter in the country on the Middle Volga was undoubtedly due to Seima-Turbino relations with the east Baltic coast.

The Abashevo tribes retreating before the Srubnaya advance crossed the Volga and settled in the region about sixty miles north of Kazan, where a larger group of Abashevo remains has been investigated (Map XXVI). The group survived there for some centuries, then gradually merged into the local culture, which was related to both the Kazan Bronze Age and the Kama-Turbino cultures. Abashevo elements are also clearly distinguishable in the Ananino culture of the Early Iron Age, which developed out of the two latter cultures.

In the meantime the Kazan/Lower Kama bronze industry began a new period of development lasting until the ninth to eighth centuries B.C., during which it changed gradually into the Ananino bronze industry. The double-looped celts of the hoard from Sabancheevo, mentioned previously, were characteristic of the new trend. Besides these, the industry produced a series of new types, one of which was the single-looped celts, derived from the Seima socketed axes, and called the 'Derbeden' type of celt. Other locally evolved types were socketed celts with a single loop on the wider, front, side of the axe, and hoes with a folded open-socket. Of special interest were dart- or spear-heads with openings on the blade, which belonged to a widespread type; similar lance-heads have been found in Ireland. In Eastern Europe three main but somewhat differing types of lance-head have been distinguished, chiefly in three regions: Kazan, the South Urals, and the Ukraine south of Kiev. The origin of these lance/or spear-heads has not been established, though they might have developed in the Kazan area by the end of the second millennium B.C.[59] They were taken over by the Ananino culture.

WEST SIBERIA

THE WEST SIBERIAN BRONZE INDUSTRY

The Siberian bronze industry evidently played an important role in the events and developments in Eastern Europe during the period after about 1300 B.C.; some attention should therefore be given to its origin and its further evolution.

Copper is found in many regions east of the Urals—in Kazakhstan, in the Altai mountains—and in some areas tin is also available (Map XXVII). The deposits were exploited during the Bronze Age and the Early Iron Age, until the third century B.C. The Andronovo culture was mainly responsible for their exploitation[60] (Map XIX). It has been estimated that in the Karkaralin mountains south-east of Karaganda around 200,000 tons of copper ore were exploited during the period; but the mines further to the south-west in the region of Dzhezkazgan, about 310 miles north-east of the Sea of Aral in the centre of Kazakhstan and about 620 miles south-east of Cheliabinsk, are said to have produced about one million tons of copper ore in the same period.

Recently, S.S. Chernikov called for a more cautious estimate of the total output of ancient mines. His doubts arose from the results of his own investigations of tin mines. The tin-mining area (Map XXVII) covered a wide stretch in the region south-east of Semipalatinsk, which extended over a distance of about 220 miles, from the northern slopes of the Kalbinskii ridge south-eastwards up to the Chinese border. No large mines have been uncovered, so mining was evidently all open-cast; a very large number of shafts, twenty-six to fifty-two feet in diameter, were examined. They lay close to each other and seem to have been worked by groups of eight to ten miners. No settlements have been found near any of the shafts, which implies that mining was probably a seasonal, summer, occupation. Galleries were seldom found, though a human skeleton was uncovered in one; evidently a miner was trapped by a fallen roof.

It had been previously estimated that three to five tons of tin ore were taken from one of the larger tin mines every year; but a new study of the heaps[61] has shown that only about 130 tons of tin ore were taken from all the mines of this region during the whole period of their exploitation. No more than five to ten tons of bronze, therefore, could have been produced yearly from this tin. So the figures relating to the estimated production of copper mines quoted previously seem greatly exaggerated. Nevertheless, the output was big enough to satisfy the demand of the people throughout a large area.

At Stepniak in Northern Kazakhstan traces of ancient copper and silver mines and of gold mining and goldsmith workshops have been

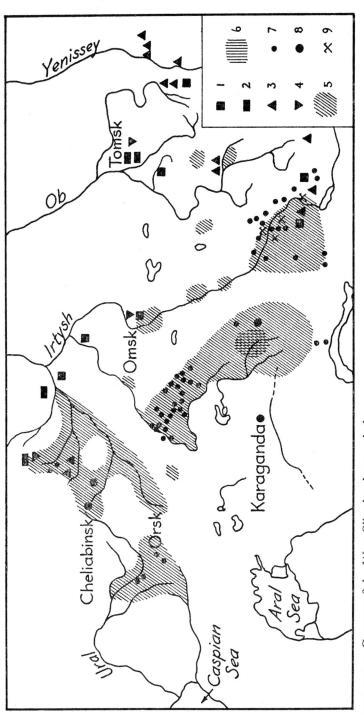

MAP XXVII Centres of the West Siberian bronze industry.
(1) socketed axes with no loops; (2) their moulds; (3) socketed axes with one or two loops; (4) their moulds; (5) territories containing pottery of the Alakulskii type; (6) areas of 'ribbed' pottery; (7) ancient copper mines; (8) larger concentrations of copper mines; (9) ancient tin mines.
After S. V. Zotova (KSIAM No. 101, 1964, p. 62, fig. 18).

discovered. They were active during the Andronovo period, and probably also in the Scytho-Sauromatian period.

The beginnings of the Siberian mining and bronze industry were modest, and its roots evidently lay in the west. Its pioneers must have come from the Urals, as is suggested by the earliest products of the industry, which are of North Caucasian types widely diffused throughout the east European steppe industry (Fig. 71). The western links of the Siberian industry have been confirmed by the investigation of a newly discovered mine of copper ore (malachite and azurite) in the north-western part of the Altai mountains near Ust-Kan, 7,550 feet above the sea level. Many perforated stone hammer-axes and wedges were found, plus wooden tools, leather straps, elk hides and other equipment; all the objects made of organic matter, having been deep-frozen for millennia, were well preserved. The stone equipment has been connected with the Catacomb culture; [62] the mine was probably an enterprise of western prospectors, either from the Caucasus or the Urals, most probably in the sixteenth century B.C. It seems to have been soon abandoned, probably because ore deposits were found in more hospitable regions.

During the second period of the Andronovo culture a local industry began to develop, and a number of local bronze types—socketed lance-heads and celts of the Seima-Turbino type (Fig. 67)—evolved out of those taken mainly from the Ural centre.

The fact that the Seima-Turbino celts were found in the forest zone west and east of the Urals has already been referred to, but moulds for casting them occur only east of the mountains. The diffusion of the celts [63] implies that they were produced mainly in four centres, all situated on the southern border of the forest zone on the banks of large rivers that evidently connected them with the mining districts and served as waterways for the transport of the bulky ores. The forests around provided the necessary fuel for smelting the ore, alloying metals, and casting. The main centres were the region of Sverdlovsk in the southern division of the Middle Urals, and the regions of Tobolsk, Omsk, and Tomsk. Spectral analyses of a large number of Seima-Turbino celts from the whole area of their diffusion revealed their very similar chemical composition, and this makes it difficult to say exactly in which region they were made.

The settlement at Samus, on the Middle Ob in the region of Tomsk (Map XXVII), was especially important. It belonged to a culture entirely different from the Andronovo culture, which was called the Samus culture after the site and was characteristic of the forest zone. It was kindred to the Gorbunovo culture. Scores of moulds for casting Seima-Turbino celts and lance-heads, and other objects, were found at the site. Some scholars [64] believe it to be the primary centre of

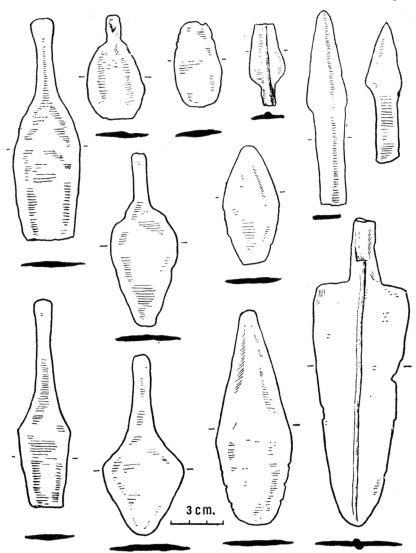

FIG. 71 Bronze daggers, or knives, from West Siberia of the earliest stage of the metallurgical development, representing western (Caucasian) types.
After S. S. Chernikov (MIA 88, 1960, p. 97, fig. 18).

Seima-Turbino metallurgy, the centre in which the Seima-Turbino axes and lance-heads originated. However, they do not mention how and whence the knowledge of alloying bronze and of the complicated technique of casting reached the area. The Samus centre was evidently a secondary one, and its growth and development were obviously the outcome of its very advantageous position on the southern border of the forest zone and close to the foothills of the Kuznetsov Altai, a mountain ridge very rich in copper deposits, tin and other metals. Several rivers of the area, the Ob and its tributaries, offered an easy access to the metalliferous ridges.

However, probably the most important ancient metallurgical centre had developed in the area south-east of Semipalatinsk the tin mines of which were investigated, as mentioned above (Map XXVII). The area was also rich in copper ores, and the adjoining steppe in gold. Traces of gold mining have been found there, and implements and pottery from these imply that they were exploited by the Andronovo people,[65] and later probably by those of the Karasuk culture.

During the second period of Andronovo development the valley of the Yenissey in the region of Minusinsk in Southern Siberia was (according to S.V. Kiselev) the 'westernmost province of the western metal industry'. However, only one Seima-Turbino celt has been found in that area, and that belonged to the subsequent Karasuk period. During the Karasuk period a variety of Seima-Turbino celts evolved there and were still in use in the following Tagarskii period.

An entirely different picture of this region is revealed by Map XXVIII, which shows the diffusion of bronze objects within the Andronovo territory during the third and fourth periods of the development of the culture. A striking feature of the concentrations that appear in the ancient centres of industry was that most of the objects were entirely new types, unknown to the preceding period; in the western division of the area Karasuk bronzes (see p. 305) were found in large numbers. All the products of the bronze industry of the Andronovo culture of that period show the very high skill and technique of their foundry-masters. Furthermore, most of the copper and tin mines described above were opened during this period.

All these changes, which were repeated at the same period in the countries further west were evidently connected with the advance of the Karasuk people and their seizure of the Minusinsk valley in the thirteenth or twelfth centuries B.C. This event poses the immediate problem of the origin of that culture, and especially of its highly evolved bronze industry, which had considerably influenced the west Siberian and Ural bronze industries, and also affected wide areas of Eastern Europe.

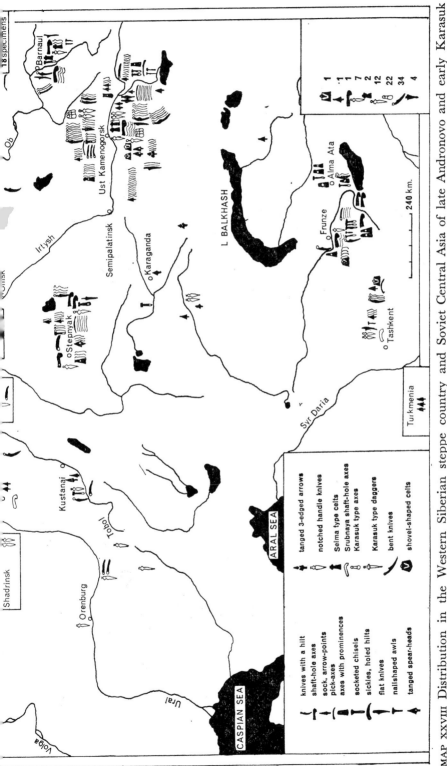

MAP XXVIII Distribution in the Western Siberian steppe country and Soviet Central Asia of late Andronovo and early Karasuk bronze tools and weapons. *Lower right*: numbers represent relative quantities of specimens found in the Yenissey area. After S. S. Chernikov (MIA 88, 1960, p. 76, fig. 16).

FIG. 72 Stone 'enclosures' round Karasuk tribal burial grounds (Berazy in central Kazakhstan; after L. R. Kyzlasov and A. Kh. Margulian, KSIIMK No. 32, 1950, p. 127) and Karasuk sculptured menhir-statues ('baby') from the central Siberian Minusinsk steppe (after M. P. Griaznov, S.A. vol. XII, 1950, p. 154).

THE KARASUK CULTURE

In the thirteenth century B.C., an important change took place in the Minusinsk valley on the Yenissey. The local branch of the Andronovo culture was then ousted by the new and entirely different Karasuk culture. The name of the latter is derived from a small tributary of the Yenissey. The new culture soon spread westwards up to the Ob. The local Andronovo tribes were partly subdued and absorbed by the newcomers, while the rest retreated westwards, displacing other tribes in their turn.

The culture is known almost entirely from its cemeteries, which were mainly large, often with over a hundred graves. These were square or rectangular enclosures of upright stone slabs, grouped close together (Fig. 72); in some areas circular enclosures appear, evidently a throwback to the preceding Andronovo period. In each enclosure was a single, and occasionally a double, burial containing a man and his wife (or a child) in a shaft lined with stone slabs; sometimes two or even three graves were placed in a single enclosure. Most skeletons lay extended, seldom crouched, with their heads mainly to the east. No cremations were found. Many graves had a sabre-shaped stone stele, the upper part of which was carved to represent a human face, usually combined with some animal features. Stelae have also been found with ram-head carvings on their tops.

The majority of Karasuk graves were ransacked in antiquity, the looters mainly looking for large bronze weapons and other bronze objects. Grave goods (Fig. 73) consisted of bronze axes, battle-axes, flat tanged arrow-heads and flat lance-heads, knives of three main types, daggers, and personal ornaments. Elbow-shaped or inward-curving knives reminiscent of Chinese bronze 'coin-knives' were characteristic. Many knives and daggers had the top of the hilt adorned by the head of a ram or a bull. Daggers were provided with two prominences to form a kind of guard. Objects of personal adornment consisted of finger-rings, bracelets, small plates sewn on garments, and a variety of long bronze tubular beads, plain or segmented. Also very common were small beads of white paste, and once a carnelian bead was found. Each grave contained two or three vessels made of a thin-walled sand-gritted and well fired ware. Vessels had a rounded base and short neck and were decorated only on their upper part, but occasionally spherical flat-based vases appeared. The decorative patterns, incised or comb-stamped, consisted mainly of rows of hanging hatched triangles or lozenges and horizontal zigzag bands, motifs common to the pottery of the Andronovo culture and taken over from the native population. Only about a quarter of the graves contained animal bones, and these were mainly of sheep, sometimes cattle, and exceptionally horses.

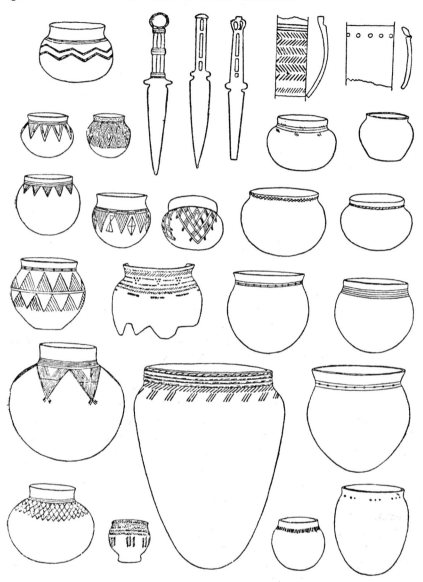

FIG. 73 Bronze daggers and pottery of the Karasuk period in the valley of the Yenissey near Minusinsk.
After S. V. Kiselev (*Drevnyaya Istoria Iuzhnoi Sibiri*. Moscow 1951, p. 123, pl. XIII).

The population of the Karasuk culture was not homogeneous, but was a mixture of the native Andronovo people with the Karasuk immigrants. This is well illustrated by the cranial material: it was partly of Europoid type, which did not differ from that of the Andronovo culture and its preceding Afanasievo culture, but it also contained a large proportion of the elements characteristic of the population of Fergana and Pamir in Soviet Central Asia, and had also a marked admixture of Mongoloid elements. The pottery and its decoration, and many features of the burial ritual, indicate that a large proportion of the indigenous population must have been absorbed by the newcomers, who adopted several features of the native culture.

The economy of the Karasuk people was based mainly on stock-rearing, with seasonal summer migrations to maintain pastures. No permanent settlements have been found. No stone tools or weapons were in use; which is hardly surprising considering the abundance of stray bronze weapons and tools found all over the country, as well as in graves.

The bronze industry of the Karasuk culture was well developed, demonstrating a great advance in the technique of metallurgy, with greatly improved methods of casting. However, the bronze objects were not produced in large foundries, for products are not standard-ized and numerous traces of casting have been found all over the country. The knowledge of casting must have been common among the Karasuk people, and only copper miners seem to have been skilled artisans. Copper was got from open-cast mines. Remains of primitive furnaces for smelting copper were found in several sites.

The Karasuk people were well armed intruders who subdued and assimilated the native population and disrupted its ancient connec-tions. Where did they come from?

The Karasuk culture shows close connections with the contem-porary cultures to its east and south-east—the Baikal country, Mongolia, and the area further south up to the Great Wall of China. Some authors[66] seek the origin of the culture somewhere in Mongolia, or even further south,[67] and are of the opinion that their advanced bronze technique was acquired by their ancestors from the Chinese of the Shang Yin period; the Anyan forms of the fifteenth and four-teenth centuries B.C. are thought to have been the prototypes of many Karasuk bronzes. Accordingly, in contrast to the preceding period, the Minusinsk valley now became the westernmost province of the east Asiatic assemblage. However, it has been shown by other scholars[68] that knowledge of metallurgical techniques reached China from outside, evidently from the west. This was followed by a rapid mastery of the bronze technique in the time of the Shang dynasty, but some forms, like the socketed axes and socketed lance-heads, were not a Chinese invention; they must be credited to the 'West', and could not have reached the Shang culture before the thirteenth century B.C.

It seems most likely that the original country of the Karasuk people was on the eastern foothills of the Tien-Shan mountains in North-west China, and credit should be given to the theories put forward by N.L. Chlenova. [69] She demonstrates several inconsistencies and discrepancies in the theory of an eastern or south-eastern origin of the Karasuk people, and points out that several characteristic features of the Karasuk culture (such as similar pottery) can be found in the culture of the preceding period in North Iran and South Turkmenia. Many prototypes of the Karasuk bronzes can also be found in Iran, and the advanced bronze technique might easily have been acquired by the proto-Karasuk people in the Pamir-Fergana region, near centres of the highly evolved bronze metallurgy of Iran. The results of the anthropological study of the cranial material, already mentioned, is also in favour of the theory that the original country of the Karasuk people lay somewhere in the mountains of the south and south-east of Soviet Central Asia, close to the Iranian border; the Fergana-Pamir racial type played an important role in the population of the Karasuk culture. N.L. Chlenova is inclined to consider the people as a branch of the Tocharians.

The culture lasted up to the seventh century B.C., and was then replaced by the Tagarskaya culture, which was of the 'Scythian' type.

The Consequences of Karasuk Expansion

The Karasuk invasion of the valley of the Yenissey must be regarded as an event of the utmost importance, not only in the history of Siberia, but also of Eastern Europe. For millennia the valley formed the boundary between the peoples of Mongoloid stock to the east, and the peoples of Europoid racial type who dwelt in the steppe country to the west. The seizure of the region, irrespective of the origin of the Karasuk culture, was the starting point of the western advance of the Mongoloid racial type and of the gradual retreat of the Europoid stock from Siberia. The Sarmatian-Alan tribes were the last Indo-European peoples of mostly Europoid stock to abandon, in the third and fourth centuries of the Christian era, the westernmost part of the Siberian steppe country. It was taken over by the Turkish Huns, among whom the Mongoloid racial type was predominant. Subsequently the Mongoloids, whether Turks or Mongols, established themselves in the south of Eastern Europe and even penetrated deep into Europe. It was only by the end of the sixteenth century of our era that the process was reversed by the Russians.

The seizure of the Minusinsk valley, hitherto held by the Andronovo tribes, caused a considerable upheaval in West Siberia. It would, however, be futile to try to reconstruct in detail the events that followed and reshaped the picture of West Siberia and East Europe, for the information available is still very fragmentary. Only the outlines of this very important historical process can be grasped; its final results have been briefly summarized here.

The Minusinsk valley and the country westwards up to the Ob were not the only regions invaded by the Karasuk people. It seems very likely that the region south-east of Semipalatinsk was also lost by the Andronovians, together with the metalliferous region of the Altai mountains and its copper, gold and tin mines. The Karasuk invaders might have seized the country even before their conquest of the Minusinsk valley, when their northern advance took them along the western edge of the Tien-Shan mountains. The Karasuk culture of this area absorbed many elements of the local branch of the Andronovo culture, which gave it a hybrid character; some authors[70] look upon the group as an Andronovo branch of the late period. The bronze industry of the group was predominantly Karasuk (Map XXVIII).

We have said that part of the native Andronovo people remained in the countries concerned, being ultimately absorbed by the Karasuk newcomers. But a large proportion of the population fled westwards before the invaders. Their withdrawal started what may be called a chain reaction, the retreating tribes setting in motion the tribes bordering on them whose country had been encroached upon. Some of the Andronovo tribes migrated southwards, which resulted in the formation of the Tazabagyabskaya culture in the area of the Aral Sea; another Andronovo group established itself on the Upper Syr-Daria and further south in Soviet Central Asia.[71] Another group of Andronovians moved northwards and seized the forest-steppe country between the Irtysh and the Tobol. The many tribes of the Sacae (Sacians), whose names have been recorded by ancient authors, were descendants of the southern migrants; the common name of the Eastern Scythians has been usually given to the descendants of the northern branches.

These changes and movements mark the beginning of the third, the Alakulskii, period of Andronovo development, which lasted from the twelfth century till the ninth century B.C. This period was followed by a transitional stage preceding the formation of the 'Sauromatian' culture, which is dated possibly to the turn of the seventh and sixth centuries, but more likely to the sixth century B.C.

The characteristic feature of the third Andronovo period was its pottery, which differed from that of the preceding period mainly by somewhat changed decorative patterns. But the bronze objects characteristic of the period were markedly different from those of the preceding one. The leading types were inward-bending knives, knives with a ring-shaped terminal of the handle, flat tanged arrowheads, daggers, most of these being either of genuine Karasuk type or of a Karasuk-inspired East Kazakhstan (Semipalatinsk) type. This period was the summit in the development of the West Siberian bronze industry; all the copper, tin and gold mines were exploited, and many new mines came into existence during this period.

The high quality of the products of the industry, their abundance, and, presumably, their cheapness, on the one hand, and lack of iron ores in the country, on the other hand, led to the manufacture of bronze tools and weapons in many parts of West Siberia until the fifth or fourth centuries B.C., at a time when bronze had already been replaced by iron in other areas of the country. Herodotus[72] reports that the Massagetae, who lived on the eastern side of the Aral Sea, in present-day Soviet Central Asia, were still armed with bronze weapons when fighting against the Persians around 529 B.C.

Nevertheless, the country does not seem to have been able to absorb the whole output of the West Siberian bronze industry, and part of it was most likely exported to the west. A number of bronzes of Karasuk or 'East Kazakhstan' type found in the Urals, and inward-curved bronze knives, adorned with animal figurines on their handles, found in the cemeteries of Turbino on the Middle Kama and in the Seima cemetery on the Lower Oka (Pl. XXXIX) are evidently products of East Kazakhstan or Altai centres (see pp. 250, 288).

The Account by Aristeas of Proconnesus

Some light has been thrown on circumstances in parts of Western Siberia by the account of Aristeas of Proconnesus on his journey to these countries.[73] The journey was undertaken about the middle of the seventh century B.C., at the very end of the era with which we are concerned here, but similar conditions undoubtedly prevailed during the centuries preceding the journey. The archaeological material of the area reflects no marked changes after the twelfth century B.C., after the disturbances of that time had quietened down.

The account has been discussed by many scholars, who differ considerably in reconstituting the route followed by Aristeas, and in placing all the countries and peoples mentioned in the account. It seems that the study by J.D.P. Bolton[74] shows the proper solution of the dilemma, though it needs correction in view of more recent archaeological discoveries and publications. This especially relates to the peoples which presumably lived east of the Urals. In placing them the well defined groups of the Andronovo culture of the Late

Bronze Age, and those of the early Scythian period must be taken into account. They must be considered in the light of the details furnished by the account of the journey relating to the respective peoples.

Let us begin to trace the route taken by Aristeas from the border of Eastern Europe from the country of the Thyssagatae. These were 'a numerous and distinct race' (from the Budini), who lived from hunting and whom we may identify with the people of the Kazan Bronze Age culture on the Middle Volga and the Lower Kama, or perhaps with the people of the earliest stage of the Ananino culture, which was the heir and successor of the Kazan. Next was the country of the Ircae, a people related to the Thyssagatae, who lived in a 'thickly wooded country' evidently in the Middle Urals on the eastern side of the mountains, and the area further east up to the river Tobol (Map XXVII); the report also mentions that they rode horses, and when hunting often lay in ambush in trees. The description of the Ircae and their country suggests that their archaeological equivalent was most probably the branch of the Andronovo culture that seized the southern part of the Middle Urals and absorbed many elements of the local Gorbunovo culture. It later developed into the Cheliabinsk group of the Sauromatian culture.

The next people visited were the 'Other Scythians'. We may identify them with the Andronovo group that was forced to migrate northwards at the time of the Karasuk invasion, and established itself on the border of the steppe and forest-steppe country between the Ishim and the Irtysh. The area was rich in copper deposits, and also in gold; traces of gold mining and gold workshops have been uncovered there near Stepnyak (Maps XXVII; XXVIII). Their southern neighbours were the Issedones, a people also of Iranian-Aryan stock. They may be placed in the region of the town of Karaganda extending eastwards up to the Irtysh, somewhere south and beyond the town of Pavlodar. However, some authors[75] are of the opinion that they lived further south, east of lake Balkhash and on the river Ili; the position of that country and its archaeological remains of the pre-Scythian period do not fit into the report by Aristeas.

The Issedones were the remotest people reached by Aristeas, but according to his account, this was not their original country; it says that the peoples just mentioned continually encroached upon their neighbours. Thus the Issedones were expelled from their country by the Arimaspians, and the 'Other Scythians', in turn, by Issedones. The archaeological material of the area above, the remains of the relative branches of the Andronovo culture (Map XIX, see p. 261) well attest to these migrations.

The women of the Issedones 'have equal authority with the men', which seems to echo a former social organization of the people based on a matriarchy. They also practised a ritual cannibalism, traces of which have also been noticed among the Sauromatians. These features seem to have been common to all peoples descended from the Andronovians.

Another people mentioned in the report on the journey were the Argippaei, most probably a Finno-Ugrian people. They lived east of the 'Other Scythians' from whom they were separated by 'a considerable extent of the rugged country', most probably the hilly country west and north-west of the Upper Ob. The remark that they lived 'at the foot of the lofty mountains' places them close to the High Altai, presumably in the valley of the Ob in the region of the towns of Barnaul and Biisk (Map XIX: II). The account says that they were flat-nosed, 'bald from their birth', and had 'large chins'; they were evidently of the Mongoloid race. They spoke 'a peculiar language, and the western traders (Scythians) who go to them transact business by means of seven interpreters and seven languages'. They 'wear the Scythian costume' (probably trousers) and had not many cattle as the pastures were not good. The account also mentions that the people were considered as 'sacred'; they did not possess any weapons, and 'they determine the differences that arise among their neighbours'. The country lay close to the metalliferous region (see p. 298), very rich in copper, tin and gold deposits. The Argippaei might have been skilled bronze founder-masters, but above all fine goldsmiths, and this probably accounts for their special position and sacrosanctity. The region must have been an important gold trading centre, as suggested by the fact that it was visited by western traders in spite of the distance and of language difficulties. Trade must evidently have flourished well before the time of Aristeas, and probably even before the turn of the second and first millennia B.C.

To the west, the Argippaei bordered on the Issedones. A fabulous account relates to their eastern neighbours, the inhabitants of the 'lofty and impassable mountains' (evidently the High Altai), who are said to have been 'men with goats' feet'. South of the Argippaei, on the other side of the Lower Altai ranges, in the valley of the Upper Irtysh, presumably lived the Arimaspians. They seem to have been either one of the early Turcoman peoples, or more likely a Tocharian people (see p. 308), and may be identified with the men of the hybrid Andronovo-Karasuk group in east Kazakhstan east of Semipalatinsk; the country was rich in metals and an important centre of the bronze industry (Map XXVIII). The hostile relations between them and the Iranian Issedones, their western neighbours, which evidently go back to the time of the expulsion of the latter (Map XIX: III), were undoubtedly responsible for the absence of any knowledge of this people

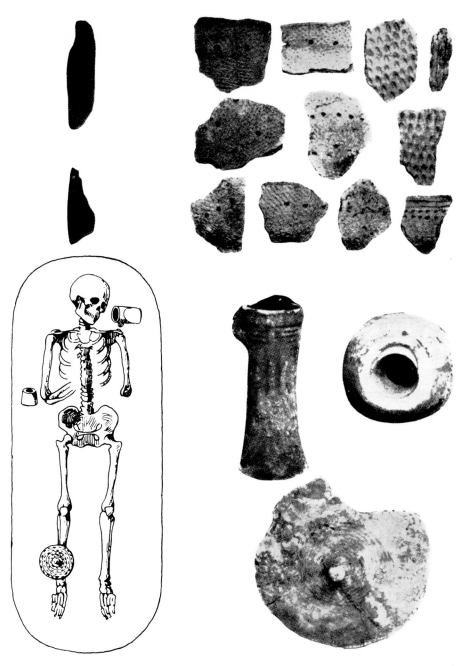

XL Grave 9 of the 'Late Volosovo' cemetery, with Scandinavian imported bronze tutulus and 'Mälar' celt.
After A.M. Tallgren, ESA vol. XI, 193, p. 37, fig. 58.

XLI Pots from late Srubnaya barrow graves at Kalinovka on the lower Volga.
Archaeological Institute of the Academy of the U.S.S.R. in Leningrad.
After V.P. Shilov, MIA 60, 1959, p. 419, fig. 36: 3, 7.

XLII Pottery and an iron knife from settlements of the Holihrady culture.
Large vase from Lesieczniki (before Second World War at the Museum at Zaleszczyki) ; ι
from Śniatyn (before the Second World War at the Dzieduszycki Museum in Lwów) ;
remaining objects are from a settlement investigated by the author at Holihrady.

being reflected in the account of Aristeas. The only remark relating to them is that they were 'men with only one eye', who lived close to the 'gold-guarding griffins'. Traces of gold mines were in fact recorded in that region (see p. 302).

The account of the expulsion of the Issedones by the Arimaspians, and of other tribal displacements following this event, fits in well with the archaeological material and evidently reflects the upheaval of the thirteenth and twelfth centuries B.C. (see p. 261). The sudden blooming and the high technique of the east Kazakhstan bronze industry, with its predominantly Karasuk character (Map XXVIII), suggests that the country had been seized by some newcomers whom we may identify with the Arimaspians. The former inhabitants of the country, the people of the local branch of the Andronovo culture, were probably the Issedones, the bulk of whom yielded to the invaders' pressure and moved westwards. The formation at that very time of a new Andronovo group between the Ishim and the Irtysh, in the region of Stepnyak, may well be connected with the migration of the 'other Scythians' whose country was invaded by the retreating Issedones.

Tribal displacements and the upheaval caused by these movements in the countries further to the west, in Eastern Europe, will be discussed in Chapter V.

SUMMARY

The easternmost part of the East European forest zone, the region east of the Middle Volga and the Urals, was the territory of the cultures of the Eastern assemblage, which differed in many respects from those of Central Russia. By the middle of the second millennium the ancient Neolithic Kazan and Middle Kama cultures had been transformed into the Bronze Age Kazan and Turbino cultures. A similar evolution occurred, a little earlier, on the eastern side of the Middle Urals, where the Early Gorbunovo gradually changed into the Middle Gorbunovo culture (Table 4). Further south, in the steppe country on the Lower Volga, the ancient Yamnaya culture, exposed to the strong influence of the Catacomb culture (in fact an aftermath of the Corded-Ware/Battle-axe assemblage), evolved first into the Poltavka culture and then, by the mid-millennium, into the fully formed Srubnaya culture.

During the second half of the millennium a very important development began with far-reaching effects upon the whole of Eastern Europe. Its starting point seems to have been the expansion of trade between Eastern Europe and various distant countries, in particular the maritime trade with the Aegean countries. The Aegean, or rather Trojan traders and prospectors (from the Sixth City) penetrated deep

22

into the country most probably in search of metals, reaching the Urals and even West Siberia (Map XX).

The prospectors, coming from the highly evolved culture of the Aegean, undoubtedly influenced the culture of the natives of the countries they travelled in. But the most important effect was their introduction into the metalliferous region of the South Urals their highly evolved bronze technique. It resulted in the sudden growth of the South Urals metallurgical centre and similar centres in Western Siberia, based on rich deposits of metal ores—tin as well as copper in some regions. Table 6 summarizes the results of the study of the diffusion in Eastern Europe of metal objects, of copper, arsenic and tin-bronze, during the period from the fourth millennium to the beginning of the first millennium B.C. It illustrates the close relation between the expansion of the Mycenaean trade of the mid second millennium via the sixth city of Troy, and the sudden appearance in the South Urals and West Siberia of a new metal industry, the tin-bronze industry, which replaced the arsenic bronze industry of North Caucasian origin (Table 9).

The abundance of metal allowed the peoples of the area to equip themselves with bronze weapons of good quality, and gave them superiority over their less well equipped neighbours. Their pressure began to be felt in the areas around the Urals.

The turning point in the history of the West Siberian and East European peoples was, however, the thirteenth century B.C. At that time an alien people of the Karasuk culture invaded the valley of the Yenissey, the Minusinsk valley, and a wide area further west, hitherto held by the Andronovians. The Karasuk people most probably advanced from the south-west, from an area somewhere near the border of Iran, where they had acquired a superior bronze technique. Their arrival caused the westward retreat of the Andronovians, whom we may identify with some proto-Iranian tribes, the ancestors of the Sarmatians and Alans. The wave soon reached the eastern borders of Europe, causing further tribal displacements and movements. Ultimately Eastern Europe was completely transformed; the western preponderance came to an end. But this will be discussed in Chapter V.

References

1 N.Ia. Merpert, MIA 61, 1958.
2 N.F. Kalinin, A.Kh. Khalikov, MIA 42, 1954.
3 O.N. Bahder, MIA 99, 1961.
4 E.N. Chernykh, PEB, pp. 195–213. See also: L.Ia. Krizhevskaya, N.A. Prokoshev, IA, 1961.
5 V.N. Chernetsov, MIA 35, 1953.
6 A.V. Shmidt, A.A. Yessen, *Izvestia* GAIMK 110, 1935.

7 A.A. Kachalova, ASE, Vol. 5, 1961; KSIAM 112, 1967.

8 M. Gimbutas.

9 M.W. Thompson in the translation of the work by L. Mongait.

10 O.A. Krivtsova-Grakova, MIA 46, 1955; A.E. Alikhova, MIA 80, 1960.

11 A.M. Mandelshtam, KSIAM 112, 1967.

12 S.S. Chernikov, MIA 88, 1960.

13 M.N. Komarova, ASE, Vol. 5, 1961.

14 A.A. Formozov, KSIIMK 39, 1951.

15 M.F. Kosarev, SA 1965–2.

16 M.F. Kosarev, as above.

17 A.A. Formozov, *op. cit.*, note 14; S.P. Tolstov, S.V. Kiselev.

18 S.P. Tolstov.

19 V. Dumitrescu, *Hăbășești*. Bucharest 1954, p. 435 ff.

20 A.A. Yessen, 1947.

21 J. Kantor, 'The Aegean and the Orient in the Second Millennium B.C.'. *American Journal of Archaeology*, Vol. 51, 1947, pp. 1–103.

22 C.W. Blegen, *Troy and the Trojans*, London, 1963. Ancient Peoples and Places series. See also: J. Bouzek, *Památky Archeologické*, Vol. LVII, 1966, pp. 242–76.

23 V.G. Childe, *Prehistoric Migrations in Europe*. Oslo, 1950, pp. 145, 174 ff.

24 R.H. Dyson in *Chronology in Old World Archaeology*, Chicago, 1965, pp. 241 f. D.H. Gordon, *Iraq*, Vol. XIII, 1951, proposes the date c. 1700–1550 B.C.

25 E.g. M.F. Boltenko, KSIIMK 12, 1940, p. 164.

26 J.F. Stone and L.C. Thomas, 'The Use and Distribution of Faience in the Ancient East and Prehistoric Europe'. *Proc. Prehistoric Society*, Vol. XXII, 1956.

27 O.A. Krivtsova-Grakova, *Trudy* GIM, Vol. XVII, 1948, figs. 35, 36; A.M. Orazbaev, Severnyi Kazakhstan v Epokhu Bronzy. TIIAEK, Vol. 5, 1958, Pl. V: 17; S.S. Chernikov, KSIIMK 53, 1954 (gold mines at Stepnyak); M.P. Griaznov, Zoloto Vostochnogo Kazakhstana i Altaya. *Izvestia* GAIMK 110, 1935.

28 E.S. Sharafutdinova, KSIAM 112, 1967. S.N. Bratchenko, in *Arkheologicheskie Otkritia 1966 goda*. Moscow 1967, pp. 66 f.

29 See K. Horedt, 'Săbiile de tip 'micenian' din Transilvania'. *Studii și Communicari*, Vol. IV, 1961, p. 9 ff., Fig. 2 (map); T. Sulimirski, 'Barrow-grave 6 at Komarów'. *Bulletin No. 4 of the Institute of Archaeology*, London, 1964, p. 171 ff., Fig. 3 (map); and J. Bouzek, 'The Aegean and Central Europe. An Introduction to the Study of Cultural Interrelations, 1600–1300 B.C.' *Památky Archeologické*, Vol. LVII, 1966, pp. 242–76.

30 E.H. Minns, 'Trialeti', *Antiquity*, Vol. XVII, 1943, p. 129 ff.; C.F.A. Schaeffer, *Antiquity*, Vol. XVII, 1943, p. 183 ff.; and *La Stratigraphie comparée et chronologie de l'Asie occidentale, III–IIe Millénaire*. London, 1948.

31 T. Özgüç, *The Golden Period of Early Anatolian Art: Hittite Art and the Antiquities of Anatolia*. London, 1964.

32 K.F. Smirnov, SA 1961–1, pp. 46–72; A.M. Leskov, SA 1964–1, pp. 208–303. Carbon–14 date of its upper (Holihrady) layer is 540 B.C. (LE–573) and that of its lower (Noua) layer is 1430 B.C. (LE–489).

33 B.G. Tikhonov, E.N. Chernykh, S.S. Chernikov.

34 E.E. Kuzmina, AO for 1965, p. 84 f.; AO for 1966, p. 113.

35 O.N. Bahder, 1964.

36 S.S. Chernikov.

37 C.F.A. Schaeffer, *op. cit.* ref. 30.

38 B.G. Tikhonov.

39 B.G. Tikhonov.

40 V.G. Childe, 'The Socketed Celts in Upper Asia', *Tenth Annual Report, Institute of Archaeology*. London, 1954, pp. 11–25.

41 V.G. Childe, *op. cit*, ref. 40, p. 11.

42 V.M. Raushenbakh.

43 V.G. Childe.

44 E.N. Chernykh.

45 V.G. Childe, M. Gimbutas, B.G. Tikhonov.

46 E. Šturms, 'Die ältere Bronzezeit im Ostbaltikum', *Vorgeschichtliche Vorschungen*, Vol. 10, 1936.

47 K. Jettmar; B. Kalgren, *Bulletin No. 17*, The Museum of Far Eastern Antiquities, Stockholm 1945, p. 143.

48 A good review of the recent literature relating to the culture has been given by A. Häusler, *Ethnographisch-Archäologische Zeitung*.

49 K.V. Salnikov, KSIIMK 67, 1957; A.P. Smirnov, MIA 58, 1957.

50 N.N. Bortvin, ESA, Vol. III, 1928.

51 A.P. Smirnov, to 51 MIA 95, 1961; F.V. Kakhovskii, SA 1962-1.

52 A.Kh. Khalikov, MIA 97, 1964.

53 P.N. Tretiakov, *Památky Archeologické*, Vol. 52, 1962; P.P. Efimenko and P.N. Tretiakov, MIA 97, 1961; O.N. Evtiukhova, MIA 97, 1961.

54 K.V. Salnikov, *op. cit.* ref. 49.

55 K.V. Salnikov, as above.

56 O.N. Evtiukhova, MIA 130, 1965.

57 P.N. Tretiakov, *op. cit.* ref. 53.

58 N.Ia. Merpert, MIA 97, 1961.

59 B.G. Tikhonov.

60 S.S. Chernikov, S.B. Zolotova, KSIAM 101, 1964; A.K. Maksimova, TIIAEK, Vol. 7, 1959.

61 A.G. Timofeev, S.S. Chernikov.

62 L.R. Kyzlasov, MIA 130, 1965.

63 B.G. Tikhonov, M.F. Kosarev, S.V. Zolotova.

64 M.F. Kosarev, SA 1963-4.

65 M.P. Griaznov, *Zoloto Vostochnogo Kazakhstana i Altaya*. Izvestia GAIMK 110, Moscow Leningrad 1935, pp. 192 f.

66 M.P. Griaznov.

67 S.V. Kiselev.

68 W. Watson, *China Before the Han Dynasty*. London, 1961. Ancient Peoples and Places series.

69 N.L. Chlenova, Karasukskaya Kultura na Yenisseye. *Istoria Sibiri*, Vol. I, Ulan-Ude 1964.

70 S.S. Chernikov.

71 S.S. Chernikov.

72 I, 215.

73 Herodotus IV, 13, 22–7.

74 J.D.P. Bolton, *Aristeas of Proconnesus*, Oxford, 1962.

75 S.I. Rudenko, *Sibirskaya kollektsiya Petra I*. Moscow-Leningrad, 1962, Svod Archeo logicheskich Istochnikov—Map fig. 108, p. 175—S.P. Tolstov in *Sovetskaya Etnografiya*, Vol. 1963 (2), map fig. 2, p. 29—A.N. Bernshtam, in MIA, Vol. 26, 1952, map fig. 87 p. 209.

5

The Late Bronze and Early Iron Ages

The Thirteenth to Seventh Centuries B.C.

THE FOREST ZONE

THE events in the valley of Minusinsk and in Eastern Kazakhstan, which probably started around 1300 B.C., affected the steppe peoples, the Andronovians, and subsequently the Srubnaya tribes and other peoples of the East European south. They also affected the inhabitants of the West Siberian forest zone, who were pressed by the Karasuk culture, and whose southern borders were encroached upon by the Andronovians. Archaeological evidence in the region of Stepnyak (Map XXVIII), on the southern border of the forest zone, implies that some Andronovo tribes, evidently retreating before the advancing Karasuk people, displaced the indigenous inhabitants of the area. Consequently, the latter moved northwards and westwards, threatening their western neighbours up to the Urals.

The advance of the Andronovians is also reflected in the archaeological material of the southern part of the Middle Urals, where the victims were the people of the local branch of the Gorbunovo culture (see p. 311). The same conditions prevailed on the other, the western, side of the Urals. Both the Srubnaya and Andronovo tribes advanced northwards into that region, along the Middle Volga and the western slopes of the mountains respectively (Map XXIX); on reaching the Lower Kama and the region near Kazan, they drove out some of the peoples of the East European forest zone.

The Gorbunovo Culture

The pressure of the kindred peoples of the West Siberian forest zone, the impact of the vigorous Andronovo culture, and the loss of the richest metalliferous region, must have affected the further development of the Gorbunovo culture. These events mark the beginning of the third and last period in its evolution.

Among the notable features of the age was the appearance of domesticated animals in the Gorbunovo settlements, undoubtedly under the influence of the Andronovians, though hunting and fishing

317

MAP XXIX Eastern Europe *c.* 1200 B.C.
(I) Ches-Tyi-Iag group; (II) Late Gorbunovo culture; (III) Late White
Sea culture; (IV) Late Karelian culture; (V) Late Kargopol culture;
(VI) 'Textile pottery' groups; (VII) Late Balakhna-Volosovo culture;
(VIII) Pozdniakovo culture; (IX) Galich (Seima) culture; (X) Late
Turbino culture; (XI) Balanovo-Abashevo territory; (XII) Late Kazan
culture; (XIII) Balanbash (Abashevo) group; (XIV) Andronovo culture;

still remained at the basis of the economy. Their gradually diminishing role, however, is well illustrated by the osseous material from two sites: at Annin, one of the early sites of the period, bones of wild animals prevailed over the domesticated, whereas at Palkino, one of the latest sites, the position was reversed. Traces of agriculture are said to have been noticed, but no saddle-querns, sickles, or similar implements connected with agriculture, have been found, except for a few stone tools considered to have been hoes.

There were marked changes in the equipment of the hunters and fishermen. Arrow-heads, mainly of flint, show a great variety of types, and seem to have been used for hunting some specific type of game. Fish-hooks were mostly of copper or bronze, and bone harpoons were much thicker. Tools were still made mainly of stone (schist, flint) in spite of the well developed metallurgy. Traces of the casting of metal objects have been found in nearly all sites (moulds, slag, bronze or copper drippings), but only special types of tool were made of metal —socketed celts and knives in particular. A mould for casting socketed

(XV) original territory of the Srubnaya culture; (XVI) territories seized by the Srubnaya culture; (XVII) Kuban-Catacomb culture; (XVIII) Koban culture; (XIX) Kayakent-Khorochoi culture; (XX) Abkhasian-Eshery (Colchidic) culture; (XXI) Central Transcaucasian culture; (XXII) Kizil-Koba culture; (XXIII) Sabatynivka culture; (XXIV) Noua culture; (XXV) Bilohrudivka culture; (XXVI) Bondarykha culture; (XXVII) Proto-Yukhnovskaya culture; (XXVIII) Proto-Milograd culture; (XXIX) Wysocko culture; (XXX) Holihrady-Komarów culture; (XXXI) Lusatian culture; (XXXII) East Baltic Bronze Age groups.

● Numbered sites listed below; △ 'Cimmerian' foundries or bronze foundry hoards (after O. A. Krivtsova-Grakova, MIA 46, 1955, map p. 164).

SITES: (1) Ches-Tyi-Iag; (2) Vis; (3) Gorbunovo; (4) Razboinichyi; (5) Palkino; (6) Turbino; (7) Borovoe Ozero; (8) Bui; (9) Fedorovskaya; (10) Galich; (11) Boran; (12) Kubenino; (13) Tomitsa; (14) Babya Guba; (15) Seima; (16) Volosovo; (17) Maloe Okulovo; (18) Pozdnia-kovo; (19) Alekanovo; (20) Abashevo; (21) Zaimishche; (22) Penkino; (23) Urnyak; (24) Verknii Kizil; (25) Suskan; (26) Sabancheevo; (27) Mokshan; (28) Sosnovaya Maza; (29) Skatovka; (30) Khutor Lyapichev; (31) Kobiakovo; (32) Elisavetovskoe; (33) Kislovodsk; (34) Nalchik; (35) Verkhnaya Rutkha; (36) Koban; (37) Khorochoi; (38) Kayakent; (39) Khodzhal; (40) Samtavro; (41) Gomi; (42) Sukhumi; (43) Kamyanka-Bilozerska; (44) Lukianivka; (45) Zvonetska Balka; (46) Berislav; (47) Zmiivka; (48) Koblevo; (49) Illinka; (50) Sabatynivka; (51) Bilohrudivka (Belogrudovka); (52) Pechora; (53) Kievka; (54) Bondarykha; (55) Kruchowicze; (56) Voytsekhivka; (57) Krzemienna; (58) Nowosiółka Kostiukowa; (59) Holihrady; (60) Ostrivets; (61) Mahala; (62) Holercani; (63) Borodino; (64) Komarniki.

lance-heads of a type derived from the Seima specimens was excavated in the upper layer of Section Six of the Gorbunovo peat-bog. However, all the metal objects, though manufactured locally, are based on types adopted from neighbouring cultures, mainly from the Abashevo and the Kama-Kazan Bronze Age culture; no local forms had evolved in the country. The pottery of the Gorbunovo culture of this period shows a marked tendency towards the flattening of the rounded base, which tendency, together with the style of decoration reflects a strong influence of the Andronovo culture.

The period lasted till about the eighth or seventh centuries B.C. (Table 5), as suggested by iron slag found in one of the sites of the Gorbunovo peat-bog, and has been divided into two stages.[1] Site Razboinichyi on lake Karasie was characteristic of the earlier stage; and the Palkino site and the upper layer of Section Six of the Gorbunovo peat-bog were of the later stage.

There is no common agreement as regards the end of the Gorbunovo culture. Some scholars think that it ceased to exist abruptly, destroyed by alien intruders. Others believe that the influx of the alien people was gradual, although it likewise resulted in the ultimate absorption and assimilation of the Gorbunovians by the newcomers, who were more advanced culturally.

The people of the culture, which extended eastwards probably up to the river Tobol,[2] may be identified with the Ircae in the account by Aristeas of Proconnesus[3] (see p. 311).

THE TURBINO AND KAZAN CULTURES

The western neighbour of the Gorbunovo culture was the Turbino culture (see p. 249), which extended over the area on the Middle Kama on the western side of the Middle Urals (Map XXIX: X). Around 1200 B.C. a new period began in the development of the culture, called the Borskii[4] period (Table 5); it lasted till about the eighth century B.C., being followed by a transitional period, by the end of which the Ananino culture of the Early Iron Age was formed. The latter, which fell entirely in the Scythian Age, extended over the area of the Late Bronze Age Turbino and Kazan cultures—the regions on the Kama and the Middle Volga—and was in fact a further development of these. The Srubnaya culture, which by the end of the Garinskii period of the Turbino culture advanced northwards up to the Lower Kama, and the Abashevo culture both contributed considerably to this evolution and most probably even brought it about.

The characteristic feature of the Borskii period was the breakdown of communications with the South Ural industrial centre, consequent upon the seizure of that region by the advancing Andronovo tribes.

The date of the Andronovian advance, the thirteenth century B.C., marks the beginning of the Borskii period, though some authors[5] erroneously date it to the fourteenth century. The strong impact of the Srubnaya culture, which at that time bordered the culture to the south, is well attested by the presence of Srubnaya pottery in many sites in the southern division of the area.

Another specific feature of the period was the development of the local metal industry on the Middle Kama, based on copper refined from local copper ores. Its products were mainly of pure copper because of the absence of tin or its substitutes in the country. The number of these products considerably increased and were diffused over the area, but the local industry never attained the high output of the South Ural (Seima-Turbino) industry or of the West Siberian centres. The development of the local metal industry was evidently forced upon the culture by the severance of its South Ural connections.

The second cemetery of Turbino may be attributed to the beginning of this period. It lay close to the first one, but has been almost completely ruined by the modern village built over it. A copper axe and a bronze inward-curved knife (or dagger) of Karasuk type were found there; the top of the hilt of the latter was adorned with three ram figurines (Pl. XXXIX). The knife, like one from Seima, was of Siberian workmanship, probably from the region near the Altai mountains. The Karasuk knives cannot be dated to before 1100 B.C.,[6] so this knife gives a later date to the second Turbino cemetery than that of the first, though both were usually considered to be contemporary (see p. 250).

It was stated in Chapter IV that during the second half of the second millennium significant changes took place in the country on the Middle Volga near Kazan and on the Lower Kama. The ancient Neolithic culture had gradually changed into a new one (see p. 246), called the Kazan Bronze Age culture (Map XXIX: XII). This was effected under a strong impact from the Srubnaya culture, which spread northwards along the Volga and penetrated into the country.

The impact of the Srubnaya culture grew stronger during the last quarter of the second millennium (Table 5). Under its pressure the Abashevo people abandoned the country south and west of the Volga bend and migrated northwards. The Kazan Bronze Age culture eventually began to disintegrate. South of the junction of the Kama, Srubnaya pottery was found in all sites and accounted for up to 20 per cent of the pottery excavated. The tendency towards flattening the hitherto rounded bases of the local pottery, and the adoption of some Srubnaya, and also Andronovo, decorative patterns were among the clearly distinguishable traces of the influence exercised by their southern neighbours on the local tribes. At the same time the 'textile' pottery, characteristic of the northern part of Central Russia, also appeared in sites of this culture.

The mode of life of the population underwent further changes. Hunting and fishing were gradually losing their position to stock-breeding and some sort of primitive agriculture. Settlements did not differ from the earlier ones, a typical site being the upper layer of Zaimishchi III, about eleven miles west of Kazan (see p. 248). 'Textile' pottery (Pl. XXX) and a few lumps of iron were found there, and iron lumps were also found in another site of the culture, Kartashinka I, south of the Kama. The investigators of these[7] wrongly dated them to the turn of the second and first millennia B.C. In the north Caucasus, close to the earliest centres of the iron industry, the metal did not appear before the ninth century, and was not widely used before the eighth century B.C. Iron objects of the Kazan culture cannot be dated earlier than the eighth century B.C. Traces of copper smelting and of bronze casting have been found in several sites.

The culture formed the main substratum from which sprang the Ananino culture about the seventh century B.C. Its main development took place during the subsequent Scythian Age;[8] but some authors claim that the Kazan culture played the main role in its formation. The analysis of bronze objects revealed that the Ananino socketed celts and spear-heads derived from the Seima-Turbino industry; but in the countries west of the Urals the diffusion of the products of the Turbino industry ceased in the twelfth century, well before the formation of the Ananino culture. A Middle Ural or West Siberian element in the formation of the latter must, therefore, be taken for granted. The traditions of the industry must have survived in the ancient centres east of the Urals, and then were implanted in the Ananino culture. This is also corroborated by the results of the anthropological study of the cranial material which shows a strong admixture of Mongoloid elements in the Ananino population.

THE COUNTRY NORTH OF THE MIDDLE VOLGA

Different and contradictory views have been expressed by various authors as regards the conditions during the second part of the second millennium B.C. in the wide country north of the Volga that extends east of the Vyatka and northwards up to the junction of the Oka and Kostroma. During the first half of the millennium, fishing and hunting tribes lived there—those of the Eastern assemblage nearer the Vyatka, those of the Balakhna culture of Volga-Oka Neolithic parentage further west. There was no clear-cut boundary line between the two distinct complexes.

The position began to change considerably around the twelfth century B.C. It has been already mentioned that some of the Balanovo and Abashevo tribes who lived south of the Middle Volga in the eastern part of the area left their country under the pressure of the Srubnaya tribes. After crossing the Volga the Abashevians settled in a restricted area about six miles north of Kazan, where a large group of their barrow graves has been investigated.[9] Some of the Balanovians must have settled north of them, as indicated by a number of their flat and barrow-grave cemeteries and settlements in that region.[10]

Considerable changes also took place about the same time in the western division of the country. An example of the new era was the cemetery of Seima (see p. 288), of the fourteenth to twelfth centuries B.C.; it was placed within the area of the Balakhna culture, but had no connections whatever with that culture. Many authors compare it with sites investigated north of the Middle Volga, including the site and hoard of Galich (Fig. 74; Map XXIX: 10) about 155 miles north of Seima which was of a later date. The name of the 'Seima' culture has been given to these remains in spite of the fact that, first, the remains were of a later date than the cemetery, and secondly, that the cemetery lay in fact outside the territory of the culture called after it. The cemetery was most probably the burial place of a group of eastern traders in the products of the Seima-Turbino bronze industry (see p. 284). Its final date, the eleventh century B.C., is indicated by a knife-dagger of Karasuk type, adorned with the horse figurines (Pl. XXXIX).

THE VOLOSOVO CULTURE

The end of the Seima trading post coincides with the seizure of the Balakhna territory by the Volosovo tribes, and was possibly connected with this development. Most of the Volosovo tribes, pressed by the advancing Srubnaya people in the south, expanded northwards, first into the Balakhna country on the Lower Oka and then further north and west. The tribes that remained managed to survive to the seventh century B.C. at least, according to grave goods of the 'Late Volosovo' cemetery described later. The culture was succeeded by that of the Gorodets earthworks, a culture typical of the Scythian Age. The large section of the Volosovo population that left their country under the Srubnaya pressure left sites with typical Volosovo pottery throughout the former territory of the Volga-Oka culture (Map XXX). The Volosovians were most probably of Finno-Ugrian stock. P.N. Tretiakov points out that the area covered by the Volosovo remains coincides almost exactly with that of the Finno-Ugrian peoples, before the east Slavonic expansion into it about the middle

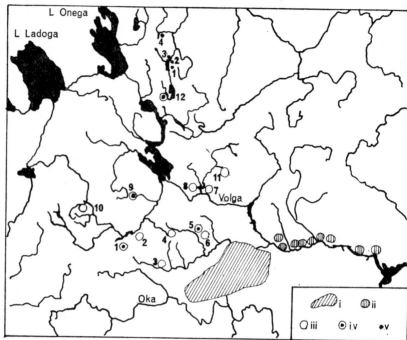

MAP XXX Distribution of sites of the Volosovo culture in the first half of the first millennium B.C.
(I) The original territory of the Volosovo culture; (II) (III) western and eastern sites of the culture; (IV) sites in which amber objects were found; (V) sites with pottery of Modlona II type.
SITES MENTIONED IN THE TEXT: (5) (6) Sakhtysh; (8) Boran; (11) Fedorovskaya; (12) Modlona. Northern sites (*black points*): (1) Kinema. After S. N. Oshibkina (S.A. vol. 1966–4, p. 30, fig. 2).

of the first Christian millennium. A few remains from the late Volosovo cemetery are shown in Fig. 76.

The Volosovo tribes were not the only ones to enter the Balakhna territory. They met there with that part of the Balanovians who had retreated north-westwards from their former country. A mingling and blending of the three ethnical elements, the local Balakhna people with the intrusive Volosovians and Balanovians, resulted in the formation of a new culture called the 'Late Balakhna' culture, or the 'Bolshoe Kozino' culture after a site on the Lower Oka (Table 5). The inclusion of new peoples with a different type of economy changed the local economy into one based on stock-rearing and agriculture.

The new culture, which bore a predominantly 'eastern' character evidently given it by its strongest element, the Volosovo culture, soon spread over the whole northern part of Central Russia (Map XXIX: VII).

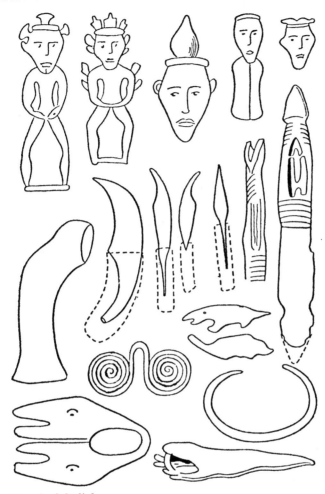

FIG. 74 Hoard of Galich.
After E. I. Goriunova (MIA 94, 1961, p. 20, fig. 5).

THE GALICH CULTURE

A similar blending of different elements—local survivors from the earlier people and some eastern newcomers—took place in the wide area on the Middle Volga east of Gorkii and Kostroma, up to the Vyatka. Some scholars call the new culture 'Seima-Chirkovskaya' culture,[11] but it seems that the term 'Galich' culture, proposed by others, is the right one (Table 5). The new wave of eastern immigrants seems to have proceeded westwards by a northerly route along the Vychegda and the Sukhona, as suggested by the appearance in the relevant sites of the culture of objects characteristic of the Ust-Poluy culture, the successor to the Ches-Tyi-Iag culture in the

Northern Urals and the region along the Lower Ob. Traces of the culture have also been discovered in the late stage of the 'Arctic' cultures (see p. 328). The Ananino elements, which also appeared in many later sites, imply that the Galich culture must have survived to the Scythian Age.

One of the most important sites of the culture, after which it in fact should be called, is that at Turovskoe on lake Galich, where the famous 'Galich' hoard was found. The hoard (Fig. 74; Map XXIX: 10), discovered in 1836 hidden in a clay vessel, consisted of a large number of various metal objects. Among these were small silver buttons, a bronze shaft-hole axe of a Late Kama type, bronze knives with decorated handles, daggers with viper-shaped hilts, bronze arrow-heads, bronze bracelets, small bronze plaques, a 'spectacle' pendant of bronze wire, and bronze and silver beads. The most striking objects were a small animal figurine and five copper 'idols', namely figurines of naked men with their heads decorated with axes, birds or streams of flame; they possibly derive from the Eastern deities like the Sun-god Shamas.[12] Most of the objects were of Ural or West Siberian origin. Some authors put the date of the hoard to the fourteenth–thirteenth centuries, which is evidently erroneous. The ninth century B.C. as proposed by others,[13] or even later, would be more accurate. A late date is indicated by the very fact that the settlement in which the hoard was hidden had only been in existence since the twelfth century and was inhabited until the Scythian Age.

The settlement of Galich, situated in fact at Turovskoe, was investigated by several scholars. It was stratified, the hoard belonging to its upper layer. The inhabitants lived on hunting and fishing, and no traces of any animal husbandry or agricultural activities have been noticed. Nine semi-subterranean huts and traces of four hearths have been uncovered. Tools, axes, shaft-hole axes, knives, scrapers, arrow-heads, etc. were made of stone and flint. Only a few metal objects were found—a copper knife, a small pendant made of bronze wire, and a small bronze plaque; they were all of the same type as those forming part of the hoard. An important discovery was that of iron objects in the occupation layer: a flat dagger, a fragment of a socketed axe, and lumps of iron slag. The latter suggests that iron was smelted locally from bog ores. Iron work and connections with the Ananino culture of the Scythian Age imply that the settlement must have been inhabited till the mid-first millennium B.C. The pottery found in the settlement was the so-called 'net ware'; its name derives from its decoration, which consists of wide cross-hatchings, zigzags, lozenges, and similar motifs, impressed by a comb-like stamp (Fig. 75). 'Textile' pottery characteristic of the Early Iron Age of Central Russia was also excavated.

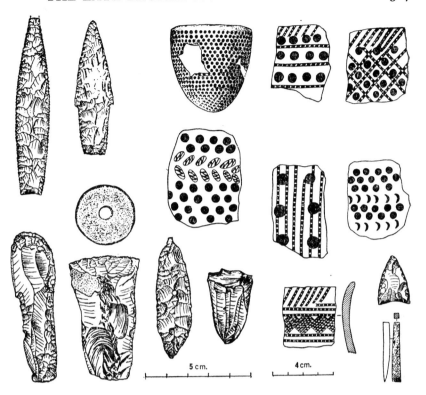

FIG. 75 Remains of the Galich culture: pottery from the settlement of Fedorovskaya; flint and slate disc from the Umilenie site on Lake Galich. After M. E. Foss (MIA 29, 1952, p. 163, fig. 84; and KSIIMK No. XXVI, 1949, p. 37, fig. 13).

Several sites of the Galich culture have been recorded in the region north-east of Kostroma and also further south (Fig. 75). The settlement called 'Fedorovskaya', situated on lake Chukhlomskoe (Map XXIX: IX; 9), nearly thirty-one miles north of Galich, is one of the northernmost sites of the culture known so far. Semi-pit dwellings were uncovered round in plan and about ten feet in diameter. Tools were of stone and flint and were similar to those of the Kargopol culture, a pointer to connections with the latter. A fragment of a bronze object was found, but an iron fragment that was also discovered might have belonged to a medieval settlement, traces of which were uncovered on the same site. Bones of cattle found in one of the dwellings imply a knowledge of animal husbandry. The pottery was mostly archaic in character, related to the pit-comb ware of the Kargopol culture, but Ananino pottery was found also. The latter precludes a late date for the settlement.

Vessels of the Ananino culture have often been found in sites around lake Galich.[14] These vessels, and those in which the 'textile' style of the Diakovo culture of Central Russia in the Scythian period prevails, give the final date of the Galich culture. It was succeeded by the Dyakovo culture.

THE ARCTIC CULTURES

Considerable changes also occurred in the 'arctic' region of north Russia at the very end of the period under review, probably in the seventh or even sixth centuries B.C., but definitely not earlier than the eighth century B.C. They ushered in a new period in the development of the area, which has been incorrectly dated by some authors[15] to 1000–700 B.C. The period belonged almost entirely to the Scythian Age, which lies outside the scope of our study. Nevertheless, the changes which might have begun at the end of our era, and were evidently the outcome of events around the eighth century B.C., deserve to be outlined here (Table 5).

It has been emphasized by several scholars[16] that at the time just mentioned a new wave of eastern immigrants must have reached the arctic area (Map XVIII). Their arrival cut across the development of almost all the 'arctic' cultures; a study of the relevant archaeological material revealed that there was no continuity in development between the cultures of the area of the preceding period and that with which we are concerned here (Map XXIX: III–V).

The territory of the Kargopol culture was taken over by tribes from the east (Table 14). They seem to have advanced by the northern route. Ananino pottery soon appeared there—round-based vessels decorated with rows of horizontal cord-impressed lines, pits and short incisions. Flat-based vessels were also common, and the 'net' and 'textile' pottery of the Central Russian Diakovo culture appeared soon in many sites. Tools were mostly of bone and antler—harpoons, arrow-heads, etc.—but differed from those of the preceding period by being heavy and clumsy. A few bronze objects, including a Mälar socketed axe (Fig. 77), probably of Kama or Ural origin, were found, and in some sites there were clay moulds for casting bronze wire. At the Olskii Mys site on lake Lacha, ten and a half miles south of Kargopol, a primitive oven for smelting iron and a set of iron tools were found. Iron slag and potsherds lay around. The pottery was of a late date, similar to that of the Scythian-period earthworks on the Middle Volga and the Vetluga, though pottery of an early period was found alongside it. The site has been dated to the first half of the first millennium B.C.,[17] but, in fact, as shown by other finds, its correct date is probably the beginning of the Christian era.

Lumps of iron, iron knives and other small iron objects have been found in at least two other sites of the culture. The economy of the population was still based on fishing and hunting.

A change in the population has also taken place in the country further north, within the territory of the White Sea culture. Some features of the new culture suggest that the newcomers arrived there from the region north of the Ananino culture—the Upper Pechora, North Urals, and the Lower Ob. They were people of the Ust-Poluy culture, the successor of the Ches-Tyi-Iag culture (Map XXIX: 1). A number of imported objects found in the area imply that the new period did not begin earlier than the seventh or more likely the sixth century B.C. Several crucibles and other utensils of a bronze foundry were found in a number of sites, along with copper slag and drippings, which imply the local casting of bronze tools. Copper was most probably brought from the region on the Lower Kama or from the Middle Urals in exchange for furs and other arctic products. The hunting of water birds, elk, bear, reindeer, seal, and whale, were the basis of the economy.

No such clear-cut break between the two subsequent periods, around 1300 B.C., has been noticed in Karelia, though there was a marked difference between the remains of the 'Second' and the 'Third' stages of the second Karelian cultures (Tables 4, 15, 16). The number of settlements considerably increased in the later period, probably because of an increase in the population. Among the standard sites are Voy-Navolok and Orov-Navolok, both in the northeastern corner of Lake Onega.

Settlements were long-lived. Winter dwellings were sunk in the ground; they were round in plan with a corridor entrance that was always placed on the side facing the river or stream. Light summer huts and traces of temporary encampments, probably summer camps, have been recorded in several sites. Pottery characteristic of the preceding period was still in use, though the bulk of the pottery was 'asbestic' pottery, an asbestos-gritted ware. Vessels were mainly round-based, but flat bases also appear. The decoration was restricted to the upper part of the vessels, and consisted mainly of rows of short incisions, comb impressions, and irregularly scattered pits. Many vessels were undecorated.

There was no difference between the tools of the two periods. However, bronze seems to have been used more widely in the later period, though bronze tools were never very important. Some moulds for casting bronze socketed axes indicated their local production. Raw material was probably imported from the Urals or the regions on the Kama—from the territory of the Ananino culture. However, the Karelian culture, unlike the Kargopol and the White Sea cul-

23

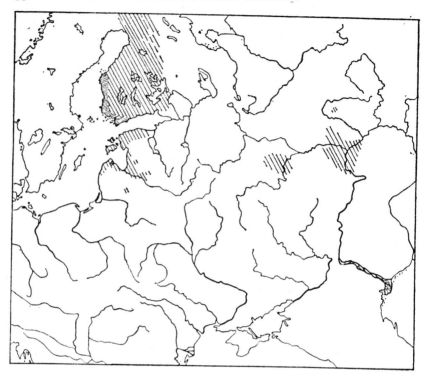

MAP XXXI Map showing the Swedish eastwards expansion in the Late Bronze Age, early in the first millennium B.C.
Hatched areas: Regions in which objects of Swedish origin (including axes of the Mälar type) were found, or Swedish influence was well marked in local cultures.
After B. Nerman (*Fornvännen,* 1954, p. 265, fig. 1).

tures, does not seem to have had any close contact with the Ananino culture of the East Russian forest zone.

Remains of a bronze foundry found at Tomitsa on the western coast of lake Onega (Map XXIX: 13) and of another one at Babya Guba, where remains of an ironworks have also been uncovered, were of a still later period, which began about 700 B.C. Among the objects excavated were crucibles, pestles, stone hammers for crushing ore, and an oven for smelting iron. Iron was evidently smelted from local bog ores, and its importance grew as it was easily accessible. The Babya Guba site has been dated around 1000–500 B.C. However, Carbon-14 dates (LE. 331, 365, 378) imply that the neighbouring sites and the ironworks should be dated from about the end of the first millennium B.C. to the beginning of the Christian era.

The Scandinavian Trade

One very important event of the early first millennium B.C. in Eastern Europe was the development of the Scandinavian trade. The trade and its extent were studied and discussed thirty years ago by A.M. Tallgren,[18] and new finds and research have added little to the results of his investigations.

During the Late Bronze Age, a Gotland colony was in existence in East Curland in Latvia.[19] 'Ship' tombs of Scandinavian type were uncovered there, and a large family tomb with Swedish-imported objects of the early first millennium B.C. was investigated near Riga. Scattered finds and tombs of Scandinavian type in the coastal part of Estonia, and also Swedish-imported objects found further inland, point to close connections with Scandinavia at that time.

The extent of Scandinavian influence is shown by the diffusion of axes of the Mälar type (Map XXXI). They were found in all the East Baltic countries up to Estonia, and in the northern part of Byelorussia; and thirty odd specimens or local imitations of them have been found in many points of the northern part of Russia. Nine specimens were excavated in the 'Late' cemetery of Volosovo on the Lower Oka (Fig. 76). In the same cemetery were bronze tutuli typical of the Swedish Middle Bronze Age of 1100–700 B.C.[20] (Pl. XL). Other Scandinavian-imported objects are a dagger from Galich and an East Scandinavian palstave (bronze celt) from Murom on the Oka. All these objects illustrate Scandinavian trade expansion into the northern part of Eastern Europe during the early first millennium B.C. The Karelian petroglyphs, counterparts of which exist in the Scandinavian countries, are another indication of the strong Scandinavian influence of that period (Figs. 53, 54; Map XVI).

The rather small number of these finds, scattered over very wide distances, cannot be looked upon as traces of actual migration.[21] This was evidently an undertaking aiming at safeguarding the trade routes and creating new trade conditions. The Scandinavians reached only the junction of the Kama with the Volga, and their colonies—Volosovo on the Lower Oka, and another most likely in the region of Kazan or near the junction of the Kama (Fig. 77)—lasted for about two centuries at the most (Map XXXI). Scandinavian traders gradually lost their identity by merging with the local population, which seems to be indicated by the fact that they developed no pottery of their own. That found in the graves at Volosovo was a local ware, typical of the late stage of the Volosovo culture.

The 'Late' Volosovo cemetery differed substantially from the early one investigated in the same village and called the 'Early' cemetery. Its manifold remains suggest a very important role for the people who

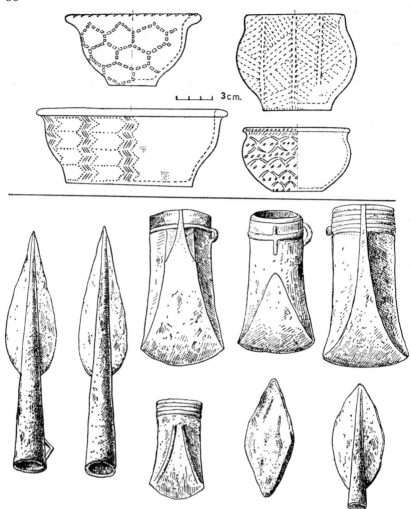

FIG. 76 *Upper:* Pottery from late Volosovo settlement at Podboritsa-Scherbininskaya on the lower Oka.
After I. K. Tsvetkova, s.a. vol. 1961–2, p. 180, fig. 8.
Lower: Bronze weapons found in graves of the 'Late Volosovo' cemetery.
After A. P. Smirnov (MIA 28, 1952, p. 38, pl. x).

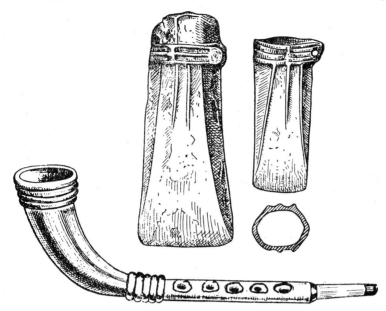

FIG. 77 Two bronze celts of the Mälar type from the region of Kargopol and from the region of Kazan (after M. E. Foss, MIA 29, 1952, p. 195, fig. 100:4, 5); and a reconstructed flute with a bronze terminal found at Boran (after N. N. Gurina, MIA 110, 1963, p. 107, fig. 18).

were buried there, the inhabitants of the nearby settlement. The cemetery consisted of nine graves only. It has been considered to belong to the very end of the Volosovo development. Flints were found in four graves only, but the other five burials yielded a variety of objects (Fig. 76; Pl. XL). They were bronze socketed axes of Scandinavian Mälar type; decorated bronze tutuli of Scandinavian (Swedish) origin; and a socketed spear-head with a loop on the socket, and another one with it, both representing somewhat evolved Seima forms. A bronze mirror characteristic of the Tagar culture of the Minusinsk valley must have been imported from Siberia; it was either of the late seventh, or, more likely, the sixth century B.C. A similar date is also suggested by a small rhomboid plate (or point) of iron found in one of the graves (Fig. 76: 7).

The Volosovo axes of Mälar type differed somewhat from the genuine Swedish axes of this type. They were cast of metal from Kazan, and were probably products of a bronze foundry in that region. According to B.G. Tikhonov all axes of this type, whether provided with a loop or not, were of the eleventh to ninth centuries, but their Scandinavian affinities point to the ninth or eighth centuries B.C.

Copper and other metals were probably the commodities sought by the Scandinavians. The Scandinavian bronze industry of the early first millennium B.C. seems to have depended to a large extent on this source of supply. The upheaval in Central Europe, as shown by the large number of bronze hoards hidden at that time, no doubt greatly interfered with Scandinavian trade with Central Europe and the regular delivery of the raw material, if it did not prevent it.[22] And possibly the increase in trade at that time between the Scandinavian countries and the British Isles, where tin was sought, was caused by the Scandinavian search for a new source of supply.

The range of the Scandinavian trade with the eastern countries[23] at that time is indicated by the bronze horse head on a processional requisite of Chinese origin found at Svartarp in Västergötland; and, among the same group of finds, a bronze knife with the handle in the form of a human figurine, found in Holstein in north-west Germany and supposed to be of Annamese origin. These objects suggest Scandinavian trade, though undoubtedly indirect, with the Far East. East European outposts evidently formed an important link in these trade connections It is also worth while mentioning in this context that a South German sword of 1200–1000 B.C. has been found in a peat-bog in South Finland.[24]

No one knows what the Scandinavians exchanged for the metal and other commodities they imported from the east. It was evidently not amber; the few amber finds recorded in Eastern Russia were all of the preceding, Seima-Turbino, period, and no amber was found in the cemetery of Volosovo.

Scandinavian penetration was the main factor in the further development of trade between the Urals and the Baltic and Scandinavian countries in the mid-first millennium B.C. The main role in this development was played by the Ananino culture, which also enjoyed close relations with the Scythians of the Pontic area and the North Pontic Greek colonies.

When discussing Scandinavian trade with east Europe, one must emphasize the striking similarities in shape between some East European bronze objects and those of the Late Bronze Age in the British Isles, and in Scotland and Ireland in particular. This related especially to socketed spears and lance-heads with openings on the blade, which appeared in the British Isles about 800 B.C. Their replicas in the Ukraine and eastwards up to the Urals were of an earlier date, approximately 1000 to 800 B.C. Socketed axes, including the double-looped celts, were also of an earlier date than those in the west. It seems very probable, therefore, that the idea was introduced into the British Isles from Eastern Europe; and the Scandinavian trade connections with East Russia and with the Caucasus via the Ukraine on the one hand (Map XXXII), and with the British Isles on the other, might have acted as the intermediary.

The east–west connections at that time may also be confirmed by a bronze terminal of a flute found in the remains of a settlement of the Galich culture at Boran, north of Kostroma (Fig. 77; Maps XXIX: 11; XXVIII). The instrument calls to mind the modern Russian 'zhaleyka',[25] but is also remarkably similar to the Scandinavian bronze horns that were introduced into Ireland from Scandinavia about the eight century B.C. The instrument from Boran might have also been of Scandinavian origin[26] of the same date, the early first millennium B.C. The evidence is inconclusive, however, for in an earlier layer of the same settlement at Boran a fragment of a clay flute was found, obviously not Scandinavian. A much earlier musical instrument was found about 500 miles south-east of Boran in a Yamnaya barrow grave, probably of the end of the third millennium B.C., at Skatovka near Saratov, on the Lower Volga. It consisted of five small tubular bird bones of different lengths, which lay close to each other. The smallest, two inches long, lay at one end of the row, and the longest one, nearly five inches long, at the other end. They evidently formed part of a kind of harmonica.[27]

THE EAST EUROPEAN STEPPE COUNTRY

As mentioned at the beginning of this chapter, the steppe peoples of Eastern Europe were also among those affected by the events in Western Siberia. In the thirteenth century B.C. the pressure of the Andronovo tribes on those of the Srubnaya culture in the region on the Lower Volga considerably increased, and eventually a number of Andronovo tribes entered the country. Some of the Srubnaya tribes remained and were ultimately absorbed by the newcomers, who imbued them with much of their culture. These changes mark the beginning of the third ('C') period of the Srubnaya development on the Volga, and the hybrid culture formed has often been called the Srubnaya-Khvalinsk culture.

Other Srubnaya tribes, mainly in the west of their territory, gave way before the newcomers and moved to new homes. Some of them advanced northwards, into the territory of the Kazan Bronze Age, the Abashevo, and the Balanovo cultures; others pushed westwards and conquered the territory of the Catacomb culture. A small group of the Srubnaya people advanced into the borderland of the forest-steppe and forest zones of Central Russia, forming the hybrid Pozdniakovo culture, and forcing some of the Volosovo tribes to retreat northwards.

The Srubnaya-Khvalinsk Culture

On the Lower Volga the third period of the Srubnaya-Khvalinsk culture was marked by an increase in West Siberian, Andronovo, influence.[28] No major changes have been recorded in the burial ritual —skeletons still lay, mostly crouched, in rectangular shafts, but cremations have been recorded, especially in the region of Volgograd, Decorated bowls with a more or less carinated body were still in use; but they were being rapidly replaced by dark, thick-walled, mostly undecorated, pots or deep bowls with straight sides and wide open at the top (Pl. XLI). The large pots often had a single raised band around the neck with its terminals pointing down, leaving a narrow interval; this band was usually punctured or finger-tipped.

Bronze tools and ornaments seldom appear in graves of this period, and only a small number of stray bronze objects have been found within the confines of the culture. They include small simple bracelets of the Andronovo type, flat tanged knives-daggers of the 'Srubnaya' type also common in graves of the Andronovo culture, and some sickles with hooked handles, similar to specimens from Kuban. Socketed axes were of little use on the steppe, but some were found on the border of the forest-steppe zone, mainly in hoards.

The bronze hoard found at Sosnayaya Maza near Khvalinsk, on the western side of the Volga, was one of the most important. It consisted of sixty-five objects of a total weight of sixty-four pounds. The bulk of its contents consisted of fifty complete and five broken knives or sickles of a special type. There were also two daggers with perforated handles, a socketed gouge, and two knives reminiscent of Karasuk specimens. The three socketed axes found were asymmetric, and provided with two loops—one on the narrow side, the other on the wide, front side of the axe. One socketed axe had one loop only. The hoard has been usually dated to the tenth–eighth centuries,[29] though some authors wrongly date it to the thirteenth–twelfth centuries B.C. Chemical analysis of some of the socketed axes (96 per cent copper, 3.5 per cent iron) confirms the later date for the hoard.

West Asiatic records of the ninth century B.C. report a new wave of steppe nomads menacing the frontiers of Urartu and other kingdoms. The archaeological material of the Andronovo culture shows some changes in the ninth century, possibly due to tribal movements. No such changes have been noticed for that time in the Srubnaya culture on the Lower Volga, although they are well reflected on the Srubnaya remains of the country on the Lower Dnieper (see p. 341). It may be that their absence is simply due to an error in dating the relevant remains.

The bronze industry of the Srubnaya culture on the Lower Volga was well developed; moulds for casting sickles, ornaments and other objects have been found in the region of Saratov and in other sites along the Volga. The industry in its earlier stage was linked with the Seima-Turbino industry, but later with that of the Andronovo culture.

The diffusion of barrow graves of various periods implies that an important development took place during the second half of the second millennium in the country on the Lower Volga.[30] The earlier barrow graves of the Yamnaya, Catacomb and Poltavka cultures in that region kept relatively close to the river valleys, and have never been found any deeper into the steppe; but those of the Srubnaya culture and succeeding periods appear almost all over the steppe land. The gradual change of climate, from the dry sub-Boreal of the earlier period to the damp sub-Atlantic stage, undoubtedly fostered this evolution: under the new climatic conditions the arid steppe east of the Lower Volga became a rich grassland that could provide pasturage for larger herds. The migratory steppe pastoralism began to develop, and the increased use of the horse for riding enabled the nomads to move quickly over large distances. The consequences of this evolution were soon felt in the countries west of the Volga.

The number of settlements along the valleys of the main rivers, near the mouth of the Don, and in the forest-steppe zone in the north, greatly increased during the late stage of the Srubnaya culture. Several of these were investigated. One of them at Khutor (Farm) Lyapichev on the Tsaritsa (Fig. 78), where the river closely approaches the Volga, was founded during the second period, but was still in existence during the third period. Seven semi-subterranean huts about thirty feet square, and three large houses about sixty-five feet by twenty-six feet, were uncovered. The houses probably served some communal purposes and had no hearths. The inhabitants of the village were engaged in stock-rearing, like those who lived in the open steppe, but agriculture and fishing were of importance for their economy. The osseous material from the settlement at Khutor Khailovshchina on Lake Chernotske (basin of the Don) shows that of the 376 individual animals identified, 56 per cent were cattle, 17 per cent sheep, 14 per cent pigs and 13 per cent horses. The latter were kept mainly for milking or for providing meat. In a settlement at Voronezh there were the bones of a camel, which had evidently come from the Andronovians who reared it in west Siberia.

The settlements of the Lower Don and the Don delta bore the marked character of fishing villages. Agriculture played no part in an economy that depended on fishing and the gathering of molluscs. A few villages had already been founded in the Catacomb period. Among these were the long-lived Elisavetovskoe and Kobiakovo[31] earthworks, both situated near the mouth of the Don; their defensive

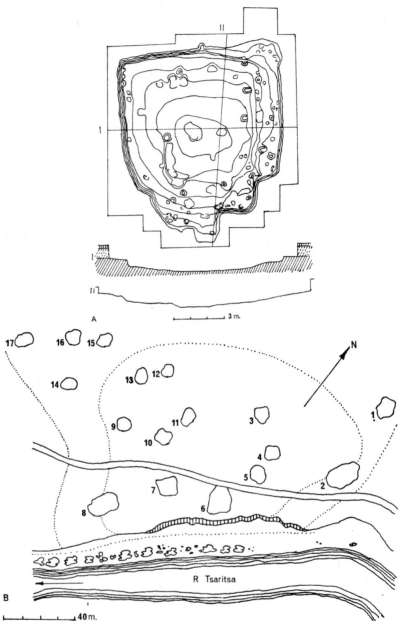

FIG. 78 (A) Plan and cross section of the largest hut in a settlement of the Late Srubnaya culture at Khutor Lyapichev on the R. Tsaritsa in the basin of the Middle Don. Probably used as a communal centre.
(B) Settlement at Khutor Lyapichev.
After A. P. Kruglov and G. V. Podgaetskii (*Izvestia Gaimk* No. 119, 1935, pp. 121, 122, figs. 24, 25).

constructions were built by the end of the Srubnaya period. They were inhabited until about the fourth century B.C. In the filling of a pit-dwelling at Kobiakovo, there was a fragment of a talc mould for casting socketed celts similar to those of the pre-Ananino period of the Kazan-Kama region. The Elisavetovskoe earthwork contained Greek pottery of the sixth to fourth centuries B.C. it was certainly an important Greek trading centre during that period and acquired a Scytho-Greek character.

The steady influx of the Andronovians into the Srubnaya territory, and also the permeation of some Srubnaya tribes in the West Siberian steppe, gradually destroyed the differences between the two cultures in the steppe east of the Lower Volga and in West Siberia. This blending resulted in the emergence, around the seventh century B.C., of the Sauromation people.[32]

Originally the western boundary of the Srubnaya culture was the Middle Don, up to Voronezh—remains of the Poltavka culture have been recorded in the region of Tambov, north-east of Voronezh[33]—its presence in that region during the fourteenth century is attested by a number of settlements, and other further to the north-west.

A barrow grave at Kievka is of special interest. A vessel found in it was strikingly reminiscent of the Trzciniec-Komarów bowls, and similarly decorated; and there was a mould for casting shaft-hole axes of the Caucasian type.[34] And contacts linking the Srubnaya culture with the countries around the Carpathians around 1300 B.C. have also been confirmed by an early Srubnaya bronze dagger found in a barrow grave of the early stage of the Komarów culture at Komarów.

THE POZDNIAKOVO CULTURE

In the thirteenth century the Srubnaya tribes began to move west and north. Those from the region on the Upper Don invaded the territory of the Riazan culture on the Middle Oka, and also seized the southern part of the Volosovo territory. They soon mingled with the local population, a large section of which remained where they were, and ultimately the hybrid Pozdniakovo culture was formed (Table 11). The site after which it was called lay near Murom, nearly in the centre of the Volosovo territory. Also located in this area was the barrow-grave cemetery of Maloe Okulovo; its earliest graves were of the Early Srubnaya type, but the later ones contained pottery similar to that found in the cultural layer of the 'Late' Volosovo cemetery.

The Pozdniakovo culture has not been thoroughly investigated, a few settlements only having been excavated. Some authors divide its development into two periods. The pottery was a kind of Srubnaya ware, with bulging pots and carinated bowls, and a Srubnaya type of decoration, but it also retained many features from the indigenous culture of the preceding period. The Pozdniakovo culture survived up to the Scythian Age. In the settlement of Alekanovo near Riazan,[35] a fragment of a socketed axe of the Mälar type and a few other bronze objects were found. Among them was a crucible, implying that bronze objects were cast locally. Another important find was a bronze pin of the same type as those found in graves of the Wysocko culture in West Podolia, probably of the seventh century but definitely not earlier than the eighth century B.C.

THE COUNTRY WEST OF THE DON

The event of crucial importance for the steppe country west of the Don was the westward retreat, about the mid-thirteenth century B.C., of a large section of the Srubnaya people before the Andronovians. In crossing the Don the Srubnaya tribes invaded the territory of the Donetz groups of the Catacomb people. The archaeological material reflects no links whatever between the invaders and the invaded in the two subsequent cultures of that region, which means that the invaders must have driven out their predecessors (Table 4).

Another wave of the Srubnaya tribes proceeded southwards and took possession of the territory on the Lower Don and the Manych occupied by the local branch of the Catacomb culture; some of the latter tribes were overrun, while others retreated southwards into the North Caucasian foothills. The Srubnaya wave next seized the steppe country north of the Sea of Azov, where they absorbed the local Catacomb population, though they themselves were influenced by the people they absorbed. By the end of the second millennium B.C. the whole territory of the Catacomb culture west of the Don and up to the Inguletz had been captured. Only in the Crimea did a few small Catacomb tribes manage to survive.

The Srubnaya advance reached the Dnieper in the thirteenth century; and some Srubnaya burials of a relatively early type within the Usatovo territory imply that they moved still further west, though they do not seem to have settled there. Srubnaya elements have also been found in the remains of the early stage of the Noua culture of Moldavia, west of the Pruth.[36]

The advance of the culture towards the Carpathians must have been a bloody business, according to the number of bronze swords of the Naue II type—the earliest bronze swords in that area and dated to this very period, 1250–1200 B.C.[37]—that have been found, near Iași in Rumania, on the western border of West Podolia south-east of Lwów (Lvov), and near Kiev. Further warlike evidence is a number of 'Hungarian' bronze battle-axes and other weapons. The advance of the Srubnaya tribes into the countries west of the Dnieper evidently caused some upheaval there, as evidenced by a number of bronze hoards hidden at that time. The outcome of the invasion was the loss to the Transylvanian and 'Hungarian' centres of the bronze industry of the whole country up to the Dnieper.

The famous silver hoard of Borodino must also have been hidden away during this invasion. The hoard has been dealt with and described by many scholars.[38] It comprised two lance-heads of the early Seima type and the socket of a third one, all decorated in the 'Mycenaean' style; a dagger and a pin with a rhomboid head, similarly decorated; three stone mace-heads; and four fine nephrite battle-axes. The hoard must have been the property of a local chief or princeling who lost his principality and was unable to recover his property.

The Srubnaya culture of the Ukrainian grassland differed from its contemporary that remained in the original country on the Lower Volga (Fig. 62). It was a further development in the new environment of the ancient culture of the early stage, with no traces of the Andronovo elements characteristic of the Srubnaya-Khvalinsk culture on the Lower Volga. It absorbed some Catacomb elements, and was also affected by Central European influences—all of which added to its individual development.

The burials of the Ukrainian steppe were in timber-log chambers, like those on the Lower Volga. In the Donetz area about 60 per cent of the Srubnaya burials were unfurnished, whereas 92 per cent of the Catacomb graves of the same area contained grave goods. The Srubnaya pottery, mainly carinated vases with an incised or comb-stamped decoration of horizontal bands of meanders, lozenges, triangles, etc., was plentiful; but other grave goods were few and far between and consisted almost exclusively of small flat copper daggers of the Srubnaya type and small personal ornaments. The grave goods do not reflect any considerable social differences among the Srubnaya population.

Two periods in the development of the Srubnaya culture in the steppe country east of the Dnieper have been distinguished (Table 5). The earlier of these lasted till about the eighth century B.C., when considerable changes occurred, evidently through the arrival in the country of a wave of kindred tribes from the east, from the original region of the culture on the Lower Volga. Graves during this later period were mainly secondary burials in ancient mounds and had no timber constructions. On the Lower Dnieper up to thirty burials have been uncovered in a single mound. Their pottery was dark, thick-walled, and often had a finger-tipped band round the vessel; it was of the same type as that found in Srubnaya graves on the Lower Volga and settlements of the region on the Middle Volga of the time preceding its appearance in the west (Pl. XLI). Also very common were simple undecorated pots, straight-sided and wide-mouthed, or beakers with a wide base.

The Srubnaya graves on the Lower Dnieper and in the steppe west of the river up to the Inguletz differed in many respects from those further east. No timber constructions were found in the graves, which for the most part were secondary burials in ancient mounds. A common practice was to cover the grave with a stone pavement or a small cairn (Fig. 79), and this was the rule in flat graves, many of which were discovered within or near the settlements of that period. The pottery included vessels alien to the Srubnaya culture east of the Dnieper, but characteristic of the cultures of the steppe or forest-steppe west of the river (see p. 344). In graves later than the eighth century B.C., pottery of the late Srubnaya character appeared—mainly low, wide-mouthed and straight-sided undecorated pots, with a wide base.

The Srubnaya population in the Ukrainian steppe country depended mainly on a pastoral economy. Animal bones found in barrow graves near Izium on the Donetz are divided 55.6 per cent to cattle and 44.4 per cent to sheep. Horses' bones were very seldom found in burials, though sometimes a skull and occasionally entire skeletons were excavated; horses must have been kept for transport. Agriculture was practised mainly by the inhabitants of the settlements in the river valleys.

A number of settlements west of the Don have been attributed to the Srubnaya culture.[39] The early settlements lay exclusively in the valley of the Upper Don, but those of the second stage moved further west, though still keeping to the forest-steppe zone on the Upper Donetz or the coast of the Sea of Azov in the south. Most of the settlements of that period in the Dnieper valley and in the valley of the Southern Bug (the Boh) belonged to a somewhat different culture called the Sabatynivka culture. Only a few settlements near Dnepropetrovsk and one on the southern bank of the Dnieper (Bilozerka liman), south of Nikopol, belonged to the Srubnaya culture; they have been called the Bilozerka type of settlement. In one of these, at Kamyanka-Dniprovska, a semi-subterranean rectangular dwelling was uncovered. It was large, thirty-six feet wide and very long, though its exact length has not been established, and several cobbled hearths lay along the axis; it contained a large number of stone tools, potsherds, bronze knives, and wrought bronze awls; and the animal bones discovered in it were identified as those of horses, cattle, sheep, and pigs.

THE SABATYNIVKA CULTURE

Most of the settlements of the Srubnaya period in the valley of the Lower Dnieper, and in the valleys of other rivers further west in the steppe country, were not of the Srubnaya culture. These settlements, about a hundred of which have so far been recorded and many investigated, formed part of the Sabatynivka culture, called after a settlement on the Boh near Pervomaisk. The culture differed in many respects from the Srubnaya. The construction of its dwellings, its pottery, and also the character of the graves associated with its settlements, imply that the inhabitants were for the most part the descendants of the indigenous population, the parentage of which may be traced back to the Neolithic. The preponderant influence, however, came from the newcomers of the Srubnaya culture, some of whom settled in the valley and mingled with the aboriginal population, though most of them lived on the steppe.

The settlements of the Sabatynivka culture lay on the edge of the river valleys. Their dwellings differed from those of the Srubnaya culture east of the Dnieper, some huts being semi-subterranean, though most of them were built on the surface. The lower part of the latter was of stone, or had at least a kind of stone foundation, and the upper part was of pisé—following the style of the dwellings of the Usatovo settlement of the preceding period. In some cases (Zmiivka), the walls were of wattle mounted on a frame of vertical paling plastered with clay and resting on a foundation of irregularly quarried stones. Dwellings were rectangular; some were large, up to forty-six feet by twenty-six feet in area, and had several apartments, while others, considered to be of a later date, were smaller, with a single apartment. Huts were mostly arranged in one or two rows, forming small villages. The largest known so far (Zvonetska Balka) consisted of eighteen huts in two rows, which lay at a distance of forty feet from each other.

The culture has been divided into two periods (Table 5). The earlier one, to which the settlement of Sabatynivka belonged, began by the end of the thirteenth century B.C. and ended probably in the eighth century B.C. It has often been called the 'Cimmerian' period and has usually been divided into the Sabatynivka and Bilozerka stages.[40] In fact, however, the Sabatynivka settlements were characteristic of the country west of the Dnieper, and those of the Bilozerka type, found only in the valley of the Dnieper, were closely related to the Srubnaya settlements east of the river. The second period which lasted to the Scythian Age, the end of the seventh century B.C. has mostly been called the 'pre-Scythian' period.

The turn of the two periods was marked by the destruction of a large number of settlements, probably by a North Caucasian people who invaded the country via the Crimea and then proceeded further north into the country of the Middle Dnieper. There, on the southern border of the forest-steppe zone, a new culture, the 'Chornii-Lis' culture, was formed (see p. 378); and its founders were presumably the North Caucasian newcomers.

The period from 850 to 700 B.C. was relatively calm. The arrival at the turn of the seventh and sixth centuries B.C. of the west Asiatic Scythians, and their splendid culture, hardly affected the Srubnaya tribes east of the Dnieper or the Sabatynivka people west of the river. For at least another two centuries they kept to their ancient culture.

The pottery of the two periods of the Sabatynivka culture shows some differences. Typical pots of the earlier period were fashioned with a widened belly, a slightly everted rim, and a relatively wide base. Their usual decoration consisted of one or more bands in relief, plain or with oblique incisions placed under the rim. Many vessels had incised or stamped rows of short oblique lines or zigzags, sometimes rows of horizontally shaded triangles or some other more sophisticated pattern, reminiscent of the pottery of the Catacomb culture. Handled cups and dippers and straight-sided pots were also common. A few vessels had black, slightly polished surfaces. Tools found in huts consisted of saddle-querns, stone hammers, grinders, bone implements (points, pins, awls, etc.), and often a few small bronze knives and awls. Moulds for casting bronze objects were found in many settlements. Several types of vessels and tools are very like those of the Bilohrudivka culture (see p. 375), which bordered the Sabatynivka culture to the north.

The pottery of the second period included many vessels of the earlier period, but the leading types were now vessels with nearly cylindrical necks and undecorated pots of the flower-pot type; straight-sided cups replaced handle cups and dippers. The pottery of this period reflects close connections with the Srubnaya settlements of the Bilozerka type (see p. 342). Among the stone implements found were composite sickles of the same type as those of the Bilohrudivka culture. Bone implements were rare, but there were more bronze objects than during the first period, and among them were now bronze pins. In some cases, iron knives and awls were excavated. The remains of the second period reflect an impoverishment of the population.

Many graves and small cemeteries of the Sabatynivka culture have been investigated. They were just inhumations, without mounds over the grave, and only a few barrow graves are attributable to the culture. One of these, at Lukianivka near Kakhivka on the Lower Dnieper, contained a small grey vase with a high neck and its lower

XLIII 'Villanova' bronze helmet found at Krzemienna near Kamenetz Podolskii.
After A. Szlankówna, *Swiatowit* vol. XVII, 1936–7, p. 296, fig. 2.

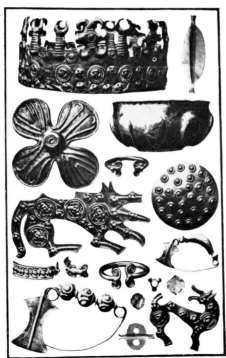

XLIV Objects from the gold hoard of Michałków on the Dniester.
After K. Hadaczek, *Złote skarby Michałkowskie*, Kraków 1904, pl. I–XIII, and L. Kozłowski, *Zarys pradziejów Polski południowo-wschodniej*, Lwów 1939, p. 76, pl. XXI.

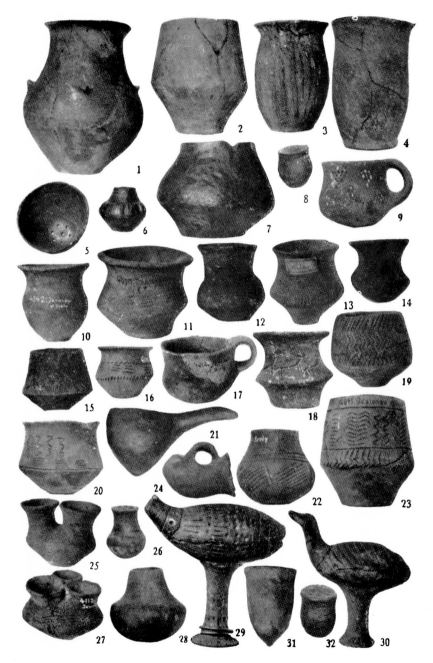

XLV Vessels characteristic of the cemeteries of the Wysocko culture. After T. Sulimirski, *Kultura Wysocka*. Kraków 1931, pl. XI–XXIII; and L. Kozłowski (as pl. XLIV, p. 64, pl. XVII).

part decorated with a few small bosses; bronze tutuli; amber and glass beads; and a bronze brooch. The brooch, of Sub-Mycenaean type (the eleventh to ninth centuries B.C.), must have been imported either from the Balkans, or from Italy. The grave evidently belonged to the earlier period of the culture. Three barrow graves were excavated at Pechora on the Boh (Southern Bug), south of Vinnitsa. They contained only pottery of the same type as that of the upper layer of the Sabatynivka settlement, which suggests that the Sabatynivka culture extended westwards up to that area. The pottery also exhibits many features characteristic of the early Scythian ware, of the sixth century B.C., and may be regarded as transitional to the latter.

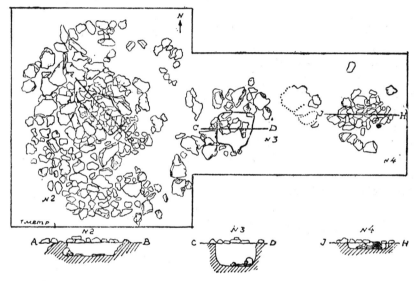

FIG. 79 Burials with 'stone covers' (kamyana zakladka) at Balka Bashmatka near the Dnieper rapids.
After O. Lahodovska (P.A. vol. II, 1949, p. 177, fig. 10).

Burials under so-called 'stone-covers', consisting of an area ten feet by twenty-six feet three inches cobbled with irregularly quarried stones, were characteristic of the culture (Fig. 79). Usually a single grave was placed under each 'cover', but quite often two or three were uncovered. In a few instances, a cairn was raised over the grave. Graves under the 'covers' were mostly in shallow shafts and each contained a single corpse; often, however, slab-cists were found. Stone 'covers' sometimes appear in groups of up to seven, forming small cemeteries. Skeletons sometimes lay supine, or, more often, crouched. Their endowment was poor: a single vessel, a few flints, occasionally a hoe of antler or a clay whorl.

24

Stone 'covers' were typical of the Srubnaya period on the Lower Dnieper, but similar constructions had already appeared in the region of the Dnieper rapids during the Catacomb period. Vessels typical of the Scythian period appeared in the latest 'covers'. The persistence of this type of burial implies the survival of the ancient indigenous population of the valley throughout several subsequent periods, during which it always managed to adapt itself to changing circumstances. Pottery and other features of the Srubnaya barrow graves of the surrounding steppe show how the culture of the new-comers had been influenced by that of the local population. For this reason the Srubnaya branch on the Dnieper differed from its kindred groups further east, and from the Srubnaya-Khvalinsk culture in particular.

The economy of the population was based on agriculture and animal husbandry. Bones excavated in the settlement of the earlier period at Zmiivka were identified as 45 per cent of cattle, 26 per cent horses, 18 per cent sheep, and 18 per cent pigs; they all belonged to young animals. A large number of moulds for casting bronze objects were found in settlements of the early period in the valley and along the sea coast, and suggest the existence of a developed bronze in-dustry based on imported raw material that must also have played an important role in the economy of the population. Once about seventy moulds were excavated in a single hut, which implies that the products of the foundries were destined for distribution among the pastoral tribes of the surrounding steppe.

THE 'CIMMERIAN' BRONZE INDUSTRY (Table 6)

The Sabatynivka bronze industry was not the only one in the valley of the Dnieper and the country west of the river. Traces of local foundries have been found in several points north of the steppe. The industry of the whole area deserves some attention, as it also reflects the great changes which occurred in the country during the second and early first millennia B.C.[41]

During the Middle Bronze Age, the Catacomb period, a very meagre bronze (copper) industry existed in the north Pontic area west of the Dnieper, based on raw material probably imported from Transylvania. Most of its products—small weapons and tools, per-sonal ornaments—represent slightly modified 'Hungarian' types, and many objects were simply imported from Central Europe.

The position was different after the arrival of the Srubnaya people in the thirteenth century B.C., for one of the consequences of this event was the growth of a new metallurgy on the Dnieper, closely related to and evidently derived from the bronze industry of the region of Kazan and the Lower Kama. Bronze objects of this period, up to about the eighth century B.C., found in the regions along the Middle and Lower Dnieper show unmistakable derivation from the east Russian Seima-Turbino types. However, only a few of these can be regarded as having actually been imported from the east; the bulk were evidently the products of local foundries of the Cimmerian bronze industry using imported raw material. Stone (talc) moulds for casting bronze objects were found in settlements of almost all the cultures of this period investigated in the valley of the Dnieper (Fig. 80), from Kiev down the river to the Black Sea coast, and also outside the valley. The great foundries of the Sabatynivka culture, with up to seventy moulds, were concentrated mainly in the valley of the Lower Dnieper, and near the estuaries of the rivers along the Black Sea coast further west, up to the Dniester (Map XXII: I).

Foundries in the northern part of the area, such as that at the settlement of Bondarykha, and possibly also those along the valley of the Middle Dnieper, were presumably provided with raw material from the Kazan-Kama region or the Urals. This seems to be indicated by the discovery of bronze hoards consisting of 'eastern' types of objects within the area. The route probably led through the forest-steppe country, over the territory containing the earliest settlements of the Srubnaya culture that appeared west of its original country. On the other hand, chemical analyses of the Cimmerian bronzes produced by the large southern foundries of the Sabatynivka culture revealed that they were cast of bronze of 'Balkan-Carpathian' origin.

The products of all the foundries of the Cimmerian stage, the twelfth to eighth centuries B.C., exhibit a remarkable degree of uniformity (Fig. 81), which implies that the industry must have been well organized and the delivery of the raw material well regulated. The industry must have been started by foundry-masters from the Kazan-Kama region or the Urals, for no contacts existed with the industry of the south Urals and that of the Andronovo culture. Among the typical products were varieties of single and double-looped socketed axes, spear-heads with semicircular openings on the blade, chisels, sickles, and numerous personal ornaments. Daggers with the opening on the hilt, similar to those from Sosnovaya Maza in the Volga region, and sickles with hooked pivots, seem to have been introduced at the very end of the Cimmerian stage.

The products of the Cimmerian bronze industry of the Ukraine differ markedly from their prototypes of the Kazan-Kama region. They skilfully combine characteristics of the original eastern types with those of the 'Hungarian' types common in the country during

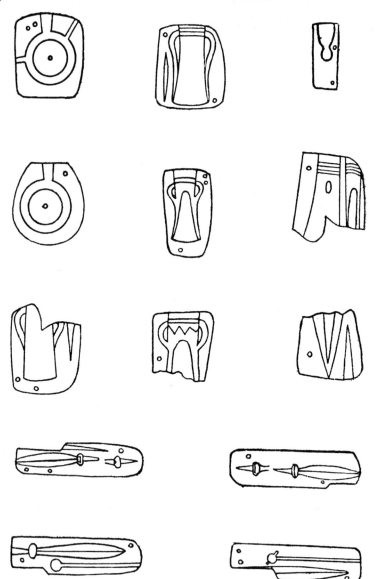

FIG. 80 Thirteen talc moulds for casting sixteen bronze objects of the 'Cimmerian' type from the settlement of the Sabatynivka culture at Novo-Oleksandrivka on the Lower Dnieper.
After A. V. Dobrovolskii (A.K. vol. IV, 1950, p. 165, pl. 1).

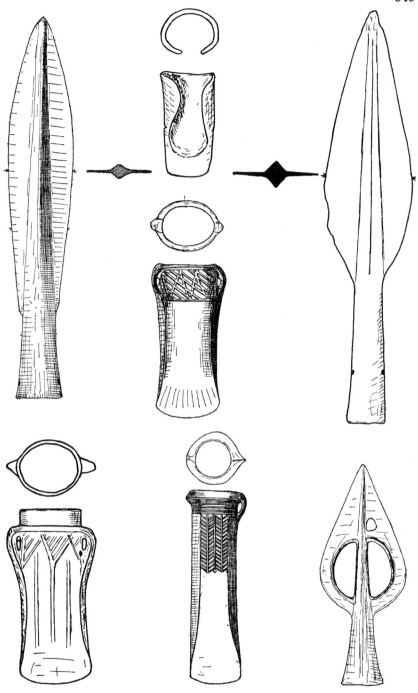

FIG. 81 *Top right:* Bronze lance-heads of the Seima type and axe with an open socket (Karabczyjów near Kamenets Podolskii); objects typical of the 'Cimmerian' bronze industry (lance-head with an oblong blade from Bybolush on the Perekop, socketed axes: *(in the middle)* Bukryn near Kanev, *(lower row left)* from the Ukraine, *(middle)* from Khmilna near Cherkassy, lance head with open blade from Tripolye).

the preceding period. The local bronze-founders evidently adapted the eastern types to the taste of the local population, which must have survived from earlier times.

The industry served several cultures of the period in the North Pontic area. Cimmerian bronze tools and weapons have been found throughout the territory of the Srubnaya culture west of the Don; small numbers also appeared in the steppe country of the Caucasus, but not the mountains; they were occasionally found in the Ukraine west of the Boh (Southern Bug), but more frequently in the coastal strip; and they reached the Sub-Carpathian area.

Apart from the products of the local Cimmerian industry, many Central European bronze objects found their way into the North Pontic area west of the Dnieper. Socketed axes and other objects of 'Hungarian' type were found in West Podolia and the sub-Carpathian area, giving this region the character of a 'Hungarian' province. Several 'Hungarian' bronzes were found along the sea coast, and also a number of 'Transylvanian' and 'Rumanian' types of socketed axes (Pl. XXVII) and sickles reached the same regions. They illustrate well the extent of the 'western', Komarów-Costişa penetration into the Ukraine. On the other hand, in the northern part of the country several objects (mainly personal ornaments) of Lusatian type have appeared, and a genuine Lusatian socketed axe of the Great Polish type, characteristic of the Bronze Age period IV (1000–800 B.C.), reached as far south as Koblevo near Odessa (Map XXIX: 48; Fig. 82).

The conditions during the later period were different. The Cimmerian bronze industry came to an end in the eighth century B.C.; and its moulds, made exclusively of talc, were found heaped and abandoned in the ruins of the destroyed Sabatynivka settlements, the main centres of the industry. Only meagre traces of its revival have been noticed in the second period; at Illinka near Odessa a foundry oven of this period was uncovered. The new industry differed substantially from that of the preceding period; its Caucasian links, unknown previously, came to the fore. The large hoard from Berislav on the Lower Dnieper contained bronze objects characteristic of this period—Koban and Kuban shaft-hole axes (Pl. XXVII) and bent sickles with a hooked hilt-tang. Most of these objects seem to have been cast locally on Caucasian models.

The centre of the North Pontic bronze industry of the period from the eighth to seventh centuries B.C. moved from the Sabatynivka region northwards, into the territory of the Chornii-Lis culture (see p. 381). It was closely connected with and dependent on the industry of the North-west Caucasus. A similar industry, called the 'Thraco-Cimmerian', sprang up in Rumania and the Hungarian plain.

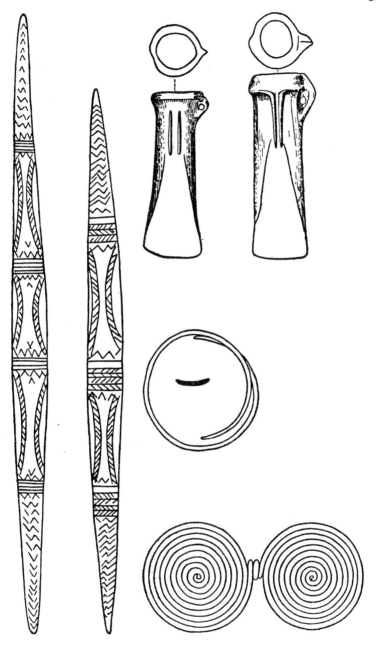

FIG. 82 Lusatian bronze objects found in the Ukraine: decorated arm-bands from Babychi near Cherkassy and Marianówka in Podolia (*on the right*); Lusatian type socketed axe from the hoard of Koblevo near Odessa (*left*) and from an unknown location in Podolia (*right*); a double spiral from the environment of Zhitomir.
After T. Sulimirski (*Wiadomości Archeologiczne*, vol. xiv, 1936, pls. x, xi).

THE SOUTH-WESTERN BORDERLAND

Before describing the further development of the North Pontic area, attention must first be given to the border area between Eastern and Central Europe, to West Podolia and West Volhynia in particular. There, several cultures characteristic of these two parts of Europe met and overlapped late in the second and early in the first millennia B.C., thus giving us an opportunity for comparing their development (Table 5). Then the Caucasian, and especially the Transcaucasian, developments must be dealt with, for these played a decisive role in the later cultural evolution and history of Eastern Europe.

The Srubnaya conquest of the steppe country of the Ukraine around 1200 B.C., and its expansion further west, considerably affected the countries on the south-western confines of Eastern Europe and the adjoining areas. Among its consequences was the replacement in Moldavia of the Costişa culture by the Noua culture, which seems to have been formed under Srubnaya impact.[42] Objects characteristic of the Srubnaya culture, for example bronze knives of a special type, have been found in some sites among the remains of the Noua culture. On the other hand, a number of pot-forms point to Noua connections with the Komarów and the Bilohrudivka cultures (see p. 377)—high pots with a row of perforations under the everted rim, and a raised band around the shoulder of the vessel.

Another consequence of the impact of the Srubnaya culture was the development of a specifically Transylvanian bronze industry; for its bent and hooked sickles and some types of socketed axe were obviously derived from the Dnieper and even the Kama industries, where similar objects were common at a much earlier date. The Transylvanian and the Noua industries also evolved several local types.

THE NOUA CULTURE

The consequences of the new development in Rumania were soon felt further north. In moving northwards the Noua culture (Map XXIX: XXIV) spread along nearly the whole course of the Dniester, from the region north of Chernivtsi (Cernauţi) down to the region north-west of Kishinev (Chişinau). The northernmost site was the settlement and cemetery at Ostrivets, near Horodenka on the Dniester,[43] with its 156 poorly endowed interments. Skeletons, all crouched, were accompanied by up to four vessels and occasionally some simple bronze ornaments, chiefly pins, sometimes small rings or small discoid beads of white paste. Pots with a raised band round the shoulder, cups, and double-handled vases, were the usual pottery finds. In a hut of the settlement stone moulds were found for casting bronze socketed celts, spear-heads, small mirrors and other small objects typical of the culture.

An important stratified settlement was investigated at Mahala, near Chernivtsi[44] (Map XXIX: 61). Its lower layer was of the Noua culture, and the upper of the Holihrady culture, which hitherto had been looked on as earlier than the Noua culture. Huts were quadrangular in shape and built on the surface, with several posts supporting the roof. They had either an open hearth or an oven built of clay with some kind of vaulted overstructure, probably of ozier plastered with clay. An ashy mound (zolnik) adjoined the settlement; a large number of potsherds were found in its layer, and also stone and bone tools and several bronze objects—a socketed spear-head, pins, sickles of Transylvanian type, and pendants. The pottery was either a thin-walled 'table' ware (dippers and double-handled vases) or a thick-walled 'kitchen' ware (mostly simple pots) made of quartz-gritted paste.

Similar settlements and ashy mounds (zolniks) have been recorded in several sites along the Dniester. That investigated at Holercani, north-east of Kishinev,[45] was of the same type as the settlement at Mahala and its ashy mound was similar. So also was its pottery and the other remains found in the settlement. Ashy mounds of the Bilohrudivka culture were of the same type. This circumstance, and also the fact that they were found only in the Uman group of the culture, indicate that the custom of raising them was taken over from the Noua culture.

Small groups of the Noua people must have crossed the Dniester and entered West Podolia; for double-handled vases characteristic of the culture have been found in some sites in west Podolia and in the central part of Volhynia (Dubno), and even in the barrow-grave cemetery of Voytsekhivka on the Sluch (Pl. XXVI). The newcomers seem to have soon been assimilated by the indigenous population of these countries, but they nevertheless influenced them to some extent. The double-handled vases which at that time appeared in the Komarów culture and also in Volhynia, and several bronze socketed axes and sickles of Transylvanian types, found mainly in West Podolia, were undoubtedly connected with the activities of the Noua people.

THE HOLIHRADY CULTURE

Considerable changes took place about the eleventh century B.C. in the southern part of Podolia and also in Bessarabia and Moldavia (Table 5). At that time these countries became the domain of the 'Thracian Hallstatt' or 'Holihrady' culture[46] (Map XXIX: XXX), called after a settlement in West Podolia excavated by the author.

The culture has been almost entirely deduced from forty odd recorded settlements, which in their character, type of house, etc. did not differ from those of the preceding period, or even from those of the Tripolye culture. One characteristic of the culture was its very fine, black, polished, often fluted pottery of excellent quality, which compares well with the best Tripolyan ware (Pl. XLII). Another feature of the culture, especially in West Podolia, was the large number of stray bronze objects and also hoards, all of 'Hungarian' type: bronze socketed axes, spear-heads, ornaments, and sickles. They simply flooded the country at that time, giving it the character of a Hungarian Bronze Age province.

The origin of the Holihrady culture and the reason for its sudden appearance are disputable. I.K. Sveshnikov seems to be right in connecting it with an invasion or immigration of a people from the other side of the Carpathians, from the Hungarian plain. The culture must have spread rapidly over the whole country, superseding the Noua culture. In West Podolia, the Biały Potok group disappeared, but the few slab-cist graves of a later date seem to imply the survival of the ancient traditions of its ruling class. The Komarów culture was now confined to the sub-Carpathian area only.

The founding of the culture can be dated by two bronze brooches of a late variety of the Peschiera type found in the remains of a burnt hut of the culture at Nowosiółka Kostiukowa near Zaleszczyki (Map XXIX: 58). The brooch cannot be dated later than 1000–1100 B.C.

The current responsible for the formation of the Holihrady culture reached further east, up to the Dnieper. Several vessels of the Bilohrudivka culture (see p. 376) reflect its influence; and bronzes of the 'Hungarian' type of that period have been found in several sites, especially in the region on the Lower Dnieper and near the sea coast —such as the hoard of Novogrigorievka (Pl. XXVII).

A new and troublesome period returned in the eighth century B.C. A large number of bronze hoards were hidden then, especially in West Podolia, where also twenty-odd bronze swords of the period were found—twelve of them in a single hoard at Komarniki near Turka, in a Carpathian pass. The weapons well illustrate the precarious situation of the Holihrady people, which was evidently the outcome of the events in the country on the Lower and Middle Dnieper, and with the formation there of the Chornii-Lis culture. We shall return to these events on p. 378.

The assault on West Podolia seems to have been repulsed, but it was followed by a gradual decline of the culture, which is well illustrated by the advance of the Wysocko culture deep into Podolia. Hungarian connections were probably still maintained, and a few east Alpine or Italian bronze objects reached the country most probably via those sources. One of these was a Villanova bronze helmet, found at Krzemienna near Kamenetz Podolskii (Pl. XLIII; Map XXIX: 57), which dated from the very end of this period. However, the centre of events gradually shifted to Moldavia and Transylvania, where the 'Thraco-Cimmerian' bits, cheek-pieces and other pieces of horse harness made their appearance. The gold hoard found at Michałków on the Dniester (Pl. XLIV) reveals wide connections southwards to the Balkans (Bulgaria) and also with the eastern part of the Hungarian plain.[47]

The Michałków hoard above gives the final date of the Holihrady culture. It consisted of vessels, a diadem, plaques, brooches of several types, thousands of beads of various types and sizes, bracelets, a torque, and of bars, all made of electron, an alloy 83 per cent of gold and 13 per cent of silver—plus some large lumps of amber. Brooches derived from Greek fibulae of the eighth–seventh centuries B.C. point to close relations with the Balkans, and others shaped like fantastic animals suggest North Caucasian, Koban connections. The hoard weighed over thirteen pounds and was one of the outstanding finds of the 'Thraco-Cimmerian' type, most of which were discovered within the limits of the Hungarian Plain. It was evidently the property of the wealthy ruling family, collected by several subsequent generations, and so contained objects made at various periods. It was most probably hidden about 600 B.C. during the Scythian assault on West Podolia and the surrounding area. We may guess that the principality ruled by the owner of the hoard was conquered by the Scythians and that he was unable to recover his property, which, even by present-day standards, was of very considerable value (see p. 384).

THE WYSOCKO CULTURE

North of the Holihrady culture extended the territory of the Wysocko culture (Map XXIX: XXIX), called after a cemetery near Brody that was excavated by the author. It lay near the sources of the Styr and the Bug, on the watershed between the Baltic and the Black Sea.

The Wysocko culture was formed probably in the ninth century B.C., about the middle of period IV of the Bronze Age.[48] It developed out of the local substratum, though the main agent in its development was the Central European Lusatian culture, typical of the Polish Bronze Age. Formed in the north, the Wysocko culture later spread southwards into West Podolia, and after 800 B.C. reached deep into that country; it survived at least to the fourth century B.C.

Some of the cemeteries of the Wysocko culture, such as Wysocko itself, contained over 150 burials, about 10 per cent of which were cremations, some in urns and some not. The commonest grave goods

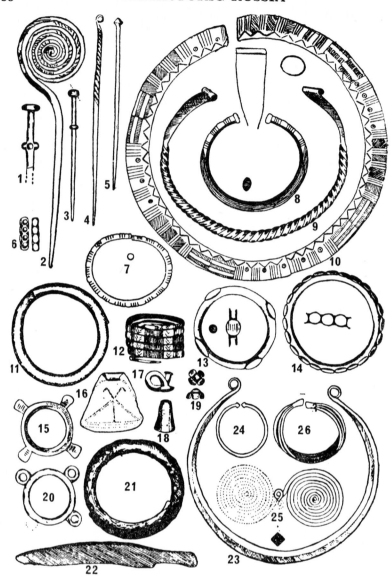

FIG. 83 Bronze and iron ornaments characteristic of the Wysocko culture. After T. Sulimirski and L. Kozłowski (*Zarys pradziejów Polski poludniowo-wschodniej.* Lwów 1939, pl. xviii).

were pottery, one to four vessels but seldom more. They were mostly high tulip-shaped pots, often with a row of perforations under the rim and a raised, mostly finger-tipped band round the shoulder (Pl. XLV); they did not differ much from those of the Bilohrudivka culture, and hardly at all from the Chornii-Lis pots (Table 23). Other common vessels were dippers, cups and bowls. Personal ornaments were often found, and several graves were richly endowed with them; they consisted of bronze and iron pins, rings, temple ornaments, neck-rings, necklaces of a variety of beads, bronze and iron bracelets and armlets etc. Small iron knives (Fig. 83) were also common. Stone

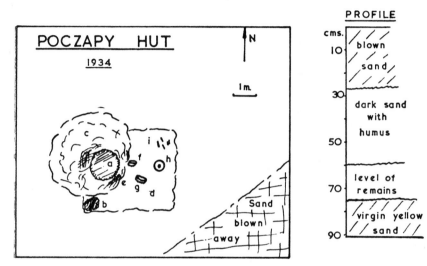

FIG. 84 Plan of a hut of the Wysocko culture (about 13 ft. wide and 16 ft. 6 in. long), excavated in 1934 by the author at Poczapy near Złoczów, West Podolia.
(a) hearth; (b) heaped fine gravel; (c) layer of fine gravel mixed with sand, probably from the destroyed overstructure of the hut; (d) layer of dark earth marking the floor of the hut, on which lay sherds of several vessels and objects quoted below; (e) iron roll-headed pin; (f) (g) bases of two vessels; (h) clay whorl; (i) small accumulation of charred animal bones.

hammer-axes (battle-axes), flint knives and arrow-heads were a sur-vival from the past. In late graves bronze temple ornaments and arrow-heads of the Scythian type were found. A bronze brooch of the Hallstatt B-C type found in the cemetery of Złoczów and a few bronze razors of the Benacci type were important for dating purposes, and they also pointed to connections with the distant Alpean countries.
One of the few settlements of the Wysocko culture recorded was

on a sand-dune near Złoczów (Poczapy Fig. 84). The huts were quadrangular, about thirteen feet by sixteen feet six inches, and built on the surface. They had either an oven built of clay, or a circular hearth over forty inches in diameter, placed in the middle of the narrow side. Potsherds scattered on the floor, whorls, and once an iron roll-headed pin, were found in the debris. The pin dated the settlement to the seventh century B.C.

The Wysocko culture owed its formation to small groups of Lusatian colonists who entered the country and mingled with the aboriginal population. Lusatian influence, probably through trade and not actual colonization, had penetrated as far east as the Dnieper by about 900 B.C. Stray bronze objects, palstaves, winged axes, and an arm-ring—all of Lusatian types of the middle of period IV of the Bronze Age—have been found in the northern part of the Ukraine up to Kiev, and in the valley of the Dnieper down to the Black Sea coast. A genuine Lusatian bronze socketed axe formed part of the foundry hoard discovered at Koblevo near Odessa[49] (Fig. 82). It is interesting to note that pottery almost identical with the Lusatian ware of the fourth period of the Bronze Age has been found on sand-dunes near Kherson, south of the Dnieper.

THE CAUCASUS

The movement of the Srubnaya tribes in the thirteenth century B.C. forced several tribes of the Manych group of the Catacomb culture to retreat into the North Caucasian foothills (Map XXIX: XVII). Under renewed pressure they retreated into the Kuban country and the plateau near Nalchik, where they survived up to the eighth or seventh centuries B.C.[50] Considerable changes also occurred in the Caucasian highland; however, the ancient division into three main areas, each with a somewhat different culture, remained.

In the central part, in Northern Ossetia and Kabarda, together with the highland region called Digoria, the North Caucasian culture of the Middle Bronze Age was succeeded by the 'Digorian' culture (Table 4). Slab-cists were the usual type of grave and contained mostly a single, exceptionally, a double burial. The skeletons were in a slightly crouched position, heads to the east, and female skeletons were strewn with ochre. They were accompanied by bronze earrings with flattened ends overlapping; bronze bracelets; pins of the 'Digorian' type with flattened and spirals on both sides to give them the shape of a ram's head; and small cylindrical beads of white paste. Flint or bone arrow-heads, shaft-hole axes of bronze, or knives were often found. At Verkhyaya Rutkha, among the grave goods, were a mould for casting spear-heads, and two iron shaft-hole axes of the 'Koban' type; and many burials included pottery.

The Koban Culture

By the end of the second millennium B.C. the Digorian culture fell under a very strong Transcaucasian influence, which gradually transformed it into the Koban culture (Map XXIX: XVIII), called after a village near Orjonikidze (Vladikavkaz) in the Central Caucasian highland (Table 5).[51] The close ties connecting the new culture with the Colchidic culture of Georgia has already been referred to (see p. 236).

The newly formed Koban culture soon spread throughout the central part of the north Caucasus, and also affected the neighbouring areas. The absorption of the Late Bronze Age groups in these regions led to the formation of three more or less differing branches of the Koban culture[52]—the proper Koban, or highland branch; the Kabardino-Piatigorsk branch to the north-west of the former; and the Checheno-Ingush branch in the north-eastern foothills.

The Koban culture has been variously dated. According to recent research it was formed approximately in the eleventh century and continued till about 400 B.C. Three periods in its development have been distinguished. The first, formative, period lasted till the ninth or perhaps the eighth century B.C.; the second period ended around 650 B.C., and close contact throughout it was maintained with the Scythians in Transcaucasia (see p. 339), who became a great power at that time in Western Asia; and the third period, called the 'Scythian' period, lasted till the fourth century B.C.

The cemeteries of the Koban culture were rather small, consisting of a few graves only; the large ones, like that at Verkhnaya Koban after which the culture has been called, with its 800 to 1,000 burials, were an exception. Burials in slab-cists sunk in the ground were typical, often containing several subsequent interments. The highland graves were richly furnished with bronze weapons and ornaments, and occasionally with pottery. Bronze objects were usually large in size, and many of them decorated—especially the bronze belts, belt-buckles, shaft-hole axes of the 'Koban' type (Fig. 85) and pins.[53] The latter often had the head fashioned in the shape of a human or animal figurine. The favourite decorative motif, engraved on axes and other objects, was the 'Koban' animal, which seems to be the greatly distorted figure of a horse. There were also temple ornaments, bracelets of many types, a variety of brooches, and necklaces of carnelian beads and of other varieties of stone. A large number of pieces of horse harness were found: bits, and cheek-pieces often decorated with figurines (Pl. XLVI). At a later stage the bits and many weapons were made of iron. The pottery included bowls, handled cups and dippers, usually decorated with incised patterns consisting of hatched

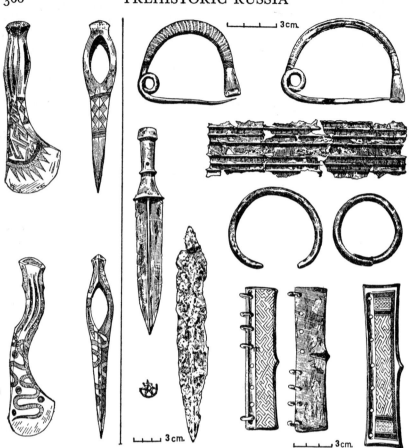

FIG. 85 Bronze weapons and ornaments, and an iron dagger, of the Koban culture, excavated in grave 16 at Til in South Ossetia. After B. M. Tekhov (s.a. vol. 1960–1, p. 163, figs. 4, 5).

triangles or rows of hatched lozenges; the incisions were often filled in with white paste.

The burials of the two other groups of the culture (for example, Kislovodsk) were also mostly in slab-cists, or were surrounded and covered by stones. Those in the Kabardino-Piatigorsk group were usually square, unlike those of the highland branch, which were quadrangular. Tubular bronze beads, pins, bracelets, small cylindrical beads of white paste, and iron pendants, were among the grave goods. Vessels, mainly bowls, were made of well silted clay paste, their surfaces polished, smoothed and decorated by incised triangles, squares and oblique lines; some of the decorative patterns and also the shapes call to mind the Srubnaya pottery of the region on the

XLVI Decorated bronze objects of the Koban culture. Bronze cheek-piece (no. 70587); bronze armband from the Faskau cemetery (no. 111 d 2311); a bronze decoration from the North Caucasus (no. 111 d 3948); zoomorphic bronze buckle from Koban (no. 27216).
Museum für Vor- und Frühgeschichte, Berlin-Charlottenburg; the latter at the Musée St Germain-en-Laye.

XLVII A decorated vase of the Gandzha-Kara-
bagh culture (no. 111 d 5151).
Museum für Vor- und Frühgeschichte, Berlin-
Charlottenburg.

XLVIII Decorated oval bronze armbands of the Chornii-Lis culture;
of unknown location in the Ukraine. *Upper:* (no. 32705, 5 in. long;
lower: (no. 32611), 4½ in. long.
State Archaeological Museum, Warsaw.

Lower Volga, though there are big differences. The grave goods and the burial ritual of these groups were typical of the Koban culture, but their pottery differed to some degree from that of the highland graves.

The fine genuine bronze objects of the Koban culture, their unusual abundance, the very large size of some, and their decorative style, have given rise to a great interest, and they have often been the source of discussion and special studies. The products bear witness to the great skill of the Koban master-smiths, and their knowledge of bronze alloying. The industry undoubtedly developed under the guidance of the Colchidic industry, but later evolved independently and produced a series of weapons and other objects, especially personal ornaments, which have no counterpart in the Colchidic culture. Some armlets or anklets made of a wide band of bronze sheet with spiral terminals, some very large raquet pins, and a few other similar ornaments, are strikingly reminiscent of products characteristic of the Central European Middle Bronze Age, and at least two daggers typical of the Hungarian Middle Bronze Age must have been imported from that area; several vessels from Verkhnaya Koban and other cemeteries are almost replicas of vessels from the Trzciniec and Komarów cultures. It seems very likely that the Trzciniec influence reached the Caucasus at the beginning of the Digorian period, and implanted Central European ideas in the Koban culture. Pottery similar to that of the Digorian culture with western features appeared also in the barrow-grave cemetery of Nalchik of the Middle Bronze Age.

The most characteristic types of the Koban metal industry however, were developed locally. The shaft-hole axes of the 'Koban' type (Fig. 85) are one of these, and they are regarded as deriving from the Piatigorsk stone battle-axes of the preceding period. The brooches, which show a great variety of types, are a development of Aegean brooches of the proto-geometric period (the eleventh–tenth centuries B.C.); they probably reached the Central Caucasian highland via Transcaucasia at a very early stage of the Koban culture. Many variations of cheek-pieces, bit, and other parts of a horse's harness, were evidently Transcaucasian borrowings.

The wealth displayed in Koban graves was of a different type from that of the Maikop or Trialeti barrow graves. No gold or silver objects were found in any of the Koban graves, and no marked disparity existed between the endowment of burials of the same cemetery; this fact suggests that Koban society was not divided into sharply differentiated social classes. On the other hand, the rather unusual abundance of metal, expressed especially by the size and extravagant shape of many bronze objects and the considerable waste

25

of material by the practice of depositing a large mass of metal in graves, implies that copper, at least, was cheap. The Koban territory, particularly the highland region, was very rich in copper deposits, but tin was available only in small quantities on the southern side of the main ridge, in South Ossetia; arsenic and lead were mainly substituted for it.

No such display or waste of metal has been noticed in any other of the rich metalliferous regions of East Europe and West Siberia, so it seems that this was due to special circumstances. Copper was already exploited in the Central Caucasian highland during the Digorian period, and probably exported via Transcaucasia to distant countries including the Aegean, as suggested by the brooches. But by the ninth century B.C. conditions must have changed considerably. This was a troublesome period in Caucasian history, as is shown by the exceptionally high number of weapons found in Koban graves of that time. The wide use of iron weapons since the ninth century B.C. in Western Asia, and also in Transcaucasia, must have cut the demand for copper, leaving large supplies available to the local population.

The earliest iron objects seem to have reached the Koban culture by the ninth century B.C., but it is only later, probably after the seventh century, that locally wrought iron objects—knives, axes, and daggers—began to appear in Koban burials. Nevertheless, the cheapness of copper, the high quality of the products of local coppersmiths, and probably also the inborn conservatism of the population and its ancient traditions, allowed bronze tools and weapons to be manufactured and used in the Koban territory for several centuries more.

The Kayakent-Khorochoi and Late Kuban Cultures

The two other north Caucasian cultures of the Late Bronze Age and Early Iron Age differed from the Koban culture. That in Dagestan in the North-east Caucasus, called the Kayakent-Khorochoi culture, developed out of the reaction between the local culture of the preceding period and invading Srubnaya tribes.[54] It had many features in common with the contemporary culture of Azerbaijan, and was also considerably influenced by the Koban culture. Fifty graves were investigated at Khorochoi, mainly slab-cists, though some were timber chambers similar to those of the Srubnaya culture. The skeletons were crouched and the usual grave goods consisted of pottery, beads, bronze brooches and other personal ornaments, characteristic of the Koban culture (Map XXXII).

The pottery found in the other important cemetery, at Kayakent, was different. Many of its vessels call to mind those of the late corded ware of Central Europe, and some are reminiscent of the

Trzciniec-Komarów types. A slab-cist grave at Berekey, one of which bore an incised drawing of a chariot, was of particular interest.

A different culture developed at the western end of the North-west Caucasus, in the region on the river Kuban. During the Late Bronze Age up to the ninth century B.C. the country was the home of the Catacomb culture, which had retreated southwards under the pressure of the Srubnaya tribes and absorbed the survivors of the local branch of the North Caucasian culture of the Middle Bronze Age. The further development of this group ran parallel to, and was closely connected with, that of the Kabardino-Piatigorsk branch of the Koban culture, which bordered it to the east. The Catacomb elements probably contributed to the similarity of the two groups.

The culture of the North-west Caucasus of the Early Iron Age developed under a considerable influence from the Koban culture, which is clearly reflected by the bronze objects found within that territory. Some of these—shaft-hole axes, sickles, and personal ornaments of various types—were purely Koban and were undoubtedly brought there from the Central Caucasian highland. But most of the bronze objects of this period found in the area were evidently locally developed varieties of Koban types. Some of these were cast of pure copper, which was abundant, as no tin was available in the country. Traces of copper mining have been recorded in at least ten sites in the metalliferous mountains near the sources of the river Kuban and its tributaries. A few of these mines were caves dug out of the rock during the exploitation of the ores; the earliest dates from the Early Bronze Age, but several belonged to the Koban period or were still in operation during the Early Iron Age.

The people of the North-west Caucasian culture may be considered as ancient Sindians, a people mentioned by Herodotus.[55] The Sindians, whose territory included the Taman peninsula, are regarded as a branch of the Maeotians. The latter lived in the broad coastal strip of the Sea of Azov, the Maeotis of the Ancients, north of the Caucasus up to the delta of the Don; and were distinct from the Scythians, and also from the Sauromatians or Sarmatians, with whom they ultimately merged. They might have been a branch of the Cimmerians.

Two barrow graves of the seventh century B.C., the one on the Taman Peninsula called the Tsukur barrow, and the other near Kerch in the Crimea called 'Temir Gora', have been for long regarded as Cimmerian.[56] The latter contained several secondary interments. In its original burial were found a Rhodian oinochoe of the second half of the seventh century B.C., a few bone objects, a 'beak-head', and a ring-shaped pieces with an animal curled around —considered to be the earliest specimens decorated in the 'Scythic Animal' style in Europe.

One of the hallmarks of the period was the sudden appearance, perhaps in the eighth century but more likely in the ninth, of a relatively large number of bronze bits, cheek-pieces, and other pieces of horse-harness. They were found in graves, in hoards, and also as stray objects, within the Kuban country, the territory of the Koban culture, and further east. These objects could not have been introduced from the steppe, as no metal cheek-pieces or bits were known there before this period. Their origin must be sought in West Asia, and though the North Caucasian specimens differ from earlier specimens found in Transcaucasia and Western Asia, they were evidently a local development of the latter.

The appearance of a large number of horse-trappings in the North Caucasus faces us with the problem of their purpose and use. They were not needed for the small steppe horses of the Srubnaya, Andronovo, or other steppe peoples, but they were indispensable for harnessing the better-bred horses used for chariots in Western Asia. They were found in large quantities in all the countries that fought mainly in chariots at that time. A bronze model of a chariot with two horses and two warriors found in a barrow grave at Lchashen in Armenia, mainly of the thirteenth and twelfth centuries B.C.,[57] and bronze bits of an early west Asiatic type, imply the introduction of chariots into Transcaucasia at an early date. This is confirmed by drawings of chariots on a clay vessel from Dilizhan in Armenia, on the bronze belt from Akhtala near Leninakan, and on the stele from Berekey in Dagestan. It seems very likely that the Koban and probably the Kuban tribes of that period fought not only on horseback but also in chariots, like their neighbouring peoples in Transcaucasia. Presumably, only wealthy chieftains were in the possession of chariots.

Several types have been distinguished among the North Caucasian bits and cheek-pieces of the period from the eighth to the fifth century B.C.[58] Some of these were widely scattered, both within the North Caucasus and outside that country. Those of the earliest type, from the eighth century, were found mainly in the North Caucasus—the Koban area and the Kuban country—and also in the Crimea, the Ukraine, and the country on the Lower Don. But a variety of the early bits and cheek-pieces (called Type II) were also found in the Danubian countries of Central Europe, which formed part of the 'Thraco-Cimmerian' assemblage. Bronze cheek-pieces and bits, and also other objects of Caucasian type and origin, which were found in the Ukraine in the remains of the Chronii-Lis culture, and those found in some areas of Central Europe, especially Hungary, seem to indicate a western migration of some of the North-west Caucasian tribes around the eighth century B.C. We shall return to this subject on p. 382.

KOBAN TRADE

It has already been emphasized that one of the consequences of the western drive of the Srubnaya tribes in the thirteenth century B.C. was the isolation of the Caucasus and its well developed bronze industry from its wide markets in Eastern Europe (Map XXII). And it was not until centuries later that the North Caucasian bronzes, mainly products of the Koban industry, began again to be exported into the north Pontic steppe country and far beyond it.

Bronze objects of Koban origin found north or north-west of their original country were of several different classes. It is interesting to note that the diffusion of each of these classes was different, and depended on the distance from the Caucasus (Map XXXII). The steppe country in the south took Koban shaft-hole axes almost exclusively. One human figurine reached the province of Kiev, and others as far as the amber coast in East Prussia. The Late Bronze Age bronze figurines from Sweden, and from Kl. Zastrov in Mecklenburg,[59] most probably had some Caucasian connections, though they were not imported from the Caucasus. The class of Caucasian objects that travelled furthest was personal ornaments—circular or wheel-shaped pendants, belt-clasps, racquet pins, pins with a ram head, etc.; they were either imported from the Caucasus or were made locally on Caucasian models. They formed part of hoards or were found among grave goods in East Prussia, the island of Gotland, and on the Swedish mainland.[60] A bowl of the Luristan type also must have reached Sweden via the Caucasus. All these objects have been dated to period V of the Scandinavian Bronze Age, around 700 B.C. They were evidently of a somewhat later date than the Scandinavian objects found in Central Russia, which were of period IV (see p. 331); they suggest that the Koban relations with East Prussia and Scandinavia were later than the Scandinavian connections with the Urals. In this context it may be added that Koban and Caucasian contacts in general with Luristan and Iran have been pointed out by F. Hančar;[61] they are confirmed by a number of Luristan daggers found in the eastern part of Transcaucasia, and also within the Koban territory.[62]

The geographic diffusion of Koban objects (Map XXXII) evidently marks the important trade route by which connections must have been maintained between the Caucasus and the East Prussian amber coast and Sweden. It ran along the Donetz, the northern part of the Ukraine east of the Dnieper, and then along the water network of the Dnieper, the Pripet or the Niemen, and the Vistula. It is significant that it avoided the territory of the Chornii-Lis culture.

The concentrations of Koban finds in Sambia in East Prussia,

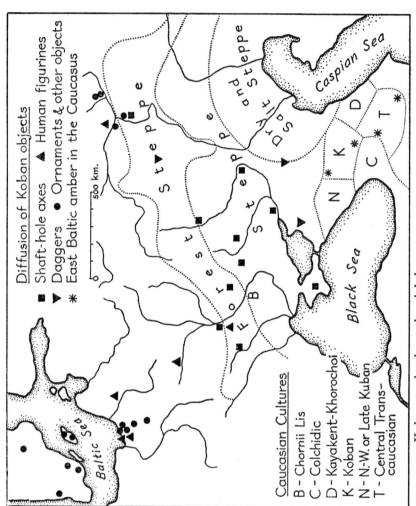

Diffusion of Koban objects
■ Shaft-hole axes   ▲ Human figurines
▶ Daggers   ● Ornaments & other objects
✳ East Baltic amber in the Caucasus

Caucasian Cultures
B - Chornii Lis
C - Colchidic
D - Kayakent-Khorochoi
K - Koban
N - N.-W. or Late Kuban
T - Central Trans-
      caucasian

MAP XXXII Koban trade about the eighth century B.C.

the very centre of the amber industry, is evidence for the object of the Caucasian trade. Actually, a considerable number of amber ornaments, pendants and beads, were found in the graves at several cemeteries of the Koban culture, and also in burials of the Central Transcaucasian culture dealt with under the next heading. The trade route had been long established: amber beads were found in Early Bronze Age graves of the Dnieper-Desna culture in Byelorussia, and also in those of the Sofiivka group further south, and Caucasian copper had already reached these regions at that time.

It seems that the Koban bronzes were not the sole commodity exported northwards; another was most probably *Cauris* shells, found in a number of graves in East Prussia and in those of the Pomeranian (Face-urn) culture in Northern Poland. They were imported from India or some other country on the Indian Ocean, most probably via the Caucasus. *Cauris* shells were found in several graves in various parts of the Northern Caucasus—at Kislovodsk and Nesterovskaya Stanitsa, for example.

Koban products also found their way to the country on the Middle Volga; two shaft-hole axes of the Koban type were found there and two others on the Don. A bronze dagger was found further north in Penza, and the northernmost find was a human figurine at Bolgar near Kazan.

Nothing can be said about the commodities received in exchange for these objects, but their small number seems to indicate that there was no intensive trade at that time between the Caucasus and the countries along the Volga. Trade connections between these areas with the Ananino culture developed considerably later, in the mid-first millennium B.C., during the Scythian Age. The few Koban objects just mentioned might have had some connection with the Scandinavian trade with the Urals.

THE CENTRAL TRANSCAUCASIAN CULTURE

Three main cultures of the period have been distinguished in Transcaucasia. The easternmost of these was the 'Khodzhaly-Kedabek' culture, also called the 'Gandzha-Karabagh' culture,[63] the development of which has usually been dated from the tenth to seventh centuries B.C. It extended over the steppe country of west Azerbaijan, south of the river Kura to the Karabagh mountains in the south (Pl. XLVII). It has been pointed out recently, however, that very similar remains have been found over the whole central part of Transcaucasia, though these come from slightly differing regional groups, as, for example, the 'Lelvar' culture near Leninakan. Accordingly, the present tendency is to group all these remains together under the heading of the 'Central Transcaucasian' culture (Maps XXIX; XXI; XXXII).

The Central Transcaucasian culture bordered on the Koban and Kayakent-Khorochoi cultures, and the Colchidic culture to the west, roughly along the line Tbilisi-Leninakan. In the south, the region around lake Sevan and the Karabagh mountains was within its territory, and its eastern limits did not go far beyond the town of Mingechaur.

This large territory was far from being homogeneous, nor were the remains of the main culture of the country. Burials in slab-cists were common in all parts of the country, but graves in simple shafts, frequently with an earthen or stone mound raised above them, often appeared alongside them. As a rule, graves contained a single corpse, but there were also many communal burials. Skeletons lay mostly crouched, though they were found sitting in many slab-cists. In some graves a horse skeleton was found beside the buried person. The grave goods consisted chiefly of pottery, up to twenty-three vessels having been found in a single grave. Vessels were of two types, either black polished, or dark-grey with an incised white inlaid ornament. The decorative motifs consisted of a variety of geometric patterns and of schematic human and animal (mainly stag) figures. The pottery was evidently a development of the former local ware, but the shape and decoration of a large number of bowls and other vessels call to mind those characteristic of the Srubnaya culture and, perhaps even more, those of the Andronovo culture.

Other common grave goods were axes, weapons, and personal ornaments. Swords and daggers were mostly local varieties of the common Transcaucasian type, and the same applies to the shaft-hole axes (battle-axes). Daggers often had hilts in openwork. Wide bronze belts made of thin sheet were usually decorated with hunting or battle scenes, or with animal figures. Among the personal ornaments were bracelets, armlets, temple and forehead ornaments, necklaces of carneol, and glass and bronze beads; bird-shaped pendants were common, but no brooches were found. Parts of horse harness were occasionally found.

All these objects were products of the well developed Transcaucasian bronze industry, which was based on rich deposits of copper, lead, zinc, silver and, later, iron, in the main northern ridge of the Caucasian mountains and various parts of the southern Anti-Caucasus, including the Karabagh mountains. The main centres of this industry were established in the period around 1300–1100 B.C.[64] The industry had close relations with that of Luristan further south in Iran,[65] and some of the Transcaucasian daggers were modelled on Luristan prototypes.

In the twelfth century B.C. the earliest iron objects began to appear in Armenia, but it was not until the ninth and eighth centuries B.C.

that their number showed any significant increase. These early iron objects—tools and weapons—were mostly modelled on their bronze prototypes. From the eighth century onwards iron gradually super-seded bronze in the manufacture of weapons and tools in Trans-caucasia.

Several settlements of the culture were investigated. The huts were mostly of the semi-subterranean type, with sides lined with stones, and often divided into four compartments, each with a hearth inside.

The people of the culture were the indigenous tribes, the names of some of which have been passed down to us by Urartian rock in-scriptions and by other records. Those in the south, in Soviet Armenia, were akin to the Urartians. The tribes who lived north-west and probably also to the north of these, the Colchians, were the ancestors of the modern Georgians and their kindred peoples. The men of the Khodzhaly-Kedabek culture have often been regarded as Scythians, who are said to have entered Transcaucasia in the ninth century B.C.; but the remains suggest that neither this culture nor the Central Transcaucasian culture can be looked upon as Scythic, though at the time of their development the Scythians undoubtedly lived within that territory.

During the ninth and eighth centuries B.C., the southern tribes were subdued by the kings of Urartu. Subsequently several strong-holds were built by the Urartians within this area, which was then incorporated into their kingdom. The tribes fought against Urartian expansion; Urartian inscriptions on rocks, many of which survived, boast of victories over these tribes and of the numbers of cattle, horses and slaves, taken. Thus Sardur II (764–735 B.C.) reports the capture of 10,000 youths, 4,600 men, and 23,200 women; he also says that he carried off from north Azerbaijan 3,500 horses, 40,000 oxen, and 214,700 sheep. The figures give an idea of the density of the local population, and of their developed animal husbandry. The 'Cyclo-paean' fortress at Lchashen (Lake Sevan) was constructed at that time (see p. 400).

The economy of the Transcaucasian peoples, as indicated by the Urartian inscriptions and the study of their remains, was based chiefly on stock-breeding. Agriculture played a subordinate role. They seem to have had winter seats with permanent huts in the plain; and in the summer they pastured their flocks in the mountains, where only light shanty-like huts were built. They were organized in small indepen-dent clans, which in case of danger united under the leadership of the strongest of them.

Imported objects found in various parts of the country, mainly in graves, imply that contacts were maintained with the neighbouring countries. Weapons and ornaments of the Koban and Colchidic types were common. And the similarities of many objects with types from the Luristan culture of Iran, pointed out by some authors, also suggest a contact with that people. Of importance is an Assyrian bead with the name of Adadnirari (763–755 B.C.) inscribed on it, found in a grave at Khodzaly.[66]

THE COLCHIDIC CULTURE

The western part of Transcaucasia during the Late Bronze Age and the Early Iron Age was ruled by the men of the 'Colchidic' culture (Map XXIX: XX), and the name of their country, Colchis, is recorded in ancient sources. The culture is known mainly from its bronze weapons, tools, and ornaments, but only a few settlements and cemeteries have been investigated. The description by Herodotus[67] of the Colchian contingent in the Persian army that invaded Greece in 480 B.C. gives a notion of their armament, which most probably did not much differ from that of the ninth to seventh centuries B.C., two centuries before. They had wooden helmets, small shields of raw-hide, short lances, and swords. Actually, many long and short bronze swords, lances or spear-heads, and battle-axes were found in the country; those dating to the fifth century B.C. were made of iron. The settlements of the Colchidic culture, such as that at Gomi, near Samtredi on the Rion, were for the most part founded during the 'Aeneolithic', and were continuously inhabited up to the time of the Greek colonization in the sixth century B.C. Their inhabitants were engaged in agriculture and horticulture, and they reared domestic animals—cows, sheep, goats, and pigs. Horses must have been kept, too, for they appear on pottery, but they were probably used just for transport. The pottery was a wheel-made ware produced in special potteries. Large storage vessels called *pithoi* were common; they were dark brown in colour and decorated with animal figures. Large dishes or bowls, and other fine, yellow well polished vessels were also common. Many bronze and some iron tools were found; the latter were of an archaic type, being replicas in iron of bronze originals.

The culture was closely related to the Koban culture of the Caucasian highland, some authors[68] even considering them as branches of a single 'Colchidic-Koban' culture. But although a number of almost identical bronze objects were common to both cultures, many others were typical of only one of them; the burial ritual of the two groups was different; and other features were specific to one group only. All these circumstances are opposed to the idea of their forming a single culture.

Bronze objects of Colchidic type, and other elements characteristic of the culture, have also been found in West Georgia, nearly up to

Tbilisi, where the Colchidic culture overlapped the Central Trans-caucasian culture; the remains were a kind of hybrid, with a pre-ponderance of Colchidic elements. The population of the area lived mainly on agriculture and stock-breeding, and partly on hunting, though an important branch of its economy was mining and foundry-work.

A few settlements, like Dvani on the Kura, and cemeteries were excavated throughout the region. The famous cemetery at Samtavro, in which about 1,800 graves were uncovered, was one of these; its earliest burials can be dated to the end of the second millennium and the latest to the eighth century B.C. Burials were in shafts, the skele-tons almost always crouched. In the early graves of the period under review, the grave goods were mostly Colchidic or Koban in style—bronze shaft-hole axes decorated in the Koban style, bronze daggers, and hoes—but they also contained objects from the Central Trans-caucasian culture, and this was still more apparent in graves of the advanced stage.

The contents of the cemetery at Beshtasheni, west of Tbilisi, was still more mixed. Its early graves corresponded with the earlier burials of the Samtavro cemetery, containing Koban-type objects and others characteristic of the North Caucasian workshops; but once a bronze dagger of Gandzha-Karabagh type was found in association with Koban objects. Another grave contained a conical bronze helmet, made of two bronze sheets with cheek-pieces affixed.

Similar grave goods were also found further south in the cemeteries of the Lelvar group near Leninakan. Many of these graves were from the Early Iron Age, containing iron objects never found in earlier graves. The latest graves were slab-cists, and their grave goods con-sisted of spear-heads, knives, iron daggers with bronze hilts, long tanged bronze arrow-heads, and bronze and blue-paste beads.

North of the Colchidic culture, in Abkhazia, the westernmost ex-tremity of Transcaucasia, another culture developed in the Late Bronze Age roughly covering the area of the ancient 'Dolmen' cul-ture. One of its characteristics was the secondary interment of bones in large vessels after the corpse had decayed. Its utensils and weapons were similar to those of the Koban or Colchidic cultures. Cemeteries usually lay close to settlements, and the inhabitants of many of the latter—for example, one situated on the top of a hill near Sukhumi on the Black Sea coast—were engaged in smelting copper from nearby mines, and producing bronze tools and weapons. Greek pottery of the sixth century B.C. found in these industrial settlements, implies that they were still flourishing at the time of the Greek colonization of the coast. The Greeks began to visit the Transcaucasian coast in the seventh century, according to the earliest samples of Greek pottery found thereabouts, and to establish permanent colonies in the sixth century B.C.

From the eighth century onwards important economic and political changes began to take place in Transcaucasia, partly through the gradual replacement of bronze by iron in the production of weapons and tools, which considerably affected many old and prosperous centres of the bronze industry, and partly through changing political conditions and events in the countries of Western Asia, including Iran, with which Transcaucasia had many ties. One of the factors responsible for these changes was the rise of the Scythians (see p. 400).

The confusion of that time is well reflected in the archaeological remains in Transcaucasia; many 'Cyclopaean' fortresses were built in Georgia,[69] and several Transcaucasian cultures were displaced.[70] These events strongly influenced the history and fate of the ancient West Asiatic kingdoms, and subsequently affected the peoples throughout the south of Eastern Europe, and those in Central Europe.

The troubles of the ninth century B.C. most probably had their source in the East European steppe on the Lower Volga, or in West Siberia. However, as stated previously, no changes have been noticed at that time in the Srubnaya culture on the Volga, though they are reflected in the remains of the Andronovo culture further east. Nevertheless, some steppe tribes, presumably including those of the Srubnaya culture, must have crossed the Caucasus and entered Transcaucasia—there to be confronted and strongly influenced by peoples of the ancient Oriental civilization and highly organized Oriental states. This amalgam was the embryo of the 'Scythian' culture, which was later carried by the 'Royal Scythians', the descendants of the Srubnaya-Andronovo invaders in Western Asia, into the North Pontic steppe country. The culture subsequently exercised an enormous influence on all peoples of the east European south and its neighbouring areas.

THE PONTIC LANDS AT THE END OF THE PREHISTORIC ERA

THE CRIMEA

A culture very similar to that of the North-west Caucasus, described in the preceding section, evolved in the southern part of the Crimea (Map XXIX: XXII).

During the Neolithic and most of the Bronze Age the Crimea was a backwater. The steppe of the Central and northern parts of the peninsula was peopled first by the Yamnaya and later by the Catacomb tribes, the same who dwelt further north on the Lower Dnieper; and in the Taurian mountains of the south lived tribes of the Kemi-Oba culture of Mesolithic ancestry (Table 22). Conditions changed during the Late Bronze Age. In the eighth century B.C. a new Crimean culture appeared, called the Kizil-Koba culture (Table 5) after a cave near Simferopol, in the lower occupation of which Palaeolithic remains were excavated. This culture has been recently renamed the 'Taurian' culture, the term Kizil-Koba being restricted to its earliest stage. The culture extended over the foothills and mountains of the Crimea, and more than ninety sites and settlements and over fifty cemeteries have been recorded.

The settlements[71] lay mainly on the terraces of rivers and streams and extended over an area of two and a half to twelve and a half acres. The inhabitants also lived in caves and rock-shelters, the more inaccessible being used as refuges in times of trouble. One of these at Osipovaya Balka had a wall built of large stones enclosing an area forty feet wide and twenty feet deep in front of an overhanging cliff; its date was of the seventh–sixth century B.C. Not many settlements have been investigated. But holes up to five feet six inches in diameter and two feet eight inches deep have been uncovered in those that have; some of these holes served for the storage of corn and food, and some as potter's kilns, but most were hearth-holes, over which probably some light constructions were built. Only once was a pit-dwelling uncovered. Many potsherds, flint implements, and fragments of saddle-querns, were found in all the occupation layers.

The pottery was of two categories. There was a coarse, grey or brownish undecorated kitchen ware, comprising wide tulip-shaped pots, bowls and flat-based dishes; and another group consisting of well made brown, red, or black, polished vessels. The characteristic decoration of both was horizontal rows of round hollows with groups of oblique or vertical lines beneath them; and also common were grooved rows of hatched triangles and groups of vertical lines. Large vessels with narrow bases and apertures, bowls, cups, and handled cups, were also discovered.

The flint implements uncovered were mainly microlithic in character and included small cores, small narrow blades, knives, and inlays of composite sickles. Bone and bronze arrow-heads and small iron objects have been found in a series of sites. The sickles and saddle-querns point to a knowledge of agriculture. Wheat, barley, and peas, were cultivated. Bones found in the settlement were identified as those of cattle, sheep, pigs, and horses, though the two latter were not present in all sites. In the coastal sites the bones of sea fishes and dolphins were most frequent.

The usual form of burial was in a grave-shaft lined with stone slabs and covered with a larger one.[72] Most of the graves had been looted in the past; for instance, in the valley of Baidary, fifteen and a half miles south-east of Sevastopol, only six graves out of fifty-two investigated were intact. In some regions small mounds were raised over the grave. The skeletons lay in a crouched position. The usual grave goods consisted of similar pottery to that found in the settlements, though sometimes horse harness and double-edged socketed bronze arrow-heads were found, and late graves contained iron objects and Greek pottery.

Around Simferopol, close to the steppe border, Kizil-Koba interments were often dug into ancient mounds of the Yamnaya culture. The skeletons in these graves lay supine with knees upwards, like those of the Yamnaya culture, and they differed only by their furniture from the burials of the latter. One very richly furnished grave deserves mention. The shaft was lined with wattle, supported by posts on which the cover also rested. The grave goods consisted of thirty-three bronze and iron double-edged arrow-heads, mostly rhomboid in shape; conical and pyramidal bone arrow-points; bronze buttons; bits; cheek-pieces characteristic of the Piatigorsk group of the Koban culture; a short iron sword recalling North Caucasian specimens of the eighth century B.C.; and some very fine decorative plaques of horse harness with carved spiral ornamentation (Fig. 86), very like bronze plaques from the Piatigorsk group of the Koban culture. The grave's date was around 700 B.C.

The development of the culture has been divided into three stages;[73] the earliest stage embraced the eighth and seventh centuries B.C., the next the sixth and fifth centuries, and the final stage is said to have lasted to the first century B.C. The origin of the culture is enigmatic. Some scholars[74] think that it represents the archaeological equivalent of the Cimmerians who were forced by the Scythians to retreat to the Crimea, and accordingly date the beginning of the culture to the ninth century B.C.; while others[75] place its beginning in the second millennium. However, the earliest remains of the culture, so far as is known, do not go back beyond the seventh century B.C.[76]

Remains of the first stage appear only in the northern foothills. Most of the cheek-pieces, bits, bronze arrow-heads, and ornaments, found in settlements and graves, do not differ from similar specimens found in the North-west Caucasus or in the remains of the Chornii-Lis culture in the Ukraine, and Crimean pottery is also similar to that of these two cultures; which points of agreement imply a close relation between the three groups, the Crimean group forming a link between the two others. It seems very probable that the Kizil-Koba (Taurian) culture was formed by the North-west Caucasians who entered the peninsula on their way to the Ukraine, the iron sword from the secondary burial near Simferopol seeming to support this assumption.

During the two following stages the same intimate connections were maintained with the steppe country and the North-west Caucasus; and later, close relations were established with the Crimean Greek colonies. Nevertheless, the culture always had its own distinguishing features.

The people of the culture were undoubtedly the Taurians, who are often mentioned in ancient records, and with whom several Greek legends were connected, though their organizing element might have been the north-west Caucasian Cimmerians. According to Herodotus and other ancient writers the Taurians were pirates and wreckers, and lived mainly by war and rapine; their peaceful pursuits were agriculture and, mainly, stock-rearing. They were ruled by kings; sacrificed any shipwrecked persons they captured to their virgin goddess Deve or Orsiloche, whom they declared to be the daughter of Agamemnon; and raised the heads of their captives on tall poles above their huts. They must have been a rude and cruel people.

THE BILOHRUDIVKA CULTURE

The conditions in the steppe country of the Crimea and on the Lower Dnieper after its seizure by the Srubnaya tribes have been already dealt with (see p. 340). The forest-steppe country further north, which bordered to its north on the Sabatynivka territory (see p. 343), was the territory during the period under review of the Bilohrudivka culture (Belogrudovka in Russian), called after a forest in the region of Uman (Table 5; Map XXIX: XXV).

The Bilohrudivka culture was known at first from its flat mounds, twenty inches to six feet in height and forty-nine to sixty-five feet six inches in diameter, called 'zolniks' (ashy mounds). The mounds consisted of one to three layers of ash, twelve to sixteen inches thick, which also contained a great variety of remains, potsherds, animal bones and skulls, fragments of stone and flint implements, occasional bronze objects, bronze slag, and, once, iron slag. On the original surface under the mound, traces of hearths in the form of holes filled in with charcoal were uncovered, and fragments of tools and bronze personal ornaments were scattered around.

The mounds of the Bilohrudivka culture appear only round Uman. They were placed on high ground at least 550 yards from the nearest well or stream; they usually formed groups of two or three mounds, and the groupings often lay several hundred yards apart. The purpose of the ashy mounds is disputable. At first, they were classed as burial mounds, but the fact that no cremations or inhumations were found in any of them disposed of this theory. Some authors[77] consider them to have been connected with the worship of fire, which presumably involved depositing ashes from the households in some selected sites; and others[78] believe that the constructions are remains of small farmsteads. Their riddle is complicated by the fact that many mounds had no ashy layers, and in many sites the remains of small hamlets, or single huts, were covered with a layer of ashes that formed no mound; again, in other Bilohrudivka settlements no accumulations of ashes have been found.

The ideas of ashy mounds and an accumulation of ashes into which many entire objects were thrown were evidently of south-western origin, and must have been adopted from the Noua culture.[79] Ashy mounds or 'zolniks', or ashy layers, have not only been found over the remains of a series of settlements of the Noua culture, or raised close to them, in Rumania and Bessarabia[80] on the Middle Dniester; but also further to the north-west in the Bucovina.[81] The lower occupation stratum of the settlement of the Sabatynivka culture at Ashkalka, on the Lower Dnieper, was overlaid by an ashy layer that extended over an area of about one acre. Its upper occupation stratum was also covered with a similar layer of ashes, but that layer was thinner and covered a smaller area. The custom, taken over from the Bilohrudivka culture, survived into the Scythian period in the forest-steppe zone east of the Dnieper, near Poltava. There, the 'zolnik' mounds of the seventh to fourth centuries B.C. that were investigated by I.I. Lyapushkin were of about the same size and construction as those near Uman.

The pottery of the culture was not uniform (Table 23). High tulip-shaped pots with an everted rim and a raised band under the rim or around the shoulder were characteristic; and bowls or deep dishes, and handled cups and dippers were also common. Vessels of the latter group mostly had their surfaces well polished and lustrous, often decorated with cord impressions, incised lines, or with other simple decorative patterns impressed with a thin stamp; the grooves were often filled in with a white paste. There were undecorated miniature cups and bowls, which presumably had some ritual purpose, similar to those found in graves of the Wysocko culture. The later remains also included rough zoomorphic, and occasional human figurines that call to mind similar specimens of the Tripolye culture. Among broken tools were flint blades of composite sickles, fragments of stone battle-axes, bracelets made of narrow bronze bands, and bronze ornaments made of wire, usually with spiral terminals. Once a fragment of a mould for casting socketed axes was excavated.

Pottery of the Bilohrudivka type has been found in many settlements outside the Uman region, in most of which no ashy layers appear; and they show the limit of the culture. Eastwards, the culture reached the Dnieper, and a site near Kiev marked its north-eastern-most extent. In the south the culture bordered the true Sabatynivka culture of the steppe country, in the north it extended over east

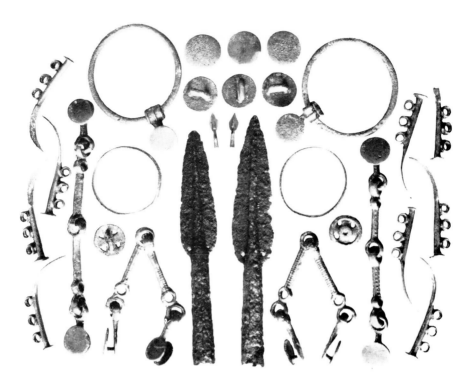

XLIX Bronze grave goods and lance-heads made of iron from a cremation grave at Butenki on the Vorskla.
After H.T. Kovpanenko, *Plemena skifskoho chasu na Vorskli*, Kiev 1967, fig. 18.

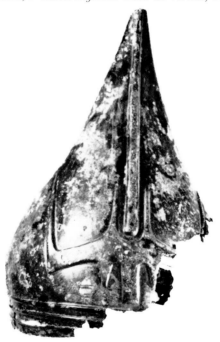

L An Uratian bronze helmet found at Rutchi Tig in the North Caucasian highland, in a cemetery of the Koban culture.
Museum für Vor- und Frühgeschichte, Berlin-Charlottenburg (no. 111 d 4882).

Volhynia, and westwards it probably reached the border of West Podolia.

Only a few graves of the culture have been recorded—exclusively inhumations, some were furnished with simple ornaments made of bronze wire, spiral pendants, and bronze bracelets.

The economy of the population was based on agriculture and stock-breeding. Mainly cattle and sheep were kept, bones of pigs and horses having seldom been found.

The origin of the culture is debatable: some authors[82] seek it in the area of Uman and further east, which does not seem likely; while others[83] point to the north-west and emphasize the important role played by the Trzciniec culture in its formation. A gradual transition from the Middle Bronze Age remains of the Trzciniec-Voytsekhivka type to those of the Bilohrudivka culture may be observed in several sites. The settlement at Voroshilivka near Zhitomir[84] belonged to this category; it consisted of about a dozen quadrangular huts thirty-three feet by twenty-six feet. Some of the potsherds excavated recall the Trzciniec-Voytsekhivka pottery, but their bulk is typical of the Bilohrudivka culture. Clay zoomorphic figurines were also typical Bilohrudivka products, and a bronze pin was similar to one found at Sabatynivka. A few crucibles imply the local production of small bronze objects. No ashy mounds were recorded in any of the east Volhynian settlements of the Early Bilohrudivka culture.

The culture was formed soon after 1200 B.C., after the arrival of the Srubnaya tribes in the steppe country west of the Dnieper. It extended over most of the territory previously held by the eastern groups of the Tripolye culture, and its most characteristic remains were found within the area of the former Uman group.

The Uman group of the Tripolyte culture (see p. 176) presumably survived till about the middle of the second millennium B.C.; and its final disappearance, like that of other neighbouring groups of the culture, poses a problem. The turbulence of that period must have contributed to their decline, but it seems that climatic conditions were among the main causes; for the mid-second millennium was the climax of the dry and very warm sub-Boreal climate, which must have adversely affected the agriculture in that semi-steppe country. The fact that animal figurines and some features characteristic of the Late Tripolyan kitchen ware of that area were found in the Bilohrudivka remains suggests that some links had existed between the two succeeding cultures; no remains have been found to fill the gap between them.

It seems that by the end of the second millennium, when the climatic conditions had improved, small groups of northern colonists began to move gradually southwards. They absorbed the few sur-

26

viving Tripolyans scattered over the country, and formed the new Bilohrudivka culture. The various elements contributing to its formation are well reflected in its remains: tulip-shaped pots evidently inherited from the Trzciniec culture; bowls from the Komarów culture; ashy mounds adopted under the influence of the Noua culture; Tripolyan clay figurines and some pottery; in moulds for casting socketed axes and some other elements from the Sabatynivka culture in the south and the Srubnaya culture east of the Dnieper; and stone battle-axes, flanged bronze axes (Sandraki on the Boh), and a bronze spear-head from the Catacomb culture of the preceding period.

The Bilohrudivka culture lasted until about the eighth century B.C., the time of the formation of the Chornii-Lis culture. In some regions, especially in the northern part of its territory, however, the culture seems to have survived into the Scythian period, the sixth-fifth centuries B.C.

THE CHORNII-LIS CULTURE

Around 800 B.C. disturbances in the Ukraine greatly affected its peoples, especially those of the Sabatynivka culture in the steppe country (Map XXIX: XXIII), and of the Bilohrudivka culture further north (Table 5). Sabatynivka settlements were burnt to the ground, and the Bilohrudivka culture was overrun.

About that time the open settlements of the Bilohrudivka culture on the border of the steppe and forest-steppe zones were replaced by earthworks; the latter were concentrated especially within a strip of land stretching west of the Dnieper near Kremenchug for sixty-odd miles, chiefly along the river Tiasmin. The remains found in these earthworks differ from those of the Bilohrudivka culture, and show strong affinities with the North-west Caucasian culture (see p. 363). They have been allocated to the Chornii-Lis culture,[85] called after an earthwork in a large forest near the sources of the Inguletz. The culture was formed in the south and soon spread northwards along the Dnieper up to Kiev. The Dnieper was its eastern border, but the western limits have not been established.

Many of the weapons, parts of horse harness, and other objects, found in the Chornii-Lis earthworks, were evidently modelled on North-west Caucasian prototypes, and many were of North Caucasian origin. A decorated bronze belt from the hoard of Podgortsa, near Kiev, was Transcaucasian. However, elements of the preceding Bilohrudivka culture are even more prevalent, which seems to show that there was no break in the settlement of the country in spite of its conquest by newcomers from North Caucasia.

The Chornii-Lis earthworks were mostly small in size, 45–110 yards in diameter, and seem to have been inhabited solely by the newcomers. Among the largest earthworks was that at Chornii-Lis, which consisted of a small citadel situated within a larger area enclosed by a rampart; in the latter area lay a number of ashy mounds or 'zolniks'. A larger earthwork containing a settlement was found at Subbotovka near Chigirin; it was ninety-three yards wide by 110 yards long and formed part of a nearly triangular enclosure with sides about 220 yards long, surrounded by steep ravines. The settlement showed two stages of habitation:[86] pit-dwellings of the very short earlier stage containing remains characteristic of the Bilohrudivka culture; whereas huts of the second stage built of pisé on the original ground level were typical of the Chornii-Lis culture. Potsherds of the Middle Bronze Age, that were found in the remains of this settlement show that the site was inhabited during the Catacomb period.

Only a few graves attributable to the culture have been recorded; they were mostly cremation burials, and only a few were inhumations. Small bronze personal ornaments were found in some graves. The most richly furnished of these was a recently published[87] barrow grave from Nosachevo near Smila, in which three pairs of bits, seven cheek-pieces, bronze arrow-heads, an iron sword and lance-head, and also several bronze ornaments of horse harness were found. All objects were of the same type as those excavated in the barrow grave of Simferopol (see p. 374), and those from the area on the river Vorskla (see p. 387) (Pl. XLIX).

The pottery of the Chornii-Lis culture, known almost exclusively from its settlements, was a hand-made ware of two categories (Table 23). The first was a quartz-gritted ware, comprising elongated tulip-shaped pots with a raised finger-tipped band around the shoulder and often a row of perforations below the rim, bowls with an inverted rim, and a series of miniature pots. This pottery was evidently inherited from the preceding Bilohrudivka culture. The second category was made of well silted clay paste, with a well polished surface, and black, brownish or yellow in colour; it was similar to the pottery of the Holihrady culture. Large pear-shaped vases, usually with a narrow base and an everted rim, undecorated or adorned with a single row of grooved triangles or horizontal lines, were typical of this class. Also important were large vases of the 'Villanova' type. Other vessels were mostly decorated cups, goblets, handled cups and dippers, and bowls with an inturned rim usually covered with horizontal or oblique fluting.

Stone axes and similar tools were now obsolete throughout the culture. Smaller tools, horse harness, and ornaments, were made of bone and antler. Pyramidal-shaped socketed arrow-heads, square in section, were also fashioned of bone (Fig. 86). Bronze objects were found in most of the earthworks investigated, and the moulds for

FIG. 86 Weapons of iron, some of bronze, and parts of horse harness of bronze and bone, from the Simferopol barrow grave and the burial from Butenki.
After A. I. Terenozhkin (S.A. 1965–1, p. 77, fig. 6).

casting them that were also found imply a developed bronze industry. In some earthworks bronze objects were hidden in clay vessels (Subbotov, Zalivki); such hoards consisted mainly of personal ornaments, pins, pendants, and beads, but also occasional implements. A typical feature of the culture was its cast bronze armlets, made of wide bands intricately decorated in relief with spirals, circles, and dotted lines (Pl. XLVIII). Other objects typical of the culture were long, narrow socketed axes decorated in relief under the thickened outlet (Fig. 81). Small iron knives, iron pins, and chisels, were found in all the sites investigated; and once an iron flat axe with two prominences on the narrow sides was discovered.

Unlike its pottery, which exhibits some links with that of the preceding period, the bronze industry of the Chornii-Lis culture shows a definite break with the past. No Cimmerian bronzes were now in

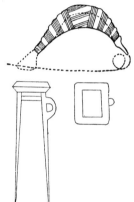

FIG. 87 Bronze boat-shaped brooch found at Hrebeny, in the district of Rzhyshchev south of Kiev, and a socketed axe of the Brittany type found in the Ukraine.
After T. Sulimirski and A. Szlankówna (*Swiatowit* vol. XVII, 1936–37, pp. 299, 303, fig. 3, 8).

use, and the technique of casting bronze objects was different. The stone (talc) moulds of the preceding period were replaced by those made of clay, and the technique of casting *à cire perdue* in clay moulds formed on wax models was also widely used.

Bronze objects found in the area connect the culture with several distant countries, and also point to the origin of its bronze industry. Bronze cheek-pieces and bits found in the settlements (earthworks) or outside follow North-west Caucasian or Koban models, as do iron daggers with bronze hilts in openwork; but many other tools and ornaments have obviously been influenced by the local bronze industry of the preceding period.

By the end of the eighth century B.C. trade connections had been established with the Central European countries, the Hungarian Plain in particular, and through their intermediary with the countries further west[88] (Table 5). Several long, socketed axes of the Brittany type, quadrangular in section, which were found in the Kiev country on the Middle Dnieper, were of West European origin; and boat-shaped bronze brooches found in the same area were probably of Italian or east Alpine derivation (Fig. 87). Brooches of the same type were also found on the sea coast in the south, in a pre-Greek layer of the Greek colony of Olbia. A bronze sword with an antennae pommel, which was found at Romny east of Kiev, outside the territory of the Chornii-Lis culture, also came from Central Europe. Swords of this type were later imitated locally, as indicated by specimens being found as far apart as West Podolia (Jazłowiec), the region of Poltava (Aksiutyntsi), and the Caucasian threshold (Sennaya on the Taman Peninsula).

The most striking result of this Central European influence was perhaps the Chornii-Lis adoption, probably through the intermediary of the Holihrady culture, of the black polished 'Hallstatt' ware, combined with the liking for the large 'Villanova' type vases (Table 23). Once introduced, this pottery survived the upheaval in the country around 600 B.C., and was in great vogue in the early Scythian culture of the Ukraine.

The Chornii-Lis culture seems to have extended over a smaller area than its predecessor, the Bilohrudivka culture. Its settlements, almost all undefended, have been placed within a strip of land, nearly sixty-two miles wide and about 155 miles long, stretching along the western side of the Dnieper south of Kiev down to the steppe border. And there, along the steppe border, was a concentration of seventeen earthworks. Locally evolved bronze objects produced by the Chornii-Lis foundries are very widely diffused, especially the long socketed celts mentioned previously which reached the sea coast in the south and West Podolia in the west.

The appearance of North Caucasian weapons and horse harness in the Crimea and the Middle Dnieper, and also further west, in the eighth century B.C. was most likely due to the pressure of the Transcaucasian Scythians (see p. 364) on the people who lived in the North-west Caucasus. Some of these people seem to have retreated westwards, via the Taman Peninsula and the Crimea, and ultimately to have reached the country on the Middle Dnieper. They contributed to the formation of the Taurian (Kizil-Koba) culture in the Crimean mountains, and brought about the decline of the Sabatynivka culture in the steppe west of the Lower Dnieper.

We may conjecture that they also advanced further north and that the Chornii-Lis culture was formed by the North-west Caucasian newcomers who conquered the country; they introduced the types of tools, weapons and other bronze and iron objects current in their original country; but did not annihilate the aboriginal population, into which they subsequently merged. The Caucasian objects give the date of the beginning of the Chornii-Lis culture to the early eighth century B.C.

A few of the earliest earthworks on the southern border of the forest-steppe zone were probably built at the time of the seizure of the country, and were the centre of power of the newcomers. Later, however, a long chain of strongholds was erected along the steppe border, which suggests that some aggressors were advancing from the south. These strongholds were not long-lived, most of them falling to an enemy by the end of the seventh or the beginning of the sixth century B.C. and many others being abandoned. And the Chornii-Lis culture came to an end at that time. The only conclusion to be drawn from these facts is that the culture collapsed before the southern aggressors, and the date of this collapse coincides with the appearance of the Scythian culture in the Ukraine. The country was then conquered by the 'Royal Scythians', who initiated the new, Scythian Age in the north Pontic area (see p. 402).

The identity of the newcomers is unknown. They might have been a Maeotian people, or a Sindian tribe, or, alternatively a branch of the Cimmerians. A passage in Herodotus relating to the Cimmerian kings buried near the river Tyras (the Dniester) suggests that a branch of the Cimmerians may have retreated westwards. Herodotus expressly links the royal Cimmerian graves on the Dniester with the ousting of the Cimmerians by the Scythians immediately after their crossing the Volga (see p. 395).

THRACO-CIMMERIAN FINDS

The retreating North-west Caucasians seem now to have proceeded even further west. By the end of the Hallstatt B period, North-Caucasian-type horse harness and weapons appeared in the countries on the Middle Danube, where the culture formed part of the so-called 'Thraco-Cimmerian' complex of the Hallstatt C period. Among the weapons were daggers (swords) of a special type—mainly of iron, some of bronze—with a bronze guard and bronze hilt either plain or in open-work, the earliest examples of which have been found in the Caucasus.

It has been widely agreed that the presence of Thraco-Cimmerian finds in Central Europe was the result of an invasion of an East European people, either horsemen or, perhaps, charioteers.[89] The hiding of a large number of bronze hoards at the turn of periods IV and V of the Bronze Age early in the eighth century B.C. in west Podolia and the Hungarian plain was evidently the outcome of this aggression. The Northern Caucasians who eventually crossed the

Carpathians were unable to proceed further west, being halted most probably by the well armed people of the Alpine Hallstatt culture. Consequently, they settled in the Hungarian plain. Their remains in that area are characteristic of the Hallstatt C period.[90]

Two relatively peaceful centuries followed the turbulent time just described. During this period the newly formed Chornii-Lis and Early Taurian (Kizil-Koba) cultures blossomed. The Wysocko culture developed in Volhynia and the northern part of West Podolia. Further south, chiefly south of the Dniester, extended the 'Thraco-Cimmerian' area represented by the famous golden hoard of Michał-ków. Wide commercial relations developed between the north-Pontic lands and the east Alpine and Italian centres. The Hallstatt-Koban connections, discussed by many scholars,[91] were undoubtedly the outcome of mutual trade. Koban commerce covered large areas of Eastern Europe and reached as far as Scandinavia. A gradual blending of the various elements in the area on the Middle Volga and the Kama laid the foundations for the development, in the following period, of the important Ananino culture, the centre of commerce with the arctic cultures.

The period ended with the arrival, around the turn of the seventh and sixth centuries B.C., of the west Asiatic Scythians, who were forced to retreat northwards and so entered the Ukraine. Their arrival brought about the downfall of the Chornii-Lis culture, to which we are indebted for the large number of hoards hidden at that time, including the golden hoard of Michałków (Pl. XLIV; see p. 355).

The establishment of the rule of the Royal Scythians throughout the north Pontic territory is a landmark in the past of Eastern Europe, and the beginning of the new Scythian Age.

THE COUNTRY EAST OF THE DNIEPER (Table 6; Map XXVII)

Partly contemporary with the Bilohrudivka, but mainly with the Chornii-Lis culture in the forest-steppe country on the eastern side of the Dnieper was the Bondarykha culture, called after a settlement excavated on a sand-dune near Izium on the Donetz.[92] It was formed later than the Bilohrudivka culture and survived to the early first millennium B.C.

Its rectangular huts were one of its main characteristics; they were about thirty-three feet long by thirteen feet wide and sunk about sixteen inches into the ground (Fig. 89). The hearth was on one of the shorter sides. In all settlements and all huts, saddle-querns, animal bones, flint sickles, scrapers, and a large volume of pottery, were found. Vases with a flat narrow base, a wide aperture, and a slightly bulging body, were characteristic of the culture; their scanty decoration, consisting of rows of small dimples and small incisions,

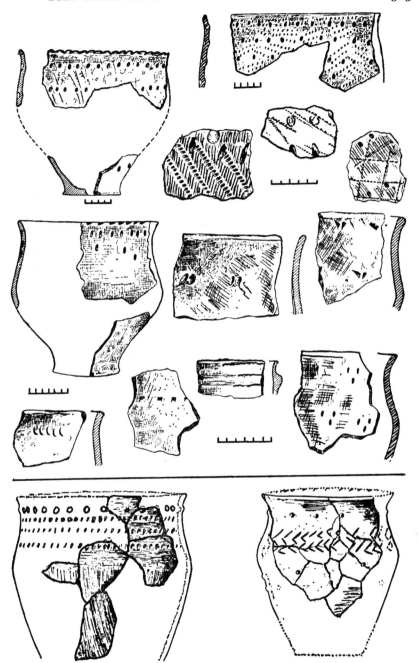

FIG. 88 *Upper row:* Pottery of the Bondarykha culture from Malye Budki on the Sula.
Middle row: Pottery from Bondarykha near Izium.
Lower row: Vessels from the Studenok 5 site.
After D. Ia Telegin (KSIAK No. 8, 1959, p. 75, fig. 2).

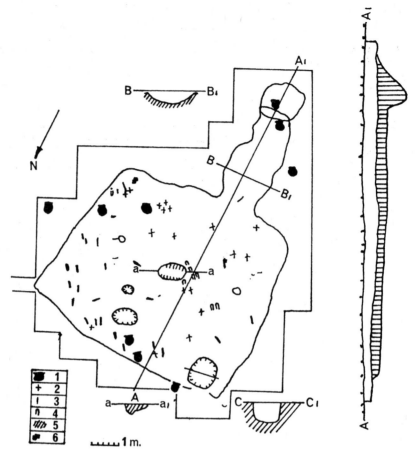

FIG. 89 Plan and cross-section of a hut of the Bondarykha culture at Studenok 5.
(1) pots; (2) flints; (3) animal bones; (4) lumps of fired clay; (5) fire-pit (hearth); (6) mould for casting socketed axes.
After D. Ia. Telegin (as fig. 88, p. 74, fig. 1).

covered mainly the upper part of the vessel (Fig. 88). Some settlements also contained moulds for casting bronze socketed axes and daggers of the Srubnaya type.

The Bondarykha culture extended over the forest-steppe country west of the Donetz up to the Middle Dnieper (Map XXIX: XXVI). It was evidently descended from the Neolithic and Bronze Age culture of that area—the Dnieper-Donetz culture[93]—and bore a strong Srubnaya imprint. Settlements of the Bondarykha type have also been recorded further east on the Oskol (Studenok 5; Fig. 89), but the Srubnaya element in these was much stronger (Fig. 88, lower row); they may be considered transitional between the two cultures. The Caucasian development and the Koban culture did not influence the Bondarykha culture, but the Srubnaya tribes further south, in the steppe and forest-steppe east of the Dnieper, were affected by them. Bronze bits, cheek-pieces and other parts of horse harness, characteristic of the north Caucasus in the eighth and seventh centuries B.C., have been found in two regions in the steppe east of the Dnieper.

The country on the Vorskla, a tributary of the Dnieper, near Poltava was one of these. Two richly furnished graves have been recorded there, containing objects of the Chornii-Lis type, one north of Poltava (Likhachevka), and the other south-west of it at Butenki.[94] The latter was a cremation burial. Calcinated human bones were found in a small shallow shaft, along with several pieces of horse-harness, six pairs of bronze bits, twelve cheek-pieces, two large rings with buttons affixed, eight round buttons, two bronze bracelets made from a wide, thick band, thirty bronze arrow-heads, and two iron lance-heads (Pl. XLIX). The objects had close affinities with the equipment of the grave from Simferopol in the Crimea; with the hoard found in the earthwork of Zalivki near Smila, belonging to the Chornii-Lis culture and about 125 miles west of the Butenki grave; and also with the hoard of Novocherkassk on the Don. The objects listed are characteristic of the Piatigorsk group of the Koban culture, and the grave has been dated around the eighth–seventh centuries B.C.

Two barrow graves with a similar content have been uncovered on the Lower Donetz, about 185 miles east of the Poltava group. Both the graves, at Kamyshevakha and Chornohorivka (Chernogorovka in Russian), north-east of Stalino, contained bronze bits and cheek-pieces, and bronze socketed arrow-heads with rhomboid-shaped edges—all of the same type as those of Butenki and Simferopol (Pl. XLIX; Fig. 86)—plus a bronze dagger with a bronze grip, and small decorative plates. Arrow-heads of the same type, bronze bits and cheek-pieces, were also found in another barrow grave at Stanitsa Chernyshevskaya on the Chir, a tributary of the Lower Don, about 185 miles east of the two graves on the Lower Donetz; but this grave was dated to the sixth century B.C. by the presence of a three-edged 'Scythian' arrow-head.

Both the latter grave and those on the Donetz lay about 125 miles north-east and north-west, respectively, from Novocherkassk on the Lower Don, where an important bronze hoard was found.[95] It comprised two pairs and fragments of another pair of bits, a pair of cheek-pieces, fragments of a point, a bronze mould for casting socketed two-edged arrow-heads, and a shaft-hole axe of the Koban type; and has been dated between 750 and 650 B.C. To the same group of remains belong two sets of horse harness found together with an iron socketed lance-head in barrow-grave 'Gireeva Mogila' near Rostov-on-the-Don;[96] each set consists of a pair of bronze bits with double-ring terminals and of pair of tutuli, larger rings and cheek-pieces of a special type. All objects specified above evidently had formed parts of harness of horses put in pairs to chariots. Supposedly, the chariots had been used by the local princelings only who adopted them from the Caucasian chieftains (see p. 364).

The east-of-the-Dnieper finds just quoted above, including the hoard from Novocherkassk, are of the Koban-Piatigorsk type, whereas those of the Chornii-Lis culture were related to the North-west Caucasian type. The finds in question, scattered over a distance of over 400 miles, bear a special character: they were found in graves that were evidently those of the rulers of a number of late Srubnaya tribes. Their equipment, consisting of improved types of weapon and horse harness, was obviously imported from the North Caucasus. The harness was needed for harnessing good quality horses, which were most probably also imported from the North Caucasian studs, for drawing chariots. We may guess that the hoard from Novocherkassk belonged to a North Caucasian trader, who was able to cast arrow-heads from the mould, possibly for his own needs.

The conditions in this area did not change in the early period of the Scythian Age. The local rulers must have still maintained intimate connections with the North Caucasus, as indicated by the grave goods found in the barrow grave at Krivorozhe on the Kalitva, a tributary of the Lower Donetz, north-east of the mouth of the Don.[97] A golden band or wreath, and the silver terminal of an object of unknown shape, in the form of a bull head, were found there. The latter object was of Oriental origin, of the seventh or early sixth centuries B.C., and must have been acquired through the agency of Caucasian Koban, north-west Caucasian, or Scythian traders. The local hand-made ware found in the barrow grave shows no Scythian influence.

SUMMARY

Events in Western Siberia in the thirteenth century B.C. had far reaching consequences for the further development and history of Eastern Europe (Tables 4, 5). The Karasuk seizure of the Minusinsk valley and parts of the adjoining steppe marked the end of the advance of the western peoples, and of their influence and preponderance. From that moment began a gradual retreat from the West Siberian steppe country of the Andronovo peoples and their successors—peoples of the Indo-European, North Iranian stock. The process ultimately resulted in Siberia being entirely abandoned in the second century A.D. to peoples of Turkoman origin.

The retreating tribes set in motion their threatened neighbours, who crossed the European border. Then came the expansion of the Srubnaya tribes, who during the thirteenth century B.C. reached and crossed the Dnieper. At the same time, a parallel development took place in the west Siberian forest zone (Map XXIX). Some of the retreating tribes of that zone entered Europe, and, after proceeding across Central Russia, nearly reached the East Baltic coast. The effect of their drive was that Eastern and Central Russia, and the whole east European north, came under the aegis of the Finno-Ugrian peoples.

We have traced these movements and discussed their bearing on the indigenous peoples. Some ancient cultures disappeared and new ones were formed. But the disturbances soon died down and the evolution of the peoples started again; new relations were entered into. A significant process was the tendency towards blending smaller cultures into larger units—like the late-Balakhna/Volosovo culture in Central and Northern Russia, or the Ananino culture in the east, which however, sprang up only by the very end of the period.

Less stable conditions prevailed in the southern part of the country, in the steppe. The upheaval of the thirteenth–twelfth centuries was followed by a rather short period of relative stability during which a series of new cultures developed in various parts of the country—the Srubnaya culture in the steppe east of the Dnieper, the Sabatynivka culture west of the river, and the Bilohrudivka culture north of it; and also the Caucasian cultures, among them the Koban, Colchidic, and the Central Transcaucasian.

The development in the south was disturbed again in the ninth–eighth centuries B.C., when a new wave of West Siberian nomads entered Europe. Their advance was mainly directed towards the Caucasus, but it ultimately affected the whole East European steppe and forest-steppe zones. One of its consequences was the expansion of the North-west Caucasian culture, with the formation of the Chornii-Lis culture on the border of the steppe and forest-steppe west of the Dnieper; and there were also disturbances in the countries further to the west, including the Hungarian plain and the formation of the 'Thraco-Cimmerian' complex there. All these changes and their consequences are summarized in Table 5.

Another characteristic feature of the period, especially of its second half, was the development of wide commercial relations by the main metallurgical centres of Eastern Europe (Map XXII). Very notable was the considerable expansion of the North Caucasian trade, which reached the East Prussian amber coast and Scandinavia (Map XXXII). It must also have had commercial relations with the west Asiatic countries and India. But perhaps more far-reaching was the expansion of the Scandinavian trade in Eastern Europe (Map XXXI). Scandinavian colonies have been found on the East Baltic coast, and presumed traces of small Scandinavian trading depots have been found deep in Russia, at the junction of the Kama with the Volga. Some finds in Sweden even suggest that Scandinavian trade reached as far east as China.

The period ended with the arrival of the 'Royal Scythians' in the Ukraine about 600 B.C. or at the very end of the seventh century. And this is dealt with in Chapter VI.

References

1 M. Gimbutas, PPS, XXIV, p. 155.
2 N.P. Kiparisova, SA, 1962–2.
3 Herodotus IV, 22.
4 O.N. Bahder, MIA 99, 1961.
5 O.N. Bahder, as above.
6 K. Jettmar.
7 N.F. Kalinin, A.Kh. Khalikov, MIA 42, 1954; see also A.P. Smirnov, MIA 28, 1952; MIA 95, 1961.
8 A.V. Zbrueva, MIA 30, 1952; MIA 80, 1960.
9 A.Kh. Khalikov, MIA 61, 1958.
10 O.N. Bahder, 1963.
11 O.N. Bahder.
12 A.M. Tallgren.
13 V. Gorodtsov, Trudy RANIION, Vol. 3, 1928.
14 A.V. Zbrueva, 1952.
15 M.E. Foss.
16 M.E. Foss, N.N. Gurina.
17 O.V. Ovsyannikov, G.V. Grigorieva, KSIAM 102, 1964.
18 A.M. Tallgren, 'The Arctic Bronze Age in Europe', ESA, XI, 1937, p. 1 ff.
19 B. Nerman, *Fornvännen*, 1954, p. 257 ff.; and the literature quoted.
20 M. Stenberger, *Sweden*, London 1962, p. 90.
21 A.M. Tallgren, ESA, Vol. XI, 1937.
22 E. Sprockhoff, *Zur Handelsgeschichte der germanischen Bronzezeit*. Berlin, 1930.
23 B. Nerman, *op. cit.*
24 H. Salmo, SMYA, Vol. LXII, 1955, p. 71 ff.
25 N.N. Gurina, MIA 110, 1963.
26 J.V.S. Megaw, *Antiquity*, Vol. XXXIV, 1960, pp. 6–13.
27 I.V. Sinitsyn, KSIIMK 63, 1956, p. 79.
28 P. Rykov.
29 B.G. Tikhonov.
30 V.P. Shilov, ASE 5, 1962.
31 E.S. Sharafutdinova in *Arkheologicheskie Raskopki na Donu*. Rostov-on-the-Don, 1962; and KSIAM 103, 1965; 112, 1967.
32 K.F. Smirnov, *Savromaty*. Moscow, 1964.
33 T.B. Popova, 1955.

34 A.M. Tallgren, ESA, II, 1926, p. 70, Fig. 47.
35. A.Ia. Briusov.
36 A. Florescu, *Arheologia Moldovei*, Vols. II-III, Iaşi, 1964, p. 145 ff.
37 J.D. Cowen, *Bericht über den V. Internationalen Kongress für Vor und Frühgeschichte* (1948). Berlin, 1961, p. 207 ff., Fig. 6.
38 In English lately by M. Gimbutas, PPS, Vol. XXII, 1956, p. 143 ff.
39 O.A. Krivtsova-Grakova.
40 O.A. Krivtsova-Grakova, *op. cit.*, Map; A.M. Leskov, PEB.
41 O.K. Krivstova-Grakova, *op. cit.*; E.N. Chernykh, KSIAM 106, 1966; A.M. Leskov, PEB.
42 A. Florescu, *op. cit.*; and M. Petrescu-Dimboviţa, *Dacia*, Vol. NS IV, 1960, p. 139 ff. and *Arheologia Moldovei*, Vols. II-III, 1964, p. 251 ff.
43 E.A. Balaguri, AK, Vol. XIII, 1961; MDAPV, Vol. 5, 1964.
44 G.I. Smirnova, KSIIMK 70, 1957; *Soobshch. Gos. Ermitazha*, Vols. XIII, 1956; XVI, 1959. Carbon-14 date of its upper (Holihrady) layer is 540 B.C. (LE-573), and that of its lower (Noua) layer is 1430 B.C. (LE-489).
45 A.I. Meliukova, MIA 96, 1961.
46 I.K. Sveshnikov, MDAPV, Vol. 5, 1964.
47 K. Hadaczek, 1904; I.K. Sveshnikov, SA 1968-1, pp. 10-27.
48 T. Svlimirski, 1931; M.I. Kanivets, KSIAK 4, 1955; Z. Bukowski, *Archeologia Polski*, Vol. XI, 1966; L.I. Krushelnytska, AK, Vol. XIX, 1965.
49 T. Sulimirski, *Wiadomosci Archeologiczne*, Vol. XIV, 1936, Pl. XI: 1.
50 A.A. Yerusalimskaya, SA, 1952-2.
51 The material has been published by many western scholars. See A.M. Tallgren, *Reallexikon* (Ebert), Vol. VII, p. 11 ff.; and C.F.A. Schaeffer, *La Stratigraphie comparée et chronologie de l'Asie occidentale, III-IIe Millénaire.* London, 1948, p. 525 ff.
52 E.I. Krupnov, *Drevnyaya Istoria Severnogo Kavkaza.* Moscow, 1960. *Idem*, SA, 1969-1, pp. 13-18; Carbon-14 dates are quoted there of all the periods distinguished in the development of the culture.
53 F. Hančar, ESA, Vol. VII, 1932; *Wiener Prähist. Zft.*, Vol. XXI, 1934.
54 A.P. Kruglov, MIA 68, 1958; E.I. Krupnov, MIA 23, 1954; KSIIMK 5, 1940, 13, 1946.
55 IV, 28.
56 E.H. Minns, *Art of the Northern Nomads. Proceedings of the British Academy*, Vol. XXVIII, 1942.
57 O. Mnatsakhanian, SA 1957-2; KSIAM 85, 1961; *The Illustrated London News*, April 1967.
58 A.A. Yessen *Voprosy Skifo-Sarmatskoy Arkheologii*, Moscow 1954.
59 T.J. Arne, *Fornvännen*, 1909, pp. 184, 337.
60 B. Nerman, *op. cit.*
61 F. Hančar, ESA, Vol. IX, 1934, pp. 47-112.
62 M.N. Pogrebova, KSIAM 103, 1965.
63 F. Hančar, *op. cit.*
64 A.A. Martirosyan, SA, 1964-3.
65 F. Hančar, *op. cit.*; M.N. Pogrebova, *op. cit.*
66 A.M.Tallgren, ESA, Vol. IX, 1927; F.Hančar, ESA,Vol.IX, 1934.
67 VII, 79.
68 B.A. Kuftin, 1943, 1944.
69 B.A. Kuftin, 1944. Carbon-14 date of the fortress built at Lchashen is 890±60 B.C. (LE-689).
70 E.I. Krupnov.
71 C.I. Kris in *Istoria i Arkheologiya Drevnego Krima*; A.A. Shchepinskii, SA, 1966-2.
72 A.M. Leskov, G.D. Belov.
73 A.M. Leskov.
74 A.I. Terenozhkin.
75 A.A. Shchepinskii.
76 Kh.I. Kris, KSIAM 112, 1967.
77 S.S. Berezanska, AK, Vol. XVI, 1964.
78 A.I. Terenozhkin.
79 A. Florescu, *op. cit.*
80 A.I. Meliukova, MIA 96, 1961.
81 G.I. Smirnova, *op. cit.*, note 44.

82 A.I. Terenozhkin.
83 S.S. Berezanska.
84 E. Makhno, AP, Vol. II; S.S. Berezanska, *op. cit*, note 77.
85 A.I. Terenozhkin.
86 A.I. Terenozhkin.
87 G.T. Kovpanenko, AK, Vol. XX, 1966.
88 A. Szlankówna, *Swiatowit*, Vol. XVII, 1936–7, pp. 293–306.
89 S. Gallus and T. Horvath, *Un Peuple cavalier préscythique en Hongrie*. Budapest, 1939; and M. Parducz, *Acta Archaeol. Hungarica*, Budapest, Vol. II, 1952, pp. 143–69, and Vol. IV, 1954, pp. 25–89.
90 To these also belong three iron swords with bronze grips from Leibnitz in Styria, Austria, from Komorno, Czechoslovakia, and from Neundorf near Görlitz in Lusatia, East Germany. See: M. Jahn, Schlesiens Vorzeit in B.u.Schr. vol. NF IX, 1928, p. 23, Fig. 17; Z. Podkowińska, Swiatowit Vol. XV, 1932, p. 121, Figs. 2, 3; A.I. Terenozhkin, 1961, p. 135 ff., Fig. 91.
91 E.g., F. Hančar, *Mitteilungen der anthropologischen Gesellschaft*, Vienna, Vols. LXIII–LXIV, 1947, pp. 152–67.
92 D.Ia. Telegin, AK, Vol. IX, 1954.
93 V.A. Ilinskaya, AK, Vol. X, 1957, SA, 1961–1.
94 G.T. Kovpanenko, KSIAK 12, 1962.
95 A.A. Yessen, *op. cit.*, note 58.
96 A.N. Melentiev, KSIAM 112, 1967.
97 T.N. Knipovich, *Izvestia* GAIMK, Vol. 104, 1934.

6
Conclusion

We have come to the end. The hundred of millennia of human development in Eastern Europe during the prehistoric era have moved rapidly along before our eyes. The very slow pace of evolution throughout the enormous time span of the Glacial Age accelerated in post-glacial times. Several ages and periods of very different duration have been distinguished in this evolution (Tables 1–5).

The earliest hunters of the Lower and Middle Palaeolithic—even if some of their descendants survived at all to the later periods—had no influence whatever on Eastern Europe in the post-glacial era; and the same virtually applies to the Upper Palaeolithic men. The foundations for the post-glacial racial and cultural division of Eastern Europe were laid during the Mesolithic (Map IV); the main cultural provinces established then were easily discernible during the Neolithic (Map VIII) and the Bronze Ages, and are even recognizable now.

The 'Neolithic Revolution', which reached Eastern Europe at the turn of the fifth and fourth millennia B.C. (Map VI), made slow progress during the following two thousand years. The real breakthrough came at the end of the third millennium B.C., with the expansion of the early steppe dwellers of the Yamnaya culture; and, it was continued at the beginning of the second millennium B.C. by the great drive of the Central European peoples of the Corded Ware/Battle-axe assemblage and the Globular Amphora culture (Map XIV).

The second millennium must be considered the most fateful in the prehistoric past of Eastern Europe. Its weighty events had a lasting bearing on further development both in Eastern Europe and in countries further to the west. The spread of the western (Central European) peoples and their ideas resulted in the awakening of the energy of local peoples. Another factor that likewise contributed enormously to the new development was the penetration of the Aegean and Oriental traders and prospectors, and the consequent growth of skilled local metal industries. The swing of the pendulum at the end of the second millennium saw the retreat of the western wave and western influence, and the invasion of the central and northern parts

393

of Russia by peoples of eastern origin (Map XVIII). In the south the recurrent expansions of the East European and West Siberian steppe peoples first became menacing; they were to continue right up to the Middle Ages.

The successful expansion of the Siberian steppe peoples into Eastern Europe, which contributed to the revolution of that area (Map XXIX), depended on several important innovations. One was the development of a highly mobile, mounted nomad pastoralism, not tied any longer to restricted pastures. Another, perhaps still more important, was their change to a warlike way of life—training from early youth in warfare and spending most of their lives in fighting and skirmishing. And a third factor that enabled the advancing eastern peoples to defeat their western opponents was the development of a special tactic: assaulting the enemy with large groups of mounted bowmen who were consummate horsemen and had perfected the art of shooting from the gallop. This tactic, characteristic of the Scythians in the second half of the first millennium B.C., evidently developed in the Eurasiatic steppe well before the Scythian feats in Western Asia and Europe.

One other reason for their success by the end of the second millennium B.C. was the growth of a bronze industry in Western Siberia based on rich local deposits of copper and tin (Map XXVII). It provided the peoples of Siberia—both the forest-dwellers and the steppe pastoralists—with a range of tools and effective weapons. The inhabitants of the threatened countries in east Europe had for the most part no proper organization nor adequate arms to resist the eastern invaders.

During that period iron came into general use in Western Asia, but was still almost unknown in the countries north of the Caucasus. Single iron objects imported from the south began to appear in our area from the eighth century B.C. onwards, but it was not until the sixth century, the Scythian Age, that iron weapons and, later, tools became sufficiently prevalent to oust those made of bronze.

The eastern incursions did not annihilate the native population; some tribes retreated, setting in motion other peoples, but most remained in their own country and mingled with the newcomers, giving rise to new hybrid cultures. Another effect of the eastern advance was the disruption of age-old trade connections, and the establishment of new ones, mainly with different countries and centres. All these factors revolutionized the cultures concerned.

THE CIMMERIANS

The effects of the unrest and tribal movements in the Eurasiatic steppe country were also felt in Western Asia, in the countries of the ancient Oriental civilization. The mounted nomads must have penetrated deep into the south at an early date, as is suggested by the earliest representations of mounted bowmen, disguised in the form of shooting centaurs, found on Babylonian boundary stones of the end of the thirteenth century B.C. (Fig. 90; Table 4). From that time onwards, written records continued to report the growing menace of the northern nomads (Table 5).

The Cimmerians were one of these nomadic peoples, the earliest of Eastern Europe whose name has come down to us. Herodotus in his *History*[1] reports that the Scythian nomads who dwelt in Asia, being harassed by the Massagetae, crossed the river Araxes (the Volga) and entered Cimmerian territory. The Cimmerians did not dare to fight against the invaders and abandoned their land. Thus the Scythians 'coming up took possession of the deserted country'.

The date of the retreat of the Cimmerians before the Scythians has not been established, but historical and archaeological data imply that it must have taken place well before the tenth century B.C. A hint of the date is furnished by the journey of Aristeas of Proconnesus[2] (see p. 310) to the countries north-east of the Black Sea, which took place sometime in the middle of the seventh-century B.C. His report clearly indicates that the Cimmerians had been driven out of their homeland some hundreds of years before, and the disaster remained as a vague memory among the peoples whom he met. Another indication is provided by the study of Hesiod and Homer. Hesiod, who lived not later than the eighth century B.C., knew the mare-milking Scythians, and also speaks of a tribe of milk-drinkers who had wagons for houses, but he does not know the Cimmerians; for their tenure of the east European steppe country had been forgotten. Homer leads us to the same conclusion when he mentions the mare-milkers.[3] His account on the Cimmerians[4] reflects an ancient tradition of a country and people that were known some time ago but are now forgotten. This seems to confirm that by the time of Homer—not later than the eighth or ninth centuries B.C.—the Scythians had lived in the Pontic steppe for so long that the Cimmerians' occupation of that area was hardly remembered.

The sudden replacement, in the thirteenth century B.C., of the Catacomb culture in the Don-Donetz area by the Srubnaya culture expanding from beyond the Volga (Map XXIX) seems to fit in neatly with Herodotus's account of the advent of the Scythians into the Pontic steppes. Other data relating to the early Scythians, which

FIG. 90 The earliest representation of the northern mounted steppe nomads: a shooting centaur from a Babylonian boundary stone of the thirteenth century B.C. (British Museum).

can be deduced from the Herodotus' account suggests that they belonged to the Srubnaya culture.

It would seem, at first sight, that the Catacomb culture can be identified with the early Cimmerians. However, difficulties arise when this possibility, which is suggested by the archaeological research, is confronted with the well established chronology of the Cimmerians in Western Asia. Herodotus says[5] that the Cimmerians, being driven from their seats by the Scythians, 'fled constantly by the sea-coast (the Black Sea coast) and possessed themselves of all Sardia' (a country in the eastern part of Asia Minor). In fact, the Cimmerians of Asia Minor were often mentioned in Assyrian and Greek records, though they were sometimes confused with the Scythians. They were first mentioned by the Assyrians at the time of Sargon II (722–705 B.C.) when, about 714 B.C., they assaulted the Urartian kingdom in the region of Leninakan, on the south-western border of Transcaucasia. In 705 B.C., being repulsed by Sargon II, they turned aside into Asia Minor, into Cappadocia in fact. In 696–695 B.C. they defeated Midas and conquered Phrygia, and in 679 B.C. they were driven by Esarhaddon from the Assyrian border. They reached the summit of their fortunes in 652 B.C., by taking Sardis, the capital of Lydia, which was situated on the Aegean coast; but soon afterwards, in 637 or 626 B.C., they were routed by Alyattes of

Lydia, and disappeared from the stage of history.

A gap of five centuries separates the appearance of the Cimmerians on the Urartian border from the time of the defeat of the Catacomb culture and its ejection from the East European steppe country. The small groups of the Catacomb culture which according to some scholars[6] managed to survive in the North-west Caucasus up to the eighth or seventh centuries B.C. (Map XXIX: XVII) could not have been the powerful Cimmerians who threatened the mighty Urartian kingdom, and even Assyria. At the time of the Cimmerian exploits in Asia Minor, they still lived in the North-west Caucasus. No archaeological remains have been found so far in Asia Minor that could be attributed to the invading Cimmerians and connect them with the respective remains in the areas north of the Caucasus. Perhaps the remains of so-called 'Thraco-Cimmerian' type found in the North-west Caucasus and in the country along the Sea of Azov up to the Don may be connected with the Cimmerians. These remains have been attributed to the Sindians or Maeotians, but the origin of these peoples is unknown, and one or the other, or both, might have been a branch of the Cimmerians. Further studies and research are undoubtedly needed to solve this dilemma.

THE EARLY SCYTHIANS

The other people mentioned alongside the Cimmerians were the Scythians, who, by the end of the seventh century B.C., had, among others, contributed greatly to the destruction of the ancient Oriental empires. According to Herodotus,[7] the Scythians pursued the retreating Cimmerians into Transcaucasia, 'keeping the Caucasus on the right', and evidently proceeding along the coast of the Caspian Sea. He says that they subsequently entered the Median territory and overthrew the empire of the Medes. They then ruled 'over Upper Asia for twenty-eight years' when, being defeated by an uprising of the Medes, they were forced to retreat northwards back into Europe.

An Assyrian bas-relief from the north-western palace of Nimrud, built by Ashurnazirpal II (885–859 B.C.) seems to be the earliest evidence of the Scythians in west Asia. It shows two mounted bowmen fleeing at a gallop. The bowmen, wearing pointed caps, soft top boots and trousers, cannot represent Urartians, Medes, or Cimmerians. They probably were nomad tribesmen, most likely the Scythians, who had just arrived from the East European steppe. The bas-relief also gives the date of their arrival. It is true that the Scythians were not mentioned by name in this battle scene; but it was not necessary to reveal their identity if they had fought against the Assyrians as auxiliaries or allies of their opponents.

FIG. 91 Black polished pottery with white encrusted ornament. According to M. P. Griaznov (KSIAM No. 108, 1966, p. 33).
Upper row: Transcaucasia.
Middle row: Kazakhstan.
Lower row: Yenissey steppe country, north of the Altai Mountains.

An Urartian helmet of the eighth–seventh centuries B.C., which was found at Rutchi Tig in north Ossetia, in the Caucasian highland (Pl. L) and within the territory of the Koban culture, points to warfare between the Transcaucasian tribes and the Urartians. And warfare with the Assyrians is indicated by an Assyrian votive bead or seal, with an inscription of Adad-nirari (763–755 B.C.), which was excavated at Khodzhal (see p. 370).

The Scythians who entered Transcaucasia early in the ninth century B.C. may be identified as a mixed people of Srubnaya and Andronovo descent. Their progress southwards along the Caspian coast is marked by Srubnaya features in the remains of the Late Bronze Age cultures in Dagestan in the North-east Caucasus; and the presence of some Andronovo tribes is suggested by characteristic bronze objects and pottery of that culture found along the Caspian coast (Fig. 91). More definite evidence of Andronovo influence is supplied by a number of Late Bronze Age graves in the cemetery of Beshtasheni, which contained gold and silver pendants, beads, and bracelets, of types unknown to Transcaucasia but common to the Andronovo burials in Kazakhstan.[8] Furthermore, it has been emphasized[9] that the place-names of Transcaucasia, and some topics of Avesta, suggest that the nomads who invaded Western Asia in the eighth–seventh centuries originated from the Kazakhstan steppe.

The newcomers must soon have adopted many elements of the much higher cultures surrounding them in their new country, and gradually transformed their own culture into the 'Scythian' culture characteristic of the 'Scythian Age'. An important role in the final formation of the Scythian culture was played by the splendid Oriental civilization with which they came into close contact during their sojourn in Iran. It would be futile trying to follow this evolution step by step, as no relative material is available; but its outlines can be sketched in as follows.

Ancient Greek and Assyrian records furnish ample evidence that the time between the ninth and seventh centuries B.C. was a very troublesome period in the history of Western Asia. We hear that in 815 B.C. the forefathers of the ancient Persians entered the valley of Zagros in South-western Iran, having been forced to leave their previous seats in Parsua, east of Lake Urmia. One of the main causes of the disturbances and displacements was most probably the influx and pressure of the Cimmerians and Scythians, who at that time appeared on the northern border of Western Asia. The introduction into the regular Assyrian army of mounted archers was undoubtedly one indication of the pressure of the steppe nomads; for up to the ninth century B.C. the main mobile force of the Assyrian army, and of other Oriental armies consisted of chariots, which were far less effective than mounted cavalry against the northern horsemen. The presence of the latter at that time on the Assyrian border is well illustrated by the bas-relief of Nimrud, mentioned previously. The dress of its two bowmen was typical of the nomads of the Pontic and Asiatic steppes, as was also the bow. The art of shooting backwards at a gallop, was peculiar to the steppe nomads and this tactic was widely used by the Scythians.

During the ninth and eighth centuries B.C. the frontiers of the Urartian kingdom were pushed northwards up to Lake Sevan, and strongholds were built in order to protect the new acquisitions. The Urartian king Manua, son of Ispuini (810–778 B.C.), erected many fortresses on his northern border, and Manuaki (Tashburun) and the first fortress of Karmir-Blur was founded at that time. The main aim of these measures was undoubtedly to secure the kingdom from the inroads of Transcaucasian tribes, and also the Scythians. At that very time also the people of the Transcaucasian culture built many 'Cyclopaean' fortresses in the western part of Transcaucasia (see p. 372).

The advance of the mounted nomads was probably checked in the eighth century by the Urartians and Assyrians. Eventually, the newcomers settled in the steppe of west Azerbaijan, in the ancient country of Sakasene, which was named after them; it lay close to the northeastern border of the kingdom of Urartu.

The furniture of Transcaucasian burials after the ninth century B.C., and the ritual performed, reflect changes in the social structure of the population. In the second millennium, differences in the endowment of graves did not indicate any particular social distinction between the persons buried; but from the eighth century onwards, richly furnished graves of chieftains, some with human offerings, contrast strongly with the burials of ordinary people, and imply a considerable social differentiation. Furthermore, anthropological study of the osseous material has revealed that serfs were of a different racial type from their masters, on whose graves they were put to death. Some indigenous peoples must have been subject to alien tribes, and the Scythians may well have been among the latter.

The Scythians undoubtedly contributed to all these changes. They seem to have subjugated at least some of the Transcaucasian indigeneous tribes, and thus built up their strength for future conquests in the seventh century B.C. in the countries of Western Asia. This view seems to be supported by princely 'Scythian' graves excavated in some parts of Transcaucasia—such as the barrow graves at Mingechaur, on the Kura in Eastern Azerbaijan, which contained iron and bronze weapons of the Scythian type, daggers of the 'akinakes' type, iron spear-heads, bronze belts, and iron and bronze three-edged Scythian arrow-heads. In the settlement associated with these burials, a clay model of a two-wheeled Scythian cart was found. The barrow graves were most probably the burial places of Scythian princelings; though the settlement, which was contemporary, was inhabited by the indigenous population of local origin, as indicated by its remains, which were a further development of the local culture of the preceding, pre-Scythian period. Some authors[10] also attribute to the Scythians the barrow-graves of the Gandzha-Karabagh culture.

Graves with Scythian-type weapons—iron daggers, battle-axes, iron and bronze three-edged arrow-heads—were also found in other parts of Transcaucasia, especially in Georgia and Abkhasia. They have all been dated to the seventh and sixth centuries B.C., and attributed to the Scythians. A relatively large number of similar objects have been found outside graves. They also appear in cemeteries—in many graves associated with objects typical of the Colchidic culture (Kolkhida near Gagri), or in graves belonging to one of the branches of that culture, and their appearance in such graves marks a new stage in the development of the Colchidic culture. The earliest of these objects were from the eighth century, and it is doubtful whether they were deposited by the Scythians; they might originally have belonged to the indigenous population of the country and been subsequently adopted by the Scythians.

It has been pointed out by several scholars[11] that the iron daggers of the 'akinakes' type were probably a local, Transcaucasian invention, presumably Central Georgian. The earliest specimens, in their fuller shape and decoration, resemble the Transcaucasian daggers of the Late Bronze Age, and were undoubtedly derived from these. The same applies to the Scythian iron battle-axes, the earliest specimens of which were closely related to the South-western Transcaucasian bronze battle-axes (shaft-hole axes). The three-edged arrow-heads of the Scythian type were also a Transcaucasian invention; the earliest datable specimens being found exclusively in Transcaucasia.[12] The 'typical Scythian' armament was in fact Transcaucasian. The Scythians seem to have availed themselves of the new and more effective weapons invented, or improved, by the highly skilled Transcaucasian master-smiths. Later, they introduced them to the North Pontic steppe country.

During the seventh century B.C. the Scythians again made their presence widely felt in Western Asia. About 674 B.C. they seem to have become powerful enough for their king Bartatua to ask for and receive an Assyrian princess in marriage; she was the daughter of Esarhaddon (680–669 B.C.). They seem to have been recruited as mercenaries by the kings of Manna, the country in the central part of Iran; and the power of the Mannaean kingdom in the first half of the seventh century B.C. most probably rested on them.[13] Later, they probably made themselves masters of the country and ultimately subdued the Medes and the kingdom of Urartu. Their presence was recorded in Palestine, on the Egyptian border. Presumably they also took part in the final assault and destruction of Niniveh in 612 B.C., and in the liquidation of the last remnants of independent Assyria in 610 B.C.

The date of the zenith of Scythian power—the twenty-eight years of their rule 'over Upper Asia'—is disputable. The reign of Bartatua (680–652 or 678–648 B.C.) has been proposed by some scholars, but it seems more likely to have been the reign of his son, Madyas, estimated variously within the period from 653 to 609 B.C. The Scythian rule left a bad reputation. Herodotus says 'everything was overthrown by their licentiousness and neglect. Besides the usual tribute, they extracted from each whatever they chose to impose, and in addition to the tribute, they rode the country and plundered them of all their possessions'.

Scythian domination came to an end with their defeat by the Medes, who thrust them out of Asia back into Europe. The struggle is said to have taken place shortly before the war of the Medes against the Lydians, which began about 590 B.C. and ended in 585 B.C.

During their stay in Western Asia the Scythians, especially their rulers, were greatly affected by the Oriental civilization. They absorbed many Oriental features into their culture, which accordingly acquired a marked west-Asiatic character. This is well reflected in 'Scythian' art, the earliest examples of which, dating from the seventh century B.C., have been found in Iran (for example, Ziwiye-Sakkez) and in Kars, close to the southern border of Transcaucasia (Zakim). The Scythian animal style, whether taken over from the Mannaeans[14] or the Urartians,[15] was of west Asiatic origin. All the animals that appear on early Scythian masterpieces—stags, ibexes, lions—do not live in the steppe and were unknown to the Srubnaya-Andronovo Scythians in their original country on the Volga.[16] Scythian art, with its scenes of battle and struggle, and its griffins, shows no connections with the art of the northern forest zone, with its restricted range of stationary animals—bears, elks, water birds.[17]

The impact of Oriental civilization on the Scythians is well reflected also in their remains of the sixth century B.C. in the Ukraine—the period after their retreat from Western Asia and Transcaucasia. The costume, armour and funeral fitments were purely Oriental,[18] as was the style and technique of the objects found in their early tombs; even the names of the Scythian gods were most probably of west Asiatic or Anatolian origin.[19]

At the turn of the seventh and sixth centuries B.C., the Scythians were driven out of Asia. In retreating northwards, they conquered the whole north Pontic steppe country and destroyed the Chornii-Lis and other cultures of the area; their arrival marks the beginning of the new, Scythian Age in the history of Eastern Europe.

GREEK COLONIZATION

Another factor in the establishment of the new order was Greek colonization, which played by no means a less important role than that of the Scythians.

During the several centuries that had elapsed since the era of Mycenaean trade with the north Pontic countries no regular commercial relations had apparently been maintained between the two areas. The new period of Aegean—now Greek—commercial activity in the north Pontic region began not later than in the ninth century B.C., when the Asiatic Greeks already seem to have been well acquainted with the countries round the Black Sea. Hesiod, who lived around 800 B.C., was the first to mention the Scythians. He knew the mare-milking Scythians, and also speaks of a tribe of milk-drinkers who have waggons for houses. Homer speaks of them when he mentions the Maremilkers, and he also mentions the Cimmerians; both his poems were written not later than the eighth century B.C.

Aristeas of Proconnesus travelled to the countries situated northeast of the Black Sea about the middle of the seventh century B.C., and seems to have reached the steppe of Eastern Kazakhstan. His account shows how deeply the Greeks had already penetrated into the hinterland of the Black Sea by the seventh century B.C., and how much they knew about the very remote countries far inland (see p. 310).

In the seventh century B.C. the Asiatic Greeks, mainly Milesians, began to trade more regularly with the North Pontic countries and to visit the northern coast of the Black Sea frequently. Greek pottery of the end of the seventh century has been found in several sites along the Caucasian coast and in the Cimmerian barrow graves of Temir Gora near Kerch and Tsukur, on the Taman peninsula. Trading posts sprang up all along the coast, most of them placed in the settlements of the local population. Suitably placed posts, with favourable communications with the hinterland, undoubtedly attracted the produce and population of a wide area;[20] and so permanent Greek colonies arose in the sixth century B.C., after the conquest of the Ukrainian steppe country by the Scythians who retreated from Iran and Transcaucasia; most of these towns or cities survive to the present day. The Scythian might, which secured the necessary peace and security for the growth of commerce, was one of the important pre-conditions for this development.

But the appearance of Greek colonies on the Black Sea coast had another, no less important, significance. It brought the countries of Eastern Europe into close contact with the ancient civilized world, with the result that the names of its peoples, often of their leading personalities, and their doings began to be recorded. The archaeological material of the following periods can be supplemented by written records. The era of the dark prehistoric past has run out; the Proto-Historic Era has begun. It will be dealt with in another volume.

References

1 IV, 11–13.
2 Herodotus IV, 13.
3 *Iliad* XIII, 4–8.

4 *Odyssey* XI, 14–19.

5 I, 15.

6 A.A. Yerusalimskaya, SA, 1962–1.

7 IV, 12.

8 B.A. Kuftin, КSIIМК 8, 1940, p. 17.

9 S.S. Chernikov.

10 S. Ter-Avestiian.

11 M.M. Trapsh, КSIIМК, 53, 1954; E.I. Krupnov.

12 T. Sulimirski in *Artibus Asiae*, Vol. XVIII, 1954.

13 G.A. Melikishvili.

14 R. Ghirshman, *Artibus Asiae*, Vol. XIII, 1950, pp. 181–206.

15 R.D. Barnett, *Iranica Antiqua*, Vol. II, 1962, pp. 77–95.

16 N. Tchlenova, 'L'Art animalier de l'époque scythique en Siberie et en Pontide', *Les Rapports et les Informations des Archéologues de l'URSS. VIe Congrès International des Sciences, Préhistoriques et Protohistoriques*. Moscow, 1962. *Eadam*, 'Le cerf scythe', *Artibus Asiae*, Vol. XXVI, 1963, p. 27 ff.

17 N. Tchlenova, as above.

18 M. Rostovtzeff, *Iranians and Greeks in South Russia*. Oxford, 1922, p. 57.

19 L.E. Elnitskii in *Vestnik Drevney Istorii*, Vol. 2 (24), 1948, p. 99.

20 Ch.M. Danoff, 'Pontos Euxeinos', *Pauly-Wissowa Realencyclopädie*, Vol. IX, 1962

Geological Periods	Main Fauna	Archaeological periods and important sites		
Würm Glaciation LG1 2	Fauna of: Rangifer tarandus (reindeer)	**10,000 B.C.** VII: Bugorok, Gontsy lower horizon, Babin I layer 3, Moldova V-2-4, Sokol I	*Periods by P.I. Boriskovskii*	Other important sites of the Upper-Palaeolithic:
		VI: Chulatovo I, Suponevo, Timonovka	Magdalenian	Medvezha on the Pechora
Inter-Stadial LG1 1/2	Late period of fauna of Elephas primigenius (mammoth)	V **15,000 B.C.**: Kostionki II, III, Mezin, Kirillovskaya lower layer, Moldova V-6, Borshevo I, Amvroslevka		Kapova Cave in the Urals
		IV **21,000 B.C.**: Pushkari I, Gagarino		Chusovaya near Perm
		III: Kostienki I upper layer	Aurignatian-Solutrean	
		II **23,000 B.C.**: Moldova V-9, 10, Kostienki I lower layer, Telmanskaya upper layer		
	–25,000 B.C.–	I: Telmanskaya lower layer, Babin I, layer 1, Moldova V-10a layer		Siuren I lower layer
Würm (Valdai) Glaciation LG1 1	Elephas primigenius Rhinoceros antiquitatis	Mousterian: Akhtyrskaya cave (upper Mousterian) 35,000 B.P. (Mo 337 and 342); Chusovaya junction near Perm; Sukhaya Mechetka near Stalingrad; Derkul on the middle Donets; Kodak, region of the Dnieper rapids; Moldova V on the Dniester, layers 11, 12; Vykhvatyntsi on the middle Dniester; Chorkurcha (Crimea); Kiik-Koba (Crimea) upper horizon; Ilskaya (Caucasus)		
Riss-Würm Inter-Glacial LIG 1	Elephas trogonterii	Late Acheulean: Environments of Kuibyshev; Luka Vrublevetskaya on the Dniester; Environment of Zhitomir; Kruglik, region of the Dnieper rapids; Nenasytets, region of the Dnieper rapids		
Riss (Volga-Dnieper) Glaciation PG 1	Elephas antiquus Rhinoceros Merkii	Early Acheulean: Amvrosievka, north of the Sea of Azov; Kiik-Koba (Crimea) lower horizon; Sites in Ossetia (Central Caucasus); Sites in the region of Maikop (NW Caucasus); Region of Sukhumi (Georgia) many sites; Satani-Dar cave (Armenia) upper layer		
Inter-Glacial Mindel-Riss	Hippopotamus Elephas meridionalis Rhinoceros etruscus	Chellean: Luka-Vrublevetskaya ?; Satani-Dar (Armenia)		

TABLE I. Chronological scheme of the Palaeolithic, based mainly on works by P.P. Efimenko and P.I. Boriskovskii.

Date B.C.	Climate	Period	Caucasus	Crimea	Lower Dnieper	Podolia and the South-west	Middle Dnieper and Desna	Byelo-russia	Donetz	Central Russia	Don	Kama Urals	East Baltic	North
4000	Atlantic	Late Mesolithic / Tardenoisian	Sosruko M2 – M1	Siuren II upper, Murzak-Koba graves; Shan-Koba layers 2-3	Kamyana Mohyla lower layers; "Early neolithic" cemeteries; Igren 5,8 lower layer	Zankivtsi	Pishchanyi Riv	Grensk upper level	sites on sand – dunes	Sobolevo; Elin-Bor middle layer	Tardenoisian sites on the lower Don	Nizhnee Adishchevo Borovoe Ozero I		Pogostishche I
5000												Ogurinskaya Shigir culture		
		Spread of the Tardenoisian industry					Smyachka XIII			Skniatino				Arctic "Pal-aeolithic"
6000	Boreal	Early Mesolithic	Sosruko M3 – M5	Siuren I, Siuren II lower upper Kukrek; Shan-Koba layers 4-6	Voloske	Vladimirovka upper layer; Moldova V upper	Smyachka XIV		semi-desert ?	Elin-Bor lowest layer	semi – desert ?		Kunda culture	
7000	Pre-Boreal				Osokorivka upper layer; Cemeteries Vasylivka III, Amvrosievka		Zhurovka				Borshevo II upper layer			
8000			Sosruko			Vladimirovka lower layer; Lisichniki	Spread of Swiderian elements	Rogalik						
9000	Final Glacial / Alleröd / Upper Drias	Epi-Palaeolithic			Osokorivka lower layer		Kirillovskaya upper Gonsty upper layer Chulatovo II				Borshevo II lower and middle layers	Talitskii site on the Chusovaya South Ural cave sites		
10 000														

TABLE 2. Tentative chronological scheme of the East European Epi-Palaeolithic and Mesolithic.

3500	3000	2500	2000	Date B.C.
Atlantic		Sub-Boreal		Climate
1 2 3 — EARLY NEOLITHIC	MIDDLE NEOLITHIC	LATE NEOLITHIC		Periods
Danubian I / South-Bug	Tripolyan B-1 A A	Tripolian B-2		Chernozem country
Surskii I	Surskii II	Sobach-ky Seredni Stog		Lower Dnieper
Dnieper – Elbe Assemblage		Dnieper-Donetz culture		Kiev-Donetz region
Shan-Koba upper level	Pre-pottery Neolithic			Crimea
		Yamnaya		Dnieper-Don-steppe
	Yamnaya			Volga steppe
		Maikop culture Maikop Novosvo-bodnaya		North Caucasus
Kyul - Tepe I	Kura - Araxes	Sachkhere		Trans-caucasia
	Dnieper-Elbe Assemblage Valdai	Comb-pricked pottery culture		West
Lialovo culture Belev culture		Lialovo culture Balakhna culture		Central Russia
Late Kunda culture	Sperrings Narva culture	Sarnate Pit-comb ware Akali II		Eastern Baltic
	Sperrings	Early Karelian culture Oleni Ostrov		Karelia
Pre-pottery Neolithic Pogostishche Veretie		Kargopol I culture		South-east
Nizhnee Adishchevo?		Kama-Kazan Neolithic Borovoe Ozero I and Observatoria III		Middle Volga Kama
	Early Gorbunovo culture Stage I Strelka	Stage II Section 6 lowest level		Middle Urals
	Chebarkul I lower	Chebarkul II upper level		South Urals
Namazga I Namazga II		Namazga III Kelteminar	Late Kelteminar	West-Siberia Cent. Asia

Far-right vertical region labels: South-west, South-east, Forest-zone, The North, The East.
Far-left vertical labels: Mesolithic cultures.

TABLE 3. Tentative chronological scheme of the East European Neolithic (the fourth and third millennia B.C.).

2000	1900	1800	1700	1600	1500	1400	1300	1200	Date B.C.	
Neolithic		Br. Age I		Bronze Age II			III		Montelius	
Bronze Age A-1			Br. Age A-2	Bronze Age B-2			C–D		Reinecke	
Early stage			Middle		Late	VII-a			Troy VI	
Aegean trade		Mycenean		Koszider bronzes						
Cypriote Middle		trade		Füzesabony Babylon.					Equations	
Bronze Age		Irish trade		boundary						
Laibach–Vučedol				stones						
Late Neolithic		Bronze Age stage I		Bronze Age stage II		stage III		Late Br.Age	East European stages	
Barrow-grave culture I		Barrow-grave culture II		Barrow-grave culture III (Rusiłów)		Komarów culture			Sub-Carpathian	
Tripolye culture C-1		Werteba	Koszyłowce–Tovdry		Komarów	Noua			West Podolia	
Globular Amphorae stage I	stage II			stage III		Biały-Potok				
Tripolye culture γ-1 Vykhvatyntsi			Pechora-Gorodsk Globular Amphorae		Komarów Costişa	Noua			Middle Dniester	
Tripolye culture C-1 Volodymirivka			Sabatynivka II		Komarów	Bilo-hrudivka			Uman region	South–west
Globular Amphorae stage I	stage II		Gorodsk culture		Trzciniec current Voytsekhivka				Volhynia	
Tripolye culture C-1 Sofiivka–Evminka			Marianivka culture		Bilohrudivka Sosnitsa culture				Kiev country	
Middle Dnieper culture period I	period II			period III		period IV				
Usatovo culture			Sukleia		Komarów Hungarian bronzes	Borodino Sabatynivka Srubnaya			Steppe	
Yamnaya	Usatovo settlement			Mikhailivka II	Mikhailivka III					
Seredni Stog 2 Yamnaya culture		Catacomb influence		Durna Skela		Srubnaya			Lower Dnieper & Rapids	
Yamnaya culture		Catacomb culture				Srubnaya culture			Steppe up to the Don	South–east
Yamnaya culture		Poltavka culture			Srubnaya culture		Srubnaya Khvalinsk culture		Volga steppe	
North – Caucasian Bronze Age culture period I Novosvobodnaya	(Kuban culture) period II			period III		Digorian culture			Caucasus & Trans-caucasia	
Transcaucasian Early Br. Age				Trialeti XV		Catacomb culture				

TABLE 4a. Tentative chronological scheme of the East European Early and Middle Bronze Age (the second millennium B.C.).

2000	1900	1800	1700	1600	1500	1400	1300	1200	Date B.C.
Neolithic			Br. Age I		Bronze Age II			III	Montelius
Bronze Age A-1			Br. Age A-2		Bronze Age B-2		C-D		Reinecke
Early stage			Middle			Late	VII-a		Troy VI
Aegean trade / Cypriote Middle Bronze Age / Laibach-Vučedol			Mycenean trade / Irish trade		Koszider bronzes / Füzesabony Babylon. boundary stones				Equations
Late Neolithic	Bronze Age stage I			Bronze Age stage II			stage III	Late Br. Age	East European stages
I (Early)	Dnieper - Desna culture period II / Globular Amph. elements / Strelitsa					III (Late) / Trzciniec influence			West
Early Balakhna	Volga - Oka assemblage / Balakhna culture II / Fatyanovo I / Early Volosovo		Late Balakhna culture / Early textile pottery / Fatyanovo II / Volosovo II			textile pottery / Seima cemetery / Volosovo III			Central Russia
Eastern assemblage	Balanovo I / Globular Amphora elements			Balanovo II		Balanovo III / Srubnaya advance / Abashevo			Middle Volga
Combed ware culture	Local groups of Combed ware / Boat-axe culture / Early textile pottery					Bronze Age culture			East Baltic
Early Karelian (combed ware) culture	Second Karelian culture. / I stage II stage					Late Karelian flint sculptures			Karelia
	Early White Sea culture					Second White Sea culture / Siberian elements			White Sea
First Kargopol culture	Second Kargopol culture / East Baltic elements / Modlona I					Third Kargopol culture / Siberian elem. / Flint sculpture			South-east
Middle Kama Late Neolithic culture				Turbino culture / Garinskii period Bor period / cemetery I / II					Middle Kama
Kazan Neolithic culture / stage I II / stage III				Early Bronze Age / Srubnaya elements / Abashevo culture			Late Br. Age		Kazan area
Early Gorbunovo culture stage II			Middle Gorbunovo culture / Site section six - middle layer				Late Gorbunovo culture		Middle Urals
Neolithic culture			Andronovo culture / Formative period		Fedorovskii period		Alakulskii period		South Urals

(Right vertical labels: Forest-zone · The North · The East)

TABLE 4b. Tentative chronological scheme of the East European Early and Middle Bronze Age (the second millennium B.C.).

28

1200	1100	1000	900	800	700	600	Date B.C.	

Br. III		Br. IV		Br. V		Br. VI	Montelius	
Br. C/D		H.A.		H.B.		H.C.	Reinecke	

Pilin Egyek Noua	Val I Velatice Thracian Hallstatt	Val II 	Thraco-Cimmerian remains	Central European	Equations
	Nomad menace Uratian expansion	Cimmerians Scythic summit		West Asiatic	

Komarów Biały-Potok Noua advance	Lusatian advance Holihrady (Thracian Hallstatt)	W y s o c k o c u l t u r e c u l t u r e Thraco-Cimmerian finds	West Podolia & Volhyn	
Bilohrudivka culture "Thracian Hallstatt" "Cimmerian" bronze industry	Chornii – Lis culture		Chernozem country	South –west
Sabatynivka culture "Cimmerian" bronze industry "Cimmerian period" Lukianivka	Settlms. destr.	"Pre-Scythian" period Late Sabatynivka Illinka – Pechora	Scythians	Steppe	South
		Kizil-Koba culture Simferopol		Crimea	
Srubnaya culture earlier period Bondarykha culture	Srubnaya culture later period Bilozerka settlements		Dnieper- Don country	
Srubnaya – Khvalinsk culture Andronova elements	Sosnovaya Novo- Saurom- Maza cherkassk atians	Volga steppe	South – east
Late Catacomb culture Koban culture I Kaya -Kent – Khorochoi culture	Koban trade Koban Koban culture II culture Iron weapons III	North Caucasus	
Khodzhala –Kedabek (Gandzha – Karabagh) culture Central Transcaucasian culture Nomad invasion New nomad tribes Scythic domination Colchidic culture Samtavro	Trans- Caucasia	
Textile pottery Late Volosovo Volosovo III – Late Balakhna culture cemetry Bolshoe-Kozino Scandinavian trade	Central Russia North	Forest zone
Early Pozdniakovo culture	Late Pozdniakovo culture	Central Russia South	
Seima-Galich culture (Seima -Chirikovskaya) Galich Balanovo – Abashevo survivals hoard	Fedorovskaya settlements	Central Russia North-East	
East Baltic Bronze Age culture Scandinavian colonies	East Baltic	The North
Late Karelian culture Third Kargopol culture Mälar Second White Sea culture axes	Latest Karelian & Late Kargopol & White Sea cult- ures Wave of eastern tribes	Arctic cultures	
Kazan Late Bronze Age culture Srubnaya elements Balanovo – Abashevo survivals in North Turbino culture Borskii period	Zaimishche III upper level Scandinavian connections Transition to Ananino	Ananine culture	Kazan	The East
				Kama	
Late Gorbunovo culture Stage I – Razboinichyi Stage II Andronovo elements Section Six upper Lev.	Middle Urals	The East
Andronovo culture Alakulskii period	Uphe laval	Andronovo culture Zamaraevskii period Saurom- atians	South Urals	

TABLE 5. Tentative chronological scheme of the East European Late Bronze Age and the Earliest Iron Age (end of the second and early first millennia B.C.).

Date B.C.	Caucasus		North-Pontic area			Country on the Volga				The Urals		West Siberia	Equations						
	Trans-Caucasia	North Caucasus	The West	Middle and lower Dnieper	Don	Lower	Middle	Upper	West and Kama	South		Troy	Aeg. trade	Reinecke	Montelius	China	The South-west		

TABLE 6. Chronological scheme of the use of copper and bronze in Eastern Europe up to the early first millennium B.C. After E.N. Chernykh (MIA 132, 1966, p. 92, fig. 26), with additions and a few alterations.

Legend:
- Copper
- Arsenic bronze
- Tin bronze
- * Faience beads & other Mycenean objects

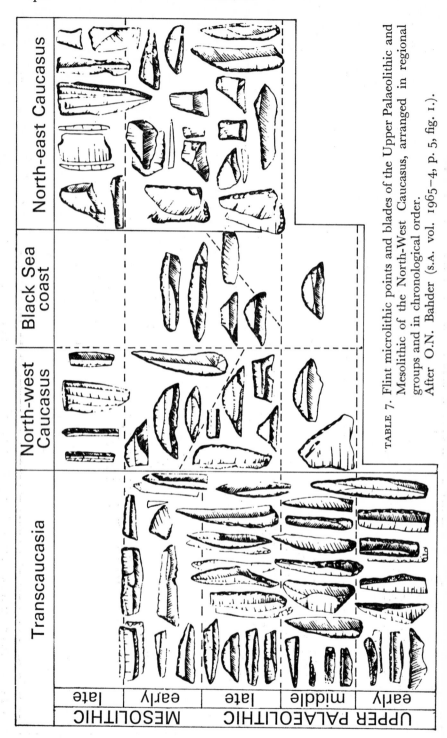

TABLE 7. Flint microlithic points and blades of the Upper Palaeolithic and Mesolithic of the North-West Caucasus, arranged in regional groups and in chronological order.
After O.N. Bahder (s.A. vol. 1965–4, p. 5, fig. 1.).

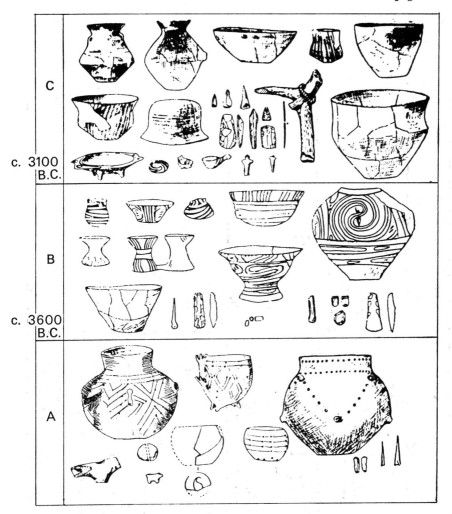

TABLE 8. Pottery and other objects typical of the three superimposed
levels of the lower occupation layer at the Nezvysko site.
After E.K. Chernysh (MDAPV vol. 2, 1959, p. 76, pl. I.).
(A) Danubian I level; (B) Tripolyan B–1 level; (C) Tripolyan
B–2 level.

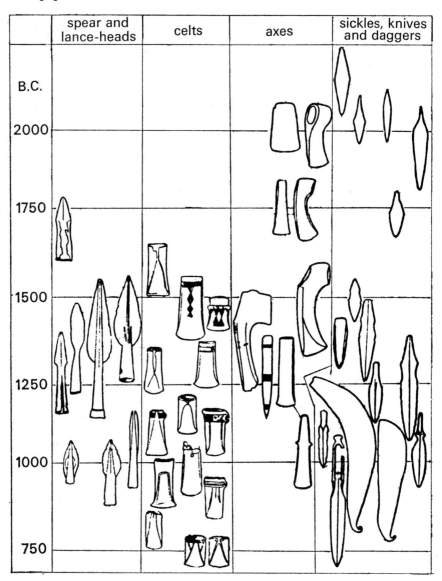

TABLE 9. Scheme of the typological and chronological development during
the Bronze Age of metal weapons and tools found in the Middle
Urals and the Kama country.
After B.G. Tikhonov (MIA 90, 1960, p. 114, pl. xxv.).

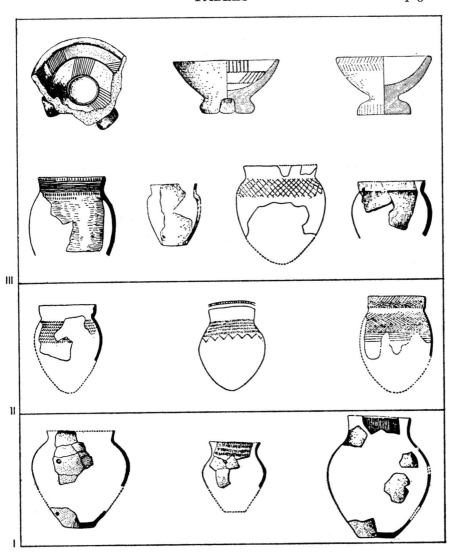

TABLE 10. Vessels typical of the three superimposed layers of the settlement at Mykhailivka (Mikhailovka).
After O.F. Lahodovska, O.G. Shaposhnikova and M.L. Makarevych (*Mykhailivske Poselennya,* Kiev 1962, pp. 32, 86, 100 and 113; p. I, VII, XI; fig. 33.).
(I) lower layer of Tripolyan period B–2; (II) middle layer of the turn of the third and second millennia B.C.; (III) upper layer of the Catacomb period, to which also the pedestalled bowls belonged.

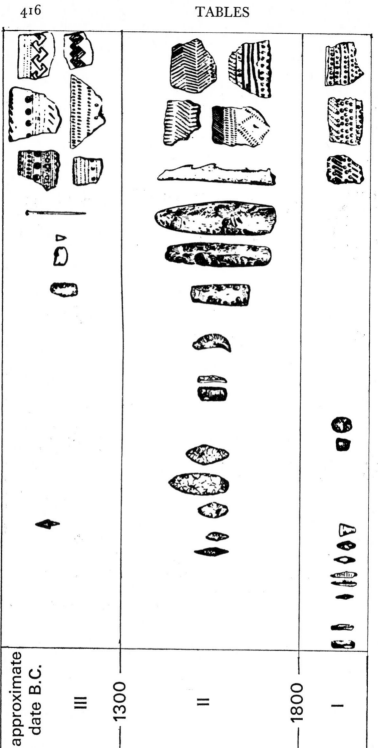

TABLE 11. Stages in the prehistoric development of the country of Riazan.
After A.Ia. Briusov (*Ocherki po Istorii Plemen*. Moscow 1952, p. 69, fig. 11.).

(I) the early stage (the Lialovo culture); (II) the Riazan culture of the Volga-Oka assemblage, with elements of the Catacomb and Volosovo cultures; (III) period of the Pozdniakovo culture.

TABLE 12. Stages in the prehistoric development in Estonia.
After L. Jaanits (*Poselenia Epokhi Neolita*. Tallin 1959, p. 293, fig. 63),
with dates of the later periods slightly modified.

B.C.	pottery	flints	other kind of stone, bone, metals

TABLE 13. Stages in the development of the country on the Vychegda in North-East Russia.

After G.M. Burov (*Vychegodskii Kraj*. Moscow 1965, p. 56, fig. 19).

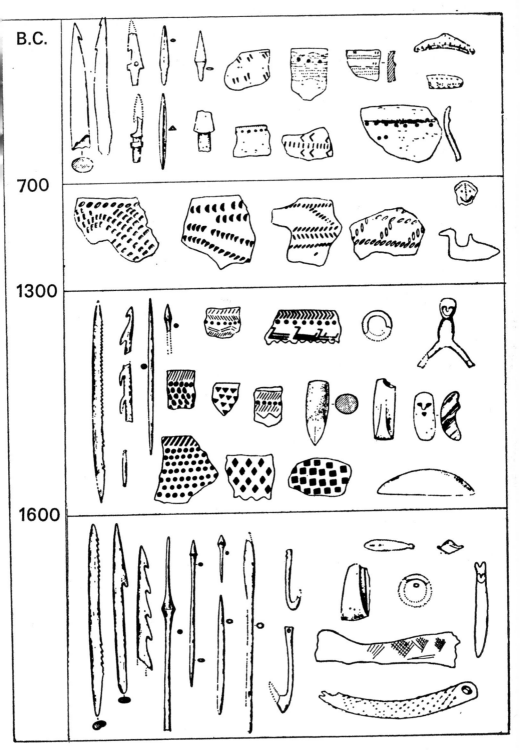

TABLE 14. Stages in the prehistoric development of the Kargopol area.
After M.E. Foss (MIA. 29, 1952, p. 118, fig. 68).

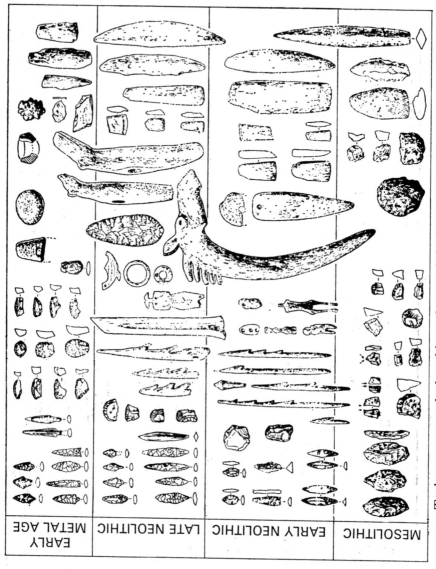

EARLY METAL AGE	**LATE NEOLITHIC**	**EARLY NEOLITHIC**	**MESOLITHIC**

TABLE 15. Tools, weapons, and other objects, characteristic of the subsequent periods of the prehistoric development in Karelia and the Leningrad region, from the Mesolithic to about 300 A.D. After N.N. Gurina (MIA 87, 1961, p. 47, fig. 11) with dates and the names of periods

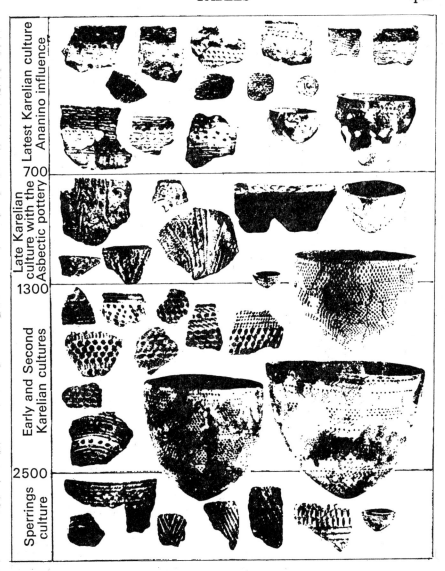

TABLE 16. Pottery characteristic of the periods distinguished in Table 15 in Karelia and the Leningrad region.
After N.N. Gurina (as Table 15.).

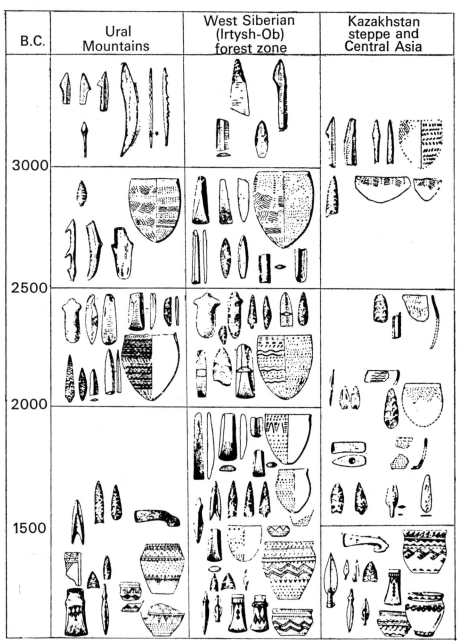

B.C.	Ural Mountains	West Siberian (Irtysh-Ob) forest zone	Kazakhstan steppe and Central Asia
3000			
2500			
2000			
1500			

TABLE 17. Stages in the Neolithic and Bronze Age development of three distinct regions east of the Urals.
After V.N. Chernetsov (MIA 35, 1953, p. 56, pl. xx.).

B.C.	period	type of burials	settlements	pottery	ornament	stone tools	metal objects
800 — 1100	KHULA-SIUKHINSKII						
1100 — 1300	OSH-PANDINSKII						
1300 — 1500	ATLI-KASINSKII						
1500 — 1800	BALANOVSKII		open settlements				

TABLE 18. Stages in the development of the Balanovo culture.
After A.Kh. Khalikov and E.A. Khalikova (MIA 110, 1963, p. 239 ff., fig. 16.).

TABLE 19. Stages in the development during the second millennium B.C. of the Piatigorsk group of the North Caucasian culture.

After V.I. Markovin (MIA 93, 1963, p. 102, fig. 46) with the dates modified.

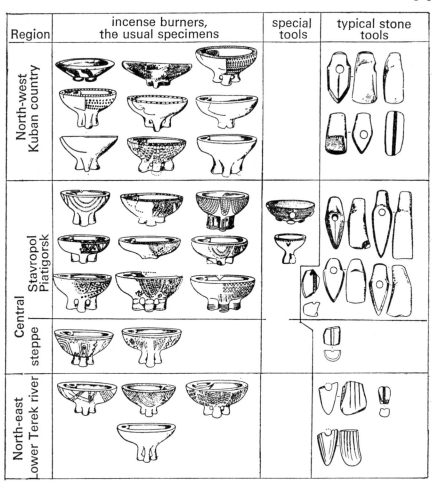

Region	incense burners, the usual specimens			special tools	typical stone tools
North-west Kuban country					
Central Stavropol Piatigorsk					
steppe					
North-east Lower Terek river					

TABLE 20. Development of grave goods of the Catacomb culture, including the cross-footed vessels ('incense-burners'), from different parts of the North Caucasus.
After V.I. Markovin (as Table 19, p. 72, fig. 31.).

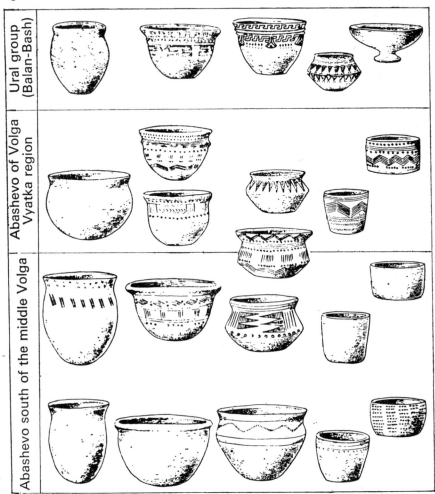

TABLE 21. Pottery characteristic of the different groups of the Abashevo culture.
After A.Kh. Khalikov (MIA 97, 1961, pl. XIII.).

	type of grave	pottery	copper and bronze	stone	flint	bone	stelae and engravings
Yamnaya culture							
Kemi-Oba culture							
1800							
Catacomb culture							
Srubnaya culture							
1250							

TABLE 22. Scheme of the development of the steppe and highland cultures in the Crimea during the late third and second millennia B.C.
After A.A. Shchepinskii (S.A. vol. 1966–2, p. 11, fig. 1.), with dates added.

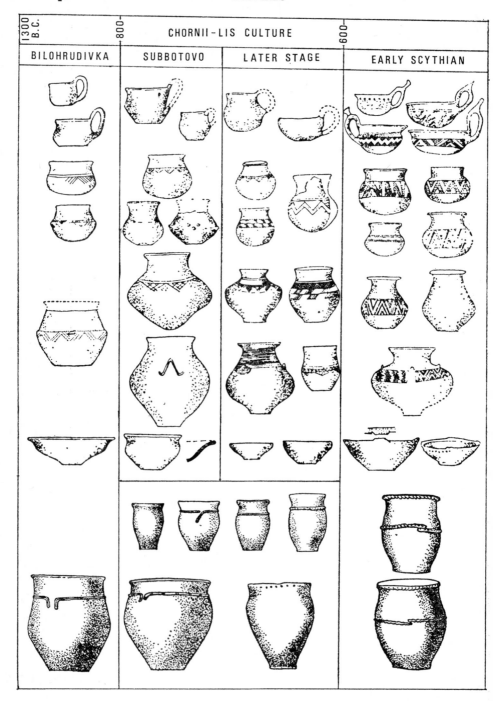

1300 B.C.	800	CHORNII-LIS CULTURE		600
BILOHRUDIVKA	SUBBOTOVO	LATER STAGE	EARLY SCYTHIAN

TABLE 23. Main types of pottery of the Ukrainian forest-steppe country west of the Dnieper of the Bilohrudivka, Chornii-Lis, and Early Scythian cultures.

After A.I. Terenozhkin (*Predskifskii Period.* Kiev 1961, pp. 75, 77, figs. 50, 51.).

Bibliographies

BOOKS AND ARTICLES BY THE AUTHOR
ON TOPICS DISCUSSED IN THIS VOLUME

'The Neolithic of the U.S.S.R. A Guide to the Recent Literature on the Subject', *Bulletin* no. 6 for 1966, pp. 94–1291.

'The Bronze Age of the U.S.S.R. A Guide to the Recent Literature on the Subject', *Bulletin* no. 7 for 1967, pp. 43–83.

'The late Bronze Age and Early Iron Age of the U.S.S.R. A guide to the Recent Literature on the Subject', *Bulletin* no. 8 for 1968.

Corded Ware and Globular Amphorae North-East of the Carpathians (University of London Athlone Press, London 1968).

Polska przedhistoryczna [Prehistoric Poland, in Polish], parts I and II (London 1955 and 1959).

'Climate and Population', *Baltic Countries*, vol. I (Toruń 1935), pp. 1–18.

'The Climate of the Ukraine during the Neolithic and the Bronze Age', *Archeologia*, vol. XII (Warszawa 1961), pp. 1–18.

'The Problem of the Survival of the Tripolye Culture', PPS, vol. XVI for 1950, pp. 42–51.

'Tripolyan Notes', PPS, vol. XXX for 1964, pp. 56–65.

'Copper Hoard from Horodnica on the Dniester', *Mitteilungen d. Anthropologischen Ges.*, vol. XCI (Wien, 1961), pp. 91–7.

'Die schnurkeramischen Kulturen und das indoeuropäische Problem', *La Pologne au VIIe Congrès Intern. des Sciences Historiques* (Warszawa 1933), 22 pages.

'Thuringian Amphorae' PPS, vol. XXI for 1955, pp. 108–122.

'On the Polesian Cradle of the Slavs' [in Polish], *Z Otchłani Wieków*, vol. XIV (Poznań 1939), pp. 33–42.

'Das Hügelgräberfeld in Komarów und die Kultur von Komarów', *Bulletin Internat. de l'Académie Polonaise* (Kraków 1936), pp. 172–82.

'Barrow-Grave 6 at Komarów', *Bulletin* no. 4 for 1964, pp. 171–88.

'Troy's Trade with Europe' [in Polish, with a summary in English], *Teki Historyczne*, vol. XV, (London 1968), pp. 3–27, 357–8.

'Eine kobaner Prachtaxt von Winniza, Ukraine', *Mitteilungen d. Anthropologischen Ges.*, vol. XCII (Wien 1962), pp. 269–71.

'Bronze Hoards of Kamionka Wielka and Potoczyska' [in Polish, with a summary in French], *Memorial Book, Prof. W. Demetrykiewicz* (Poznań 1930), pp. 177–88.

'The Problem of the Expansion of the Lusatian Culture in the Ukraine' [in Polish, with a summary in German], *Swiatowit*, vol. XIV (Warszawa 1936), pp. 40–55.

'The Bronze Hoard from Niedzieliska' [in Polish, with a summary in German], *Swiatowit*, vol. XVII (Warszawa 1938), pp. 255–82.

'The Cimmerian Problem', *Bulletin* no. 2 for 1960, pp. 45–64.

'Die thrako-kimmerische Periode in Südostpolen', *Wiener Prähistorische Zft*, vol. XXV (1938), pp. 129–151.

'Les archers à cheval—Cavalerie légère des anciens', *Revue Internationale d'Histoire Militaire*, vol. 3 (Paris 1952), pp. 447–61.

Kultura Wysocka [The Wysocko Culture, in Polish, with a summary in German] (Kraków 1931).

Scytowie na zachodniem Podolu [Scythians in West Podolia, in Polish, with a summary in German] (Lwów 1936).

'Scythian Antiquities in Western Asia', *Artibus Asiae*, vol. XVII (Ascona 1954), pp. 282–18.

SELECTED BIBLIOGRAPHY

NOTE: Only books and a few larger contributions have been taken into account. It was not practicable to quote here the hundreds of articles consulted, published mainly in periodicals listed further below. The authors of some of these, which seemed to be of particular importance for the questions discussed, have been mentioned in the references in the respective chapters of the volume.

Z.A. ABRAMOVA, 'Paleoliticheskie iskusstvo na territorii S.S.S.R. svod A-4-3 (1962).

I.I. ARTEMENKO, *Plemena Verkhnego i Srednego Podneprovya v epokhu bronzy*. MIA 148 (1967).

A. ÄYRÄPÄÄ, 'Uber die Streitaxtkulturen in Russland', ESA VIII (1933).

O.N. BAHDER, *Balanovskii Mogilnik* (Moscow, 1963); *Drevneyshe metallurgi Priuralya* (Moscow, 1964); *Poseleniya Turbinskogo tipa v Srednem Primkamie*, MIA 99 (1961).

N.A. BEREGOVAYA, *Paleoliticheskie mestonakhozhdeniya S.S.S.R.*, MIA 81 (1960).

S.S. BEREZANSKA, *Bronzovyi vik na Ukraini* (Kiev, 1964).

S.N. BIBIKOV, *Ranne tripolskoe poselenie Luka-Vrublevetskaya na Dnestre*, MIA 38 (1961).

P.I. BORISKOVSKII, *Paleolit Ukrainy*, MIA 40 (1953); and its French translation: *Le Paléolithique de l'Ukraine* (Paris, 1958). Annales du Service d'Information geologique.

P.I. BORISKOVSKII and N.D. PRASLOV, Paleolit basseyna Dnepra i Priazovia, SVOD A-1-5 (1964).

A.IA. BRIUSOV, *Ocherki po istorii plemen evropeiskoi chasti SSSR v neoliticheskuyu epokhu* (Moscow, 1952); and its German edition: *Geschichte der neolithischen Stämme im europäischen Teil der UdSSR* (Berlin, 1957).

A.IA. BRIUSOV and M.P. ZIMINA, Kamennye sverdlenye voyevye topory na territorii evropeiskoy chasti SSSR, SVOD B-4-4 (1966).

G.M. BUROV, *Vychegodskii Kraj. Ocherki drevney istorii* (Moscow, 1965).

K.W. BUTZER, *Environment and Archaeology. An Introduction to Pleistocene Geography* (Chicago, 1964).

J.K. CHARLESWORTH, *The Quaternary Era, with a Special Reference to its Glaciation*, vol. II (London, 1957).

V.N. CHERNETSOV, V.I. MOSHINSKAYA and I.A. TALITSKAYA, *Drevnyaya Istoria Nizhnego Priobia*, MIA 35 (1953).

S.S. CHERNIKOV, *Vostochnyi Kazakhstan v epokhi bronzy*, MIA 88 (1960).

E.N. CHERNYKH., *Istoria drevneyshey metallurgii Vostochnoy Evropy*, MIA 132 (1966).

A.P. CHERNYSH, *Pozdnyi Paleolit Srednego Pridnestrovia* (Moscow, 1959).

K.K. CHERNYSH, *Ranno tripolske poselennya Lenkivtsi na Serednemu Dnistri* (Kiev, 1959).

V.G. CHILDE, *The Dawn of European Civilisation* (5th ed. 1950; 6th ed. 1957); *Prehistoric Migrations in Europe* (Oslo, 1950); *New Light on the Most Ancient East* (4th ed. London, 1952).

T.N. CHUBINISHVILI, *The Earliest Culture of the Region between the Rivers Kura and Araxes* [in Georgian, with a summary in Russian] (Tbilisi, 1961); *Amiranis Gora* [in Georgian, with a summary in English] (Tbilisi, 1963).

J.G.D. CLARK, *The Mesolithic Settlement in Northern Europe* (Cambridge, 1936); *Prehistoric Europe. The Economic Basis* (London, 1952).

V. DUMITRESCU, *Hăbăşeşti* (Bucureşti, 1954).

O.M. DZHAPARIDZE, *On the History of the Georgian Tribes during the Early Stage of the Copper-Bronze Culture* [in Georgian, with a summary in Russian] (Tbilisi, 1961).

A.I. DZHAVAKHISHVILI and A.I. GLONTI, *Urbnisi I* [in Georgian, with a summary in Russian] (Tbilisi, 1962).

P.P. EFIMENKO, *Pervobytnoe obshchestvo*, 3rd ed. (Kiev, 1953).

A.A. FORMOZOV, *Kamennyi vek i eneolit Prikubanya* (Moscow, 1965); *Peshchernaya stoyanka Starosellye i ee mesto v paleolite*, MIA 71 (1958).

J.E. FORSSANDER, *Der ostskandinavische Norden während der ältesten Metallzeit Europas* (Lund, 1936); *Die schwedische Bootaxtkultur und ihre kontinental-europäischen Voraussetzungen* (Lund, 1933).

E.M. FOSS, *Drevneyshaya istoria Severa Evropeyskoy chasti SSSR*, MIA 29 (1952).

M.M. GERASIMOV, *Ludi kamennogo veka* (Moscow, 1964).

M. GIMBUTAS, *Bronze Age Cultures in Central and Eastern Europe* (The Hague, 1965); *Prehistory of Eastern Europe*. Part I, *Mesolithic, Neolithic and Copper Age Cultures in Russia and the Baltic Area* (Cambridge, Mass., 1956); articles in PPS XIX for 1953; XXII for 1956; XXIV for 1958.

E.I. GORIUNOVA, *Etnicheskaya Istoria Volgo-Okskogo mezhdurechia*, MIA 94 (1961).

Ya.Ya. Graudonis, *Latviya v Epokhu Pozdney Bronzy in Rannego Zheleza*. (Riga, 1967).

M.P. GRIAZNOV, *Istoria drevnikh plemen Verkhney Obi po razkopkam bliz s. Bolshaya Rechka*, MIA 48 (1956).

IA.I. GUMMEL, *Arkheologicheskie ocherki* (Baku, 1940).

N.N. GURINA, *Drevnyaya istoria Severo-Zapada evropeyskoy chasti S.S.S.R.*, MIA 87 (1961); *Oleneostrovskii mogilnik*, MIA 47 (1956); *Iz istorii drevnikh plemen zapadnykh oblastei S.S.S.R.*, MIA 144 (1967).

F. HANČAR, *Urgeschichte Kaukasiens* (Wien-Leipzig, 1937); *Das Pferd in prähistorischer und früher historischer Zeit* (Wien-München, 1956). Articles in: ESA VII–1932; IX–1934; *Quartär* IV–1942, *Mitteilungen d. Anthropol. Ges. Wien*, LXXIII–LXXVI–1947.

K. HADACZEK, *Złote skarby michałkowskie* (Kraków, 1904).

A. HÄUSLER, Articles in: *Wissenschaftliche Zft d. Martin-Luther Universität, Halle*, VIII–1959, IX–1960, XI–1962, XV–1966; *Jahresschrift f. mitteldeutsche Vorgeschichte*, 47–1963; 48–1964; 50–1966.

R. INDREKO, R., *Mesolithische und frühneolithische Kulturen in Osteuropa und Westsibirien* (Stockholm, 1964).

A.IA. JAANITS, *Poselenya epokhi neolita i rannego metalla v priustie r. Emaiygi* (Tallin, 1959).

S.V. KISELEV, *Drevnyaya Istoria Sibiri* (Moscow, 1951).

V.G. KOTOVICH, *Kamennyi vek Dagestana* (Makhachkala, 1964).

D.A. KRAINOV, *Pamyatniki Fatyanovskoy kultury*, SVOD B-1–19, 1963; B-1–20 (1964); *Peshchernaya stoyanka Tash-Air I*, MIA 91 (1960).

O.A. KRIVTSOVA-GRAKOVA, *Stepnoe Povolzhe i Prichernomorie v epokhu pozdney bronzy*, MIA 46 (1955).

L.IA KRIZHEVSKAYA, *Neolit Iuzhnogo Urala*, MIA 141 (1968).

A.P. KRUGLOV and G.V. PODGAETSKII, *Rodovoe obshchestvo stepey Vostochnoy Evropy* (Moscow-Leningrad, 1935), Izvestia GAIMK. 119.

E.I. KRUPNOV, *Drevnyaya istoria Severnogo Kavkaza* (Moscow, 1960).

B.A. KUFTIN, *Arkheologicheskie Raskopi v Trialeti I* (Tbilisi, 1941) [with a summary in English]; *O dreveyshikh kornyakh gruzinskoy kultury na Kavkaze* (Tbilisi, 1944); *Urartskii 'Kolumbarii' u podoshvi Ararata i Kuro-Araksskii eneolit* (Tbilisi, 1943). See also its translation provided with commentaries, by R.D. Barnett, 'The Urartian Cemetery at Igdyr', *Anatolian Studies* XIII (1963), pp. 153–98.

IU.V. KUKHARENKO, *Pervobytnye pamyatniki Polesya*, SVOD b-1–18 (1962).

E.E. KUZMINA, *Metallicheskie izdelia eneolita i bronzovogo veka v Sredney Azii*, SVOD B-4–9 (1966).

O.F. LAHODOVSKA, O.G. SHAPOSHNIKOVA and M.L. MAKAREVYCH, *Mikhailivske poselennya* (Kiev, 1962).

B.A. LATYNIN, 'Molotochkovidnye bulavki, ikh kulturnaya atributsiya i datirovka' (Leningrad, 1967), ASE 9, 95 pages.

A.M. LESKOV, *Gornyi Krym v pervom tysyacheleti do nashey ery* (Kiev, 1965).

P.D. LIBEROV, *Plemena srednego Dona v epokhu bronzy* (Moscow, 1964).

J. MACHNIK, *Studia nad kultur ceramiki sznurowej w Małopolsce* (Wrocław-Warszawa-Kraków, 1966).

V.I. MARKOVIN, *Kultura plemen Severnogo Kavkaza v epokhu bronzy*, MIA 93, 1960; *Dagestan i Gornyaya Chechnyaya v Drevnosti* MIA 122 (1969).

A.A. MARTIROSYAN, *Armeniya v epokhu bronzy i rannego zheleza* (Erevan, 1964).

V.M. MASSON, *Srednyaya Aziya i drevnii Vostok* (Moscow-Leningrad, 1964).

O.N. MELNIKOVSKAYA, *Plemena Iuzhnoy Belorussii v Rannem Zheleznom Veke* (Moscow, 1967).

E.H. MINNS, *Scythians and Greeks* (Cambridge, 1913); 'The Art of Northern Nomads', *Proceedings of the British Academy*, vol. XXVIII (1942).

A.L. Mongait, *Archaeology in the U.S.S.R.*, translated by V.M. Thompson (Penguin Books, 1961).

H. Moora, *Die Vorzeit Estlands* (Tartu, 1932).

R.M. Munchaev, *Drevneyshaya kultura Severo-Vostochnogo Kavkaza*, MIA 100 (1961).

J. Ozols, *Ursprung und Herkunft der zentralrussischen Fatjanovo Kultur* (Berlin, 1962). Berliner Beiträge zur Vor- und Frühgeschichte 4.

G.A. Pankrushev, *Plemena Karelii v epokhu neolita i rannego metalla* (Moscow-Leningrad, 1964).

T.S. Passek, *Periodizatsiya tripolskikh poselenii*, MIA 30 (1949); *Rannezemledelcheskie (tripolske) plemena Podnestrovya*, MIA 84 (1961).

T.S. Passek and E.K. Chernysh, 'Pamyatniki kultury lineyno-lentochnoy keramiki na territorii S.S.S.R.', SVOD b–1–11 (1963).

J. Pasternak, *Arkheologiya Ukrainy* [Archaeology of the Ukraine, in Ukrainian, with a summary in English] (Toronto, 1961).

S. Piggott, *Ancient Europe from the Beginnings of Agriculture to Classical Antiquity* (Edinburgh, 1965).

B.B. Piotrovskii, *Vanskoe Tsarstvo (Urartu)* (Moscow, 1959); *Iskusstvo Urartu, VIII–VI v. v. do N.E.* (Leningrad, 1962).

T.B. Popova, *Dolmeny Stanitsy Novosvobodnoy* (Moscow, 1963); *Plemena katakombnoy kultury* (Moscow, 1955), Trudy GIM 24.

V.M. Raushenbakh, *Srednee Zauralie v epokhu neolita i bronzy* (Moscow, 1956), Trudy GIM 29.

A.N. Rogachev, *Aleksandrovskoe poselenie drevne kamennogo veka u sela Kostenki na Donu*, MIA 45 (1955).

Iu.A. Sabbataev, *Rirunki na skalakh.* (Petrozavodsk, 1967).

I.H. Shovkoplyas, *Arkheologichni doslidzhennya na Ukraini*, 1917–1957 (Kiev, 1957).

A.P. Smirnov, *Ocherki Drevney i srednevekovoy istorii narodov Srednego Povolzha*, MIA 28 (1952); *Zheleznyi vek Chuvashskogo Povolzhya*, MIA 95 (1961).

K.F. Smirnov, *Savromaty. Rannaya istoriya i kultura Sarmatov* (Moscow, 1964).

V.S. Sorokin, *Mogilnik bronzovoy epokhi Tasty-Butak I v Zapadnom Kazakhstane*, MIA 120 (1962); [Editor], *Andronovskaya kultura*, SVOD B–3–2 (1966).

E. Sturms, *Die älteste Bronzezeit im Ostbalticum* (Berlin-Leipzig, 1938).

I.K. Sveshnikov, *Megalitychni pokhovanya na Zakhidnom Podilli* (Lviv, 1957); *Pamyatniki plemen bronzovogo veka Prikarpatya i Zapadnoy Podolii* (Moscow, 1958); *Pidsumki doslidzhennya kultur bronzovoi doby Prikarpattya i Zakhidnoho Podilla* (Lviv 1958).

A.M. Tallgren, *La Pontide préscythique après l'introduction des meteaux* (Helsinki, 1926), ESA II; many articles and larger contributions in the volumes of ESA and in other periodicals.

D.Ia. Telegin, *Dnipro-donetska Kultura* (Kiev, 1968).

A.I. Terenozhkin, *Predskifskii period na Dneprovskom Pravoberezhye* (Kiev, 1961).

B.G. Tikhonov and Iu.S. Grishin, *Ocherki po istorii proizvodstva v Priurale i Iuzhnoy Sibiri v epokhu bronzy i rannego zheleza*, MIA 90 (1960).

S.P. Tolstov, *Po drevnim deltam Oksa i Yaksarta* (Moscow, 1962).

P.N. Tretyakov, *Vostochnoslavyanske plemena*. 2nd ed. (Moscow, 1953); *Finno-Ugry, Balty i Slavyane na Dnepre i Volge* (Moscow-Leningrad, 1966).

V.I. Tsalkin, *Drevnyee Zhivotovodstvo, Plemen Vostochnoy Evropy i Sredney Azii*, MIA 135 (1966).

R. Vulpe, *Izvoare. Săpăturile din 1936–1948* (Bucureşti, 1957).

W. Watson, *China before the Han Dynasty* (London, 1961), Ancient Peoples and Places.

A.A. Yessen, *Grecheskaya kolonizaciya Severnogo Prichernomorya* (Leningrad, 1947).

A.V. Zbrueva, *Istoria naseleniya Prikamya v Ananinskuiu epokhu*, MIA 30 (1952).

E.F. Zeuner, *Dating the Past*. 4th ed. (London, 1958); *The Pleistocene Period; its Climate, Chronology and Faunal Succession* (London, 1959).

G.P. Zinevich, *Ocherki Paleoantropologii Ukrainy* (Kiev, 1967).

COLLECTIVE WORKS

Absolutnaya geokhronologiya chetvertichnogo perioda (Moscow-Leningrad, 1963).
Arkheologicheskie Otkritiya 1965 goda (Moscow, 1966).
Arkheologicheskie Otkritiya 1966 goda (Moscow, 1967).
Arkheologicheskie Raboty Akademii na Novostroykakh, vol. II (Moscow-Leningrad, 1935).
Arkheologicheskie Razkopki na Donu (Rostov-on-the-Don, 1962).
Arkheologiya i Estestvennye nauki (Moscow, 1965).
Contributions to the Physical Anthropology of the Soviet Union. Russian Translations
Series I. Peabody Museum (Cambridge Mass., 1960).
L'Europe à la fin de l'âge de la pierrre (Praha, 1961).
Issledovaniya po Arkheologii S.S.S.R. (Leningrad, 1961).
Istoriya i Arkheologiya Drevnego Kryma (Kiev, 1957).
Istoriya S.S.S.R., vol. I (Moscow, 1966). Editors S.A. Pletneva and B.A. Rybakov.
*Materialy i Issledovaniya po Arkheologii Iugo-Zapada S.S.S.R. i Rumynskoy Narodnoy
Respubliki* (Kishinev, 1960).
Materialy i Issledovaniya po Arkheologii S.S.S.R. Volumes:

1, 1940, 'on the Neolithic and Bronze Age of the Urals and the country on the Kama', N. Prokoshev, D. Eding, K. Salnikov, G. Podgaetskii.

2, 1941, 'on the Palaeolithic and Neolithic sites', P.P. Efimenko, N.A. Beregovaya, P.I. Boriskovskii.

3, 1941, 'on the North Caucasus', A.K. Kruglov, B.B. Piotrovskii, G.V. Podgaetskii, A.A. Yessen, E.Iu. Krichevskii, B.E. Degen.

13, 1950, 'on the Mesolithic and Neolithic of the region on the Upper Volga', O.N. Bahder, P.N. Tretiakov, L.Ia. Krizhevskaya.

20, 1951, 'on the Neolithic and Bronze Age of North Russia', A.Ia. Briusov, N.N. Gurina.

21, 1951, 'on the Urals and the country east of the Urals', P.A. Dmitriev, K.V. Salnikov, O.A. Krivtsova-Grakova, E.M. Bers, O.N. Bahder.

22, 1951, 'on site Borovoe Ozero I', O.N. Bahder.

23, 1951, 'on the Bronze Age of the North Caucasus', E.I. Krupnov, A.A. Yessen.

24, 1952, 'on West Siberia', M.N. Komarova, K.V. Salnikov.

27, 1952, 'Material to the archaeological map of the basin of the Kama', I.A. Talitskaya.

39, 1953, 'on the Upper Palaeolithic and Neolithic, including site Borshevo II', P.I. Boriskovskii, P.P. Efimenko, A.N. Rogachev, M.Z. Panichkina, E.A. Vekilova. Its French translation: *Paléolithique et Néolithique de l'U.R.S.S.* (Paris, 1957).

58, 1957, 'on the Urals and West Siberia', A.P. Smirnov, V.I. Moshinskaya.

59, 1957, 'on the Palaeolithic and Neolithic of the U.S.S.R.', A.N. Rogachev, G.I. Lazurkov, P.I. Boriskovskii, P.P. Efimenko, E.A. Velikova.

60, 1959, 'on the country on the Lower Volga', I.V. Sinitsyn, V.P. Shilov, V.V. Ginzburg.

61, 1958, 'on the country on the Middle Volga', A.Kh. Khalikov, N.Ia. Merpert, A.E. Alikhova, N.V. Trubnikova.

68, 1958, 'on the North Caucasus', A.P. Kruglov, R.M. Muchaev, E.P. Krupnov.

78, 1960, 'on the country of the Lower Volga', I.V. Sinitsyn, K.F. Smirnov,
79, 1960, 'on the Palaeolithic and Neolithic of the U.S.S.R.', V.P. Ayubin. A.D. Kolbutov, O.N. Bahder, S.I. Rudenko.

96, 1961, 'on the pre-Scythian period in Bessarabia', A.I. Meliukova.

97, 1961, 'on the Abashevo culture in the country on the Middle Volga', O.N. Evtiukhova, A.P. Smirnov, P.P. Efimenko, P.N. Tretiakov, N.Ia. Merpert, A.Kh. Khalikov.

102, 1962, 'Neolithic and Aeneolithic of West Podolia, the Crimea and the Caucasus', E.K. Chernysh, N.V. Ryndina, A.A. Formozov.

110, 1963, 'on the Middle Volga', Gorki, P.N. Tretiakov, N.N. Yablokova,

L.Ia. Krizhevskaya, I.V. Gavrilova, I.K. Tsvetkova, N.N. Gurina, A.L. Nikitin, A.Kh. Khalikov, E.A. Khalikova.

111, 1962, 'on the Srubnaya culture in the Chuvash country', N.Ia. Merpert.

115, 1962, 'on pre-scythian (and Scythian) barrow-graves on the lower Dnieper', O.A. Krivtsova-Grakova.

126, 1966, 'on the Mesolithic of the U.S.S.R. and Central Europe', by 20 authors.

130, 1965, 'Novoe v Sovetskoy arkheologii', by over 60 authors.

131, 1965, 'on the Palaeolithic and Neolithic of the U.S.S.R.', V.P. Lubin, I.I. Korobkov, L.M. Tarasov, N.N. Gurina, I.V. Gavrilova, P.N. Tretiakov, V.P. Levenok.

135, 1967, on 'the origin and development of agriculture', by several authors.

Narysy Starodavnoi Istorii Ukrainskoy RSR (Kiev, 1957).

Ocherki Istorii S.S.S.R. Pervobytno-obshchynnyi stroy i drevneyshie gosudarstvana territorii SSSR (Moscow, 1962).

Pamyatniki Epokhi Bronzy Iuga Evropeyskoy Chasti S.S.S.R. (Kiev, 1967).

Les Rapoorts et Informations des Archéologues de l'URSS (Moscow, 1966). VIe Congres International des Sciences Prehistoriques et Protohistoriques.

Relief and Stratigraphy of the Quaternary Deposits in the North-Western Part of the Russian Plain (Moscow, 1961). Publication for the Sixth Congress of Inqua 1961.

Sbornik po Arkheologii Vologodskoy Oblasti (Vologda, 1961).

Trypilska Kultura, vol. 1 (Kiev, 1940).

Tsentralnaya Aziya v Epokhu Kamnha i Bronzy (Moscow-Leningrad, 1966).

Voprosy Etnicheskoy Istorii Estonskogo Naroda (Tallin, 1956).

Voprosy Skifo-Sarmatskoy Arkheologii (Moscow, 1954).

Vozniknovenie i Razvitie Zemledeliya (Moscow, 1967).

PERIODICALS

Arkheologicheskii Sbornik (Leningrad), (Ermitage).

Arkheologichni Pamyatky URSR (Kiev), [in Ukrainian].

Arkheologiya (Kiev), [in Ukrainian].

Eurasia Septentrionalis Antiqua (Helsinki).

Kratkie Soobshcheniya Instituta Arkheologii (Kiev).

Kratkie Soobshcheniya Instituta Materialnoy Kultury (Moscow-Leningrad). As from issue no. 81: *Kratkie Soobshcheniya Instituta Arkheologii* (Moscow).

Materialy z Arkheologii Pivnichnogo Prichenomorya (Odessa), [in Ukrainian].

Materialy i Doslidzhennya z Arkheologii Prykarpattya i Volyni (Kiev), [in Ukrainian].

Sovetskaya Arkheologiya (Moscow).

Zapiski Odesskogo Arkheologicheskogo Obshchestva (Odessa).

THE FOLLOWING ARE THE CHIEF ABBREVIATIONS USED IN THIS VOLUME:

AK	—Arkheologiya (Kiev), [in Ukrainian].
AO	—Arkheologicheskiye Otkritiya (Moscow).
AP	—Arkheologichni Pamyatky U.S.S.R. (Kiev), [in Ukrainian].
ASE	—Arkheologicheskii Sbornik Gos. Ermitazha (Leningrad).
ESA	—Eurasia Septentrionalis Antiqua (Helsinki).
IA	—Issledovaniya po Arkheologii SSSR (Leningrad, 1961).
KSAMO	—Kratkie Soobshcheniya Arkheologicheskogo Muzeya (Odessa).
KSIAK	—Kratkie Soobshcheniya Istituta Arkheologii (Kiev).
KSIAM	—Kratkie Soobshcheniya Instituta Arkheologii (Moscow).
KSIIMK	—Kratkie Soobshcheniya Instituta Materialnoy Kultury (Moscow).
MDAPV	—Materialy i Doslizhdeniya z Arkheologii Prykarpattya i Volyni (Kiev), [in Ukrainian].
MIA	—Materialy i Issledovaniya po Arkheologii S.S.S.R. (Moscow-Leningrad).

PEB —Pamyatniki Epokhi Bronzy Iuga Evropeyskoy Chasti SSSR (Kiev, 1967).

PPS —Proceedings of the Prehistoric Society (Cambridge).

Rapports et
Informations —Le Rapports et Informations des Archeologues de l'URSS, VI Congrès International des Sciences Préhistoriques et Protohistoriques (Moscow, 1962).

SA —Sovetskaya Arkheologiya (Moscow).

SV —Sbornik po Arkheologii Vologodskoy Oblasti (Vologda, 1961).

SVOD —Svod Arkheologicheskikh Istochnikov. Arkheologiya SSSR (Moscow-Leningrad).

Symposium—L'Europe à la fin de l'age de la pierre (Praha, 1961).

TIIAEK —Trudy Instituta Istorii, Arkheologii i Etnografii Akademii Nauk Kazakhstanskoy SSR, Alma-Ata.

Trudy GIM —Trudy Gosud. Istoricheskogo Muzeya (Moscow).

Indexes

AUTHORS CITED IN THE TEXT

ABIBULAEV O.A., 77, 78, 145
Alikova A.E., 146, 181, 315
Antoniewicz J., 243
Arne T.J., 391
Artamonov M.I., 225, 243
Artemenko I.I., 87, 146, 192, 193, 242, 243

BAHDER O.N., 28, 34, 54, 105, 201, 202, 243, 251, 252, 314, 315, 390, 412
Balaguri E.A., 391
Barnet R.D., 404
Belov G.D., 391
Berciu D., 145
Beregovaya N.A., 16
Berezanska S.S., 189, 242, 391
Bernjakovič K., 242
Bernshtam A.N., 316
Bibikov S.N., 69
Blegen C.W., 315
Boltenko M.F., 315
Bolton J.D.P., 310, 316
Bóna I., 242
Boriskovskii P.I., 23, 54, 405
Borvin N.N., 316
Bouzek J., 315
Bratchenko S.N., 315
Briusov A.Ia., 50, 54, 93, 145, 146, 206, 242, 243, 391, 416
Budko V.D., 18, 42, 54
Bukowski Z., 391
Burov G.M., 28, 418

CHERNETSOV V.N., 146, 242, 314, 422
Chernikov S.S., 262, 286, 298, 301, 303, 315, 316, 404
Chernykh E.N., 124, 145, 278, 279, 314, 315, 391, 411
Chernysh A.P., 12, 20, 22–5, 54
Chernysh E.K., 62, 63, 75, 413
Chiguryaeva A.A., 54
Childe V.G., 123, 146, 227, 242, 243, 270, 285, 315
Chlenova N.K., 308, 316, 404
Chmielewska M., 54
Chubinishvili T., 145
Coon E.S., 54
Cowen J.D., 391

DANOFF Ch.M., 404
Danylenko V.M., 81, 145
Dobrovolskii A.V., 177, 348
Dubynin A.F., 242
Dumitrescu V., 146, 315
Dyson R.H., 315
Dzhaparidze O.M., 146, 243
Dzhavakhishvili A.I., 110, 145

EFIMENKO P.O., 9, 11, 23, 31, 316, 405
Elnitskii L.E., 404
Esipenko A.P., 145
Evtiukhova O.N., 292, 316

FLORESCU A.C., 242, 391
Formozov A.A., 10, 12, 28, 39, 79, 119–21, 130, 146, 315
Foss M.E., 46, 47, 146, 214, 243, 327, 333, 390, 419

GADZYATSKAYA O.S., 94, 145, 146
Gallus S., 392
Gardawski A., 145, 242
Gavrilova I.V., 145
Ghirshman R., 404
Gimbutas M., 145, 146, 243, 315, 390, 391
Glonti L.I., 110
Gordon D.H., 315
Goriunova E.I., 325
Gorodtsov V., 390
Griaznov M.P., 304, 315, 316, 398
Grigorieva G.V., 390
Gromov V.I., 11, 54
Gurina N.N., 54, 91, 92, 145, 146, 216, 333, 390, 420, 421
Guslitzer B.I., 16

HADACZEK K., 391
Hančar F., 146, 365, 391
Häusler A., 316
Horedt K., 315
Horvath T., 392

ILINSKAYA V.A., 242, 392
Indreko R., 50, 90, 145

JAANITS L., 28, 145, 146, 243, 417

Jahn M., 392
Jettmar K., 315, 390

KACHALOVA N.K., 255, 315
Kakhovskii N.F., 203, 316
Kalgren B., 315
Kalinin N.F., 247, 314, 390
Kanivets M.I., 391
Kanivets V.I., 16, 17
Kantor J., 315
Khalikov A.Kh., 43, 44, 106, 146, 247, 290,
    314, 316, 390, 423, 426
Khvalina N.Ia., 54
Khvalyuk P.I., 65
Kilian L., 242
Kiparisova N.P., 390
Kiselev S.V., 302, 306, 316
Klein L.S., 145
Knipovich T.N., 392
Kolosov Iu.G., 145
Komarova M.N., 264, 315
Kosarev M.F., 315, 316
Kovpanenko G.T., 392
Kowalczyk J., 242
Kozhin P.M., 192, 243
Kozłowski L., 172, 356
Kraynov D.A., 54, 94, 145, 242, 243
Kris C.I., 391
Krivtsova-Grakova O.A., 197, 243, 258,
    259, 315, 319, 391
Krizhevskaya L.Ia., 106, 145, 146, 242, 314
Kruglov A.P., 235, 338, 391
Krupnov E.I., 146, 243, 391, 404
Krushelnytska L.I., 391
Kuftin V.A., 243, 391, 404
Kukharenko Iu.V., 146
Kuzmina E.E., 315
Kyzlasov L.R., 304, 316

LAHODOVSKA O.F., 146, 345, 415
Leskov A.M., 315, 391
Levenok V.P., 28, 33, 54, 97, 146
Levytskii I., 161
Lisitsyna G.N., 54, 146
Lyapushkin I.I., 376

MAKARENKO N., 146
Makarevych M.L., 145, 146, 415
Makhno E., 391
Maksimova A.K., 316
Mandeshtam A.M., 315
Margulian A.Kh., 304
Markevych V.I., 65
Markovin V.I., 233, 243, 424, 425
Martirosyan A.A., 391
Masson V.M., 101, 146
Matiushin G.I., 32, 54, 146
Megaw J.V.S., 390
Melentiev A.N., 392

Melikishvili G.A., 404
Meliukova A.I., 391
Mellaart J., 36
Merpert N.Ia., 132, 146, 256, 314, 316
Minns E.H., 243, 315, 391
Mnatsakhanian O., 391
Mongait L., 315
Moora H., 28, 145, 195, 210, 242, 243
Munchaev R.M., 146

NANDRIS J., 145
Nerman B., 330, 390, 391

OHULCHANSKII O.Ia., 168
Okladnikov A.P., 17
Orazbaev A.M., 180
Oshibkina S.N., 146, 324
Ossowski G., 128
Ovsyannikov O.V., 390
Özgüç T., 315

PANKRUSHEV G.A., 146
Parducz M., 392
Passek T.S., 67, 73, 75, 145, 171, 181, 182,
    242, 243
Peshchanov V.F., 222
Petkov N., 242
Petrescu-Dimboviţa M., 145, 391
Pittioni R., 242
Podgaetskii G.V., 235, 338
Podkowińska Z., 392
Pogrebova M.N., 391
Popova T.B., 222, 226, 228, 243, 391
Prox A., 242

RAUSHENBAKH V.M., 54, 103, 315
Rosenfeldt I.G., 146
Rostovtzeff M., 404
Rudenko S.I., 316
Rudynskii M., 54, 226
Rybakov V.A., 175
Rykov P., 390

SALMO H., 390
Salnikov K.V., 316
Schaeffer C.F.A., 243, 315, 391
Schild R., 54
Sergeev G.P., 145
Shackleton M.R., 4
Shaposhnikova O.G., 146, 222, 415
Sharafutdinova E.S., 315, 390
Shchepinski A.A., 391, 427
Shilov V.P., 390
Shmaglii M.M., 242
Shmidt A.V., 314
Siedov V.V., 243
Sinitsyn I.V., 390
Smirnov A.P., 316, 331, 390
Smirnov K.F., 146, 275, 315, 391

Smirnova G.I., 391
Spitsyn I.V., 146
Sprockhoff E., 390
Stenberger M., 146, 243, 390
Stepanov P.D., 243
Stolyar A.D., 38, 54
Stone J.F., 315
Šturms E., 242, 315
Sulimirski T., 60, 158, 275, 315, 351, 356, 281, 391, 404
Sveshnikov I.K., 188, 194, 242, 391
Szlankówna A., 381, 392

TALLGREN A.M., 146, 243, 270, 274, 275, 331, 390, 391
Tchlenova—see Chlenova
Tekhov B.M., 360
Telegin D.Ia., 28, 37, 39, 54, 83, 89, 111, 114, 115, 145, 146, 385, 386, 392
Ter-Avestiian S., 404
Terenozhkin A.I., 380, 391, 392, 428
Thomas L.C., 315
Thompson M.W., 315
Tikhonov B.G., 280, 282–4, 315, 333, 390, 414

Tolstov S.P., 146, 315
Toporov V.N., 243
Trapsh M.M., 404
Tretiakok P.N., 95, 145, 241, 243, 293, 316, 323
Trubachev O.N., 243
Tsvetkova I.K., 146, 243, 332
Tymofeev E.M., 16, 316
Tyuremov. SN., 54

VULPE A., 242

WATSON W., 316
Wiślański T., 242

YERUSALIMSKAYA A.A., 243, 391, 404
Yessen A.A., 145, 146, 314, 315, 391, 392

ZAMYATNIN S.N., 54, 217, 219
Zbrueva A.V., 390
Zeuner F.E., 145
Zolotova S.V., 299, 316
Żurek J., 242

ABASHEVO, 319
Adzhiask, 268
Akali, 140, 153, 211, 218
Akbuta, 106
Akhshtyrskaya cave, 8
Akhtala, 364
Akkermen, 129
Aksiutyntsi, 382
Alaca-Hüyük, 153, 271
Alekanovo, 319, 340
Aleksandriya, 114
Aleksandrovka—see Oleksandrivka
Aleksandrovskaya (Kostienki IV) 25
Alekseevskaya Zasukha, 80, 85
Alekseevskoe, 263, 264, 296
Algaski 291
Alishar 237, 295
Amiranis Gora, 79, 85, 145
Amvrosievka, 8, 19
Annin, 319
Anosovka, 54
Antrea, 49
Arzamas, 85, 96
Ashkalka, 376
At-Bash, 80

BABYA GUBA, 319, 330
Babychi, 351
Baia-Hamangia, 107, 131
Baidary valley, 373
Balakhna, 153, 209, 246
Balan-Bash, 169, 276, 295
Balanovo, 153, 169, 204
Balka Bashmatka, 345
Bashkiv Ostriv, 60
Belev, 85
Bele Ozero (lake), 138
Belogrudovka—see Bilohrudivka
Belynets, 194
Bełz, 275
Berazy, 304
Berdychev, 151
Berdysh, 18
Beregovaya, 39, 153, 169, 253, 387
Beregovskoe, 296
Berekey, 362, 364
Berezhnovka, 131
Berislav, 319, 350
Bernovo-Luka, 70
Beshtasheni, 371, 399
Biały Potok, 165
Bilcze Złote, 153, 172, 173, 188
Bilohrudivka, 319
Biolozerka, 342, 343
Bireti, 17
Bobrikino, 263
Bolgar, 367

Bolgrad, 85
Bondarykha, 85, 86, 319, 347, 385
Bor, 250
Boran, 85, 96, 137, 217, 319, 324, 333, 335
Borisovka, 68
Borodino, 159, 274, 319, 341
Borovoe Ozero, 104, 105, 288, 319
Borshevo, 29, 39, 40, 50
Briansk, 7, 194
Bui, 319
Burkryn, 349
Buranovskaya cave, 45
Butenki, 380, 387
Bybolush, 349
Byzovaya, 17

CHAGALLY, 146
Chapli, 114
Chatal-Hüyük, 36
Chebarkul, 85, 107, 130
Cheboksary, 289
Cheliabinsk, 264, 277, 280, 284, 311
Cheremoshnik, 7
Ches-Tyi-Iag, 153, 169, 253, 318, 319, 325, 329
Chokh, 29, 35
Chornii-Lis, 379
Chornohorivka (Chernogorovka), 387
Churachiki, 200, 203
Chusovaya river sites, 16, 40, 44, 104
Chyngul, 222
Ćmielów, 173
Corbuna, 71, 72, 85, 267
Cucuteni, 85

DEBOLOVSKOE, 26
Desna river sites, 40, 50
Dilizhan, 364
Djebel cave, 45, 85, 99, 130
Dolgoe, 47, 85, 96, 97
Dolinskoe, 121, 226, 232
Don river sites, 50
Dubno, 164, 353
Dubosishche, 167
Durna Skela, 135
Dvani, 371

ELIN BOR, 29, 44, 45, 153, 205
Elisavetovskoe, 319, 337, 339
Elista (Stepnoe), 153, 223, 224, 230
Esbo, 218
Evminka, 186

FATMA KOBA, 36
Fatyanovo, 153
Fedorovskaya, 47, 319, 324, 327

Floreşti, 60, 61, 82, 85
Folteşti, 153, 186

GAGARINO, 19, 32
Galashki-Pervomaiskoe, 236
Galich, 319, 323, 325, 326, 331
Gari, 250
Gîrbovaţ, 176
Girevaya Mogila, 388
Gomel, 41, 167, 190, 273
Gomi, 319, 370
Gorbunovo, 45, 49, 85, 91, 153, 220, 269, 270, 281, 319, 320
Gorodsk, 153
Grechaniki, 178
Gremayachee, 26, 29, 42, 85, 91
Grensk, 26, 27, 29, 41, 42, 92
Grishchintsy, 178
Gródek, Nadbużny, 153, 173, 185
Gubskii Naves, 35
Gvardzilas-Klde, 29, 34

HĂBĂŞTI, 72, 85, 267
Hamangia, 85
Hlynyshche, 60, 64, 65
Holercani, 319, 353
Holihrady, 319
Horodiştea, 153, 186
Horodnica, 85, 109, 267
Horodyszcze, 160
Horozheno, 183
Hrebeny, 381

IDRISOVSKAYA CAVE, 45
Ihren, 80, 134
Illinka, 319, 350
Ilmurzino, 32
Ilskaya, 10, 12
Ivanovo, 209
Izium, 29, 39, 86, 89, 112, 342

JACKOWICA (YATSKOVITSA), 153, 178
Janisławice, 50
Jazłowiec, 382

KALENSKE (MOSTVA), 85, 86, 108, 112
Kalinovka, 131, 254, 280
Kalmatskii Brod, 153, 169, 252
Kamiana Mohyla, 26, 29, 37, 80
Kamyanka aelozerska (Dniprovska), 319, 342
Kamyshevakha, 387
Kanev, 153, 167, 276
Käpää, 91
Kapova cave, 21
Karabalykty, 263

Karabczyjów, 349
Karachanovo, 32
Karavaikha, 47, 138, 213
Kargopol, 49, 333
Karmir-Blur, 399
Kars, 402
Kartashinka, 322
Kasperowce, 167, 186
Kaury, 29, 37, 113, 114
Kazan, 44, 217, 288, 333
Kazanska, 39
Kayakent, 262
Khalepie, 176
Kherson, 358
Khmilna, 349
Khodovichi-Moshka, 112, 192
Khodzhaly, 319, 370, 398
Khorochoi, 319, 362
Kriashchevka, 248
Khutor Khailovshchina, 337
Khutor Lyapichev, 319, 337, 338
Kiev-Kirillovskaya, 19
Kievka, 319, 339
Kiik-Koba, 8–12
Kinema, 47, 324
Kslovodsk, 319, 360, 367
Kittilä, 220
Kizlevyi Ostriv, 29, 37
Klein Zastrov, 365
Klynivka, 226
Koban (Verkhnaya), 273, 319
Kobiakovo, 257, 274, 319, 337, 339
Koblevo, 313, 350, 351, 358
Kochishche, 92
Kolkhida, 401
Kolodnoe, 176
Kolomishchyna, 74, 153, 154, 171, 176
Koltubanka, 254
Komarniki, 319, 354
Komarów, 153, 159–61, 174, 339
Kostianets, 188
Kostienki, 17, 21, 25, 54
Kostroma, 138, 208, 214
Koszyłowce, 167, 173
Krasnostavka, 68
Krivoluchie, 131, 200, 267
Krivorozhe, 388
Kruchowicze, 287, 319
Kruglyk, 8, 11
Krupol, 153, 229
Krzemienna, 319, 355
Kubenino, 47, 138, 217, 319
Kuibyshev, 8
Kuibyshev-Postnikov Ovrag, 29, 40
Kukrek, 29, 36
Kullamägi, 140, 211
Kültepe, 275
Kunda, 29, 47–50

Kurgan, 47
Kvatskhelebi, 79, 85, 109
Kyul-Tepe, 85

LCHASHEN, 364, 369
Lenkivtsi, 68
Leontinivka, 222
Levina Gora, 7
Levshino, 106
Lialovo, 85, 95, 416
Liventsovka, 274
Likhachevka, 387
Losiatyn, 178
Luka Vrublivetskaya, 8, 68–70
Lugovoe, 117
Lukianivka, 319, 344

MAHALA, 319, 353
Maiaki, 242
Maikop, 8, 85, 117, 118, 125, 237, 267, 361
Malye Budki, 385
Malyi Kizil, 295
Malyi Ostrovok, 167, 198
Makushinskoe, 252
Malta (Siberia), 17
Manuaki (Tashburun), 399
Marianówka, 351
Marievka, 114
Mariupol, 113–115, 267
Markina Gora (Kostienki XIV), 21, 54
Maloe Okulovo, 47, 319, 339
Medvezha cave, 17
Meliopol, 160
Meshoko, 117, 118
Mezin, 7, 16, 19, 32
Miass, 47
Michałków, 355, 384
Mikhailovka (Dnepropetrovsk), 268
Mingechaur, 400
Modlona, 47, 153, 212–14, 217, 218, 220, 324
Mokshan, 260, 319
Moldova, 12, 19, 20, 22–5, 54
Moshka (Khodovichi), 192–4
Moshna, 161
Murom, 331
Murak Koba, 29, 36
Mykhailivka (Mikhailovka), 134–6, 153, 154, 179, 267, 268, 271, 415
Mykilska Slobidka, 85, 86, 88, 108, 109, 112
Mykolske (Nikolskoe), 114, 115, 133, 267
Mytishchi, 197, 199, 208

NALCHIK, 121, 131, 153, 224, 267, 273, 358, 361
Narodychi-Pishchane, 161, 188
Narva, 29, 49, 85, 218

Nenasytets, 8, 11
Nesterovskaya Stanitsa, 367
Nezvysko, 60–4, 68, 74, 75, 413
Nimrud, 397, 399
Niniveh, 401
Nizhnee Adishchevo, 29, 44, 45, 105
Nizhnee Veretye, 47
Nizhne-Shilovskaya, 122
Nosachevo, 379
Novaya Kazanka, 133
Novgorod Siverskii, 16
Novi Arshi, 117
Novocherkassk, 387, 388
Novogrigorievka, 354
Novo-Oleksandrivka, 348
Novosvobodnaya-Tsarskaya, 118, 125, 201, 232, 237, 268
Nowosiołka Kostiukowa, 319, 354

OBSERVATORIA III, 85, 104–6, 245, 246
Odishi, 79, 85
Ogurinskaya, 44, 45
Olbia, 382
Oleksandrivka, 70, 71
Oleni Ostrov, 47, 139, 140, 145, 153, 216
Olskii Mys, 328
Omsk, 236
Orlivka, 153, 167, 168
Orenburg, 130
Orov-Navolok, 329
Osipovaya Balka, 373
Osokorivka, 26, 29, 37
Ostapie, 269
Ostrivets, 319, 352

PALKINO, 319, 320
Pamfilovo, 207
Pärnau-Pärnii, 47
Pechora river sites, 16, 17
Pechora (Vinnitsa), 68, 85, 153, 167, 186, 319, 345
Pekliuk (Bulgaria), 162
Penizhkova, 74
Penkino, 291, 319
Penza, 217, 367
Perm, 44, 104
Peshchernyi Log, 10, 11
Petreyny, 175
Piatigorsk, 121, 153, 232
Pilava, 112
Piros lake, 85, 92, 217
Pishchanyi Riv, 29, 42
Pleshcheevo, 96
Poczapy, 357
Podboritsa-Shcherbinskaya, 332
Podgortsa, 378
Podluzhie, 26
Pogon, 19

Pogostishche (Modlona), 47, 51, 85, 137
Pogrebennaya, 29, 34
Pogurdino, 29
Pokrovsk, 273
Polivaniv Yar, 68, 74, 85
Polotsk, 86
Poltavka, 153
Poludenka, 85, 103
Popudnia, 109, 176, 271
Pozdniakovo, 319
Prelipce, 269
Privolnoe, 260, 286
Pushkari, 16, 19, 32

RADZIMIN, 188
Razboinichyi, 319, 320
Rayki, 188
Rechista, 153, 190
Remontnoe, 224
Repin Khutor, 133, 135
Rezina, 29
Rogachev, 167
Rogalik, 29, 39
Romny, 382
Rusiłów, 193
Russo-Lugovskaya, 41, 44
Rutchi-Tig, 398
Rybinskoe lake, 138
Ryżanówka, 128

SABANCHEEVO, 288, 296, 297, 319
Sabatynivka, 71, 153, 176, 177, 319, 345, 377
Sakhtysh lake, 93, 94, 96, 153, 167, 169, 196, 198, 209, 324
Samchyntsi, 60, 66
Samtavro, 274, 319, 371
Samus, 300
Sandermokha, 139
Sandraki, 378
Sārnate, 91
Satani-Dar, 8, 9
Savran, 66
Seima, 248, 288, 289, 310, 319, 323
Seliger lake, 85, 92
Seltso, 93, 95
Semipalatinsk, 286, 302, 309, 310, 312
Sennaya, 382
Seredni Stog, 133, 153, 167
Šernai (Schernen), 272, 276
Shandasha, 264
Shan-Koba, 29, 35, 36, 80, 85
Shigir, 29, 45–7, 49, 85, 277
Shurskol, 7
Simferopol, 36, 373, 374, 379, 380, 387
Siuren, 16, 26, 29, 36
Siwki, 188
Skala, 118
Skatovka, 319, 335

Skniatino, 29, 42, 44
Smyachka, 29, 42
Sobachky, 114
Sobolevo, 29, 42, 44, 45
Sofiivka, 187, 188, 239, 276, 367
Solomenka, 232, 235
Solonceni, 68, 71
Soroki, 54, 145
Sosnovaya Maza, 319, 336, 347
Sosruko, 29, 35, 36
Sozh river sites, 112
Stanitsa Chernyshevskaya, 387
Stanok, 169
Starosele, 14
Staryi Kodak, 129
Stepnyak, 263, 298, 311, 313, 315, 317
Strelcha Skela, 133
Strelitsa, 153, 191, 193, 288
Stubło, 269
Studenok, 86, 385, 386
Subbotov, 381
Subbotovka, 379
Sukhaya Mechetka, 10, 12
Sukhodolskaya cave, 45
Sukhumi, 319, 371
Sukleia, 183
Surskii island, 82, 84, 85
Suskan, 258, 319
Svartarp, 334

TAMBOV, 339
Tamula, 153, 218
Tashburun, 399
Tasty-Butak, 263
Temir Gora, 363, 403
Tepe Hissar, 125, 270
Tepe Sialk, 99
Til, 360
Timonovka, 16, 19
Tiraspol, 181, 183
Tobol river sites, 273
Tolstik, 253
Tomashivka, 271
Tomitsa, 319, 330
Trialeti (Tsalki), 153, 236–8, 268, 274, 285, 361
Trifautskii Forest, 65
Tripolye, 85, 141, 153, 166, 177, 349
Troy II, 76, 123, 125, 268; VI, 147, 271, 273, 276, 314
Troyaniv, 188
Truşeşti, 72, 85
Tsiurupinsk, 274, 275
Tsukur barrow, 363, 403
Turbino, 249–52, 284, 288, 310, 319, 321
Turgau river sites, 130
Turovskoe, 326
Tutayevo, 7
Tyrvala, 216

UCH-TEPE, 122
Ufa, 32, 44
Ulskii, 153, 232, 233, 236, 237, 270
Uman, 375, 377
Umilenie, 327
Uralsk, 273
Urnyak, 295, 319
Urup, 109
Usa river sites, 28
Usatovo, 153, 175, 182–4, 237, 271, 343
Us-Kan, 300
Ust-Ayskaya, 153, 169
Ustie-Oskola, 85, 86
Ust-Rybezhno, 139, 146

VARVAROVKA, 145
Vaskin Bor, 138
Västerbjers, 140
Vasylivka, 29, 37, 38
Vaulovo, 196
Veretie, 85, 137
Verkhnii Kizil, 250, 291, 295, 319
Verkhnyaya Koban, 153, 236, 359, 361
Verkhnyaya Rutkha, 153, 236, 219, 358
Vilnyi, 83, 115
Vinnitsa, 165
Vis, 44, 54, 153, 209, 319
Vita Litovska, 86
Vladichino, 208
Volgograd, 336
Volodary, 206
Volodymirivka (Vladimirovka), 26, 29, 40,
    73, 74, 85, 108, 153, 176
Vologda, 51
Voloske, 29, 37
Volosovo, 47, 153, 206, 207, 319, 324, 331–
    4, 339
Voronezh, 162, 337
Voroshilivka, 377
Vorskla river sites, 379, 387

Vovnykhy, 85, 114, 115
Voy-Navolok, 329
Voytsekhivka, 163, 166, 319, 353
Vozhe lake, 51, 138
Vtoraya Vilovatovskaya, 290
Vučedol, 175, 271
Vychegda river sites (and basin), 44, 45,
    209, 325, 418
Vyg river petroglyphs, 220
Vykhvatyntsi, 153, 154, 181
Vystelizhna, 250

WITÓW, 31

YAGODNOE, 256
Yagorba, 137
Yaila Mountains sites, 80
Yakimovskaya, 39
Yangelka, 45

ZAIMISHCHI, 153, 245, 246, 248, 319,
    322
Zakim, 402
Zaleszczyki, 74
Zalivki, 381, 387
Zaman-Baba, 129, 130
Zamil-Kova cave, 80
Zankivtsi, 29, 40, 64
Zavalie, 112, 167, 169
Zedmar (Serovo), 47, 86
Zhitomir, 8, 163, 351
Zhurovka, 29
Zhury, 71
Ziwiye-Sakkez, 402
Złoczów, 357
Zmiivka, 319, 343, 346
Zolotoi Bugor, 205
Zolotoruchie, 29, 42, 93, 95, 198
Zvenigorod (Moscow), 7, 26
Zvonetska Balka, 319, 343

ABASHEVO culture, tribes, 204, 249, 250, 253, 289, 290, 291, 294, 296, 318, 320, 321, 323, 335, 426
bronze industry, 249, 277, 279, 284, 291-6
Abkhasian Dolmen culture, 123, 125, 126, 153, 202, 237, 371
Acheulian Age, 8, 11, 52
Aegean basin, 156, 175, 183, 223, 224, 314, 362
impulse, 271, 272, 276
trade, traders, 270, 273-5, 313, 393, 402
Afanasievo culture, people, 100, 265, 266, 307
Alps, 173, 174
Alpine Bronze Age, 183
trade, imports, 266, 269, 270, 382
Altai Mountains, 6, 240, 252, 254, 261, 277, 300, 302, 312
metallurgy, 6, 285, 298, 310, 321
Amber, 141, 178, 183, 184, 187, 191, 196, 209, 212, 214, 216, 218, 270, 390
route 273, 276, 288, 345, 355, 367, 390
Ananino culture, 249, 294, 297, 311, 320, 322, 326-30, 334, 367, 384, 389
Anatolia (Asia Minor), connections, influence, imports, 76, 116, 123, 155, 175, 183, 234, 236-8, 268, 270, 271, 275, 396, 397, 402
Anau culture, 99, 143
Andronovo, culture, tribes, 100, 106, 153, 202, 246, 248, 249, 258, 261-6, 273, 275, 280, 285, 287, 289, 295-8, 300, 302-5, 307, 309-14, 317-20, 335, 336, 339, 340, 347, 364, 368, 372, 388, 398, 399
style, 253, 260, 294, 336
metallurgy, 263, 280, 286, 337
Annam, 334
Arctic, Palaeolithic culture, 28, 51, 215
Neolithic cultures, 138, 199, 212, 213, 215, 241, 326, 328
Aristeas of Proconnesus, 310-3, 395, 403
Arrow-straighteners (smoothers), 178, 191, 196, 198, 223, 234, 252, 266, 270, 288
Arsenic bronze, 6, 79, 191, 231, 268, 277, 278, 281
Art, paintings, engravings, sculptures, 21, 103, 123, 213, 214, 216-21, 238, 252, 304, 359, 402
Assyrians, 397-400
records, 396, 397, 399
traders, imported objects, 275, 370
Aurignacian-Solutrean Age, 17, 25, 35
Azilian period, 36, 37
industry, 31, 32, 34-6

BALAKHNA culture, tribes, 105, 136, 153, 206, 208, 209, 246, 318, 322-4, 389
Balan-Bash group, 290, 291, 294, 295, 318, 426
Balanovo people, 105, 202, 204, 294, 323, 324
culture, 153, 154, 199-203, 239, 269, 290, 293, 318, 335, 423
Balkans, 55, 70, 155, 345
Baltic coast, 151, 191, 196, 198, 200, 287, 297, 389
Balts, 156, 241, 242
Belev culture, 84, 96, 98, 112, 139, 208
Biały Potok group, 165, 174, 354
Bilohrudivka culture, 188, 319, 344, 352-4, 357, 375-9, 382, 384, 389, 428
Bodrog-Keresztur culture, 109
Boian-Giuleşti culture, 61, 82
Bondarykha culture, 319, 384-7
Boat-axe culture, 141, 153, 195, 209-13, 218, 219, 239, 241, 242
British Isles, 193, 334, 335
imported objects, 193
Brittany type bronze axes, 381, 382

CARBON-14 dates, 7, 25-7, 36, 42, 48, 49, 61, 66, 71, 72, 76, 79, 91, 96, 99, 102, 104, 131, 132, 154, 173, 263, 330
Catacomb culture, 132, 135, 149, 153, 178, 179, 184-8, 193, 196, 198, 200, 208, 222-31, 234, 236, 239, 240, 253-7, 260, 265, 266, 269-71, 274, 277, 288, 291, 294, 300, 313, 319, 335, 337, 340, 341, 363, 372, 378, 395-7, 416, 425, 427
period, 96, 115, 129, 132, 224, 346, 379, 415
graves 182, 230, 273
Carts, wagons, 129, 132, 223, 224, 237, 238, 400
Caucasian copper, 267, 268, 280, 367
metallurgical centre, 5, 125, 191, 230, 234, 236, 237, 254, 266, 268, 273, 287, 314
bronze types and imports, 196, 199-202, 223, 227, 228
trade and prospectors, 266, 267, 269, 273, 367, 388, 389
Cemeteries, mesolithic and neolithic, 37, 38, 82-4, 114-8, 121, 122, 125-34, 139, 140
Central Europe, 8, 13, 14, 21, 30, 32, 41, 42, 148-51, 154, 155, 162, 173, 191, 200, 201, 208, 232, 240, 271-273, 362, 364, 374, 381-3, 393
Central European current, 240, 341, 381
bronze industry, 161, 162, 176, 178, 182,

183, 187, 196, 212–4, 221, 223, 225, 260, 266, 277, 297, 334, 346, 350, 361
Central Asia (Soviet), 34, 90, 98–100, 107, 113, 129, 130, 141–3, 240, 266, 303, 307–10, 422
Central Transcaucasian culture, 318, 367–71, 389
Chariots, charioteers, 183, 276, 364, 383, 388, 399
Chebarkul culture, 84
Chellean Age, 8, 52
China, 307, 308, 390
  objects of Chinese origin, 334
Chornii-Lis culture, 344, 350, 354, 357, 364, 365, 374, 378, 379, 382–4, 387–9, 402, 428
  bronze industry, 382
Cimmerians, 363, 374, 375, 383, 395–7, 399, 403
'Cimmerian' period, 343
  bronze industry, 279, 346–50
Climate and climatic condition, 2, 3, 17, 19, 25–8, 31, 32, 35, 36, 38, 39, 42, 48–51, 53, 57, 58, 64, 70, 99, 107, 127, 154, 176, 245, 252, 253, 329, 337, 377
Colchians, 369, 370
Colchidic culture, 319, 361, 368, 370, 371, 389, 400, 401
  bronze industry, 361, 370
Comb-pricked ware, 66, 86–8, 107, 109, 112–6, 191, 194
  culture, 108, 112, 140, 144, 229
Combed ware (East Baltic) culture, 140, 141, 212, 213, 218, 239, 241, 242
Corded Ware (Battle-axe) assemblage, people, 133, 134, 148, 150, 151, 154–7, 160, 166, 169, 170, 176–80, 185, 188, 190, 194–6, 198, 199, 201, 204, 205, 225, 227–9, 231, 239, 240, 269, 294, 313, 393
Costişa culture, 160, 165, 174, 175, 350, 352
Cremations, 62, 157, 163, 187, 188, 191, 193, 194, 263, 336, 355, 379, 387
Crete, 70, 270
  Cretan culture, 271, 273
Criş-Körös culture, 62, 64–6, 82, 91, 141, 142
Cromlechs (Stone circles), 118, 129, 135, 180, 182, 224, 263
Cucuteni culture, 66, 67, 71, 109, 173, 175
'Cyclopean' fortresses, 369, 372, 400
Cyprus, 175
  Cypriot culture, 271
  bronze pins, 176, 177

DANUBIAN I, culture, 60–4, 68, 141
  pottery, 66, 88, 90, 413

Deformation of skulls, 224, 228
Diakovo culture, 328
Digorian culture, 236, 358, 359, 361
Dnieper river, 1, 8, 16, 32, 33, 37, 65, 66
Dnieper-Desna culture, 153, 161, 167, 179, 188, 190–6, 198, 200, 211, 229, 239, 241, 242, 273, 367
Dnieper-Elbe culture, 84, 86, 90–2, 95, 96, 109, 113, 114, 142, 151, 194
Dnieper-Donetz culture, 84, 86, 89, 105, 109, 11–4, 135, 140, 144, 189, 194, 239, 386
Dniester river, 16, 19, 34, 64
Dolmen culture, see Abkhasian Dolmen culture
Don river, 6, 16, 19, 32–4, 40
Donetz river, 6, 16, 34
Donetz-Volhynian mesolithic group, 28, 39

EASTERN Assemblage, see Kama-Ural culture
East Baltic Bronze Age culture, 319, 417
East Prussia, 86, 91, 191, 196, 210, 211, 214, 276, 365, 367
Elbe river, 151
Encampments, palaeolithic, 9, 11, 12, 16, 17, 19, 20
  mesolithic, 41
  neolithic, 79, 88, 95, 133, 151, 329
Erteb∅lle culture, 90, 91
Eshery culture, 126, 153, 237, 319
Evminka-Sofiivka group, 153, 186

FAIENCE beads, 121, 157, 191, 223, 236, 272–4
Fatyanovo culture, 105, 153, 154, 167, 191, 195–202, 204, 207, 208, 210, 232, 239, 246, 269, 270, 272, 278
Fino-Ugrian peoples, 155, 156, 241, 242, 312, 323, 389
Funnel-Beaker pottery, influence, 157, 173, 186
Füzesabony culture, 148, 159

GALICH culture, 318, 325–8, 335
Gandzha-Karabagh culture, 367, 371, 400
Germany, 191, 193, 334
Globular Amphora culture, 112, 150, 153, 161–7, 169, 170, 173–6, 178, 184, 186, 193, 198, 201, 202, 229, 230, 234, 294, 317, 393
  people, 148, 154, 184, 186, 239, 240, 276
  potsherds, decoration, 133, 157, 167, 193, 198, 201, 202, 253, 254, 294
Gold, 118, 123, 159, 167, 193, 236–8, 263, 270, 274, 284, 355, 388, 399
  mining, 298, 302, 309–13
Gorbunovo culture, 45, 47, 84, 86, 90, 91, 103–5, 107, 113, 143, 153, 213,

220, 221, 245, 250, 252, 253, 280, 285, 311, 313, 318, 320
Gorodets earthworks, 323
Gorodsk culture, 151, 153, 166, 167, 174, 184–6, 239
Gotland, 365
Greece, 285, 370
Greek colonies, North Pontic, 334, 370, 371, 375, 382, 402, 403
trade, 339, 402
finds of pottery, 339, 363, 371, 374, 403
Gumelniţa culture, 72

HAMANGIA culture, 71
Holihrady culture, 319, 353–5, 379, 382
Hungary, 62, 129, 364
Hungarian Plain, 148, 269, 350, 355, 381, 383, 384, 389
bronze industry, types, 341, 346, 347, 350, 354, 361
Huts, palaeolithic, 12, 17, 18–20
mesolithic, 44, 45
'ploshchadka' type, 71, 73, 170, 186

INDIA, 123, 367, 390
Indo-Europeans, 147, 154–6, 241, 242, 265, 389
Iran, 76, 98, 116, 123, 125, 202, 267, 268, 276, 286, 308, 314, 365, 368, 372, 399, 402, 403
Iranians (Arians), 156, 265, 311, 389
Ireland, 334
Iron objects, lumps, slag, 6, 199, 202, 230, 270, 322, 326–30, 357, 359, 360, 369–72, 374, 375, 381, 394, 400, 401
Irtysh river, 106, 253, 261, 309, 311, 313
Italy, 345
Italian bronzes, 354, 382

JEITUN culture, 99, 146
Jutland, 129, 151

KAMA Neolithic culture, 104, 105, 107, 113, 143, 240, 277, 313
Kama-Ural region, 40, 149
culture, 199, 200, 204, 205, 207–9, 220, 221, 241, 244, 322
bronze industry, 5, 276, 352, 414
Kama-Turbino culture, see Turbino culture
Karelian culture, 137–9, 145, 153, 199, 211, 213, 214, 218, 220, 318, 329, 420, 421
bronze foundries, 330
Kargopol culture, 137–9, 145, 153, 199, 212, 214, 215, 218–21, 318, 327–9, 419
Kayakent-Khorochoy culture, 319, 362, 368
Kazakhstan steppe, 275, 317, 398, 422

Kazan Neolithic culture, 84, 104–6, 113, 143, 153, 204, 205, 245, 246, 248, 277, 313, 321
Kazan Bronze Age culture, 246–9, 260, 294, 296, 297, 311, 313, 318, 320–2, 335
metallurgy, 249, 296, 297, 321, 322, 333, 347
Kelteminar culture, 84, 100–2, 104, 107, 113, 130, 143, 265
Kemi Oba culture, 372
Khodzhaly-Kedabek culture, 367, 369
Kizil-Koba culture, 319, 373, 374, 382, 384
Koban culture, 162, 236, 319, 359–64, 367, 368, 370, 371, 374, 387, 389, 398
bronze industry, types, 350, 358, 361, 365, 371
trade, connections, 355, 365–7, 384
Køkkenmødding culture, 90
Kola peninsula, 51
culture, 137, 215
Komarów culture, 148, 158–60, 165, 175, 188, 225, 229, 240, 257, 294, 319, 350, 352–4, 361, 378
Komsa culture, 51
Kostienki-Borshevo group, 16, 27, 39, 40
Koszider type bronzes, 159, 160, 269
Kuban culture, 231, 239, 364
types, 350
trade, connections, 365–7
Kunda culture, 28, 49–51, 90, 91, 211, 221
Kura-Araxes culture, 77, 79, 84, 109, 110, 116, 117, 120, 122, 123, 142, 146, 231, 267
Kuyavia, 162, 164
Kyul-Tepe culture, 76–8, 141, 142

LELVAR culture, 367, 371
Lialovo culture, 42, 84, 95, 96, 98, 136–9, 198, 199, 207, 215
Lublin Painted pottery culture, 109
Luristan, 365, 368, 370
Lusatian, culture, 319, 355
bronze types, 350, 351, 358

MAEOTIANS, 363, 383, 397
Magdalenian period, 19–21, 25, 35
Maglemose culture, 49, 50
Maikop culture, 84, 115, 117, 119–23, 125, 126, 131, 136, 142, 144–6, 226, 231, 232, 268, 270
Mälar type axes, 328, 330, 333, 340
Manna, 401, 402
Manych river, 34, 40
Marianivka culture, 153, 188, 189
Maritime trade, 147, 149, 175, 184, 240
Masovian culture, 84, 86, 151, 194
Massagetae, 310, 395

Medes, 397, 401, 402
Mediterranean links, borrowings, trade, 32, 34, 36, 126, 147, 223, 225, 236, 238, 270, 273, 274, 285
Mesopotamia, 125, 267
Metallurgical regions, centres, 5, 6, 167, 240, 254
Middle Dnieper Barrow-grave culture, 153, 176–9, 188, 190, 191, 194, 229, 239, 270, 276
Middle Kama Pre-pottery culture, 84
Middle Ural metal industry, 281, 289, 296, 414
Migratory steppe pastoralism, 337, 342
Milograd culture, 194, 319
Mining, copper, 26, 126, 276, 277, 298–300, 307, 363, 371
gold, 298, 302, 309–13
flint, 5
Minusinsk valley, steppe, 284, 302, 304, 305, 307–9, 317, 388
Moldavia, 61, 62
Mostičarska culture, 135, 175, 271
Moulds for bronze casting, 78, 79, 200, 252–4, 264, 280, 291, 300, 319, 339, 344, 346–8, 350, 352, 358, 376, 378, 381, 386, 387
Mousterian Age, period, 8, 11–3, 16, 25, 52
encampments, 12
flint industry, 11
Mycenaean trade, penetration, prospectors, 214, 238, 260, 270, 273–6, 285, 314, 345, 402
'Mycenaean' ornament, 183, 272, 274, 275, 341

NAMAZGA culture, 99, 143
Narva culture, 84, 86, 91, 92, 142
pottery, 90, 91
Neanderthal racial type, 13, 14
Netherlands, 132, 154
North Caucasian culture, people, 135, 153, 196, 225, 227, 231, 232, 234, 236, 237, 239, 268, 271, 273, 291, 358, 363, 383, 424, 425
metallurgy, 191, 268
North Pontic province, mesolithic, 34, 38, 40
neolithic, 74, 130, 131
North-west Caucasian culture, 363, 364, 378, 389
Noua culture, 176, 188, 319, 340, 352–4, 376, 378
Novosvobodnaya culture, 126, 226, 267

OB river, 102, 148, 253, 302, 305, 312, 326, 329
Obsidian tools, 61, 121
'Ochre graves', 127

Oder river, 157
Oriental civilization, 98, 266, 372, 395, 399, 402
trade, prospectors, influence, 123, 237, 388, 393, 402
Orkneys, 11
Otomani culture, 148, 158

PALESTINE, 285
Persia, 202, 236
Pecsel culture, 227, 271
Peschiera bronze pins, 354
Petroglyphs, 214, 216–20
Pit-comb ware, 91, 93, 95, 139, 140, 155, 327
culture, 96, 153, 195, 198
Poland, 160, 162, 193
Pollen analysis, 99, 104, 138, 220
Poltavka culture, 132, 153, 245, 254–7, 263, 265, 266, 267, 269, 277, 280, 285, 313, 337, 339
Pomerania, 191
Pomeranian Face urn culture, 367
Pozdniakovo culture, 198, 318, 335, 339, 340, 416
Pre-pottery Neolithic, 64, 86, 137
'Pricked ware', 107

RACIAL types, 13, 14, 21, 36–8, 48, 50, 52, 115, 131, 140, 144, 166, 198, 202, 211, 224, 256, 307, 308, 312, 322, 400
Riazan culture, 153, 208, 339, 416
Rock engravings, see Petroglyphs
Romania, 126, 129, 132, 155, 162, 165, 167, 201, 269, 350, 352, 376
Rzucewo culture, 151, 196, 200

SABATYNIVKA culture, 319, 343, 347, 348, 376, 378, 382, 389
people, 344, 375
bronze industry, 346, 347, 350
Sachkhere culture, 116, 117
Sambia, 276, 365
Samus culture, 265, 300
metallurgical centre, 302
San river, 61, 157
Sarmatians, Sarmatian-Alan tribes, 308, 314, 363
period, 224
Sauromatian culture, 309, 311, 312
Scandinavian relations, 198, 201, 220, 330, 331, 384, 390
trade, 330, 331, 334, 365, 367
imported objects, types, 167, 168, 208, 331, 333, 335, 365
colonies, 331, 390
Schneckenberg culture 165.

Scotland, 334
Scythian Age, period, 178, 311, 322, 323, 326, 328, 340, 343, 346, 376, 378, 382, 384, 388, 394, 399, 402
culture, 372, 382, 383, 399, 428
Scythians, 3, 311–3, 334, 344, 355, 363, 369, 372, 374, 384, 390, 394–7, 399–403
Seima culture, 318
Seima-Chirikovskaya culture, 325
Seima-Turbino period, 334
bronze industry, 279, 281, 282, 284, 285, 287, 289, 296, 300, 321, 323, 337, 347
types (Seima types) 248, 250, 252, 253, 283–7, 297, 300, 302, 333, 341, 349
Seredni Stog period, 108, 115, 133, 134
Shang-Yin period, 307
culture, 308
Shigir culture, 45, 47, 48, 50, 103
bone points, 44, 46, 47, 49, 93, 137, 138
Siberia, 6, 17, 32, 55, 150, 213
pottery, 107
flint industry, 108
metal industry, 252, 276, 286
tribes, 219, 244
Sindians, 263, 283, 397
Single-graves culture, 154
Slab-cist graves, 118, 125, 126, 162–5, 180, 184, 201, 234, 263, 276, 345, 358, 359, 368, 373
Slavonian culture, 135, 136, 227, 271
Slavs, 242, 323
Slovakia, 173
metal industry, 269
'Small tranchet' flint industry, 28, 42, 88
Sobachky period, 113, 115
Social organization, stratification, 19, 122, 145, 166, 184, 202, 223, 265, 287, 312, 400
Solutrean period, 22, 25, 35
Sosnitsa culture, 161, 189, 194
Southern Bug culture, 60, 64–6, 68, 70, 88, 141, 142, 145
South Urals, 16, 244
Neolithic culture, 100, 102, 106, 107, 113, 130, 264
metallurgical centre, 260, 264, 273, 277, 278, 280, 285, 287, 293, 295, 314, 320, 321
Sperrings culture, 84, 86, 139, 142
pottery, 90, 91, 104, 139, 140
Srubnaya (Timber-grave) culture, 132, 149, 184, 204, 206, 207, 229, 230, 236, 245, 246, 248, 254, 256–63, 273, 275, 285, 288, 291, 293, 294, 296, 313, 319–21, 335–9, 341–3, 346, 347, 350, 352, 358, 360, 362, 364, 365,

368, 371, 372, 377, 378, 386–9, 395, 396, 398
tribes, 274, 280, 287, 295, 317, 323, 339, 340, 375, 427
bronze industry, 279, 295
Srubnaya-Khvalinsk culture, 162, 257, 335, 336, 341, 346
Strzyżów culture, 151, 153, 166, 273
Studenok culture, 189
Sub-Carpathian barrow grave culture, 129, 151, 153, 156–60, 167, 174, 179, 180, 239
Suomusjärvi culture, 28, 49, 90
Surskii culture, 65, 66, 80, 81, 88, 113, 142
Sweden, 365
Swiderian culture, 27, 28, 41
flint industry, 31, 32, 36, 42
flint arrow-heads, elements, 31, 32, 44, 45
Syr-Daria river, 309
Syria 236, 238, 274
objects imported, 125, 273, 276, 285

TAGARSKII period, 302
culture, 308, 333
Talysh (Persian), 285
Tardenoisian period, 30, 36
culture, 44, 50
flint industry, 28, 32, 34, 35, 37, 38, 40, 41, 64
Taurians, 375
Taurian culture, 373, 374, 382, 384
Tazabagyabskaya culture, 265, 266, 309
'Textile' pottery, early, 198, 207, 208, 212
late 318, 322, 326, 328
'Thracian Hallstatt' culture, 353
Thraco-Cimmerian culture, 364, 383, 389
bronze industry, types, 350, 355, 383, 397
Thuringia, 151, 191, 269
'Thuringian' amphorae, 134, 135, 154, 157, 173, 176, 178, 180, 183, 187, 190, 196, 197, 199–202, 232
Timber-grave culture, see Srubnaya culture
Tin, 5, 6, 254, 276, 277, 312, 314
mines 299
Tobol river, 261, 309, 311, 320
Tocharians, 308, 312
Transcaucaisa, 3, 8, 11–13, 35, 202
Bronze Age culture, 153
bronze industry, 116, 368
imported objects, 223
Transylvania, 62, 70, 148, 165, 167, 173
current, 160
metal industry, 267, 269, 270, 341, 346, 350, 352, 353
Tripolye culture, 40, 61, 66, 67, 84, 108,

109, 170, 173, 176, 188, 267, 271, 277, 278, 354, 376–8
people, 184, 239
stages in the development, 67, 68, 151, 176, 179, 180, 415
pottery, 116, 133, 134, 144, 154, 172, 174, 175, 178, 180, 182, 185, 186, 413
Troyan trade, current, 183, 184, 238, 244, 260, 268, 270, 275
agents, prospectors, 266, 274, 276, 285, 313
Trzciniec culture, 148, 159–62, 174, 188, 189, 240, 257, 294, 361, 377, 378
pottery, 162, 179, 190, 193, 194
Trzciniec-Komarów current, types, 188, 260, 339, 362
Turbino (Middle Kama) culture, 153, 245, 248–50, 253, 279, 288, 294, 297, 313, 318, 320
Turkey, 237

UGRIANS, 265
Unetice types, 183, 196, 199, 200, 208, 213, 269, 272, 273
Ural river, 107
Urals, 16, 17, 32, 44, 45, 90, 149, 155, 167, 169, 220, 244, 261, 277, 278, 314, 317, 365, 422
metallurgical centre, 5, 252, 273, 276, 281, 284–6, 289, 314, 322
Urartu, Urartians, 336, 369, 397–402
Usatovo, culture, 153, 179–81, 184, 185, 228, 239, 276, 340
pottery, 135, 181
Ust-Poluy culture, 325, 329

VALDAI culture, 84, 86, 92, 93, 98, 140, 142
Vistula river, 157, 162
Volga river, 1, 6, 8, 16, 43
Volga-Oka Neolithic assemblage, 86, 93, 95, 96, 104, 105, 112, 138, 140, 142, 195, 198, 199, 204, 205, 207–9, 212, 213, 239, 241, 322, 323, 416

Volosovo culture, Early, 153, 198, 204, 205, 207–9, 220
Late, 310, 323, 324, 332, 339, 389, 416
tribes, 323, 324, 335
Voytsekhivka culture, 161, 188, 377
Vykhvatyntsi group, 179, 180, 184, 185, 239
pottery, 182

WESTERN ASIA, 8, 13, 32, 34, 35, 40, 55, 82, 99, 116, 123, 132, 326, 372, 390, 394–6, 399–402
West Siberia, 17, 45, 102, 105–7, 144, 215, 236, 240, 241, 244, 284, 309, 310, 335, 372, 373, 388, 393, 422
metallurgical industry, 6, 284, 287, 296, 298–303, 310, 312, 314
mining, 298–300
products diffused, 268, 289, 326
White Sea culture, 153, 214, 215, 219, 221, 318, 329
Wysocko culture, 319, 340, 354–8, 376, 384

YAMNAYA culture, 84, 107, 113, 115, 127, 134, 142, 144, 147, 151, 156, 157, 170, 176, 178, 221, 225, 229, 230, 239, 254, 265, 271, 291, 294, 313, 374, 393
people, 107, 132, 134, 142, 155, 158, 175, 177, 184, 269, 372
barrow graves, 121, 122, 127, 130, 131, 155, 223, 335, 357, 427
'Yamnaya position' of skeletons, 121, 122–7, 128, 130, 131, 133–5, 150, 163, 165, 178, 180, 190, 195, 196, 200, 209, 225, 255, 291, 294
Yenissey valley, 17, 261, 302, 314
steppe, 398
Yukhnovskaya, 319

ZOLNIKS (ashy mounds), 353, 375, 376, 379